# COLLECTED OPINIONS

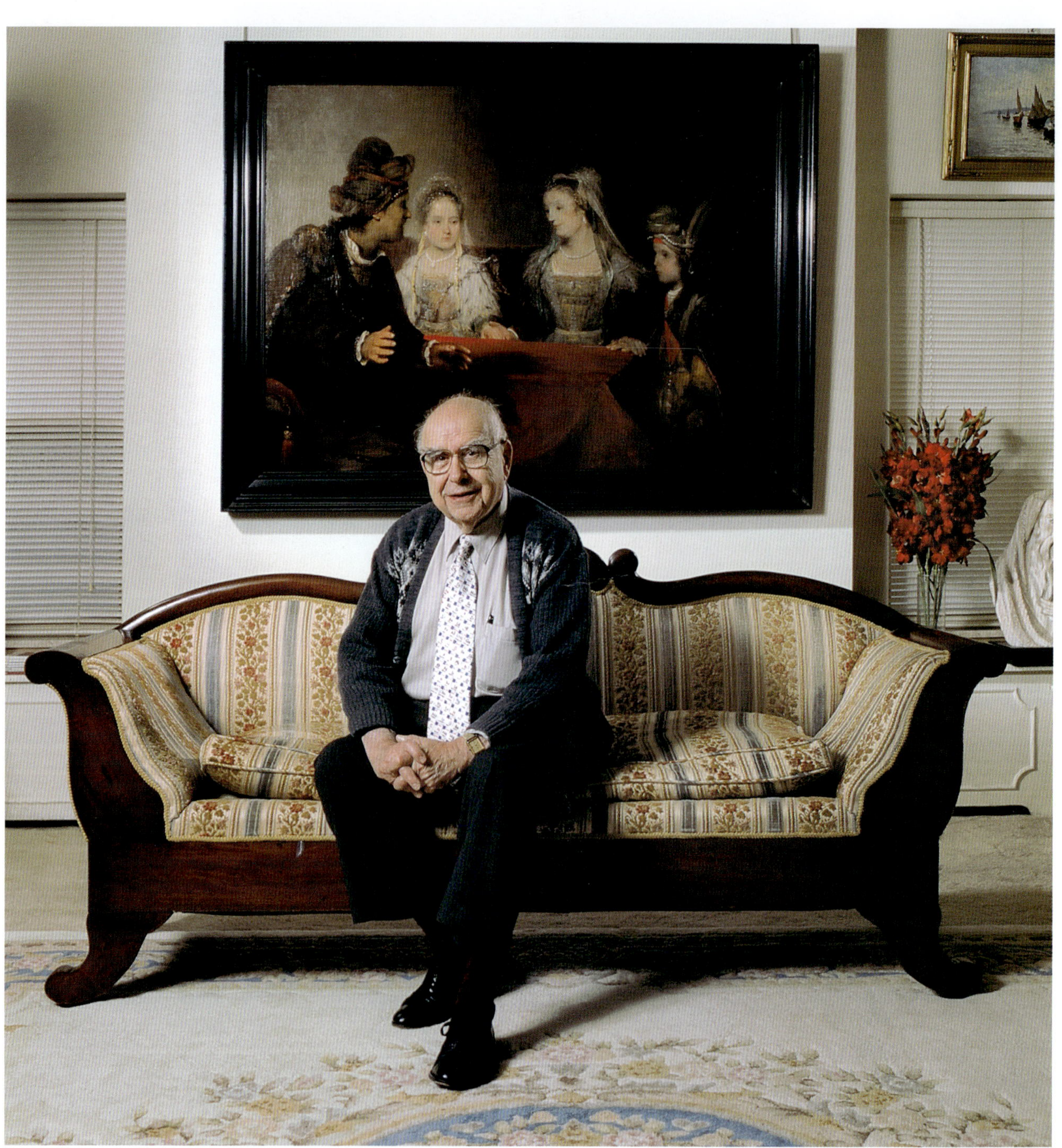

# COLLECTED OPINIONS

## Essays on Netherlandish Art
## in Honour of Alfred Bader

EDITED BY

VOLKER MANUTH AND AXEL RÜGER

Paul Holberton publishing

LONDON 2004

First published by Paul Holberton publishing 2004
www.paul-holberton.net

Copyright © Paul Holberton publishing



ISBN 1 903470 35 8

*British Library Cataloguing in Publication Data*
A catalogue record for this book is available from the British Library

Produced by Paul Holberton publishing
37 Snowsfields, London SE1 3SU
www.paul-holberton.net

Designed by Philip Lewis
Typeset in Monotype Van Dijck
Printed in Verona, Italy

Distributed in USA and Canada for Paul Holberton publishing by
University of Washington Press: www.washington.edu/uwpress

ILLUSTRATION ON PAGE 8:

Charles Munch
*Alfred looks at Rembrandt*, 2003
Pencil on paper, 62 × 50 cm

# CONTENTS

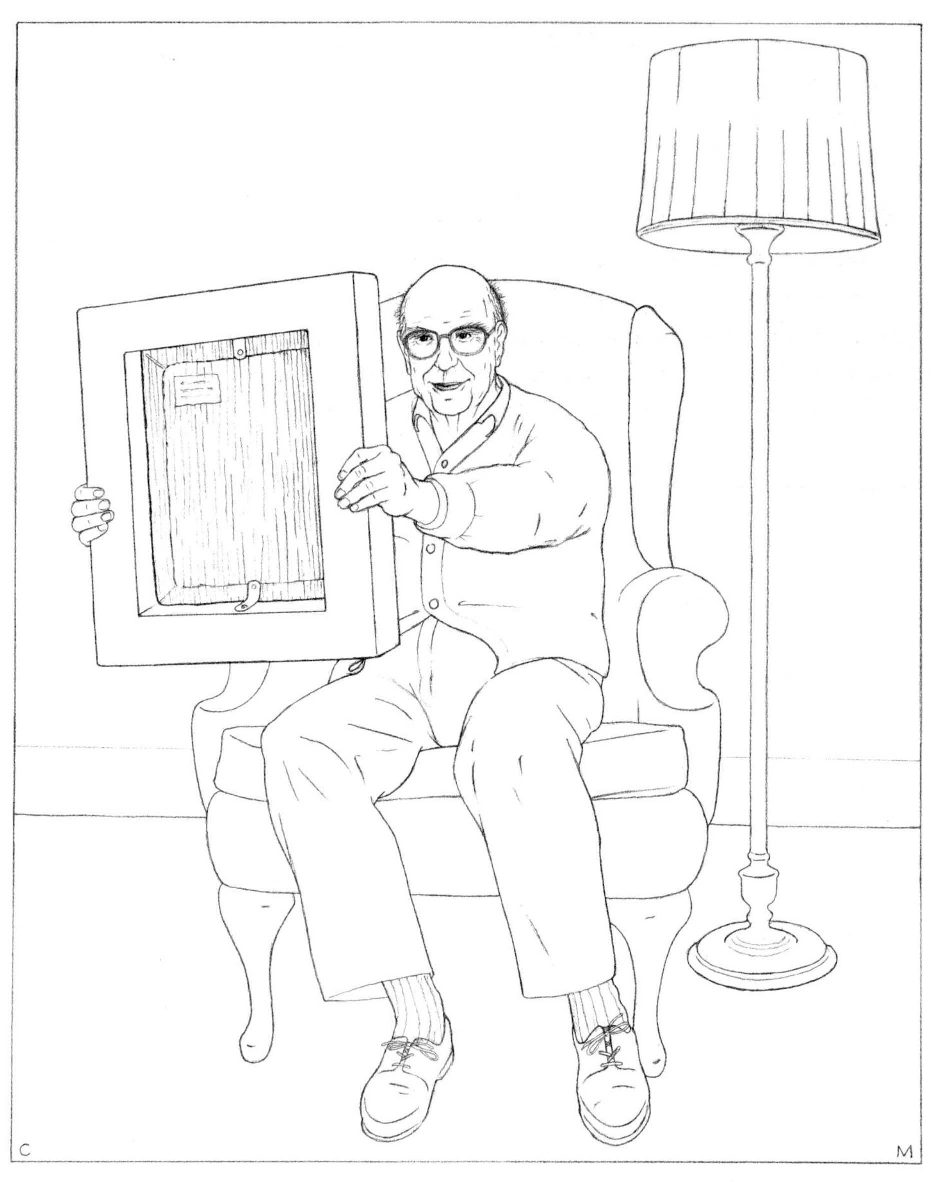

ALFRED LOOKS AT REMBRANDT

# FOREWORD

A few years ago, while still the Bader Professor of Northern Baroque Art at Queen's University in Kingston, Ontario, Volker Manuth mentioned that he was planning to prepare a *Festschrift* for Alfred's eightieth birthday. I was delighted. The love of paintings has played a central role in my husband's life. It is impossible to imagine Alfred without paintings. His tireless engagement in the lives of students and friends of art has been a deep source of encouragement to many over the years. I know that Alfred will be deeply touched and honoured by this expression of appreciation for his contribution to art history.

The mere mention of a good painting, the arrival of an Old Master paintings catalogue or a letter from a fellow art lover still generate in Alfred a rush of adrenalin. He is a man who finds great joy in paintings. The hours he has spent with art historians, whether in person, on the telephone, through letters or pouring over their publications, have truly informed and enriched his life. He clearly misses the great scholars who have gone, but yet he is still eager to work with a new generation of scholars and with those who share his enthusiasm and love for paintings.

I am most grateful to Volker, the current Chair of Art History of the Early Modern period at the University of Nijmegen, who conceived this project, and to Axel Rüger, Curator of Dutch paintings at the National Gallery in London, for their commitment of time and energy. To them and to those who have generously contributed to this *album amicorum* on the occasion of Alfred's eightieth birthday, my sincere thanks.

ISABEL BADER
Milwaukee, January 2004

# FOREWORD

We are pleased to honour our father's eightieth birthday by joining some of the world's finest art historians in this tribute to a remarkable man. Our father is a man of many talents and skills. But, more than anything, our father is a man of passion. His passion for art, chemistry and the Bible (the ABCs of life) has driven many others to share his enthusiasms in equal measure. The articles in this book reflect his passion for Baroque art. We are grateful to all those that have put so much work into making this tribute a reality.

If you are wondering what it is like to be the son of a man who is so very passionate about art, let us give you some insight.

There was no switching subjects with him the way you would have done with most fathers to, say, a ball game or a great new car. He wouldn't let us stray from the arena of art no matter how badly we wanted to. As soon as we could speak intelligently – maybe by age five – our conversations with our father went something like this:

- "Could you help me hang some paintings, please?"

- "Would you like to help me clean and varnish this painting?"

- "What is the subject of this painting?"

- "Would you please pack this painting for me?"

- "What century and what country is this painting from?"

- "Do you like this painting?"

- "What is the condition of the painting? Is it a fragment? Is it a copy?"

- "How much would you pay for this painting? After a reply he would always say, 'How much? You've got to be kidding.'"

- "Go to the auction and bid on these paintings. Don't let anyone know you are bidding for me."

- "This gentleman is always interested in these sorts of paintings."

- "The painting is at the restorer, and he/she has cleaned it. All the over-paint and dirt has come off and it is most beautifully painted and in excellent condition as well."

– "Can you find the signature or a monogram? Is it dated?"

– "Does this painting remind you of anything? The paint handling is very similar to this other painting by this artist."

– "Would you please be quiet; I am concentrating on this painting."

– "You want to eat lunch. What for? We have to go look at that painting auction preview."

– "Don't take a taxi – take the Tube."

It took us many years to appreciate this particular set of questions. Our father was not simply trying to drive us crazy – but was persistently teaching us how to look at paintings, judge their condition and, with luck, learn when they were of good value. "Don't pay too much," he would always say.

DAVID AND DANIEL BADER
Erwinna and Milwaukee, January 2004

# EDITORS' FOREWORD
# AND ACKNOWLEDGEMENTS

Goennern reiche das Buch und reich' es Freunden und Gespielen,
Reich es dem Eilenden hin, der sich vorüber bewegt.
Wer des freundlichen Worts, des Nahmens Gabe dir spendet,
Häufet den Schatz holden Erinnerns dir an.

(J.W. VON GOETHE, Motto for the album of his son August, 1800)

For any lover and scholar of seventeenth-century Dutch painting a visit to the collection of Alfred and Isabel Bader in Milwaukee is a rather special – and never casual – event. While the study and enjoyment of a remarkable collection of paintings lie at the heart of the visit, it is accompanied by a prolonged and rigorous art-historical discussion with the enthusiastic host in front of the originals. These debates often also include the intensive study of comparative photographic material. Upon the in-depth analysis of the condition and the qualities of a particular painting follows the inevitable – and often feared – moment of truth. With the words, "Yes, a nice picture indeed, but who painted it?" uttered almost in passing, Alfred opens the discussion around the attribution of the picture in question. Neither the advancing time of day nor the possible onset of exhaustion on the part of those visitors who have travelled a great distance will bring these passionate discussions about art and connoisseurship to a speedy end. Of course, a satisfying answer is not always reached, but nevertheless these conversations never fail to be most stimulating and thought-provoking.

It is indeed a joy and privilege for the visitor to experience the passion, interest and care Alfred invests in his activities as a collector. This passion for collecting Old Master paintings, especially those of Rembrandt and the Rembrandt-school, and the debates around them have always gone hand in hand with a deep interest in the discipline of art history and the institutions and individuals involved in it. This enduring relationship is reflected not only by Alfred and Isabel's hospitality towards their 'art-historical houseguests', but also by their considerable generosity towards numerous institutions, such as New York University, Harvard University and the Fogg Art Museum, the Allen Memorial Art Museum at Oberlin College, the Milwaukee Art Museum and, most importantly, Queen's University and the Agnes Etherington Art Centre in Kingston, Ontario. In addition to numerous other projects at Queen's, in the field of art history Alfred has generously endowed several academic chairs and funded a programme of travel and research bursaries for students, as well as numerous acquisitions for the art library. The university's museum has received financial support for building an extension as well as a position for a Bader Curator of European Art. Furthermore, over the years numerous paintings from the collection of Alfred and Isabel have been donated to the museum – including the recent spectacular gift of Rembrandt's *Bust of an Old Man in a Cap* of around 1630 (illustrated on the cover of this book) – and eventually the Agnes Etherington Art Centre will be host to the entire Bader collection.

As a result of his activities as a keen collector and picture dealer Alfred has also developed close relationships – which have often turned into friendships – with some of the most eminent scholars in the discipline of art history. It is this close involvement with scholars and students in the field that has prompted us to think of a *Festschrift* as the most appropriate gift to honour Alfred on his eightieth birthday in 2004. A *Festschrift* is typically a gift presented to a distinguished academic on the occasion of a significant event in that person's life or career, be it a special anniversary or the moment of retirement from an academic position. The tradition of the *Festschrift* goes back to that of the *album amicorum* which emerged in sixteenth-century Germany. At that time these autograph books became fashionable among students who moved from university to university over the course of their studies. Professors and fellow students were asked to contribute short and witty inscriptions, sometimes accompanied by drawings. How highly they were valued becomes clear from the words of the eminent humanist Philip Melanchthon (1497–1560), cited in translation in M.A.E. Nickson, *Early Autograph Albums in the British Museum*, London 1970, pp. 9–10:

> These little books certainly have their uses: above all they remind the owners of people, and at the same time bring to mind the wise teaching which has been inscribed in them, and they serve as a reminder to the younger students to be industrious in order that the professor may inscribe some kind and commendatory words on parting so that they may always prove themselves brave and virtuous during the remainder of their lives, inspired, even if only through the names of good men, to follow their example. At the same time the inscription itself teaches knowledge of the character of the contributor, and quite often significant passages from otherwise unknown and little-read authors are found in albums.

While the character of the present volume with its scholarly essays follows more closely the format of a present-day *Festschrift*, it is in the sense of Melanchthon and Goethe also an *album amicorum*, a reminder of the many colleagues and students Alfred has encountered and befriended throughout his career as a collector and scholar.

How close these relationships are is reflected by the immediate, overwhelmingly positive response we received from all those friends and colleagues whom we invited to contribute. We are particularly pleased that the contributors include both long-standing friends of Alfred's and eminent scholars in the field of Dutch art as well as a number of younger art historians who have benefited greatly from the financial support Alfred has provided for their research. Several of them are now working in important universities and museums around the world. The list of authors also reflects Alfred's wide-ranging interest in and involvement with the various aspects of our discipline, that is to say the university, the museum and the art trade.

The book presents a wide array of subject matter, ranging from sixteenth-century Flemish altarpieces to the heroes of seventeenth-century Dutch painting such as Rembrandt, Gerrit Dou and Jacob van Ruisdael, as well as the works of lesser known Dutch and Flemish – and two Italian – painters, draughtsmen and printmakers. Two very personal contributions come in the form of a pair of short stories by Astrid Tümpel and a portrait drawing of Alfred himself by Charles Munch. Given that Alfred is fluent in both German and English and that written texts almost inevitably lose something of their character in translation, the editors have decided to publish the German contributions in their original language. As is the tradition with academic *Festschriften*, in the back of the book we have included a bibliography of Alfred's art historical publications. The editors, however, have refrained from including a biography of Alfred in this volume as he has already published his autobiography, *Adventures of a Chemist Collector*, in 1995.

Publishing a book of this kind is of course impossible without support from many sides. The editors would first like to thank the authors, who have not only readily agreed to contribute but who have also been exceptionally speedy and punctual in their delivery. We are also extremely grateful to our editor and publisher, Paul Holberton, who enthusiastically agreed to take on the project and who shepherded it through its various stages with great care and attention to detail and deadlines! Our designer, Philip Lewis, provided us with the elegant type and layout of the book. The successful collaboration of authors, editors, designers and publishers, however, does not guarantee the final publication of a book like this. The financial burden is considerable and the history of *Festschrift* publication is littered with delayed and abandoned projects as a consequence. We would therefore like to express our deep gratitude to Isabel, David and Daniel Bader, who immediately agreed to fund the publication fully when we first presented the idea to them. Their support took a great weight from our shoulders and freed us to concentrate on the production of the book.

As always, when taking on something one has never done before, one does not grasp the full extent of the undertaking. We have greatly benefited from the expertise and professional and logistical support provided by our colleagues at the National Gallery in London. Besides the staff in the curatorial department and the library, we owe a debt of gratitude to Kate Bell, Tom Windross and Xenia Corcoran of the National Gallery Company. Kate, in particular, has been enormously helpful in the initial stages of the project, advising on scope and format, the financial implications, illustrations, paper and a myriad of further details. It was also she who put us in contact with our publisher. Further, we would like to thank our colleagues at the University of Nijmegen for their support. Finally, thanks are due to our friends and colleagues in other institutions and libraries who provided us with the essential pieces of information, references and photographs we needed.

This volume is a token of friendship, gratitude and respect offered to Alfred on the occasion of his eightieth birthday by those who share his passion for art, especially painting of the Dutch Golden Age.

VOLKER MANUTH, AXEL RÜGER
Nijmegen and London, January 2004

# COLLECTED OPINIONS

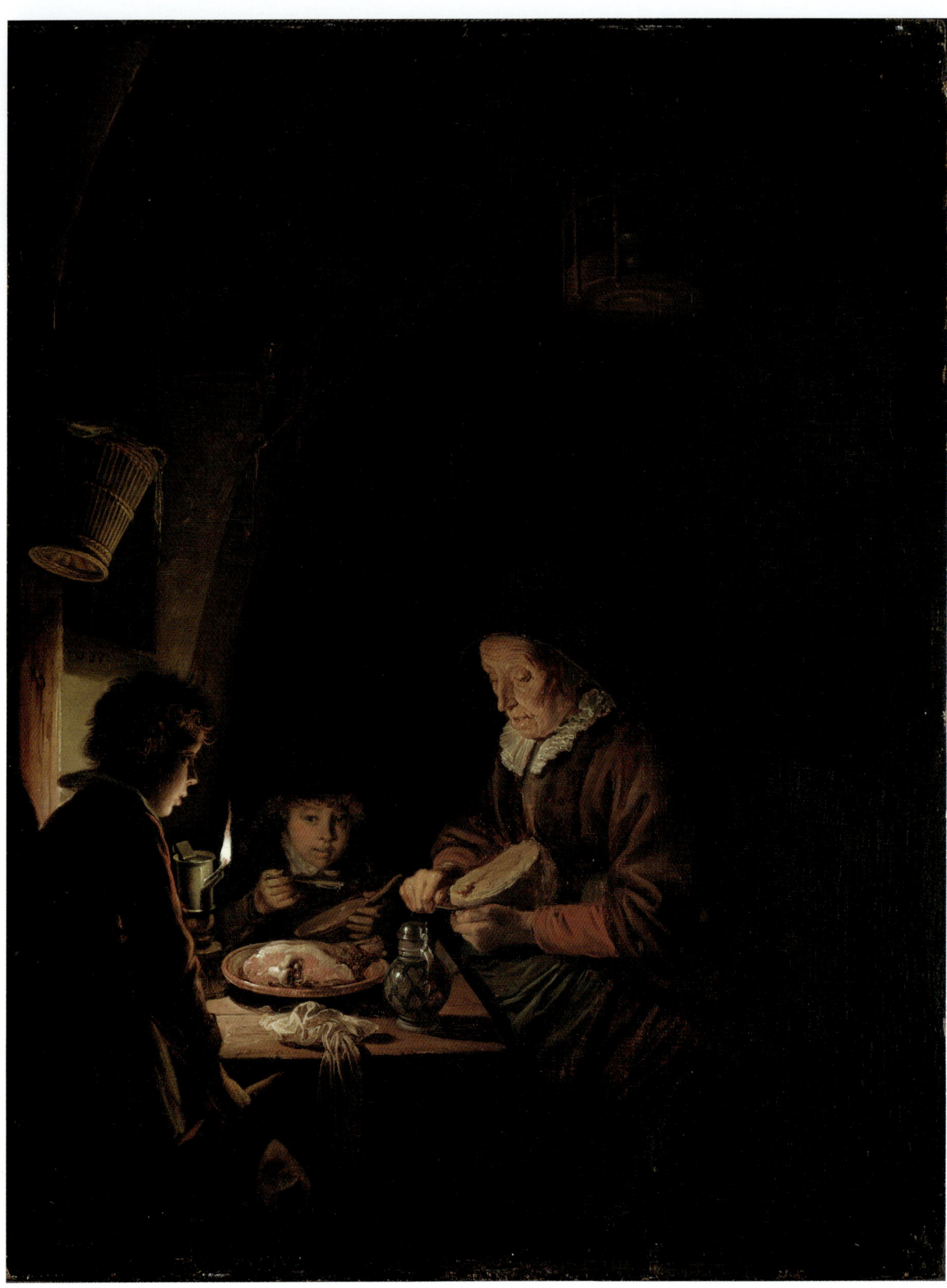

# A Dou for Boston

RONNI BAER

Gerrit Dou (1613–1675), Rembrandt's first pupil and founder of the Leiden school of *fijnschilderij*, was among the most successful artists of the seventeenth century. His painstaking, jewel-like works were highly sought after by royalty and affluent Dutch burghers alike, and critical appreciation for his production only dissipated in the mid nineteenth century.[1] *Old Woman cutting Bread*, recently acquired by the Museum of Fine Arts, Boston, is a significant example of the meticulous yet flowing style that made the artist so famous (fig. 1). Since Alfred Bader funded the scholarship at the Institute of Fine Arts for study in Holland that enabled me to research and write a monograph and catalogue raisonné of Dou's paintings as the subject of my doctoral dissertation, it seemed appropriate, if not felicitous (Dou is not among Bader's favourite Dutch artists), to write on this subject for his *Festschrift*.

The provenance of Dou's *Old Woman cutting Bread* can be traced back to the large collection of paintings assembled in the seventeenth century by Elector Johann Wilhelm von Pfalz-Neuburg (1658–1716).[2] Dou's work subsequently passed by descent to King Ludwig I of Bavaria (1786–1868), who, in 1836, opened the Pinakothek in Munich for the display of the royal painting collection. A century later, Dou's painting was among those deaccessioned by the museum in order to buy pictures by early German masters.[3] The Boston museum was recently able to acquire the painting from descendants of the private collector who purchased it in 1937 from the Alte Pinakothek.

The Museum of Fine Arts has few significant Dutch genre paintings and, of these, *Twelfth-Night Feast* by Jan Steen (1626–1679) and *The Usurer* by Gabriel Metsu (1629–1669), do not depict ordinary domestic activities. Dou's work, with its typical and quotidian subject-matter, thus adds an important facet to the collection. The small scale of the painting, measuring 27.9 × 21.6 cm, corresponds to that of Boston's *Artist in his Studio* by Rembrandt (1606–1669), executed while Dou was apprenticed to the master. It also serves as an instructive comparison to the earlier candlelit scene in Boston, *The Wedding Night of Tobias and Sarah*, by Rembrandt's teacher Pieter Lastman (1583–1633). Providing a beautiful and apposite bridge between Lastman and Rembrandt on the one hand and the later

fig. 1 GERRIT DOU
*Old Woman cutting Bread, ca.* 1655
Oil on panel, 27.9 × 21.6 cm
Boston, Museum of Fine Arts,
Henry H. and Zoe Oliver
Sherman Fund (2003.71)

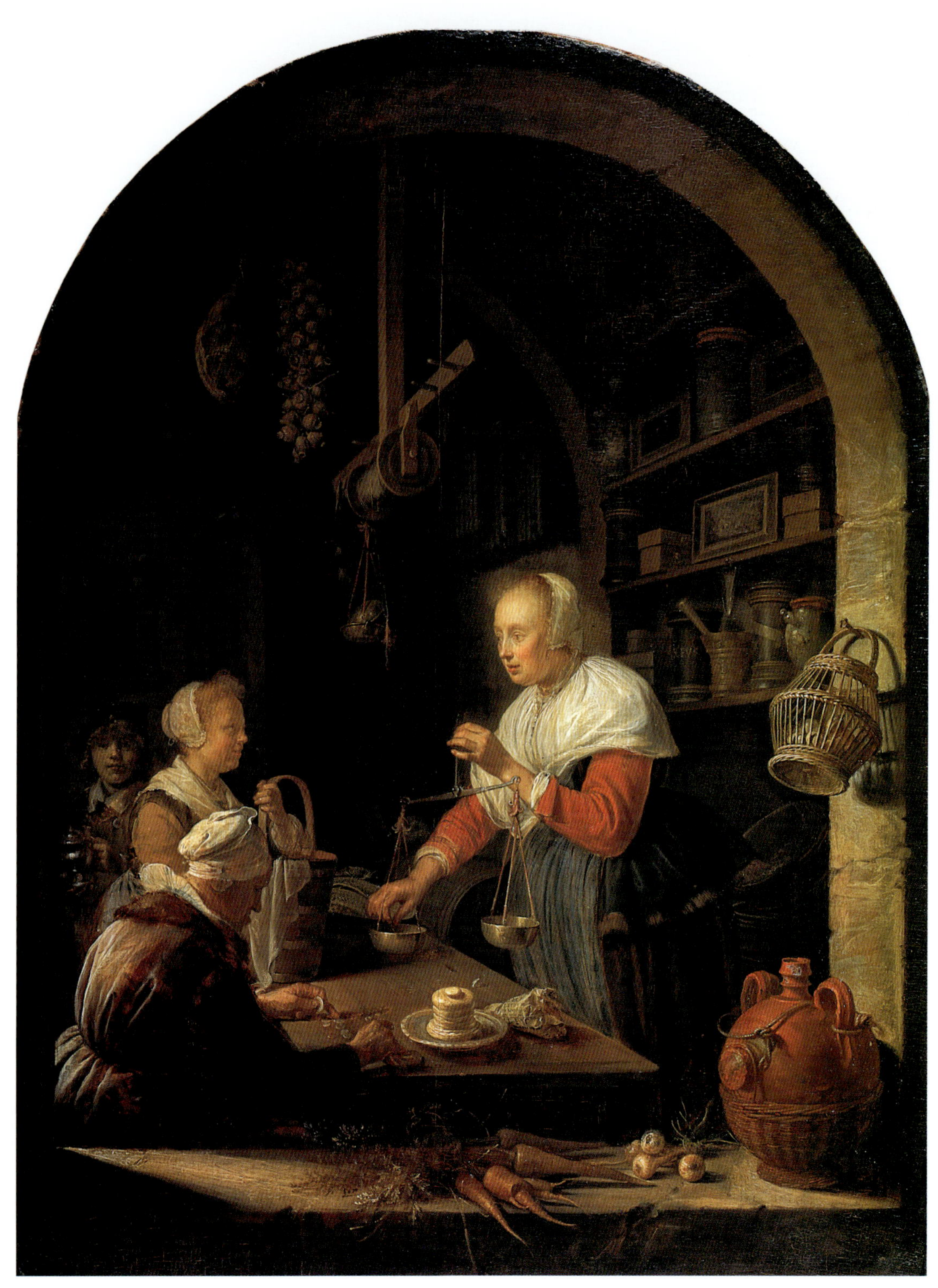

*fijnschilders* on the other, it is the first major picture of its type to enter the collection.[4]

*Old Woman cutting Bread* is signed under the window on the left in Dou's typical manner.[5] The work depicts three figures illuminated by an oil lamp, gathered around a table. To the right is an elderly woman concentrating on her task. Throughout his long career, Dou portrayed such women praying, reading from the Bible, merely standing at a window or, as here, performing their domestic duties. Beside her to the rear is a young boy who pauses, spoon halfway to his mouth, to look out at the viewer. On the left against the light is a youth standing with hat in hand. A joint of meat, an earthenware jug and a piece of white linen are arranged on the wide planks of the table.

For the composition Dou adapted elements from his *Grocery Shop* of 1647, now in the Louvre, Paris (fig. 2). Shared motifs in the two paintings include the table placed perpendicular to the picture plane, the *repoussoir* figure in the left foreground, the protagonist anchoring the composition just to the right of centre, and the young boy in the rear, who, like the boy in the Boston painting, makes eye contact with the viewer. *Old Woman cutting Bread* features the humble interior and figure types characteristic of Dou's mature genre works of the 1650s. Its composition and execution are most closely related to the *School by Candlelight* in the Metropolitan Museum of Art, New York (fig. 3). This work probably pre-dates by only a few years Dou's famous lost *Triptych* of about 1660, which featured a similar school scene on its left wing. A date of about 1655 for the Boston painting is further corroborated by related compositions by the artist's followers executed at about that time.[6]

The support is a roughly worked oak panel bevelled on all sides. The painted surface reveals that Dou applied a warm brown underlayer of translucent paint over a smooth white ground. He used this toning imaginatively in the jug, for example, where the upper paint layers add to the illusion of the vessel's textured surface while the brown underlayer visible around its handle and far side implies its recession into shadowed depth. A reddish underlayer in the jacket of the standing youth gives it warmth, and a granular greenish-grey layer under the small boy's face tempers the effect of light on it. Alligator craquelure evident in the background, encountered in many of Dou's works, may be due to his use of a bituminous pigment or to the lack of sufficient drying time for one of the dark paint layers.[7]

Infra-red reflectography reveals that Dou made use of substantial under-drawing.[8] With a broad brush he boldly blocked in the layout of the composition, including the position of the table, the architectural elements, and the standing youth. He used a quite different method of careful drawing to outline the old woman's cloak and went so far as to apply fine hatching in the area of her upper left sleeve. Despite this preparation, Dou made several changes during the painting process. He adjusted the position of the youth's right arm once, if not twice. At some point it seems to have been bent at the elbow, his hand extending out towards the oil lamp. Dou might also have tried placing the youth's hand on the table. The white cloth hanging over the table edge was originally either larger or moved to the right of its initial position, alterations that are obvious to the naked eye.[9]

Dou often varied his brushwork to suggest the ages of his figures. As one would expect, the youth's relatively impasted face is smoothly rendered, his tousled curls picked out in tiny red flicks of the brush. Dou softened the contour of his profile by extending the areas of light paint ever so slightly over the darker background, thereby creating a blurred, wispy effect. Exceptionally, the young boy has been painted roughly, his features rapidly sketched in; the artist's adoption of this technique probably has less to do with the boy's years than with his placement furthest back in space. The old woman's visage is, in terms of Dou's work, quite broadly painted. It has not been described by the tiny individual brushstrokes the artist often used for the faces of his elderly figures. Rather, he has juxtaposed more broadly painted multi-coloured strokes – yellowish ochre, dark ochre, grey-green, dark brown – over the warm underlayer. The woman's hands, too, are relatively broadly painted, with slashing brushwork delineating the structure of the forms rather than careful horizontal or vertical striations representing the individual wrinkles of her aged skin. A memorable passage of brushwork is the execution of her ruff collar, for which Dou used a very thin, dry brush. The resulting white feathery squiggles serve as a foil to her sunken cheeks in much the way that the painting of the white cloth functions as a calligraphic counterpoint to the summarily executed planks of the table.

This is perhaps the earliest of Dou's twenty or so extant paintings of scenes lit by candle- or lamplight, a type of work for which he would become particularly renowned.[10] The presence of an oil lamp in *Old Woman cutting Bread* functions to indicate a specific time of day – most likely that this is an evening meal, although it would have been dark both at the beginning and at the end of the school day. It was most certainly, however, also included to illustrate the painter's virtuosity. Dou seized on any opportunity to display his artistic gifts, whether in his use of illusionism, his meticulous replication of materials and fabrics or, as here, his uncanny ability to capture the poetic effects of artificial illumination, even in the most mundane of subjects.

Dou's painting is related to the themes of 'The Schoolboy's Meal' and 'Grace,' popular subjects for both paintings and prints in the seventeenth century.[11] The two subjects are imaginatively combined in the engraving by Jan Saenredam (*ca.* 1565–1607) after *Morning* from *The Four Times of Day* by



RONNI BAER

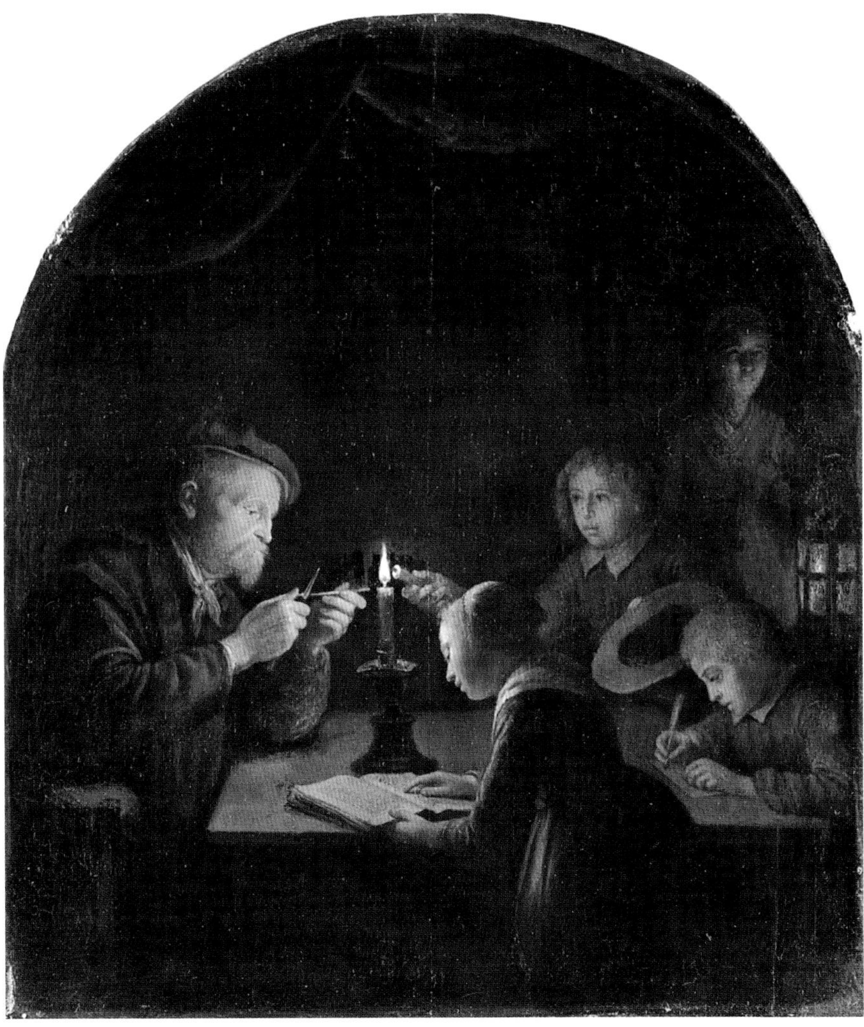

fig. 3 GERRIT DOU
*School by Candlelight, ca.* 1655–57
Oil on wood, 25.4 × 22.9 cm
New York, The Metropolitan
Museum of Art, Bequest of Lillian
M. Ellis, 1940 (40.64)

Hendrick Goltzius (1558–1617) and, in a more naturalistic manner, in the adaptation of it by Gillis van Breen (active 1588–1602).[12] Dou's painting departs from established tradition, however, in the absence of prayer or any reference to school and in the concentrated attention of the old woman on her task.[13]

There are no veiled or emblematic allusions in this anecdotal image, in contrast to Dou's genre paintings that feature split views, where the background scene was included to comment on the action in the foreground, or to the *kas* still-lifes that provided a moral gloss on the paintings (initially) housed inside.[14] Rather, the artist here depicts a plausible and recognizable reality that would have been familiar to his public. The scene embodies associations of domesticity and virtue that were core values in the seventeenth century. On the most general level, the woman is providing food, virtuously fulfilling her domestic role as nurturer. She is also responsible for the training of the children, for their correct behavior and courteous manner, for which meal-times provided ample exercise. Good manners were expected, among them the postponement of eating until a blessing was said.[15] Meal-times afforded the opportunity to promote godliness through prayer, and thereby to instil virtue and piety in children.[16] The humble scene, in which the woman discharges her domestic and familial duties on the occasion of a frugal repast – to nourish and teach propriety and gratitude to those in her care – is elevated by Dou's art into an exquisite image that extolls the virtues of simplicity, rectitude and moderation. The acquisition by the Museum of Fine Arts of Dou's painting both reflects a new-found appreciation and taste for his style and underscores the appeal of his subject-matter to early twenty-first-century viewers.[17]

1 On Dou's patronage, see Ronni Baer, 'The Life and Art of Gerrit Dou', in Ronni Baer, *Gerrit Dou 1613–1675: Master Painter in the Age of Rembrandt*, exh. cat., ed. Arthur K. Wheelock, Jr, National Gallery of Art, Washington, D.C.; Dulwich Picture Gallery; Mauritshuis, The Hague, 2000, pp. 30–32; on the vagaries of taste for his fine painting, see Wheelock, 'Dou's Reputation', pp. 12–24.

2 In 1687, Johann Wilhelm purchased a painting by Dou at auction for 250 *gulden*. The inventory of his collection published in 1751 by Johan van Gool lists seven paintings by Dou, among them *Old Woman cutting Bread*.

3 The *Young Girl at a Window* and *The Quack* in the Museum Boijmans Van Beuningen, Rotterdam, the *Hermit* in the National Gallery of Art, Washington, D.C., and the *Self-Portrait* in the Nelson-Atkins Museum, Kansas City, are other paintings by Dou sold by the Alte Pinakothek in the 1930s. The Munich museum retained three paintings by the artist, including the superb *Spinner at Prayer*, set in an interior very much like the one in *Old Woman cutting Bread*.

4 The museum owns genre-like portraits by Dou's followers Pieter Cornelisz. van Slingeland (1640–1691) and Eglon van der Neer (*ca*. 1634–1703), and a niche painting of children blowing bubbles by Dou's student Matthijs Naiveu (1647–1726).

5 The signature, all in capital letters, has the initial *G* and *D* in ligature; the final letter in Dou's signature always takes the form of a *v*. Rarely does he include the emphatic point after his name.

6 Otto Naumann dated *The Lesson* by Frans van Mieris (1635–1681) in the Corcoran Gallery of Art, Washington, D.C., to about 1650–55; the figure in that painting of the old woman cutting bread is closely related to Dou's. See Otto Naumann, 'The Lesson (Reattributed)', in *The William A. Clark Collection*, The Corcoran Gallery of Art, Washington, D.C., 1978, pp. 69–71. *Old Woman slicing Bread, with Two Children* by Quiringh van Brekelenkam (after 1622–1668 or after) of about 1658 in the Frits Lugt Collection, Paris, one of a series of paintings by the artist of family scenes, depends on Dou's prototype; see Angelika Lasius, *Quiringh van Brekelenkam*, Doornspijk 1992, pl. 35.

7 Recently, much attention has been focused on Dou's working method and technique: see Christoph Schölzel, 'The Technique of the Leiden *Fijnschilders*', in *The Leiden Fijnschilders from Dresden*, exh. cat., Stedelijk Museum De Lakenhal, Leiden, 2001, pp. 16–24; Annetje Boersma, 'Dou's Painting Technique', in Baer, *op. cit.* (note 1), pp. 54–63; L.M. Struick van der Loeff, 'Problemen, Overwegingen en Beslissingen bij de Conservatie en Restauratie van het Schilderij door Gerard Dou "Jonge Moeder"', *Centraal Laboratorium Themadag*, vol. 12, 1987, pp. 40–50; Raymond White, 'Brown and Black Organic Glazes, Pigments and Paints,' *National Gallery Technical Bulletin*, vol. 10, 1986, pp. 58–71.

8 Since no secure compositional drawings by Dou have survived, it has long been thought that he must have worked directly on his panels. Our findings and

those of Jørgen Wadum ('Dou doesn't
paint, oh no, he juggles with his brush',
*Art Matters*, no. 1, 2002, pp. 62–77)
corroborate this assumption.

9   I am greatly indebted to Jim Wright and
Rhona MacBeth, painting conservators
at the Museum of Fine Arts, who shared
and discussed their technical findings
with me.

10   His skill in this respect is mentioned
specifically by Samuel van Hoogstraeten
in 1678; see Samuel van Hoogstraeten,
*Inleyding tot de Hooge Schoole der
Schilderkonst*, Rotterdam 1678; reprint
Doornspijk 1969, p. 262.

11   For a discussion of the theme of grace in
Dutch art, a subject Dou painted in the
background of his *Maidservant at a Window*
in the Museum Boijmans Van Beuningen,
Rotterdam, of about 1657–63, see Pieter
J.J. van Thiel, 'Poor parents, rich children
and family saying grace: two related
aspects of the iconography of late
sixteenth- and seventeenth-century Dutch
domestic morality', *Simiolus*, vol. 17,
no. 2/3, 1987, pp. 90–149; Wayne Franits,
'The family saying grace: a theme in
Dutch art of the seventeenth century,'
*Simiolus*, vol. 16, no. 1, 1986, pp. 36–49;
Mary Frances Durantini, *The Child in
Seventeenth-Century Dutch Painting*, Ann
Arbor 1983, pp. 47–58.

12   Van Breen replaced the allegorical
component in the background of
Saenredam's print with a solid wall
behind the figures; see Eddy de Jongh
and Ger Luijten, *Mirror of Everyday Life*,
exh. cat., Rijksmuseum, Amsterdam,
1997, p. 72, fig. 1 and p. 74, fig. 6.

13   Ter Borch painted an old woman and
young boy at a humble meal sometime
before 1650 (known today through a copy
in Dessau); see S. J. Gudlaugsson, *Gerard
Ter Borch*, 2 vols., The Hague 1959–60,
cat. 72. This painting is the first that
depicts the theme without reference to
school or prayer. However, Ter Borch's
work does not present the image of
concentration so key to Dou's conception
of the subject. The centrally placed ham
on a plate with a bit of cloth beneath it,
a similar jug, and the man's gesture of
removing his hat as a sign of respect are

found in Jan Steen's *Prayer before the Meal*
of 1660 in the Morrison Collection,
Sudeley Castle, Gloucestershire; see
Peter Sutton, *Masters of Seventeenth-
Century Dutch Genre Painting*, exh. cat.,
Philadelphia Museum of Art; Gemälde-
galerie, Berlin; Royal Academy of Arts,
London, 1984, cat. 102, pp. 307–08.

14   Most of the paintings by Dou owned by
Johan de Bye that were exhibited in
Leiden in 1665 had cases (the seventeenth-
century Dutch word for this type of case
is '*kas*'), some of which had painted
covers. In addition to their iconographic
function, such 'shutters' had both a
practical, protective purpose and served
to signal the preciousness of the painting
within. (For more on this subject see
also Arthur Wheelock's essay in this
volume, pp. 232–39.) For this idea, and
Dou's tendency to employ vignettes
metaphorically, see Baer, *op. cit.* (note 1),
p. 40.

15   Plutarch's idea that good manners and
outward appearance constitute evidence
of good morals and inward virtue was a
commonly held principle; see Durantini,
*op. cit.* (note 11), p. 112. It is tempting
to see in Dou's painting an intended
contrast between the boy who waits
patiently and respectfully for his bread
to be cut and the boy who is already
eating, not waiting for grace to be said.

16   Franits, *op. cit.* (note 11), pp. 36–37, 43.
The woman's action evokes the passage
in the Lord's prayer, "[Give us this day]
our daily bread . . .", which is actually
inscribed on the *belkroon* in Jan Steen's
painting of the *Prayer before the Meal* in
Belvoir Castle, Grantham; see Karel
Braun, *Alle tot nu toe bekende schilderijen
van Jan Steen*, Rotterdam 1980, no. 174.

17   Contemporary collectors in Boston
seem to be particularly drawn to fine
painting. Six of the seventeen figure
paintings that were exhibited in a recent
show featuring works borrowed from
local individuals were influenced by
Dou's example and one was by the master
himself; see Ronni Baer, *The Poetry of
Everyday Life: Dutch Painting in Boston*,
exh. cat., Museum of Fine Arts, Boston,
2002, pp. 69, 76–81.

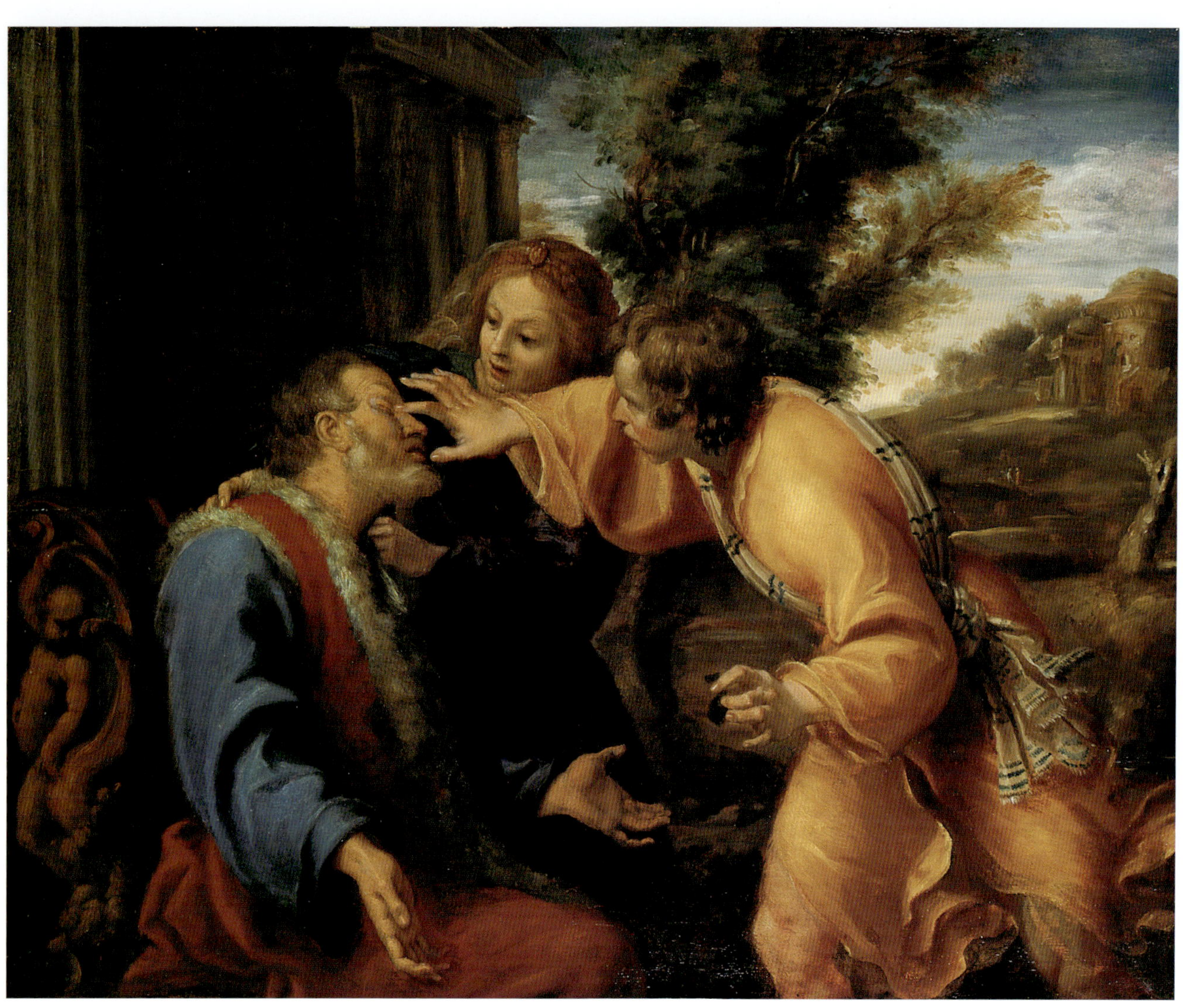

# Balthasar Coymans's Italian Paintings and Annibale Carracci's Melancholy

JONATHAN BIKKER

While the situation would change in the second half of the seventeenth century, in the first half few Dutch collections contained Italian paintings.[1] A notable exception was the collection of the brothers Jan (1601–1646) and Gerard (1599–1658) Reynst, the core of which was formed in one fell swoop around 1627 with the purchase of some 140 pictures once owned by Andrea Vendramin (died 1547) in Venice.[2] Although some of the paintings later acquired by the Reynst brothers were by contemporary Italian artists, such as Guido Reni (1575–1642), Guercino (1591–1666) and Bernardo Strozzi (1581–1644), the sixtcenth-century Venetians acquired from Vendramin made up the bulk of their collection. Even earlier, when Jan and Gerard Reynst were still children, another collection of Italian paintings that would find its way to Amsterdam was being formed, that of the wealthy merchant Balthasar Coymans (1555–1634). Coymans was born in Antwerp and came via Hamburg to Amsterdam in 1592, where he founded a trading company and was active as an international banker.[3] His fortune was assessed in 1631 at 400,000 guilders, making him one of the three wealthiest citizens of Amsterdam. In 1625, he moved to a new house across from the Westerkerk on Keizersgracht (now no. 177), that had been built in the latest Italianate classicizing style.[4] Later in the century, this house was described as "like a church in appearance" and admired for the "exquisite paintings and other decorations" it contained.[5] Balthasar Coymans stands out as a collector because he was not only one of the first Dutchmen to acquire Italian paintings, but because all of these "exquisite paintings" were apparently by contemporary artists. Coymans, the sources indicate, amassed his collection during his business travels in Italy, where he seems to have been on familiar terms with a number of leading artists.

In his *Teutsche Academie* of 1675, Joachim von Sandrart (1606–1688) claims that the best place to see paintings by Bartolomeo Manfredi (1582–1622) was in

fig. 1 Circle of
ANNIBALE CARRACCI
*Tobias healing his Father's Blindness*
Oil on poplar, 52.8 × 66.5 cm
Cassel, Staatliche Museen Kassel,
Gemäldegalerie Alte Meister

the house of "the art-loving Coymans" in Amsterdam.[6] Sandrart would have seen these paintings himself when he was a pupil of Gerard van Honthorst (1592–1656) in Utrecht in the 1620s, or during his stay in Amsterdam between 1637 and 1644. His claim sounds utterly fantastic, but we do know that Balthasar Coymans owned works by Manfredi. In 1709, the paintings in Coymans's house on Keizersgracht were put on the block after one of his grandsons, Jan Coymans (1645–1703), disinherited half of his family and died childless.[7] The catalogue itself of the 1709 auction has, unfortunately, not survived, but the advertisement listing the artists whose works were in the sale has, and indeed one of them was "Manfredo".[8] The advertisement also informs us that many of the paintings in the sale had been acquired in Italy and that they had been with the family for more than sixty years. Other artists in the 1709 advertisement whose paintings are likely to have been acquired by Balthasar Coymans and remained with his heirs are Paul Bril (*ca.* 1554–1626; twelve works), Caravaggio (1571–1610; three works), and Annibale Carracci (1560–1609; seven works). Some of the items in the 1709 sale must have remained unsold, for they show up in an anonymous sale of pictures, which we know to have come from the Coymans family, that took place in Amsterdam on 16 May 1725.[9] Lot 8 was made up of eight views of Rome by Bril of, among other things, the Campo Facino, Tivoli and the Tiber. Lot 9 contained two more landscapes by Bril. These paintings, one can readily imagine, had been acquired by Balthasar Coymans as souvenirs of his time in Rome. The 1725 sale no longer contained any works by Manfredi, making it impossible to verify Sandrart's claim about the quantity of paintings by that master Coymans owned. Nor do the three Caravaggios reappear. Paintings by other artists mentioned in the 1709 advertisement do, however, feature in the 1725 sale, amongst them two paintings by Michelangelo Cerquozzi (1602–1660) and a *Mocking of Christ* by the Milanese artist Francesco del Cairo (1607–1665). Their work would have been a bit too recent for Balthasar Coymans to have been able to acquire it, and it is more likely to have reached Amsterdam through his son Joan (1601–1657), who, like his father, had extensive business dealings in Italy. On the other hand, the *Prometheus Bound* by "Mennitti" could well have been one of Balthasar Coymans's acquisitions, as the artist in question is probably the Sicilian follower of Caravaggio Mario Minniti (1577–1640).

As far as the reconstruction of Balthasar Coymans's collection is concerned, it is very fortunate that the seven paintings by Annibale Carracci listed in the 1709 advertisement reappear in the 1725 sale. These paintings illustrated the Seven Acts of Mercy, and the story related by Sandrart of how they came into Coymans's possession seems even more unusual than what he has to say about Manfredi's paintings. According to Sandrart, the series was given to Balthasar

Coymans by Annibale in gratitude for the material assistance he had awarded to the Bolognese artist.[10] Annibale, Sandrart relates, experienced a terrible bout of melancholy while he was working on what was undoubtedly his most important commission, the Farnese Gallery. The cause of his gloom was the stinginess of a certain Don Giovanni, a Spanish courtier in charge of the finances of Annibale's patron, Cardinal Odoardo Farnese (1573–1626). In an attempt to please the Cardinal, who was always extremely reluctant to untie his purse strings, Don Giovanni gave a platter with the paltry sum of five hundred gold *scudi* to Annibale as his reward for ten years of work. Annibale's melancholic state was to last until Balthasar Coymans "found him in Rome, took him in, and by alleviating his poverty made his desperate soul happy once more".[11]

Not only does this story of how Coymans acquired the paintings seem incredible, the series itself was most unusual, too, as at least four of the Seven Acts were represented by Old Testament subjects: Refreshing the Thirsty by *The Angel appearing to Hagar in the Wilderness* (Genesis 21: 17–19), Visiting the Sick by *Tobias healing his Father's Blindness* (Tobit 11: 13–15), Feeding the Hungry by *Abraham and the Angels* (Genesis 18: 2–5), and Burying the Dead by *The Prophet taking the Body of the Man of God back to Bethel to be Buried* (I Kings 13: 29). While this way of representing the Seven Acts was possibly a first in the history of art, the first three Old Testament subjects in themselves are not uncommon in Italian art. The most unusual subject, and one, as far as I know, not depicted by any other Italian artist, is the episode from the story of the man of God used to illustrate Burying the Dead.[12] The man of God, who had preached in Bethel, was tricked into accepting a Prophet's invitation to eat and drink in his house, thereby unwittingly disobeying God's command not to return to Bethel. As the result of his disobedience, he was slain by a lion after leaving his host. Although a frightful story involving disobedience, gullibility and deceit, it is rich in allusions to other acts of mercy (Harbouring the Stranger, Feeding the Hungry and Refreshing the Thirsty) and the fact that the Prophet goes out to recover the body of the man of God and buries him in his own grave is very moving.

At the 1725 sale the series of the Seven Acts began to be broken up. Five of the paintings apparently came back once again to a descendant of Balthasar Coymans, as they show up in the 19 March 1760 sale of his eponymous great-grandson.[13] This Balthasar (1699–1759) was the last member of the Coymans family to live in the house on Keizersgracht.[14] In the 1760 sale, the five paintings fetched significantly less than in the 1725 sale, and it is stated in the catalogue that the paintings were to be sold individually. Four of them were purchased by the art dealer Jan Yver. The fifth, representing Ministering to Prisoners, was acquired by the Leyden Burgomaster Johan Aegidiusz. van der Marck for

61 guilders, and shows up again in his 1773 sale, where it is described as showing six knee-length figures in a landscape.[15] From the description we also know that the painting was on panel. In the 1725 catalogue, the measurements of the paintings are not given. But from the 1760 sale catalogue and that of the Van der Marck sale we know that they were 20 by 25 *duim*, or about 51 × 64 cm. Ministering to Prisoners was purchased at the Van der Marck sale by the collector Hendrik van Maarseveen for 88 guilders. It does not show up in his 1793 sale.[16] Yver sold two of the paintings he had purchased at the 1760 Coymans sale, *Abraham and the Angels* (Feeding the Hungry) and *The Angel Appearing to Hagar in the Wilderness* (Refreshing the Thirsty), to Pieter Leendert de Neufville; they appear as pendants in his 1765 sale, where they were purchased by the artist/ dealer Jan Matthias Cock for 210 guilders each.[17]

Although no longer part of a series, these individual Acts of Mercy found homes in some of the best eighteenth-century Dutch collections. This holds true as well for the most expensive painting of the series at the 1725 auction, *Tobias healing his Father's Blindness*. It was sold for 500 guilders to Adriaan Bout, in whose collection it was given a '*faux pendant*' in the form of a *Liberation of St Paul* by Annibale Carracci. At the 1733 sale of Bout's paintings, the famous Delft collector Valerius Röver acquired the *Tobias* for 405 guilders.[18] Röver also purchased the *Liberation of St Paul*, but paid only 105 guilders for it. He must have considered it a lesser painting, and probably did not regard it as a suitable pendant to the *Tobias*. At any rate, he appears to have disposed of it, as it is not listed in the inventory of his paintings.[19] In 1750, the *Tobias* was acquired by Landgrave Wilhelm VIII of Hesse-Cassel (1682–1760) with the rest of Röver's collection.[20] The painting is still in Cassel today (fig. 1). It is hoped that the 're-discovery' of this Act of Mercy will lead to that of the other paintings in the series.

*Tobias healing his Father's Blindness* was considered an authentic Annibale Carracci until the late nineteenth century, when Eisenmann cast the attribution into doubt and wondered whether the painting should not be ascribed to Annibale's school.[21] In the twentieth century, some scholars still maintained that the painting had been executed by Annibale himself. Herzog, for example, considered it to be a work from Annibale's "Venetianizing period", around 1590–95.[22] The scholarly consensus now, however, is that the painting is from Annibale's circle, and it is as such that it appears in the most recent catalogue of the Cassel collection.[23] If Annibale himself did not paint the *Tobias*, Sandrart's story about how Balthasar Coymans acquired his Seven Acts of Mercy would appear to be fanciful. Or did Annibale perhaps design the paintings, leaving their execution largely or entirely to assistants? Even if this could be proven, one would still be left wondering whether Sandrart, or perhaps one of Balthasar



JONATHAN BIKKER

Coymans's sons, or perhaps Balthasar Coymans himself, did not simply make up the wonderful story of their acquisition.

The story of Annibale's melancholy was certainly not an invention. Sandrart's version of it is a literal translation of the account written by Baglione in 1642, and from other, contemporary, sources it is known that Annibale fell ill in the beginning of 1605.[24] An account written in 1599 suggests that the eventual illness was not brought on merely by the meagre reward he received after his ten years of labour for Cardinal Farnese, but that his lot during those ten years had not been an enviable one either: "M. Annibale Carracci receives from his [cardinal] no more than ten *scudi* per month, and portions for himself and a servant, and a little room under the roof. And for this he toils and pulls a cart the whole day like a horse and does loggias, rooms and salons, pictures and altarpieces, and works that are worth a thousand *scudi*. He is worn out with hard work and has little taste for such servitude."[25] At some point, Annibale moved out of the small room in the Palazzo Farnese and found quarters first on the Quirinal Hill and later in the neighbourhood of San Lorenzo in Lucina. Balthasar Coymans, perhaps, financed one of these new addresses and gave the artist money. But if the Amsterdam merchant did indeed alleviate Annibale's melancholy it was not of lasting effect. On 15 July 1609, Annibale Carracci died, according to some of his contemporaries as the result of his melancholy.[26] And in a letter written the night of his death by his friend Giovanni Battista Agucchi, it is stated that from the time he left the Palazzo Farnese he "was barely able to work on anything at all".[27]

1 Jaap van der Veen, 'Schilderijencollecties in de Republiek ten tijde van Frederik Hendrik en Amalia', in *Vorstelijk verzameld: de kunstcollectie van Frederik Hendrik en Amalia*, exh. cat., ed. Peter van der Ploeg and Carola Vermeeren, Mauritshuis, The Hague, 1997, p. 91. For a good recent overview of the collecting of Italian paintings in the United Provinces in the seventeenth century see Bert W. Meijer, 'Italian paintings in 17th century Holland: Art market, art works and art collections', in *L' Europa e l'arte italiana*, ed. M. Seidel, Venice 2000, pp. 377–415.

2 For the Reynst collection and Andrea Vendramin's paintings see Anne-Marie S. Logan, *The 'Cabinet' of the brothers Gerard and Jan Reynst*, Amsterdam, Oxford and New York 1979; and for further recent archival research on Vendramin Stefania Mason, "'Di mano di questo maestro pochissime sono le cose che si vedono": Giorgione nel collezionismo veneziano', in *Giorgione: Le maraviglie dell'arte*, exh. cat., Accademia delle Belle Arti, Venice, 2004, pp. 64–71, esp. p. 66.

3 For Balthasar Coymans's biography see J.E. Elias, *De vroedschap van Amsterdam 1578–1795*, 2 vols., Haarlem 1905, II, pp. 761–62.

4 Inigo Jones's Banqueting House for Whitehall Palace in London was the direct model for Coymans's house, which was designed by Jacob van Campen. See Koen Ottenheym, 'Architectuur', in *Jacob van Campen: het klassieke ideaal in de Gouden Eeuw*, ed. Jacobine Huisken, Koen Ottenheym and Gary Schwartz, Amsterdam 1995, pp. 158–60.

5 The description is Melchior Fokken's from 1662. See J.F.L. de Balbian-Verster, 'Het Huys van Coymans', *Maandblad Amstelodamum*, XVI, 1929, p. 30.

6 A.R. Peltzer, *Joachim von Sandrarts Academie der Bau- Bild- und Mahlerey-Künste von 1675*, Munich 1925, p. 277.

7 For Jan Coymans see Luuc Kooijmans, *Vriendschap en de kunst van het overleven in de zeventiende en achttiende eeuw*, Amsterdam 1997, pp. 204–05.

8 S.A.C. Dudok van Heel, 'Honderdvijftig advertenties van kunstverkopingen uit veertig jaargangen van de Amsterdamsche Courant: 1672–1711', *Jaarboek Amstelodamum*, LXVII, 1975, p. 170, no. 125.

9 Gerard Hoet, *Catalogus of naamlyst van schilderyen…*, 2 vols., The Hague, 1752, II, pp. 307–08. For evidence that the collection in this sale did indeed belong to the Coymans family see note 19 below.

10 Peltzer, *op. cit.* (note 6), I, p. 274.

11 *Ibid.*: "Ihn in Rom gefunden, zu sich genomen und durch Vorschiessung aller Nohtdurft seinen verlassenen Geist wieder erfreuet".

12 Dutch artists did, occasionally, depict this scene. See Judith van Gent, 'De tijd van de koningen en de profeten', in Christian Tümpel *et al.*, *Het Oude Testament in de Schilderkunst van de Gouden Eeuw*, exh. cat., Joods Historisch Museum, Amsterdam, and Israel Museum, Jerusalem, 1991, p. 101.

13 An annotated catalogue for this sale held in Amsterdam is preserved in the Bibliothèque Nationale, Paris.

14 Kooijmans, *op. cit.* (note 7), p. 297.

15 Sale catalogue (Bibliothèque Nationale, Paris), sale Johan Aegidiusz. van der Marck, Amsterdam, 25 August 1773, lot 41.

16 Sale catalogue (Netherlands Institute for Art History, RKD), sale Hendrik van Maarseveen, Amsterdam, 28 November 1793.

17 Sale catalogue (Netherlands Institute for Art History, RKD), sale Pieter Leendert de Neufville, Amsterdam, 19 June 1765, lots 16 and 17.

18 Sale catalogue (Netherlands Institute for Art History, RKD), sale Adriaan Bout, The Hague, 11 August 1733, lots 9 and 10.

19 Röver's catalogue is reproduced in E.W. Moes, 'Het Kunstkabinet van Valerius Röver te Delft', *Oud Holland*, XXXI, 1913, pp. 4–24; for the catalogue see pp. 16–24. The *Tobias* is listed on p. 23, no. 105. Röver states that he acquired this painting from Bout, who had acquired it from "Mr. Coymans in Amsterdam". The *Liberation of St Paul* was likely the painting sold as lot six in Gerard Bicker van Zwieten's sale held in The Hague on 12 April 1741 (sale catalogue, Netherlands Institute for Art

  JONATHAN BIKKER

History, RKD). It was purchased by the artist Philip van Dyck for only 18 guilders.

20  For the purchase of Röver's collection by the Landgrave see Moes, *op. cit.* (note 19), pp. 5–6.

21  Oscar Eisenmann, *Katalog der Königlichen Gemälde-Galerie zu Cassel*, Cassel 1888, p. 329, no. 529.

22  Erich Herzog, *Die Gemäldegalerie der Staatlichen Kunstsammlungen in Kassel*, Hanau 1969, p. 91, no. 76.

23  Bernhard Schnackenburg, *Gesamtkatalog Gemäldegalerie Alte Meister Kassel*, 2 vols., Cassel and Mainz am Rhein 1996, I, pp. 78–79, no. GK 568; see also Jürgen M. Lehmann, *Staatliche Kunstsammlungen Kassel, Katalog I, Italienische, französische und spanische Gemälde des 16. bis 18. Jahrhunderts*, Fridingen 1980, p. 78, and Erich Schleier's review of Jürgen M. Lehmann's catalogue in *The Burlington Magazine*, CXXVII, September 1985, p. 627. The painting is not included in and, therefore, not accepted by Donald Posner, *Annibale Carracci: A Study in the Reform of Italian Painting around 1590*, 2 vols., London and New York 1971.

24  Giovanni Baglione, *Le vite de' pittori, sculttori et architetti*, Rome 1642, p. 102. For Annibale's melancholy see Rudolf and Margot Wittkower, *Born under Saturn. The Character and Conduct of Artists: A Documented History from Antiquity to the French Revolution*, New York and London 1969, pp. 113–15.

25  This account was given by a pupil of Annibale, Giovanni Battista Boncourt, and is recorded in Carlo Cesare Malvasia, *Felsina pittrice. Vite de' pittore bolognesi*, ed. Giampietro Zanotti, 2 vols., Bologna 1841 (*editio princeps* Bologna 1678), I, p. 574. The English translation is taken from John R. Martin, *The Farnese Gallery*, Princeton, New Jersey, 1965.

26  This was the diagnosis of, for example, the medical doctor Giulio Mancini; see his *Considerazioni sulla pittura*, ed. Adriana Marucchi and Luigi Salerno, 2 vols., Rome 1956, I, p. 218.

27  The English translation is taken from Anne Summerscale, *Malvasia's Life of the Carracci*, University Park, Pennsylvania, 2000, p. 227. For Annibale's last years see Posner, *op cit.* (note 23), pp. 146–49.

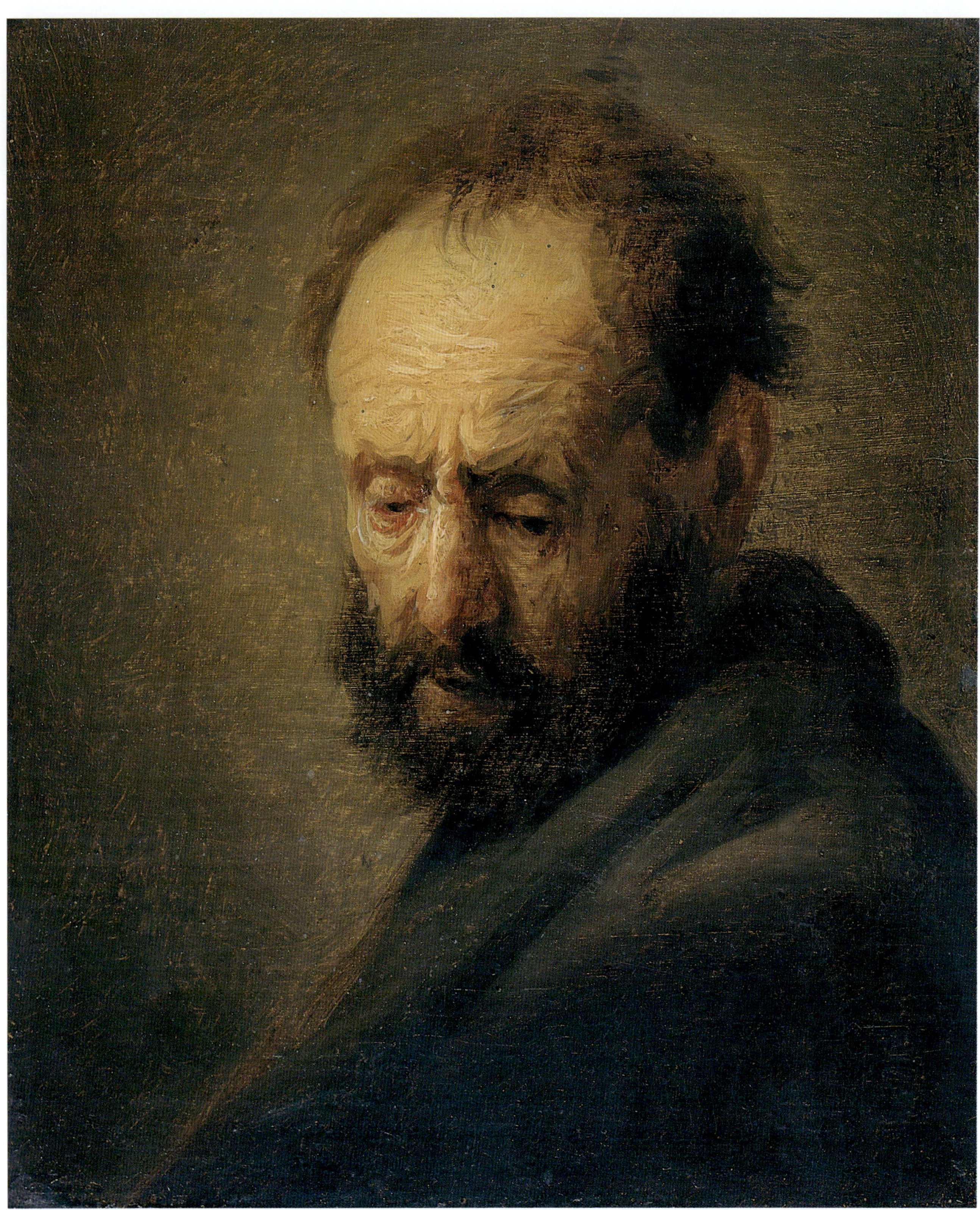

# Rembrandt in Oxford

CHRISTOPHER BROWN

Alfred and Isabel Bader were frequent visitors to my office when I was at the
National Gallery in London, often returning from sales with Alfred carrying the
latest Rembrandt-school painting under one arm. Since I left my post there and
moved as Director to the Ashmolean Museum in Oxford, I have sadly seen them
less frequently and find it hard to tempt them to Oxford. I suspect this is
because they are under the false impression that there is little in Oxford to
attract the Rembrandt scholar. I therefore thought that an appropriate contribution to this *Festschrift* would be a survey of the Rembrandt and Rembrandt-
school holdings in the Ashmolean – paintings, drawing and prints – in the hope
that Alfred and Isabel – and indeed other Rembrandt scholars – will make their
way to the Ashmolean Museum, which is better known for Raphael (1483–1520)
and Michelangelo (1475–1564) than Rembrandt (1606–1669).

Like many institutions, the Ashmolean did have a painting by Rembrandt
until Horst Gerson published his third edition of Bredius's catalogue (fig. 1).[1]
Painted on panel, it shows an old bearded man: the face is freely painted and there
is a strong fall of light on the forehead. There are two other versions of this
composition and the Ashmolean painting has usually been thought of as the best
of the three.[2] There is also an etching of the same head which has been attributed
to Jan van Noordt (1624– after 1676), which may point to the existence of a
Rembrandt original.[3] The Rembrandt Research Project followed the lead of Gerson,
noting the similarity of the work to Rembrandt and Lievens's style of around 1630
but suggesting that its origin was to be found outside Rembrandt's circle at a later
date.[4] My predecessor, Christopher White, in his eminently balanced discussion
of the painting, opted for "style of Rembrandt". I had hoped that this painting,
long ago relegated to the picture store, might reveal formerly undreamt-of qualities
to the new Director of the Ashmolean. Sadly, however, having spent a considerable
amount of time examining it, I find myself broadly in agreement with recent
criticism. The treatment of the features is too broad to be Rembrandt's, the
puckered skin around the eyes too slackly drawn. It may well have been painted
substantially later than Rembrandt's lifetime: an inscription on a label on the back
suggests that it may have been in France in the eighteenth century.

fig. 1 Style of REMBRANDT
*Head of a Bearded Man*
Oil on panel, 16 × 13 cm
Oxford, Ashmolean Museum

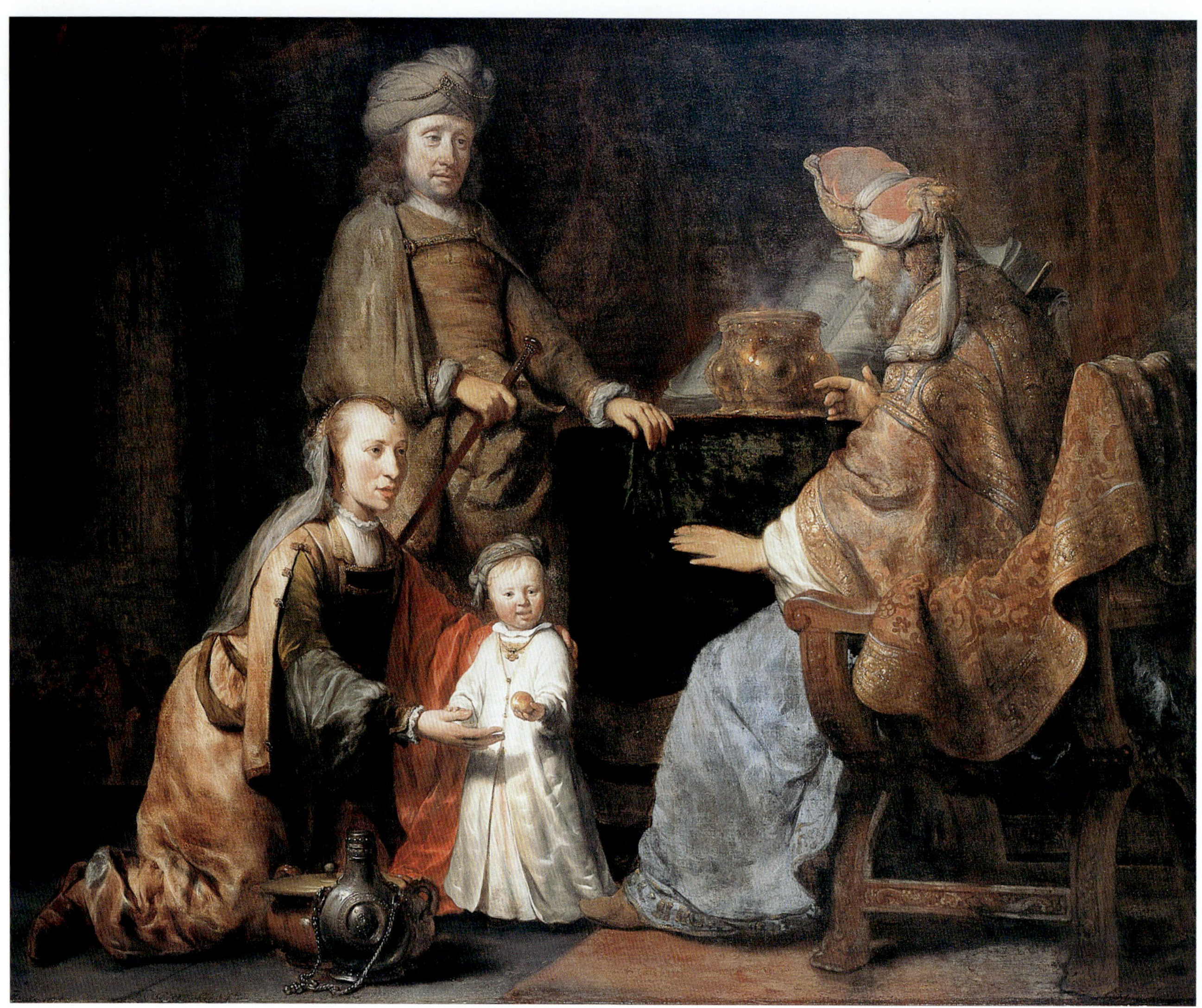

fig. 2 GERBRAND VAN
DEN EECKHOUT
*The Infant Samuel brought by Hannah
to Eli*, early 1660s
Oil on canvas, 110 × 135 cm
Oxford, Ashmolean Museum

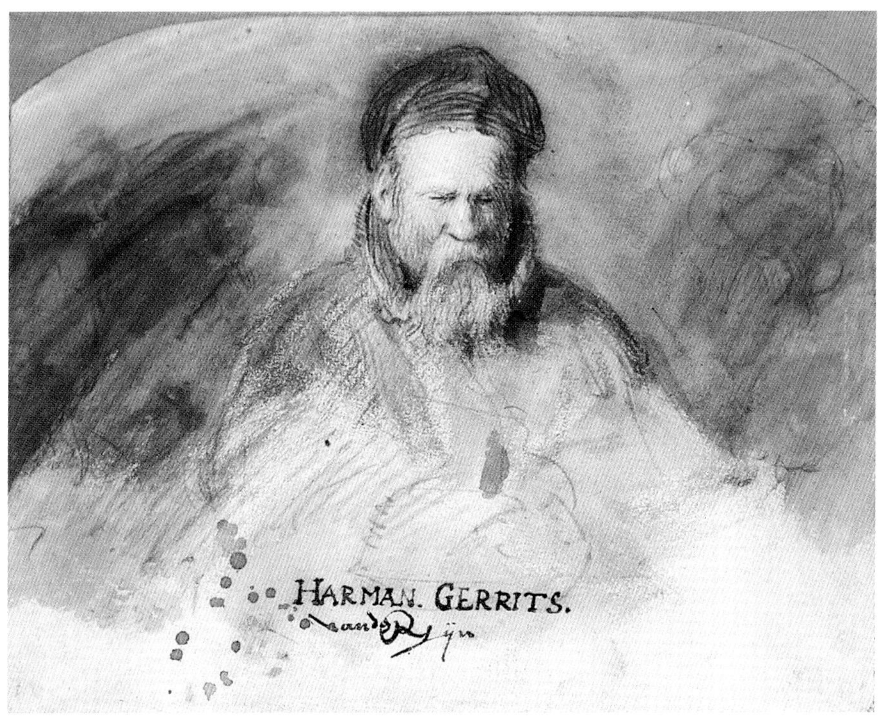



fig. 3 REMBRANDT
*Portrait of the Artist's Father*
Red chalk, strengthened with
black chalk and washed with bistre,
189 × 240 mm
Oxford, Ashmolean Museum

So, while this painting may not cause a stampede of Rembrandt scholars to Oxford, there are major Rembrandt-school paintings which should. The *Ruth and Naomi* by Willem Drost (1633–1659) is one of the key works by this artist whose oeuvre has recently been carefully assessed in a monographic study.[5] Its relationship to a drawing in the Kunsthalle, Bremen, which (to quote my predecessor) "is reasonably but not incontestably attributable to Drost" has made it one of the few secure points in the mapping of his early work. The Museum also owns a major historical work, *The Infant Samuel brought by Hannah to Eli* – a profoundly Baderesque subject – by Gerbrand van den Eeckhout (1621–1674) from the early 1660s (fig. 2) and a *Portrait of a Young Man wearing a Wreath of Vine Leaves* by Jacob Backer (1608–1651).[6]

Our drawings present a challenge for the Rembrandt scholar. There are on the Museum's database no fewer than twenty-six sheets classified as by, attributed to, style of, follower of, Rembrandt. They include some of the greatest of all Rembrandt drawings, such as the study of his father (1568–1630), inscribed *HARMAN. GERRITS. van de Rhijn* in a seventeenth-century hand (fig. 3); the well-known study of the artist's studio; several landscape drawings made by the artist on his walks outside Amsterdam; one of the studies of Saskia sleeping;

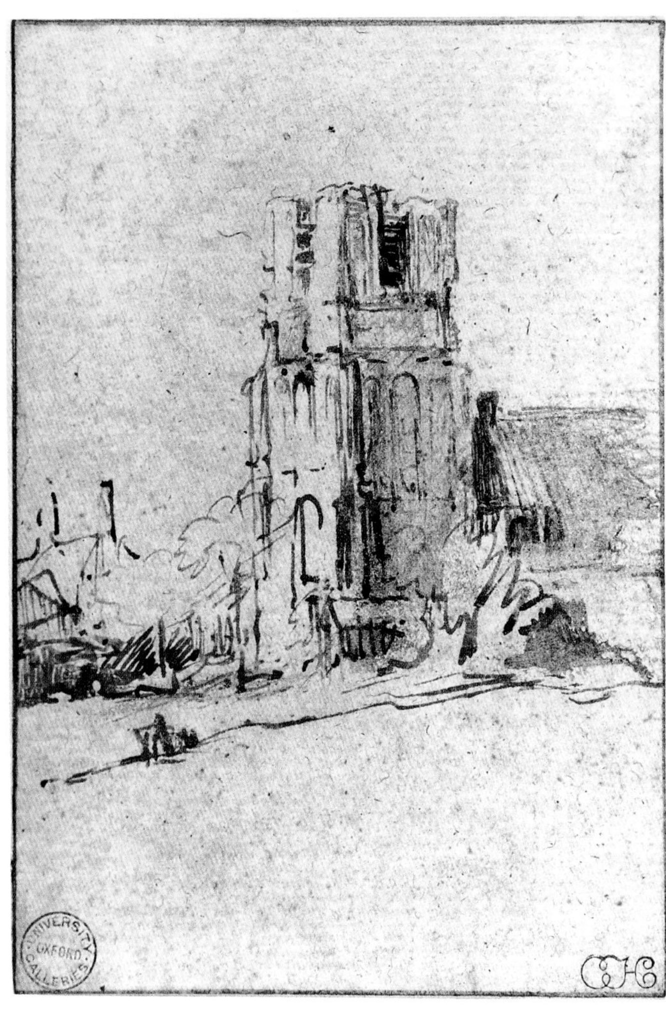

*Jael and Sisera*; *Christ and the Woman of Samaria*; as well as several sheets of head and figure studies.

The Ashmolean Printroom is, of course, best known for its holdings of Italian Renaissance drawings, including the richest of all collections of Raphael drawings and one of the three great collections of Michelangelo drawings as well as sheets by Guercino (1591–1666) and other Bolognese seventeenth-century drawings, eighteenth-century French and nineteenth-century French and British drawings. The Dutch drawings have received far less critical attention and were last catalogued by Sir Karl Parker (himself a specialist in Italian and French drawings) in 1938.[7] Perhaps for this reason the presence of a significant group of Rembrandt and Rembrandt-school drawings in Oxford is less well-known than it should be.



CHRISTOPHER BROWN

Particularly important was the gift of the collector Chambers Hall (1786–
*ca.* 1855) in 1855: he specialized in landscape drawings – and also donated to the
Ashmolean, for example, a Dürer watercolour of the Alps – and gave the
museum no fewer than nine landscape drawings which he believed to be by
Rembrandt. More than half of these have not survived modern critical judgement, but among them are *View of the Church at Ransdorp in Waterland* (fig. 4)
and *View from the Amsteldijk*. The entire group would reward further study and
analysis. Chambers Hall's drawings were catalogued by Parker but the six sheets
acquired subsequently have only been inventorized and not fully catalogued.

However, perhaps the greatest Rembrandt surprise in Oxford is the superb
quality of the etchings, which make it one of the most important of all holdings
of the artist's prints. The states were identified and recorded in Hollstein by
Christopher White,[8] but, as with the drawings, I have the sense when speaking
to colleagues that the significance of the holding is not appreciated. My
colleague, Christian Rümelin, Curator of Prints at the Ashmolean, is currently
preparing a publication on the group which will include the latest scholarship
and watermark analysis, but in the meantime I append a list of rare and
outstanding impressions made by him.

I hope that in this brief note I have done enough to tempt Alfred and Isabel
and many other scholars and enthusiasts for the work of Rembrandt and his
circle to Oxford. Alfred with his wide knowledge and infectious enthusiasm has
been a great inspiration to those of us who have had the privilege to know him
well in recent years and it is with great pleasure that I join the other authors of
this volume in honouring his achievement.

Rembrandt's rare and outstanding impressions (listed according to their numbers in Adam Bartsch, *Catalogue raisonné de toutes les estampes qui forment l'œuvre de Rembrandt, et ceux de ces principaux imitateurs*, Vienna 1797)

B. 11    *The Artist's Son Titus*: printed with surface tone on European paper

B. 13    *Self-Portrait open-mouthed, as if shouting*: bust: first and second state

B. 22    Self-portrait drawing at a window: all five states in the collection (the first especially of interest)

B. 29    *Abraham entertaining the Angels*: impression on Japanese paper (as in London, St Petersburg, Amsterdam, Paris and Vienna)

B. 36    Four illustrations to a Spanish book, a) *The Image seen by Nebuchadnezzar*; b) *Jacob's Ladder*: first state with only the upper part of the ladder visible; c) *David and Goliath*: first state with the broken contour of the hill top right (on Japanese paper?), d) Daniel's vision of four beasts: first state

B. 38    *Joseph's Coat brought to Jacob*: first state

B. 39    *Joseph and Potiphar's Wife*: first state

B. 41    *David in Prayer*: first state

B. 42    *The Blindness of Tobit*: the larger plate: two impressions of first state

B. 47    *The Circumcision in the Stable*: two impressions of the first state (one on loan, the other Chambers Hall), the Chambers Hall impression with surface tone; just for comparison B. 48 small plate as well

B. 49    *The Presentation in the Temple*: first and second state

B. 64    *Christ disputing with the Doctors*: only state, impression on Japanese paper (as London, Cambridge, Berlin)

B. 65    *Christ disputing with the Doctors*: a sketch: first state

B. 66    *Christ disputing with the Doctors*: small plate: first state

B. 67    *Christ preaching*: two impressions, one on Japanese paper (Chambers Hall)

B. 71    *Christ and the Woman of Samaria among Ruins*: both states (Madan Bequest: first state; Chambers Hall: second state, this impression on Japanese paper)

B. 72    *The Raising of Lazarus*: unrecorded state before the burnishing out of the three lines behind Lazarus, plus first state

B. 76    *Christ presented to the people*: first state on Japanese paper

B. 83    *The Descent from the Cross by Torchlight*: on Japanese paper (Chambers Hall)

B. 92    *The Beheading of St John the Baptist*: first state

B. 104    *St Jerome in an Italian Landscape*: first state with an inscription in red chalk (*7 op de plaat*): at present in McAlpine Gallery

B. 110    *The Phoenix* or *The Statue overthrown*: impression on Japanese paper

B. 123    *The Goldsmith*: first state on Japanese paper

B. 125    *The Golf-player*, first state

B. 203    *Jupiter and Antiope*: the larger plate, impression on Japanese paper

B. 223    *Landscape with Trees, Farm Buildings and a Tower*: first state and third state

B. 224    *Landscape with a Hay Barn and a Flock of Sheep*: both states and the drawing related to this print



CHRISTOPHER BROWN

B. 226   *Landscape with a Cottage and a large Tree*: only state and counterproof
(as in Amsterdam, London and Paris)

B. 234   *Bleaching fields near Haarlem*: only state on Japanese paper

B. 235   *Canal with an Angler and two Swans*: both states

B. 237   *Landscape with a Cow*: both states

B. 265   *Old man with a Divided Fur Cap*: first state

B. 266   *Jan Cornelis Sylvius, Preacher*: first state

B. 270   *Faust*: first state

B. 272   *Clement de Jonghe, Printseller*: two impressions of first state

B. 276   *Jan Lutma, Goldsmith*: two impressions of first state, one (Farrer Bequest)
on Japanese paper

B. 277   *Jan Asselyn, Painter*: first and second state

B. 285   *Jan Six*: third state on white paper

B. 320   *Self-portrait in a Cap, open-mouthed*: uneven plate edges (as in London
and Vienna)

B. 321   *Bust of a Man wearing a High Cap, three-quarters right*: the artist's father?:
first state

B. 349   *The Artist's Mother with her Hand on her Chest*: small bust: first state

B. 363   *Sheet of studies: Head of the Artist*, *A Beggar Couple*, *Heads of an Old Man
and an Old Woman etc.*: first state

1   Abraham Bredius, *Rembrandt, The Complete Edition of the Paintings*, revised by Horst Gerson, London and New York 1969, p. 124, no. 138a.

2   For the most recent discussion of the painting see Christopher White, *Dutch, Flemish and German Paintings before 1900*, Ashmolean Museum Oxford, Catalogue of the Collection of Paintings, Oxford 1999, pp. 102–04, ill., inv. no. A804. The other two versions are in the Museum of Fine Arts, Houston, and in a French private collection.

3   F.W.H. Hollstein, *Dutch and Flemish Etchings, Engravings and Woodcuts, ca. 1450–1700*, 57 vols., Amsterdam 1949–2001, XIV (1956), p. 183, no. 9, ill., as by Joannes van Noort IV.

4   Josua Bruyn, Bob Haak, Simon H. Levie, Pieter J.J. van Thiel, Ernst van de Wetering, *A Corpus of Rembrandt Paintings*, vols. I-, Foundation Rembrandt Research Project, The Hague, Dordrecht, Boston and London 1982–, I, pp. 619–22, no. C 31.

5   For the painting see White, *op. cit.* (note 2), pp. 33–35, inv. no. 390. The recent study of Drost is Jonathan Bikker, 'Willem Drost (1633–1658): A Rembrandt pupil in Amsterdam, Rome and Venice', Ph.D. thesis, Universiteit Utrecht, 2001 (to be published by Yale University Press in 2004). The picture is discussed under no. 1, pp. 63–66. The author has more recently amended the death date to 1659. For the documents see pp. 6, 49 and 60. See also Jonathan Bikker, 'Drost's end and Loth's beginnings', *The Burlington Magazine*, CXLIV, no. 1188, March 2002, pp. 147–56.

6   White, *op. cit.* (note 2), pp. 48–50, inv. no. A 714 (Van den Eeckhout); pp. 8–10, inv. no. A 668 (Backer).

7   Karl T. Parker, *Catalogue of the Collection of Drawings in the Ashmolean Museum*, 2 vols., Oxford 1938, I, Netherlandish, German, French and Spanish Schools.

8   See Hollstein, *op. cit.* (note 3), XVIII and XIX (1969), Rembrandt, compiled by Christopher White and Karel G. Boon.

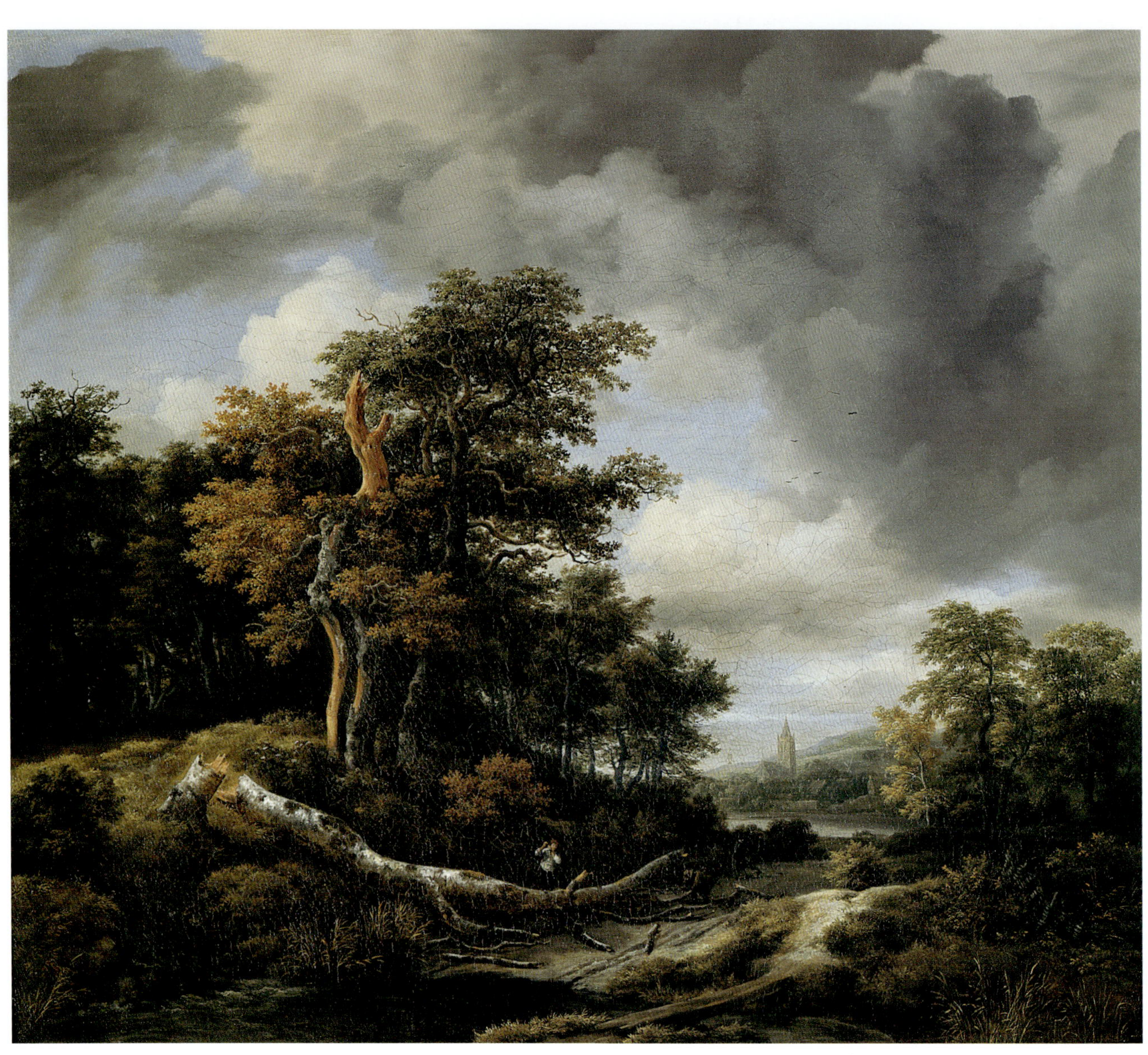

# Reflections on Three Landscapes
# by Jacob van Ruisdael

GEORGE S. KEYES

Amid their remarkable collection of Dutch religious paintings Alfred and Isabel Bader possess two lovely landscapes by Jacob van Ruisdael (1628/9–1682). This artist's sensitivity to nature projects a profundity consonant with the religious pathos conveyed by so many Dutch history painters in their representation of biblical subjects. Therefore, it seems fitting to focus on Ruisdael as the subject of my essay in honour of Alfred Bader.

By complete chance, since my return to North America in 1984 on three separate occasions I became intimately involved with three Ruisdael paintings which engaged my attention as a museum curator. The first, *A Wooded Landscape* (fig. 2) from the mid 1660s, is a masterpiece that I had hoped to acquire for the Minneapolis Institute of Arts.[1] Frustratingly, the museum was unable to raise sufficient funds and the picture was lost to us. Its present location is unknown. As a consolation the Minneapolis Institute of Arts was subsequently, in 1988, able to purchase Ruisdael's *Castle by a Torrent and a Water Mill in a Mountainous Landscape* (fig. 6).[2] This well-preserved, upright landscape is an unusual variation on one of Ruisdael's most celebrated themes – his Scandinavian-inspired waterfall subjects. In the end the Minneapolis Institute of Arts did secure a fine example of Ruisdael's art and a subject singularly befitting this part of the United States with its early influx of Swedish immigrants.

As part of my responsibilities upon assuming my position as Curator of European paintings at the Detroit Institute of Arts, I undertook my share of the project to produce a scholarly catalogue of the seventeenth-century Dutch paintings in the museum's collection. Among the most important of those assigned to me is the remarkable group of pictures by or associated with Jacob van Ruisdael. Chief among these is the celebrated Detroit version of *The Jewish Cemetery*. However, the Ruisdael painting that particularly captivated me is *A Pool in a Wooded Landscape* (fig. 4),[3] the third of my triad. This tranquil and rather discreet picture tends to be overlooked, particularly when pitted against the thrilling theatricality of the vastly larger *Jewish Cemetery* in the same gallery.

fig. 1 JACOB VAN RUISDAEL,
*Entrance to a Wood*
Oil on canvas, 57 × 65 cm
Paris, Musée du Louvre,
Bequest of Léon Moreaux

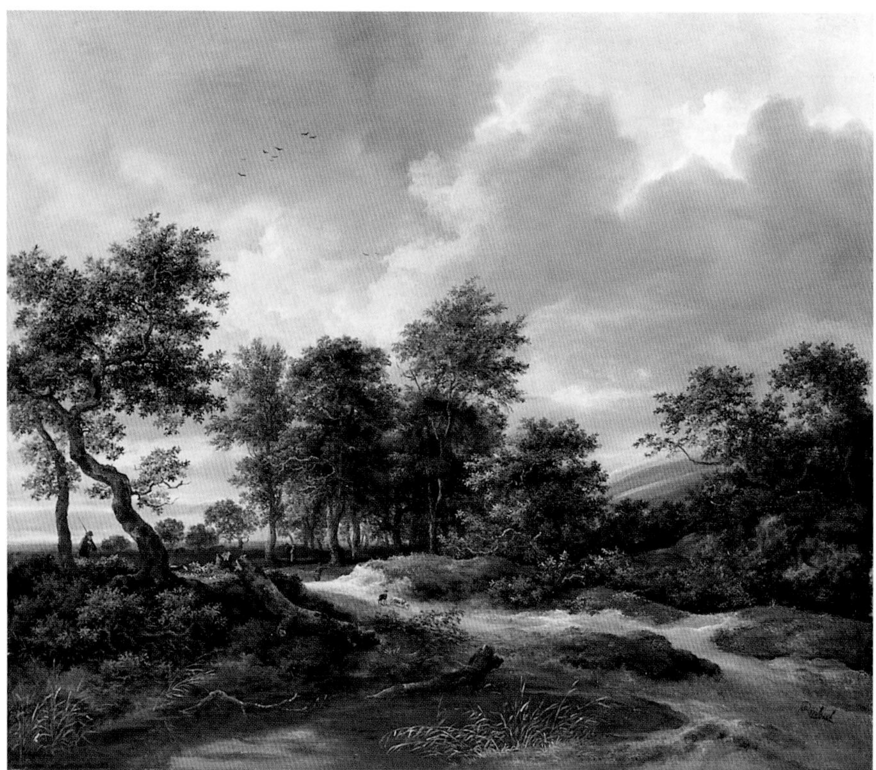



fig. 2 JACOB VAN RUISDAEL
*A Wooded Landscape*
Oil on canvas, 53.3 × 59.6 cm
Present whereabouts unknown

In considering these three pictures I sensed a thread that connected them and recognized that all raised the wider issue of Ruisdael's chronology, particularly involving works which postdate the 1650s. This has led me to address two related questions. The first is the complex issue of dating Ruisdael's paintings during the latter half of his career. The second concerns a category of landscape subject-matter in which Ruisdael represents nature in its tranquillity. The artist evokes a serenity that is rare in his work yet which is appealing and notable. Those paintings which project this mood constitute a hitherto somewhat overlooked and underestimated aspect of his art. Central to this group is the *Pool in a Wooded Landscape* in Detroit (fig. 4).

During the 1660s Ruisdael evolved a more refined painting style that superseded the vigorous and heroic character of his landscapes of the 1650s, exemplified by his two versions of the *Jewish Cemetery*, in Detroit and Dresden, and his *View of Bentheim Castle*, now in Dublin (see fig. 3, p. 180, in this volume).[4]

The *Wooded Landscape* (fig. 2) that initiated my inquiry is notable for its stately format. It is a complex composition predicated on the harmonious intersection of diagonals. A sandy path moves from the right foreground into the left distance. In contrast, the general slope of the land leads from the left foreground to fields rising beyond trees at the right. A grove of trees in the centre mid-distance



GEORGE S. KEYES

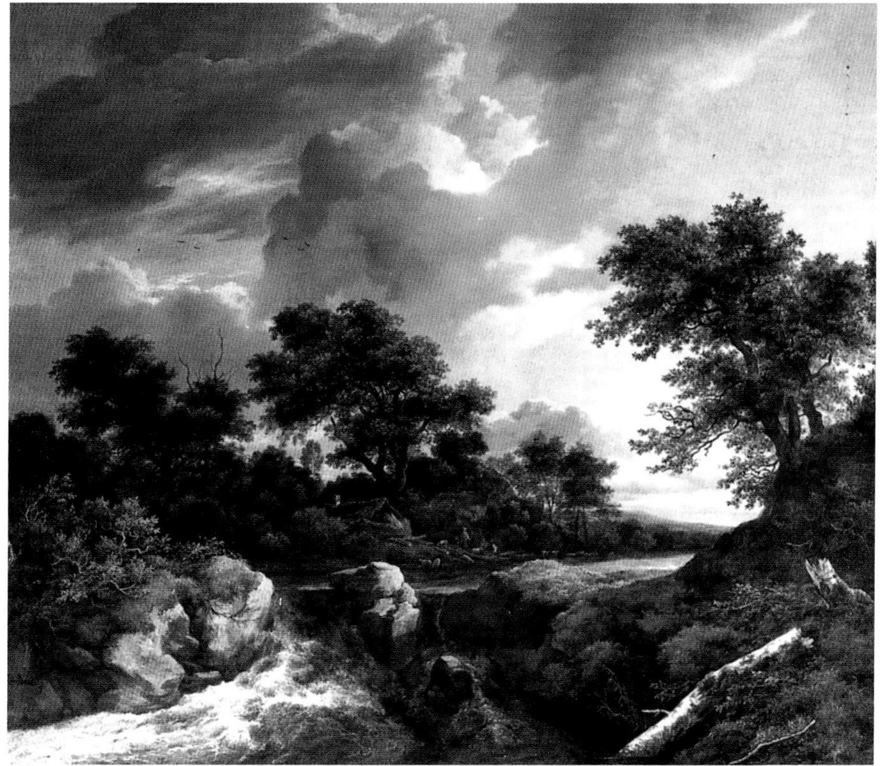



serves to lock these diagonals into place almost functioning as a kind of hub. Ruisdael represents the trees with great refinement. Although diminutive in scale these trees are individually characterized and subtly differentiated. The superb and harmonic sense of balance is further reinforced by the refined pattern of clouds. Ruisdael modulates the shifting grey coloration of the clouds with great subtlety. They become a dynamic visual counterpoint to the wooded landscape below.

This refined contrapuntal balance – a kind of harmonic equipoise – finds close parallels in related works, four of which seem particularly close in style and spirit. *A Waterfall in a Wooded Landscape* in the Residenzgalerie in Salzburg (fig. 3) contains similarly scaled trees under a canopy of beautifully modulated clouds.[5] These clouds form a bold diagonal accent, which becomes an effective visual counterpart to the tranquil vista formed by the stream that leads to low lying hills in the right distance.

The second analogous picture is *Entrance to a Wood* in the Musée du Louvre in Paris (fig. 1).[6] Here the clouds seem to broil up into the right foreground. They become a splendid, dramatic foil to the stately trees below on either side of a sandy path. These trees, like those in *A Wooded Landscape* (fig. 2) are refined in their characterization and diminutive scale. These same qualities are found in

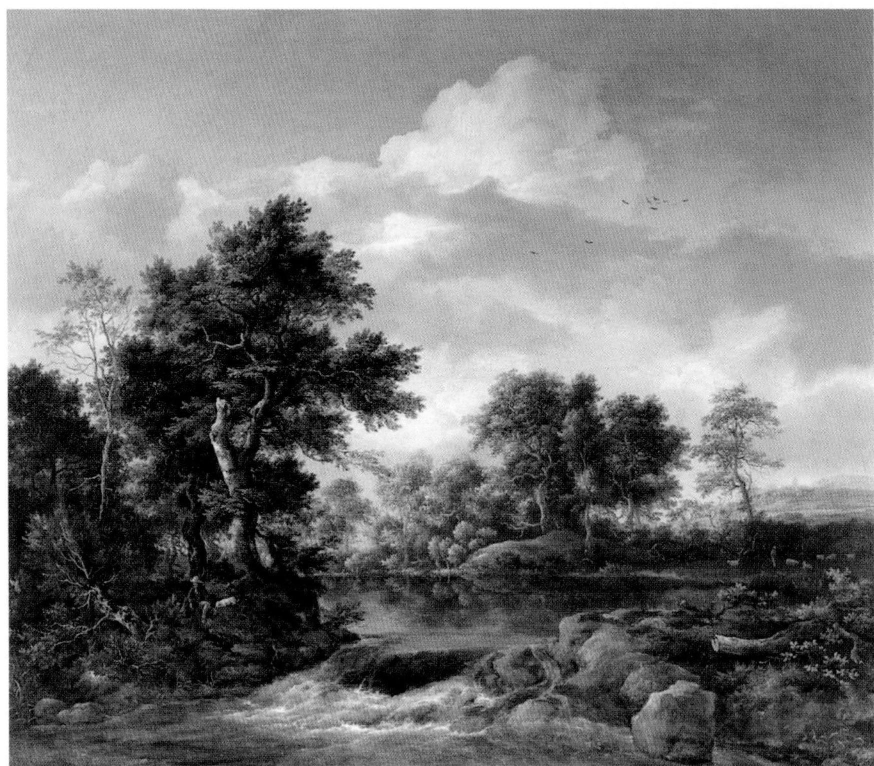



Ruisdael's *Wooded Landscape with a Stream*, now in the Staatsgalerie in Stuttgart.[7] The trees in this picture offer particularly close parallels in their refined characterization and in the way their trunks are silhouetted against distant sky along the horizon. Ultimately the syntax of these pictures evolved from Ruisdael's earlier paintings of the 1650s. Of these his *Landscape near the Ruins of the Old Church in Muiderberg* in the Ashmolean Museum in Oxford is a remarkable premonition of what would follow.[8] The trees comprising the grove are boldly characterized yet diminutive. Ruisdael silhouettes their trunks against the glowing light. The dynamic energy of the clouds echoed in the contrast between patches of light and shadow playing across the landscape is much more powerful and declarative in comparison to Ruisdael's more refined landscapes of the 1660s.

The fourth related picture is *A Ford in a Wood* in the Krannert Art Museum in Urbana.[9] As in the *Wooded Landscape* (fig. 2) the trees in this painting are diminutive yet fully characterized. At the right trees appear silhouetted against a low, open vista in a manner analogous to the left-hand section of the *Wooded Landscape*. Ruisdael's delineation of space is complex in *A Ford in a Wood*, with sandy tracks moving in many directions beyond the ford.

*Pool in a Wooded Landscape* in the Detroit Institute of Arts (fig. 4) is remarkable for its pervading sense of calm and serenity. The waterfall is gentle in



GEORGE S. KEYES

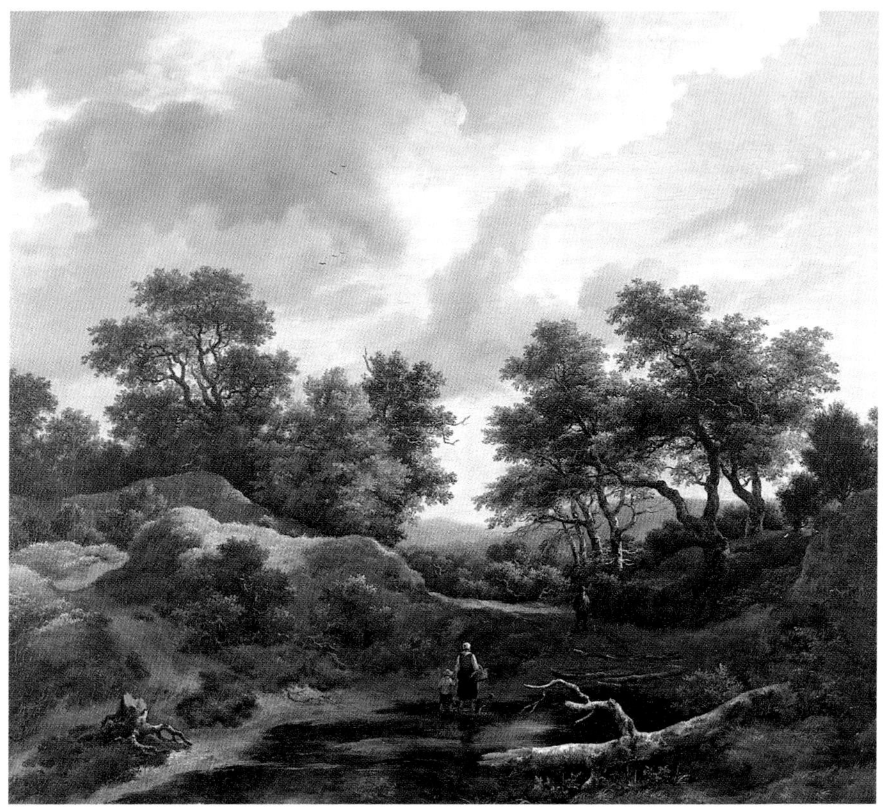



comparison to Ruisdael's more celebrated 'Scandinavian' counterparts. The modest display of white water offers a subtle visual contrast to the unruffled surface of the pool beyond, which reflects the distant trees. Ruisdael's cloud configuration in this picture is also unusual. At the upper centre a cumulus cloud rises above a thin horizontal band of darker clouds that extend across virtually the entire sky. Yet above the clouds blue sky fills the entire upper section of the canvas.[10] The trees in the Detroit painting are diminutive and relatively squat, yet refined in characterization. The dominating tree to the immediate left of the waterfall is thick-trunked. This marks a genuine shift from Ruisdael's works of the earlier 1660s such as the *Wooded Landscape* (fig. 2), and represents an important component of Ruisdael's oeuvre from later in the decade.

In mood and style the *Waterfall in a Wooded landscape* in Salzburg (fig. 3) is analogous to *Pool in a Wooded Landscape* in Detroit (fig. 4). Both contain an expanse of tranquil water beyond the foreground waterfall. The clouds in the Salzburg painting, although more dramatic in effect, are relatively thin and are set off by substantial expanses of blue sky. This painting, in turn, relates closely to Ruisdael's *Wooded and Hilly Country* in the Cleveland Museum of Art (fig. 5).[11] This landscape, evoking the approach of early evening, is remarkably serene in mood. The deepening yet transparent shadows underscore the complex delineation of space setting off a path that leads to a distant hilly vista. The diminutively scaled trees are relatively squat and thick-trunked. Ruisdael silhouettes the trunks of the right-hand trees whereas those to the left of the path in the centre form an impenetrable mass. The clouds provide a powerful diagonal accent yet are counterbalanced by much blue sky. Although the Cleveland painting ultimately relates in style more closely to the *Wooded Landscape* (fig. 2), in its serene mood it adumbrates *A Pool in a Wooded Landscape* in Detroit (fig. 4) even though it precedes it in date by about five years.

*A Wooded Landscape with a Pond*, of which the current location is unknown,[12] contains squat, thick-trunked trees that are similar in character to those in the Detroit *Pool in a Wooded Landscape* (fig. 4). A solitary angler stands before still, reflecting water. The pervading calm of this scene is enhanced by the unruffled water that extends all the way from the distant hills into the entire foreground. Ruisdael produced several landscapes, apart from his celebrated images of swamps, that contain expanses of still water but lack waterfalls of any sort. Typifying these is a *Wooded Landscape with a River and Anglers* in the collection of Edinburgh University.[13] Here Ruisdael depicts a tranquil woodland scene closer to midday. The water gleams in strong sunlight and lacks the deepening shadows so evident in the *Wooded Landscape with a Pond* of unknown location.[14]

*Oaks near a Low Waterfall* in the Alte Pinakothek in Munich,[15] although more majestic and heroic in character, contains squat, thick-trunked trees that are analogous to those in *A Pool in a Wooded Landscape* in Detroit (fig. 4). Much of the landscape rests in shadow, which adds a somewhat brooding and dramatic accent to the subject. Yet, like the painting in Detroit, this large canvas in Munich contains rushing water, figures seated on the ground and a shepherd tending his flock of sheep before a distant vista containing a spire and a wind-mill. This picture would appear to be close in date to that in Detroit, from the late 1660s.

Ruisdael produced a group of large-scale, oblong landscapes which contain waterfalls in open, hilly country. At least three of these contain expanses of still water above the waterfalls. In style and mood these pictures relate closely to the tranquil landscapes of the 1660s and probably date from the same period. In terms of lighting and the energized counterpoint between land and cloudy sky these pictures relate most closely to the *Wooded and Hilly Landscape* in Cleveland (fig. 5) and *Waterfall in a Wooded Landscape* in Salzburg (fig. 3). In particular the paintings in the Wallace Collection in London[16] and in the Philadelphia Museum of Art,[17] with lengthening shadows across the water, suggest a moment late in the day similar in effect to the picture in Cleveland. The same might be said for the picture in Indianapolis,[18] even though the light is much colder.[19] All contain

fig. 6 JACOB VAN RUISDAEL
*Castle by a Torrent and a Water Mill in a Mountainous Landscape*
Oil on canvas, 68.6 × 57.2 cm
Minneapolis, Minneapolis Institute of Arts, The John R. Van Derlip Fund and Gift of Margaret Weyerhaeuser Harmon, by exchange, inv. no. 88.43



GEORGE S. KEYES

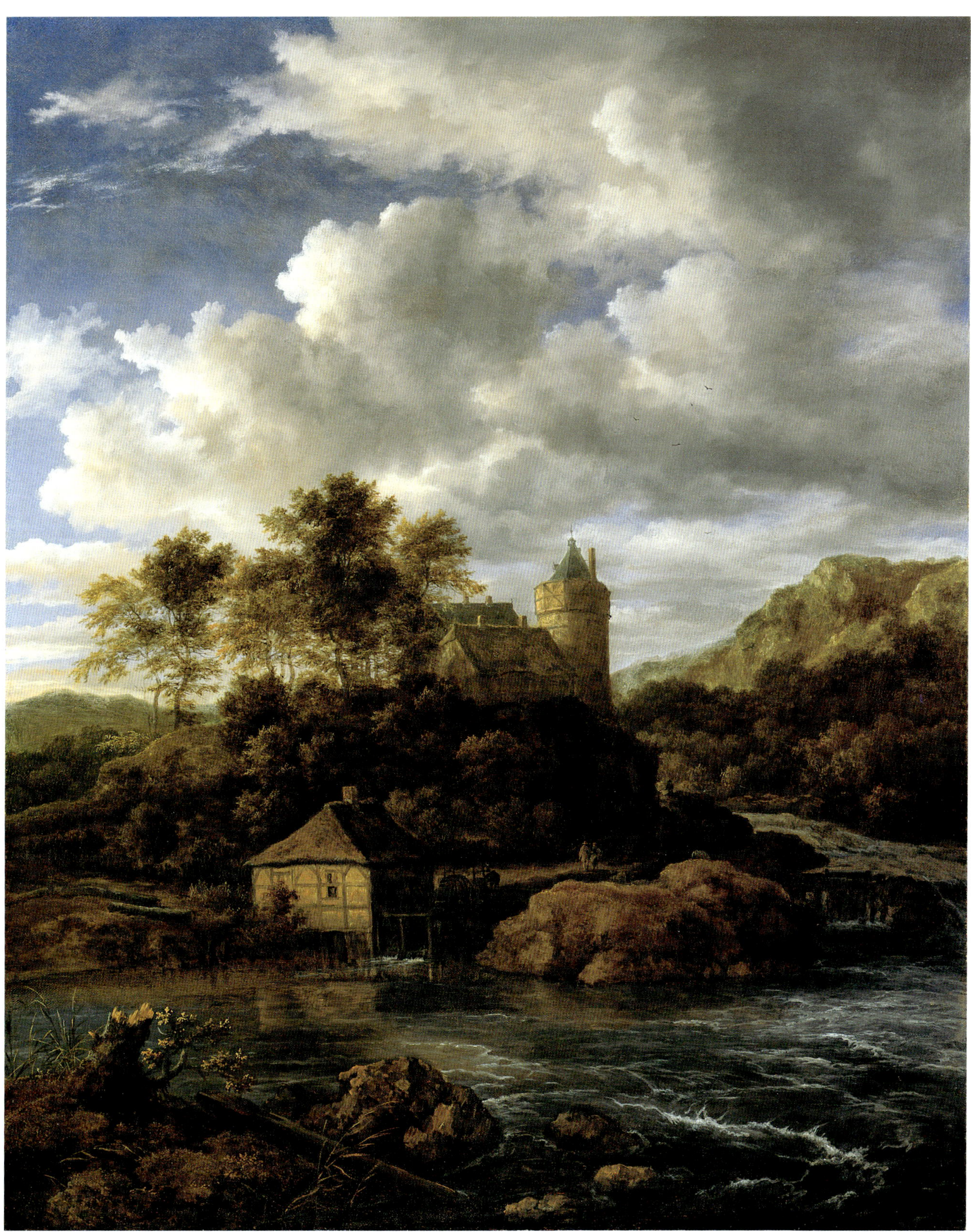

clouds that are beautifully modulated. Shifting values of gray contrast with the highlights caught in the fading sunlight. In patterning and coloration these clouds recall those in *Wooded and Hilly Country* in Cleveland (fig. 5) and the *Waterfall in a Wooded Landscape* in Salzburg (fig. 3).[20]

The last painting in my triad, *Castle by a Torrent and a Water Mill in a Mountainous Landscape* in Minneapolis (fig. 6)[21] clearly belongs to the last great phase of Ruisdael's activity – the first half of the 1670s. Several features distinguish this painting: its pronounced upright format, the unusual representation of rapidly flowing but still reflecting water, and the muted late afternoon light with its concomitant cool deep shadows. The clouds are also noteworthy because their contours no longer consist of relatively broadly curving edges. Instead, each is defined by a much more complex pattern of small curving contours interspersed with more ragged edges as clouds seem to dissipate into the surrounding blue sky. This concept clearly supersedes that found in Ruisdael's group of serene works from the 1660s such as *Wooded and Hilly Country* in Cleveland (fig. 5). On a majestic scale this highly complex patterning and layering of clouds finds its most grandiose expression in Ruisdael's celebrated marine painting at the Museum of Fine Arts in Boston, *Vessels in a Choppy Sea*.[22]

During the 1670s Ruisdael produced a large number of landscapes in an upright format. These tend to be of a standard size measuring roughly between 68 and 71 cm in height and 52 to 55 cm in width.[23] Certain of these pictures, such as *Waterfall with a Wooded Hill* in Berlin,[24] *Waterfall in Hilly Country* in the Mrs Amir Pakzad Collection in Hanover,[25] *Low Waterfall in a Wooded Landscape* formerly in Stockholm,[26] and *Pond at the Edge of a Wood* in the Niedersächsische Landesgalerie in Hanover[27] all contain cloudy skies that are analogous to that in the Minneapolis picture. All are notable for the refined patterning of the clouds with their diminutively shaped, irregular curving contours.

Other paintings in this group feature exotic buildings in the mid-distance similar to the castle in the Minneapolis landscape (fig. 6). Three examples seem particularly germane – *Waterfall before a Castle* in the Dayton Art Institute,[28] *Landscape with a Castle and a Waterfall* in a German private collection,[29] and *Waterfall in a Landscape with Two Churches* in a private collection.[30] The clouds and the trees silhouetted against the horizon in the last-cited of these three pictures are strikingly close in treatment to the corresponding features of *Castle by a Torrent and a Water Mill in a Mountainous Landscape* in Minneapolis (fig. 6).

In format and in their particular interest in representing landscapes below a dramatic cloud canopy these pictures invite comparison with Ruisdael's contemporary panoramic views of Haarlem. The celebrated examples in Amsterdam[31] and Zurich[32] contain clouds characterized almost identically to those in *Castle by a Torrent and a Water Mill in a Mountainous Landscape* in



GEORGE S. KEYES

Minneapolis (fig. 6), although the artist devotes considerably more of the over-all composition to the exhilarating expanse of clouds floating above the flat panorama below. These clouds filter the sunlight, generating patches of land in strong light versus other areas left in shadow. This similar characterization of clouds confirms a dating of these two views of Haarlem (or *Haarlempjes*) to the earlier 1670s, very much in keeping with the larger series of upright subjects typified by the picture in Minneapolis.

John Walford places the celebrated *Panoramic View of Haarlem* in the the Mauritshuis in The Hague slightly earlier than the examples in Amsterdam and Zurich – to the 1660s.[33] In its stately, somewhat square format this picture shares much with many of the serene landscapes from the 1660s, not least of which are *Wooded and Hilly Country* in Cleveland (fig. 5), the *Waterfall in a Wooded Landscape* in Salzburg (fig. 3) or *The Entrance to a Wood* in Paris (fig. 1). Such comparisons may indeed argue in favour of a slightly earlier dating of the *Panoramic View of Haarlem* in the Mauritshuis relative to the two in Amsterdam and Zurich.

Ruisdael's concept of landscape during the 1660s became more refined. If these works lack the sheer vitality and robustness of his landscapes from the 1650s, one detects a wider range of moods which the artist explores. Although the number of landscapes one could classify as serene is restricted in number, their importance should still not remain underestimated. This aspect of Ruisdael's creativity led to a striving for progressively greater refinement both in characterization and sentiment that would find its most perfect realisation in his later panoramic views of Haarlem and the numerous upright waterfall subjects that preoccupied the artist during the earlier 1670s.

1 Seymour Slive, *Jacob van Ruisdael. A Complete Catalogue of His Paintings, Drawings and Etchings*, New Haven and London 2001, p. 329, no. 443 (as early 1660s).

2 *Ibid.*, p. 392, no. 543 (as late 1660s or early 1670s); George S. Keyes, 'Hobbema's *Wooded Landscape with a Water Mill*', *Bulletin of the Minneapolis Institute of Arts*, vol. 67, 1995, pp. 42–57, esp. p. 53, fig. 15.

3 Slive *op. cit.* (note 1), p. 185, no. 179. This painting, in turn, has been closely associated with a similarly sized canvas, *A Low Waterfall in a Wooded Landscape* (*ibid.*, p. 237, no. 282). Like the picture in Detroit, this painting was also once in the collection of Sir John Foley Grey. Both were dispersed in the same sale – Christie's, London, 15 June 1928, lots 95 and 96 respectively. This *Low Waterfall in a Wooded Landscape* recently appeared at auction in New York – sale Christie's, New York, 24 January 2003, lot 20, repr.

4 Slive, *op. cit.* (note 1), pp. 179–85, no. 178 (Detroit); pp. 186–88, no. 180 (Dresden); pp. 31–32, no. 15 (Dublin).

5 *Ibid.*, p. 233, no. 274 (as early 1670s).

6 *Ibid.*, p. 303, no. 399 (as early 1660s).

7 *Ibid.*, p. 320, no. 427 (as early 1660s); E. John Walford, *Jacob van Ruisdael and the Perception of Landscape*, New Haven and London 1991, p. 117, fig. 117 (as late 1650s).

8 Slive, *op. cit.* (note 1), pp. 102–03, no. 77 (as later 1650s); Walford, *op. cit.* (note 7), p. 91, fig. 83 (as *ca.* 1652–53).

9 Slive, *op. cit.* (note 1), p. 323, no. 432 (as early 1660s).

10 This emphasis on so much uninterrupted blue sky that appears above clouds finds close parallels with the earlier marine paintings of Willem van de Velde the Younger (1633–1707) from the early to mid 1660s.

11 Slive, *op. cit.* (note 1), pp. 340–41, no. 463 (as *ca.* 1660–65); Walford, *op. cit.* (note 7), p. 173, fig. 175 (as earlier 1670s). Wolfgang Stechow, 'Ruisdael in the Cleveland Museum', *Bulletin of the Cleveland Museum of Art*, vol. 55, no. 8, 1968, p. 252, dates this picture to about 1663–65 and characterizes the painting as a "characteristic example of the most intimate trend in which silence becomes eloquent".

12 Slive, *op. cit.* (note 1), p. 321, no. 429 (as about 1665).

13 *Ibid.*, pp. 271–72, no. 341 (as mid 1660s).

14 A number of analogous subjects by Ruisdael indicate that his representations of still water in wooded settings comprise a substantial corpus. These include *A Wooded Landscape with a Broad Stream* in the Gemäldegalerie, Berlin, see Slive, *op. cit.* (note 1), p. 257, no. 316 (as first half 1660s); *Edge of a Wood with a flooded Path*, *ibid.*, p. 257, no. 317 (as late 1650s); *Woods near a Pool with two Swans* in the Städelsches Kunstinstitut in Frankfurt-am-Main, *ibid.*, p. 274, no. 346 (early to mid 1660s); *Wooded Landscape with a River*, *ibid.*, p. 298, no. 391 (early 1660s); *River Landscape with a Quarry*, Collection of Alfred and Isabel Bader, Milwaukee, *ibid.*, p. 371, no. 506 (as about 1660 or a little later); and *Ruins of a Castle on a Hill*, *ibid.*, p. 389, no. 536 (1660s). Although these vary considerably in mood, the majority convey a pervading tranquillity that relates to that projected in the pictures in Cleveland and Detroit.

15 Slive, *op. cit.* (note 1), p. 215, no. 236 (as *ca.* 1670); Walford, *op. cit.* (note 7), p. 116, fig. 116 (as late 1650s).

16 Slive, *op. cit.* (note 1), pp. 207–08, no. 218 (late 1660s or early 1670s).

17 *Ibid.*, p. 225, no. 259 (late 1660s or early 1670s).

18 Indianapolis Museum of Art, see Slive, *op. cit.* (note 1), pp. 201–02, no. 205 (early 1670s).

19 A fourth painting in a Scottish private collection, – *ibid.*, pp. 234–35, no. 278 (late 1660s or early 1670s) – is similar to that in Indianapolis in mood and coloration but its torrential waterfall and the boulders flanking it dominate the subject.

20 Another picture displaying these qualities is the *Waterfall with a Low, Wooded Hill* in the Uffizi Gallery in Florence, Slive, *op. cit.* (note 1), p. 192, no. 188 (as 1670s). I believe that this painting comes late in this sequence and could well date from about 1670.

21 *Ibid.*, p. 392, no. 543 (late 1670s or early 1670s); Keyes, *op. cit.* (note 2).



GEORGE S. KEYES

22  Museum of Fine Arts, see Slive *op. cit.*
    (note 1), pp. 451–52, no. 640 (*ca.* 1670);
    Walford, *op. cit.* (note 7), pp. 154–55
    (1660s).

23  Slive, *op. cit.* (note 1), nos. 10, 150, 158,
    163, 165, 170, 175, 176, 177, 193, 197, 203,
    229, 233, 239, 246, 251, 260, 262, 265,
    266, 269, 271, 281, 286, 298, 302, 303,
    304, 305, 323, 360, 419 and 559 (all
    reproduced and datable to the 1670s).

24  *Ibid.*, pp. 162–63 (1670s); Walford, *op. cit.*
    (note 7), pp. 175–76, fig. 178.

25  Slive, *op. cit.* (note 1), pp. 200–01,
    no. 203 (1670s).

26  *Ibid.*, pp. 236–37, no. 281 (1670s).

27  *Ibid.*, p. 280, no. 360 (1670s).

28  *Ibid.*, p. 178, no. 177 (1670s).

29  *Ibid.*, pp. 195–96, no. 193 (1670s).

30  *Ibid.*, p. 247, no. 302 (1670s).

31  Rijksmuseum, see *ibid.*, pp. 62–63, no. 35
    (early 1670s).

32  Kunsthaus, Stiftung Prof. Dr. L. Ruzicka,
    see *ibid.*, pp. 93–95, no. 70 (as
    *ca.* 1670–75); Walford, *op. cit.* (note 7),
    pp. 153–54, fig. 159 (as late 1660s).

33  Walford, *op. cit.* (note 7), pp. 128–29,
    fig. 134; Slive, *op. cit.* (note 1), pp. 68–69,
    no. 40 (early 1670s).

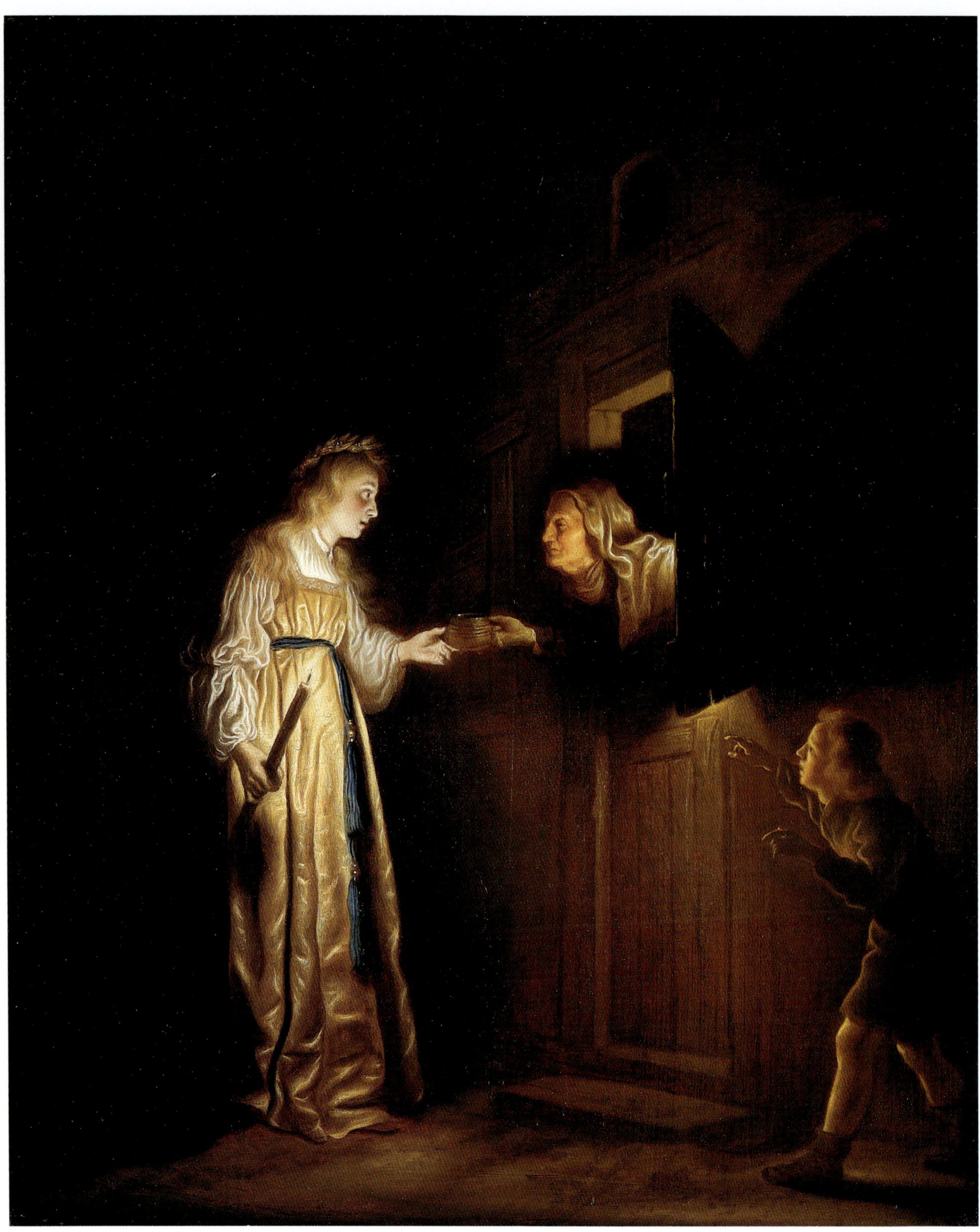

# Adam Elsheimer – Bemerkungen zur Rezeption seiner Kunst im Norden

RÜDIGER KLESSMANN

Adam Elsheimer (1578–1610), der das kleine Format liebte, war ein Meister der Erzählung. Peter Paul Rubens (1577–1640) und Rembrandt (1606–1669), aber auch viele andere Künstler, haben ihn wegen dieser Fähigkeit bewundert, sie mögen ihn auch als einen Nachfolger der großen Meister der Dürerzeit gesehen haben. Carel van Mander (1548–1606) in seinem *Schilderboek* von 1604 lobt ihn als einen Figurenmaler, der wenig zeichnete, aber die Bilder der italienischen Meister genau studierte. Joachim von Sandrart (1606–1688) hat mit Recht in seiner *Teutsche Academie der edlen Bau-, Bild- und Mahlerey-Künste* (1675) das neue Verständnis für die Natur und die genaue Wiedergabe der Landschaft betont, Giovanni Baglione (*ca.* 1566–1643) hat in seinen *Vite de' Pittori . . .* von 1642 mehr noch die wunderbare Harmonie hervorgehoben ("*mirabile armonia*"), in welcher Elsheimers Figuren mit der naturgetreuen Landschaft verbunden sind. Elsheimers Leben, das er zum größten Teil in Rom verbrachte, war nur kurz. Da auch – wie seine Freunde wußten – eine Melancholie seine Schaffenskraft begrenzte, ist das Lebenswerk Elsheimers klein geblieben. Trotzdem war seine Wirkung auf die Malerei in Italien und mehr noch in den Niederlanden beträchtlich. Der Umstand, daß schon früh zahlreiche Kopien seiner Bilder angefertigt wurden, die – abgesehen von Kupferstichen – zur Verbreitung seiner Kunst beigetragen haben, macht es nicht leicht, die Spuren der Originalwerke zu verfolgen. Auf welchen Wegen sind Elsheimers Schöpfungen bekannt geworden?

Zunächst war es wohl Elsheimers Erfindung der Figuren und die von ihnen ausgehende poetische Stimmung, welche die Aufmerksamkeit der Zeitgenossen erregte. Zu der Zeit seiner Niederlassung in Rom, die spätestens für den Monat April 1600 gesichert ist, könnte sein *Hl. Christophorus* entstanden sein, eine Annahme, die nur durch stilistische Vergleiche gestützt wird.[1] Das kleine, in St. Petersburg (Eremitage) bewahrte Gemälde verrät noch die altdeutsche Schulung des Künstlers in Frankfurt, die Kenntnis graphischer Werke von

Abb. 1 SALOMON KONINCK
*Die Verspottung der Ceres*, 1645
Öl auf Holz, 66 × 55.5 cm
Milwaukee, Wisconsin, Sammlung
Drs Alfred und Isabel Bader

Albrecht Dürer (1471–1528) und Albrecht Altdorfer (*ca.* 1480–1538), gleichzeitig aber auch seine in Venedig empfangenen Eindrücke von den Bildern und der Malweise Tizians (*ca.* 1490–1576) und Jacopo Tintorettos (1519–1594), die er bei seinem Aufenthalt dort kennengelernt hatte. Das monumentale Christophorus-Fresko Tizians im Dogenpalast wird ihm in Erinnerung geblieben sein. Es gelang ihm ein Werk zu schaffen, von dem trotz seines kleinen Formats eine starke Wirkung und eine typenprägende Kraft für die Gestalt des Heiligen ausging. Es gehörte offenbar zu den ersten Bildern, die den jungen, damals 22-jährigen Deutschen in Rom bekannt gemacht haben.

Der gleichaltrige Orazio Borgianni (1577/78–1616), der um 1605 aus Spanien nach Rom zurückkehrte, hat verwandte Christophorus-Bilder gemalt, welche die Kenntnis von Elsheimers Vorbild voraussetzen. Hier ist vor allem das um 1610/15 geschaffene Gemälde Borgiannis in Edinburgh zu nennen, in welchem der schwere Weg des Heiligen eine fast dramatische Steigerung erfährt.[2] Auch Rubens hat während seiner römischen Aufenthalte die Komposition Elsheimers kennengelernt und verwendete danach angefertigte Zeichnungen[3] für die monumentale Gestalt des Heiligen auf den Außenflügeln seines Kreuzabnahme-Altars in der Antwerpener Kathedrale (um 1613). Rubens assoziiert mit seiner Figur bewußt die antike Skulptur des Herkules Farnese, ist aber dennoch von Elsheimers Gemälde ausgegangen. Seine in München bewahrte Ölskizze für den Altar läßt erkennen, daß Rubens Korrekturen an der Haltung des Heiligen vornahm. Wie Röntgenaufnahmen zeigen, folgte er zunächst in dem Festhalten des Kindes am Kopf des Heiligen der Erfindung Elsheimers bevor er den heutigen Zustand mit dem Motiv des erhobenen Gewandes festlegte.[4] Rubens's gezeichnete Studien auf dem Blatt in London, das nach Held erst um 1611–13 entstanden ist, bestätigen diesen Ausgangspunkt auf seinem Wege zur endgültigen Gestalt des Christophorus. Held vermutet, daß Rubens vielleicht noch frühere, aus seiner römischen Zeit stammende Studien von Elsheimers Gemälde ausgewertet hat, die heute verloren sind.

Es ist ungewiß, wie lange Elsheimers *Christophorus* in Rom geblieben ist, doch möchte man dieses für das dritte Jahrzehnt annehmen. Zwei Gemälde des Heiligen in nächtlicher Landschaft von Cornelis van Poelenburch (1594/95–1667), der von etwa 1617 bis 1625 in Rom und Florenz lebte, zeigen die enge Anlehnung an Elsheimers Vorbild. Zwar nimmt die Stimmung der Landschaft einen breiteren Raum ein, doch bleibt die Monumentalität der schreitenden Figur erhalten.[5] Die Spur des bewunderten Werkes von Elsheimer verliert sich. Vielleicht gelangte es schon früh in eine englische Sammlung, da mehrere alte Kopien, darunter eine aus dem Besitz des Earl of Arundel, sich heute in England befinden. Andrews betont mit Recht, daß nur das Bild der Eremitage als Elsheimers Original in Betracht kommt. Wann und wo dieses erworben wurde, ist unbekannt, es wird 1797 erstmals in St. Petersburg erwähnt.

Elsheimers *Judith* in London (Apsley House, Wellington Museum), die er
in den ersten römischen Jahren malte, stellt eine konsequente Fortsetzung
des Stils und der erzählerischen Kraft der Christophorus-Legende dar, wirkt
aber noch reicher in den eingesetzten Mitteln.[6] Es verwundert nicht, daß
Rubens von diesem Werk nicht weniger gefesselt war. Seine sogenannte 'große
Judith', ein heute verschollenes Gemälde, das nur durch einen Kupferstich
(im Gegensinne) von Cornelis Galle (1576–1650) überliefert ist,[7] zeigt einen
ganz ähnlichen Ablauf des Geschehens wie bei Elsheimer, obwohl hier vier Engel
als himmlische Zeugen der Bluttat hinzukommen. Rubens übernahm von
Elsheimer die ganzfigurige Anlage der Komposition mit der an den vorderen
Bildrand verlegten Handlung, den sachlichen Ernst der schönen, von rechts mit
dem Schwert zuschlagenden Frau, die komplizierte Bewegung des im Tode
zuckenden Holofernes und die dramatische Lichtführung. Es ist wahrscheinlich, daß Rubens' erster Entwurf zur Zeit seines römischen Aufenthalts
entstanden ist, als er Elsheimers Bild direkt vor Augen hatte. Später, vermutlich nach 1626, konnte Rubens dieses sogar erwerben, von wem ist freilich
unbekannt. In einem Brief vom 14. Januar 1611 hatte er noch beklagt, daß sich
bisher kein Werk Elsheimers in Flandern befände.[8] Als Rubens 1640 starb, wird
Elsheimers *Judith* erstmals im Inventar seiner Sammlung erwähnt.[9] Damals,
jedenfalls vor 1645, hat König Philip IV. von Spanien (1605–1665) das Bild aus
dem Nachlaß erworben, und es verblieb in Spanien bis es 1813 als Kriegsbeute
in den Besitz des Herzogs von Wellington (1769–1852) gelangte, der es in seine
private Galerie nach London überführte. Die lange Abgeschlossenheit in Spanien
hat einer späteren Rezeption des Bildes im Norden natürliche Grenzen gesetzt.

Der *Hl. Laurentius vor seinem Martyrium* in London (National Gallery) gehört
zu den erstaunlichsten Leistungen der frühen Jahre.[10] Der junge Maler verläßt
sich nicht auf die traditionelle Schilderung der Passion des Heiligen, die er
gewiß in Tizians Altarbild in der Gesuiti-Kirche in Venedig bewundert hatte,
sondern erweitert das Geschehen durch eigene Erfindungen. Daß Elsheimer
nicht das Martyrium, sondern die Vorbereitung dazu in den Mittelpunkt stellte,
war schon ungewöhnlich genug. Aber – nach einer Deutung von Bachner[11] –
verlieh er auch dem heidnischen Götterbild, über dessen Zugehörigkeit zum
Thema hinausgehend, eine neue inhaltliche Position, welche die Kraft des
Herkules als Tugendheld gleichnishaft einschließt. Auch formal bildet die Trias
von Opfer, Kläger und Götterbild das beherrschende Motiv der Komposition.
Anregungen aus Elsheimers Darstellung mag Nicolas Poussin (1594–1665) in
seinem 1628 geschaffenen Erasmus-Martyrium in Rom (Pinacoteca Vaticana)
aufgenommen haben, worauf Andrews hingewiesen hat. Sollte dieses zutreffen,
müßte Elsheimers *Laurentius* noch um die Mitte der zwanziger Jahre in Rom
gewesen sein. Für das zweite Viertel des 17. Jahrhunderts kann man mit

einiger Sicherheit die Anwesenheit des Bildes in Antwerpen vermuten, wie sich aus zahlreichen Kopien und Derivaten ergibt, unter denen auch Bilder von und aus dem Kreis von Frans Francken d. J. (1581–1642) und ein Kupferstich von Pieter Soutman (*ca.* 1580–1657) zu nennen sind. Zu einem unbekannten Zeitpunkt gelangte das Bild in die bedeutende Sammlung des Antwerpener Juweliers und Kunsthändlers Diego Duarte (vor 1616–1691), in dessen Inventar von 1682 es erwähnt wird.[12] Zum Bekanntwerden der Werke Elsheimers bei den Kunstkennern Antwerpens hat der werbende Einsatz von Rubens, der sich nach seinen eigenen Worten bemühte, Bilder des deutschen Malers für Flandern zu gewinnen, gewiß wesentlich beigetragen.[13]

Wie stark das Neue und Eigenartige der Kunst Elsheimers seine Freunde und Zeitgenossen beeindruckte, läßt sich an der Wirkung seines um 1603–04 geschaffenen *Martyriums des Hl. Stephanus*, heute in Edinburgh, verfolgen.[14] Auch hier ist an erster Stelle Rubens zu nennen, der es wohl in Rom kennenlernte und mehrere Figuren des Bildes in einer in London bewahrten Zeichnung (um 1606–08) festgehalten hat.[15] Pieter Soutman, der wahrscheinlich bei Rubens in der Lehre war, reproduzierte das Blatt in einem Kupferstich, der im ersten Zustand Elsheimer als Inventor bezeichnet. David Teniers d. Ä. (1582–1649), der vor 1605 wahrscheinlich als Mitarbeiter in Elsheimers Atelier tätig war, hat das Stephanus-Thema in einem heute verlorenen Gemälde behandelt, das durch einen Kupferstich von Egbert van Panderen (*ca.* 1581–1637) überliefert ist.[16] In seiner Komposition ist die Nähe des Vorbildes leicht erkennbar, darüber hinaus hat Teniers zahlreiche Einzelheiten aus dem Werk seines Meisters später noch in anderen Gemälden verwendet (darunter seine *Anbetung der Könige* in Aachen).[17]

Unter den holländischen Künstlern, die um 1605/07 in Rom in Elsheimers engstem Umkreis lebten, sind die Brüder Jan (1581/2–1631) und Jacob Pynas (1592/3–nach 1650) sowie Pieter Lastman (1583–1633) zu nennen. Sie haben nach ihrer Rückkehr – wie auch in Rembrandts Frühwerk erkennbar – zur Verbreitung von Elsheimers Stil beigetragen. Ob Claes Moyaert (1591–1655), wie allgemein angenommen, ebenfalls Italien besuchte, ist nicht gesichert. Zu den frühesten Beispielen der Wirkung Elsheimers in Amsterdam gehört Lastmans *Flucht nach Ägypten*, datiert 1608, in Rotterdam, welche die Kenntnis von Elsheimers Bild des gleichen Themas in Fort Worth (Kimbell Art Museum) voraussetzt, sowie Lastmans um 1607/08 gemalter *Bethlehemitischer Kindermord* in Braunschweig[18], auf dem in der Landschaft und der Reitergruppe Beziehungen zum *Stephanus-Martyrium* erkennbar sind. Lastman hielt sich auch an den herbei-fliegenden Engel dieses Bildes als er um 1612 sein *Opfer Abrahams* in Amsterdam (Rembrandthuis) konzipierte. Die Reiterfigur findet man auch in der 1617 von Jacob Pynas gemalten *Anbetung der Könige* in Hartford.[19]

Elsheimers *Stephanus-Martyrium* blieb über das 17. Jahrhundert in Rom, zunächst im Besitz von Paul Bril (1554–1626) und nach seinem Tod bei dessen Witwe und seiner Tochter. Es ist nicht bekannt, ob Bril das Bild von Elsheimer selbst und wann er es erworben hat. Dieser Umstand ist bei der engen stilistischen Verwandtschaft der beiden Künstler in ihrem Verhältnis zur Landschaft besonders bemerkenswert, zumal Bril in seiner Spätzeit dem kleinen Format den Vorzug gab.[20] Schon in dem 1659 aufgezeichneten Inventar der Tochter von Bril glaubte man, daß dieser beim *Stephanus-Martyrium* die Landschaft hinzugefügt hatte.[21] Es waren aber eben diese Naturausschnitte, wie auch jener im Hintergrund der schon früher entstandenen *Taufe Christi* in London, welche den Blick der Zeitgenossen auf Elsheimers poetische Kunst lenkten und sein hohes Ansehen als Landschaftsmaler begründeten. Sein Ruf auf diesem Gebiet hat schon bald dazu geführt, eine immense Zahl von Landschaftsbildern aus der Nachfolge und Umgebung des Malers fälschlich mit Elsheimers Namen zu verbinden. Dadurch wurde das Wissen um seine besondere Begabung und Bedeutung als Erzähler und Figurenmaler zurückgedrängt. Bei der Elsheimer-Ausstellung in Frankfurt 1966/67 hat die Konfrontation der bekanntesten ihm zugeschriebenen Landschaften vor Augen geführt, daß in Wahrheit nur ganz wenige Werke seiner Hand existieren, bei denen die Landschaft die Hauptrolle übernimmt, wie es etwa bei der *Aurora* in Braunschweig oder den *Tobias*-Bildern der Fall ist – nach Van Gelder und Jost das wichtigste Ergebnis der Schau.[22] Dieses Resultat hat den Weg freigemacht, Elsheimer als Historienmaler neu zu würdigen.

Die um 1608 geschaffene *Verspottung der Ceres* gehört zu jenen beispielhaften Meisterwerken Elsheimers, deren Bedeutung sofort von den Zeitgenossen erkannt wurde, wie aus den zahlreichen Reflexen und Kopien hervorgeht.[23] Zur Verbreitung der Wirkung dieses Bildes hat der hervorragende Kupferstich beigetragen, den Hendrick Goudt (1583–1648), im Todesjahr Elsheimers, in Rom geschaffen hat. Der weitere Weg des Gemäldes, das der Maler durch Zeichnungen sorgfältig vorbereitete, soll hier kurz skizziert werden. Mit großer Wahrscheinlichkeit befand es sich noch 1628 in Italien, wie dem in diesem Jahr von Johannes Faber (1574–1629) publizierten Buch *Animalia Mexicana* zu entnehmen ist. Faber, der mit Elsheimer befreundet war, berichtet dort von dem Aufsehen, daß das Bild in Rom erregte, und daß es bei seinem Verkauf einen enormen Preis erzielte. Faber mag den Namen des Käufers, der ihm als Kunstfreund gewiß bekannt war, nicht nennen. Sollte es der berühmte Bildersammler Kardinal Scipio Borghese (1576–1633) gewesen sein, dem Hendrick Goudt 1610 den Stich der *Ceres* gewidmet hatte ? Faber würde wohl erwähnt haben, wenn das Werk damals die Stadt verlassen hätte. Der sienesische Stecher Bernardino Capitelli (1590–1640), der häufig für römische Auftraggeber

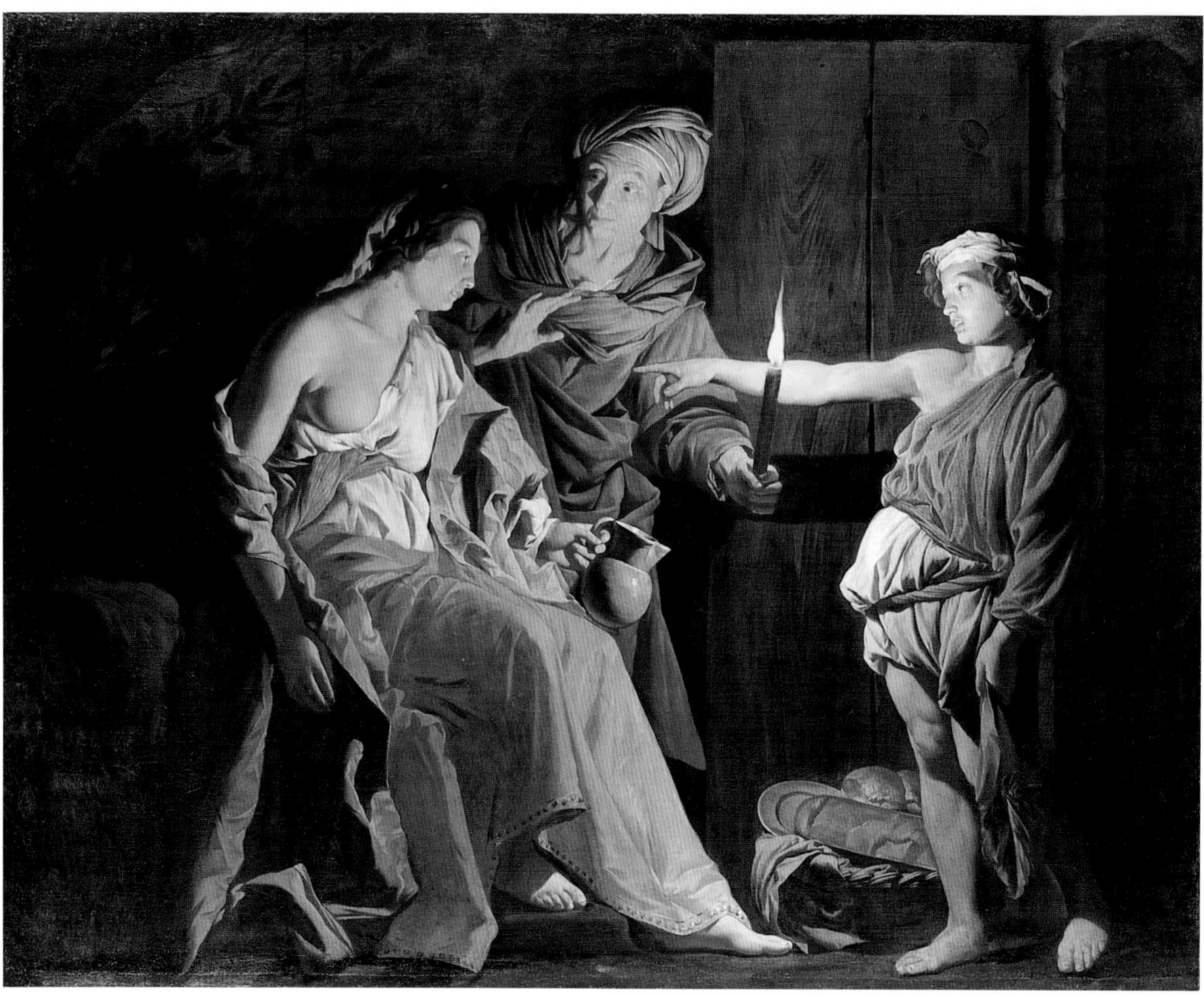



arbeitete, hat 1633 eine Radierung von Elsheimers Darstellung herausgegeben, gewiß auch, weil das Bildthema viele Kunstfreunde beschäftigte.

Das zu dieser Zeit ungewöhnliche Bildthema, das auf Ovids *Metamorphosen* (V, 446–461) zurückgeht, impliziert die Warnung, daß die Fruchtbarkeit der Erde von den Menschen mit Respekt zu behandeln sei. Elsheimers Erzählung verdankt ihre geheimnisvolle Stimmung den verschiedenen, im Bildraum verteilten Lichtquellen, welche für die Handlung bedeutungsvoll sind. Da es sich um eine nächtliche Begebenheit handelt, sind der Vollmond oben links und die Kerze in der Hand der Bäuerin Hinweise auf die Stunde der Begegnung. Anders die links auf dem Wagenrad abgelegte Fackel, welche die Göttin bei Beginn ihrer Wanderung am Feuer des Aetna entzündet hatte, um ihre entführte Tochter Proserpina auch im Dunkeln suchen zu können. Die Fackel wie auch die von einem Feuer beleuchtete Szene im Hintergrund mit einer melkenden Frau

sind Hinweise auf die Göttin der Landwirtschaft und Fruchtbarkeit und ihre
lebensspendende Bedeutung, ebenso das Ackergerät und die üppigen Pflanzen
hinter ihr. Das Wirken der Göttin duldet keine Verspottung, auch nicht durch
einen vorwitzigen Knaben. Stellio (auch Abas genannt) muß deshalb bestraft
werden. Es folgt seine (auf dem Bilde nicht dargestellte) Verwandlung in eine
Eidechse, in ein Kriechtier, das der Erde zugeordnet ist.[24] Elsheimer schildert
die Szene als ein moralisches Exemplum, Carel van Mander folgend, der den
Künstlern den Gebrauch der *Metamorphosen* in diesem Sinne empfohlen hat.

Der in Italien lebende niederländische Maler Matthias Stom (*ca.* 1600–
nach 1652) hat in seinem Gemälde in München (Alte Pinakothek) Elsheimers
Komposition aufgenommen und variiert (Abb. 2).[25] Stom war der erste, der die
*Verspottung der Ceres* in einem monumentalen Format gemalt hat. Er wählte für
den herausfordernd auftretenden Stellio die gleiche Haltung wie bei seinem
Vorbild, der ausgestreckte Arm des Jungen kreuzt in ähnlicher Weise den Arm
der Frau, die ihn zurückzuhalten sucht. Allerdings verzichtet Stom auf die
provozierend dargebotene Nacktheit des Knaben, mit der Elshcimer vielleicht auf
die kommende Verwandlung zur Eidechse anspielte, und zeigt Stellio bekleidet.[26]
Stom, ein Nachfolger von Gerard van Honthorst (1592–1656) und wohl auch
dessen Schüler, muß die Lichtführung in Elsheimers *Ceres* besonders angezogen
haben. Seine als Querformat angelegte Komposition ist im Unterschied zu
seinem Vorbild wesentlich vereinfacht und auf eine Lichtquelle reduziert, die
Fackel in der Hand der Bäuerin. Auch die Handlung selbst hat sich verändert,
sie ist in ihrem Ablauf um einen Augenblick weiter fortgeschritten als bei
Elsheimer. Die Göttin, die mit entblößtem Busen die Fruchtbarkeit verkörpert,
hat nach dem Trinken den Krug abgesetzt und richtet den Blick fest auf den
Jungen, der ihr in Augenhöhe gegenüber steht. Die Vereinfachung der Szene
bei Stom macht deutlich, mit welchem geistigen Reichtum Elsheimer das
Thema behandelt.

Stom hat sich nachweislich in den Jahren 1630–32 in Rom aufgehalten und
hat damals wahrscheinlich Elsheimers *Ceres* kennengelernt. Er zog später nach
Neapel; sein Gemälde ist vielleicht erst in den vierziger Jahren entstanden.
Es ist unbekannt, wann Elsheimers Original Italien verlassen hat, und ebenso
wenig wissen wir, wann es die Niederlande erreichte. Seine Rezeption im
Norden kann auch von Kopien des Bildes oder von Goudts Kupferstich ausgegangen sein. Eine Kopie, die sich 1628 in der Sammlung des Antwerpener
Kaufmanns Cornelis van Geest befand, ist wahrscheinlich identisch mit jener
im Besitz von Rubens, welche aus dessen Nachlaß vor 1645 für König Philip IV.
von Spanien erworben wurde und später in den Prado gelangte.[27]

Man darf annehmen, daß sich Elsheimers Originalbild spätestens in den
vierziger Jahren in Holland befand. Rembrandt und einige Künstler aus seinem

Umkreis haben die Anregung der Komposition aufgenommen. Eine verlorene Zeichnung Rembrandts, die durch Kopien überliefert ist, kann zwar auch auf Goudts Kupferstich zurückgeführt werden, bezeugt aber jedenfalls das Interesse des Malers an dem Bildthema.[28] Von der Hand des Rembrandt-Nachfolgers Salomon Koninck (1609–1656) ist ein 1645 datiertes Gemälde der *Verspottung der Ceres* in Privatbesitz bekannt (Milwaukee, Slg. Dr. Alfred und Isabel Bader, Abb. 1), von Jacob Pynas eine 1648 datierte Zeichnung in Rotterdam.[29] Eine Zeichnung von Leonard Bramer (1596–1674) und ein Gemälde Jan Steens (1626–1679) dieses Themas gehören ebenfalls in diesen Zusammenhang.[30] Eine Kopie niederländischen Ursprungs in Berlin, die wahrscheinlich das originale Werk Elsheimers wiedergibt, befand sich bereits am Ende des 17. Jahrhunderts im Besitz der mit Holland eng verbundenen Kurfürsten von Brandenburg.[31] Auch Gerard Dou (1613–1675) soll eine Kopie der *Ceres* gemalt haben. Der Radierer und Kunstliebhaber Christian Ludwig von Hagedorn (1713–1780) schreibt 1755, ohne Angabe einer Quelle, Dou hätte Elsheimers Gemälde kopiert, bevor dieses nach England geschickt wurde.[32] Dort sei Elsheimers Werk bei einem Brand des Whitehall Palastes verloren-gegangen. In einem Inventar der Gemälde von König Jakob II. (1633–1701) wird noch 1758 ein *Ceres*-Bild von Elsheimer erwähnt. Es ist möglich, daß das zur Zeit Gerard Dous nach England gebrachte Bild mit jenem identisch ist, das sich heute in der Sammlung von Alfred und Isabel Bader in Milwaukee befindet.[33] Dieses, in London erworben, ist zwar auf Grund schwerer Schäden, welche wahrscheinlich auf einen Brand zurückzuführen sind, nicht leicht zu beurteilen, aber die Qualität einzelner erhaltener Partien der Malerei und die mit der Bild-genese eng verbundenen Pentimenti, desgleichen die für den Künstler charakte-ristische Tafel mit der rückseitigen Inschrift, machen es sehr wahrscheinlich, daß Elsheimer selbst es geschaffen hat.

Wenn wir Elsheimers Weg verfolgen, der ihn zur ausgebreiteten, zunehmend selbständigen Landschaft führt, in welcher die handelnden Figuren eher an die Seite gerückt werden, sind vor allem seine Gemälde *Aurora* in Braunschweig, *Apollo und Coronis* in Liverpool und der sogenannte 'kleine *Tobias*' in Frankfurt zu betrachten, die etwa um 1606–08 entstanden sind. Nur für das letzte gibt es einen *terminus ante quem* durch den in Rom geschaffenen und 1608 datierten Kupferstich von Hendrick Goudt. Gerade bei diesen Bildern hat sich eine ungewöhnlich große Zahl von Kopien und Derivaten erhalten, welche die Darstellungen populär gemacht haben, ohne daß sich im Einzelfall sagen läßt, von welchen Elsheimers Stil weitergetragen wurde. Für eine Prüfung der Rezeption der Bilder besteht hier eine andere Ausgangslage. Über den Weg der Originalwerke, nachdem sie das Atelier des Malers verließen, ist abgesehen von der *Aurora* fast nichts bekannt.

Die *Aurora*-Landschaft gehört zu jenen Werken, die Hendrick Goudt nach dem Tode Elsheimers als seinen Anteil aus dem Nachlaß betrachtete und 1611 nach Holland überführte.[34] Goudt, aus vermögenden Verhältnissen stammend, bewahrte die Bilder in seinem Haus in Utrecht, wo er sie gelegentlich auch Besuchern zeigte, und hat in den Jahren 1612 und 1613 vier davon in meisterhaften Kupferstichen reproduziert, darunter auch die *Aurora*. Joachim von Sandrart, der Goudt um 1625/26 mehrfach besuchte, berichtet von dessen Geisteskrankheit, die schließlich nach dem Tod von Goudts Vater (1628) zur Auflösung seines Besitzstandes führte. Wahrscheinlich wurde schon damals Elsheimers *Flucht nach Ägypten* (München, Alte Pinakothek), die sich in Goudts Sammlung befand, an Kurfürst Maximilian I. von Bayern (1573–1651) verkauft. Goudt starb 1648, aber wir wissen nicht, was er damals noch besessen hat.[35] Das im Todesjahr aufgestellte Inventar seines Nachlasses ist bisher nicht gefunden worden. Spätestens in diesem Jahr verteilten sich die in Goudts Händen gebliebenen Reste von Elsheimers Nachlaß auf andere, zunächst vermutlich holländische Interessenten. Sicher lenkten die Verkäufe in Utrecht aufs neue den Blick auf die Kunst Elsheimers; bei Künstlern und Sammlern glaubt man nach 1650 ein "Elsheimer-revival" (Van Gelder und Jost) zu erkennen, wozu nicht zuletzt die Bilder und Kopien von Cornelis van Poelenburch und Dirk van der Lisse (?1607–1669) beigetragen haben. Dennoch bleibt es schwierig den Weg der Originalwerke aus Goudts Besitz zu verfolgen. Es ist unklar, wo sich das von ihm gestochene *Philemon und Baucis*-Bild,[36] das 1754 erstmals in Dresden erwähnt wird, nach dem Tode von Goudt befand, wobei auch eine englische Sammlung in Betracht kommt. Das Original des sogenannten 'großen *Tobias*' ist bis heute verschollen, aber durch Goudts Stich und die bekannten Wiederholungen von anderer Hand in Kopenhagen und London überliefert.[37] Für die *Aurora* möchte man Den Haag als zeitweisen Aufbewahrungsort vermuten, bis sie nach Antwerpen gelangte, wo das Bild 1682 im Inventar der Sammlung des Kunsthändlers Diego Duarte verzeichnet ist.[38] Es ist bemerkenswert, daß sich in derselben Sammlung ein Gemälde Van Poelenburchs befand, das mit den folgenden Worten beschrieben wird: „*Een lantschapken. Het auroraken naer Elshamer maer met verandering.*"

Es hat den Anschein, daß sich die Auseinandersetzung mit der Kunst Elsheimers in den Niederlanden hauptsächlich von Antwerpen und Utrecht ihren Ausgang nahm, und daß das Interesse in der Scheldestadt unter der Ausstrahlung von Rubens sich mehr dem Erzähler und Figurenmaler zuwandte, während man in Utrecht eher den poetischen Landschaftsmaler entdeckte. In Holland gehört Cornelis van Poelenburch zu den wichtigsten Vermittlern von Elsheimers Kunst, insbesondere von dessen Bildern der lichterfüllten Natur. Der Utrechter Poelenburch hatte schon vor seiner Abreise nach Italien um 1617 Gelegenheit die Werke des Frankurter Malers zu studieren, die sich seit 1611 in der Sammlung von Hendrick Goudt befanden.[39] Die in Amsterdam tätigen, sogenannten 'Praerembrandtisten,' wie Pieter Lastman oder Jan und Jacob Pynas, die in Rom mit Elsheimer selbst in Verbindung gestanden hatten, folgten zwar dem neuen Stil des Figurenmalers, sind aber – abgesehen von Jacob Pynas – trotz ihrer persönlichen Beziehung nicht dauerhaft als Vermittler der Kunst Elsheimers hervorgetreten.

Jacob Pynas war der einzige, welcher der Darstellung der Landschaft größere Bedeutung beimaß. Die Entwicklung des Malers, der um 1608 aus Rom zurückkehrte und lange in Delft wie auch in Den Haag lebte, ist nicht leicht zu beurteilen.[40] Seine *Büßende Magdalena* in Berlin, vermutlich in der Zeit um 1615–20 entstanden, seine Gemälde des barmherzigen Samariters in Paris und Nancy, sowie die *Landschaft mit Merkur und Battus* in Kassel, welche alle einmal Elsheimers Namen trugen, sind unverkennbar von dessen Vorbild geprägt.[41] Durch einen 1623 datierten Kupferstich von Magdalena de Passe kennen wir von ihm ein neuerdings aufgefundenes Gemälde *Salmacis und Hermaphroditus* (Abb. 3), in welchem das mythische Paar in einer ganz mit Elsheimers Augen gesehenen Landschaft geschildert ist.[42] Der ausgebreitete Naturprospekt und die Anbindung der Figuren an das Dickicht der Bäume erinnern an Elsheimers Bilder des 'kleinen *Tobias*' und *Apollo und Coronis*, auch hinsichtlich des für diesen charakteristischen Figurenmaßstabs. Die diagonal aufgebaute Komposition ist der ersten Fassung des Aurora-Bildes (*Acis und Galatea*) in Braunschweig vergleichbar. Ein anderer Stich der Künstlerin, *Die Rache der Latona* darstellend, scheint ebenso auf Pynas (ob Jan oder Jacob ist unklar) zurückzugehen, obwohl Elsheimer als Inventor genannt wird.[43] Es erscheint wenig glaubhaft, daß es von diesem ein Originalwerk dieser Komposition, welche eher an Waldbilder von Paul Bril erinnert, gegeben hat. Das mit dem Stich verbundene Gemälde aus der Sammlung Graf Seilern in London (Courtauld Institute) kann nur von einem Nachfolger Elsheimers geschaffen sein.[44] Hingegen hat Wenzel Hollar (1607–1677) in einer 1649 datierten Radierung eine andere *Latona*-Darstellung unter Elsheimers Namen reproduziert, die sich damals in der berühmten Sammlung von Lord Arundel befand. Das Gemälde (im Gegensinne), noch 1655 im Besitz der in Holland lebenden Witwe Arundels, wurde vor kurzem wiederentdeckt und als eigenhändiges Werk Elsheimers erkannt (Köln, Wallraf-Richartz-Museum).[45] In der Gestaltung des Naturraumes, der Anordnung der Figuren und in der Beobachtung des über die Baumkronen fließenden Sonnenlichts steht das Bild den *Tobias*-Landschaften und jener vom *Reich der Venus* in Cambridge nahe.[46] Es verwundert nicht, daß es die holländischen Italianisanten angezogen hat. Eine Kopie in englischem Privatbesitz läßt sich nach Andrews wahrscheinlich Cornelis van Poelenburch zuschreiben.

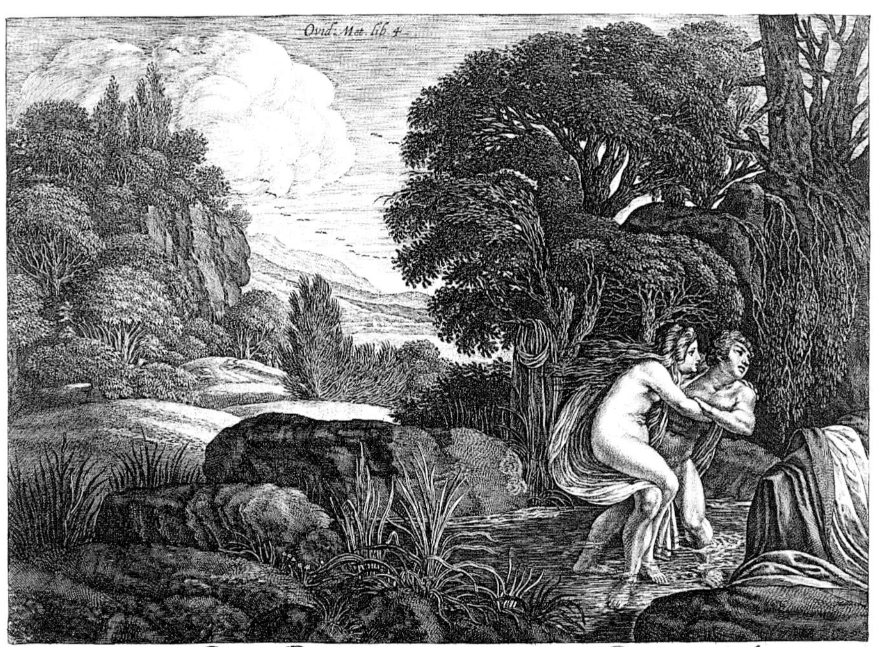


Abb. 3 MAGDALENA DE PASSE
*Salmacis und Hermaphroditus,*
Kupferstich nach Jacob Pynas
Amsterdam, Rijksmuseum

Magdalena de Passe (um 1596–1638), eine Tochter des Zeichners und Stechers Crispijn de Passe I (1564–1637), lebte mit ihrem Vater, der sie wohl als erster unterrichtete, seit 1611 in Utrecht.[47] Sie wird dort nicht nur die Werke Elsheimers im Besitz von Hendrick Goudt kennengelernt haben, sondern könnte auch bei diesem in die Lehre gegangen sein, da der Stil ihrer graphischen Arbeiten den Stichen von Goudt sehr nahe kommt. Sie hat auch einen Nachstich von Elsheimers *Apollo und Coronis* geschaffen (mit der irrtümlichen Unterschrift als 'Tod der Procris', aber der richtigen Angabe des Malers),[48] sodaß man sich fragen muß, wo die Künstlerin das Gemälde gesehen hat. Gehörte es zu Elsheimers Werken im Hause von Goudt? Dieser hatte nach 1613 – vielleicht auf Grund seiner beginnenden Erkrankung – keine Stiche nach Elsheimer mehr angefertigt. Das Blatt Magdalenas trägt eine Widmung an Rubens, der aus früherer Zeit mit ihrem Vater verbunden war und 1613 Utrecht besuchte.[49] Rubens wird ihr als Freund und Verehrer von Elsheimer bekannt gewesen sein. Die Künstlerin mag gefühlt haben, daß ihr – angesichts der Krankheit von Goudt – die Chance und Aufgabe zufiel, den Utrechter Teil von

Elsheimers Nachlaß bekanntzumachen. Ihre meist undatierten Stiche sind wahrscheinlich in den zwanziger Jahren entstanden, jedenfalls vor 1634, dem Jahr ihrer Heirat.

In Antwerpen war es neben Lucas Vorsterman (1595–1675) und dem Rubens-Schüler Pieter Soutman vor allem der Radierer Wenzel Hollar, der in den vierziger Jahren erneut den Blick auf Elsheimer lenkte. Man darf annehmen, daß die Rezeption von Elsheimers Kunst weniger von Amsterdam, der Stadt der holländischen Augenzeugen, als von Utrecht und Antwerpen ausgegangen ist, und daß selbst die eher bescheidenen Wirkungen von Elsheimers Werk in Deutschland durch niederländische Künstler vermittelt wurden.

In diesem Zusammenhang muß der Nürnberger Maler Johann König (1586–1642) genannt werden, der sich in seiner Frühzeit eng an Elsheimers Landschaftskunst anschloß.[50] Vermutlich erhielt er (nach 1606) seine Ausbildung in Augsburg bei Johann Rottenhammer (1564–1625), der schon in seiner venezianischen Zeit Elsheimer (um 1599) kennen gelernt hatte. König reiste um 1609 nach Italien, arbeitete zunächst in Venedig und anschließend in Rom, wo er von 1610 bis 1613 nachweisbar ist. Es ist möglich, daß er Elsheimer, der im Dezember 1610 starb, dort noch begegnete. Königs voll signierte *Verfolgung der Nymphe Arethusa* in Augsburg (Abb. 4)[51] überrascht durch ihre künstlerische Nähe zu Elsheimers Gemälden *Apollo und Coronis* (Liverpool)[52] und des 'kleinen *Tobias*' (Frankfurt),[53] besonders hinsichtlich der Einbindung der Figuren in den Naturprospekt, ohne daß direkte Übernahmen von Motiven erkennbar sind. Die eilenden Schritte des Flußgottes Alpheus am vorderen Bildrand und die Figuren zwischen den spiegelnden Wasserflächen unter kugelförmigen Bäumen im Hintergrund sind dem *Tobias*-Bild nahe verwandt. Die in der linken Ecke kauernde Nymphe vor einem blühenden Busch, hinter dem sich ein abgestorbener Baum erhebt, erinnert trotz ihrer ganz anderen Körperhaltung an Elsheimers diagonal gelagerten Akt der Coronis unter herabhängenden Zweigen. König hat das Thema der Nymphe Arethusa mit einer ähnlichen Komposition in einem 1615 datierten Gemälde in Privatbesitz behandelt, von dem eine Wiederholung, die früher Elsheimer zugeschrieben war, heute in Berlin bewahrt wird.[54] Man möchte annehmen, daß die Augsburger *Arethusa*, die sich durch die primäre Reflektion der Naturpoesie Elsheimers von späteren Landschaften Königs unterscheidet, ebenfalls im zweiten Jahrzehnt entstanden ist. In kaum einem anderen seiner Bilder kommt König dem Stil von Elsheimers Landschaftskunst so nahe. Seine signierte *Landschaft mit der Versuchung Christi* in Köln[55] zeigt zwar einen ähnlichen Aufbau des Prospekts und der Stimmung der Natur, dürfte aber dennoch etwas später entstanden sein, zumal die im Unterschied zu Elsheimer nur kleinen Figuren eine andere Distanz zum Bildraum bewirken.

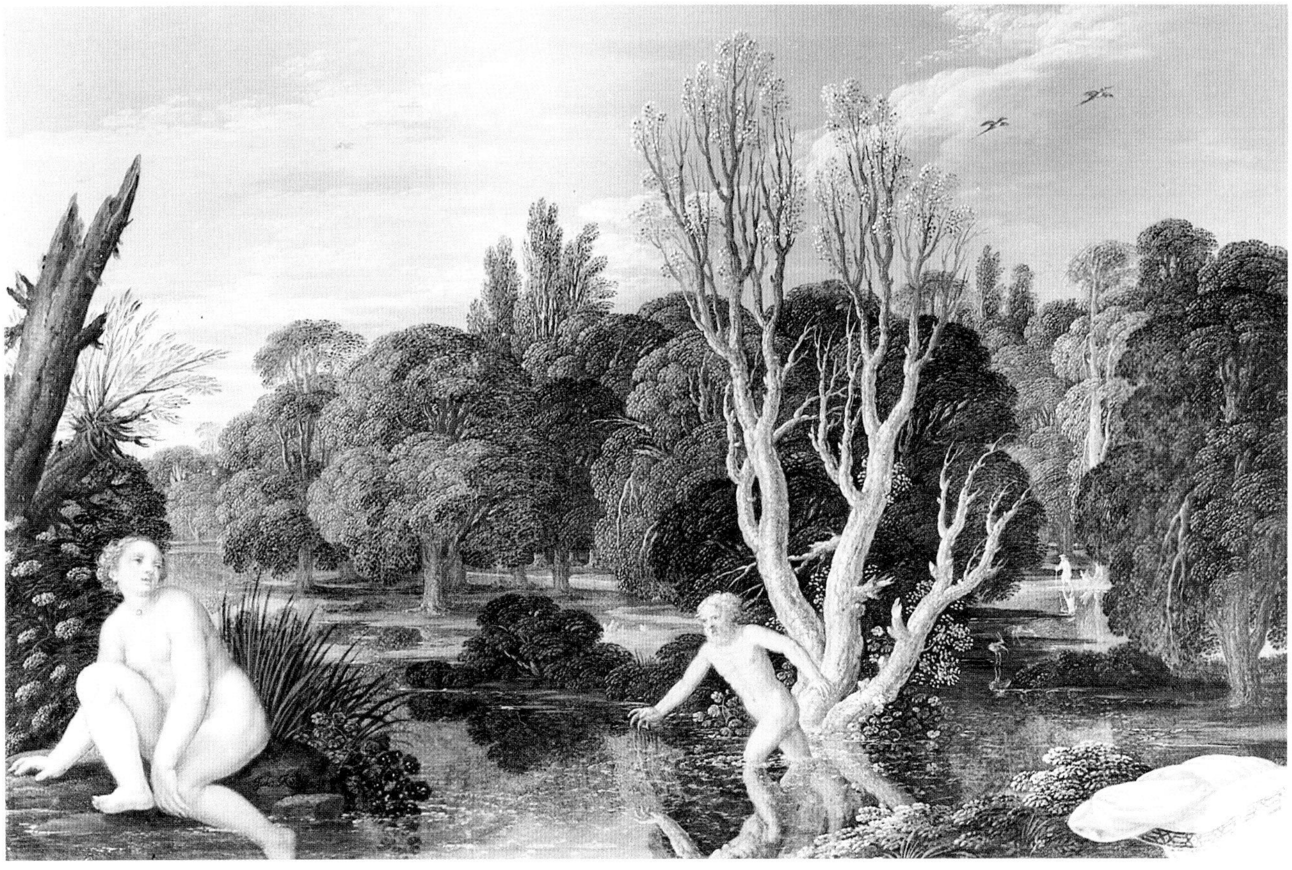

König kehrte 1614 aus Italien nach Augsburg zurück, wo er die Meisterwürde erhielt und die folgenden fünfzehn Jahre tätig war. Das Erbe der originären Landschaftskunst Elsheimers, das er mitgebracht hatte, ist schnell verloren gegangen und erschöpfte sich in einer etwas formelhaften Wiedergabe südlicher Natur, da den offiziellen Auftraggebern und Kunstsammlern der schwäbischen Reichsstadt offenbar der Sinn für die Stimmung und das Poetische der Natur fehlte. Bei König trat nun eine steife Figurenmalerei zunehmend in den Vordergrund, für die man auf seine 1619 datierte *Minerva mit den Musen* in Darmstadt verweisen kann,[56] ein Bild, das sich im Stil schon weit von der Augsburger *Arethusa* entfernt hat.

Schwieriger stellt sich das Problem, wie die Rolle des süddeutschen Malers Jacob Ernst Thoman von Hagelstein (1588–1653) zu bewerten ist, über den Sandrart ausführlich berichtet.[57] In Lindau am Bodensee 1588 geboren, in Konstanz und Kempten ausgebildet, zog er 1605 nach Italien, besuchte Mailand, Genua, Rom und Neapel, um schließlich in Rom bei Elsheimer sein Handwerk zu perfektionieren. Hier habe er gemeinsam mit den holländischen Künstlern um Lastman und Jan Pynas Studien in der freien Natur unternommen und sich der Darstellung der Landschaft gewidmet. Er soll erst um 1620 in seine

Abb. 4 JOHANN KÖNIG
*Die Verfolgung der Nymphe Arethusa*
Öl auf Kupfer, 21 × 33 cm
Augsburg, Städtische
Kunstsammlungen

Heimat zurückgekehrt sein, wo er in Lindau zunächst als Maler (besonders von Landschaften) tätig blieb, dann aber in den Kriegsdienst eintrat, um als Kaiserlicher Kommissar und Proviantmeister zu dienen. Von Jacob Thoman, der damit die Malerei aufgab, sind heute gesicherte Werke nahezu unbekannt,[58] und doch muß es manche Bilder gegeben haben, die Beachtung fanden, wie aus Sandrarts Worten hervorgeht. Schon in Italien und auch später in Deutschland habe man seine Bilder mit denen Elsheimers verwechselt. Ein Topos vielleicht, oder doch ein Hinweis, daß Thoman ein spezielles Talent besaß, von Elsheimers Werken hervorragende Kopien zu schaffen? Zu dieser Zeit war für einen Maler die Anfertigung guter Kopien eine durchaus geachtete Tätigkeit. Dieser Gedanke, obwohl nur spekulativ solange Dokumente fehlen, hat seine Berechtigung angesichts der Existenz von vielen Kopien hoher Qualität, die nur mit Elsheimers Original vor Augen entstanden sein können, und deren Urheber absolut unbekannt sind. Hier sei nur erinnert an die beachtlichen Versionen des *Apollo und Coronis*-Bildes, welche die Forschung lange beschäftigt haben, oder die hervorragende Kopie der *Ceres*, die sich einmal in Rubens' Besitz befand (heute Madrid). Daß Elsheimer selbst Wiederholungen seiner Werke gemalt hätte, wie man früher glaubte, darf man im Hinblick auf seine Mentalität und psychische Befindlichkeit ausschließen. Zu der Überlegung einer vorwiegenden Tätigkeit Jacob Thomans als Kopist würde es passen, daß er nach seiner Rückkehr aus Italien das Malen aufgab, vielleicht weil eine eigene Erfindungskraft fehlte und Elsheimers Originale nicht länger zur Verfügung standen.

Trotz des Brückenschlags Johann Königs von Rom nach Augsburg und trotz des (noch unklaren) Beitrags des Thoman von Hagelstein ist eine angemessene Rezeption der Kunst Elsheimers auf deutschem Boden ausgeblieben. Das lag gewiß nicht nur an den im zweiten Viertel des Jahrhunderts einsetzenden Gewalttaten des Dreißigjährigen Krieges, sondern auch an der im Unterschied zu den Niederlanden nur schwach entwickelten Reproduktionsgraphik, die zur Verbreitung neuer Kunstströmungen hätte beitragen können. Die höchst individuelle und stille Kunst Elsheimers, die nicht zuletzt dank des Einsatzes von Rubens in den Niederlanden schnell Aufnahme fand, blieb in Deutschland, abgesehen von gelegentlichen Übernahmen aus der Graphik, weitgehend unbeachtet. Schon Sandrart hat dieses resümiert[59] und ließ seinem Ärger über seine und Elsheimers Geburtsstadt freien Lauf, als er 1675 feststellte, in Frankfurt sei von Elsheimer „nicht das geringste zu sehen, noch seines Namens gedacht, ohnangesehen man daselbst darzu genugsame Mittel und Gelegenheit so wol vorzeiten gehabt, als noch heut zu Tage hätte".

   

1 Keith Andrews, *Adam Elsheimer. Paintings – Drawings – Prints*, Oxford 1977, S. 140, Nr. 5. Die von Andrews vorgeschlagene Datierung um 1598/99 erscheint zu früh, angesichts der Wirkung des Bildes in Rom möchte man eine Entstehung nach 1600 annehmen. Vgl. auch Jürgen Rapp, 'Adam Elsheimer, *Aeneas rettet Anchises aus dem brennenden Troja*, Ein Stammbuchblatt in Deckfarbenmalerei', *Pantheon*, Bd. 47, 1989, S. 112–32, bes. S. 126 f.

2 Hugh Brigstocke, *Italian and Spanish Paintings in the National Gallery of Scotland*, Edinburgh 1978, S. 19f., Nr. 48.

3 Ludwig Burchard und R.-A. d'Hulst, *Rubens Drawings*, Brüssel 1963, Nr. 43; Julius S. Held, *Rubens. Selected Drawings*, London 1959, Nr. 30 (2. Auflage, Oxford 1986, S. 98, Nr. 73).

4 Konrad Renger mit Claudia Denk, *Flämische Malerei des Barock in der Alten Pinakothek*, München 2002, S. 342, Nr. 72; Hubert von Sonnenburg, 'Rubens. Bildaufbau und Technik', in Hubert von Sonnenburg und F. Preußer, *Rubens. Gesammelte Aufsätze zur Technik*, München 1979, S. 6, 18f., 21.

5 *Adam Elsheimer. Werk, künstlerische Herkunft und Nachfolge*, Ausst. Kat., Frankfurt a. M., 1966, Nr. 79, 80. Die beiden Gemälde, im Besitz der Collectie Stichting P. en N. de Boer, Amsterdam, und in der Sammlung Dr. Alfred und Isabel Bader, Milwaukee, von denen das erstere monogrammiert ist, sind als Varianten anzusehen. Sie sind in der Komposition sehr ähnlich, jedoch in Einzelheiten nicht übereinstimmend.

6 Andrews, *op. cit.* (Anm. 1), S. 144, Nr. 12.

7 F.W.H. Hollstein, *Dutch and Flemish Etchings, Engravings and Woodcuts*, 57 Bde., Amsterdam, 1949–2001, VII, Nr. 31.

8 R. Saunders Magurn, *The Letters of Peter Paul Rubens*, Cambridge, Mass., 1955, S. 53, Nr. 21.

9 Jeffrey M. Muller, *Rubens: The Artist as Collector*, Princeton 1989, S. 102, Nr. 35.

10 Andrews, *op. cit.* (Anm. 1), S. 142, Nr. 12.

11 Franziska Bachner, 'Gleichartigkeit und Gegensatz. Zur Figurenbildung bei Adam Elsheimer', *Städel-Jahrbuch*, N.F. 16, 1997, S. 249–56.

12 G. Dogaer, '*De inventaris der schilderijen van Diego Duarte*', *Jaarboek van het Koninklijk Museum voor Schone Kunsten Antwerpen*, 1971, S. 212 , Nr. 105. Bei dem Wortlaut der Eintragung ist nicht ganz auszuschließen, auch das kleine Bild in Montpellier in Betracht zu ziehen (Andrews, *op. cit.* (Anm. 1), Nr. 171). Dieses gehörte jedoch zu Elsheimers Folge der Heiligenbilder in Petworth House, die wahrscheinlich schon im zweiten Viertel des Jahrhunderts in England war.

13 Vgl. Rubens's Brief in Saunders Magurn, *op. cit.* (Anm. 8), S. 53, Nr. 21.

14 Andrews, *op. cit.* (Anm. 1), S.145, Nr.15.

15 Ingrid Jost, 'A newly discovered painting by Adam Elsheimer', *The Burlington Magazine*, CVIII, 1966, S. 3f.; Julius S. Held, *Rubens. Selected Drawings*, Oxford 1986, S. 78, Nr. 31; die Zuschreibung der Zeichnung, die von Pieter Soutman gestochen wurde (Hollstein, *op. cit.* (Anm. 7), XXVII, Nr.16), ist nicht unbestritten. Anne-Marie Logan (Review of Rubens exhibition 1977, *Master Drawings*, Bd. 15, 1977, S. 412) hält sie für eine den Stich vorbereitende Arbeit Soutmans. Falls dieses zutrifft, setzt das Blatt dennoch eine Zeichnung von Rubens als Vorlage voraus, da Elsheimers Bild zu dieser Zeit in Italien war.

16 Hollstein, *op. cit.*, (Anm. 7), XV, Nr.14; J.G. van Gelder und Ingrid Jost, 'Elsheimers unverteilter Nachlaß', *Simiolus*, Bd. 1, Nr. 3, 1966/67, S. 150.

17 Eric Duverger und Hans Vlieghe, *David Teniers der Ältere. Ein vergessener flämischer Nachfolger Adam Elsheimers*, Utrecht 1971, S. 42; Van Gelder und Jost, *op. cit.* (Anm. 16), S. 146.

18 Keith Andrews, 'A rediscovered Elsheimer', *The Burlington Magazine*, CXXVIII, 1986, S. 795–97; Rüdiger Klessmann, in *Landscape of the Bible. Sacred Scenes in European Master Paintings*, Ausst. Kat., Redaktion Gil Pessach, Israel Museum, Jerusalem, 2000, Nr. 18; Rüdiger Klessmann, *Die holländischen Gemälde. Kritisches Verzeichnis. Herzog Anton Ulrich-Museum*, Braunschweig 1983, S. 118 f.

19  Astrid Tümpel und Peter Schatborn,
    *Pieter Lastman. Leermeester van Rembrandt*,
    Ausst. Kat., Rijksmuseum, Amsterdam,
    1991, S. 66, Abb. 12; S. 19, Abb. 2.
20  Zur Beziehung von Elsheimer und Bril in
    der Behandlung der Landschaft vgl. auch
    Nicolette C. Sluijter-Seijffert, *Cornelis van
    Poelenburch*, Enschede 1984, S. 44.
21  Andrews 1977, *op. cit.* (Anm. 1), S. 145.
22  Van Gelder und Jost, *op. cit.* (Anm. 16),
    S. 44 f.
23  Andrews 1977, *op. cit.* (Anm. 1), S. 152,
    Nr. 23; Rüdiger Klessmann, 'Elsheimers
    *Verspottung der Ceres* – zur Frage des
    Originals', *Städel-Jahrbuch*, N.F. 16, 1997,
    S. 239–48.
24  Elsheimer hat die Situation nach der
    Verwandlung mit der am Boden kriechen-
    den Eidechse zu Füßen der beiden
    Frauen in einer Gouache dargestellt, vgl.
    Andrews 1977, *op. cit.* (Anm. 1), Nr. 51.
    Die gleiche Szene zeigt ein Stich von Jan
    van de Velde II nach Willem O. Akersloot,
    vgl. Hollstein, *op. cit.* (Anm. 7), Bd. I,
    Nr. 18.
25  Nr. 112, vgl. Erich Steingräber (Hrsg.),
    *Alte Pinakothek München. Erläuterungen zu
    den ausgestellten Gemälden*, München 1983,
    S. 508.
26  Zur mythologischen und sinnbildlichen
    Bedeutung der Eidechse vgl. L. Stauch,
    in *Reallexikon zur deutschen Kunstgeschichte*,
    hrsg. Otto Schmidt *et al.*, Bd. 1–,
    Stuttgart 1937–, IV (1958), Sp. 931.
27  Muller, *op. cit.* (Anm. 9), S. 101, Nr. 32.
28  Wilhelm R. Valentiner, *Rembrandt. Des
    Meisters Handzeichnungen II*, Klassiker der
    Kunst, Stuttgart und Berlin 1934, Nr. 606.
29  Milwaukee, Slg. Dr. Alfred und Isabel
    Bader; Werner Sumowski, *Gemälde der
    Rembrandt-Schüler*, 6 Bde., Landau
    1983–94, III, Nr. 1088, S. 1643; Astrid
    Tümpel, *The Pre-Rembrandtists*, Ausst.
    Kat., E.B. Crocker Art Gallery,
    Sacramento, 1974, S. 34, 152, Abb. 49.
30  *Selections from the Drawing Collection of Mr.
    and Mrs. Julius S. Held*, Ausst. Kat., State
    University of New York at Binghamton,
    1970, Nr. 23; Cornelis Hofstede de Groot,
    *Beschreibendes und kritisches Verzeichnis der
    Werke der hervorragendsten holländischen
    Maler des 17. Jahrhunderts I*, Esslingen
    und Paris 1907, Nr. 72; Baruch D.

Kirschenbaum, *The Religious and Historical
Paintings of Jan Steen*, New York 1977,
S. 140, Nr. 72; Karel Braun, *Alle tot nu
toe bekende schilderijen van Jan Steen*,
Rotterdam 1980, S. 145, Nr. A 30;
M. Bellamy, *Three Eyes. The Old Master
Painting from different Viewpoints*, Heim
Gallery, London, 1990, S. 36, Nr.7 mit Abb.
31  Helmut Börsch-Supan, *Die Gemälde im
    Jagdschloß Grunewald*, Berlin 1964, S. 62,
    N. 78.
32  Christian L. von Hagedorn, *Lettre à un
    Amateur de la Peinture*, Dresden 1755, S. 179.
33  Klessmann 1997, *op. cit.* (Anm. 23), S. 247.
34  Andrews 1977, *op. cit.* (Anm. 1), S. 148,
    Nr. 18; Rüdiger Klessmann, 'Elsheimers
    Aurora-Landschaft in neuem Licht',
    *Nederlands Kunsthistorisch Jaarboek*, Bd.38,
    1987, S. 158–71.
35  Hierzu vgl. Klessmann 1987, *op. cit.*
    (Anm. 34), S. 168f., Anm. 7.
36  Andrews 1977, *op. cit.* (Anm. 1), S. 153,
    Nr. 24.
37  Andrews 1977, *op. cit.* (Anm. 1), S. 154,
    Nr. 25. Eine genaue Analyse der unter-
    scheidenden Merkmale der beiden
    *Tobias*-Kompositionen bei Werner
    Sumowski, 'Varianten bei Elsheimer',
    *artibus et historiae*, XXV, 1992, S. 145–49.
38  Vgl. Dogaer 1971, *op. cit.* (Anm. 12),
    S. 212, Nr. 106
39  Vgl. Albert Blankert, *Nederlandse 17e
    Eeuwse Italianiserende Landschapschilders*,
    Ausst. Kat., Centraal Museum, Utrecht,
    1965, S. 63f., Anm. 6.
40  Vgl. Tümpel, *op. cit.* (Anm. 29), S. 26f.
41  Rüdiger Klessmann, 'Die Landschaft mit
    der büßenden Magdalena von Jacob
    Pynas', *Jahrbuch der Berliner Museen*, N.F.
    15, 1965, S. 7ff.; Ausst. Kat. Frankfurt
    1966, *op. cit.* (Anm. 5), Nr. 88, 91; Albert
    Brejon de Lavergnée, Jacques Foucart,
    Nicole Reynaud, *Catalogue sommaire illustré
    des peintures du Musée du Louvre. Ecoles
    flamande et hollandaise*, Paris 1979, S. 109,
    Nr. 1269; Bernhard Schnackenburg,
    *Staatliche Museen Kassel. Gemäldegalerie Alte
    Meister, Gesamtkatalog*, Mainz 1996, S. 224,
    Nr. GK 611.
42  Hollstein, *op. cit.* (Anm. 7), XVI, Nr. 7.
43  Hollstein, *op. cit.* (Anm. 7), XVI, Nr. 6;
    Ausst. Kat. Frankfurt 1966, *op. cit.* (Anm. 5),
    Nr. 289.

  RÜDIGER KLESSMANN

44 Andrews 1977, *op. cit.* (Anm. 1), S. 166,
Nr. A 2.

45 Gustav Parthey, *Wenzel Hollar.
Beschreibendes Verzeichnis seiner Kupferstiche*,
Berlin 1853, Nr. 272; Andrews 1986,
*op. cit.* (Anm. 18), Nr. 21A; Antje Repp-
Eckert, in *I Bamboccianti. Niederländische
Malerrebellen im Rom des Barock*, Ausst.
Kat., Redaktion D.A. Levine, E. Mai,
Wallraf-Richartz Museum, Köln;
Centraal Museum, Utrecht, 1991, Nr. 13.
Das vom Wallraf-Richartz-Museum
erworbene Bild befindet sich leider in
einem schlechten Erhaltungszustand.

46 Andrews 1977, *op. cit.* (Anm. 1), Nr. 22.

47 Vgl. Ilja M. Veldmans Eintrag in Jane
Turner (Hrsg.), *The Dictionary of Art*, 34
Bde., London 1996, Bd. 24, S. 236; I.M.
Veldman, *Crispijn de Passe and his Progeny*,
Rotterdam 2001, S. 199f.

48 Hollstein, *op. cit.* (Anm. 7), XVI, Nr. 5.

49 J.G. van Gelder, 'Rubens in Holland in
de zeventiende eeuw', *Nederlands Kunsthistorisch Jaarboek*, Bd. 3, 1951, S. 103 f.

50 Es fehlt bis heute eine monographische
Bearbeitung des Oeuvres von Johann
König, welche im Hinblick auf seine
von Elsheimer geprägte Frühzeit ein
dringendes Desiderat darstellt.

51 Städtische Kunstsammlungen Augsburg,
Nr. L 834. *Deutsche Barockgalerie. Katalog
der Gemälde*, 2. Auflage, bearbeitet von
Gode Krämer, Augsburg 1984, S. 160f.
Die hier vorgeschlagene Datierung des
Bildes um 1625 erscheint zu spät. Für
die Beschaffung einer Fotografie habe
ich Gode Krämer zu danken.

52 Andrews 1977, *op. cit.* (Anm. 1), S. 151,
Nr. 21. Es sind zahllose Versionen oder
Wiederholungen der Komposition
bekannt, aber nach der Qualität und
malerischen Handschrift kann man
nur dem Gemälde aus Corsham Court,
heute in Liverpool, Walker Art Gallery
(Nr. 10329), die Eigenhändigkeit
zuerkennen.

53 Andrews 1977, *op. cit.* (Anm. 1), S. 150,
Nr. 20. Die Eigenhändigkeit des häufig
kopierten Gemäldes in Frankfurt ist
erst spät erkannt worden, dabei kann –
abgesehen von der charakteristischen
Malweise – Sandrarts Beschreibung und
Goudts Nachstich von 1608 nur auf
dieses bezogen werden.

54 Vgl. G. Biermann, *Deutsches Barock und
Rokoko. Jahrhundert-Ausstellung deutscher
Kunst 1650 – 1800*, Ausst. Kat., 2 Bde,
Darmstadt und Leipzig, 1914, II,
S. XXVII; I, S.132 (Slg. Fürst Reuß ä. L.);
*Gemäldegalerie Berlin. Gesamtverzeichnis,
Staatliche Museen zu Berlin, Preußischer
Kulturbesitz*, Redaktion R. Grosshans,
Berlin 1996, S. 44, Nr. 664A.

55 Wallraf-Richartz-Museum, Nr. 2520;
Ursula Erichsen-Firle, Horst Vey, *Katalog
der deutschen Gemälde von 1550 – 1800*,
Köln 1973, S. 59, Nr. 2520.

56 Darmstadt, Hessisches Landesmuseum
Johann König, *Minerva und die Musen*,
Inv. Nr. GK 1152, datiert 1619, vgl.
Gerhard Bott, *Die Gemäldegalerie des
Hessischen Landesmuseums in Darmstadt*,
Hanau 1968, S. 43, Nr. 65; Götz Adriani,
*Deutsche Malerei im 17. Jahrhundert*,
Köln 1977, S. 31.

57 Vgl. A.R. Peltzer (Hrsg.), *Joachim von
Sandrarts Academie der Bau-, Bild- und
Mahlerey- Künste von 1675*, München 1925,
S. 163.

58 Ein als gesichert anzusehendes Bild, eine
monogrammierte und 1607 (oder 1609 ?)
datierte *Judith*, in Friedrichshafen,
Städtisches Bodensee-Museum, zeigt
Entlehnungen von Elsheimers *Ceres*.
Wenn die undeutliche Jahreszahl richtig
gelesen ist, wäre damit ein *terminus ante
quem* für Elsheimers Gemälde gegeben.
Vgl. auch Malcolm Waddingham, 'Adam
Elsheimer and His Circle at Frankfurt',
*The Burlington Magazine*, CIX, 1967, S. 48.

59 Peltzer 1925, *op. cit.* (Anm. 57), S. 163.

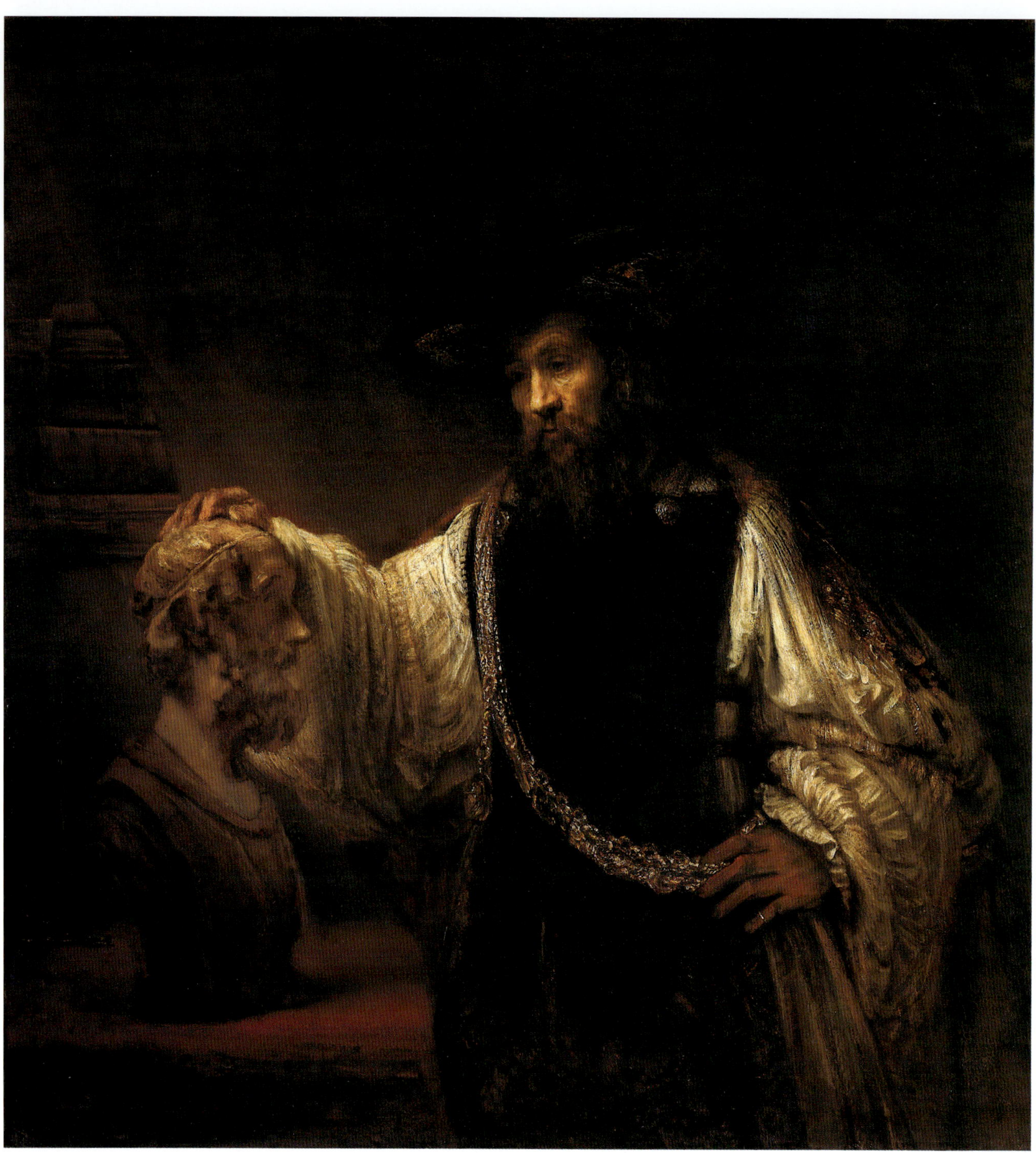

# The Meaning of Rembrandt's
## *Aristotle with a Bust of Homer*

WALTER LIEDTKE

It is a rare form of homage when scholars think of the essential literature on a great work of art mainly in terms of a single essay, such as 'Rembrandt's *Aristotle*' by Julius Held.[1] The painting we no longer call 'Aristotle contemplating the Bust of Homer' (fig. 1) changed in meaning with that publication of 1969.[2] When Held presented his study as a lecture in 1966 Erwin Panofsky declared it the best he ever heard at Princeton.[3] And in thirty-five years no one has improved upon our understanding of a picture that may be considered one of Rembrandt's most significant works.[4]

Held's explanation of the subject has been restated so frequently that it would be wise to start with what he actually wrote.[5] He begins by questioning the familiar title (introduced by Bredius in 1936) and by reviewing recent interpretations, such as Saxl's idea that Aristotle (384–322 BC) and Homer represent the kinship of Philosophy and Poetry. In Held's opinion, most commentaries fail to clarify "the specific nature of the confrontation" between the figure and the bust (p. 18). Some readings require no discussion: Neumann's notion of a "silent dialogue" between the savant and his sculpture; Schmidt-Degener's perception of a melancholy poet who "looks into the eyes" of the marble head. As is well known, the main figure went by other names – an unknown poet, Virgil (70–19 BC), Torquato Tasso (1544–1595), P.C. Hooft ('the Dutch Homer', 1581–1647) – until 1916, when the account books and correspondence of Rembrandt's patron, the Sicilian nobleman Antonio Ruffo (1610/11–1678), were published and identified the subject as Aristotle.[6]

The widely accepted hypothesis advanced by Held is that the philosopher contemplates not only the bust of his distant predecessor Homer but also the magnificent chain given (in Rembrandt's imagination) to Aristotle by his royal pupil Alexander the Great (356–332 BC). Alexander's portrait, evidently, appears on a medallion suspended from the cascading strands of gold. For Held, these motifs establish a "contrast between two sets of values" (p. 54): everything that Aristotle would have admired in Homer, as opposed to the wealth and

fig. 1 REMBRANDT
*Aristotle with a Bust of Homer*, 1653
Oil on canvas, 143.5 × 136.5 cm
New York, The Metropolitan
Museum of Art

worldly honour that are announced by the chain. This interpretation is supported by Held's erudite remarks on what the Greek authors, gold chains and princely patrons meant to seventeenth-century artists, and by his impressions of what such themes as blindness, sight, inner vision, material riches, mortality and lasting fame meant to Rembrandt in his life and art.

However, readers who remember Held's essay in a golden haze may wish to reconsider his closing lines, which refer to the "deeply religious [artist's] attitude towards the value of secular honor"; to Homer as perhaps subconsciously "a transfigured image of [Rembrandt's] own father"; and to the painter as someone "who never compromised, who never permitted himself to be burdened with a chain of honor [not that one was offered], and fiercely maintained both the integrity of his art and his freedom as a man" (pp. 57–58). Sauerländer cites this article as an example of how subjectively Held responded to Rembrandt, as opposed to Rubens: "Hinter der kunstgeschichtlichen Deutung wird die Lebensspur eines Interpreten sichtbar, der selbst vor der Tyrannis hatte flüchten müssen."[7]

The period flavour of Held's study is most evident in his assumption that the *Aristotle* can be understood as the painter's own manifesto. Rembrandt chose the subject and "whatever thoughts went into the creation of the work, they were not shaped by the wishes or instructions of the Italian collector" (p. 27). Comparisons are made with other images by Rembrandt that involve moral issues, such as his representations of the blind Tobit and of Bathsheba. The latter figure, in the Louvre canvas of 1654, is also "alone with her thoughts, pondering a decision of far-reaching implications" (p. 44).

Much of this is *ben trovato* when not manifestly true. But when Held observes that Rembrandt, following "age-old pictorial conventions", shows Aristotle touching Homer with his right hand raised into the light, while his left hand strokes the chain in a lower and more shadowy part of the picture (p. 53), one wonders what Ruffo would have made of such symbolism. There must have been less 'embarrassment of riches' in Messina than in Amsterdam, especially in the grand *palazzo* where Ruffo kept a few hundred paintings and perhaps a few gold chains. Similarly, when Held relates *Aristotle with a Bust of Homer* to portraits of male figures holding skulls, one might question whether Ruffo would also have detected the concept of "survival" after life or in the face of death (pp. 41–42), ideas that were conveyed more clearly in his painting by Anthony van Dyck (1599–1641), *Saint Rosalie interceding for the Plague-Stricken of Palermo* (Metropolitan Museum of Art, New York), and in many Italian works of art.

Here we touch upon a problem with Held's approach. On the one hand, there are meanings that Rembrandt may have intended, or that are plausible for his time and place. On the other hand, there is the patron's likely response, which in this case would reflect a rather different culture and level of society. To what extent can personal or profound thoughts be read into a picture made for export, as opposed to a drawing, an etching, or a painting destined for a sympathetic collector in Amsterdam?

It would be useful to learn a little more about Antonio Ruffo than is found in Held's article. He was born in 1610 or 1611 into one of the great aristocratic families of southern Italy, although as clerics (and patrons) the Ruffos were influential in places as far away as Ferrara. Antonio was the posthumous son of the Duke of Bagnara, Carlo I (1566–1610). The widowed duchess (Antonia Spadafora, died 1619) moved to Messina, where the majestic palace she commissioned was completed in 1646. Antonio purchased paintings aggressively from that year onwards (at his death he had 364). He also collected silver, coins and medals and tapestries (two after designs by Peter Paul Rubens), but pictures by sixteenth- and seventeenth-century masters were his main concern. Money was never a problem but price was frequently an issue, as in 1649, when one of his favourite artists, Guercino (1591–1666), informed Ruffo that "as Your Excellency has restricted Yourself to 80 ducats, you will have just a bit more than half of one figure".[8] Another priority was size. As Haskell explains, Ruffo's paintings "were arranged according to a symmetrical pattern, and he was often anxious to make up pairs – either from the same artist or two different ones – and this concern naturally involved the actual composition".[9] Almost all of Ruffo's collecting was done through agents, friends and family members such as his brother in Rome, the abbot Flavio Ruffo (died 1656), and his nephews Tommaso Ruffo in Bologna and Fabrizio Ruffo (1619–1692) in Naples. In comparatively provincial Messina, from which he rarely travelled, Ruffo learned of living artists mostly through correspondence and word of mouth.[10]

Ruffo came into contact with Rembrandt through his agent in Messina, Giacomo di Battista, who did business with the wealthy Amsterdam merchant Cornelis Gijsbertsz van Goor (*ca.* 1600–1675). In a letter to Battista dated 19 June 1654, Van Goor reports on a shipment of goods by sea which will include (in the care of the captain) "a square crate with the picture for your friend". The letter includes a bill for five hundred guilders "for the painting by Rembrandt as per invoice", and fifteen guilders for crating and shipping expenses.[11]

The earliest known references to the picture's subject are found on a single page in Ruffo's ledger or 'account book', and read as follows: "1654 on 1 September – Rembrant – Palmi 8 × 6 – half-length figure of a philosopher made in Amsterdam by the painter named Rembrant (it appears to be Aristotle or Albertus Magnus)"; and (within a paragraph listing various expenses) "1657. 8 January . . . 3 ounces [coinage] for a frame of the picture of Albertus Magnus".[12] It should be emphasized that there are no earlier known descriptions of the figure, even in the most general terms. Ruffo is not known to have requested a painting of a philosopher, as is commonly stated, nor is he known to have collected pictures of philosophers before the 1660s. The possibility remains that the patron or a middleman remarked on the subject in advance, but it appears much more likely that Ruffo (as on other occasions) simply asked for a figure painting of a certain size and approximate format.

Giltaij, after close examination of the evidence, agrees with Held that Rembrandt chose the subject of Aristotle. But the younger scholar doubts that any "intellectual ambitions" should be discerned in the work. Rembrandt probably decided that a classical subject would appeal to such a patron and turned for inspiration to his *kunstkamer*. In that room he had a number of busts or statues of Roman emperors, and busts of Socrates, Homer and Aristotle. The latter (because they stood together?) were listed consecutively as nos. 162–64 in the inventory of Rembrandt's household effects made in July 1656.[13] Held suggests reasonably that while no. 163 was "at least a plaster cast" of a famous Hellenistic bust of Homer, no. 164 was "probably a copy of a well-known and entirely imaginary Renaissance sculpture rendering Aristotle with long hair and a flowing beard" (as in fig. 3).[14] For the *Aristotle* Rembrandt may also have employed a live model, who appears in a few other works by the master and his pupils, including *A Bearded Man in a Cap*, signed *Rembrandt. f. 165*[3 or 7?], in the National Gallery, London.[15]

A prototype for the gold medallion is not known. However, the helmeted head resembles a Renaissance type of Alexander, whose portrait would of course help identify the pensive figure as Aristotle.[16] Or as Alexander's painter, Apelles (active 332–304 BC), according to a recent theory,[17] which has nothing in its favour apart from the medallion, and flies in the face of almost every Renaissance and Baroque image of the Greek artist.[18] By contrast, Rembrandt's figure is consistent in type not only with the Italian bust cited by Held and similar relief and medallion portraits of Aristotle dating from about 1500,[19] but also with pictorial examples ranging from the lively *Aristotle* (fig. 2) in the Urbino series of *Famous Men* by Joos van Gent (active *ca.* 1460–80) to the fallen philosopher clutching his *Ethics* in one of the *Desolation of Parnassus* frescoes of 1635 by Giovanni di San Giovanni (1592–1636) in the Palazzo Pitti (where the neighbouring figure of Homer is about to stumble blindly through the picture plane).[20] Van Gent anticipates Rembrandt by individualizing the Renaissance type and by recalling Aristotle's reputation for dressing up.[21]

These comparisons, combined with a survey of Dutch and Flemish scholar portraits (as opposed to pictures of Apelles's studio), would appear to resolve the issue of whether the man with a bust of Homer is an artist or a philosopher.[22] However, one should also consider the Ruffo documents of the 1660s

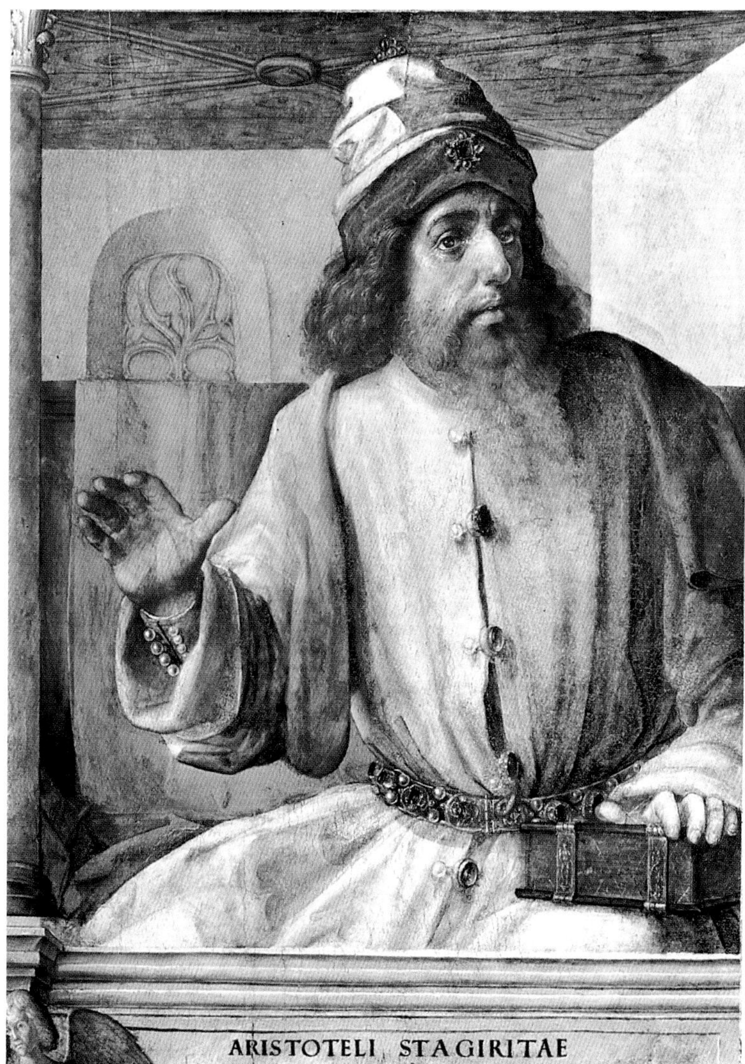



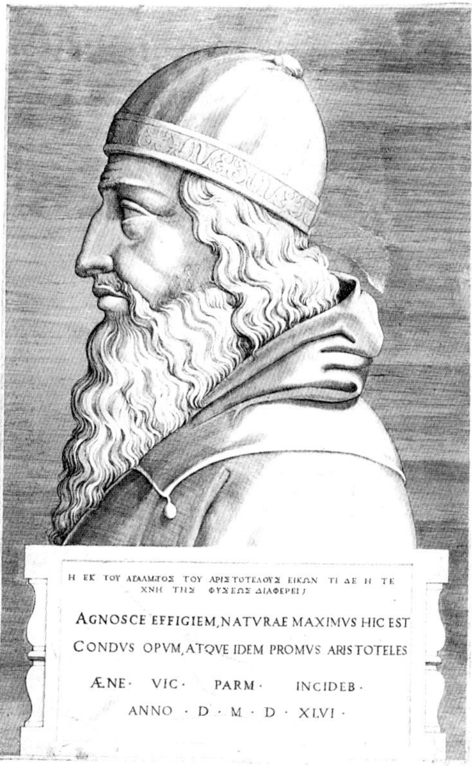



fig. 3 ENEA VICO, *Aristotle*, 1546
Engraving, 35.1 × 22.5 cm
London, The British Museum

fig. 2 JOOS VAN GENT, *Aristotle* (from the
series of *Famous Men* painted for the *studiolo*
of the Palazzo Ducale, Urbino), *ca.* 1475
Oil on wood, 100.3 × 68.5 cm
Paris, Musée du Louvre

concerning Rembrandt's Homer and Alexander and the Italian portraits of philosophers that were likewise intended to complement the canvas of 1653: Guercino's *Cosmographer*, Mattia Preti's *Dionysius*, Salvator Rosa's *Pythagoras* or *Archytas of Tarentum* and Giacinto Brandi's "*Philosopher or* [the studious] *St Jerome*".[23]

A related question has never been considered adequately. Why did Ruffo or another viewer of Rembrandt's painting in 1654 think that it might represent Albertus Magnus, that is, St Albert the Great (1206–1280), the celebrated scholar of Aristotle and teacher of Thomas Aquinas (*ca.* 1225–1274)? During the seventeenth century Albertus was such a familiar figure in Church history (he was beatified in 1622) and university curricula that almost any image of a scholar seeming to have lived some time before Ruffo's day might be thought to depict the so-called 'universal doctor.' It would not be inappropriate to portray

Albertus pondering a classical bust (which was evidently not identified in 1654), considering his eight thousand pages of commentary on Aristotle and frequent discussion of other ancient authors.[24] Ruffo may not have already known an imaginary portrait of Albertus – certainly not the clean-shaven cleric in Van Gent's series of *Famous Men*, and perhaps not any of the minor prints that show him as a beardless and balding monk or bishop. However, the collector was probably acquainted with the legend that Albertus had created a talking statue or head which was destroyed by Thomas Aquinas. A staple of the literature on automata (much more so than Leonardo's mechanical lion or Archytas's flying dove), the story circulated in contemporary publications like Selenus's *Cryptomenytices et cryptographiae* of 1624, in which the second book opens with a discussion of hidden speaking tubes. "So it is recorded in the books that Albertus Magnus constructed a talking head. There is no doubt that he produced this rare and wonderful thing through one of the above-mentioned devices."[25]

Anyone in Ruffo's cultivated circle could have proposed Albertus's name. But if the patron thought that "*Alberto Magno*" was one of two plausible identifications in 1654, why was the other "*Aristotile*"? The figure's face, perhaps the bust, and conceivably even the medallion may have led to this conclusion. But the costume was another matter. Italian artists, such as Giovanni di San Giovanni in Florence and Raphael (1483–1520) in the Vatican, were accustomed to presenting Aristotle and his contemporaries in classical drapery. Appropriate models were not lacking in Sicily, where, however, it might not have been realised that Rembrandt (unlike Rubens in the *Achilles* tapestries Ruffo owned) would take a far from archaeological approach to describing antique dress. The question deserves repetition: how is it possible that in Messina (as opposed to Amsterdam) this image of a scholar with his leather-bound volumes, his Venetian shirt and vaguely outdated tunic – looking altogether more like a contemporary of Ruffo than of Albertus – could be considered to be, if not Albertus then Aristotle?[26]

Perhaps the answer is that both philosophers were known in the seventeenth century for their discussions of the human senses, and in particular for their comparisons of touch and sight. It is not hard to imagine that Ruffo or an acquaintance would have concluded that in Rembrandt's painting touch and sight are prominent concerns. In early pictures by Jusepe Ribera (1591–1652) of the Five Senses, which were probably painted about 1613–15 in Rome, *Touch* (fig. 4) is represented by a blind man (who bears a curious resemblance to the Renaissance Aristotle; compare fig. 3) exploring with his fingers the features of a classical head. A painting of a bust-length figure lies on the table, stressing the limits of the sense of touch. Ribera's *Sight* from the same series (Museo Franz Mayer, Mexico City) shows a man holding a Galilean telescope by a window;

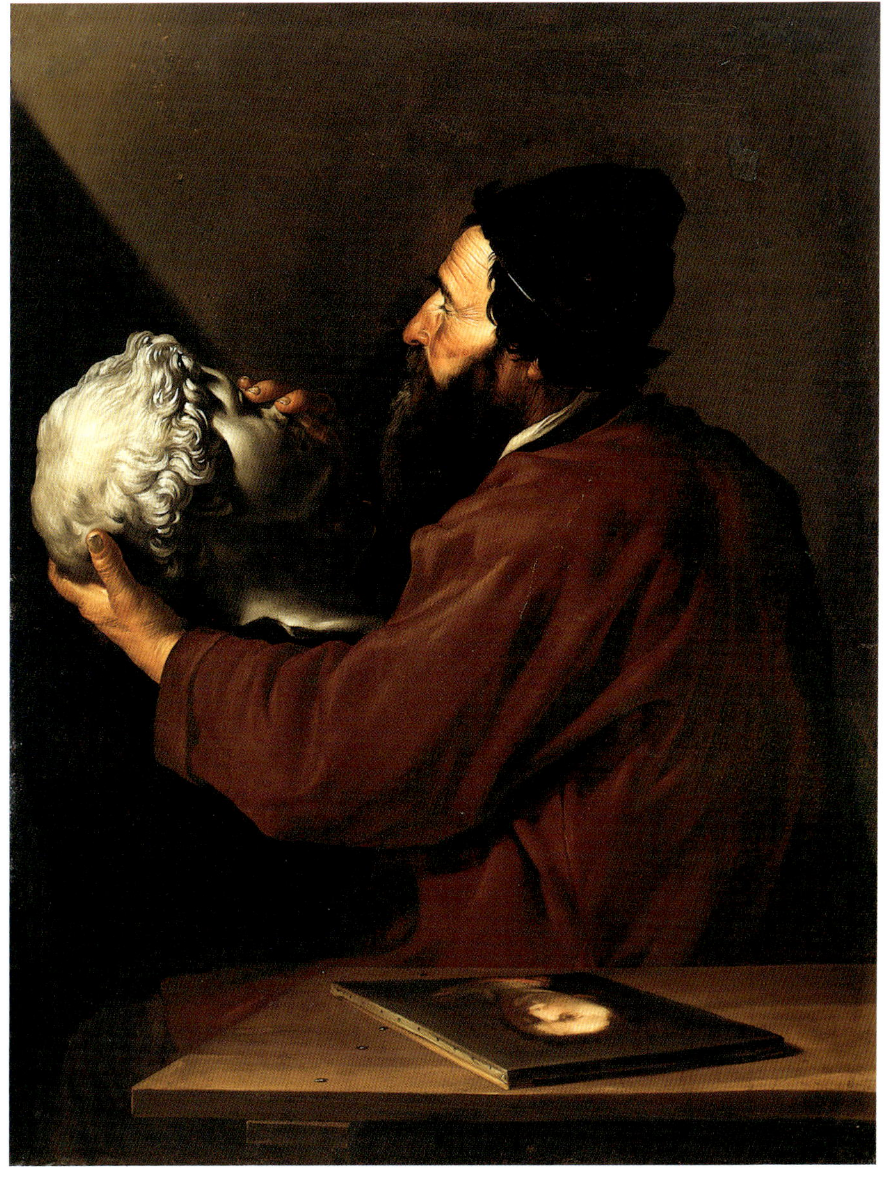

fig. 4 JUSEPE DE RIBERA
*The Sense of Touch*, *ca.* 1615–16
Oil on canvas, 116 × 88.3 cm
Pasadena, The Norton Simon
Foundation

a mirror and spectacles lie before him. The thoughtful figure does not look at anything, but with wide, unfocussed eyes appears to reflect upon what he has seen. The senses of hearing, taste and smell in Ribera's series are represented by earthier, less cognizant types accompanied by items intended solely for gratification.[27]

In his Caravaggesque presentation of single figures Ribera departed from the complex allegories favored by artists such as Jan Brueghel the Elder (1568–1625) and at the same time anticipated many Netherlandish and Italian works.[28] Among the more inventive examples are two series of the *Five Senses* painted in the 1650s by Gonzales Coques (1614/18–1684). In the set of panels at the National Gallery, London, *Sight* represents a painter with a palette and brushes, while *Touch* illustrates a young man letting blood from his arm.[29] In the second series (Koninklijk Museum, Antwerp) *Touch* depicts a man sharpening a pen, while *Sight* unexpectedly shows a spectacled sculptor carefully finishing a statuette.[30] The latter picture takes clever advantage of the role of sculpture in contemporary illustrations of the sense of touch (see fig. 4) in order to suggest that sight is more important no matter what the object perceived.

A somewhat similar *paragone* of the senses is found in the large canvas by Theodoor Rombouts (1597–1637), *The Five Senses* (Museum voor Schone Kunsten, Ghent), where the dignified figure of Sight peers through his glasses at the handicapped efforts of Touch to comprehend some fragments of sculpture. In the foreground, Sight's mirror reveals to the viewer a second perspective upon Hearing's pile of musical instruments. Quite as Touch would learn nothing from the mirror, a sculptor would be unable to match its verisimilitude or to depict all the textures, reflections, and other visual effects (water, glass, smoke, shifting colours etc) that may be appreciated in Rombouts's painting.[31]

Fittingly enough, the first known representations of the Five Senses as human figures are found in thirteenth-century Latin translations of Aristotle's "On Sense and Sensible Objects" (*De sensu et sensato*).[32] In the same period Albertus Magnus endorsed Aristotle's ranking of the senses by explaining that sight provided the most rapid, comprehensive and discriminating knowledge of the physical world. Through sight, Albertus maintained, human beings discover and create, while they teach and learn through hearing. Aquinas expanded on his mentor's remarks, suggesting that humans walk upright because their senses seek out knowledge and beauty, not just mere necessities. Animals face the ground, but man stands erect "in order that by the senses, and chiefly by sight, which is more subtle and penetrates further into the differences of things, he may freely survey the sensible objects around him, both heavenly and earthly, so as to gather intelligible truth from all things".[33]

Aristotle's judgment of the senses and his importance for the history of art theory are topics that cannot be touched upon further without losing sight of the matter at hand.[34] Rembrandt's appreciation of Aristotle probably focused on questions of observation, and with respect to painting must have been influenced by the philosopher's opinions of the senses as cited in the ongoing *paragone* debate. It will be remembered that the usual Renaissance comparisons of painting and sculpture extended the parallels drawn between painting and poetry in two classical sources, Horace's *Ars poetica* and Aristotle's *Poetics*.[35] Homer is cited repeatedly in the latter text as an authority or example for Aristotle's subject, which (it should be stressed) is not poetry *per se* but imitation (*mimesis*). He maintains, for example, that painting, poetry, music and certain non-artistic activities (child's play, mimicking sounds, and so on) are consistent forms of imitation in that they reveal an innate desire for knowledge and the experience of pleasure in response to likenesses.[36]

Here again it would be wise to consider plausible as well as possible interpretations. The bust of Homer in Ruffo's picture might be taken by some scholars as a reference to Horace's dictum, *ut pictura poesis* (as is painting so is poetry), especially since Homer's fame in Holland was unsurpassed by that of any other poet.[37] But Aristotle is not Apelles, and if Rembrandt had Horace's pronouncement in mind he probably would have meant by it only that painting, like poetry, was a learned art. As for the argument that painting is superior to sculpture as a form of imitation, this must have seemed to the artist, in his decision to portray Aristotle, an opportunity too good to miss. Rembrandt was apparently asked by Ruffo for an example of his work, a figure painting, no more. The characterization of Aristotle is so fully realised in the picture that this choice of subject surely came first, as opposed to, for example, a decision to praise *Pictura* in an unexpected way. But in thinking, reading or hearing about Aristotle Rembrandt must have realised that he had come to the very source of the concept that painting is a noble art, namely Aristotle's arguments for the primacy of sight as a means to acquire knowledge.

In this Rembrandt would have followed many artists and critics from Leon Battista Alberti (1404–1472) onwards, and especially Leonardo (1452–1519), who not only echoed Aristotle in declaring that "the eye embraces the beauty of the whole world", and that "its sciences are the most certain", but also wondered in the same passage what words could possibly express the nobility of "most excellent painting, above all other things created by God". In another part of the *Treatise on Painting* (first published in Paris in 1651) Leonardo pokes his finger in the eye of more conventional theorists by placing painting even higher than poetry, since the former originates in the light of nature, whereas the latter is born in the "*occhio tenebroso*" of the imagination.[38]

It is noteworthy that Rembrandt's primary source for the features of Aristotle was a piece of sculpture, which he apparently improved upon by employing a live model (the sort of *paragone* in practice that Rubens prescribed).[39] The bust of Homer in Rembrandt's studio became in the painting (among other things, to be sure) a reference to sculpture and touch (compare fig. 4). Except for the motif of blindness one finds an analogous conceit in Titian's early portrait of a woman, called *La Schiavona* (fig. 5). The lady looks at the viewer and rests her hand on a parapet where her own image appears in profile. This flattering portrait *all'antica* was added in the course of work.[40] Titian (*ca.* 1490–1576) evidently realised that he could compare painting with sculpture and sight with touch by showing

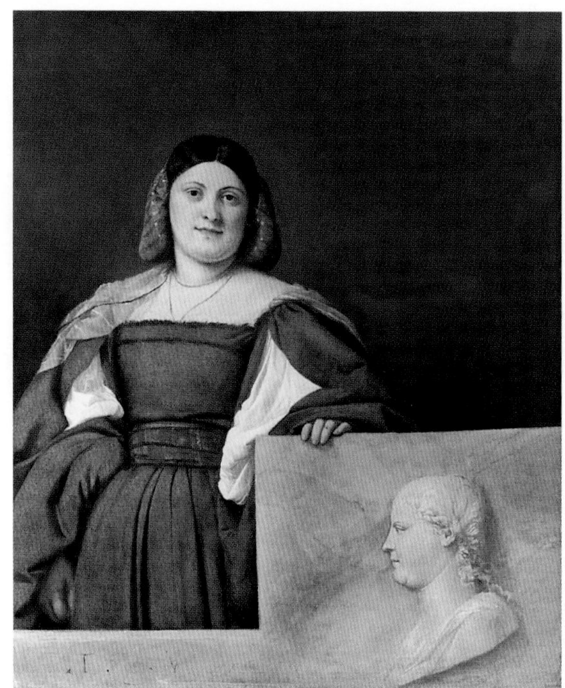



another view of the sitter as if carved in relief. Other Venetian artists had just painted simultaneous views of a single figure in response to one of the standard arguments made on sculpture's behalf.[41]

Rembrandt created something original in the same vein, as might have been expected. Acts of touch and sight take on special meaning in earlier works by the artist, such as those based on the Book of Tobit.[42] Of course, conspicuous glances and gestures are commonplace in history pictures, but the instances of looking at or touching something thoughtfully, or of looking inward, are nonetheless remarkable in Rembrandt's oeuvre (for instance, in the Louvre *Bathsheba*, *Isaac Blessing Jacob* and *The Jewish Bride*, and also in portraits such as *The Anatomy Lesson of Dr Tulp* and *The Preacher Anslo and his Wife*). In the 1640s optical and tactile qualities also appear to have preoccupied Rembrandt for their own sake, to an extent that reading about their imitation in a manuscript copy of Leonardo's *Treatise on Painting* seemed likely to Kenneth Clark.[43]

That Rembrandt would allude to the senses in a portrait of the most renowned authority on the subject seems the more probable when one considers the comparisons of sight and touch, painting and sculpture that had been drawn in recent works by his most successful pupil, Gerrit Dou (1613–1675). Not only did that painter to princes set plaster heads and stone reliefs next to everything that his own art could describe more convincingly (flesh, fabrics, metal, glass, water, shadows and so on), but his pictures also were praised as the pinnacle of that achievement in Philips Angel's *Lof der Schilder-konst*, an oration presented in 1641 to the painters' guild of Leiden and published there in the following year.



WALTER LIEDTKE

The "far-famed Rembrandt" himself is honored in the text for his close reading of history but it is "the perfect and excellent Gerrit Dou" who puts both sculptors and poets to shame, partly on the Aristotelean grounds that "the eye is the noblest of the five senses" and that "the art of painting is far more general because it is capable of imitating nature much more copiously".[44]

Aristotle is a very different subject than those treated by Dou, whose main concerns were merely subthemes for Rembrandt. The artist's insight into historical subjects may be described as one aspect of a broader ability to convey the essence of a story or character. Thus, the figure of Aristotle would not simply stand for Sight and that of Homer for Touch, or any other pair of ideas. Aristotle's responsive eyes and hands imply their proper senses, but also contemplation or philosophy. He sees without looking, and in that resembles Homer; perhaps the concept of inner vision (or imagination) is conveyed by animating the bust with fluid brushwork and light and shadow. If Rembrandt read Aristotle on the sense of sight he would have come upon his analysis of hearing, which in certain circumstances "makes the largest contribution to wisdom. For the spoken word, which is responsible for all instruction, is heard . . . . Consequently, of those who have been deprived of one sense or the other from birth, the blind are more intelligent than the deaf and the dumb."[45]

For Leonardo a man who goes blind "loses the sight and beauty of the universe, and remains like one buried alive in a tomb".[46] There is no hint of this opinion in Rembrandt's images of Homer. For the artist, as for Dutch writers of the time, Homer was "the outstanding poet of the serious kind" praised in the *Poetics*, where his effectiveness as a dramatist is explained by Aristotle. "When he composed the *Odyssey* he did not include everything which happened to Odysseus . . . ; instead, he constructed the *Odyssey* about a single action of the kind we are discussing. The same is true of the *Iliad*."[47] And of Rembrandt.[48]

In conclusion, the emphasis placed upon the senses in this article may be said to temper but not displace Held's idea of contrasting values.[49] The main comparison intended by the painter, to judge from Aristotle's expression, pose and attributes, is between worldly things such as wealth and power and the search for virtue and truth. Anyone who read Aristotle in Rembrandt's day would have known that in the *Ethics* knowledge gained through contemplation was more esteemed than information gathered by the senses, and that intellectual pursuits were placed above all others, including those of kings.[50] Perhaps the choice between an active and a contemplative life was assigned to Aristotle when Rembrandt painted companion pictures of Homer and Alexander. But this goes beyond our subject, and beyond Rembrandt's in 1653. "It appears to be Aristotle or Albertus Magnus": Ruffo's reading offers more to think about than meets the eye.

1   Julius S. Held, *Rembrandt's Aristotle and other Rembrandt Studies*, Princeton 1969, ch. 1. Held died on 22 December 2002, at the age of ninety-seven.

2   In 1972 the Metropolitan Museum changed the picture's title at the suggestion of curator John Walsh.

3   This was recalled in Willibald Sauerländer's obituary of Held in the *Süddeutsche Zeitung*, 22 January 2003, p. 13.

4   In a postscript to 'Rembrandt's *Aristotle*' published in Julius S. Held, *Rembrandt Studies*, Princeton 1991, pp. 191–92, the author convincingly refutes the observations of Michael Platt and Svetlana Alpers and the more substantial contribution of Margaret Deutsch Carroll, 'Rembrandt's *Aristotle*: Exemplary Beholder,' *artibus et historiae*, x, 1984, pp. 35–56. I am grateful to Vanessa Schmid for reviewing all published references to the painting on behalf of my department in the Metropolitan Museum.

5   In the text following, the use of notes will be minimized by citing page numbers in Held, *op. cit.* (note 4), in parentheses, and by asking the reader to consult that volume for various references.

6   What the documents actually say is considered below. See Jeroen Giltaij, *Ruffo en Rembrandt. Over een Siciliaanse verzamelaar in de zeventiende eeuw die drie schilderijen bij Rembrandt bestelde*, Zutphen 1999, ch. 5 and appendix B.

7   Sauerländer, *op. cit.* (note 3).

8   Francis Haskell, *Patrons and Painters*, New Haven and London 1980, p. 14, for the quotation, and pp. 169, 209–10, 214 on Ruffo. See also Giltaij, *op. cit.* (note 6), ch. 1.

9   Haskell, *op. cit.* (note 8), p. 209.

10  *Ibid.*, pp. 209, 214; Giltaij, *op. cit.* (note 6), ch. 2.

11  Giltaij, *op. cit.* (note 6), pp. 43–44, 160–61.

12  *Ibid.*, pp. 44, 125–26. Giltaij (personal communication, April 2003) agrees with the present writer that the 1657 reference to Albertus Magnus is probably just a shorthand repetition of the entry dated 1654, and not an instance of new thinking on the subject.

13  Giltaij, *op. cit.* (note 6), p. 81; Walter L. Strauss and Marjon van der Meulen, *The Rembrandt Documents*, New York 1979, p. 365, no. 1656/12.

14  Held, *op. cit.* (note 4), pp. 29, 31–32.

15  See Neil MacLaren (revised and expanded by Christopher Brown), *The Dutch School 1600–1900*, National Gallery Catalogues, 2 vols., London 1991, I, p. 335.

16  See Held, *op. cit.* (note 4), pp. 30–31, and Giltaij, *op. cit.* (note 6), pp. 49, 81.

17  Advanced in an unpublished paper by Paul Crenshaw (1995), which he kindly sent to the present writer. The theory is adopted in Simon Schama, *Rembrandt's Eyes*, New York 1999, pp. 582–94, 720 n. 18. In Benjamin Binstock's review another misreading by Schama of a classical subject is considered "outdone in implausibility only by his renaming" of the *Aristotle* (*Art Bulletin*, LXXXII, 2000, p. 365). The same opinion is expressed by David Freedberg in *The New Republic*, 6 December 1999, p. 50.

18  The Netherlandish Apelles is usually youthful, short-bearded (when not clean-shaven) and busy with the tools of his trade. For a few of the many examples see Zirka Zaremba Filipczak, *Picturing Art in Antwerp 1550–1700*, Princeton 1987, figs. 12, 13, 34.

19  See Leo Planiscig, 'Leonardos Porträts und Aristoteles', in *Festschrift für Julius Schlosser zum 60. Geburtstag*, Vienna 1927, pp. 137–44, figs. 59–61 (bust), 62 (relief), 63 (medallion). Planiscig (pp. 140–41) stresses that there are other versions of the relief, and examples of the type in other art forms (see fig. 3). In addition to the bust in his own collection, Rembrandt could have known the engravings of the Renaissance Aristotle in Fulvio Orsini's *Imagines et elogia virorum illustrium* (Rome 1570), in André Thevet's *Les Vrais Pourtraits et vies des hommes illustres . . .* (Paris 1584), or in a similar compendium. For Orsini's and Thevet's portraits of Homer and Aristotle, see Eugene Dwyer, 'André Thevet and Fulvio Orsini: The Beginnings of the Modern Tradition of Classical Portrait Iconography in France', *Art Bulletin*, LXXV, 1993, pp. 467–80, figs. 5, 6, 13, 14.

   

A copy of Orsini's *Imagines*, as well as Aristotle's complete works in Latin and several editions of Homer, were in the library of Jan Six, Rembrandt's principal supporter during the early 1650s (Amy Golahny, personal communication, March 2003; see also note 47 below).

20  Elizabeth McGrath, 'From Parnassus to Careggi: A seventeenth-century celebration of Plato and Renaissance Florence', in *Sight and Insight. Essays on art and culture in honour of E. H. Gombrich at 85*, ed. John Onians, London 1994, p. 197, fig. 81, for Aristotle and Homer, and p. 193, fig. 80 for Giovanni's large gold medal of Alexander in an adjacent fresco. See also Joachim von Sandrart's portrait of Aristotle (engraved by B. Kilian, 1675), which is quite consistent with Rembrandt's; J. A. Emmens, *Rembrandt en de regels van de kunst*, Utrecht 1968, p. 173, fig. 50.

21  Held, *op. cit.* (note 4), pp. 28, 48, notes that according to ancient sources the wealthy philosopher was "somewhat of a dandy" and liked to wear rings.

22  See *ibid*, pp. 36–39, on Aristotle's study and scholar portraits. Susan Koslow is researching the sources of Aristotle's gown, which she considers to be that of a doctor or academic. Carroll, *op. cit.* (note 4), pp. 55–56, defends the identification with Aristotle on various grounds. The object she describes as "a mirror on the table" (p. 40) is a silver-gilt tray supporting a book or box.

23  See Giltaij, *op. cit.* (note 6), ch. 5, on Ruffo's paintings by Rembrandt, and ch. 6 on the Italian contributions to the series. Rosa's *Archytas* of 1668 (untraced) featured the philosopher's wooden dove that could fly, a point of some interest below. Schama, *op. cit.* (note 17), p. 590, and other writers have mocked Guercino's supposition that Rembrandt depicted a physiognomist. However, the explanation found in Held, *op. cit.* (note 4), pp. 20–21, could be considerably amplified. Physiognomy and cosmography were both respected forms of natural philosophy in the seventeenth century, with deep roots in Aristotelean texts (as was kindly clarified for the

writer by David Summers, in a letter of 16 November 1995).

24  As noted by Held, *op. cit.* (note 4), p. 26, the painting's subject was described in 1678 as 'Aristotle with his right hand on a head'.

25  Gustavus Selenus, *Cryptomenytices et cryptographiae libri IX*, Lüneburg 1624, p. 16. Selenus was the pseudonym of Augustus II (1579–1666), Duke of Braunschweig-Lüneburg. His book is considered the first encyclopedia of cryptographic methods.

26  Not only Guercino (see note 23) but all the Italian painters who supplied pictures of philosophers to Ruffo failed to recognize Aristotle from the evidence that was supplied to them (see Giltaij, *op. cit.* [note 6], ch. 6). However, they obviously understood that the figure was a philosopher.

27  See Alfonso E. Pérez Sánchez and Nicola Spinosa, *Jusepe de Ribera 1591–1652*, exhib. cat., Metropolitan Museum of Art, New York, 1992, nos. 2–5.

28  As noted by Pérez Sánchez, *ibid.*, p. 64, where Frans Floris, Goltzius and other Northerners could also have been mentioned.

29  See Gregory Martin, *The Flemish School*, National Gallery Catalogues, London 1970, pp. 21–24.

30  The last panel is reproduced in Filipczak, *op. cit.* (note 18), fig. 81.

31  See Peter Hecht, 'The *paragone* debate: ten illustrations and a comment', *Simiolus*, vol. 14, no. 2, 1984, p. 132, and *idem*, 'Art beats nature, and painting does so best of all: the *paragone* competition in Duquesnoy, Dou and Schalcken', *Simiolus*, vol. 29, no. 3/4, 2002, p. 194.

32  Carl Nordenfalk, 'The Five Senses in Late Medieval and Renaissance Art', *Journal of the Warburg and Courtauld Institutes*, XLVIII, 1985, p. 2 (see also p. 6 on Aristotle and Albertus).

33  David Summers, *The Judgment of Sense. Renaissance Naturalism and the Rise of Aesthetics*, Cambridge 1987, p. 36, for this translation of a passage in the *Summa theologiae*. For a concise review of Albert the Great's extensive writing on the senses, see Nicholas H. Steneck,

'Albert on the Psychology of Sense
Perception', *Albertus Magnus and the
Sciences. Commemorative Essays 1980*, ed.
James A. Weisheipl, Toronto 1980,
pp. 263–90.

34 See *ibid.* for an excellent introduction to
these subjects. A reading of Summers's
book and correspondence with him in
1995 inspired the present article.

35 Rensselaer W. Lee, *Ut Pictura Poesis: The
Humanistic Theory of Painting*, New York
1967, pp. 5–7. For an overview of *paragoni*
and a bibliography see Claire Farago's
entry in *The Dictionary of Art*, ed. Jane
Turner, 34 vols., London 1996, vol. 24,
pp. 90–91.

36 In Malcolm Heath's translation of the
*Poetics* (London 1996), pp. xii–xv, he
defends "imitation" (as opposed to
"representation") as the closest approxi-
mation of what Aristotle meant by
*mimesis*, and outlines his philosophical
argument. Held, *op. cit.* (note 4), pp. 32–33,
counts the references to Homer in the
*Poetics* ("the last word on the rules of
poetry") but never mentions the subject
of imitation. The *Poetics* was enormously
influential from the sixteenth century
onwards, and was virtually the only known
source for Aristotle's views on Homer.

37 See Held, *op. cit.* (note 4), pp. 33–35.
Not only Hooft but also Jacob Cats
was called the Dutch Homer, quite as
numerous painters were cited as the
Apelles of their time.

38 See Summers, *op. cit.* (note 33), pp. 38, 71,
for these quotes, their sources and further
literature. On Leonardo's treatise and
Rembrandt's style see Walter Liedtke,
'The "View in Delft" by Carel Fabritius',
*The Burlington Magazine*, CXVIII, 1976,
pp. 72–73.

39 See Jeffrey M. Muller, 'Rubens's Theory
and Practice of the Imitation of Art',
*Art Bulletin*, LXIV, 1982, pp. 229–47,
where it is noted that the painter's
distinction of "matter from form",
"stone from figure" and so on derives
from Aristotle (p. 230).

40 See Harold E. Wethey, *The Paintings of
Titian, The Portraits*, London 1971, no. 95.

41 See Hecht (1984), *op. cit.* (note 31),
pp. 125–27. Perhaps the first printing

of Aristotle's *Poetics* (Venice 1508)
contributed to Venetian interest in
the *paragone* theme.

42 Held, *op. cit.* (note 4), ch. IV.
Rembrandt's earliest known paintings
may be panels depicting Hearing, Touch
and Sight (Josua Bruyn, Bob Haak,
Simon H. Levie, Pieter J.J. van Thiel,
Ernst van de Wetering, *A Corpus of
Rembrandt Paintings*, vols. I–, Foundation
Rembrandt Research Project, The Hague,
Dordrecht, Boston and London 1982–,
I, 1982, nos. B1-3), but this is less
relevant than is his attention to those
senses in works dating from throughout
his career.

43 Kenneth Clark, *Rembrandt and the Italian
Renaissance*, London 1966, pp. 64–67;
see also Liedtke, *loc. cit.* (note 38), and
Ernst van de Wetering, *Rembrandt.
The Painter at Work*, Amsterdam 1997,
pp. 186–88.

44 Philips Angel, *Praise of Painting*,
translated by Michael Hoyle, with an
introduction and commentary by Hessel
Miedema, in *Simiolus*, vol. 24, no. 2/3,
1996, pp. 238–39 (p. 246 on Rembrandt).
On Dou and Angel's *paragone* of painting
with sculpture and with poetry see Eric
Jan Sluijter, *Seductress of Sight. Studies in
Dutch Art of the Golden Age*, Zwolle 2000,
pp. 210–24, 335 n. 96. Sight is also
described as the noblest sense, and
Aristotle cited as the authority, in Cesare
Ripa (trans. by Dirck P. Pers), *Iconologia
of uytbeeldingen des Verstands*, Amsterdam
1644, p. 465.

45 *Aristotle on the Soul; Parva Naturalia;
On Breath* (trans. by W. S. Hett), p. 213
(in section I of 'On Sense and Sensible
Objects'). On 'Rembrandt and the
Spoken Word' see Held, *op. cit.* (note 4),
pp. 164–83 (p. 177 on the drawing of
Homer mentioned in note 47 below).

46 See Summers, *op. cit.* (note 33), p. 38.

47 Aristotle in Heath, *op. cit.* (note 36),
pp. 7, 15. It will be recalled that in
1652 Rembrandt drew "Homer reciting
his verses" in the *album amicorum* of
Jan Six: see Ben Broos, *Intimacies
and Intrigues. History Painting in the
Mauritshuis*, The Hague 1993,
pp. 271–73, fig. 4.

48 See Held, *op. cit.* (note 4), p. 174, on Rembrandt visualizing subjects in terms of the theatre.

49 However, the present article offers no support for the reading of Ruffo's three Rembrandts found in Emmens, *op. cit.*

(note 20), pp. 169–74 (restated as fact in Broos, *op. cit.* [note 47], p. 270).

50 See D.S. Hutchinson's chapter on the *Ethics* in *The Cambridge Companion to Aristotle*, ed. Jonathan Barnes, Cambridge 1995, pp. 204–5.

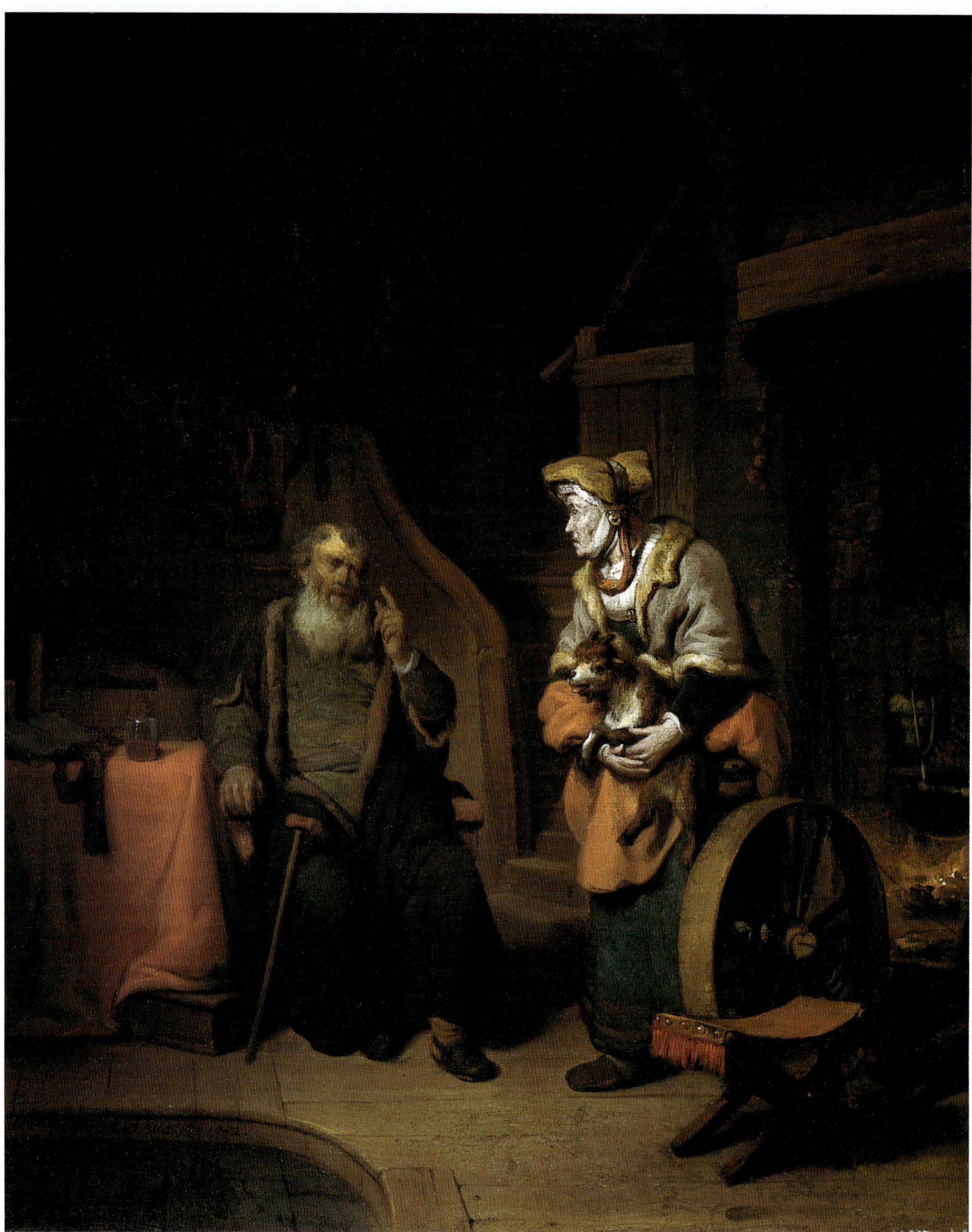

# Tobias, Anna und das Böckchen: Variationen über ein Thema aus dem Buch Tobias von Rembrandt und Gerbrand van den Eeckhout

VOLKER MANUTH

Es ist bekanntlich der ikonographische Reichtum der biblischen Historien des Alten Testaments in der holländischen Malerei des 17. Jahrhunderts, denen das besondere Interesse Alfred Baders gilt. Der Besucher seiner Sammlung kommt angesichts der Themenwahl und -vielfalt der alttestamentlichen Szenen in den Genuss, „Patriarchenluft zu kosten".[1] Dieses Interesse Alfred Baders an der Rezeption der Historien des Alten Testaments bei Rembrandt und dessen Malerkollegen fand seinen kunsthistorischen Ausdruck u.a. in dem von ihm erarbeiteten Ausstellungskatalog *The Bible Through Dutch Eyes*.[2] Bei Durchsicht des Katalogs fällt unmittelbar auf, dass es nicht allein die in den Büchern Genesis und Exodus geschilderten Taten und Verfehlungen der Erzväter und Familienpatriarchen sind, die zentral stehen. Kein anderes biblisches Buch ist mit mehr Szenen vertreten als das Buch Tobias. Der grossen Anzahl von Darstellungen aus diesem apokryphen Bibelbuch, die sich bereits in der Bader-Sammlung befinden, konnte jüngst eine weitere hinzugefügt werden. Dabei handelt es sich um ein bislang völlig unbekanntes Werk des Amsterdamer Malers Gerbrand van den Eeckhout (1621–1674). Das signierte und 1652 datierte Gemälde, das 2001 auf dem amerikanischen Kunstmarkt erworben wurde, zeigt die Szene, in der der blinde Tobias seine Frau Anna des Diebstahls eines Böckchens beschuldigt (Abb. 1).[3] Das auch in der nordniederländischen Historienmalerei des 17. Jahrhunderts eher seltene Thema, Hauptzüge der Komposition, der Erzählstil, aber auch einige Details in Van den Eeckhouts Darstellung erinnern unmittelbar an Rembrandts themengleiches Gemälde von 1626 (Bredius-Gerson 486; Corpus I, A3) im Rijksmuseum in Amsterdam (Abb. 2).[4] Das formale und ikonographische Verhältnis der beiden Gemälde zueinander und im Hinblick auf andere Darstellungen des Sujets, aber auch

Aspekte der zeitgenössischen Auffassungen zu der von beiden Malern gewählten Szene aus dem Buch Tobias, stehen im Zentrum der folgenden Ausführungen. Da Rembrandts Frühwerk seit dem Auftauchen zu Beginn des 20. Jahrhunderts in der kunsthistorischen Literatur zum unbestritten eigenhändigen Kanon seines Oeuvres gezählt wird und dementsprechend in keinem der einschlägigen Werkverzeichnisse fehlt, wenden wir uns zunächst dem weitgehend unbekannten Gemälde Van den Eeckhouts zu.

Dargestellt ist die im Buch Tobias erzählte Geschichte des frommen, aber verarmten und erblindeten Tobias, dessen Frau Anna den Lebensunterhalt durch Spinnen verdient. Zu Unrecht wird ihr von Tobias der Diebstahl eines Böckchens vorgeworfen, das sie ehrlich durch Arbeit erworben hatte. Das Aussprechen dieses Vorwurfs hat Van den Eeckhout als Thema für sein Gemälde gewählt (vgl. Tobias 2: 21). In dem sich anschliessenden Streit verspottet Anna ihren Mann wegen seiner Glaubenstreue (Tobias 2: 22–23). Tobias beklagt sein Elend und bittet Gott um Sündenvergebung und den Tod (Tobias 3: 1–6).

Van den Eeckhouts Szene spielt in einem bescheiden ausgestatteten Innenraum mit teilweise sichtbarer Balkenkonstruktion des offenen Dachstuhls. Eine geschwungene Holztreppe im Hintergrund führt in einen höher gelegenen Raumteil, der tief verschattet ist. Der unten links sichtbare Steinfussboden ist durch ein hölzernes Podest erhöht, auf dem sich die beiden Figuren befinden. Anna, das Böckchen mit beiden Armen umfassend, steht rechts vor einem Kamin, in dem ein Holzfeuer brennt. Ihr Blick ist auf den alten Tobias gerichtet, der sich mit erhobener Linker an sie wendet. Er sitzt in einem Armlehnstuhl neben einem mit einem Tuch bedeckten Tisch, auf dem ein geöffnetes Buch, ein schalartiges Kleidungsstück und ein Becher zu sehen sind. Ein Krückstock lehnt an seinem rechten Knie. Im Vordergrund erkennt man ein Handspinnrad und davor einen mit Fransen verzierten Sitzschemel. Das von links einfallende Licht hebt besonders die Figur der Anna auf dem bühnenartig beleuchteten Holzpodest hervor. Das Kaminfeuer hat auf die Beleuchtung des Raumes kaum Einfluss.

In der Literatur über den Künstler wurde das Gemälde bislang nicht erwähnt.[5] Darstellungen aus dem Buch Tobias sind im Oeuvre von Gerbrand van den Eeckhout, das reich ist an alttestamentlichen Szenen, eher selten.[6] Von der im Bild der Sammlung Bader wiedergegebenen Szene hat sich – soweit bekannt – keine zweites Beispiel von der Hand des Malers erhalten. Dennoch hat sich Van den Eeckhout offenbar mehrfach mit dem Sujet beschäftigt. Nachforschungen zur Provenienz des Bildes haben Hinweise auf die Existenz thematisch verwandter Gemälde erbracht, die ihm zugeschrieben waren. Die früheste Erwähnung eines solchen Bildes findet sich im Katalog einer Amsterdamer Versteigerung des Jahres 1761. Die dort gegebene Beschreibung des Gemäldes erinnert stark an das Bild der Sammlung Bader, ist aber letztlich doch zu summarisch für eine zweifelsfreie Identifizierung, zumal die Abmessungen auf ein horizontales Format schliessen lassen.[7] 1770 wurde eine sehr ähnliche – wenn nicht gar mit dem Bild der Versteigerung von 1761 identische – Fassung des Themas von Van den Eeckhout ebenfalls in Amsterdam versteigert. Da jedoch die Beschreibung der Szene mit Tobias und Anna in einem Interieur weder einen Hinweis auf die Auseinandersetzung der beiden um den vermeintlichen Diebstahl des Böckchens enthält noch das Tier selbst erwähnt wird, bleibt es fraglich, welche Szene aus Tobias wiedergegeben ist.[8] Denkbar wäre auch das einträgliche Nebeneinander der Eltern, die auf die Rückkehr des Sohnes warten.[9] Leichter fällt die Identifizierung des exakten Erzählmoments bei dem Van den Eeckhout zugeschriebenen Gemälde, das sich 1764 in der Sammlung des Manufakturbesitzers, Bankiers und Kunsthändlers Johann Ernst Gotzkowsky (1710–1775) in Berlin befand.[10] Gotzkowsky war lange Jahre als erfolgreicher Kaufmann und finanzieller Berater König Friedrichs II. von Preussen tätig gewesen und beriet den Monarchen auch beim Ankauf von Gemälden. Er hatte eine umfangreiche eigene Gemäldesammlung aufgebaut, die allerdings Fehlspekulationen und der nach dem Ende des Siebenjährigen Krieges in Preussen einsetzenden Wirtschaftskrise zum Opfer fiel.[11] Zwecks Begleichung seiner Schulden sah sich Gotzkowsky gezwungen, seine nahezu komplette und von ihm 1763 auf einen Wert von 316.650 holländische Gulden geschätzte Sammlung an Katharina II. nach Russland zu verkaufen. Der Erwerb der Sammlung Gotzkowsky durch die Kaiserin markierte den Beginn ihrer umfangreichen Erwerbungen von Kunstwerken, zu denen nicht selten komplette Gemäldesammlungen gehörten. Die von Gotzkowsky 1764 zwecks des Verkaufs persönlich aufgestellte „Specification meiner allerbesten und schönsten Original Gemählden bestehen in 317 Stück nebst den allergenauesten Preißen" nennt unter Nr. 579 „V:d'Eckhout, stellet den Tobiam vor, wie er seiner frau den verweiss gibt. 2 Fuss 2 Zoll [hoch], 1 Fuss 8 Zoll [breit]".[12] Die kurze Beschreibung macht deutlich, dass es sich um die auch im Bild der Sammlung Bader gezeigte Szene mit der Beschuldigung des Diebstahls gehandelt haben muss. Der Vergleich der Abmessungen schliesst allerdings auch in diesem Fall aus, dass die beiden Bilder identisch waren.[13] Das auf 300 Taler geschätzte Gemälde gelangte in den Besitz der Kaiserin nach St. Petersburg, wo es noch 1882 zusammen mit neun anderen Werken aus der ehemaligen Sammlung Gotzkowsky genannt wird, die sich „theils in der Kanzlei und den Vorrathskammern der Eremitage, sowie in einigen Wohnzimmern des Winterpalais" befanden.[14] Heute jedenfalls muss das Bild als verschollen gelten, denn in den Katalogen der Eremitage wird es nicht mehr genannt. Angesichts der hier aufgeführten Hinweise ist es sehr wahrscheinlich, dass Gerbrand van den

Eeckhout das Thema aus dem Buch Tobias in mehreren Versionen gemalt hat. Diese Praxis war für ihn nicht unüblich, denn auch von zahlreichen anderen biblischen Szenen haben sich mehrere Fassungen erhalten oder lassen sich zumindest in Dokumenten nachweisen. Leider lässt sich bislang keine der dokumentierten Fassungen mit Van den Eeckhouts *Tobias und Anna* von 1652 in der Sammlung Bader identifizieren.

Motivische Verwandtschaften mit Rembrandts *Tobias und Anna* von 1626 (Abb. 2), aber auch solche hinsichtlich der Figurenanordnung mit dem sitzenden Tobias und der rechts von ihm stehenden Anna, die das Böckchen mit beiden Armen vor ihrem Leib hält, sind offensichtlich. Sie werfen die Frage auf, ob und inwieweit nahezu dreissig Jahre nach seinem Entstehen Rembrandts Frühwerk Van den Eeckhout noch als direkte Inspirationsquelle gedient haben könnte. Die Provenienz des vom zwanzigjährigen Rembrandt in Leiden gemalten Bildes ist lückenhaft und reicht nicht weiter zurück als bis in die Mitte des 18. Jahrhunderts.[15] Eine vorbereitende Zeichnung, die hier vermittelt haben könnte, hat sich offenbar nicht erhalten. Für seine Komposition machte Rembrandt bekanntlich Gebrauch von älterer Druckgraphik. In diesem Zusammenhang ist zu Recht wiederholt auf die themengleiche Radierung des Jan van de Velde nach Willem Buytewech (1591/92–1624) von um 1619/20 verwiesen worden (Abb. 3).[16] Das Interieur mit der Holzkonstruktion des Pultdaches und dem Fenster links sowie einige andere Details zeigen deutliche Übereinstimmungen mit Rembrandts Bild. Zu klären gilt es dementsprechend auch, ob es hinreichende Parallelen zwischen der Radierung und Gerbrand van den Eeckhouts Gemälde gibt, die deutlich machen, dass der Maler – möglicherweise ohne Kenntnis von Rembrandts Version – ebenfalls das Vorbild Buytewechs benutzte. Hierfür scheint es hilfreich, um den Vergleich des Interieurs (mit Ausstattung) von dem der Figuren und der Wiedergabe des exakten Erzählmoments zu trennen. Van den Eeckhouts Inneraum ist eine vom Bildrand links überschnittene Konstruktion ohne Fenster, das sowohl bei Rembrandt als auch bei Buytewech die wichtigste Lichtquelle darstellt. Die genaue Form der Decke und der bildparallelen Rückwand des Zimmers lassen sich wegen der tiefen Verschattung nicht genauer bestimmen. Eine Treppe gibt es auf keiner der beiden anderen Darstellungen, dies gilt auch für das in der linken unteren Ecke halbkreisförmig angeschnittene hölzerne Podest bei Van den Eeckhout.[17] Lediglich Rembrandts Anna steht auf einer allerdings andersförmigen Erhöhung rechts im Mittelgrund des Raumes. Während Buytewechs Radierung ein offenes Holzfeuer im Zentrum des Hintergrundes zeigt und Rembrandt eine Feuerstelle unten rechts im Vordergrund wiedergibt, brennt bei Van den Eeckhout ein sehr viel kleineres Feuer im nahezu wandhohen Kamin im rechten Mittelgrund. Einen Hinweis auf Annas Tätigkeit gibt das im Bild der Sammlung

 VOLKER MANUTH

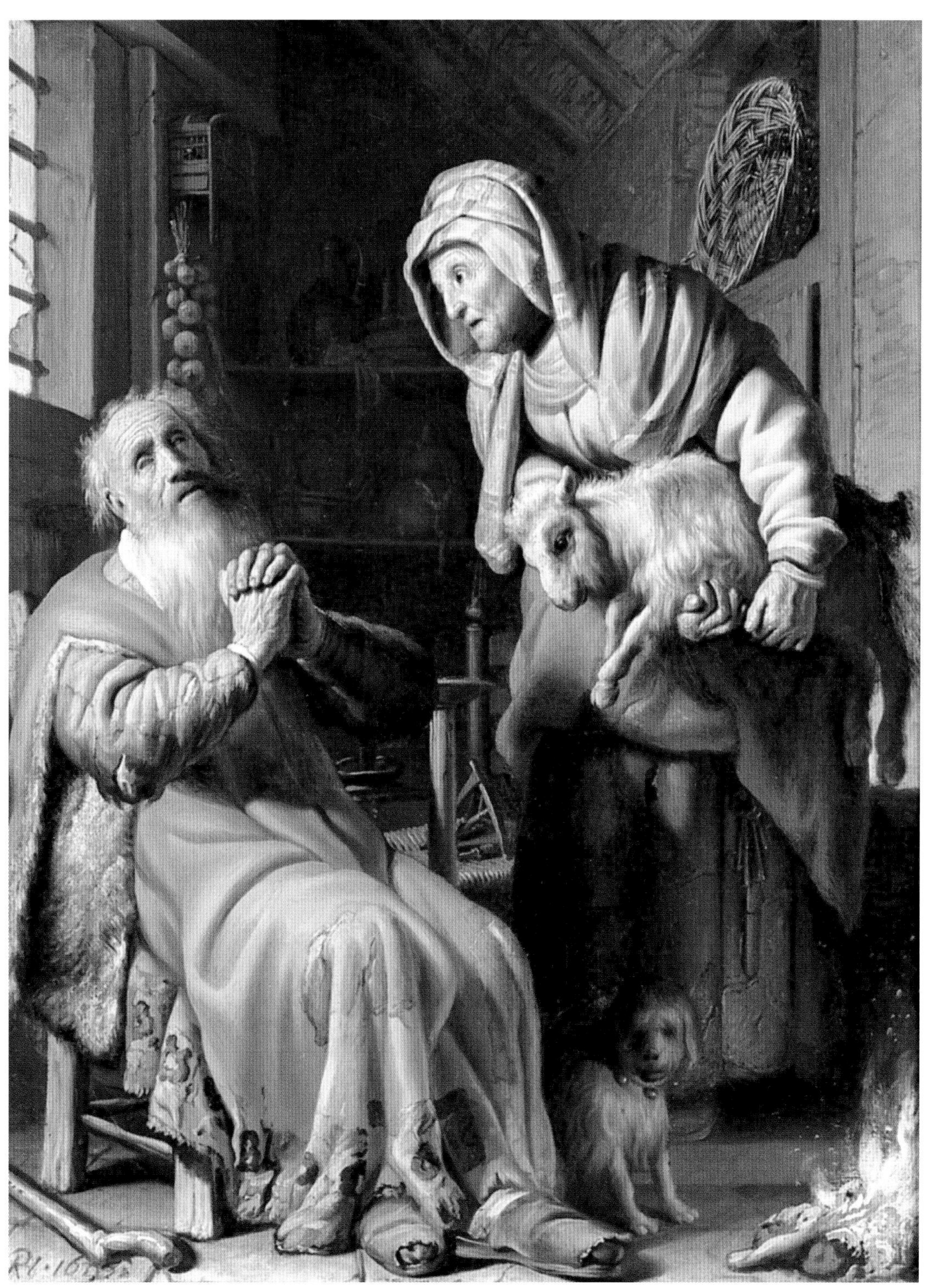

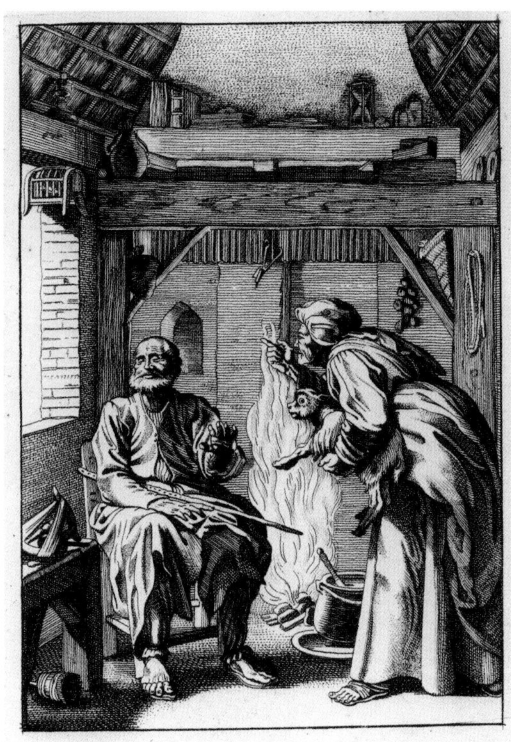



Abb. 3 JAN VAN DE VELDE
nach WILLEM BUYTEWECH
*Tobias,* Anna und das Böckchen,
um 1619/20
Radierung, 19.4 × 11.3 cm
Amsterdam, Rijksmuseum

Bader so prominent im Vordergrund dargestellte Spinnrad. Geräte zur Textilverarbeitung, wie zum Beispiel eine Garnwinde, finden sich zwar auch in der Radierung und im Gemälde von 1626, doch weder Buytewech noch Rembrandt stellen ein Spinnrad dar.[18] Betrachtet man das Mobilar und die weiteren Ausstattungsstücke in den drei Darstellungen, so gibt es wenig Parallelen. Diese beschränken sich auf Bücher (bei Buytewech und Rembrandt im Regal an der Rückwand, bei Van den Eeckhout auf dem Tisch) und das Bündel Zwiebeln, das auf Van den Eeckhouts Gemälde links neben dem Kamin aufgehängt ist. Dagegen fehlt hier der von den beiden anderen Malern wiedergegebene Vogelkäfig. Lediglich Rembrandt verweist durch die Wiedergabe des Hundes auf die bevorstehende Reise des jungen Tobias. Allen drei Darstellungen gemeinsam ist die Gegenüberstellung der beiden Alten, wobei Tobias links von der stehenden Anna sitzt. Es ist mehrfach betont worden, dass Rembrandt im Vergleich zu Buytewech einen späteren Moment der Handlung gewählt hat. Nicht der ungerechtfertigte Vorwurf an Anna und deren Reaktion, sondern das in Tobias 3:1 beschriebene Gebet wird dargestellt: „Da seufzte Tobias tief und hub an zu weinen und zu beten".[19] Van Thiel hat den Moment als Mischung

  VOLKER MANUTH

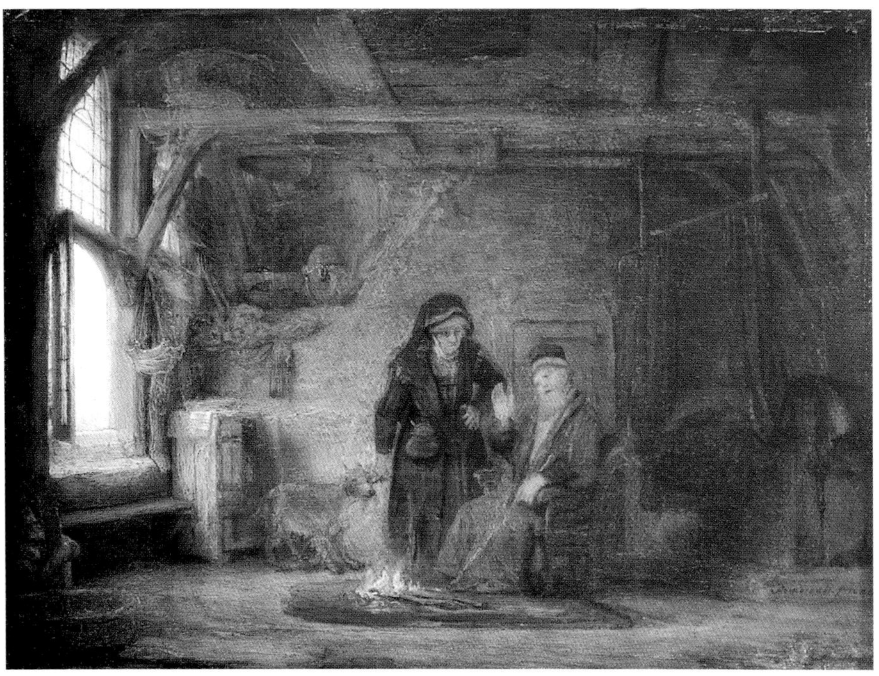

Abb. 4 REMBRANDT
*Tobias, Anna und das Böckchen*, 1645
Öl auf Holz, 20 × 27 cm
Berlin, Staatliche Museen zu Berlin,
Gemäldegalerie

aus „Verzweiflung oder Bedauern und beseeltes Gebet" charakterisiert.[20] Bei Buytewech überwiegt dagegen die unmittelbare Konfrontation der beiden Eheleute. Anna reagiert verärgert und heftig auf den Vorwurf und unterstreicht ihre verbale Rechtfertigung durch die drohend erhobene rechte Hand (Tobias 2: 22–23). Tobias reagiert mit einer abwehrenden Gebärde in Richtung seiner Ehefrau. Der an ihr vorbei gerichtete Blick unterstreicht seine Blindheit. Die Bildunterschrift der Radierung betont das innere Sehen im Glauben ohne Hilfe des Augenlichtes als Quintessenz der Szene.[21] Der von Van den Eeckhout dargestellte Erzählmoment weicht deutlich sowohl von Buytewech als auch von Rembrandt ab. In der Sequenz der fortlaufenden Ereignisse wählte er den frühesten Augenblick in der Auseinandersetzung um den vermeintlichen Diebstahl des Ziegenböckleins. Seine Profilfigur der Anna blickt – ähnlich ihrem Pendant bei Rembrandt – verblüfft und fassungslos zugleich in Richtung des alten Tobias, der seine Linke mit ausgestrecktem Zeigefinger mahnend erhoben hat. Damit unterstreicht er seine Aufforderung „Gebet's dem rechten Herrn wieder; denn uns gebührt nicht, zu essen vom gestohlnen Gut oder dasselbe anzurühren" (Tobias 2: 21). Die gestikulierend erhobene Hand des Tobias findet sich auch auf Rembrandts Gemälde von 1645 (Bredius-Gerson 514) in Berlin (Abb. 4) und einer damit in Zusammenhang stehenden Zeichnung, die sich ebenfalls in Berlin befindet.[22] Zwar sprechen dieser Gestus und die indignierte Haltung Annas dafür, dass auch in dem Berliner Bild der Moment des Vorwurfs nach Tobias 2: 21 gemeint ist, ansonsten aber weist das Bild im Vergleich zu der Darstellung Van den Eeckhouts mehr Unterschiede als Gemeinsamkeiten auf. Zusammenfassend lässt sich feststellen, dass Rembrandts

Gemälde von 1626 und Gerbrand van den Eeckhouts themengleiches Bild von
1652 in der Sammlung Bader weniger Gemeinsamkeiten haben als man vielleicht
annehmen möchte. Dass Van den Eeckhout im Hinblick auf die Lichtregie und
das dadurch entstandene kontrastreiche Gegeneinander von beleuchteten
Figuren und tief-verschattetem Hintergrund rembrandteske Stilmittel ein-
setzte, ist nicht zu bezweifeln. Dafür jedoch war die Kenntnis von Rembrandts
Original von 1626 nicht zwingend Voraussetzung. Die fraglos auf den Einfluss
seines Lehrers Pieter Lastman (*ca.* 1583–1633) zurückzuführende helle Buntfar-
bigkeit des Kolorits in Rembrandts Gemälde ist bei Van den Eeckhout einer
reduzierten Farbigkeit gewichen, in der dunkle Braun-, Grau- und Grüntöne
dominieren. Eine gewisse Verwandschaft zeigt sich – wenn auch modifiziert –
im Farbschema der Kleidung Annas, wobei die Kostümdetails der beiden
Figuren sehr verschieden sind. Dass beide Maler Tobias in einem pelzgefüt-
tertem Hausrock (*tabbaard*) wiedergeben, ist nicht ungewöhnlich, da es sich um
ein Kleidungsstück handelt, in dem traditionell besonders ältere Männer
sowohl in der Historien- als auch in der zeitgenössischen Porträtmalerei
dargestellt wurden. Auffällig dagegen ist, dass Van den Eeckhout, anders als
Rembrandt, darauf verzichtete, zur Kennzeichnung der ärmlichen Lebens-
verhältnisse, Tobias in abgerissener Kleidung darzustellen.

Bemerkenswert bleibt jedoch die Tatsache, dass – ungeachtet der fest-
gestellten Unterschiede zwischen beiden Bildern – beide Maler gerade diese so
selten wiedergegebene Szene aus dem Buch Tobias gewählt haben. Dass dies auf
Zufall beruht, lässt sich nicht ausschliessen, scheint aber auch angesichts der
langjährigen persönlichen Beziehungen zwischen Rembrandt und Van den
Eeckhout eher unwahrscheinlich. Es gibt Hinweise darauf, dass beide Maler,
auch nach der zu vermutenden Lehrzeit von Van den Eeckhout in Rembrandts
Atelier zwischen *ca.* 1635/36 und 1640/41, freundschaftlich verbunden blieben.
In seiner Biographie des Amsterdamer Landschaftsmalers Roelant Roghman
(1627–1697) bezeichnet Arnold Houbraken (1660–1719) Roghman als „in zyn
tyd, met Gerbrant van den Eekhout, een groot vriend van Rembrant van Ryn".[23]
Jüngst aufgefundene Dokumente bestätigen zumindest das freundschaftliche
Verhältnis zwischen Roghman und Van den Eeckhout. In seinem Testament
bezeichnet Van den Eeckhout Roelant Roghman als „zijn testateurs oude bekende"
und vermacht ihm 50 Gulden. Damit gewinnt auch Houbrakens Aussage über
beider Freundschaft zu Rembrandt an Glaubwürdigkeit.[24] Eine freundschaftliche
Beziehung zwischen Malern, die in derselben Stadt lebten und arbeiteten, bein-
haltete fraglos auch den Austausch künstlerischer Ideen und Erfahrungen. Dies
erklärt möglicherweise die genannten Gemeinsamkeiten, die Van den Eeckhouts
Version von *Tobias, Anna und das Böckchen* von 1652 mit der 1626 datierten themen-
gleichen Fassung seines ehemaligen Lehrers Rembrandt verbinden.

„Rembrandt illustrierte das Buch Tobias häufiger als jeden anderen Bibeltext vergleichbarer Länge.” Diese Feststellung findet sich in der Einleitung von Julius Helds Studie über die Bedeutung des Buches Tobias in Rembrandts Oeuvre.[25] Nach der beschreibenden Analyse einer Vielzahl von Werken, die seine eingangs zitierte Aussage bestätigen, wendet sich Held der Frage nach „der grundsätzlichen Botschaft” des Buches Tobias zu, die Rembrandt möglicherweise dazu geführt haben könnte, „sich immer wieder aufs neue mit der apokryphen Geschichte zu beschäftigen”.[26] Die Gründe hierfür sieht der Autor eng mit Rembrandts „religiösen Neigungen” und seiner Biographie verknüpft: einerseits nennt er des Malers angebliche Sympathien für die dissidente protestantische Gruppierung der Mennoniten (*doopsgezinde*), für die, so Held, das Buch Tobias eine besondere Rolle spielte.[27] Rembrandts konfessionelle Vorlieben und seine kirchlichen Verbindungen sind noch immer nicht überzeugend bestimmt worden. Dokumente, die hierüber eindeutige Aussagen ermöglichen, fehlen. Nach seinem Umzug nach Amsterdam wohnte er bekanntlich zunächst bei dem *doopsgezinden* Kunsthändler Hendrik Uylenburgh (1587–1661), der ihn mit Aufträgen versorgte. Auch hatte Rembrandt Kontakte zu anderen Mitgliedern der mennonitischen Gemeinde, die Porträts bei ihm in Auftrag gaben.[28] Ob und inwieweit er sich allerdings zu ihren religiösen Idealen hingezogen fühlte, ist äusserst fraglich. Dies trifft auch für Helds Aussagen hinsichtlich der besonderen Bedeutung des Buches Tobias für die Mennoniten zu. Der Gemäldebesitz von Mitgliedern dieser Gruppierung, wie er u.a. durch Inventare überliefert ist, zeichnet sich jedenfalls nicht durch eine überdurchschnittlich hohe Anzahl von Gemälden mit Themen aus dem Buch Tobias aus.[29] Weiterhin soll, so Held, Rembrandts Vorliebe für die Geschichte des Tobias auch mit der Beziehung zu seinem altersblinden Vater, Harmen Gerrits. (1568–1630; siehe Abb. 3 auf Seite 37), und dem Sohn Titus (1641–1668) zusammenhängen.[30] Es ist allerdings nachgewiesen worden, dass das starke Interesse an den Erzählungen des Buches Tobias im 17. Jahrhundert keinesfalls auf die nordniederländische Malerei und Rembrandt beschränkt blieb,[31] sondern auch und besonders im Bereich der zeitgenössischen erbaulichen Literatur ausgesprochen populär war.[32] Dies steht im Einklang mit der sich seit der Reformation in der exegetischen Literatur der verschiedenen Denominationen abzeichnenden grösseren Vielfalt in der Auslegung des Buches Tobias.

In der katholischen Kirche der Frühzeit war das Buch Tobias nicht unumstritten. Die Gründe hierfür hängen mit der problematischen Textüberlieferung zusammen, da sich kein hebräischer oder aramäischer Urtext erhalten hat. Hieronymus übersetzte das Buch schliesslich doch — ungeachtet einer gewissen anfänglichen Reserviertheit.[33] Seitdem gehört es für die Katholiken zum Kanon der Heiligen Schrift. Dies wurde im 16. Jahrhundert auch von den

Vätern des Tridentinums bestätigt, die festlegten, dass das Buch Tobias zu den „*sacri et canonici*" zu zählen sei.[34]

Kritik an der fragwürdigen Überlieferung und damit an der Glaubwürdigkeit als Wort Gottes übten dagegen die protestantischen Autoritäten. Die Aussonderung aus dem Kanon bedeutete allerdings auf protestantischer Seite nicht, dass damit auch das Interesse am Inhalt dieses so überaus populären apokryphen Buches verschwand, im Gegenteil. Gerade im Bereich der Alltagsfrömmigkeit spielte die Geschichte des alten Tobias und seiner Familie seit dem 16. Jahrhundert eine besondere Rolle. Hier waren es vornehmlich die Schriften und Kommentare Martin Luthers, in denen das Schicksal des Tobias benutzt wurde, um die allgemein menschlichen Aspekte des irdischen Daseins anhand von verständlichen Vorbildern zu erklären. Luther verbindet Unglück und Glück des Tobias mit dem Alltagsleben der einfachen Gläubigen, indem er die Hauptfigur vom geduldigen Leider „zum Vorbild des Familienvaters und des Menschen im Ehestand überhaupt" erhebt.[35] Er nennt „*Tobias exemplum est boni patris familias*".[36] Für viele der zahlreichen moralisierenden Bearbeitungen des Stoffes in der erbaulichen Literatur des 16. und 17. Jahrhunderts war dies ein wichtiger Aspekt. Auch der Umstand, dass Luther das Buch Tobias – im Gegesatz zu dem von ihm als Tragödie bezeichneten Buch Judith – als Komödie sieht, trug zur weiteren Popularisierung der Handlung bei. In der Vorrede zu Tobias in der Vollbibel von 1534 schreibt er: „Ists ein geschicht, so ists ein fein heilig geschicht, Ists aber ein geticht, so ists warlich auch ein recht schön, heilsam, nützlich geticht und spiel, eins geistreichen Poeten [. . . .] Denn Judith gibt eine gute, ernste, dapffere Tragedien, So gibt Tobias eine feine liebliche, Gottselige Comedien." Was Luther damit meint, wird deutlich, wenn er fortfährt: „Denn gleich wie das Buch Judith anzeigt, wie es Land und leuten offt elendiglich gehet, und wie die Tyrannen erstlich hoffertiglich toben, und zuletzt schendlich zu boden gehen, Also zeigt das Buch Tobias an, wie es einem fromen Baur odder Bürger auch übel gehet, und viel leidens im Ehestand sey, Aber Gott imer gnediglich helffe, und zu letzt das ende mit freuden beschliesse, Auff das Eheleute sollen lernen gedult haben, und allerley leiden, auff künfftige hoffnung, gerne tragen, inn rechter furcht Gottes und festem Glauben."[37]

Damit wird Tobias zum Vorbild der schlichten alltäglichen Frömmigkeit und des Vertrauens auf Gott, seine Ehe mit Anna zum Beispiel für den unter Gottes Schutz stehenden Ehestand. Zwar kritisiert Luther Annas Vorwürfe gegen Tobias als „*blasphemantium vox*",[38] nennt sie aber an anderer Stelle „eine liebe hausfraw, die mit irem man inn lieb und freundschaft lebet".[39] Luther unterstreicht die vielen moralisch vorbildhaften Aspekte der populären Geschichte und folgert: „Darumb ist das Buch uns Christen auch nützlich und gut zu lesen".[40] Wie nachhaltig die von ihm betonten Aspekte auch Eingang in die protestantische Volksfrömmigkeit fanden geht exemplarisch aus dem Titel eines 1576 in Magdeburg erschienenen Schultheaterstücks hervor, gemeint ist Georg Rollenhagens *Tobias, eine schöne, tröstliche Comoedia oder Spiel vom heiligen Ehestand*.[41] In der Widmung erklärt Rollenhagen, dass er es „für sehr nütz und not achte, das nicht allein junge gesellen und jungfrauen, sondern auch die Eheleute offtmals die Historiam Tobiae aus der Bibel oder in reim gefasset [. . .] uffs fleissigste ansehen und betrachten", so dass „wir allerseits dem lieben Tobiasen in unserm Ehestand seliglich folgen und gleichen segen erlangen muegen".[42] Der in den Dialogen vorherrschende Sprachgebrauch unterstreicht die Volksnähe von Rollenhagens Bearbeitung des biblischen Stückes, das Züge einer Komödie bzw. Posse trägt. Die Szene zwischen Tobias und Anna mit der Beschuldigung des Diebstahls der Ziege wird ausführlich beschrieben. Laut Regieanweisung zur 1. Szene des 1. Aktes sitzt der alte Tobias auf einer Bank vor seinem Haus und „Anna komt in gemeiner Kleidung, [und] tregt ein Böcklein im Arm".[43] Alle bislang besprochenen Darstellungen der Szene spielen sich innerhalb des Hauses ab. Das Motiv des während der Diebstahlsbeschuldigung auf einer Bank vor dem Haus sitzenden Tobias ist bei Rembrandt und seinem Kreis extrem selten. Ausnahmsweise kommt es bei Barent Fabritius (1624–1673) in dessen um 1654 geschaffenen Gemälde im Museum Ferdinandeum in Innsbruck vor.[44] Haupt-thema des Streites zwischen Tobias und Anna ist bei Rollenhagen Annas Unmut über die Freigiebigkeit und Nächstenliebe ihres Mannes. Aus Angst, er könne auch das ehrlich verdiente Böckchen mit Fremden teilen, beasichtigt sie es zu verstecken:

> Ich hab den alten blinden Mann,
> Der gar nichts mehr erwerben kan;
> Und was ich verdien mit den Hendn,
> Muss ich alles nur auff jn wendn [. . . .]
> Ach sih, der Mann sitzt für der Thür.
> Ich muss es [das Böckchen] sein heimlich verwarn
> Und es jn nicht lassen erfarn.
> Dann wann etwa ein Bettler kem,
> Gar bald er jn zu Gast auffnem
> Und steckts eim frembden in den Hals;
> Hat mir schon vor vergebn alls.[45]

Tobias entdeckt das Böckchen und fordert Anna auf, es zurückzugeben, worauf diese „fehrt mit ungestümmigkeit heraus":

Das sagt mir nie kein redlichr Mann.
Ich hab niemand ein Hellr genomm;
Aber was du hast mit mir bekomn
Und uns auch Gott selbst hat beschert,
Das hastu mit faulheit verzert
Odr uns mit deiner eigen hand
Heimlich und offentlich entwand,
Schelmen und Bubn in Hals gesteckt,
Ja auch Todten damit gedeckt.[46]

Titel und Inhalt von Georg Rollenhages Tobias-Stück stehen deutlich in Zusammenhang mit Luthers Einschätzung des apokryphen Buches Tobias. Dabei steht nicht allein der lehrhafte und moralisierende Charakter im Vordergrund, sondern auch die lebensnah geschilderten Segnungen und Verwirrungen des Ehestandes, die gerade anhand der Tobias und Anna-Szene lebhaft und nicht ohne gewisse komische Züge beschrieben werden.

Den religiös-didaktischen Wert und die grosse Popularität der apokryphen Bibelbücher machten sich auch die Autoritäten der Reformierten Kirche in den nördlichen Niederlanden zu Nutzen. In die von der Dordrechter Synode (1618–19) in Auftrag gegebene autorisierte neue Bibelübersetzung (*Statenvertaling*), die 1637 erstmals erschien, wurden auch die apokryphen Bücher integriert. Sie wurden aus dem Griechischen übersetzt, allerdings ohne dass man die für die kanonischen Bücher geforderte philologische Genauigkeit forderte. Eingeordnet wurden die apokryphen Bücher ihrem Wert entsprechend nicht am Ende des Alten Testaments, sondern ganz am Schluss der Bibel hinter dem Neuen Testament. Ein ausführliches Vorwort weist den Leser auf den umstrittenen Charakter der Schriften hin: „Warnung an die Leser der apokryphen Bücher. Apokryphe Bücher, das bedeutet: verborgene [Bücher], weil sie nicht öffentlich in der Gemeinde gelesen werden dürfen, sondern vielmehr verborgen sein sollten: und weil sie sich nicht in der Truhe [Lade] befanden, in der die Göttlichen Bücher der Juden aufbewahrt und verborgen wurden".[47] Im Vorwort zu Tobias werden zunächst Gründe für die Unzuverlässigkeit des Buches genannt, so beispielsweise die Unterschiede in den überlieferten griechischen und lateinischen Textüberlieferungen, aber auch sich widersprechende Details, wie die Behauptung des Engels, der den jungen Tobias auf seiner Reise begleitet, er heisse Azarias obwohl es sich um Raphael handelt.[48] Dementsprechend, so heisst es weiter im Vorwort,

. . . erweist sich deutlich, dass die genannten Bücher keine kanonischen,
sondern Apokryphe Schriften sind, die nicht öffentlich in der Gemeinde
gelesen werden dürfen, und aus denen, da sie von Menschen geschrieben
worden sind, keinerlei Beweise genommen werden dürfen, zur
Rechtfertigung von Glaubensartikeln, da unser Glaube auf dem
Fundament der Propheten und Apostel gebaut werden muss,
Ephes.2.20. Da sich allerdings darin auch einige gute Sprüche,
Ermahnungen und Vorbilder finden lassen, so ist es nicht ganz unnütz,
dass sie auch gelesen werden, aller-dings so wie auch alle anderen von
Menschen geschriebenen Schriften, [und deshalb] ständig geprüft
werden müssen am Prüfstein der göttlichen Lehren, welche nur beste-
hen aus den kanonischen Schriften des Alten und Neuen Testaments.[49]

Die von den Vätern der holländischen *Statenvertaling* gegebenen Gründe für
die Nützlichkeit der Lektüre der apokryphen Bibelbücher erinnern an Luthers
Ausführungen. Zwar eignen sich diese Schriften nicht als Beweis und Grund-
lage für Glaubensartikel, dennoch enthalten sie nützliche „Ermahnungen und
Vorbilder". Es war gerade das Buch Tobias, das auf unkomplizierte und nachvoll-
ziehbare Weise einfache Glaubensinhalte, deren sittlicher Wert unumstritten war,
anschaulich und unabhängig von individueller Religionszugehörigkeit zum
Ausdruck brachte. Hierzu gehörte fraglos das Vertrauen in die besondere Rolle
des Ehestandes unter Gottes Schutz, wofür sowohl die Geschichte des alten als
auch des jungen Tobias gute Beispiele lieferte. Die 1626 von Rembrandt und
1652 von Gerbrand van den Eeckhout gemalten Versionen der Szene mit Tobias,
der Anna des Diebstahls beschuldigt, machen die anhaltende Verbindung
zwischen Rembrandt und einigen seiner Schüler deutlich, auch nachdem diese
sein Atelier bereits lange verlassen hatten. Nicht immer lassen sich dabei die
oft rätselhaften Wege der Vermittlung von seltenen Themen und Motiven
vollständig erklären.

1  Johann Wolfgang von Goethe, *West-Östlicher Divan*, Buch des Sängers 4. Zitiert nach *Goethes Werke*, textkritisch durchgesehen und mit Anmerkungen versehen von Erich Trunz (Hamburger Ausgabe), Bd. II, 2. Aufl. 1952, S. 7.

2  *The Bible Through Dutch Eyes. From Genesis Through the Apocrypha*, Ausst. Kat., Introduction and catalogue by Alfred Bader, Milwaukee Art Center, Milwaukee, 1976.

3  Öl auf Leinwand, 47.6 × 39.4 cm. Signiert und datiert unten links auf der hölzernen Stufe: *G.V. Eeckhout. F. 1652*. Für die Sammlung Bader erworben auf der Versteigerung Sotheby's, New York, 25.1.2001, Nr. 119 mit Farbabb. Nach einer sorgfältigen Reinigung war das Bild 2003 erstmals auf der Rembrandt und Rembrandtschul-Ausstellung in Tokio zu sehen, vgl. *Rembrandt and the Rembrandt School. The Bible, Mythology and Ancient History*, Ausst. Kat., Tokio, The National Museum of Western Art, 2003, S. 164, Nr. 70 mit Farbabb.

4  Die Werkverzeichnisse der Gemälde und Zeichnungen Rembrandts werden wie üblich nur mit der Angabe der Autorennamen und der entsprechenden Katalognummer zitiert: Bredius-Gerson: Abraham Bredius, *Rembrandt. The Complete Edition of the Paintings*, revised by Horst Gerson, London 1969. *Corpus*: Josua Bruyn, Bob Haak, Simon H. Levie, Pieter J.J. van Thiel, Ernst van de Wetering, *A Corpus of Rembrandt Paintings*, Bde. 1–, Foundation Rembrandt Research Project, Den Haag, Dordrecht, Boston und London 1982, I: *1625–1631*; Benesch: Otto Benesch, *The Drawings of Rembrandt. A Critical Catalogue*, 6 Bde., London 1954–57.

5  Einzige Ausnahmen sind der Beitrag des Verfassers über Gerbrand van den Eeckhout, in *Saur. Allgemeines Künstler-lexikon. Die Bildenden Künstler aller Zeiten und Völker*, München und Leipzig 1992–, Bd. 23 (2002), S. 235, und *Rembrandt and the Rembrandt School, op. cit.* (Anm. 3).

6  Neben dem hier besprochenen Gemälde behandelte Van den Eeckhout lediglich die Szene *Tobias nimmt den Fisch aus* nach Tobias 6: 4–6. Das Bild befindet sich im Herzog Anton Ulrich-Museum in Braunschweig (Inv.-Nr. 259), siehe hierzu Rüdiger Klessmann, *Herzog Anton Ulrich-Museum. Die holländischen Gemälde*, Braunschweig 1983, S. 60, Nr. 259 mit Abb., und Werner Sumowski, *Gemälde der Rembrandt-Schüler*, 6 Bde., Landau 1983–90, II (1984), S. 733, Nr. 427, S. 790 mit Abb.

7  Versteigerung, Croese, de Winter, Amsterdam, 25.11.1761 (Lugt 1132), Nr. 3: „Een binnenhuis, in hetzelve zit de blinde Tobias aan tafel, naast dezelve staat een Vrouw, en verder met veel ander bywerk, zeer fraay geschildert door G. van Eekhout [*sic*], zo goed als Rembrant [*sic*], hoog 26, breed 31 duim" (für fl. 42–5 an Kalkoen). Der Bildträger ist unbekannt. Die Umrechnung ergibt Abmessungen von *ca.* 66.8 × 79.7 cm.

8  Versteigerung, de Winter, Yver, Amsterdam, 19.12.1770 (Lugt 1878), Nr. 175: „De blinde Tobias verzeld van syn huisvrouw zittende in een binnen-huis, waar in men ziet eenig Huisraad: krachtig en fraai op Doek geschildert. Hoog 26, breed 31,5 duim" (für fl. 10–5). Der Bildträger wird hier mit Leinwand angegeben. Die Umrechnung ergibt *ca.* 66.8 × 81 cm. Dies entspricht nahezu exakt den im Versteigerungskatalog von 1761 genannten Abmessungen, vgl. Anm. 7. Die beiden Bilder dürften sehr wahrscheinlich identisch gewesen sein.

9  Diese Szene kommt sowohl auf Gemälden als auch auf Zeichnungen des Rembrandtkreises häufiger vor. Erinnert sei hier an das Gerrit Dou (1613–1675) zugeschriebene Bild aus der ersten Hälfte der 1630er Jahre in der National Gallery in London (Inv.-Nr. NG 4189). Siehe hierzu *Corpus* I, *op. cit.* (Anm. 4), C3 (Dou), und Christopher Brown, in *Rembrandt. Der Meister und seine Werkstatt*, Ausst. Kat., hrsg. von Christopher Brown, Jan Kelch und Pieter van Thiel, Staatliche Museen Preußischer Kulturbesitz, Altes Museum, Berlin; Rijksmuseum, Amsterdam; National Gallery, London, 1991, S. 300–303, Nr. 55 mit Farbabb. (zugeschrieben an G. Dou). Tobias und Anna, die auf die Rückkehr des jungen Tobias warten, zeigt auch das früher zu Unrecht Rembrandt

zugeschriebene Gemälde von 1659 im
Museum Boijmans Van Beuningen in
Rotterdam, Bredius-Gerson, *op. cit.*
(Anm. 4) 520.

10  Siehe hierzu Burton P. Frederickson,
Julia T. Armstrong (Hrsg.), *The Provenance
Index of The Getty Research Institute.
Verzeichnis der verkauften Gemälde im
deutschsprachigen Raum vor 1800*, bearb.
von Thomas Ketelsen und Tilman von
Stockhausen, Bd. I (A–H), München
2002, S. 593, Nr. 579.

11  Zu Gotzkowskys Aktivitäten als
Agent und Sammler von Gemälden
siehe besonders den materialreichen
Beitrag von Christoph Frank, 'Die
Gemäldesammlungen Gotzkowsky,
Eimbke und Stein: Zur Berliner
Sammlungsgeschichte während des
Siebenjährigen Krieges', in Michael
North (Hrsg.), *Kunstsammeln und
Geschmack im 18. Jahrhundert*, Berlin 2002,
S. 117–94, bes. S. 121–47.

12  Zitiert nach Frank, *op. cit.* (Anm. 11),
S. 176. Dort (siehe Anhang 2, S. 169–194)
die bislang vollständigste Liste der
Gemälde Gotzkowskys, die er anlässlich
des 1764 vorgenommenen Verkaufs an
Kaiserin Katharina II. aufgestellt hatte.

13  Die Umrechnung der Dimensionen
des von Gotzkowsky an Katharina II.
verkauften Gemäldes mit Tobias und
seiner Frau ergibt *ca.* 67.8 × 53.4 cm.
Das Bild war somit sowohl höher als
auch breiter im Vergleich zu Van den
Eeckhouts Tobias-Szene in der Sammlung
Bader (47.6 × 39.4 cm), die nicht
beschnitten zu sein scheint. Gotzkowskys
*Specification* enthält leider keine Angabe
über den Bildträger.

14  Vgl. B. von Köhne, 'Die Gotzkowskische
Gemäldesammlung in der Kaiserlichen
Eremitage', in *idem* (Hrsg.), *Berlin,
Moskau, St. Petersburg. 1649 bis 1763. Ein
Beitrag zur Geschichte der freundschaftlichen
Beziehungen zwischen Brandenburg-Preussen
und Russland*, Schriften des Vereins für die
Geschichte der Stadt Berlin, Heft XX,
Berlin 1882, S. 141–53, Zitat S. 152.

15  Vgl. hierzu *Corpus* I, *op.cit.* (Anm. 4),
S. 87. Ob das Gemälde tatsächlich 1748
und 1759 in Amsterdam versteigert wurde,
was bis zum genannten Zeitpunkt für die

ununterbrochene Anwesenheit des Bildes
in den Niederlanden sprechen könnte,
ist zweifelhaft.

16  F.W.H. Hollstein, *Dutch and Flemish
Etchings, Engravings and Woodcuts,
ca. 1450–1700*, 57 Bde., Amsterdam
1949–2001 (im folgenden Hollstein),
hier Bd. 4, S. 77, Nr. 17. Die Verbindung
zu dem Stich wurde zuerst von Hans
Jantzen, *Rembrandt*, Bielefeld und Leipzig
1923, S. 40, gesehen. Siehe hierzu auch
*Corpus* I, *op. cit.* (Anm. 4), S. 86–87.

17  Vergleichbare Konstruktionen finden sich
in Gemälden des Malers besonders aus
den 1640er und 1650 Jahren. Zu nennen
wären hier beispielsweise „Nachden-
kender Gelehrter" von 1648 in der
Eremitage in St. Petersburg oder das
„Emmausmahl" von 1655 in der Galleria
d'Arte Antica in Rom, vgl. Sumowski,
*op. cit.* (Anm. 6), II, S. 745, Nr. 490 mit
Abb., bzw. S. 731, Nr. 419 mit Abb.

18  Ein Röntgenphoto von Rembrandts
Amsterdam Gemälde zeigt deutlich, dass
er ursprünglich die Wiedergabe eines
Spinnrades geplant und begonnen hatte.
Es zeigt sich deutlich im Hintergrund auf
Höhe des linken Ellbogens von Tobias,
vgl. *Corpus* I, *op. cit.* (Anm. 4) , S. 83 und
85 mit Abb. 2.

19  Vgl. hierzu u.a. Josua Bruyn, *Rembrandt's
keuze van Bijbelse onderwerpen*, Utrecht
1959, S. 14; Christian Tümpel, 'Studien
zur Ikonographie der Historien
Rembrandts. Deutung und Interpretation
der Bildinhalte', *Nederlands Kunsthistorisch
Jaarboek*, Bd. 20, 1969, S. 113; Pieter van
Thiel, in *Rembrandt. Der Meister und seine
Werkstatt*, *op. cit.* (Anm. 9), S. 125–26;
*Corpus* I, *op. cit.* (Anm. 4), S. 86–87, und
zuletzt Bob van den Boogert, in Ernst van
de Wetering, Bernhard Schnackenburg,
*The Mystery of the Young Rembrandt*,
Ausst. Kat., Gemäldegalerie Alte Meister,
Kassel; Museum het Rembrandthuis,
Amsterdam, 2001, S. 209.

20  Van Thiel in *Rembrandt. Der Meister und
seine Werkstatt*, *op. cit.* (Anm. 9), S. 126.

21  Die folgende Übersetzung der lateinischen
Bildunterschrift folgt Van Thiel, in
*Rembrandt. Der Meister und seine Werkstatt*,
*op. cit.* (Anm. 9), S. 125: „Komm nun,
Frau, gib die gestohlene Ziege zurück,

sagte Tobias, der mit dem Herzen sah, wenn er auch seines Augenlichtes beraubt war".

22  Benesch, *op. cit.* (Anm. 4) III, 572. Weitere Zeichnungen Rembrandts bzw. Schülerarbeiten, die mit dem Gemälde von 1645 in Berlin verbunden sind, befinden sich in Stockholm, Nationalmuseum, und in New York, Pierpont Morgan Library; siehe hierzu Julius S. Held, 'Rembrandt and the Book of Tobit', in *idem, Rembrandt Studies*, überarbeitete und erweiterte Auflage, Princeton 1991, S. 118–43, bes. S. 121–22 und Abb. 3, 4 und 5 (zuerst in *The Gehenna Essays in Art*, Bd. 2, Northampton MA, 1964). In deutscher Sprache unter dem Titel 'Rembrandt und das Buch Tobias', in *idem, Rembrandt-Studien*, Leipzig 1983, S. 78–100; zu den Zeichnungen mit dem Vorwurf des Tobias an Anna siehe S. 81–82.

23  Arnold Houbraken, *De groote schouburgh der Nederlantsche konstschilders en schilderessen*, 3 Bde., Amsterdam 1718–21, hier zitiert nach der Ausgabe Den Haag 1753, Bd. 1, S. 174.

24  Vgl. hierzu Volker Manuth in *Rembrandt. Der Meister und seine Werkstatt, op. cit.* (Anm. 9), S. 344 (Biographie Gerbrand van den Eeckhout) und *idem* in *Saur, op. cit.* (Anm. 5), S. 233–36 (s.v. Van den Eeckhout, Gerbrandt).

25  Siehe Held 1983, *op. cit.* (Anm. 22), S. 78.

26  *Ibid.*, S. 90 bzw. 91.

27  *Ibid.*, S. 92.

28  S.A.C. Dudok van Heel, 'Doopsgezinden en schilderkunst in de 17de eeuw: leerlingen, opdrachtgevers en verzamelaars van Rembrandt', in *Doopsgezinde Bijdragen* Bd. 6, 1980, S. 105–23.

29  Vgl. hierzu Gabriël Pastoor, in Christian Tümpel *et al., Im Lichte Rembrandts. Das Alte Testament im Goldenen Zeitalter der niederländische Kunst*, Ausst. Kat., Westfälisches Landesmuseum, Münster, 1994, S. 124 (*s.v.* Die Taufgesinnten). Pastoors Aussagen basieren auf „wenigen bis heute bekannten Inventaren von taufgesinnten Erblassern" (*ibid.*). Der Verfasser des gegenwärtigen Beitrages hat seitdem *ca.* 130 weitere Inventare von Mennoniten (primär wohnhaft in Amsterdam) untersucht. Die Ergebnisse bestätigen die von Pastoor gemachten Feststellungen, dass die Anzahl der Darstellungen aus dem Buch Tobias in mennonitischen Gemäldesammlungen des 17. Jahrhundert nicht grösser ist als in vergleichbaren Sammlungen von Mitgliedern anderer Denominationen. Auch in der erbaulichen Literatur der Mennoniten des 17. Jahrhunderts spielte Tobias keine besondere Rolle.

30  Held 1983, *op. cit.* (Anm. 22), S. 92–100.

31  Zur Themenwahl aus dem Buch Tobias in der holländischen Malerei des 17. Jahrhunderts vgl. Jacqueline Boonen in Tümpel *et al., op. cit.* (Anm. 29), S. 113–117.

32  Vgl. *Corpus* I, *op. cit.* (Anm. 4), S. 87.

33  Zur frühen Exegese siehe besonders Johann Gamberoni, *Die Auslegung des Buches Tobias in der griechischen-lateinischen Kirche der Antike und der Christenheit des Westens bis um 1600*, Studien zum Alten und Neuen Testament, hrsg. von Vinzenz Hamp *et al.*, Bd. XXI, München 1969, hier besonders S. 56–82. Vgl. weiterhin Friedrich Dingermann in *Lexikon für Theologie und Kirche*, Bd. 10 (1965), Spalte 215–17 (*s.v.* Tobias).

34  Zur Diskussion über das Buch Tobias in den Verhandlungen des Tridentinums siehe Gamberoni, *op. cit.* (Anm. 33), S. 219–22, Zitat S. 298.

35  *Ibid., op. cit.* (Anm. 33), S. 302.

36  Zitiert nach *ibid.*, S. 233.

37  *D. Martin Luthers Werke. Kritische Gesamtausgabe* (Weimarer Ausgabe), Bd. 12, Die deutsche Bibel, S. 108.

38  Gamberoni, *op. cit.* (Anm. 33), S. 235.

39  *D. Martin Luthers Werke, op. cit.* (Anm. 37), Bd. 12, S. 110.

40  *Ibid.*

41  Georg Rollenhagen war Rektor des altstädtischen Gymnasiums in Magdeburg; zum Text vgl. die folgende Ausgabe: *Georg Rollenhagens Spiel von Tobias 1576*, hrsg. von Johannes Bolte (Neudrucke deutscher Literaturwerke des XVI. und XVII. Jahrhunderts, hrsg. von E. Beutler, Nr. 285–87), Halle 1930.

42  Zitiert nach Rollenhagen, *op. cit.* (Anm. 41), S. 5 bzw. 6.

43  Zitiert *ibid.*, S. 16.

44 Zum Gemälde siehe D. Pont, *Barent
Fabritius 1624–1673*, Utrecht 1958,
S. 147–49, Addendum 2 (Zuschreibung
an B. Fabritius unter Vorbehalt), sowie
Sumowski, *op. cit.* (Anm. 6), II,
S. 917, Nr. 555, S. 935 mit Farbabb.
(Hauptwerk des B. Fabritius).

45 Zitiert nach Rollenhagen, *op. cit.* (Anm.
41), S. 16, I, 1, Vers 273–76 und 282–88.

46 Zitiert *ibid.*, S. 17, I, 1, Vers 289–306.

47 Zitat in eigener Übersetzung nach: *Biblia,
Dat is: De gantsche H. Schrifture, vervattende
alle de Canonijcke Boecken des Ouden en des
Nieuwen Testaments. Nu Eerst, Door last der
Hoogh-Mog: Heeren Staten Generael vande
Vereenighde Nederlanden, en volgens het
Besluyt van de Synode Nationael, gehouden tot
Dordrecht, inde Jaeren 1618 ende 1619*[. . .],
Leyden (bei Paulus Aertsz. van
Ravensteyn voor de Weduwe ende
erfgenaemen van wijlen Hillebrant
Jacobsz. van Wouw), o.J., laut der dem
Vorwort vorangestellten 'Acte van
Authorisatie' 1637 erschienen. Vorwort zu
den apokryphen Schriften: „Apocryphe
Boecken, dat is, Verborgene: ofte om
dat'se niet opentlick in de Ghemeynte
en behooren ghelesen, maer veel eer
verborghen te worden: ofte, om datse,

niet en zijn gheweest in de casse, daer
in de Goddelijcke Boecken vande Joden
bewaert ende verborgen wierden."

48 Vgl. hierzu auch Held 1991, *op. cit*
(Anm. 22), S. 118, Anm. 2.

49 Zitat in eigener Übersetzung nach: *Biblia,
Dat is*, *op. cit.* (Anm. 47): „Uyt welcken
allen klaerlick blijckt dat de voor-
verhaelde Boecken gheen Canonijke maer
Apocryphe Schriften zijn: die derhalven
niet en behooren opentlick in de
Gemeynte gelesen te worden, ende uyt
dewelcke, als zijnde menschelicke
schriften, geen bewijs-redenen en mogen
worden genomen om eenigh artijkel des
geloofs te bevestigen, alsoo ons' geloove
gebouwt moet worden op het fondament
der Propheten ende der Apostelen,
Ephes.2.20. Doch overmits in deselve
oock eenige goede spreucken, vermanin-
gen, ende exemplen gevonden worden, so
en is't niet geheel ondienstigh, dat se in 't
bysonder al te met oock gelesen worden,
alsoo nochtans dat 'se gelijck alle anderen
menschelijcke schriften, altijt getoetst
moeten worden aen den toetsteen der
Goddelicke leeringen, welcke alleen zijn
de Canonijcke Schriften des Ouden ende
Nieuwen Testaments."

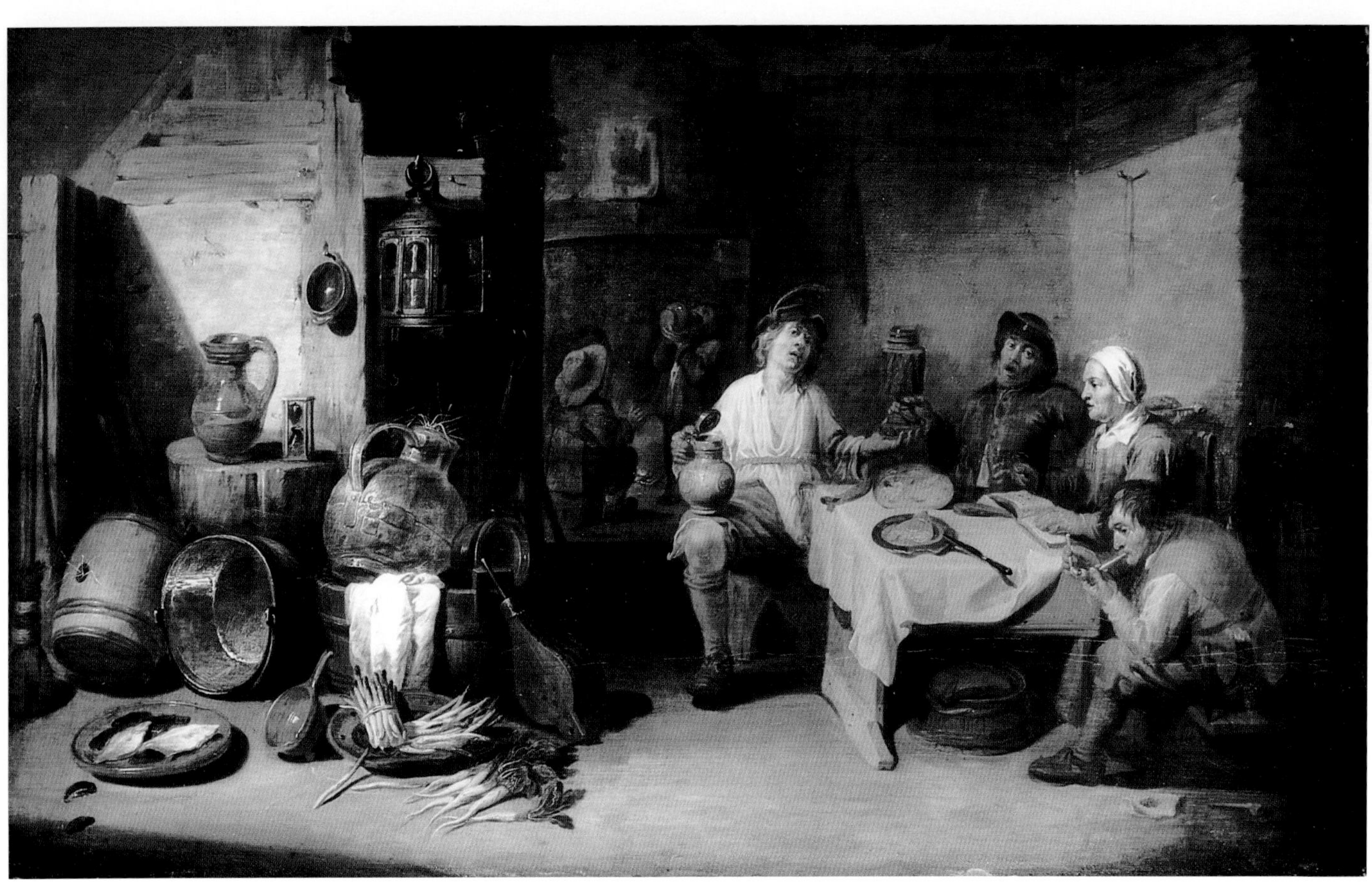

# An Early Work
# by Willem van Herp

GREGORY MARTIN

The minor, but nonetheless appealing, Antwerp master Willem van Herp (1614–1677) has received token representation in the great post-War surveys of Flemish seventeenth-century painting. In the last – the exhibition of 1993–94 at Boston and Toledo (Ohio) – Peter Sutton did Van Herp proud in the catalogue by reproducing one of his paintings in colour for the first time.[1] However, very little is known about the development of his art; indeed, as Hans Vlieghe has pointed out,[2] his early style remains obscure; thus the discovery of the artist's *Le Petit Chaudron* is timely, as it fills this gap in our knowledge.

*Le Petit Chaudron*, more explicitly entitled *A Poor Company at Table in a Rustic Kitchen* (fig. 1), has been at Tyntesfield in Somerset since the early 1840s, and will now remain there as the house and much of its contents have recently been acquired by the National Trust. The painting's first English owner, George Gibbs (died 1842) gave it to his younger brother, William (1790–1895), shortly before his death. William was the builder of the Tyntesfield we know, a magnificent neo-Gothic mansion.

At Tyntesfield, the picture was long thought to be the work of Peter Paul Rubens (1577–1640).[3] It had been bought as such on behalf of George Gibbs at the Schamp d'Aveschoot (†) sale in Ghent on 14 September 1840, lot 168.[4] The catalogue entry stated that it had been in the family for over a century. Descamps had described it in 1763: "*Rubens se vit imité de près dans quelques compositions de David Teniers . . . . Le plus beau se voit à Gand dans le cabinet de M. Lucas de Schamps* [sic]; *C'est un assemblée de Paysans qui boivent et jouent aux cartes* [sic] . . . . *Rubens s'y est si bien caché sous le masque de Teniers que les plus habiles ont cru Teniers Auteur de cet excellent morceau.*"[5] In fact, when it was offered in Ghent in 1840, notes made in catalogues of the sale by prospective purchasers – including John Smith, the celebrated dealer and taxonomist of seventeenth-century Netherlandish masters – agreed in attributing the painting to Van Herp,[6] justifiably so in view of the instantly recognizable, round-eyed protagonist and the fluid, thick handling of the brush.

fig. 1 WILLEM VAN HERP
*A Poor Company at Table in a Rustic Kitchen* (*Le Petit Chaudron*),
Oil on panel, 49.5 × 81.3 cm
The National Trust, Tyntesfield, Somerset

Not much was then known about the artist, who was wrongly thought to have been a pupil of Rubens.[7] His work seems not to have been popular with his fellow citizens, if Jean Denucé's selection of inventories of art collections in Antwerp in the seventeenth century is a reliable guide, for none is there recorded.[8] Little interest in his work seems to have been shown by the Antwerp dealers Forchondt[9] and not much more by their counterpart Matthijs Musson (1598–1678/79).[10] He was ignored in the biographical anthologies of artists compiled by Cornelis de Bie (1627– *ca.* 1715)[11] and Jean Baptiste Descamps (1715–1791).[12] Nevertheless his obscure reputation must have been given a fillip in 1764 by the publication by John Boydell (1719–1804) of a fine print, *A Flemish Entertainment*, made from an Earlom drawing[13] after one of a pair of pictures then, and still, in the collection of the Marquis of Bute.[14] His work was to appear more frequently in the auction rooms, and, some fifty years later, another pair of his paintings was engraved in the famed Stafford Gallery (now the collection of the Duke of Sutherland).[15] These are also tavern scenes, but they are more muted and restrained than the exuberant *Flemish Entertainment*. One of the Sutherland pictures is signed and dated 1654,[16] and was hitherto Van Herp's earliest known painting.

The Tyntesfield painting is dated on the drawing stuck to the wall above the fireplace *163*[?]. The last digit is obscured by the owl's perch, but it may be read as a 5 or 6;[17] the latter is to be preferred, as Van Herp only became a master in the Antwerp guild in 1637/38, at the rather advanced age of about twenty-four, having served as an apprentice to the obscure Hans Biermans for perhaps as much as nearly ten years.[18] The painting is best thought to have been executed round the time that Van Herp became a master.

Descamps's double-talk, repeated and embroidered in the 1840 sale catalogue, was due to the then high regard for the art of David Teniers (1610–1690). Although Rubens and Teniers were socially connected early, it is unlikely that Rubens would have considered the younger artist's work worthy of emulation. He is not known to have owned a painting by Teniers, whose art had reached an early distinction by 1635. Rubens was perhaps not in sympathy with his sentimental interpretation, and dilution, of the witty but unambiguous portrayal of peasant life in the raw by Pieter Bruegel the Elder (*ca.* 1524/30–1569).

In fact Rubens appreciated 'low life' scenes in the 1630s. At his death he owned seventeen paintings by Adriaen Brouwer (?1605/06–1638),[19] and he had not long before extensively reworked copies of a *Twelfth Night* and a *Feast of St Martin* after Martin van Cleve (*ca.* 1527–1581).[20] Obviously the Louvre *Kermesse* is in itself an exuberant restatement of the elder Bruegel's art,[21] probably painted in the early 1630s. Here in the bottom right-hand corner is displayed an assemblage of kitchenware, which in more compact groupings preoccupied specialists of the rustic interior in this decade. Rubens also painted figures in 'low life' scenes by Cornelis Saftleven (1607–1681).

The origin of the 'new' peasant interior (as opposed to the old formula repeated by Bruegel's younger son), with its idiosyncratic assemblage of household utensils, and its dissemination by the young Rotterdam brothers, Cornelis and Herman (1609–1685) Saftleven have been charted in detail by Margret Klinge.[22] That the 'new' peasant interior originated in the northern Netherlands in the early 1630s is clear, but how is less certain, as are the length and number of stays spent in Antwerp by the two Saftleven brothers. Further, while Herman may have been the prime mover – as was claimed some thirty years later[23] – it was Cornelis who gained the more immediate recognition, not only by the inclusion of his portrait in the *Iconography* of Anthony van Dyck (1599–1641),[24] but also by Rubens's acquisition of his work.

Rubens owned seven paintings by Cornelis Saftleven at the time of his death, in four of which he had introduced the figures;[25] Cornelis was thus singled out as the only contemporary northern Netherlandish painter with whom Rubens chose to be associated. Their joint works were chiefly 'low life' scenes, and that their execution was not regarded by Rubens as a *jeu d'esprit* but as a commercial enterprise is shown by the fact that one was on the Antwerp market in 1637.[26]

Teniers collaborated with Herman Saftleven in 1634;[27] he may also have got to know some of Rubens's work 'in collaboration' with Cornelis, as on several occasions he was to treat a subject which may have been inspired by staffage that Rubens had devised as suitable for inclusion in a painting by Saftleven. No. 297 of the 'Specification' of Rubens's collection was described as: "*Une piece du mesme* [Cornelis] *ou une femme est baissée les figures … de Rubens*".[28] Teniers returned to the subject not for the first time as late as *ca.* 1650.[29] He may also have been influenced by Cornelis Saftleven when he took up other themes that the Dutchman had made popular, in particular *The Temptation of St Anthony* and *The Rich Man led to Hell*.[30] Cornelis's stay in Antwerp is usually thought to have ended in 1634,[31] but he may have returned to the city after completing the commission for a family portrait that had required his absence.

This possibility is suggested by the *Rustic Interior with a Youth filling his Pipe* (in private hands),[32] which is on an Antwerp panel made by Michiel Vriendt, who died in 1636/37.[33] The youth seems obviously the work of Teniers, who had probably earlier used the same model for the right-hand art lover in the foreground of *Interior of the Artist's Studio* (private collection) of 1635.[34] The interior, still life and the idiosyncratic hog would seem to be the work of Cornelis. This work of collaboration was probably executed about the same time as Van Herp's picture at Tyntesfield, where the format is that developed by the Saftlevens and adopted by Teniers.

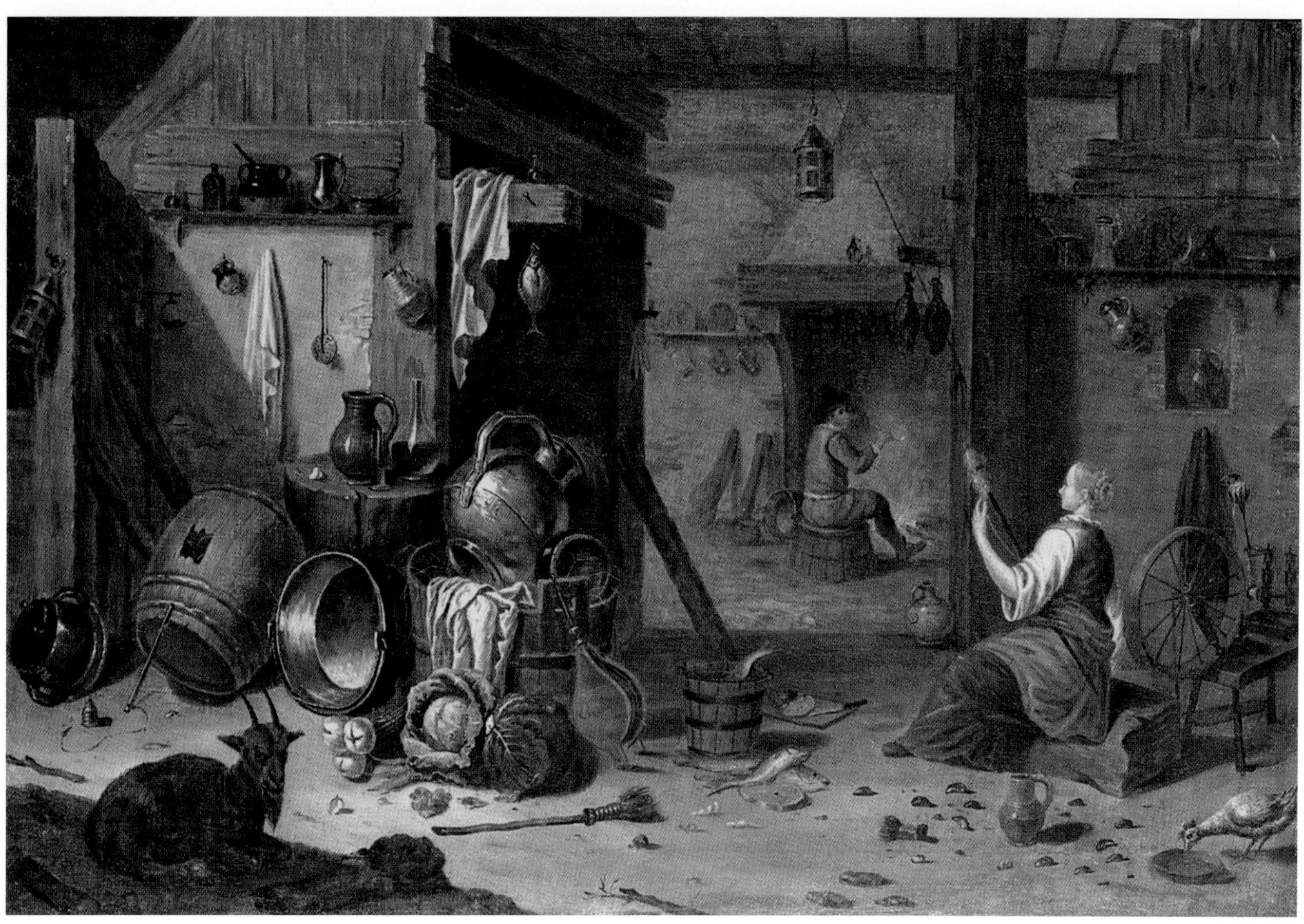

fig. 2  Copy after (?) CORNELIS
SAFTLEVEN
*Kitchen Interior with a Peasant*
*Woman spinning*
Oil on canvas, 56 × 80 cm
Sale Sotheby Mak Van Waay,
Amsterdam, 29 April 1985, lot 35

To Cornelis Saftleven's example was also probably due the compact arrangement of household utensils set against the lath-and-plaster wall. The motif appears in the left foreground in what – to judge from a photograph – may be a copy after a lost work by Cornelis (fig. 2).[35] In this rustic interior, a woman sits with a distaff, while beyond a man smokes by a fire. In the foreground is a goat, the handling of which – even in a photograph – asserts the unmistakeable characteristics of his manner. Given most prominence is the still life of a brass churn placed beside a ceramic pot on top of a draped wooden pail, against which leans a pair of bellows; between the pail and a propped-up barrel are a chopping table and a brass cauldron set on its side.

Van Herp follows this arrangement in all the main essentials, but has seen fit to replace the cabbages with asparagus in a pottery dish, to introduce flat fish on another dish nearby and an hourglass in place of the carafe. This arrangement and its setting was to prove unusually popular, for they appear – always with slight variations, usually in the foreground elements – in at least eleven other works apparently only known today from derivations, in one of which the sleeping woman may in the original have been by Teniers.[36]

The French title of the Van Herp focused on the cauldron. This motif, often viewed from the same sideways angle, was frequently depicted both in Rotterdam and in Antwerp in the 1630s. Indeed Teniers was to repeat it in his paintings as late as 1650.[37] Its meaning has not been addressed. According to Bax,[38] in the time of Hieronymus Bosch (*ca.* 1450–1519) the cauldron or 'carnival kettle' alluded (in his unvarnished phrase) to "gobbling and guzzling". That the visual association remained current in the 1630s would explain Brouwer's introduction of one such cauldron beneath the fat, dozing drinker in his Munich picture (Alte Pinakothek).[39] The hourglass and open lantern in the Van Herp presumably refer to transience and to death; their inclusion provides a moralizing warning against the protagonists' enjoyable time-wasting.

Van Herp's anti-hero (although he is anaemic in comparison) may have been inspired by the seated *Landsknecht* in Rubens's lost painting of carousing soldiers, which is known by several copies and a preparatory drawing.[40] Van Herp probably used the same model for the violinist in the Indianapolis Museum of Art *Interior*.[41] The three other figures in the Tyntesfield picture are less inspired; the woman and youth fail to engage either with each other or the spectator. For the peasants by the fire and the device of dating the work on a drawing on the back wall, Van Herp would have turned to paintings by Teniers: his *Still Life* of 1635 seems to have been the first work which he dated in this way.[42] Teniers retained as part of his repertoire a prominent display of compactly arranged household utensils until the 1650s. No such motif recurs in Van Herp's interiors, but those extant are few, and, as we have seen, none is dated again until 1654.

1 Peter Sutton, *The Age of Rubens*, exh. cat.,
Toledo Museum of Art, Toledo, Ohio,
and Museum of Fine Arts, Boston, 1993,
p. 439, no. 74

2 Hans Vlieghe, *Flemish Art and Architecture*,
New Haven and London 1998, p. 165.

3 *Catalogue of Paintings [at] Tyntesfield*,
*ca.* 1865, in the Dining Room; reference
kindly provided by the Getty Provenance
Index.

4 Information kindly provided by the
Getty Provenance Index.

5 J.-B. Descamps, *La Vie des peintres
Flamands . . .*, Paris 1763, I, pp. 313–14.

6 Information kindly provided by the
Getty Provenance Index.

7 See, for instance, J. Hobbes, *The Picture
Collector's Manual . . .*, 2 vols., London
1849, I, p. 192; but see also under note 15.

8 Jean Denucé, *Inventare von Kunstsammlungen
zu Antwerpen . . .*, Antwerp 1932.

9 Jean Denucé, *Kunstausfuhr Antwerpen . . .
Die Firma Forchoudt*, Antwerp 1931.

10 Jean Denucé, *Na Peter Pauwel Rubens . . .*,
Antwerp 1939.

11 Cornelis de Bie, *Het Gulden Cabinet . . .*,
Antwerp 1662.

12 See Descamps, *op. cit.* (note 5).

13 See Gregory Rubinstein, 'Richard Earlom
(1743–1822) and Boydell's Houghton
Gallery', *Print Quarterly*, VIII, 1991,
p. 9, note 25.

14 See Francis Russell, *John, 3rd Earl of
Bute, Patron and Collector*, forthcoming,
pls. 115–16.

15 In W.Y. Ottley, *Engravings of the Most
Noble The Marquis of Stafford's Collection*,
London 1818, III, no. 26; Ottley,
pp. 78–9, under no. 25, was less than
complimentary about the two paintings:
"The spectator . . . feels himself like
one of a party where much noise
and plenty of good fare fail to be
productive of mirth and conviviality";
he believed that the painter was a pupil
of Van Dyck.

16 *Catalogue of the Collection of Pictures . . . at
Bridgewater House* etc., privately printed,
1926, no. 181.

17 My thanks to Francis Greenacre for
having examined the date.

18 See Philip Rombouts and Theodoor van
Lerius, *De Liggeren en andere Historische

*Archieven der Antwerpse Sint Lucasgilde* etc.,
2 vols., Antwerp and The Hague
1864–76, reprint Amsterdam 1961, I,
p. 662, and II, p. 91.

19 See Jeffrey Muller, *Rubens: The Artist as
Collector*, Princeton 1989, pp. 139–42.

20 See Hans Vlieghe, 'Rubens emulating
the Bruegel Tradition', *The Burlington
Magazine*, CXLII, 2000, pp. 681ff.,
publishing the *Twelfth Night*; *The Feast of
St Martin* was published by Jeremy Wood,
'Rubens Restorations and Retouchings',
*Apollo*, CXLII, 1995, pp. 16ff.; the
whereabouts of the third in the series,
*The Lame Bishop*, remains unknown.

21 See Julius Held, *Rubens: Selected Drawings*,
2nd edn, Oxford 1986, under nos. 193
and 194.

22 See Margret Klinge-Gross, 'Herman
Saftleven als Zeichner und Maler
bäuerlicher Interieurs', *Wallraf-Richartz-
Jahrbuch*, XXXVIII, 1976, pp. 68ff.,
and Roel James, 'Van "boerenhuysen"
en "stilstaende dingen"', in *Rotterdamse
Meesters uit de Gouden Eeuw*, exh. cat.,
Historisch Museum, Rotterdam, 1994,
pp. 133–35.

23 See De Bie, *op. cit.* (note 11), p. 412.

24 See Marie Mauquoy-Hendrickx,
*L'Iconographie d'Antoine van Dyck*, 2 vols.,
Brussels 1956, 2nd edn, Brussels 1991,
I, p. 158, no. 90. Saftleven's speciality
was described not as rustic interiors
but as "*noctium phantasmatum*" – his first
interest.

25 See Muller, *op. cit.* (note 19), pp. 142–43.
The artist is there referred to only by his
surname; it is generally assumed that he
is to be identified as Cornelis and not
Herman, because the first entry is for
a *Temptation of St Anthony*, which is not
a subject that Herman is ever recorded
as having painted.

26 See Denucé, *op. cit.* (note 9), pp. 24–25.

27 See Klinge-Gross, *op.cit.* (note 22), p. 78,
fig. 18.

28 See Muller, *op. cit.* (note 19), p. 143.

29 See Gregory Martin, *The Flemish School*,
National Gallery Catalogues, London
1970, no. 862.

30 See Wolfgang Schulz, *Cornelis Saftleven,
Leben und Werke*, Berlin and New York
1978, nos. 507–11 and 515.

31  See, for instance, *ibid.*, p. 2.

32  Offered at auction, Christie's, London,
21 July 1989, lot 166.

33  See Rombouts and Van Lerius, *op. cit.*
(note 18), p. 89.

34  See Margret Klinge, *David Teniers de Jonge
. . .*, exh. cat., Koninklijk Museum voor
Schone Kunsten, Antwerp, 1991, no. 11.

35  Offered at auction, Sotheby Mak Van
Waay, Amsterdam, 29 April 1985, lot 35,
as signed; another reduced copy (?),
notably without the top and whip, was
offered at auction, Dorotheum, Vienna,
21–25 May 1987, lot 653 and later at
Christie's, Rome, 27/28 November 1989,
lot 129. I thank Judith Niessen, of
Sotheby Mak Van Waay, for having kindly
provided a photograph of the pictures
offered in 1985 and 1987 (see note 36).

36  The *Sleeping Woman in a Rustic Interior* is
recorded as in the collection of Lord
Camoys at Stonor Park, when exhibited
at the Victoria and Albert Museum in
1953/54. Three variants are known: 1) in
the Spitzer sale, Fischer, Lucerne, 10–13
May 1939, lot 1642; 2) bearing Teniers's
monogram and on an Antwerp panel
support made by François de Bout (who
became a master in the Antwerp guild in
1637/38, see Martin, *op. cit.* (note 29),
p. 272), offered at auction, Christie's,
New York, 26 March 1982, lot 136;
3) in the Musée des Beaux-Arts, Nantes,
formerly attributed to Hendrick Sorgh
(1609/11–1670) (an old reproduction is
in the Rijksbureau voor Kunsthistorische
Documentatie, RKD, The Hague.

The still life also occurs in: 1) *Interior*,
described as from the circle of Teniers,
offered at auction, Sotheby's, London,
30 October 1991, lot 51; 2) *Interior*,
described as in the manner of Ryckaert,
offered at auction, Sotheby Parke Bernet,
New York, 28 November 1978, lot 77;
and 3) *Interior with a Woman spinning*,
described as by Cornelis Saftleven,
offered at auction, Nagel, Stuttgart,
8–10 December 1970, lot 894. The still
life alone is the subject of two works:
1) offered at auction, Sotheby's, London,
27 May 1987, lot 29, as by a follower of
Saftleven; and 2) offered at auction,
Versailles, 14 November 1965, lot 55,
as attributed to Sorgh.

37  In the Hermitage *Peasant Wedding Feast*,
for which see Klinge, *op.cit.* (note 34),
no. 16.

38  See Dirk Bax, *Hieronymus Bosch: His
picture-writing deciphered*, Rotterdam 1979,
p. 234.

39  See Konrad Renger and Claudia Denk,
*Flämische Malerei des Barok in der Alten
Pinakothek*, Munich and Cologne 2002,
pp. 58–9.

40  See Held, *op. cit.* (note 21), no. 232 and
pl. 208

41  Photo in the RKD, The Hague, where
stated to be attributed to Justus van der
Nijpoort and listed in the 1942 catalogue
of the Indiana Art Institute, now the
Indianapolis Museum of Art, inv. no.
38.9, as van Herp.

42  See Klinge, *op. cit.* (note 34), no. 10.

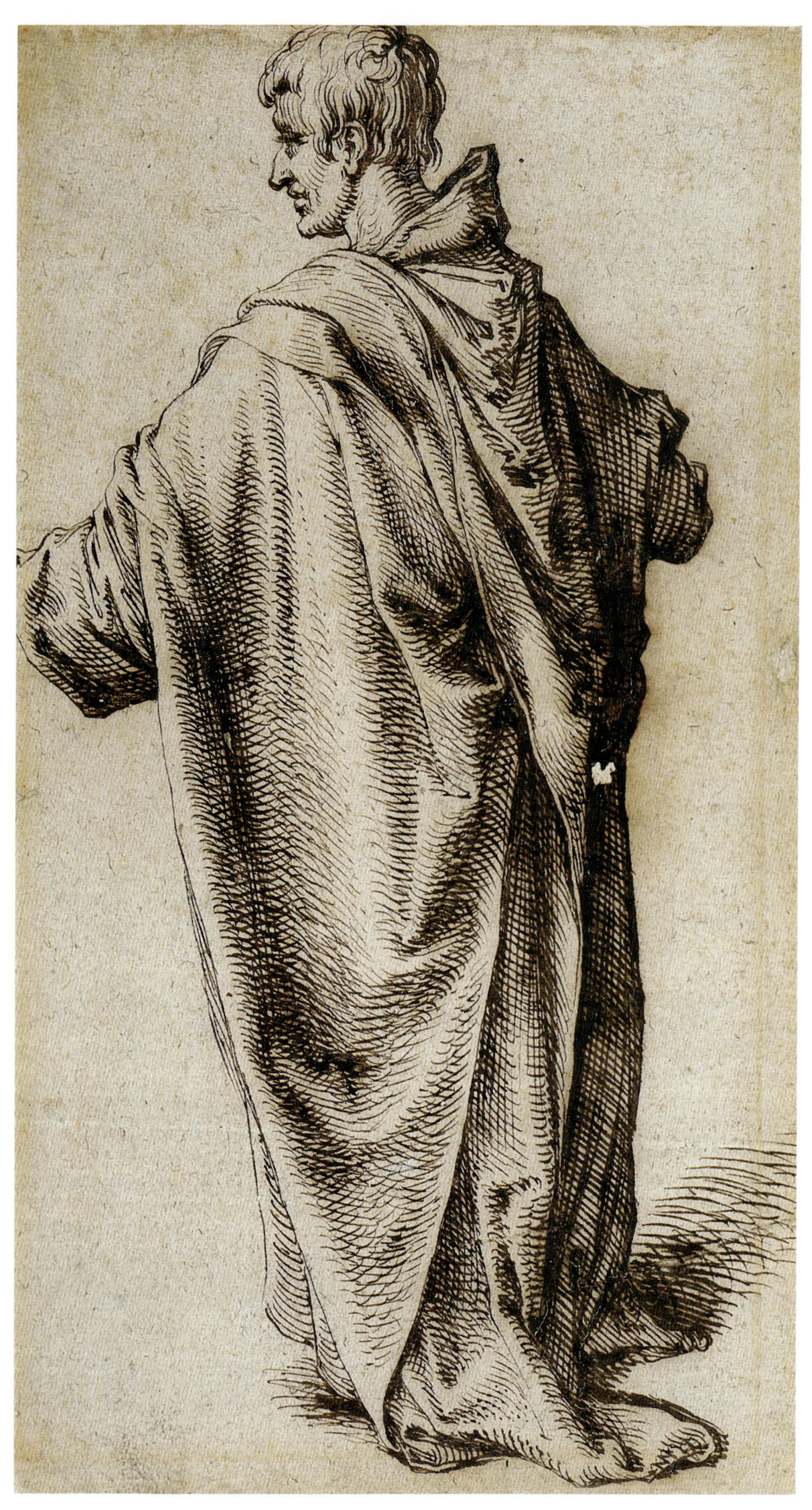

# A Newly Discovered Drawing
# by Jacques de Gheyn II

DAVID McTAVISH

The purpose of this note is to introduce a forgotten drawing in an unlikely location as the work by the Dutch draughtsman sometimes considered second only to Rembrandt.[1] And for Alfred Bader, Rembrandt remains the artist he esteems most highly.

International travel has been one of the defining features of Alfred Bader's professional life. Every year he and Isabel reserve several months for carefully planned visits to experts in the fields of chemistry and art, located in many parts of North America and Europe. They travel to wherever old pictures or new compounds are to be discovered, or an audience is waiting to be regaled by the inimitable telling of the adventures of a chemist collector.

They have travelled extensively in western Canada, but evidently they have not visited Regina, Saskatchewan, in the middle of the Canadian prairies.[2] There, in the early years of the last century, another intrepid collector – not a chemist but a lawyer – soon discovered the seductive pleasures of acquiring works of art. Not nearly as focused or as learned as Alfred Bader, and with much more modest means, the collector pursued his passion undeterred, despite an initial lack of knowledge about the field and an enduring sense of isolation.

Norman MacKenzie, the collector in question, was born in Ontario and studied law in Toronto, but, like many enterprising youths of his generation, he struck out on his own, creating a new life for himself on the recently opened-up Canadian prairies.[3] In 1891 MacKenzie established a pioneering legal practice in Regina, which at the time consisted of only 1500 inhabitants. Capital of the North-West Territories and from 1905 of the province of Saskatchewan, Regina expanded rapidly and remained MacKenzie's home for the rest of his life. On his death in 1936 he bequeathed both the major part of his collection of art and his residual estate to the University of Saskatchewan for use at Regina College. After several delays, an art gallery bearing his name was opened in Regina in 1953.

MacKenzie collected widely in various media, including minor archaeological material, paintings by local artists, and, significantly, two bronzes by Rodin

fig. 1 JACQUES DE GHEYN II
*Standing Male Figure*
Pen and brown ink, 291 × 161 mm
MacKenzie Art Gallery, Regina,
University of Regina Collection,
Gift of Mr Norman MacKenzie

which he purchased in 1916. Above all, he aimed to acquire works by well-known artists, especially of the Italian Renaissance, but, not surprisingly, given his place and period, he succumbed to unreliable advice, and his ambitions in this regard were cruelly thwarted. A few of his European drawings have, however, survived the critical scrutiny of more recent scholarship and are now acclaimed, sometimes with a change of attribution, as important works by significant artists. Such is the case with a large and handsome drawing by Federico Zuccaro (1540/42–1609) and another by Thomas Gainsborough (1727–1788).[4]

In a letter of March 1926 to J. Purves Carter, his ill-chosen advisor in Italy, MacKenzie referred to a drawing he already owned as "the little St. Francis by Guido Reni".[5] Presumably Carter had recommended the purchase of the drawing and was perhaps also responsible for the attribution, but nothing further is known about the early history of the sheet. Nor, evidently, has the drawing (fig. 1) ever been reproduced or discussed in print, though it remained with MacKenzie for the rest of his life and made its way with his collection into the art gallery named in his honour.[6]

While it cannot be proven who exactly came up with the description of the Regina drawing, as related by MacKenzie in his 1926 letter, neither the identification of the subject nor the designation of the artist carries conviction, and rightly they have both been dropped from the records of the MacKenzie Art Gallery. Now the drawing is catalogued simply as being of a monk by an unidentified Italian artist.

A work of outstanding quality, the drawing shows a standing, clean-shaven man, dressed in a heavy robe with an ample hood-like piece of drapery hanging far down his back. No indication of a setting is provided. The sheet was obviously cut down at some time, for the figure itself extends beyond the edge of the paper on three sides and its cast shadow does so on the fourth. Apart from the cowl, there is no distinguishing feature to help in identifying the male figure unequivocally, though it is possible that originally he held some informative object in his left hand.

The drawing is executed solely in pen and brown ink. Vigorous and remarkably assured, the pen line is a virtuoso performance of curved hatching, intricate cross-hatching and stippling (in the drapery at the bottom). Immediately the draughtsmanship betrays the graphic technique of an engraver and, more specifically, the characteristic hand not of an Italian but of a Dutch artist, Jacques de Gheyn II (1565–1629).

Jacques (Jacob) de Gheyn II was the most accomplished of three generations of Dutch artists with the same name. Born in Antwerp in 1565, Jacques de Gheyn II trained with his father, Jacques de Gheyn I (1537/38–probably 1581), a glass painter and miniaturist, and with Hendrick Goltzius (1558–1617) in

     

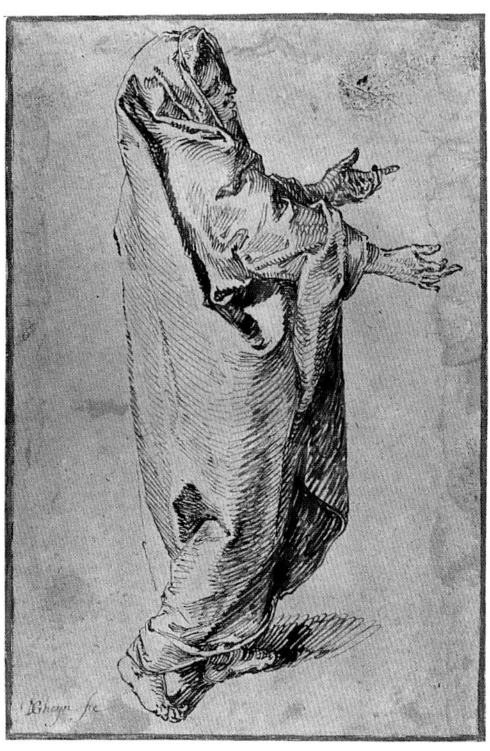

fig. 2 JACQUES DE GHEYN II
*Standing Female Figure*
Pen and brown ink, 230 × 155 mm
Yale University Art Gallery,
New Haven, Egmont Collection,
Yale Library Transfer

Haarlem between about 1585 and 1588. He then moved to Amsterdam and in 1596 to Leiden. He married well, and counted distinguished scholars and members of the court of Prince Maurice of Orange among his associates. From shortly after 1600 until his death in 1629 he lived in The Hague. Although he was also a painter, Jacques de Gheyn II is most celebrated as a printmaker and draughtsman. Hollstein catalogued 433 engravings and etchings by Jacques de Gheyn II (both after his own designs and after those of other artists), and Van Regteren Altena assembled information on 1052 drawings by the artist.[7] His son, Jacques de Gheyn III (?1596–1641), was much less prolific and is best known for the etchings done early in his career.

Not only is the overall brilliance of the barbed line typical of De Gheyn, but so too are such features in the Regina drawing as the lean profile and wavy hair. The carefully modelled and very sculptural drapery is also found elsewhere among De Gheyn's drawings, especially in his studies for biblical figures. For instance, in four drawings by De Gheyn of single standing women, which Van Regteren Altena considered to be studies of Mary and Elizabeth for a *Visitation*, similar mantles almost entirely cover the body from head to foot.[8] And again each figure casts a slight, quickly hatched shadow to the right. A sheet signed by De Gheyn in the Yale University Art Gallery (fig. 2) is typical of these drawings, though its draughtsmanship is somewhat freer than that of the

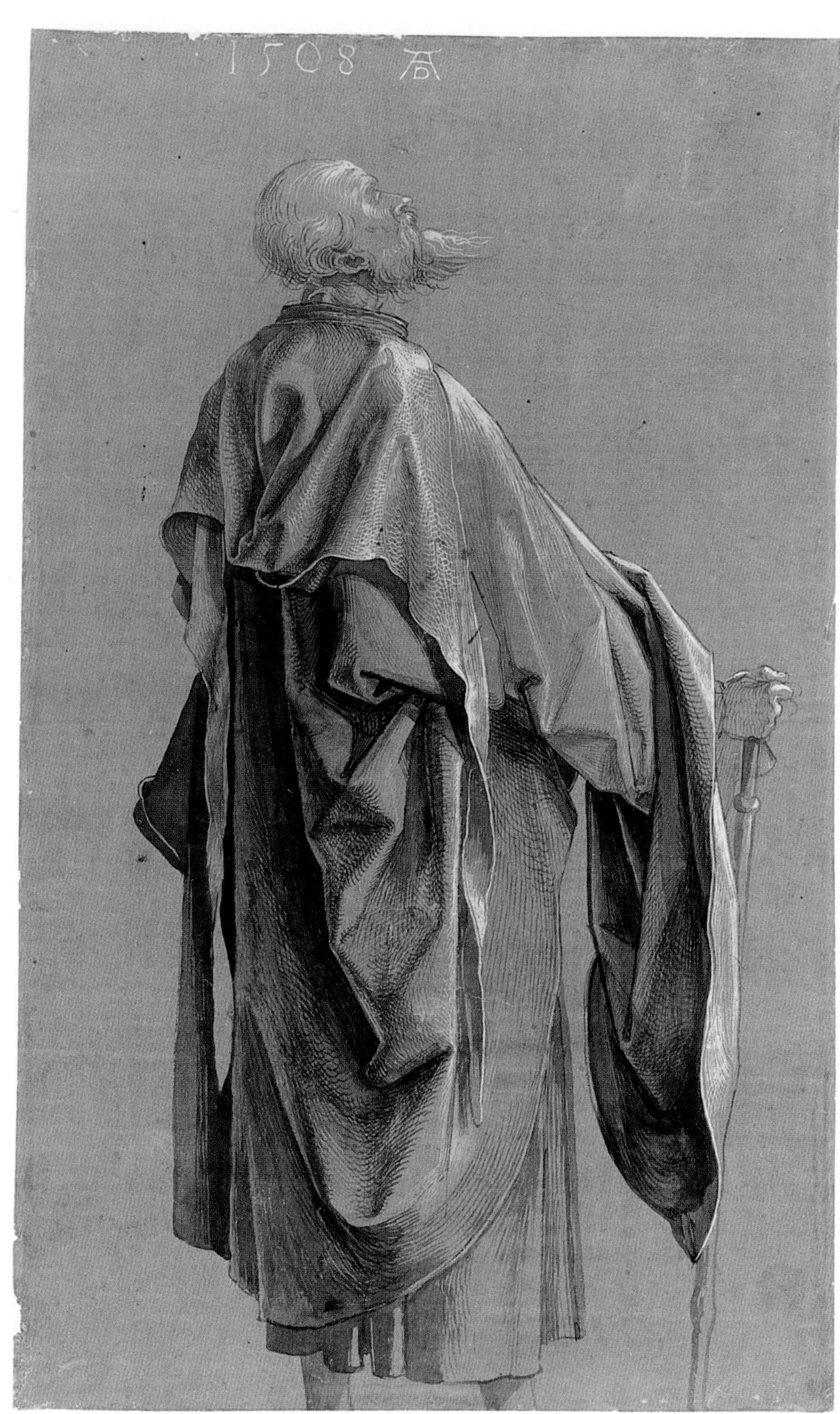


fig. 3 ALBRECHT DÜRER
*Standing Apostle*, 1508
Brush and grey wash, heightened
with white, on green prepared
paper, 406 × 240 mm
Berlin, Staatliche Museen zu
Berlin, Kupferstichkabinett

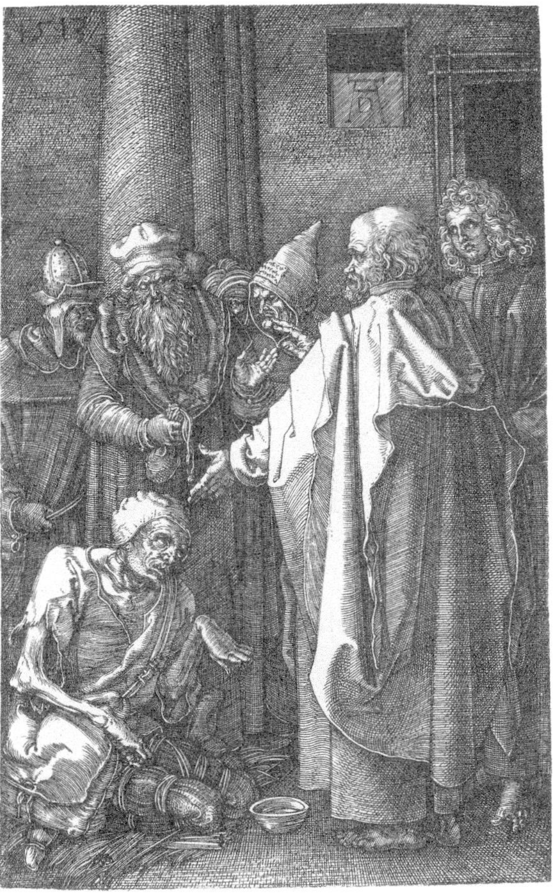

fig. 4 ALBRECHT DÜRER
*St Peter and St John healing
the Cripple*, 1513
Engraving, 11.8 × 7.4 cm
London, The British Museum

Regina sheet.[9] Of course, such voluminous cloaks have a distinguished history
as the generic garb of biblical personages, particularly in Italian Renaissance
art. De Gheyn did not travel to Italy, so he did not have first-hand knowledge of
such monumental figures in fresco or altarpieces *in situ*. He did, however, have
familiarity with some Italian sculpture (though not necessarily draped) of the
period, since the courtyard of his house in The Hague contained "two stone
figures by Michiel Angelo", unfortunately no longer identifiable.[10]

De Gheyn's monumental figure and its massive drapery are more likely to
have been heir to the more immediate Northern Renaissance tradition, particularly as transmitted through prints. In mature works by Albrecht Dürer
(1471–1528), executed after his second sojourn in Italy (1505–07), the figures
frequently exhibit a similar unadorned monumentality. This is exemplified by
the unsurpassed figure studies modelled with assured hatching and cross-
hatching, using the point of the brush, as preparation for the Heller Altarpiece.

The 1508 study in Berlin for one of the Apostles is a magnificent example (fig. 3).[11] If it cannot be certain that De Gheyn knew those drawings, he would at least have been familiar with prints containing similar figures.[12] One example could have been the 1513 engraving *St Peter and St John healing the Cripple* (fig. 4). There, St Peter stands commandingly at the right with his left arm outstretched to the lame man.[13] He is draped in a heavy robe with a cowl similar to, but not identical with, the figure in De Gheyn's drawing. Goltzius, too, placed heavily draped, standing males at the lower right in several of the episodes in his engraved *Passion* of 1596–99, though these figures are clothed in more nearly contemporary dress. In fact, large standing figures had become a much-repeated staple of such compositions, and De Gheyn himself included one at the lower left of his engraved *Crucifixion* of about 1595.[14] None of these figures is, however, exactly the same as the Regina drawing.

The third member of the family, Jacques de Gheyn III, also displayed a fondness for showing male figures enveloped in massive cloaks. Such figures are a distinctive feature of his drawings and his prints, including the *Seven Wise Men of Greece*, the 1616 series of etchings that made his reputation in his youth. However, Jacques de Gheyn III went one step further and also made pen-and-ink studies of carefully arranged drapery alone. Van Regteren Altena grouped together four such pen-and-ink drawings, the technique of which differs from his father's in that the hatching is more regular and the use of stippling more prominent.[15] The folds of drapery have now become even more ample, replacing altogether the more brittle puckers of the earlier drawings. A splendid example is the sheet from the Frits Lugt collection in the Fondation Custodia, Paris (fig. 5).[16] None of these drawings has been connected with any other work of Jacques de Gheyn III, though it has been proposed that they may have been undertaken in preparation for unexecuted etchings.[17] As studies of monumental configurations of drapery, they again recall a Renaissance precedent – the exercises done with brush and tempera on linen by Leonardo da Vinci (1452–1519) and his Florentine contemporaries after arrangements of real drapery set up precisely for the purpose. Dürer also made studies of voluminous drapery, evidently also after actual models; these drawings are generally more linear in execution but frequently they were done with the brush nonetheless.[18] It is also worth noting that during the late seventeenth century Dürer was thought to have been responsible for the large group of drapery studies now usually attributed to Leonardo or his circle.[19]

Rembrandt (1606–1669) himself fully appreciated the expressive power of heavy cloaks, and frequently heightened the solemnity of his biblical or 'timeless' figures by clothing them in just such garb, both in his paintings and in his etchings. In one early, vigorous and very sculptural chalk drawing now in Berlin,



DAVID MCTAVISH

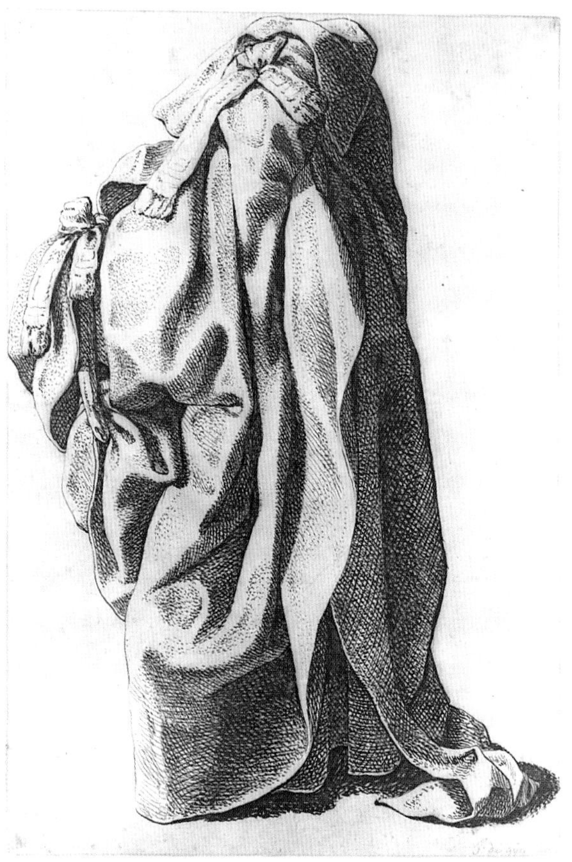

fig. 5 JACQUES DE GHEYN III
*Study of Drapery*
Pen and brown ink, 328 × 218 mm
Paris, Institut Néerlandais,
Collection Frits Lugt

he resorted to the same device, portraying an elderly bearded man seen from
behind and seated, his shoulder and the back of his chair enveloped in massive
folds of thick drapery (fig. 6).[20] The drawing is a study for the 1628 painting
in Melbourne, Australia, of two white-haired men disputing, often said to
represent Sts Peter and Paul.[21] There may not be any way of ascertaining
whether Jacques de Gheyn III (and perhaps his father) knew this particular
drawing by Rembrandt, but there can be no doubt about the related painting.
The son in fact purchased the panel from the up-and-coming young artist from
Leiden and kept it for the rest of his life. In his will of 1641 Jacques de Gheyn
III left the painting – along with another panel by Rembrandt of an old man
asleep by a fire, now in Turin, and two paintings by Jan Lievens (1607–1674) –
to Johannes Wtenbogaert (1608–1680), an Amsterdam tax collector and nephew
of the Remonstrant preacher of the same name. To Maurits Huygens (1595–
1642) he left the small portrait of himself by Rembrandt now at Dulwich.[22]
Jacques de Gheyn III is indeed to be numbered among the first collectors of

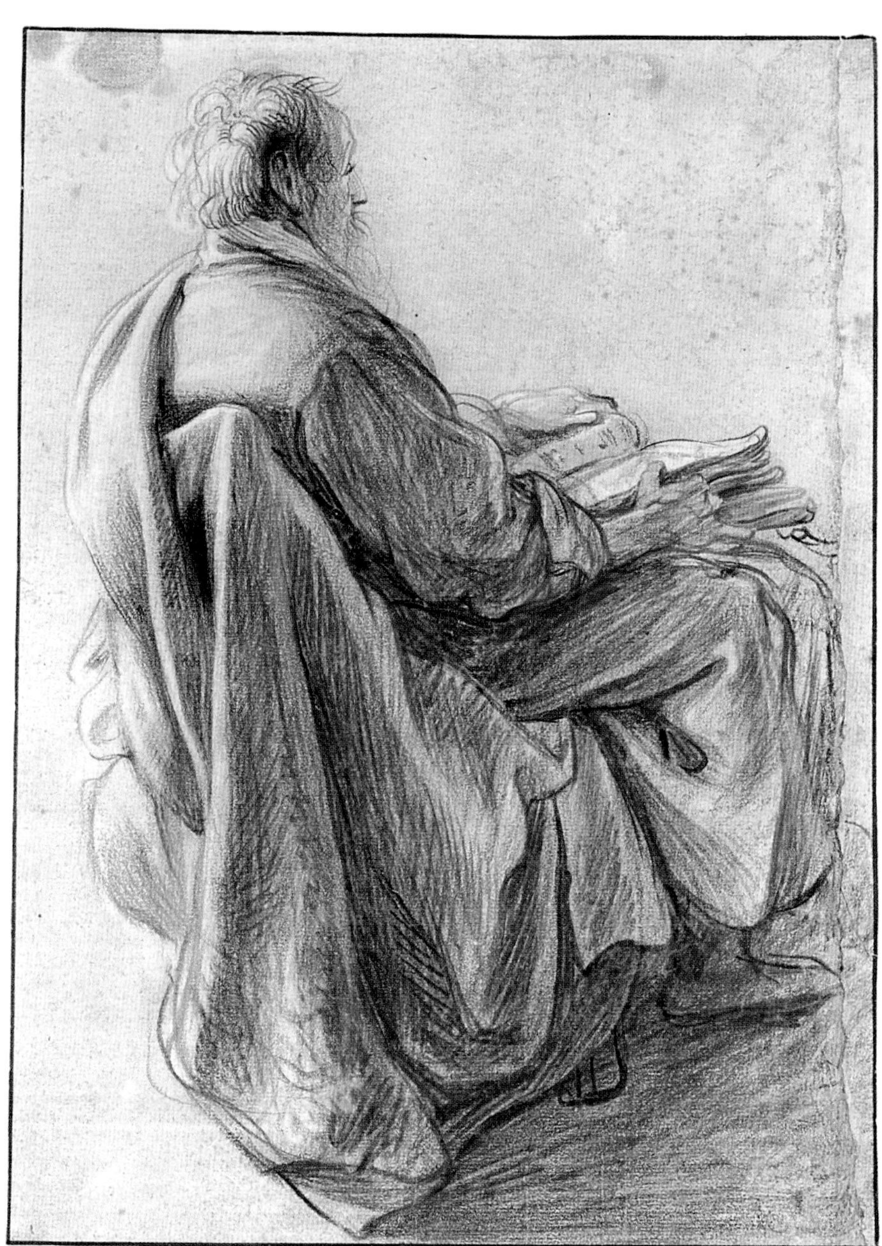



fig. 6 REMBRANDT
*Old Man with a Book, ca.* 1628
Red and black chalk, heightened
with white, and brush and ink,
on tinted paper, 295 × 210 mm
Berlin, Staatliche Museen zu
Berlin, Kupferstichkabinett

Rembrandt's work. At the same time both he and his father may have exercised a considerable influence on the young Rembrandt.[23]

To return to the father, there is no evidence that he ever undertook drapery studies unaccompanied by an underlying figure, like those by his son, though the practice would have conformed with his rational approach to recording the data of the external world. Intrigued by similarities in their graphic *oeuvres*, Van Regteren Altena explored the possibility whether De Gheyn had come into contact with Leonardo's drawings and was uniquely inspired by them, but unfortunately his research was inconclusive.[24] Certainly the range of subject-matter in De Gheyn's drawings is exceptionally wide, and his analytical investigations unusual. However, De Gheyn's drawings not only reveal a universal curiosity, they also demonstrate a graphic virtuosity distinctive of much of the finest draughtsmanship of the Northern tradition. They further display a telling stylistic evolution from late Mannerism to incipient naturalism.

Constantijn Huygens (1596–1687), who attended De Gheyn on his deathbed in 1629, wrote in his diary: "In simple drawing, whether he [De Gheyn] chose to use a pen or crayon or charcoal, he was inferior to none".[25] As a distinctive work by Jacques de Gheyn II, the drawing that Norman MacKenzie thought was by Guido Reni thus joins a distinguished Dutch oeuvre, bearing witness to intertwined traditions from both sides of the Alps.

1  J. Richard Judson, *The Drawings of Jacob de Gheyn II*, New York 1973, pp. 9, 39.

2  I am grateful to Isabel Bader for information on their travels in western Canada.

3  For MacKenzie, I have relied on W.A. Riddell, *The Mackenzie Art Gallery: Norman Mackenzie's Legacy*, Mackenzie Art Gallery, Regina, Saskatchewan, 1990, especially pp. 8–19 (by W.A. Riddell), and pp. 28–42 (by Timothy Long); and Brenda Beckman-Long, in *The Original MacKenzie Bequest*, exh. cat., MacKenzie Art Gallery, Regina, Saskatchewan, 1993.

4  For the drawing by Zuccaro, see Walter Vitzthum, *A Selection of Drawings from North American Collections / Dessins italiens aux Etats-Unis et au Canada*, exh. cat., Norman Mackenzie Art Gallery, University of Saskatchewan, Regina, 1970, pp. 24–26, no. 14; and E. James Mundy, *Renaissance into Baroque, Italian Master Drawings by the Zuccari, 1550–1600*, exh. cat., Milwaukee Art Museum, 1989, pp. 158–60, no. 46. For the drawing by Gainsborough see John Hayes, *The Drawings of Thomas Gainsborough*, 2 vols., New Haven and London 1971, I, pp. 307–08, II, pl. 232; and Ian G. Lumsden, *Gainsborough in Canada*, exh. cat., The Beaverbrook Art Gallery, Fredericton, 1991, p. 58, no. 20.

5  I owe this information to the kindness of Bruce H. Anderson, Registrar, MacKenzie Art Gallery.

6  Accession no. 1926–007. The drawing measures 291 × 161 mm, and is executed in pen and brown ink on rather rough paper, mounted on brown card. The verso of the card is inscribed in red crayon *76 A*.

7  F.W.H. Hollstein, *Dutch and Flemish Etchings, Engravings and Woodcuts ca. 1450–1700*, 57 vols., Amsterdam 1949–2001, VII (1952), pp. 109–90; I.Q. van Regteren Altena, *Jacques de Gheyn, Three Generations*, 3 vols., The Hague, Boston and London 1983, II, pp. 23–161. Both the totals are incorrectly given in the entry [by E.K.J. Reznicek] on Jacques de Gheyn II in *The Dictionary of Art*, ed. Jane Turner, 34 vols., London 1996, XII, pp. 530–31. Also see Jan Piet Filedt Kok, 'Jacques de Gheyn II, Engraver, Designer and Publisher – I', and '– II, A Catalogue', *Print Quarterly*, VII, 1990, pp. 248–81 and 370–96.

8  Van Regteren Altena, *op. cit.* (note 7), II, p. 25, nos. 26–29, III, p. 109, pls. 200–03.

9  Inv. no. 1961.63.88; pen and brown ink; 230 × 155 mm. Signed at the lower left: *IDGheijn fe*: E. Haverkamp-Begemann and Anne-Marie S. Logan, *European Drawings and Watercolors in the Yale University Art Gallery 1500–1900*, 2 vols., New Haven and London 1970, I, pp. 205–06, no. 377, II, pl. 187 (as *The Virgin under the Cross*); Van Regteren Altena, *op. cit.* (note 7), II, p. 25, no. 28, III, pl. 202 (as *St Elisabeth* for a *Visitation*). While none of these drawings can be precisely dated, they would appear to be from De Gheyn's full maturity, probably after he had settled in The Hague. The coarse paper of the Regina drawing probably argues for a later rather than an earlier date.

10  Van Regteren Altena, *op. cit.* (note 7), I, pp. 59–60, and p. 176, note 41, where the author allows that the sculptures may possibly have been the casts made after two of the '*Times of Day*' in the Medici Chapel, Florence, for Goltzius.

11  Staatliche Museen zu Berlin, Kupferstichkabinett, KdZ 12; brush and grey wash, heightened with white, on green prepared paper; 406 × 240 mm. Walter L. Strauss, *The Complete Drawings of Albrecht Dürer*, 6 vols. and 2 supplements, New York 1974, II, 1508/1.

12  A number of drawings by De Gheyn after Dürer's woodcuts have been identified; Van Regteren Altena, *op. cit.* (note 7), I, p. 49, II, pp. 156–57, nos. 1034–41.

13  Walter L. Strauss, *The Complete Engravings, Etchings and Drypoints of Albrecht Dürer*, New York 1972, p. 144, states that the figure of St Peter is actually based on the drawing of the Apostle in Berlin for the Heller Altarpiece. Herrmann Beenken, 'Zu Dürers Italienreise im Jahre 1505', *Zeitschrift des Deutschen Vereins für Kunstwissenschaft*, III, 1936, p. 91, proposed that the engraving was perhaps influenced by Masaccio's *Tribute Money* in the Brancacci Chapel in Florence.

 DAVID McTAVISH

14  Hollstein, *op. cit.* (note 7), no. 23; Filedt
    Kok, *op. cit.* (note 7), p. 392, fig. 240
    (Zacharias Dolendo as engraver after
    Jacques de Gheyn II).

15  Van Regteren Altena, *op. cit.* (note 7), I,
    p. 142, II, p. 175, nos. 83–86, and possibly
    no. 87, III, p. 255, pls. 39–41. This author
    considers a drawing evidently by Jacques
    de Gheyn II of a young man in a heavy
    cloak walking to the right (British
    Museum, inv. no. 1872.1012.3279) as the
    sort of model the son probably used in
    making his drapery studies (II, p. 93,
    no. 571, III, p. 39, pl. 5). The draughts-
    manship of the Regina drawing is
    more flexible than that of the London
    drawing.

16  Inv. no. 3037, pen and brown ink, 328 ×
    218 mm; inscribed lower left in graphite:
    *J. de gijn*. Van Regteren Altena, *op. cit.*
    (note 7), I, p. 142, II, p. 175, no. 84, III,
    p. 255, pl. 39.

17  Carlos van Hasselt, *Rembrandt and his
    Century, Dutch Drawings of the Seventeenth
    Century, from the Collection of Frits Lugt*,
    exh. cat., The Pierpont Morgan Library,
    New York, and the Institut Néerlandais,
    Paris, 1977–78, pp. 69–70, under no. 47;
    and Carlos van Hasselt and Maria van
    Berge-Gerbaud, *Le Héraut du dix-septième
    siècle: dessins et gravures de Jacques de Gheyn
    II et III de la Fondation Custodia, Collection
    Frits Lugt*, exh. cat., Institut Néerlandais,
    Paris, 1985, pp. 113–14, no. 72.

18  Annette Pfaff, *Studien zu Albrecht Dürers
    Heller-Altar*, Nürnberger Werkstücke
    zur Stadt- und Landesgeschichte 7,
    Nuremberg 1971, pp. 55–58, suggests that
    even the drawing of the Apostle for the
    Heller Altarpiece (fig. 3) is principally
    a drapery study made from a draped
    manikin. In the Albertina, Vienna, there
    are two studies for the drapery over the
    lap of God the Father in the Heller
    Altarpiece; Strauss, *op. cit.* (note 11), II,
    pp. 1046–49, 1508/16 and 1508/17.

19  These are the fourteen drapery studies
    listed in the posthumous inventory
    (1695) of Everhard Jabach's collection,
    for which see Bernadette Py, *Everhard*

*Jabach Collectioneur (1618–1695). Les
    dessins de l'inventaire de 1695*, Paris 2001,
    pp. 270–74; and Françoise Viatte, 'The
    Early Drapery Studies', in *Leonardo da
    Vinci, Master Draftsman*, exh. cat., The
    Metropolitan Museum of Art, New York,
    2003, p. 116.

20  Staatliche Museen zu Berlin, Kupferstich-
    kabinett; red and black chalk, heightened
    with white, and brush and ink on tinted
    paper; 295 × 210 mm, on the right an
    8 mm strip of paper added; Otto Benesch,
    *The Drawings of Rembrandt*, enlarged and
    edited by Eva Benesch, 6 vols., London
    1973, I, p. 5, no. 7, fig. 12.

21  Josua Bruyn, Bob Haak, Simon H. Levic,
    Acker J.J. van Thiel, Ernst van de
    Wetering, *A Corpus of Rembrandt Paintings*,
    vols. 1–, Foundation Rembrandt Research
    Project, The Hague, Dordrecht, Boston
    and London 1982–, I, pp. 159–68, no. A13.
    For a more recent discussion of the
    painting see Albert Blankert, *Rembrandt,
    A Genius and his Impact*, exh. cat., National
    Gallery of Victoria, Melbourne, 1997,
    pp. 90–95, no. 3, who draws attention
    to the fact that the two old men wear
    "loose 'antique' robes".

22  Van Regteren Altena, *op. cit.* (note 7), I,
    pp. 154–57; *Corpus, op. cit.* (note 21), II,
    pp. 219–24, no. A56; Gary Schwartz,
    *Rembrandt, His Life, His Paintings*,
    Harmondsworth 1985, pp. 91–7; Blankert,
    *op. cit.* (note 21), pp. 90–95, 108–13;
    and *The Mystery of the Young Rembrandt*,
    exh. cat., ed. E. van de Wetering and
    Bernhard Schnackenburg, Staatliche
    Museen, Cassel, and Museum het
    Rembrandthuis, Amsterdam, 2001,
    pp. 30–31, 69–70, 218–21.

23  J. Richard Judson, 'Rembrandt and Jacob
    de Gheyn II', *Album Amicorum J.G. van
    Gelder*, ed. J. Bruyn, J.A. Emmens, E. de
    Jongh and D.P. Snoep, The Hague 1973,
    pp. 207–10; Van Regteren Altena, *op. cit.*
    (note 7), I, pp. 155–57; *Corpus, op. cit.*
    (note 21), I, pp. 148, 270.

24  Van Regteren Altena, *op. cit.* (note 7), I,
    pp. 151–52.

25  Quoted *ibid.*, I, p. 152.

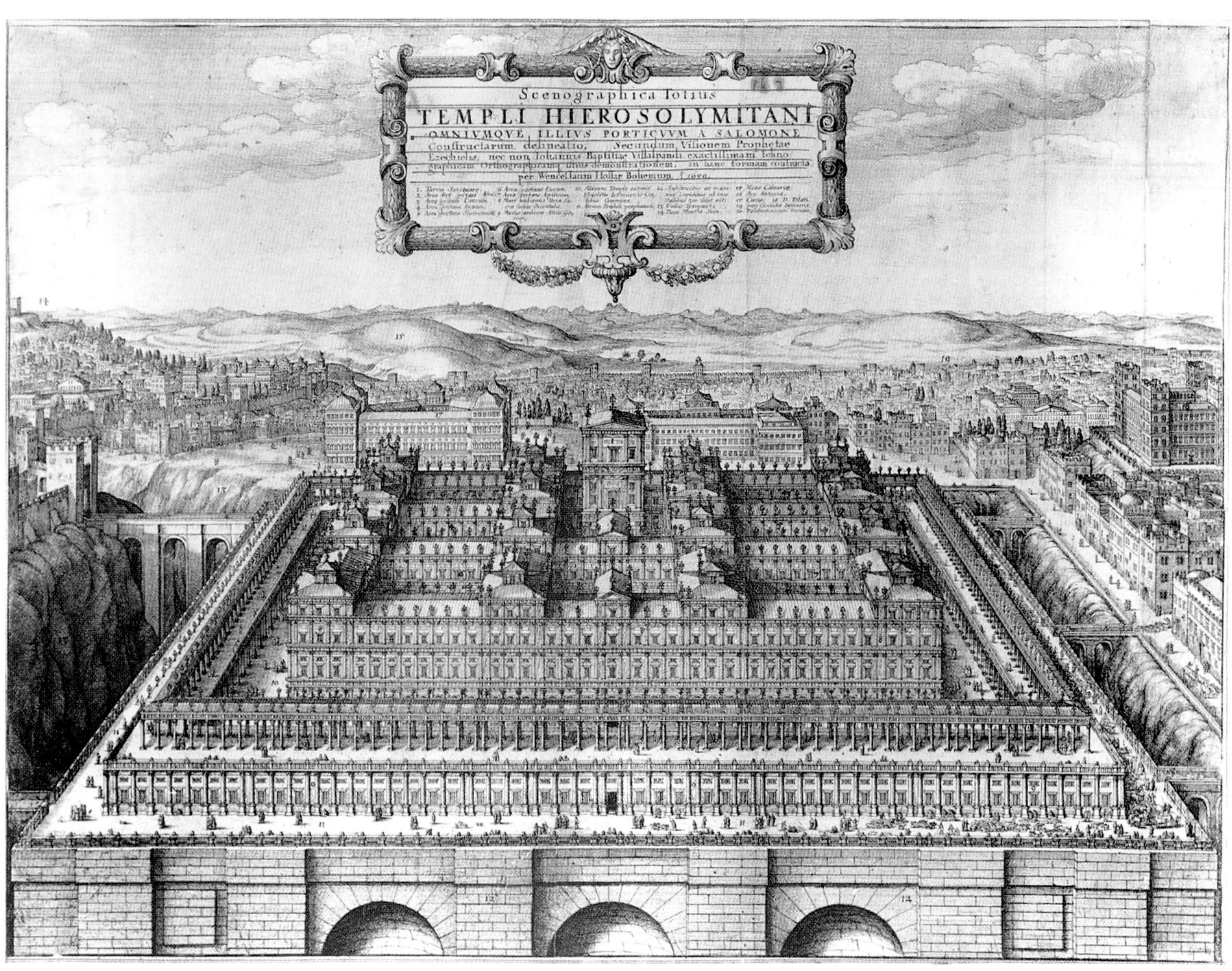


Scenographica totius
TEMPLI HIEROSOLYMITANI
OMNIVMQVE ILLIVS PORTICVVM À SALOMONE
Constructarum delineatio, Secundum Visionem Prophetae
Ezechielis, nec non Iohannis Baptistae Villalpandi exactissimam Ichno-
graphicam Orthographicamq́ue istius demonstrationem, in hanc formam contracta
per Wenceslaum Hollar Bohemum, Eures.

# Temple of Jerusalem Etchings for the Bible by Wenceslaus Hollar

PIERRE DE LA RUFFINIÈRE DU PREY

Within the Judaeo-Christian tradition, the Temple of Jerusalem stands apart from all other architectural masterpieces on account of its antiquity and its sanctity. The Old Testament discusses how the wise Jewish King Solomon was inspired by God to build this great house of worship around 950 BC. Biblical accounts elaborate on how divinely proportioned it was, how richly ornamented with gold, sweet-smelling cedar of Lebanon wood and sacred objects such as the Ark of the Covenant (1 Kings 6: 2–38; 1 Kings 7: 1–51; 2 Chronicles 3: 3–17; 2 Chronicles 4: 1–22). But the vestiges of Solomon's structure on the Temple Mount together with its two successors have all disappeared – swept away when the Roman army burned the site in the first century AD and dispersed its priceless contents. The western or "wailing" wall of the Herodian Temple alone remains to give an indication of the building's former magnificence and vastness. Despite the destruction, the image of the Temple conveyed by the Scriptures has exerted a potent force on the imagination of theologians, and of artists, one of whom was the Prague-born etcher Wenceslaus Hollar (1607–1677).

In 1995 the Agnes Etherington Art Centre of Queen's University in Kingston, Ontario, had the good fortune to acquire a collection of Temple-related material as a gift from Alfred Bader on the occasion of the fiftieth anniversary of his graduation from the university. The Bader Temple collection, as it is now known, consists of 172 items ranging in date from the invention of the printing press to the early nineteenth century.[1] It includes prints by Hollar among others and some original eighteenth-century architectural drawings. Collectively they reflect the Temple's impact on Jewish and Christian scholarship over the ages. Spanish, Dutch, German, French, and English imaginary visions of the Temple account for the collection's international breadth. Assembled originally by the renowned British antiquarian bookseller Ben Weinreb (1912–1999), the Bader Temple collection is a uniquely rich compilation of material ideally suited for study and future exhibition purposes.

fig. 1 WENCESLAUS HOLLAR after JUAN BAUTISTA VILLALPANDO *Aerial Perspective of the Temple of Jerusalem*, 1659 Etching, 32.9 × 52.5 cm Kingston, Ontario, Agnes Etherington Art Centre, Queen's University, Gift of Drs Alfred and Isabel Bader, 1995

In the friendly spirit of an essay in an *album amicorum*, I would like to begin by briefly recounting the story of the Bader Temple Collection's acquisition, in which I played the role of go-between. For more than a year beforehand a stream of letters had passed between me and Ben Weinreb, an admired mentor of mine and a personal friend.[2] Although I was not present on the day the 'deal was struck', that event took place in early July 1995 at Herstmonceux Castle in Sussex. Ben Weinreb came down from London and sat together with Alfred Bader in the castle's courtyard for what must have been fairly lengthy negotiations. At the end the prints, in addition to the drawings, and a few antiquarian and modern books about the Temple, were purchased for Queen's. The sun surely must have shone brightly that July day at Herstmonceux!

Ben Weinreb had put together the Bader Temple collection bit by bit during the previous few years, assisted by Robert Jan van Pelt, a Dutch scholar of the Bible and an architectural historian.[3] Together they wrote an unpublished catalogue of the collection's holdings, and sent it to me on approval together with a big bundle of relevant photocopies. Ben, as everyone called him, had an enviable reputation in the antiquarian booksellers' world. His bookshop stood a half block's walking distance from the British Museum — right on the corner of Gower and Great Russell Streets in London — a veritable Mecca, if I may be permitted to use such a mixed metaphor, for architectural book lovers. One of the most ardent of them, Phyllis Lambert, called it "one of the great institutions of the 20th century . . . for me one of the most delightful places in the world".[4] As the founding Director of the Canadian Centre for Architecture in Montreal she knows whereof she speaks, because much of her collection in the early days came from Ben. Over a twenty-five year period, until he closed up shop in 1986, Ben presided priest-like over the rare bookroom adjacent to his office, generously making its astonishing contents available for consultation to scholars like myself and van Pelt. Scholarly catalogues (more than fifty of them) came pouring out of Ben Weinreb Architectural Books. They made significant contributions to the bibliographic literature and have attained the status of collectors' items in themselves. Queen's University Library had acquired a selection of books from his remaining stock in 1986 with the generous support of the then Chancellor of the University, Agnes Benidickson, and the Social Sciences Humanities Research Council of Canada.[5] It was natural, therefore, that Ben would think of Queen's as an appropriate home for the Temple collection, where it now compliments so perfectly Alfred and Isabel Bader's gifts of Old Master paintings, many of them with Old Testament subject-matter.

Despite all his positive qualities, Ben had a frustrating habit of remaining singularly illusive about the sources from which his material came.[6] In the case of the Bader Temple collection, moreover, the problem of provenance is compounded a hundredfold because, in all likelihood, the various prints came from many sources, such as damaged copies of Bibles from which someone had removed the illustrations. As I hope to demonstrate, this certainly applies in the instance of the collection's six etchings of the Temple of Jerusalem prepared by Hollar from 1656 to 1660. The unpublished Weinreb and van Pelt catalogue accompanying the collection provides the following cryptic annotation regarding the source of the Hollars: "Walton's Polyglot Bible, London, 1657–[1660]". This information turns out to be only partly correct, as the remainder of this essay will set out to prove.

The first hint of Ben's problematic ascription of Hollar's plates to the Walton Bible arises over the incorrect dates he attributed to that publication, particularly the 1660 *terminus* supplied within square brackets in order to make it jibe with the latest date inscribed by Hollar on his prints. In fact, the Reverend Bryan Walton (*ca.* 1600–1661), Anglican bishop of Chester, brought out his famous six volume *Biblia Sacra Polyglotta . . .* in London between 1653 and 1657. He made a significant scholarly contribution to English Bible studies by publishing the Latin, Greek, Arabic, Syriac and Chaldaean versions of Holy Scripture in parallel columns sandwiched together for ease of textual comparison. Walton also had an entrepreneurial side. He struck on the idea of selling his Bible by subscription, a marketing device that far exceeded his best expectations. Walton enlisted the services of Hollar, who had left his native Bohemia in 1627 and eventually had settled permanently in London in 1652.[7] In addition to an aerial map of Jerusalem dated 1656 and a map of the Holy Land dated 1657, Hollar produced four similarly dated etchings representing plans, elevations and architectural details of the Temple. The information derived directly from two authorities on the Temple, the French theologian Louis Cappel (1585–1658) and the Spaniard Juan Bautista Villalpando, S.J. (1552–1608).

The Jesuit Villalpando, in collaboration with a countryman and fellow member of the Society of Jesus, Jeronimo de Prado, studied the Temple in the light of the prophetic description of it contained in the Book of Ezekiel (40–41). Their monumental three-volume *In Ezechielem explanationes et apparatus urbis ac templi Hierosolymitani commentariis et imaginibus illustratus* came out in Rome in 1605, profusely illustrated with engravings. Though hardly bedside reading, its folio volumes attained a reputation in scholarly circles for their lavish production, even though not everyone by any means agreed with its findings.[8] Walton and his advisors were aware of the book and set Hollar the task of reproducing on a much reduced scale a fairly large selection of Villalpando's engravings, all crammed together on to three plates. The fourth of Hollar's etchings derives from a separate source. Though undoubtedly contemporary with the others, it is the only one only partially dated (it lacks the last two digits). It copies Cappel's compilation of the accounts of the Herodian Temple given by the Jewish-Roman historian Flavius Josephus (AD 37–101) and in later Jewish writings, notably the Mishnah Middoth Tractate of the Babylonian Talmud, which provides the Temple's dimensions calculated down to the tiniest fraction of a cubit. Walton included in his Bible a copy of Cappel's learned text, accompanying it with Hollar's illustrations.[9] None of these Hollars has any special originality or artistry and they are not reproduced here for that reason. The same cannot, however, be said of the Hollar etching in the Bader Temple collection representing an aerial perspective view of the Temple complex seen as if by one of the sacrificial doves on the wing (fig. 1). Nothing comparable to it exists among the dry orthogonal elevations or cross-sections of Villalpando, although they still provide the ultimate source of Hollar's architectural inspiration, as his inscription admits quite plainly (fig. 2).

Hollar's breathtaking view of the Temple set amid a complex of eight courtyards cannot have come from the *Biblia Sacra Polyglotta* because it bears the date 1659, two years after the last of Walton's six volumes had left the press. Internal evidence, moreover, identifies the source as a subsequent publication, the Bible printed at Cambridge by John Field in 1660, the year of the restoration of the British monarchy, hence its nickname, the Restoration Bible.[10] Its promoter, John Ogilby (1600–1676), a publisher, mapmaker and author, knew Hollar well. The two had collaborated on a successful illustrated edition of the works of Virgil in 1654. Judging from the 1659 date on the Hollar aerial perspective, work on the Restoration Bible began during the Cromwellian period. Then, realising the change in political regime, Ogilby hastily penned a dedication to Charles II (1630–1685) and had Hollar prepare a beautiful print of the royal coat of arms as

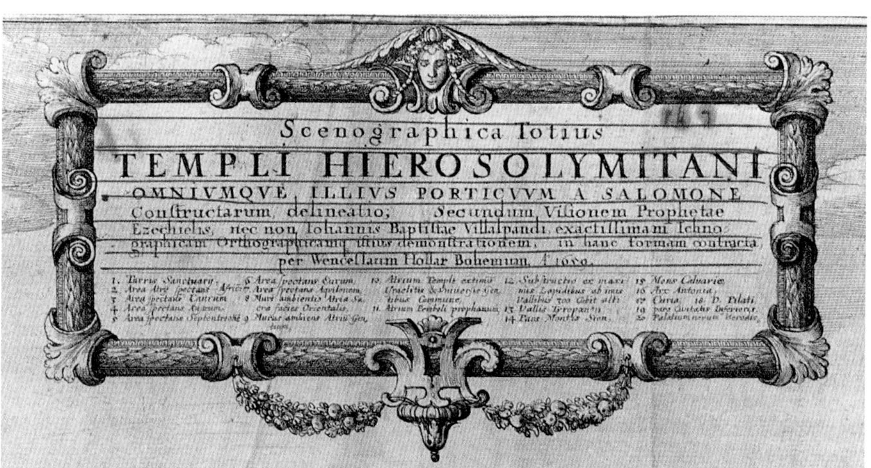

fig. 2  Detail of the cartouche in figure 1

a frontispiece.[11] With or without the permission of Walton, Ogilby reused the two maps by Hollar and his four plates after Cappel and Villalpando. Ogilby proceeded to commission new work from Hollar – the aerial perspective and coat of arms already referred to, plus an additional pair of equally magnificent and quite original etchings which I will come to shortly.

Additional internal evidence for the provenance comes in two forms. First there was the inscription in pen and ink, initially hard to decipher, placed inside the upper right-hand corner of the cloud-borne cartouche (fig. 2). This can now be securely transcribed as *1K7*, referring to the first Book of Kings, chapter 7, because that is exactly where the illustration appears in the complete copies of the Restoration Bible at Cambridge University Library and the British Library.[12] The second piece of internal evidence takes the form of double-ruled borders in red ink, hand-drawn around the print, together with similar red-ink under-lining of the text in the cartouche. The ruled borders, though present, are slightly difficult to make out in the Bader Temple collection's exemplar because its margins have been so closely trimmed to the edge of the plate. As for the underlining in the cartouche, an unfortunate slip of the scribe's pen and straight-edge under the word *omniumque* in the third line from the top underscores the hand-drawn nature of the lines.

I can only speculate as to the reason for the time-consuming process of manually inserting the red lines. No doubt they impart a richer effect. Although a two-tone colour scheme is by no means unique in print culture of the period, it could be that the regal red signified the return of the monarchy after the puritanical drabness of the Commonwealth. Underlining and bordering in red ink characterizes all illustrated copies of the Restoration Bible I have been able to find. Not all, however, conform perfectly in the quality of the hand-drawn additions. Some look relatively slapdash in execution. Others go to the opposite extreme, such as the special royal copy in the British Library. Fully bound in red Morocco leather, it has the letters *CR* stamped in gold upon it, entwined within splendid tooling in the form of flowers and crowned birds carrying a sprig of olive branch in their beaks. In terms of its illustrative content it is also the most complete copy I have found. It contains all ten of Hollar's plates, including the armorial frontispiece.[13] In this presentation copy, moreover, the plates have *triple* ruled borders instead of mere double ones. Further bibliographic research might establish whether the number of ruled borders reflects a hierarchy of copies according to client. A good place to begin the search would be with another magnificent copy, this one in the Royal Library at Windsor, recently exhibited in the Queen's Gallery at Buckingham Palace. The binding consists of blue velvet with the royal arms and monogram of Charles II embroidered in coloured silks, silver and silver-gilt wire.[14]

In addition to the aerial perspective of the Temple complex, in 1660 Hollar prepared a perspective view of the Temple proper taken from within the Courtyard of the Burnt Sacrifices, also known as the Court of the Levites (fig. 3). As in the other cases, the inscription makes no pretence of hiding the debt to Juan Bautista Villalpando's engravings (a set of forty-five of which, incidentally, figure prominently in the Bader Temple collection). But in this instance it seems to me that Hollar created a more powerful image of the lost Temple than anything produced by his Spanish source. In Villalpando's engravings the burin carefully delineates the crisp forms of the Temple, tending to flatten out the sacred structure's appearance. Hollar's consummate skill with perspective, and the softer effects and tonalities the etcher's techniques could achieve, combine to render this print three dimensional and grippingly vibrant. The figures of Levites go about their business preparing offerings for the altar of the holocaust, or cleansing with water taken from the famous bronze laver borne on the backs of oxen. The staffage adds an element of animation totally lacking in Villalpando. Hollar admittedly had some problem with getting the proportions right. According to Weinreb and van Pelt's calculations the priests would tower nearly nine feet tall.

Gustav Parthey's authoritative catalogue of all known Hollar etchings was published in Berlin in 1853. Twice reprinted, most recently in an updated version by Richard Pennington, Parthey's numbering system for the prints prevails.[15] Parthey provided partial information as to the source of most of Hollar's Temple material but failed to note systematically those cases in which it appeared in both the Walton and Restoration Bibles. Pennington sorted this out, but failed to provide a means of establishing the origin of plates removed from those books. Neither Hollar scholar paid any attention to the hand-drawn ruled borders characteristic of the Restoration Bible's illustrations. This oversight had not occurred when Ben Weinreb catalogued his prints for sale. As someone familiar with architectural drawings he had the habit of recording such draughtsman's conventions as hand-drawn ruled borders. But he drew no conclusions from their presence or absence. Their significance in distinguishing Restoration Bible illustrative material from that in the *Biblia Sacra Polyglotta* escaped his notice. With the aid of this simple tool it is now possible to pin down precisely the provenance of the six etchings in the Bader Temple collection. Besides the pair here illustrated (figs. 1, 3; Parthey nos. 1131 and 1136, respectively), another two have red borders and underlining. One is the 1656 Hollar compendium of details of the Temple's decoration and furniture taken from Villalpando (Parthey no. 1135). Another, dated the next year, compiles seven of the Spaniard's elevations and cross-sections (Parthey no. 1134). This means that of the entire six plates originally thought at their time of acquisition to have come from

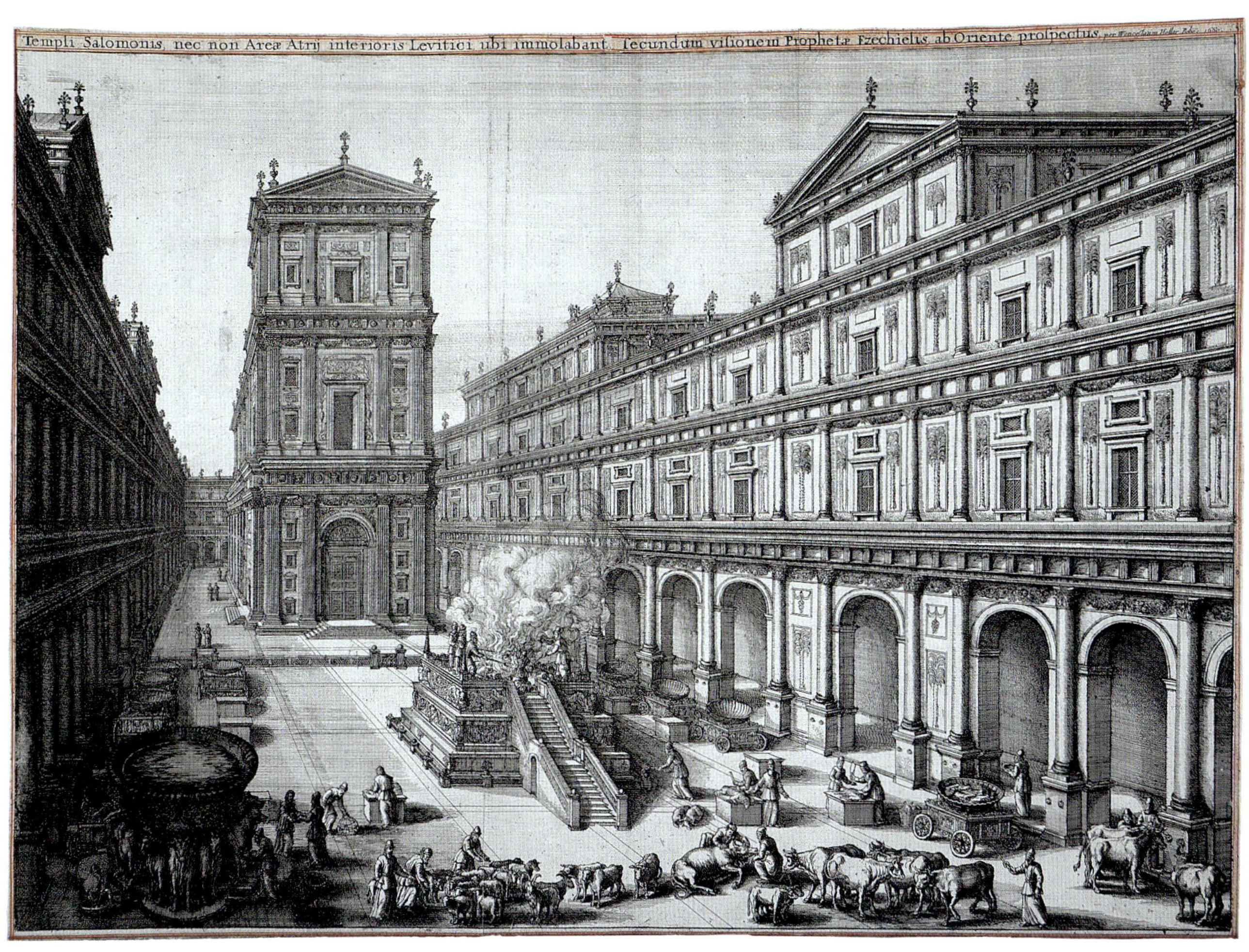


fig. 3 WENCESLAUS HOLLAR
after JUAN BAUTISTA
VILLALPANDO
*Perspective of the Temple of Jerusalem
from within the Court of the Levites*,
1660
Etching, 38.3 × 53.5 cm
Kingston, Ontario, Agnes
Etherington Art Centre,
Queen's University, Gift of
Drs Alfred and Isabel Bader, 1995

the *Biblia Sacra Polyglotta*, only the two without ruled borders actually do – one based on Cappel (Parthey no. 1132) and a second showing the plan of the Temple and other details after Villalpando (Parthey no. 1133). The Bader Temple collection's holdings of Hollars is therefore a mixed bag and incomplete. It lacks the two maps (Parthey nos. 1129, 692), and most notably Hollar's fold-out double plate showing a spectacular 105.7 cm long panorama of the entire city of Jerusalem, centering on the Temple (Parthey no. 1130).[16]

Of course it remains remotely possible that the Hollar prints circulated separately from, as well as bound together with, Walton's and Ogilby's publications. Some evidence exists to support this possibility. Four years after his death in 1736 the architect Nicholas Hawksmoor's print collection came up for auction and it numbered no less than 118 Hollars, excluding what the sale catalogue describes as "90 prints of the Bible", which could well have contained additional ones.[17] More probably, however, the Bader Temple prints at some point were bound into books. My research among copies of Hollar-illustrated Bibles rarely turned up two with exactly the same content. Some lack one plate, some another, and only one has all accounted for. So the chances are that the plates became damaged, crumpled, or dog-eared from constant opening and shutting of the Bible. On that pretext they may have been removed, and ended up decorating the walls of college libraries or country parsonages.[18] Indeed, the exemplars in the Bader Temple collection illustrated here have been creased in a whole variety of places. I measured the fold lines with the idea that they might correspond to each other and with those on copies that remained bound. But comparable ones I found within the pages of Restoration Bibles had only one vertical fold line running right down the center.

Sad though the removal of Hollar's Temple plates may be in principle, in practice they gained exposure they never would have had they remained behind the two covers of a book. Dissemination of images of the Temple in England during the generation or so before and after 1700 helps account for a veritable Temple cult that spread far beyond theologians and bibliophiles. Scientific and artistic luminaries of the age admired the Temple: Hollar etched it; Sir Christopher Wren (1632–1723) praised it; the experimentalist and natural philosopher Robert Hooke (1635–1703) discussed it; Nicholas Hawksmoor (1661–1736) puzzled over it; and Sir Isaac Newton (1643–1727) published it in his book on the subject, a copy of which came along with the Bader Temple collection.[19] The rise of Freemasonry in early eighteenth-century England gained sustenance from the prolific Temple literature and increased the demand for images as well as scale models of the structure. To many, among them the architect John Wood the Elder (1704–1754), the Temple ranked as the ninth wonder of the world, on a par with, but even more ancient (and worthy) than



PIERRE DE LA RUFFINIÈRE DU PREY

the other eight. The subtitle of Wood's 1741 book in the Bader Temple collection puts the matter very plainly by speaking of "the plagiarism of the heathens detected".[20] This is not the place to go into the long, fascinating and at times mysterious history of the Temple's influence. Suffice it to say that the Temple takes on the allure of a lost ideal, like the Garden of Eden. It stands as a symbol of all that was noble, spiritual, pure, beautiful, intangible and worthy of emulation.

I wish to thank Dorothy Farr, Curator of the Agnes Etherington Art Centre, and her Administrative Coordinator, Annabel Hanson, for their assistance. The photographs were expertly prepared by George Innes and Chris Peck of Queen's University. I would like also to mention the help I received from various librarians I have consulted, from Robert Jan van Pelt, from the late Ben Weinreb and from Howard Shubert, Curator of Prints and Drawings at the Canadian Centre for Architecture, Montreal. This essay began as a graduate student term paper I assigned to Alexandra Sharma, whose diligent research I acknowledge and commend. Julia du Prey assisted, as always, with sound editorial advice.

1   Helen Rosenau, *The Vision of the Temple: The Image of the Temple of Jerusalem in Judaism and Christianity*, London 1979, contains a useful discussion of the various imaginary architectural reconstructions of the Temple, though unfortunately not those by Wenceslaus Hollar. This text should be supplemented with the discussion in Joseph Rykwert, *On Adam's House in Paradise: The Idea of the Primitive Hut in Architectural History*, New York 1972. The general accession number of the Bader Temple collection at the Agnes Etherington Art Centre is 38-038 (the Hollars are items 001-006).

2   I have presented my entire collection of the correspondence between myself and Ben Weinreb to the Agnes Etherington Art Centre for inclusion in its acquisition files.

3   Robert Jan van Pelt has published quite extensively on the Temple of Jerusalem. He has written *Tempel van de Wereld: De kosmische symboliek van de tempel van Salomo*, Utrecht 1984. Two essays by him, 'Coccejus y el Templo sin Arquitecto', and 'Lund y el Modello en Halle', appear in *Dios, arquitecto: J.B. Villalpando y el templo de Salomon*, ed. Juan Antonio Ramirez, Madrid 1991. This volume of collected essays accompanies a two-volume translated reprint edition of Villalpando's monumental work.

4   The passages are taken from the typescript of Phyllis Lambert's introduction

of Ben Weinreb before he delivered the Queen's University Archives Lecture on 29 April 1988, at Queen's University.

5   Some of these books acquired from Ben Weinreb form the subject of a series of published essays edited by myself under the title *Architects, Books, and Libraries: A Collection of Essays*, exh. cat., Agnes Etherington Art Centre, Queen's University, Kingston, Ontario, 1995.

6   I remember in the mid 1980s trying in vain to draw Ben out on the provenance of the Ockham Park Album of Nicholas Hawksmoor's architectural drawings, acquired from Ben by Phyllis Lambert, now in the collection of the Canadian Centre for Architecture. Ben was mum on the subject. Eventually the truth came out from other eyewitness sources. It makes a fascinating story and I hope one day to publish it. As it well illustrates, Ben could be cagey in these matters.

7   Hollar's biography is succinctly provided by Richard Pennington's 'Life of Hollar', in his *A Descriptive Catalogue of the Etched Work of Wenceslaus Hollar 1607–1677*, Cambridge 1982, pp. XIX–LII.

8   For a discussion of some of the diverse opinions regarding Villalpando see Pierre de la Ruffinière du Prey, *Hawksmoor's London Churches: Architecture and Theology*, Chicago 2000, pp. 18–20, and for special reference to the English interest in reconstructions of the Temple of Jerusalem see there Appendix 1.

9   Bryan Walton, *Biblia Sacra Polyglotta*, 6 vols., 1653–57, I, pp. 1–38, the plate is opposite p. 38. For a discussion of Cappel's Temple studies see Wolfgang Herrmann, 'Unknown Designs for the Temple of Jerusalem by Claude Perrault', in *Essays in the History of Architecture Presented to Rudolf Wittkower*, ed. Douglas Fraser, Howard Hibbard and Milton J. Lewine, London 1967, p. 157.

10   For a discussion of the Field-Ogilby Restoration Bible see T.H. Darlow and H.F. Moule, *Historical Catalogue of Printed Editions of the English Bible, 1525–1961*, ed. Arthur Sumner Herbert, 2nd edn, London 1968.

11   The etched frontispiece is catalogued separately from the Hollar Temple prints

and has the number 2422 assigned to it by Gustav Parthey, see note 15 below. The colorful career of Ogilby is related by Katharine S. van Eerde, *John Ogilby and the Taste of His Times*, Folkestone 1976. On p. 44 she asserts quite plainly that Hollar's later plates appear in the British Library copy of the Restoration Bible. Hers was the only direct indication I could find of the whereabouts of a complete copy of the Bible for which the Hollar etchings were intended.

12 The copy I inspected at Cambridge University Library, one of several there, was in the Bible Society's Collection, # 201.C60. 1,2.

13 British Library, 7.h.3,4.(2.). All of the Hollars are accounted for. The only illustrative material missing from this copy is the elaborate but undated titlepage, signed by the engraver P. Lombart (an example of which is provided in another copy in the British Library, 464.h.2.1,2).

14 Jane Roberts, *Royal Treasures: A Golden Jubilee Celebration*, exh. cat., The Queen's Gallery, London, 2002, p. 378, no. 328.

15 Gustav Parthey, *Wenzel Hollar. Beschreibendes Verzeichnis seiner Kupferstiche*, Berlin 1853; Pennington, *op. cit.* (note 7).

16 The Prints and Drawings department of the Canadian Centre for Architecture, Montreal, holds in addition to the maps of the Holy Land and of the city of Jerusalem, the following four items: the aerial perspective of the Temple complex; the perspective view from inside the Court of the Levites; the elevations of the Temple after Villalpando; and the fold-out panorama of the city of Jerusalem (DR 1990:0061:001-004).

17 I made this point in my book, du Prey, *op. cit.* (note 8), p. 31, n. 59. My suggestion seems to have been adopted in Vaughan Hart's *Nicholas Hawksmoor: Rebuilding Ancient Wonders*, London 2002, pp. 91, 201.

18 In the case of a copy of the *Biblia Sacra Polyglotta* that I studied in the New York Bible Society, all that remains of one Hollar plate after Villalpando is a tiny stub of paper with a bit of the etching left on it.

19 Sir Christopher Wren's interest in the Temple is discussed in Lydia M. Soo's *Wren's "Tracts" on Architecture and Other Writings*, Cambridge 1998, pp. 122–23, and in du Prey, *op. cit.* (note 8), pp. 17–20. The same two authors also discuss Robert Hooke's fascination with the Temple. I also discuss (pp. 23–24, 128–131) Sir Isaac Newton's posthumously published book on the Temple, *The Chronology of the Ancient Kingdoms Amended . . .*, London 1728. Hart, *op. cit.* (note 17), pp. 94–96, discusses and illustrates his discovery of a Hawksmoor manuscript in the British Library devoted partly to the Temple of Jerusalem as described in the Book of Ezekiel.

20 The full title of Wood's book is *Origin of Building, or, the Plagiarism of the Heathens Detected*, Bath 1741.

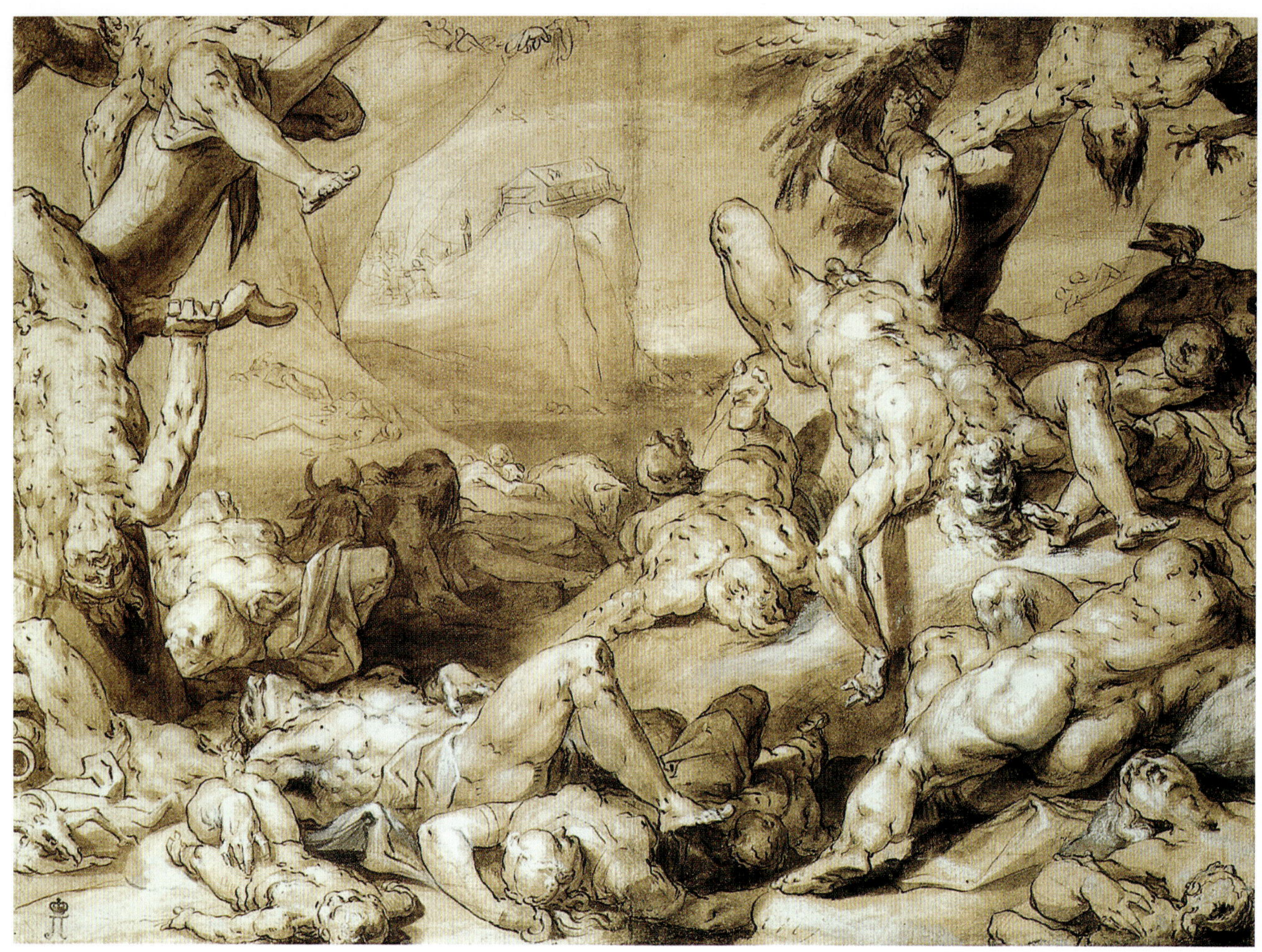

# Two Drawings by Jan Harmensz. Muller: A Tale of Two Floods?

WILLIAM W. ROBINSON

"Dutch artists, like most people, were not fascinated by Mannerism for very long," quipped Seymour Slive in 1966.[1] Four decades ago most historians of Netherlandish art probably shared Slive's view and regarded the period around 1600 with respectful reticence, if not bemused condescension. Today neither university scholars nor museum curators suffer from a short attention span when it comes to the Dutch Mannerists. Hefty catalogues raisonnés have been devoted to Cornelis van Haarlem, Abraham Bloemaert and Joachim Wtewael, while comprehensive exhibitions, such as *The Dawn of the Golden Age* (1993–94) and the 2003 Hendrick Goltzius retrospective, have brought their works before a larger public.[2] Knowing that Alfred Bader does not belong to the party of connoisseurs whose fascination with Dutch Mannerism has been short-lived, I offer this modest note on two drawings as a heartfelt expression of my sincere love and admiration for him and for Isabel.

During the 1950s and 1960s the late Professor E.K.J. Reznicek was the most prominent among the rare devotees of the art of *ca.*1600. In his landmark monograph *Die Zeichnungen des Hendrick Goltzius*, published in 1961, Reznicek ranged beyond his principal subject to address broader theoretical and practical problems raised by the study of Dutch Mannerism. Not the least of these was the task of identifying the artists responsible for the innumerable drawings then ascribed indiscriminately to Goltzius or Bloemaert. Reznicek himself had made an exemplary start in a 1956 article devoted to Jan Muller (1571–1628) as a draughtsman, to which he added supplements in 1980 and 1981.[3] With the publication of a few more sheets that have come to light since 1981, Muller's oeuvre now numbers around sixty drawings, with dated examples ranging from 1585 to 1627.[4] They affirm that this virtuoso printmaker – second only to Goltzius himself among Dutch engravers of the period – was also a versatile and highly skilled draughtsman.

Born in Amsterdam, Jan Harmensz. Muller was the son of the engraver, bookseller and publisher Harmen Muller (*ca.* 1538–1617), who undoubtedly taught

fig. 1 JAN MULLER
*After the Deluge*
Brown ink and brown wash, heightened with white gouache, 422 × 581 mm
St Petersburg, State Hermitage Museum

him both drawing and printmaking. Jan's earliest surviving works – a series of
four finished pen drawings executed when he was fourteen and fifteen years of
age – are copies after prints by Frans Floris (1519/20–1570).[5] Whether or not
he studied with Goltzius in the second half of the 1580s, Jan Muller's engraving
technique depended closely on that of the Haarlem master. By the end of the
decade Muller had joined the avant-garde circle that included Hendrick
Goltzius (1558–1616), Karel van Mander (1548–1606) and Cornelis Cornelisz.
(1562–1638) in Haarlem and Abraham Bloemaert (1566–1651) in Amsterdam.
Goltzius published a number of Jan's plates in 1588 and 1589, and shortly there-
after Muller briefly took over the role of producing reproductive prints after
Cornelis's works.[6]

His collaboration with Cornelis van Haarlem in 1589 and 1590 inspired some
of Jan Muller's most brilliant engravings and, more to the point here, precipi-
tated a crucial breakthrough in his development as a draughtsman.[7] Around
1590 he executed several drawings of biblical and mythological subjects that
represent the acme of his achievement in the medium. They not only attest to
Muller's creative engagement with Cornelis's figure style, but their technique
so closely resembles the older master's handling of ink and wash that specialists
still disagree about the authorship of a few sheets.[8]

Among those works of controversial attribution is the spectacular *After the
Deluge*, a large and fully resolved composition executed in brown ink and brown
wash with extensive heightening in white gouache (fig. 1).[9] Following a common
late Mannerist narrative strategy, the draughtsman has relegated the principal
protagonists of the story to the remote background and filled the front plane
with secondary figures depicted on an outsize scale. Far in the distance the Ark
has alighted on a puny Mount Ararat. While we can barely make out the sketchy
outlines of Noah's family attending to their burnt offering, there is no overlooking
the gigantic corpses of drowned humans and animals strewn across the foreground of the desolate landscape. Their acrobatic contortions, shown in dramatic
foreshortening, imaginatively evoke the carnage disclosed by the receding waters.
The draftsman clearly set out to invent a sequel to paintings of the biblical
Flood executed in the late 1580s and early 1590s by Cornelis van Haarlem,
Abraham Bloemaert and Joachim Wtewael (1566–1638).[10] Similar in design to the
drawing, those pictures show desperate men clambering up trees in the left
and right foreground in the vain hope of escaping the rising inundation. Both
spectacles offered a wide field for a bravura display of muscular figures *in extremis*.

*After the Deluge* entered the Hermitage in St Petersburg in 1768, when
Catherine II (1729–1796) purchased it along with the rest of the collection
formed by Count Karl Cobenzl (1712–1770), head of the Austrian imperial
administration in Brussels. The drawing was classified as an anonymous work

until the Hermitage curator Stepan P. Yaremich ascribed it to Cornelis van Haarlem in 1926. It has since been published and exhibited several times under that artist's name, most recently in 1998.[11] However, in his 1999 monograph and catalogue raisonné, Pieter van Thiel definitively rejected *After the Deluge* from Cornelis's oeuvre.[12] With the illustrations in Van Thiel's volume in hand, one can readily see that the Hermitage sheet does not belong to the small corpus of drawings attributable to Cornelis van Haarlem. In Cornelis's *Tityus* and *Olympic Games*, both of 1588,[13] the modelling of the figures is firmer, rounder and less dependent on surface effects than in *After the Deluge*, and subtle differences in the penwork distinguish the technique of the St Petersburg drawing from that of Cornelis's masterpieces. Although Van Thiel entertained the possibility that Muller might have executed the Hermitage work, in his view the drawing's style resembled neither Muller's nor Cornelis's, and its composition was too weak to justify an attribution to either master.[14]

In 1985 I tentatively attributed *After the Deluge* to Jan Muller, and I now believe it should be given to him without reservations.[15] A close comparison with drawings securely assigned to Muller confirms that the Hermitage sheet bears many hallmarks of his draughtsmanship. Specifically, it exhibits his characteristically loose application of ample white gouache highlights as well as the idiosyncratic penwork with which the artist consistently delineated the musculature and dynamic contours of his figures. As for the composition, *After the Deluge* might lack the graceful rhythms that distinguish some of Muller's drawings – including the Oxford *Brazen Serpent*, to which Van Thiel compared it – but such disciplined elegance does not govern the layout of all his works. Compositions with fewer and larger figures show remarkable similarities to the design of the St Petersburg sheet (figs. 2 and 3).

More importantly, the handling of the media in the drawings reproduced as figures 2 and 3 compellingly resembles the technique of *After the Deluge*.[16] Compare, for example, the foliage at the upper centre of *After the Deluge* with the sheaf held by the standing river-god at the left in *Peneus and the River Gods with Apollo and Daphne* in Brussels (fig. 2). Note, too, how the summary description of the landscape setting in the Hermitage work was produced with the same battery of marks in ink, wash and gouache as the backgrounds of the Brussels drawing and of *Elijah fed by Ravens at the Brook Cherith* (fig. 3). When he delineated the rippling, muscular back of the male corpse at the lower right in *After the Deluge*, the draughtsman summoned the identical combination of short ink lines in the shape of the diacritic tilde (~) and a longer arc for the spine that we find in the backs of the reclining river gods in the foreground of *Peneus and the River Gods with Apollo and Daphne*. Moreover, in both drawings he similarly enhanced the musculature with generous additions of wash for shadows and gouache for

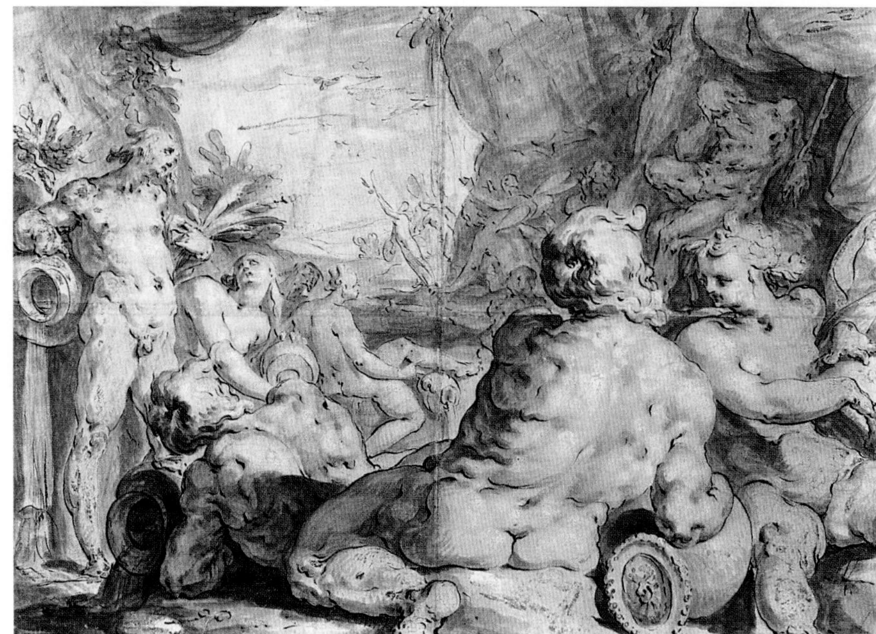



highlights. The freely applied gouache highlights in the head, torso and hand of the spread eagled male body to the right of centre in *After the Deluge* also recall the use of the opaque watercolour medium in the figure of the Prophet in *Elijah fed by Ravens*. One could go on to single out additional graphic mannerisms peculiar to Muller's technique, but these comparisons should suffice to establish that the Hermitage composition is by the same hand as those drawings and others rightly assigned to him. It should be dated to the early 1590s, although the precise chronology of Muller's drawings in Cornelis's style is by no means certain.

The second drawing I wish to consider (fig. 4) must date from the same period as *After the Deluge*, but it is smaller and sketchier in execution and presumably a working study rather than a fully resolved composition.[17] If my identification of its subject is correct, this work, too, represents an episode in one of the *Ur-*inundations in the creation literature of the ancient world. To my knowledge this sheet has been published only in the unillustrated 1956 handlist of the collection bequeathed by Sir Robert Witt to the Courtauld Institute and in Andrée de Bosque's 1985 *Mythologie et maniérisme aux Pays-Bas 1570–1630*, where it was reproduced and allotted a single sentence of text.[18] Its provenance before it came into Sir Robert Witt's possession has not been established. An earlier (eighteenth-century?) owner recorded his attribution to Cornelis van Haarlem on the verso, beside which Reznicek inscribed the name of Hendrick Goltzius, but Reznicek did not cite the work in his catalogue of that master's drawings. The current Courtauld inventory retains the attribution to Abraham Bloemaert given in the Witt handlist, and De Bosque reproduced it under Bloemaert's name.

Yet the drawing is surely by Jan Muller. The penwork of the head, back and buttocks of the river god in the foreground is indistinguishable from that of the figures seen from behind in the Brussels *Peneus and the River Gods with Apollo and Daphne* (fig. 2) and in a small sketch in a private collection of *Hercules and Deianira* (fig. 5).[19] In the latter work the technique of the branches, foliage and back-ground figures also closely resembles the execution of the Courtauld sheet. The resemblance to the *Hercules and Deianira* would have been even more striking before the Courtauld study was worked up in red chalk by a later owner or restorer intent upon giving the sketch a more finished look. Finally, the head of

fig. 3 JAN MULLER
*Elijah fed by Ravens at the*
*Brook Cherith*
Brown ink, brown wash, white
gouache, on brown prepared paper,
contours incised, 166 × 206 mm
Sale Christie's, Paris,
27 March 2003, lot 48

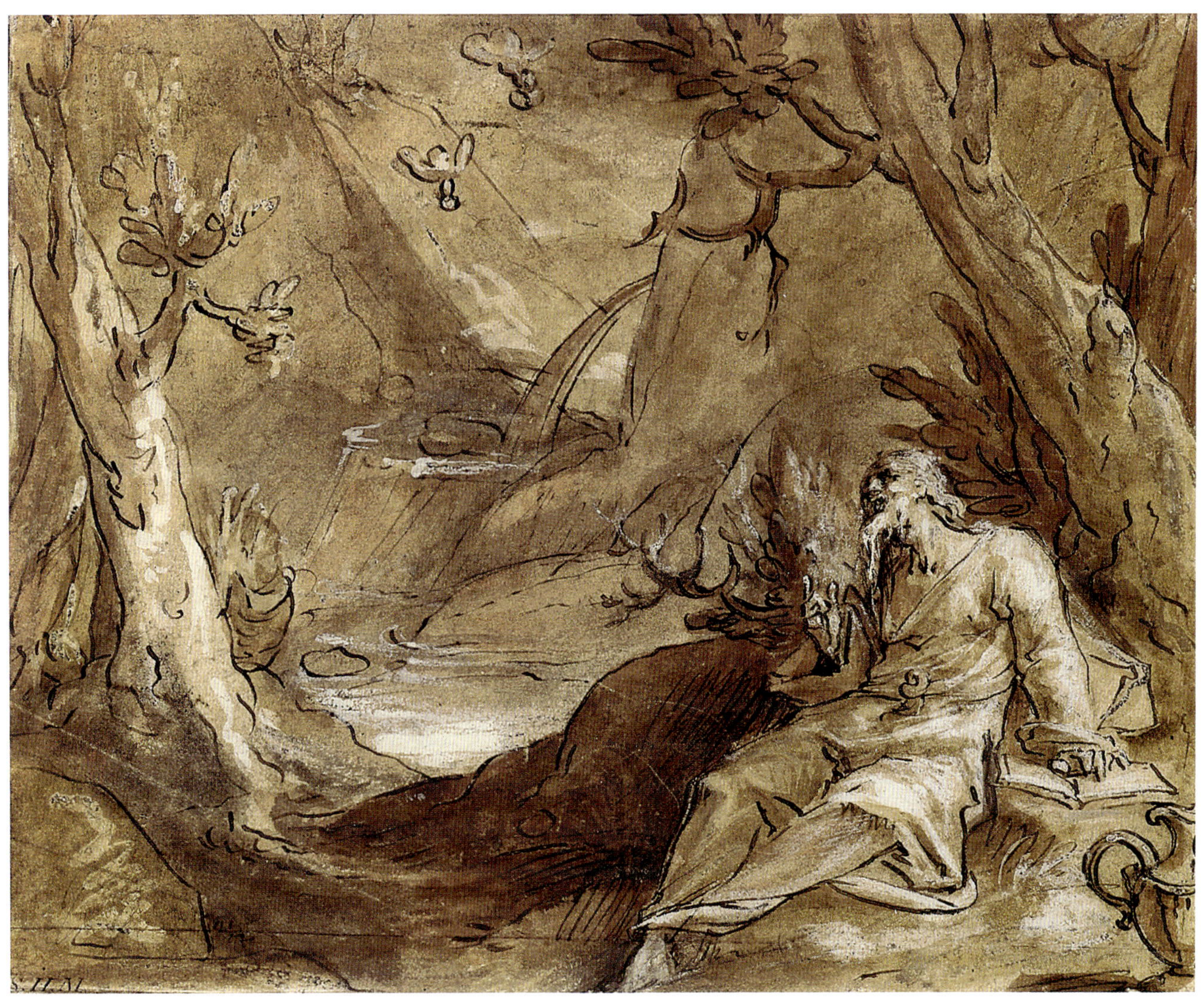

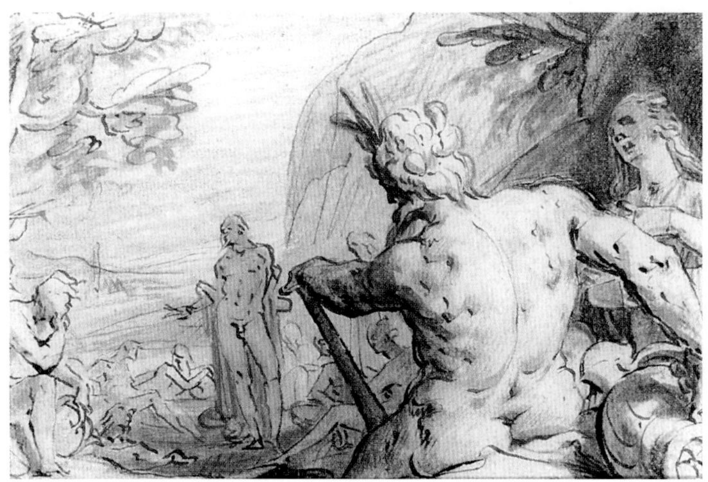

fig. 4 JAN MULLER, *Neptune commanding the Rivers to Flood the Earth*
Brown ink, brown wash, later additions in red chalk, 97 × 150 mm
London, Courtauld Gallery

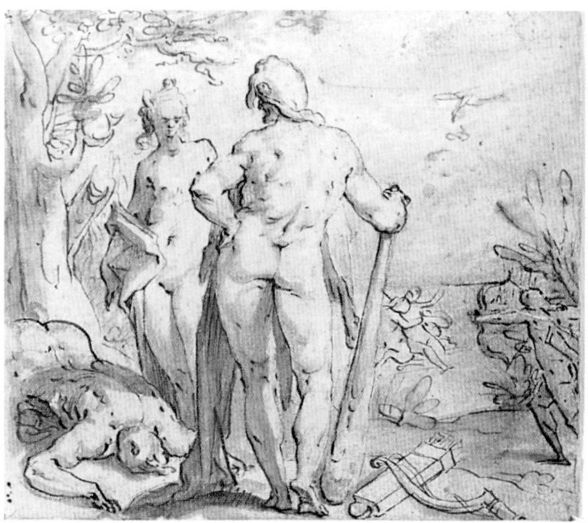

fig. 5 JAN MULLER, *Hercules and Deianira*
Brown ink, brown wash, pink and pinkish-brown
wash over black chalk, 125 × 147 mm
Cambridge, Mass., private collection

the nymph at the far right of the Courtauld drawing – with her deep, dark eye
sockets, loose hair, narrow, pursed mouth and upward gaze – belongs to a female
type that occurs elsewhere in Muller's oeuvre. Compare, for example, the
nymph in the left foreground of the Brussels drawing (fig. 2), the drowned
woman at the lower right in *After the Deluge* (fig. 1) and the head of the saint in
the *Mary Magdalene* in Brno. [20]

The subject of the London study has proved more elusive than its author. At
the foot of a rugged mountainside a nude, bearded male of heroic stature stands
in a pool and addresses a group of river gods and water nymphs, who listen
intently as they recline in a circle around him. In this working sketch Muller did
not outfit the central figure with recognizable attributes, although he clearly
enacts the principal role. The Witt handlist and De Bosque identify the subject
as *A Punishment of Tantalus*, but the drawing more plausibly represents one of
the scenes from Ovid's *Metamorphoses* illustrated in an extensive series of engravings designed and published by Goltzius in 1589. [21] In two of the plates in that
suite river gods and nymphs gather around a senior male figure.

One of the engravings after Goltzius depicts the consolation of the deity
of the River Peneus, who mourns the loss of his beloved daughter, Daphne. [22]
This is the primary subject of the Brussels drawing, where Muller conflated
Daphne's transformation into a laurel with the subsequent assembly around
Peneus of the gods and nymphs of tributary streams (fig. 2). In that composition Muller followed Ovid's text and showed Peneus seated "in a cave of over-
hanging rock". [23] He strikes a melancholy pose and pays little heed to the
condolences offered to him. In contrast, the central figure in the Courtauld
sheet stands and actively engages the assembled river gods and nymphs. Although

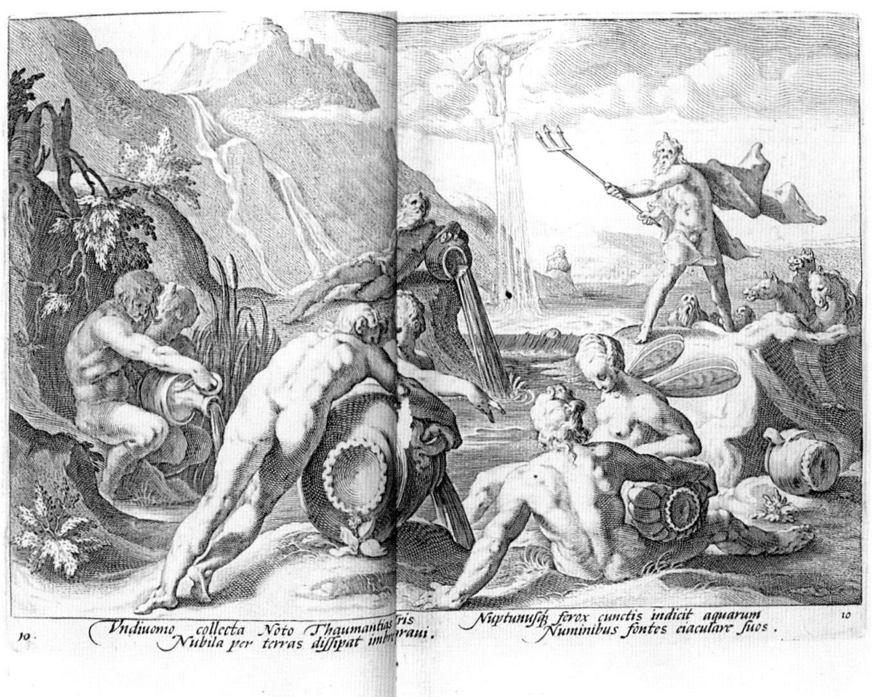



fig. 6  After HENDRICK
GOLTZIUS
*Neptune commanding the Rivers to Flood
the Earth, ca.* 1589
Engraving, 16.8 × 25 cm
London, The British Museum

the London sketch probably does not represent Peneus, it is noteworthy that
Bloemaert's 1592 painting *Peneus and the River Gods with Apollo and Daphne* evidently
provided the compositional model for both the Courtauld study and Muller's
drawing in Brussels.[24]

The London sketch more probably shows an earlier episode in Book I of
Ovid's *Metamorphoses*, in which Neptune commands the rivers to contribute to
the inundation that will destroy mankind. After Jupiter unleashes the rains that
precipitate the flood, "his sea-god brother . . . summons his rivers to council"
and orders them to gather their strength, break their dykes and send their overflowing torrents to the sea.[25] The plate in the *Metamorphoses* series after Goltzius
is one of the few works of the period that depicts this subject (fig. 6).[26] Muller's
composition shares several elements with the print. In the engraving, as in
the drawing, river gods and nymphs recline around a pool in a mountainous
landscape. The partially draped figure who addresses them in the print is
unmistakably Neptune. Alighting on a low cloud in front of his marine chariot,
he brandishes his trident as he harangues the rivers. High above him Iris, Juno's
messenger, "draws up water [from the sea] and feeds it to the clouds".[27] The
summarily sketched columnar shape in the left background of Muller's drawing
and the downward projection from the cloud above it might suggest the tower
of water raised by the cloud-borne Iris that Goltzius included in the print. In
the absence of the trident or another of the sea-god's attributes, the identification of the subject of the Courtauld work must remain tentative, but it most
probably represents Neptune commanding the rivers to flood the earth.

1 Seymour Slive, Jakob Rosenberg and E.H. ter Kuile, *Dutch Art and Architecture 1600 to 1800*, The Pelican History of Art, Baltimore 1966, p. 14.

2 Pieter J.J. van Thiel, *Cornelis Cornelisz van Haarlem 1562–1638. A Monograph and Catalogue Raisonné*, Doornspijk 1999; Marcel Roethlisberger, *Abraham Bloemaert and His Sons. Paintings and Prints*, 2 vols., Doornspijk 1993; Anne W. Lowenthal, *Joachim Wtewael and Dutch Mannerism*, Doornspijk 1986; Ger Luijten *et al.*, *The Dawn of the Golden Age. Northern Netherlandish Art 1580–1620*, exh. cat., Rijksmuseum, Amsterdam, 1993–94; *Hendrick Goltzius. Dutch Master 1558–1617: Drawings, Prints and Paintings*, exh. cat., Rijksmuseum, Amsterdam; Metropolitan Museum of Art, New York; Toledo Museum of Art, Toledo, Ohio, 2003.

3 Emil Reznicek, 'Jan Harmensz. Muller als Tekenaar', *Nederlands Kunsthistorisch Jaarboek*, vol. 7, 1956, pp. 65–120; Emil Reznicek, 'Jan Harmensz. Muller as Draughtsman: Addenda', *Master Drawings*, vol. 18, no. 2, 1980, pp. 115–33; Emil Reznicek, Letter to the Editor, *Master Drawings*, vol. 19, no. 4, 1981, pp. 460–61.

4 For some of the dated drawings, see Reznicek 1956, *op. cit.* (note 3), nos. 11, 14, 19, 23, 28–32, 36. Drawings by Muller that have come to light since 1981 include *Two Studies of Hercules*, Cambridge, Fitzwilliam Museum, inv. no. PD 53–1964; (see David Scrase, *Das Goldene Jahrhundert. Holländische Meisterzeichnungen aus dem Fitzwilliam Museum, Cambridge*, exh. cat., Staatliche Graphische Sammlung, Munich, 1996, no. 91; *Apollo and Marsyas*, Dresden, Kupferstich-Kabinett, inv. no. C 1968–610; (see Christian Dittrich, *Van Eyck, Bruegel, Rembrandt. Meisterzeichnungen aus dem Kupferstich-Kabinett, Dresden*, exh. cat., Albertinum, Dresden and Kunstforum, Vienna, 1997–98, no. 43); *Hercules and Deianira*, Cambridge, MA, private collection (see William Robinson, 'A Drawing by Jan Muller in a Modest Collection', in *Shop Talk: Studies in Honor of Seymour Slive*, ed. Cynthia P. Schneider, Alice I. Davies, William W. Robinson, Cambridge, Mass.,

1995, pp. 209–10); *Elijah fed by Ravens at the Brook Cherith*, sale, Christie's, Paris, 27 March 2003, lot 48 (fig. 3; see note 16).

5 Reznicek 1956, *op. cit.* (note 3), pp. 80–82. For the prints after Floris, see Carl van de Velde, *Frans Floris (1519/20–1570). Leven en Werken*, 2 vols., Brussels 1975, I, pp. 411–12, nos. 57–59, 61.

6 Jan Piet Filedt Kok, 'Jan Harmensz. Muller as Printmaker – I', *Print Quarterly*, vol. 11, no. 3, 1994, pp. 227–30.

7 Reznicek 1956, *op. cit.* (note 3), pp. 67–68; Filedt Kok, *op. cit.* (note 6), pp. 230–31.

8 In addition to *After the Deluge*, discussed below, see Van Thiel, *op. cit.* (note 2), p. 491, on the Getty *A Man holding a Child*.

9 422 × 581 mm, Hermitage Museum, St Petersburg, inv. no. 7510; Alexei Larionov in *Master Drawings from the Hermitage and Pushkin Museums*, exh. cat., The Pierpont Morgan Library, New York, 1998–99, pp. 94–95, no. 46, as Cornelis van Haarlem.

10 Wouter Kloek in Luijten *et al.*, *op. cit.* (note 2), pp. 379–80.

11 Larionov, *op. cit.* (note 9), p. 94.

12 Van Thiel, *op. cit.* (note 2), pp. 159, note 2, and 497.

13 *Ibid.*, pp. 441–41, nos. D6, D7. A copy of Cornelis's *Tityus* is attributed to Jan Muller; *ibid.*, p. 441.

14 *Ibid.*, pp. 159, note 2 and 497.

15 William Robinson in *The Age of Bruegel. Netherlandish Drawings in the Sixteenth Century*, exh. cat., National Gallery of Art, Washington, D.C., and Pierpont Morgan Library, New York, 1986–87, pp. 121 and 122, note 11.

16 *Peneus and the River Gods with Apollo and Daphne* (fig. 2), Brussels, Musées Royaux des Beaux-Arts de Belgique, collection de Grez, inv. no. 4060/67; Reznicek, 1980, *op. cit.* (note 3), p. 129, no. 4 ("Mythological Subject" datable "around 1590"); Roethlisberger, *op. cit.* (note 2), II, pp. 430–431, no. C12, fig. 48, as Muller and datable "within a few years after 1589". *Elijah fed by Ravens at the Brook Cherith* (fig. 3) was formerly attributed to Bloemaert, but was assigned to Muller prior to the Paris sale by Marijn



WILLIAM W. ROBINSON

Schapelhouman and Peter Schatborn.
My thanks to Emmanuel Marty de
Cambiaire of Christie's, Paris, for
providing a photograph.

17  Brown ink, brown wash, additions in
red chalk by a later hand, 97 × 150 mm;
inscribed, upper right, in brown ink: *4 1
[1?] 02 / 202*; inscribed, verso, lower left,
in graphite: *3 / C v Haerlem / 76*, and,
in graphite by Emil Reznicek: *Hendrick
Goltzius / 1558–1616 REZ Predigt im
Freien / Feder Sepia Rötel*; London,
Courtauld Gallery, inv. no. 4497. My
thanks to Joanna Selborne, Ernst
Vegelin and James Cuno for their help
and information about this drawing,
and to the Witt Library for providing
a photograph.

18  *Hand-list of the Drawings in the Witt
Collection*, ed. Anthony Blunt, Courtauld
Institute of Art, London, 1956, p. 100,
no. 4497. Andrée de Bosque, *Mythologie
et maniérisme aux Pays-Bas 1570–1630.
Peintures-Dessins*, Antwerp 1985,
pp. 261–62.

19  *Hercules and Deianira* (fig. 5): Robinson,
*op. cit.* (note 4), pp. 209–10, fig. 1.

20  For the Brno *Mary Magdalene*, see
Reznicek 1980, *op. cit.* (note 3), p. 129,
no. 3, pl. 4.

21  For this series of anonymous engravings
of scenes from Ovid's *Metamorphoses*,
published in 1589 after designs by
Goltzius, see *The Illustrated Bartsch*, ed.
Walter Strauss, III, New York 1980,
pp. 313–38, and III (Commentary), New
York 1982, pp. 354–56, nos. .031–.050.

22  Strauss 1980, *op. cit.* (note 21), p. 320,
no. 45 (105).

23  Ovid, *Metamorphoses*, I, 568–83. A drawing
of about 1588 by Karel van Mander and
a painting of 1592 by Abraham Bloemaert
also conflate the scenes of Daphne's
transformation and the river gods
consoling Peneus; Roethlisberger, *op. cit.*
(note 2), I, p. 72. Those two works and
Goltzius's engraving show Peneus seated
in a rocky cavern.

24  Roethlisberger, *op. cit.* (note 2), I, p. 72.

25  Ovid, *Metamorphoses*, I, 262–71.

26  Strauss 1980, *op. cit.* (note 21), p. 317,
no. 40 (105), with the misleading title
*Neptune plotting the Destruction of Man*.

27  Ovid, *Metamorphoses*, I, 270–71.

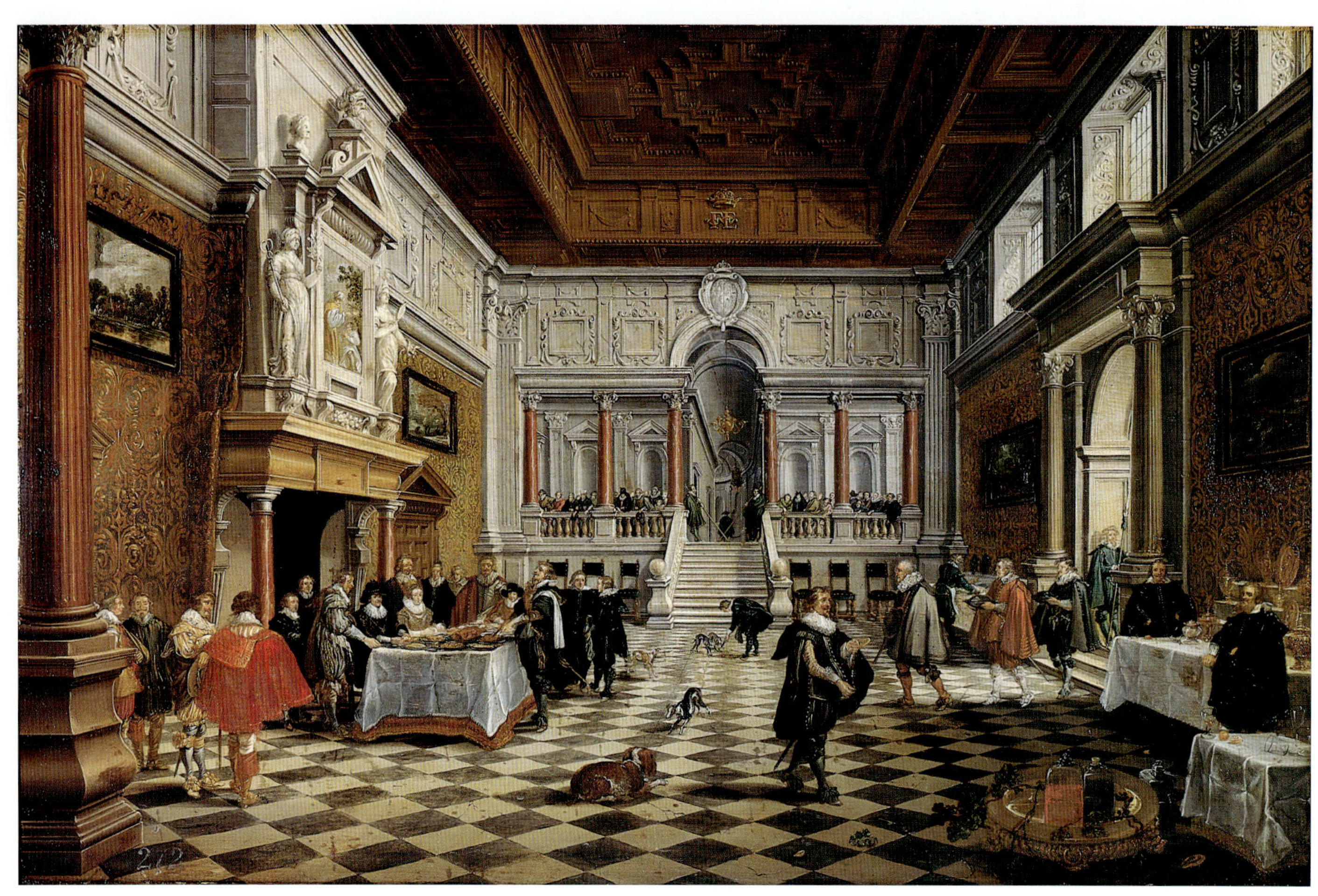

# Ein *Palastinterieur* von Bartholomeus van Bassen – Beobachtungen zur Arbeitsmethode anhand der Unterzeichnung

AXEL RÜGER

Bartholomeus van Bassen (*ca.* 1590–1652) ist einer der holländischen Künstler des siebzehnten Jahrhunderts, die in der Literatur zumeist nur marginale Beachtung finden. Dies überrascht, da er nicht nur als Maler, sondern auch als Architekt in prominenter Funktion tätig war. So erhielt er Aufträge sowohl vom Hof des holländischen Statthalters Frederik Hendrik (1584–1647) für die Paläste Honselaersdijk und Ter Nieuwburgh, als auch vom „Winterkönig" Friedrich V. (1596–1632) von Böhmen für dessen Sommerresidenz in Rhenen. In Den Haag war er als Stadtbaumeister über lange Jahre für Bauprojekte der Stadt verantwortlich.[1] Ausserdem war er ein prominentes Mitglied der Gilden in Delft und Den Haag.[2] Als Maler muss Van Bassen als der erste holländische Künstler betrachtet werden, der sich auf das Genre der Architekturmalerei spezialisierte. Zu seinen Lebzeiten wurden seine Bilder zu sehr hohen Preisen gehandelt und von Mitgliedern der höfischen Kreise und von wohlhabenden Patriziern in Den Haag und Delft gesammelt.[3] Es ist daher verwunderlich, dass keiner der zeitgenössischen Autoren, die über Kunst schreiben, Van Bassen erwähnt.[4] Erst im neunzehnten Jahrhundert, in Roeland van Eynden und Adriaan van der Willigens vierbändiger *Geschiedenis der vaderlandsche Schilderkunst sedert de Helft der XVIII Eeuw*, erschienen 1816–40, taucht Van Bassen zum ersten Mal in der Kunstliteratur auf.[5] Daraufhin erscheint sein Name allerdings in allen Handbüchern zur holländischen Malerei des siebzehnten Jahrhunderts. Die erste ausführlichere Beschreibung und Analyse von Van Bassens Oeuvre als Maler findet sich in Hans Jantzens Buch *Das Niederländische Architekturbild* aus dem Jahr 1909, wobei der Autor aber zu dem folgenden, wenig schmeichelhaften

Abb. 1 BARTHOLOMEUS VAN BASSEN
*Palastinterieur mit dem König und der Königin von Böhmen beim Schaumahl,*
*ca.* 1634
Öl auf Holz, 55.2 × 86.4 cm
The Royal Collection
© Her Majesty Queen Elizabeth II

Schluss kommt: „[...] überblicken wir das ganze Werk des Künstlers, so erscheint Bartholomeus van Bassen gewiss nicht als ein irgendwie bedeutender Maler".[6] Diese Einschätzung erfährt erst in späteren Publikationen zur holländischen Architekturmalerei eine Wandlung, und eine Reihe von Einzelbeiträgen zu Van Bassens Aktivitäten als Maler und Architekt deuten auf eine bedeutendere Rolle des Künstlers innerhalb seiner Umgebung hin.[7] 1987 hat Carla Scheffer schliesslich eine Magisterarbeit zu Van Bassen vorgelegt, die die erste, allerdings unpublizierte, monographische Studie darstellt.[8] Trotz der grösseren Bedeutung, die Van Bassen inzwischen zugemessen wird, muss er wohl dennoch als einer der holländischen „Kleinmeister" gesehen werden, dessen Werke sich noch vielfach – und zum Teil vermutlich unentdeckt – in Privatbesitz befinden und regelmässig im Kunsthandel auftauchen. Daher müsste zu diesem Zeitpunkt Scheffers Oeuvrekatalog von 129 akzeptierten Werken bereits um mindestens 30–40 Bilder erweitert werden.

Ein Aspekt, dem Scheffer in ihrer Arbeit keine Aufmerksamkeit hat schenken können, ist die Untersuchung der Arbeitsweise Van Bassens, und hier besonders die Frage nach der Vorbereitung seiner Kompositionen und der Rolle seiner Unterzeichnungen. Bislang hat auf diesem Gebiet das Hauptaugenmerk nahezu ausschliesslich auf dem wohl bekanntesten holländischen Architekturmaler, dem Haarlemer Pieter Saenredam (1597–1665), gelegen. In seinem Fall sind eine Vielzahl von losen Skizzen, vorbereitenden Zeichnungen und präzisen Konstruktionszeichnungen bewahrt geblieben, die es uns erlauben, seine Arbeitsweise Schritt für Schritt zu verfolgen. Infrarotreflektographie (IRR) hat ausserdem Aufschluss zu Saenredams Unterzeichnungen und deren Beziehung zu seinen Zeichnungen auf Papier geliefert. Die Ergebnisse dieser Studien sind in einer Reihe von Aufsätzen und Ausstellungskatalogen publiziert worden.[9] Andere holländische Architekturmaler sind zwar inzwischen auch Gegenstand einer Reihe von Einzelstudien und Ausstellungen gewesen, aber hinsichtlich der Arbeitsmethode dieser Künstler haben sich die Autoren hauptsächlich auf die Rolle der Perspektive konzentriert.[10] Technische Untersuchungen dieser Bilder haben so gut wie überhaupt nicht stattgefunden.[11]

In den vergangenen fünf Jahren ist es allerdings gelungen – mit der Unterstützung von Kollegen an der National Gallery und anderen Museen sowie aus dem Kunsthandel – eine Anzahl von Bildern von Bartholomeus van Bassen auf ihre Unterzeichnungen hin zu untersuchen. Infrarotreflektographie hat hier zu bemerkenswerten Ergebnissen geführt. Da von Van Bassen, wie auch von vielen seiner Architekturmalerkollegen, keine Zeichnungen überliefert sind, haben sich die technischen Untersuchungen als besonders aufschlussreich im Hinblick auf seine Arbeitsmethode erwiesen.[12] Im folgenden sollen einige dieser Ergebnisse anhand eines Bildes des Malers vorgestellt werden.

     AXEL RÜGER

Das *Palastinterieur mit dem König und der Königin von Böhmen beim Schaumahl* ist das einzige Bild von Van Bassen in der britischen königlichen Sammlung (Abb. 1). Es wurde von König Georg II. (1683–1760) oder Königin Caroline (1683–1737) von der Gräfin van Pomfret gekauft und kam am 12. April 1729 in den Palast in Kensington.[13] Es zeigt einen Kastenraum mit einem gefliesten Fussboden, einer kassettierten Holzdecke und reichhaltiger architektonischer und skulpturaler Dekoration. In der Mitte der linken Wand befindet sich ein mit einem Gemälde, Marmorskulpturen und –büsten bekrönter Kamin. Vor dem Kamin sitzen der „Winterkönig" Friedrich V. und seine Gemahlin Elisabeth Stuart (1596–1662) an einem mit Speisen bedeckten Tisch, dicht umringt von barhäuptigen Höflingen. Vor dem Königspaar steht ein Diener mit einem Affen vor der Brust. Auf der gegenüberliegenden Seite des Raumes, in der Mitte der rechten Wand, befindet sich ein von kanellierten Säulen flankierter offener Durchgang, durch den eine Prozession von Bediensteten Speisen auf zugedeckten Tellern hereintragen. Links und rechts des Durchgangs sind Büffets angerichtet. Auf dem Büffet rechts der Tür sind prunkvolle Stücke vergoldeten Silbers zur Schau gestellt. An den beiden Seitenwänden hängen Gemälde mit Landschaftsszenen. In der Mitte der Rückwand führt ein Treppe hinauf zu einer Art offener Loggia, von der ein tonnengewölbter Gang in die Tiefe führt. Entlang der Balustrade der Loggia drängt sich eine Vielzahl von Personen, die dem Spektakel des königlichen Mahls zusehen. Die obere Zone aller drei Wände ist mit Ornamentreliefs aus Stein verziert. Über dem Durchgang zur Loggia, eingelassen in die Decke, findet sich ein vergoldetes Monogramm, das die Initialen des Königspaars wiedergibt: *FE*. Weitere Figuren und ein paar Hunde in der Mitte des Raumes beleben die Szene.

Kurfürst Friedrich V. von der Pfalz hatte Elisabeth Stuart, die Schwester des englischen Königs Karl I. (1600–1649), 1613 geheiratet. 1619 wurde er von den freien Ständen zum König von Böhmen gewählt, verlor aber die Krone und die pfälzische Kur schon im darauffolgenden Jahr nach seiner Niederlage in der Schlacht am Weissen Berg am 8. November 1620 gegen die katholische Liga unter der Führung Maximilians I. von Bayern (1573–1651). Die kurze Dauer seiner Regentschaft hat Friedrich den Spottnamen „Winterkönig" eingetragen. In Folge dieser vernichtenden Niederlage flohen Friedrich und Elisabeth nach Holland und liessen sich in Den Haag nieder. Friedrich konnte sich hier auf die Hilfe des holländischen Hofes verlassen, da seine Mutter Luise Juliane von Oranien-Nassau (1576–1644) die Schwester des Statthalters Maurits von Oranien (1567–1625) war. Mit finanzieller Unterstützung der Oranier sowie des englischen Hofes gelang es dem Paar recht schnell, einen glanzvollen „Böhmischen Hof" in Den Haag einzurichten.[14] Einige Zeit später, im Jahr 1629, wurde Bartholomeus van Bassen beauftragt, das Kloster von St. Agniet in

Rhenen, im Osten des Landes, zu einer Sommerresidenz für das Königspaar umzubauen. Dies geschah zwischen 1630 und 1631, aber bereits 1812 wurde das Jagdschloss wieder geschleift.[15] Heute ist lediglich eine von Van Bassen 1639 ausgeführte Ansicht seines Entwurfs für das Schloss bewahrt geblieben. Van Bassen hat ausserdem eine Innenansicht der St. Cunera-Kirche, die ursprünglich zu dem Kloster gehörte, gemalt – eine seltenen Darstellungen eines tatsächlich existierenden Interieurs.[16]

Wie bereits erwähnt, zeigt dieses Bild den „Winterkönig" und seine Gemahlin bei einem öffentlichen Mahl. Diese Art des Schaumahls eines Monarchen war im Mittelalter und in der Renaissance ein äusserst seltenes Ereignis. Nur zu besonders wichtigen Anlässen, wie z.B. einer Krönung, speisten Kaiser und Könige in Anwesenheit von Publikum. Im Laufe des sechzehnten Jahr- hunderts, dem Zeitalter des aufkommenden Absolutismus, wurde es allerdings zunehmend wichtig, mit höfischen Ritualen die dynastischen Ansprüche und das Recht des Monarchen auf die Krone zu unterstreichen. Das öffentliche Mahl spielte dabei eine zentrale Rolle und wurde zu einem regelmässigen Bestandteil des Hofzeremoniells. Die Häufigkeit variierte von Hof zu Hof. Am spanischen Hof unter Karl V. (1500–1558) und Philip II. (1527–1598) fand ein öffentliches Mahl viermal im Jahr an hohen kirchlichen Festtagen statt, wobei sich die burgun- dische Etikette stark am Zeremoniell der katholischen Messe orientierte. Am englischen Hof, unter Heinrich VIII. (1491–1547), war die Etikette nicht weniger strikt, allerdings bestand keine Verbindung zum kirchlichen Zeremoniell. Während Elisabeth I. (1533–1603) nie in der Öffentlichkeit speiste, nahmen Jakob I. (1566–1625), der Vater von Elisabeth Stuart, und sein Sohn Karl I. das Ritual wieder auf. Das Phänomen des öffentlichen Mahls, bei dem der König umringt von Zuschauern alleine oder mit seiner Gemahlin speiste, hielt sich bis ins frühe achtzehnte Jahrhundert, bevor es durch eine andere, in gewisser Hinsicht weniger formelle Etikette ersetzt wurde.[17]

Das *Palastinterieur mit dem König und der Königin von Böhmen beim Schaumahl* ist ein typisches, wenn auch sehr grossartiges, Beispiel für Van Bassens Darstellungen von profanen Innenräumen. Neben Kircheninterieurs, die den grösseren Teil seines Oeuvres bestreiten, hatte Van Bassen sich auch auf die Darstellung von imaginären Palasträumen spezialisiert.[18] Charakteristisch für diese ausseror- dentlich luxuriösen Säle sind der Kastenraum, der gefliese Boden, die Kassettendecke und die überaus reichhaltige Dekoration. Keine Oberfläche bleibt unverziert, was einen gewissen *horror vacui* des Künstlers suggeriert.[19] In der Vergangenheit haben verschiedene Autoren vorgeschlagen, dass einzelne Details wie Bilder, Skulpturen, der Weinkühler im Vordergrund (ein häufig vorkommendes Motiv in Van Bassens Bildern), raufende Hunde und andere Tiere diesen Darstellungen eine symbolische Bedeutung verleihen, zumeist im

    

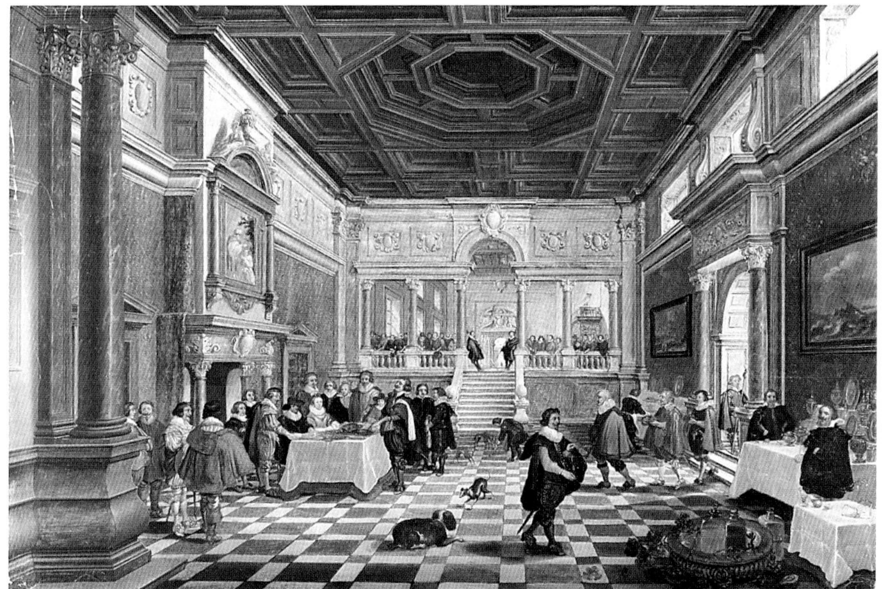



Sinne einer moralisierenden Warnung vor übermässigem Konsum weltlicher Genüsse. Insgesamt scheint es aber wohl, dass diese Bilder in erster Linie für ihre eleganten höfischen Szenen, luxuriösen Interieurs, die reichhaltigen und sorgfältig ausgeführten Details, und ihre präzisen perspektivischen Konstruktionen – was im siebzehnten Jahrhundert in Holland auf besonderes Interesse stiess – von wohlhabenden Sammlern gekauft wurden.[20] In diesem Bild kann von symbolischen Nebenbedeutungen wohl keine Rede sein, steht doch das Spektakel des öffentlichen Mahls des Königspaares im Vordergrund. Es scheint sogar, als sei hier ein ganz bestimmtes Ereignis dargestellt. Es wird berichtet, dass bei einem solchen Mahl am Hof in Prag im Jahr 1620 ein domestizierter Affe in der Tat einen der böhmischen Diener angegriffen habe.[21]

Allerdings dürfen die Identifizierbarkeit der Dargestellten sowie der Verweis auf das Ereignis mit dem Affen nicht als Hinweis verstanden werden, dass es sich bei dem dargestellten Interieur um einen Saal handelt, der tatsächlich existiert hat. Es ist, wie bei Van Bassen bis auf wenige Ausnahmen üblich, ein imaginäres Interieur. Dies lässt sich an der Tatsache festmachen, wie schon Christopher White gezeigt hat, dass es von der Szene zwei Versionen mit deutlichen Unterschieden gibt.[22] Das hier besprochene Bild stellt das aufwendigere der beiden Interieurs dar. In vielen Details folgt es aber der 1634 datierten Version Van Bassens (Abb. 2).[23] Der Verbleib des Bildes ist leider unbekannt, und gegenwärtig ist es nur aus Abbildungen bekannt. Daneben befindet sich noch eine weitere Darstellung der gleichen Szene in der britischen königlichen Sammlung, die von Van Bassens Schüler Gerard Houckgeest (*ca.* 1600–1661) gemalt wurde (Abb. 3).[24] Obwohl die Protagonisten hier der englische König Karl I. und seine Gemahlin Henrietta Maria (1609–1669) sind, folgt Houckgeest mit seiner Komposition der datierten Version Van Bassens vom Jahr zuvor

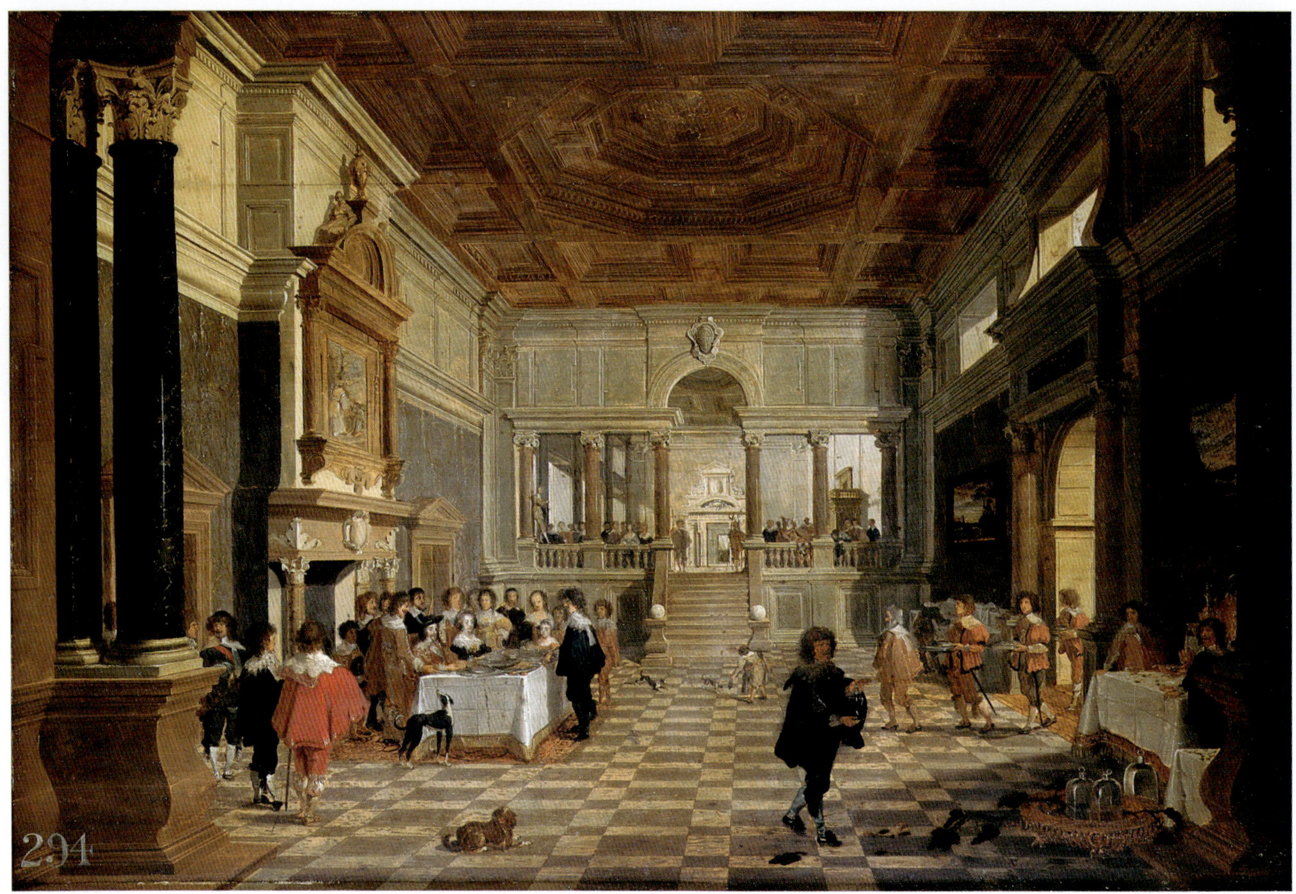



Abb. 3 GERARD HOUCKGEEST
*Karl I., Königin Henrietta Maria
und Karl, Prinz von Wales, beim
Schaumahl*, 1635
Öl auf Holz, 63.2 × 92.4 cm
The Royal Collection
© Her Majesty Queen Elizabeth II

nahezu bis in jedes Detail. Auf die Beziehung der drei Bilder untereinander und die Rolle der Figuren werden wir in Kürze noch einmal zurückkommen.

Das Mosaik des Infrarotreflektogramms des undatierten Bildes von Van Bassen zeigt deutlich die für den Künstler typische detaillierte Unterzeichnung (Abb. 4).[25] Im Fussboden, an den Wänden und an der Decke finden sich die dünnen, mit dem Lineal gezogenen Linien, die der perspektivischen Konstruktion des Raumes dienen. An der linken Wand wird besonders deutlich, dass diese Linien zur Konstruktion gebraucht werden und in der Regel nichts mit den dekorativen Details wie den Gesimsprofilen, Voluten und Kapitellen zu tun haben. Ihre Funktion ist es lediglich, die groben architektonischen Elemente festzulegen, und oft reichen sie über die Formen, die sie umreissen, wie z.B. die Säulen an der Rückwand, hinaus. Am unteren Ende der Rückwand hat Van Bassen mehrere horizontale Linien gebraucht, um die Stuhllehnen und -sitzflächen nebeneinander aufzureihen. An der Decke befindet sich eine Vielzahl von Diagonalen, die scheinbar nicht mit der endgültigen Form der Decke in Verbindung stehen. Stattdessen dienen sie der Konstruktion der perspektivisch richtigen Verkürzung der Kassetten. Mit seiner detaillierten Unterzeichnung hat Van Bassen somit die prinzipiellen architektonischen

Grundformen, wie Wände, Säulen, Durchgänge und den Fussboden, definiert. Kleinteilige Dekorationen, wie Kapitelle, Reliefs oder die Balustrade im Hintergrund, sind nahezu ausschliesslich mit lockeren Pinselzügen in der Malschicht ausgeführt worden. Diese prinzipielle Vorgehensweise findet sich in jedem Bild Van Bassens, das wir bisher untersucht haben.

In diesem Fall zeigt die Infrarotaufnahme aber, dass Van Bassen sich gelegentlich bereits im Stadium der Unterzeichnung Gedanken um einige der dekorativen Details gemacht hat. So kann man in den Kassetten am linken und rechten Rand der Decke Linien ausmachen, die ein rautenförmiges Kassettenmuster zu beschreiben scheinen, während einige der rückwärtigen Kassetten mit der freien Hand skizzierte Kreise und Ovale enthalten, die sich in der Malschicht nicht wiederfinden. Auch die Skulpturen über dem Kamin und die Konsolen, auf denen sie stehen, sind mit frei gezeichneten Linien umrissen. Die Kugeln, die die Baluster zu beiden Seiten der rückwärtigen Treppe bekrönen, sind mit skizzierten Kreisen angedeutet. Hier weicht die Position der gemalten linken Kugel deutlich von der Position in der Unterzeichnung ab. Diese Art der freien Unterzeichnung findet sich allerdings nur selten in Van Bassens Bildern. Insgesamt weisen die präzise geometrische Unterzeichnung, die Konstruktionslinien und die frei skizzierten Details deutlich darauf hin, dass Van Bassen die Komposition direkt auf dem Bildträger entwickelt haben muss ohne Zuhilfenahme einer Konstruktionszeichnung auf Papier. Hätte er zunächst eine solche Zeichnung angefertigt, hätte er diese, ähnlich der Arbeitsweise Saenredams, ohne die Konstruktionslinien direkt auf den Malgrund durchpausen können. In der Unterzeichnung wären dann aber nur jene Linien zu sehen, die direkt mit den gemalten Details des Interieurs in Verbindung stehen.

Die detaillierte Unterzeichnung macht ebenfalls deutlich, dass es sich bei diesem Bild nicht um eine direkte Kopie des Bildes von 1634 handelt. Obwohl die beiden Gemälde in ihrer Anlage sehr ähnlich sind, unterscheiden sie sich doch deutlich in ihren Dimensionen, Proportionen und vielen der dekorativen Details. Die beiden Kompositionen sind somit wohl unabhängig voneinander, jeweils direkt auf der Holztafel vom Künstler ausgearbeitet worden. Leider ist es bisher nicht möglich gewesen, das datierte Bild zu untersuchen. Es wäre sicher aufschlussreich, die Unterzeichnungen der beiden Bilder miteinander zu vergleichen. Die enge Verwandtschaft der Kompositionen weist allerdings darauf hin, dass das Bild aus der königlichen Sammlung zum gleichen Zeitpunkt wie das datierte Bild, also um 1634, entstanden sein muss. Eine solche direkte Beziehung zweier Bilder ist im Werk Van Bassens einmalig.

Dass Van Bassens Bild von 1634 auch im darauffolgenden Jahr noch zur Verfügung gestanden haben muss, wird durch das Bild von Houckgeest

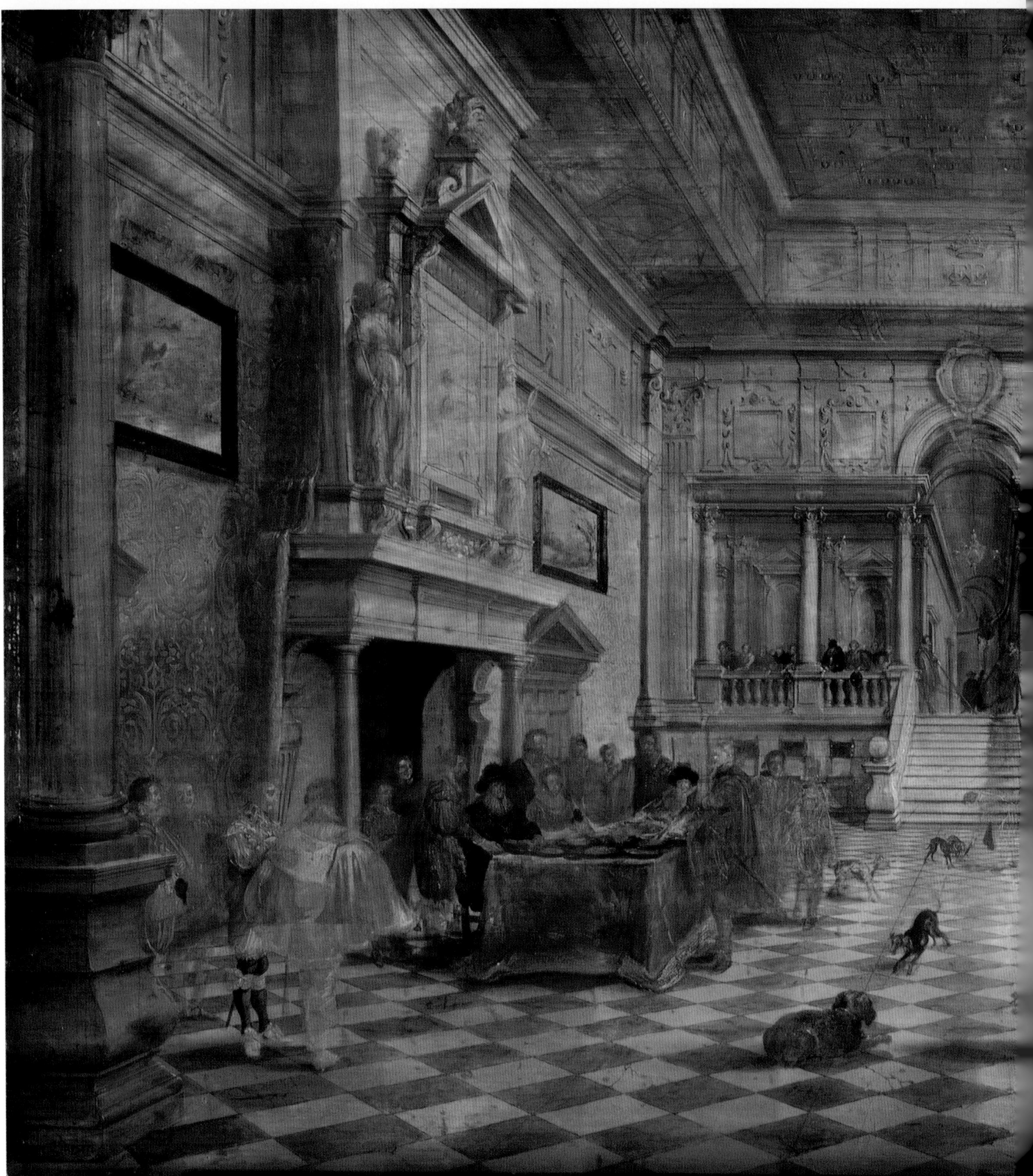

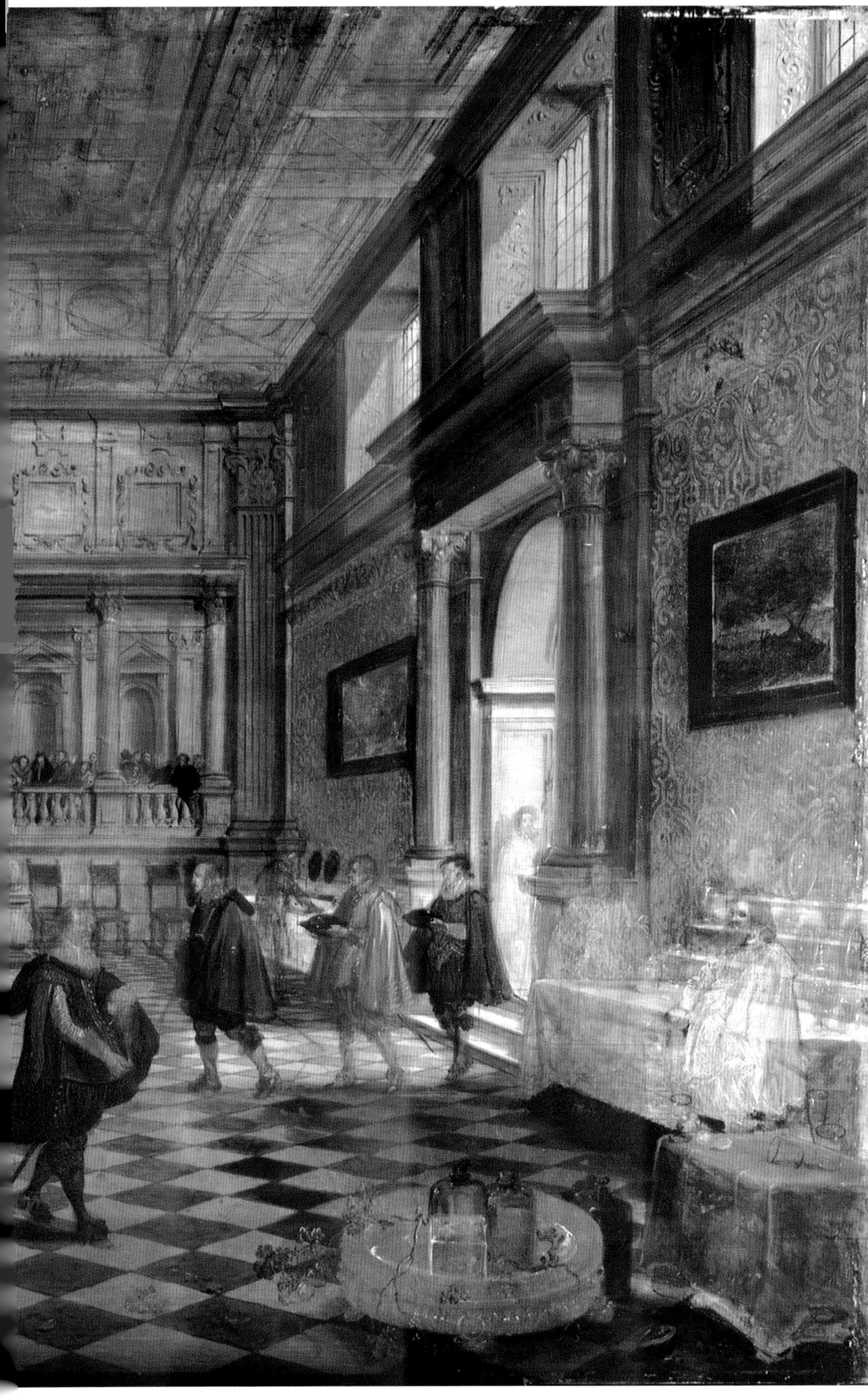

Abb. 4  Infrarotreflektogramm-
Mosaik von Abb. 1

nahegelegt. Houckgeest folgt mit seiner Komposition von 1635 dem Gemälde
seines Lehrers sehr genau. Die beiden Bilder sind nicht nur nahezu gleich gross,
sondern sie sind bis auf minimale Unterschiede in einigen dekorativen Details
und der kontrastreicheren Lichtführung auch in ihren Darstellungen nahezu
identisch. Auch wenn Houckgeest 1635 bereits von Den Haag nach Delft gezogen
war, so ist es kaum vorstellbar, dass er das Bild gemalt haben könnte, ohne Van
Bassens Version vor Augen gehabt zu haben. Wie eine erste Betrachtung des
Gemäldes von Houckgeest mit Infrarotreflektographie gezeigt hat, fertigte er
ebenfalls eine detaillierte Unterzeichnung an.[26] Im Gegensatz zu Van Bassen
gebrauchte er aber neben den geometrischen Konstruktionslinien auch für die
meisten seiner dekorativen Details, wie z.B. den Kapitellen der Säulen und der
Dekoration über dem Kamin, eine detaillierte skizzenhafte Unterzeichnung, wobei
viele dieser Linien einen eher zögerlichen, nach der Form suchenden Charakter,
aufweisen. Dies ist aber nicht die Hand eines noch unerfahrenen Schülers, denn
Houckgeest ist zu diesem Zeitpunkt bereits seit zehn Jahren als unabhängiger
Meister in der Haager Gilde registriert,[27] sondern eher das Bemühen des Malers,
eine möglichst genaue Kopie der Komposition Van Bassens anzufertigen.

Ein interessanter Aspekt ist die Tatsache, dass Houckgeests Figuren präzise
mit denen Van Bassens übereinstimmen. Mit der Infrarotkamera ist allerdings
zu sehen, dass auch die Figuren Houckgeests Unterzeichnung und Reserven
aufweisen, wie z.B. die Rückenfigur im linken Vordergrund. Das bedeutet, dass
sie nicht, wie normalerweise üblich, erst nach Fertigstellung des Interieurs über
die gemalte Architektur gemalt worden sind, sondern schon während des
vorbereitenden Stadiums eingeplant wurden. Dies scheint darauf hinzudeuten,
dass Houckgeest die Figuren selber gezeichnet und gemalt haben könnte. Der
Künstler hat dabei selbst eine kleine Veränderung vorgenommen. Die Wache,
die in den Versionen von Van Bassen im rechten Durchgang steht, ist in
Houckgeests Unterzeichnung angelegt, aber am Ende durch eine Figur, die der
Prozession der Diener folgt, ersetzt worden.

Auf der Basis der Tatsache, dass das englische Königspaar dargestellt ist, hat
White vorgeschlagen, dass Houckgeests Bild in England gemalt worden sein
könnte. Dabei bezieht er sich auf einen Vorschlag Oliver Millars, der für die
Figuren eine Zuschreibung an Jan van Belcamp (1610–1652), der in England
tätig war, angenommen hatte.[28] Dies ist aber schon deshalb nicht möglich, da
Houckgeest 1635 in Delft ansässig war, wo er im darauffolgenden Jahr heiratete.[29]
Wie bereits erwähnt, erscheint es zudem höchst unwahrscheinlich, dass Houckgeest diese Komposition hätte malen können, ohne das Original Van Bassens vor
Augen zu haben. Dabei sind die Figuren offenbar zum gleichen Zeitpunkt wie
das Bild selber entstanden und nicht nachträglich hineingesetzt worden. Bei
näherer Betrachtung des Bildes fällt aber auf, dass sich die Häupter Karls I. und

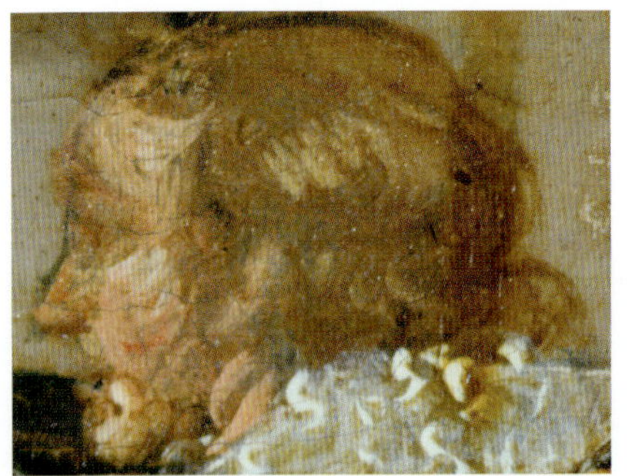

Abb. 5  Detailaufnahme von Abb. 1 unter Vergrösserung, Kopf des vor dem Tisch stehenden Mannes mit Hund

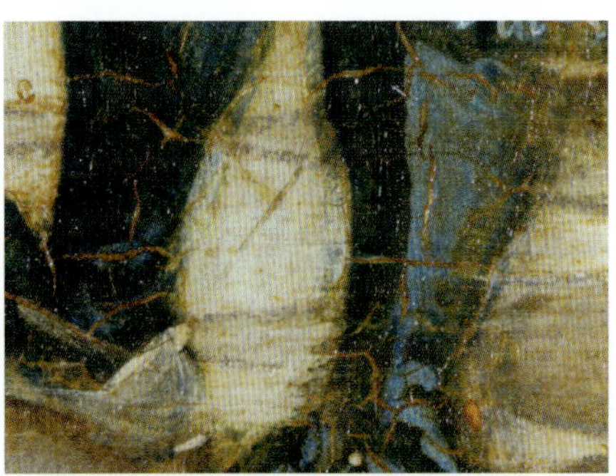

Abb. 6  Detailaufnahme von Abb. 1 unter Vergrösserung, Beine des neben dem Hund stehenden Mannes

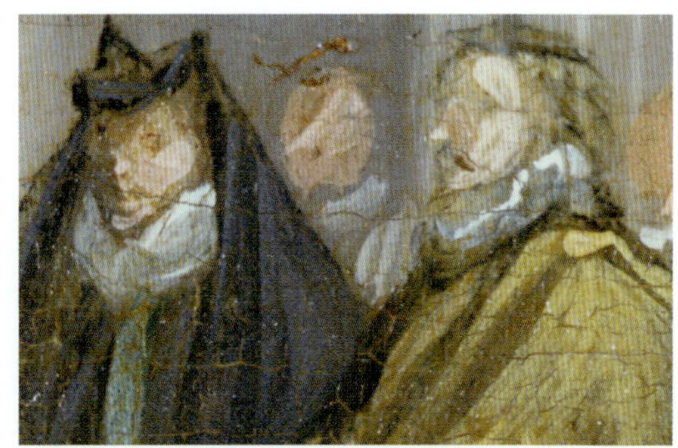

Abb. 7  Detailaufnahme von Abb. 1 unter Vergrösserung, Gruppe rechts hinter der Balustrade

seiner Gemahlin in der Ausführung und im Kolorit von den anderen deutlich unterscheiden. Hier wäre es durchaus möglich, dass diesen beiden Köpfe erst nachträglich – eventuell erst nach Ankunft des Bildes in England? – in die Komposition eingefügt worden sind. Eine genauere Untersuchung des Bildes mit dem Mikroskop und einer Röntgenaufnahme könnte dazu eventuell genaueren Aufschluss geben.

Van Bassen hat in der Regel seine Figuren nicht selber gemalt, sondern einen spezialisierten Figurenmaler beauftragt, diese seinen Interieurs hinzuzufügen. In seinen Bildern findet sich Staffage von Esaias van de Velde (1587–1630),[30] Cornelis van Poelenburgh (1594/95–1667), Anthonie Palamedesz. (1601–1673) und den Flamen Frans Francken II (1581–1642) und Sebastiaen Vrancx (1573–1647). Keyes hat die Figuren im Bild von 1634 dem holländischen Maler Adriaen van de Venne (1589–1662) zugeschrieben.[31] Die Figuren sind mit sicherer Hand gezeichnet und sehr detailliert ausgeführt. In ihren Proportionen fügen sie sich harmonisch in das Interieur ein. Die Staffage im Bild der könglichen Sammlung hingegen ist weniger scharf gezeichnet und weist gewisse Unsicherheiten auf. Auch sind viele der Gesichter weniger genau definiert, und die Figuren scheinen etwas weniger robust in ihrer Statur. Darüber hinaus ist es schwer vorstellbar, dass derselbe Künstler in einer zweiten Version eines Bildes, das sich bereits in einer Reihe von Details von der ersten Version unterscheidet, seine Figuren so haargenau wiederholen würde. Es scheint dagegen eher wahrscheinlich, dass ein anderer Künstler – oder gar Van Bassen selber? – die Figuren kopiert hat. Bei der Untersuchung des Bildes mit dem Stereomikroskop in der National Gallery hat sich gezeigt, dass der Maler der Staffage die Figuren zwar über die fertige Architektur gemalt hat, sie aber wohl zunächst mit einer lockeren Unterzeichnung mit dem Pinsel in grüner Farbe skizziert hat. An mehreren Stellen weisen die Figuren deutlich eine untere grünliche Malschicht und Konturen in der gleichen Farbe auf (Abb. 5–7). Diese Praktik ist hier zum ersten Mal im Oeuvre Van Bassens beobachtet worden. Leider ist es bisher aber nicht möglich gewesen, eine überzeugende Zuschreibung für die Figuren zu finden.

          AXEL RÜGER

Dieser Aufsatz erscheint zu Ehren Alfred Baders. Es handelt sich dabei um einen Auszug aus meiner sich in Vorbereitung befindlicher Dissertation über Bartholomeus van Bassen, die ich vor meiner Anstellung an der National Gallery an der Queen's University in Kingston, Kanada, unter der Betreuung von Volker Manuth begonnen habe. Dabei habe ich von Alfreds Grosszügigkeit gegenüber der Universität in Form eines Forschungsstipendiums für einen 15-monatigen Aufenthalt in den Niederlanden profitiert.

1 Zu Van Bassens Rolle als Architekt für den Statthalter siehe D.H. Slothouwer, *De paleizen van Frederik Hendrik*, Leiden 1945. Slothouwer zufolge war Van Bassen allerdings nicht der Architekt der Paläste, sondern lediglich mit Plänen und Ansichten beauftragt. Siehe auch H.E. van Gelder, 'Iets over Barthold van Bassen, ook als bouwmeester van het Koningshuis te Rhenen', *Bulletin van den Nederlandschen Oudheidkundigen Bond*, Bd. 4, 1911, S. 234–40; Wouter Kuyper, *Dutch Classicist Architecture*, Delft 1980, bes. S. 33–50; und Koen Ottenheym, 'The Painters cum architects of Dutch Classicism', in Albert Blankert *et al.*, *Dutch Classicism in seventeenth-century painting*, Ausst. Kat., Museum Boijmans Van Beuningen, Rotterdam; Städelsches Kunstinstitut, Frankfurt am Main, 1999, S. 34–53.

2 Siehe hierzu meine Biographie Van Bassens in Walter Liedtke *et al.*, *Vermeer and the Delft School*, Ausst. Kat., Metropolitan Museum of Art, New York; National Gallery, London, 2001, S. 222.

3 Zu den Preisen, die Van Bassens Bilder im siebzehnten Jahrhundert erzielten, siehe die Lotterie von Cornelis Cornelisz. van Leeuwen in Delft im Jahr 1626 (Abraham Bredius, *Künstlerinventare, Urkunden zur Geschichte der holländischen Kunst des XVIten, XVIIten, und XVIIIten Jahrhunderts*, Quellenstudien zur holländischen Kunstgeschichte, 7 Bde., Den Haag 1915–22, Bd. 1, S. 321–22). In der Liste der Bilder kommt Abraham Bloemaert an erster Stelle mit einem Bild für 360 Gulden gefolgt von drei Bildern von

Van Bassen für je 150, 50 und 46 Gulden. Zu Van Leeuwens Lotterie siehe auch John Michael Montias, *Artists and Artisans in Delft. A Socio-economic Study of the Seventeenth Century*, Princeton 1982, S. 198–99. Zu Preisen von Architekturbildern siehe *idem*, '"Perspectiven" in zeventiende-eeuwse boedelbeschrijvingen', in Jeroen Giltaij, Guido Jansen, *Perspectiven: Saenredam en de architectuurschilders van de 17e eeuw*, Ausst. Kat., Museum Boijmans Van Beuningen, Rotterdam, 1991, S. 19–29, bes. S. 25–29.

4 Weder Cornelis de Bie, noch Arnold Houbraken oder Jacob Campo Weyerman nehmen Van Bassen in ihre Beschreibungen der Künstler ihrer Zeit auf. Auch Dirck van Bleyswijk in seiner *Beschrijvinge der Stad Delft* von 1667 verzichtet auf eine Erwähnung.

5 Siehe Bd. 1, S. 66. Carla Scheffer hat allerdings darauf hingewiesen, dass George Vertue Van Bassen bereits 1739 – und damit zum ersten Mal – in seinen Notizbüchern erwähnt. Siehe Carla Scheffer, 'Barholomeus van Bassen (*ca.* 1590–1652), architect en schilder van architektuurstukken', unpublizierte Magisterarbeit (*doctoraalscriptie*), 2 Bde., Rijksuniversiteit Leiden, 1987, I, S. 5.

6 Siehe die 2. Auflage, Braunschweig 1979, S. 58–65, und für das Zitat S. 65.

7 Zur weiteren Literatur zu Van Bassen siehe Abraham Bredius, 'De Haagsche schilders Joachim en Gerard Houckgeest', *Oud Holland*, VI, 1888, S. 81–86; *idem*, 'Bartholomeus van Bassen, schilderarchitect', *Haagsch Jaarboekje*, Bd. 6, 1894, S. 85–90; Walter Liedtke, *Architectural Painting in Delft*, Doornspijk 1982, bes. S. 22–33, und Walter Liedtke *et al.*, *op. cit.* (Anm. 2), bes. S. 77–83 und Kat. Nrn. 6 und 7.

8 Neben einer Reihe neuer Ergebnisse zu Van Bassens wahrscheinlichen Ursprüngen umfasst die Arbeit auch einen Oeuvrekatalog. Scheffer, *op. cit.* (Anm. 5).

9 Siehe z.B. Martin Kemp, 'Construction and Cunning', in *Dutch Church Painters. Saenredam's* Great Church in Haarlem *in context*, Ausst. Kat., National Gallery of Scotland, Edinburgh, 1984; Robert

Ruurs, *Saenredam. The Art of Perspective*, Diss., Universiteit van Amsterdam, Amsterdam and Philadelphia 1986 (zur Arbeitsweise siehe Kapitel III); Gary Schwartz, Marten Jan Bok, *Pieter Saenredam. De Schilder en zijn tijd*, Den Haag 1989; J.R.J. van Asperen de Boer, Liesbeth M. Helmus (Hrsg.), *The Paintings of Pieter Jansz. Saenredam (1597–1665), Conservation and Technique*, Utrecht 2000; Liesbeth M. Helmus (Hrsg.), *Pieter Saenredam, het Utrechtse Werk, Schilderijen en tekeningen van de 17de-eeuwse grootmeester van het perspectief*, Ausst. Kat., Centraal Museum, Utrecht, 2000 (im Jahr 2002 im John Paul Getty Museum, Los Angeles).

10  Siehe u.a. Arthur K. Wheelock, Jr., *Perspective, Optics and Delft Artists around 1650*, New York und London 1977; Liedtke 1982, *op. cit.* (Anm. 7); Giltaij, Jansen, *op. cit.* (Anm. 3); Liedtke *et al.*, *op. cit.* (Anm. 2) sowie Walter Liedtke, *A View of Delft, Vermeer and his Contemporaries*, Zwolle 2000 (bes. Kapitel 3).

11  Eine Ausnahme ist die Untersuchung einiger Bilder mit IRR in der Rotterdamer Ausstellung *Perspectiven* (Giltaij, Jansen, *op. cit.*, Anm. 3) durch J.R.J. van Asperen de Boer und Jeroen Giltaij. Giltaij hat die Ergebnisse zusammenfassend in einem Artikel publiziert: Jeroen Giltaij, 'Scientific Examination of Underdrawing of Seventeenth-Century Architectural Painters', in Van Asperen de Boer, Helmus, *op. cit.* (Anm. 9), S. 32–55.

12  Einige der Ergebnisse sind vom Verfasser bereits auf einem Symposium zu technischen Untersuchungen holländischer Gemälde des siebzehnten Jahrhunderts im Rijksbureau voor Kunsthistorische Documentatie in Den Haag im Oktober 2001 vorgestellt worden. Eine detaillierte Erörterung dieser Untersuchungen wird in einem Aufsatz mit dem Titel 'Insights into the Design Practices of the Dutch Architectural Painter Bartholomeus van Bassen as revealed by Infrared Reflectography' von Rachel Billinge und Axel Rüger im *National Gallery Technical Bulletin*, Bd. 26, im Jahr 2005 erscheinen.

13  Christopher White, *The Dutch Pictures in the Collection of Her Majesty the Queen*, Cambridge und London 1982, S. 17–18.

14  Zu Friedrich V. siehe den kürzlich erschienen umfangreichen Ausstellungskatalog *Der Winterkönig, Friedrich von der Pfalz. Bayern und Europa im Zeitalter des Dreissigjährigen Krieges*, hrsg. von Peter Wolf, Michael Henker *et al.*, Ausst. Kat., Stadtmuseum, Amberg, 2003. Das hier diskutierte Bild ist Kat. Nr. 11.25, S. 355 und erwähnt mit Abb. auf S. 42, Nr. 10.

15  Ottenheym, *op. cit.* (Anm. 1), S. 34–53, bes. S. 37 und S. 52, Anm. 29. Siehe auch Marika Keblusek, 'Het Bohemse hof in Den Haag', in Marika Keblusek, Jori Zijlmans (Hrsg.), *Vorstelijk Vertoon, Aan het hof van Frederik Hendrik en Amalia*, Den Haag 1997, S. 47–57, bes. S. 54 und 220, Anm. 25.

16  Das Gemälde mit der Ansicht des Palastes ist in einer Privatsammlung in Kopenhagen, signiert und datiert 1639, Holz, 64 × 86 cm; für eine Abbildung siehe Liedtke *et al.*, *op. cit.*, (Anm. 2), S. 80, Abb. 91. Die Innenansicht der St. Cunera-Kirche, Rhenen, auf Holz, 61.1 × 80.5 cm, ist in der National Gallery, London, Inv. Nr. NG 3164. Für eine Abbildung siehe Liedtke *et al.*, *op. cit.* (Anm. 2), S. 78, Abb. 90. Für eine detaillierte Analyse dieses Kircheninterieurs und dessen Unterzeichnung, siehe Billinge, Rüger, *op. cit.* (Anm. 12).

17  Zur Geschichte des königlichen Schaumahls siehe Roy Strong, *Feast, A History of Grand Eating*, London 2003, S. 202–09, mit weiterer Literatur.

18  Siehe z.B. das *Renaissance Interieur* des North Carolina Museum of Art, *ca.* 1618–20, Holz, 57.5 × 87 cm; siehe dazu Liedtke *et al.*, *op. cit.* (Anm. 2), Kat. Nr. 7, S. 225–25, mit Abb.

19  Zu Van Bassens Palastinterieurs siehe Uwe M. Schneede, 'Das repräsentative Gesellschaftsbild in der niederländischen Malerei des 17. Jahrhunderts und seine Grundlagen bei Hans Vredeman de Vries', Diss., Christian-Albrechts-Universität zu Kiel, 1965, S. 95–101 und 178–184.

20  Siehe hierzu die Beiträge des Verfassers zu dem Interieur aus Raleigh (siehe Anm. 18) und zu der *Rückkehr des Verlorenen*

*Sohnes*, Holz, 61.6 × 92.4 cm, Detroit Institute of Arts, im Katalog der holländischen Gemälde des Museums, der für 2004 angekündigt ist.

21   White, *op. cit.* (Anm. 13), S. 18.

22   *Ibid.*, S. 18.

23   *Der Winterkönig Friedrich V. und seine Frau beim Schaumahl*, Holz, 62 × 90 cm, Verbleib unbekannt, zuletzt auf einer Auktion, Christie's, London, 27. März 1974, Nr. 119, Abb.; April 1974 nach Frankreich exportiert. Willem Jan Hoogsteder hat in seiner Magisterarbeit die Sammlung Friedrichs V. und seiner Frau rekonstruiert und ein Bild gefunden, das eine der beiden Versionen Van Bassens sein könnte. Siehe Willem Jan Hoogsteder, 'De Schilderijen van Frederik en Elisabeth, Koning en Koningin van Bohemen', unpubl. Magisterarbeit (*doctoraalscriptie*), 3 Bde., Rijksuniversiteit Utrecht, 1986, I, S. 62, Nr. 11 (Privatsammlung) und S. 63, Nr. 11.2 (Royal Collection).

24   *Karl I.*, *Königin Henrietta Maria und Karl, Prinz von Wales, beim Schaumahl*, signiert und datiert, 1635, Holz, 63.2 × 92.4 cm, Inv. Nr. 294, siehe White, *op. cit.* (Anm. 13), Nr. 87, S. 63. Die unmittelbare Abhängigkeit dieser Komposition von Van Bassens Bild ist ein Indiz, dass Houckgeest tatsächlich bei Van Bassen in die Lehre gegangen ist. Der deutlichste Hinweis auf das Lehrer-Schüler-Verhältnis der beiden Künstler ist eine Radierung Houckgeests nach einem Gemälde Van Bassens. Siehe hierzu Liedtke 1982, *op. cit.* (Anm. 7), S. 30–31. Die Radierung ist bei Liedtke abgebildet als Abb. 10. Die Abhängigkeit der Interieurs voneinander schliesst auch eine Identifikation der Darstellung mit dem Whitehall-Palast in London und dem Palast in Rhenen, wie es in der Vergangenheit gelegentlich vorgeschlagen worden ist, aus.

25   Das Bild wurde am 2. Dezember 2002 im Restaurierungsatelier der National Gallery, London, von Rachel Billinge, Rausing Research Associate, mit Infrarotreflektographie untersucht. Dabei wurde die Apparatur der National Gallery gebraucht: Hamamatsu C2400 Kamera mit einer N2606 Serie Infrarot Vidicon. Die Kamera ist mit einer 36 mm Linse ausgestattet, an die ein Kodak 87A Wratten Filter angebracht ist, um das sichtbare Licht herauszufiltern. Das Infrarotreflektogramm-Mosaik wurde mit dem Computer zusammengestellt unter Zuhilfenahme von Vips-ip Software. Für weitere Informationen zu dieser Software siehe die Vips-Website unter www.vips.ecs.soton.ac.uk. Ich bin Rachel Billinge ausserordentlich dankbar für ihre Hilfe bei diesem Projekt und für die Aufnahmen, die in diesem Artikel abgebildet sind. Ausserdem möchte ich Christopher Lloyd, Surveyor of the Queen's Pictures, danken, der uns das Bild zur Untersuchung zur Verfügung gestellt hat.

26   Die Untersuchung fand am 7. November 2003 im Restaurierungsatelier der Royal Collection in Windsor statt. Mein Dank gebührt Rupert Featherstone, Head of Paintings Conservation Royal Collection, der dies ermöglicht hat. Leider war es bei der Gelegenheit nicht möglich, eine Aufnahme der IRR-Untersuchung anzufertigen. Dies wird hoffentlich zu gegebener Zeit noch nachgeholt werden können.

27   Siehe die Biographie Houckgeests in Giltaij, Jansen, *op. cit.* (Anm. 3), S. 163, und Liedtke *et al.*, *op. cit.* (Anm. 2), S. 292.

28   White, *op. cit.* (Anm. 13), S. 63.

29   Siehe Anm. 27.

30   Siehe z.B. Liedtke *et al.*, *op. cit.* (Anm. 2), Kat. Nrn. 6 und 7.

31   George S. Keyes, *Esaias van de Velde, 1587–1630*, Doornspijk 1984, Abb. 61. Der Vorschlag Whites, dass die Figuren von Esaias van de Velde sein könnten, ist nicht haltbar, da Van de Velde zu diesem Zeitpunkt bereits nicht mehr am Leben war (siehe White, *op. cit.* [Anm. 13], S. 18).

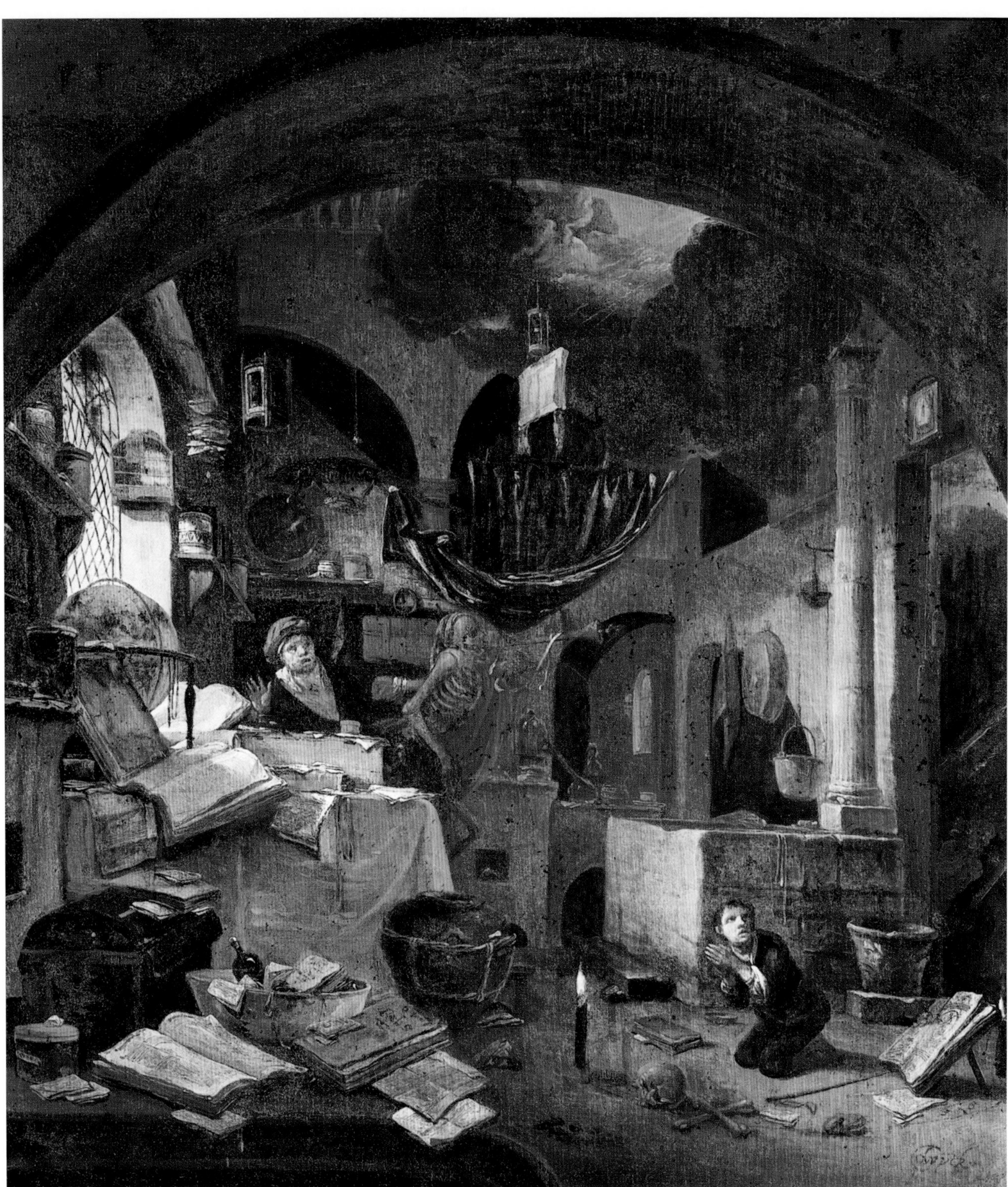

# Seeing Things: *The Alchemist and Death* by Thomas Wyck

JANE RUSSELL CORBETT

The term 'alchemy' has a complex and multi-faceted history and over time it has referred to a wide-range of practices and beliefs. Indeed, it is somewhat mis-leading to speak of alchemy as if it were a very specific enquiry or activity.[1] Both the words 'alchemy' and 'chemistry' were in usage during the seventeenth century, and there has been some confusion among historians of science as to the practices to which these terms referred. The assumption often made that they pertain to different activities, with 'alchemy' concerned specifically with the transmutation of base metal into gold and 'chemistry' to practices more closely related to modern chemistry, is misguided. Rather, there was no sharp boundary between the two and both terms related to a fairly wide range of enquiries, including but not confined to the making of gold.[2] For example, Andreas Libavius's *Alchemia* (Frankfurt 1597) is primarily concerned with the description of various laboratory procedures such as distillation and crystal-lization and has little to say about producing gold.[3] Until at least 1680 the two terms were used synonymously; this was true not only in English but in French, German and, presumably, Dutch as well. Neither word was used exclusively to refer to transmutation.[4]

Early modern alchemists engaged in a wide range of experiments; some believed in the possibility of transmutation, others did not. There were, however, specific terms for certain procedures and types of enquiry, such as 'iatrochemistry' or 'chemiatry' (medical chemistry) and 'spagirics' (the art of separation), but most of these are no longer in use. In other words, the term 'alchemy' was applied to a wide range of activities with various aims and purposes. It included the careful recording of experiments, which eventually led to a great deal of understanding regarding the nature of material substances and ultimately provided the foundation of modern chemistry.

The search for a substance, the 'philosopher's stone', that would make possible the transmutation of base metals into gold was one of the concerns most widely associated with those interested in alchemy. However, not infrequently

Abb. 1 THOMAS WYCK
*The Alchemist and Death*
Oil on panel, 55 × 49 cm
Milwaukee, Wisconsin, collection
of Drs Alfred and Isabel Bader

a certain amount of scepticism was directed at those who were engaged in efforts to make gold. For one thing, such activities were clearly vulnerable to quackery and charlatanism.[5] Secondly, transmutation was also regarded by some critics as a futile and financially risky quest. It comes as no great surprise, therefore, that in literature and in much graphic art the alchemist was presented as a figure of folly.[6] In Chaucer's *The Canon's Yeoman's Tale*, for example, the canon's assistant declares that the attempt to turn base metal into gold "will make us beggars in the end".[7]

Interest in alchemy was at an all-time high in seventeenth-century Europe. The invention of the printing press in the fifteenth century had played an important role in the dissemination of alchemical information. This had continued well into the seventeenth century, by which time almost all of the most significant alchemical treatises were available in print, many of them in collected editions. It was only in the Netherlands, however, that the alchemist at work in his laboratory became a common subject for painters. This is a consequence of two factors: first, the importance of so-called genre scenes, or scenes of everyday life, in Netherlandish art; secondly, the existence of a graphic tradition dealing with the theme. The best-known independent depiction in the visual arts of the alchemist as fool is the engraving of 1558 (fig. 2) attributed to Philips Galle (1537–1612) after a drawing in pen and brown ink by Pieter Bruegel the Elder (1525/30–1569) which was subsequently published by Hieronymus Cock (*ca.* 1510–1570). As far as is known, Bruegel's drawing was not only the earliest known Netherlandish depiction of an alchemist, but also the progenitor of satirical treatments of the theme in the visual arts. The engraving after the drawing enjoyed great popularity and the image was published in five or more different series. Moreover, it gave rise to other graphic depictions of alchemists at work in subsequent years.

Seventeenth-century painters took up the theme and adapted it in such a way as to exploit its pictorial and iconographic possibilities. The popularity of the theme in painting is a corollary of the general interest in alchemy in the seventeenth century. Depictions of alchemists flourished in certain centres; artists associated with Antwerp in the south and Haarlem in the north show the most interest in the subject. Although many commentators stress that the satirical treatment that characterized most of the earlier graphic depictions of alchemists is either significantly weakened or altogether absent in the seventeenth-century paintings, this change can be overstated. In many of the paintings the biting satire is replaced by a gentler form of didacticism. For example, in the numerous paintings of alchemists produced by the Flemish artist David Teniers the Younger (1610–1690), objects associated with the idea of *vanitas* are often displayed prominently. Other artists, such as the

Haarlemers Cornelis Bega (1631–1664) and Hendrick Heerschop (*ca.* 1620/21–after 1672), emphasize the poverty of the alchemist by showing him with bared knee. Moreover, some artists, such as Adriaen van Ostade (1610–1685) and Jan Steen (1626–1679) retain the overtly satirical depiction of the alchemist that characterizes Bruegel's drawing.[8]

In Haarlem, paintings of alchemists reached a height of popularity in the 1660s. Among the artists based there who dealt with the subject, Thomas Wyck (*ca.* 1616–1677) was certainly the most prolific.[9] Wyck travelled to Italy quite early in his career and is now perhaps best known for his numerous Italianate scenes of markets and courtyards as well as some landscapes.[10] However, in the later years of his life he turned to producing genre pictures with a Dutch style and subject matter. It is to this period that his alchemist paintings can be dated.[11] Many of them show only minor variations. The majority depict a middle-aged, bearded man seated at a desk; he is usually reading, but occasionally is shown writing or in contemplation with his head resting on his hand (fig. 3). His desk, like the entire room, is overflowing with books and manuscripts. Light pours into the room from a leaded-glass window at the left or the back wall. Recurring motifs, in addition to books and various containers, include a large globe, a bird-cage near the window, pieces of paper strung together, suspended stuffed lizards and fish, and a portrait on the wall. An arched ceiling usually frames the upper portion of the scene. These works blend aspects of the theme of the alchemist with that of the solitary scholar and they are often entitled *Alchemist in his Study* rather than *Alchemist in his Laboratory*. There is less interest in actual alchemical experiment than in many other paintings of alchemists at work. Indeed, the viewer sometimes must search the room to find evidence of alchemical experiments![12]

Wyck did produce some alchemist subjects that depart significantly from this pattern,[13] but one painting in particular stands out quite remarkably from all the others: *The Alchemist and Death* (fig. 1). A sense of the supernatural permeates this picture, the most unusual of Wyck's treatments of the theme. A boy, standing behind a desk, holds his hand up in a startled gesture. He is joined by an even younger boy shown kneeling on the floor, apparently praying before a lit candle, and a skull and cross-bones. An opened book is propped up on a stand beside him. The figure of Death, a skeleton blowing a trumpet, is behind the youths but cannot be the only cause of their alarm because both of them look towards the upper right at something not shown in the picture, with expressions that combine surprise and fear. The architectural features of the room differ from those normally shown. While the archway framing the upper portion of the picture as well as the leaded glass window at the left regularly appear in Wyck's alchemist pictures, the classical column at the right and the additional

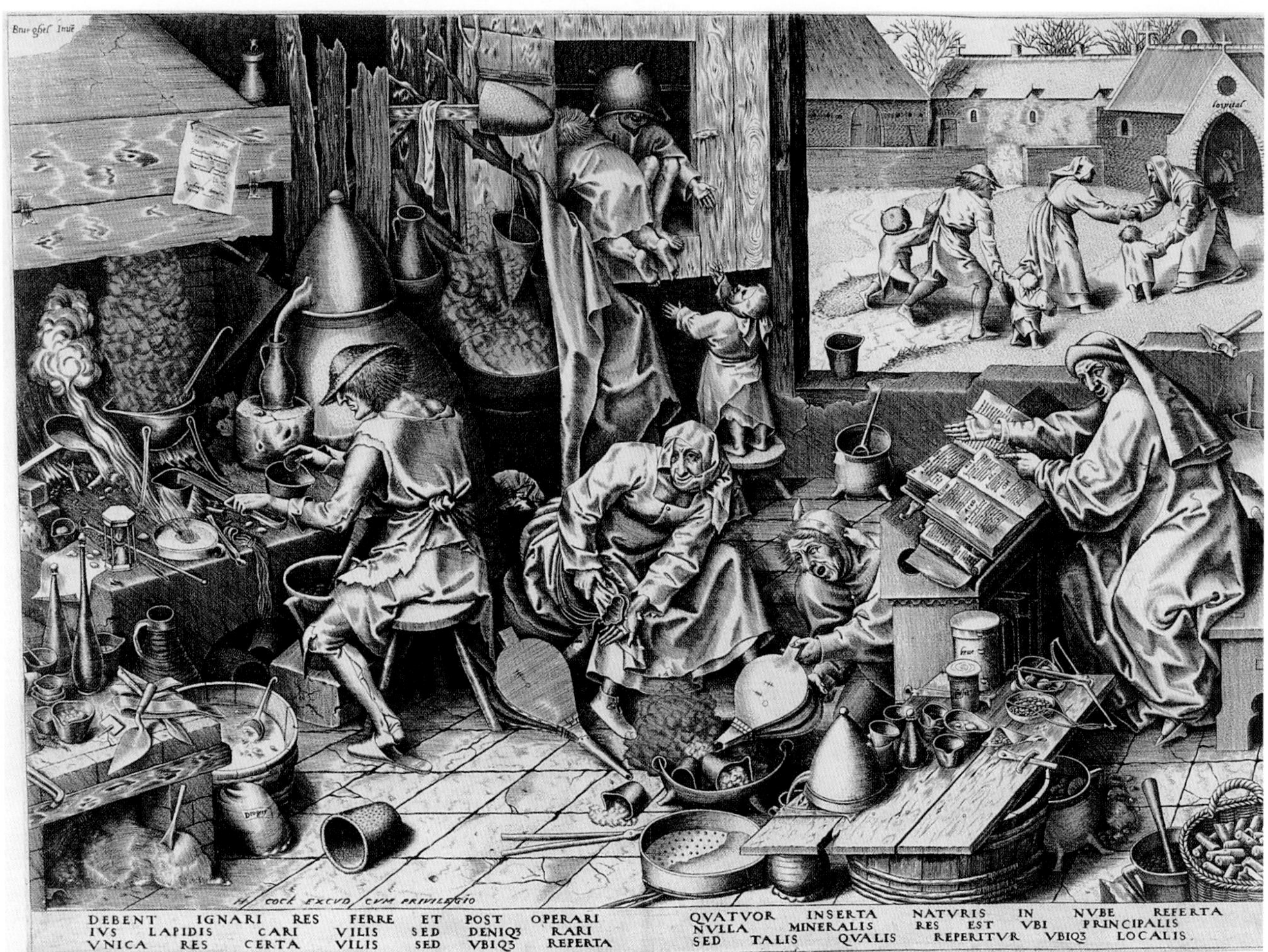



fig. 2  Attributed to PHILIPS GALLE after PIETER BRUEGEL THE ELDER
*The Alchemist*
Engraving, 34.2 × 44.9 cm
London, The British Museum

arched recesses at the back of the room do not. Moreover, there is a lack of coherence in the setting. The moon, glowing in a dramatically lit sky, shines into the room from a curious aperture in the ceiling, while a bright light enters through the opened window at the left.

The *Alchemist and Death* is a puzzling painting. It is by no means clear, first of all, that the startled figure standing behind the desk represents an alchemist, because not only does he bear little resemblance to the stock character repeated in the majority of Wyck's alchemy scenes, but he appears to be only a boy of about twelve years of age. Given his youth, it seems more likely that this is an alchemist's young assistant. The opened text, lit candle, skull and cross-bones arranged in a circle suggest the possibility that the kneeling boy is conjuring up a spell. The subject is further complicated by the presence of Death in the background. The portrayal of Death as an animated skeleton has a long history in the visual arts. It is often shown holding a scythe or an hourglass, suggesting time, and appears frequently in northern European allegories depicting young women or couples. In these images the presence of the skeleton is a reminder of the brevity of feminine beauty and of earthly life itself. Skeletons also appear in depictions of the *Dance of Death* or *Danse macabre*, the best known of which is the woodcut series designed by Hans Holbein the Younger (before 1526). Indeed, a skeleton playing on a Roman trumpet similar to that in Wyck's painting can be seen in *A Cemetery*, the fifth woodcut of the series. However, it is most unusual to find it in a painting that in other respects appears to be a genre scene.[14] Since Death as a skeleton also appears in scenes of the Last Judgment, where it is shown climbing out of a tomb or the earth, it seems possible that Wyck is making a reference here to the end of time.[15] The book that hangs from the ceiling in the painting may represent the Book of the Apocalypse with the seven seals described in the Book of Revelation: "And I saw in the right hand of him who was seated on the throne a scroll written within and on the back, sealed with seven seals; and I saw a strong angel proclaiming with a loud voice, 'Who is worthy to open the scroll and break its seals?'" (Revelation 5:1–2).[16]

The relationship between alchemical thought and religion is perhaps the most difficult aspect of the history of alchemy. Inevitably, religious issues had always informed alchemical practice to a greater or lesser degree, but there is reason to believe that they became particularly significant towards the end of the sixteenth century, when alchemy began to break down into two main branches. Bearing in mind the complexity of alchemical practice, to suggest just two 'groups' is something of a simplification.[17] But, with this *caveat*, one can talk about a significant difference in terms of the kind of questions practitioners were trying to answer.[18] One group was primarily interested in the application of chemistry to medicine ('iatrochemistry'); the other was interested in how chemical understanding could inform broader questions regarding the nature of the universe and particularly the macrocosm-microcosm relationship (a concept that was key to Paracelsus [*ca.* 1493–1541], for example).[19] Ultimately the latter were dealing with religious issues and we can refer to them as spiritual alchemists to distinguish them from those primarily interested in experimental alchemy.

Not surprisingly, in the early modern period much alchemical symbolism overlapped with Christian symbolism. Alchemical processes were often understood as cyclical in nature, involving creation, death and resurrection. The idea that new life was preceded by death and putrefaction was common. Moreover, it was supported by biblical text: "Except a corn of wheat fall into the ground and die, it abideth alone: but if it die, it bringeth forth much fruit" (John 12: 24). Thus, alchemical processes could be understood as analogous to Christian concepts of creation, purification and re-incarnation. Similarly, the result of the alchemical process was often linked to the end of time. During the sixteenth century many Protestants regarded the Reformation as a kind of purification of the Church, a necessary development which would lead precipitously to the Second Coming of Christ.[20] This idea was given explicit expression by Martin Luther (1483–1546):

> The science of alchymy I like very well, and, indeed, 'tis the philosophy of the ancients. I like it not only for the profits it brings in melting metals, in decocting, preparing, extracting and distilling herbs, roots; I like it also for the sake of the allegory and secret signification, which is exceedingly fine, touching the resurrection of the dead at the last day. For, as in a furnace the fire extracts and separates from a substance the other portions, and carries upward the spirit, the life, the sap, the strength, while the unclean matter, the dregs, remain at the bottom, like a dead and worthless carcass; even so God, at the day of judgment, will separate all things through fire, the righteous from the ungodly. The Christians and righteous shall ascend upwards into Heaven, and there live everlastingly, but the wicked and the ungodly, as the dross and filth, shall remain in Hell, and there be damned.[21]

By the seventeenth century there was a growing fatigue with religious disputes, and, in some quarters, a move away from religious dogmatism. By studying the natural world, the Book of Nature, many found a way to give expression to religious feeling. After the Reformation many of those who took up alchemy were particularly drawn to its mystical and spiritual side rather than to the more practical aspects involving laboratory experimentation. Efforts were made to determine a chemical explanation for Creation. This phenomenon

fig. 3 THOMAS WYCK
*The Laboratory of an Alchemist*
Oil on panel, 42.4 × 35.7 cm
Cassel, Staatliche Museen Kassel,
Gemäldegalerie Alte Meister

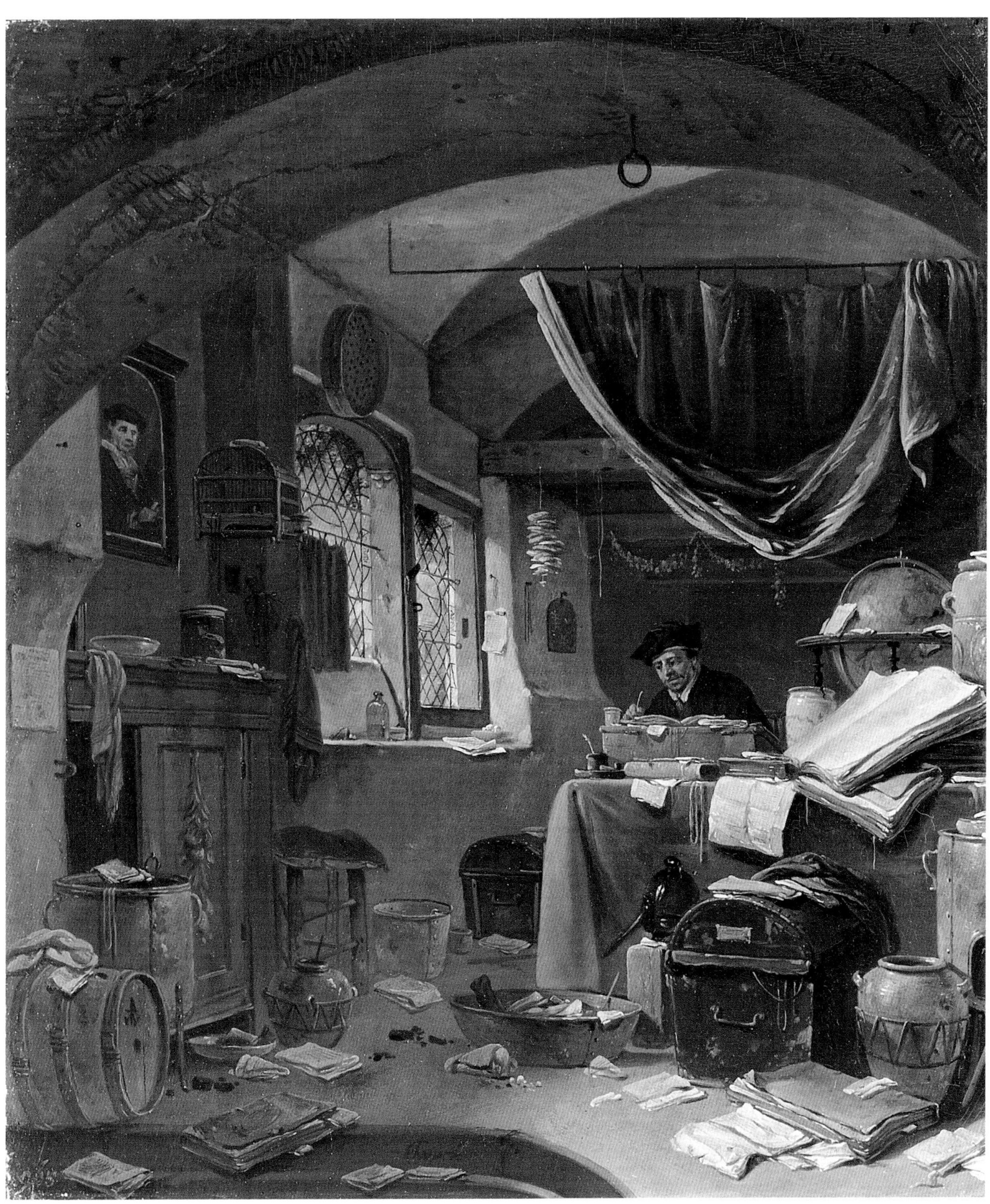

was one aspect of a general late sixteenth-century mystical movement which included alchemists, astrologers, cabalists and various other individuals interested in hermeticism.[22]

Given the extent to which *The Alchemist and Death* differs not only from the majority of Wyck's alchemist subjects, but from depictions of the theme in general, it is probable that it was painted for a particular patron rather than for the open market. Moreover, it is quite likely that it was painted for an English client. Wyck went to England around the time of the Restoration and seems to have remained there for some time.[23] Quite a few of his paintings of alchemists appear to have been produced during his stay there. For example, John Maitland, Duke of Lauderdale (1616–1682) and his duchess acquired some paintings by Wyck about 1673 or 1674, one of which was an alchemist in his laboratory.[24] Horace Walpole (1717–1797), the English antiquarian, thought that it was with alchemist subjects that Wyck excelled; certainly the great number of them attests at least to their popularity.[25] After the Restoration in 1660 an increasing number of paintings by foreign artists entered England from the Continent.[26] This may be partially due to the fact that many Royalists developed a taste for foreign art while in exile during the Civil War.[27] Certainly Charles II (1630–1685) is known to have admired the meticulous brushwork of Gerrit Dou (1613–1675), and to have tried, unsuccessfully, to entice the Dutch *fijnschilder* to the English court.[28]

If his interest in Dutch genre painting is well established, Charles II's role in supporting and advancing the interests of experimental science has not always been adequately recognized by historians of science. Not only did he grant the charter by which the Royal Society was incorporated in 1662, but he had a personal interest in scientific research, as his alchemical laboratory in Whitehall reflected.[29] Indeed, under his reign, interest in experimental science became quite fashionable among members of his court and the aristocracy, several of whom participated in the Royal Society's experiments. For example, the Scottish courtier and administrator Sir Robert Moray (1608–1673) served as the acting first president of the Society between 1660 and 1662. Moray had established a large chemical laboratory while living in exile in Maastricht, and after the Restoration he was in charge of Charles II's laboratory.[30]

Given this interest in experimental science and the new enthusiasm for Dutch genre painting, it is possible that Wyck's paintings of alchemists were quite popular with members of the English aristocracy. Certainly that was the opinion of the eighteenth-century engraver and antiquarian George Vertue (1684–1756). Vertue, Walpole relates, "supposed ingeniously" that Wyck's alchemist pictures "were in compliment to the fashion at court, Charles II and Prince Rupert having each their laboratory".[31]

While it is difficult to interpret *The Alchemist and Death* with any degree of precision, the supernatural subject-matter suggests that it was concerned with spiritual alchemy, in which there was a good deal of interest in seventeenth-century England.[32] On the one hand the presence of Death with the trumpet, the suspended, sealed book and the dramatic, fiery sky suggest a reference to the account of the Apocalypse or the end of time in the Book of Revelation. On the other, the child praying on the floor with the skull, cross-bones and lit candle is engaged in casting some kind of spell. It is not surprising that references to Christian belief should be combined with depictions of magical practice; in the seventeenth century the two could still comfortably coexist. As the historian Keith Thomas has pointed out, when magicians summoned supernatural beings, they were engaged in a religious rite, one in which prayer was a necessary element.[33] And, most importantly from the point of view of Wyck's painting, both piety and purity were considered essential for success. For example, in a deposition made in Southampton in 1631 a William Nutley is reported to have stated that "When a spirit is raised none hath power to see it but children of eleven and twelve years of age, or such as are true maids".[34] Similarly, George L. Kittredge noted that in the magical practice of crystal-gazing or mirror-magic, the screyer "was regularly a young boy, for the doctrine was that certain demons or angels – their character was equivocal – could not or would not manifest themselves except to the pure alone".[35] Since, unusually for Wyck, the middle-aged alchemist is replaced with two young boys, it is quite possible that it is to such a belief that Wyck refers in the painting known as *The Alchemist and Death*.

1 To a great extent the current problems involved in understanding those activities contained by the broad term 'alchemy' can be related to the prevalence of attitudes which have their root in the nineteenth century. At that time there was a kind of revival of interest in what might be called the spiritual aspects of alchemy. Later, the psychological interpretation of alchemy developed by Carl Jung reinforced the idea that alchemy was something separate from physical chemistry. See Lawrence M. Principe and William R. Newman, 'Some Problems with the Historiography of Alchemy', in *Secrets of Nature: Astrology and Alchemy in Early Modern Europe*, ed. William R. Newman and Anthony Grafton Cambridge, Mass., 2001, pp. 385–431. This issue is also addressed by Robert M. Schuler in 'Spiritual Alchemies of Seventeenth-Century England', *The Journal of the History of Ideas*, XLI, 1980, pp. 293–94. The term is used in this paper with the understanding that it refers to a wide range of attitudes and activities.

2 William R. Newman and Lawrence M. Principe, 'Alchemy vs. Chemistry: the Etymological Origins of a Historiographic Mistake', *Early Science and Medicine*, II, 1998, pp. 32–65, and Ferdinando Abbu, "Alchemy and Chemistry: Chemical Discourses in the Seventeenth Century', *Early Science and Medicine*, V, 2000, pp. 214–27.

3 Newman and Principe, *op. cit.* (note 2), p. 38.

4 Interestingly, though, unlike English, German or French, Dutch has retained both "chemie" and "scheikunde" to refer to chemistry, and it is the latter, which means the art of separation, that is most commonly used. J.W. van Spronsen, 'The Beginning of Chemistry', in *Leiden University in the Seventeenth Century: An Exchange of Learning*, ed. Th. H. Lunsingh Scheurleer and G.H.M. Posthumous Meyjes, Leiden 1975, p. 328. In their *100 Verbeeldingen van Ambachten* (Amsterdam 1694) Johannes and Caspaares Luiken include an illustration of a man working in a laboratory outfitted with chemical apparatus under the title *De Scheider*.

5 Pope John XXII (1316–34) issued a decree in 1317 against alchemy ostensibly in response to the amount of counterfeit gold being manufactured by charlatans, and it was completely banned by Charles V of France (1338–1380) in 1380. Other prohibitions were to follow in England and Venice: Henry IV (1367–1413) banned the practice of alchemy in 1404 as did the council of Venice in 1418.

6 Sebastian Brant (*ca.* 1457–1521) criticized the deceit that was so often associated with alchemists in the chapter entitled 'Of Falsity and Deception' in his *Narrenschiff* (1494). A woodcut illustration of an alchemist by an anonymous assistant of Albrecht Dürer (1471–1528) accompanies this chapter in the first edition of the book, published in Basle in 1494. See Sebastian Brant, *The Ship of Fools (Das Narrenschiff)*, translated by Edwin H. Zeydel, New York 1944, pp. 327–30; illustration p. 327. Petrarch (1304–1374) criticized both the charlatanism and the folly associated with alchemy in one of the dialogues in *Remedies for Fortune Fair and Foul (De Remediis utriusque Fortune, 1366)*. A woodcut illustration of an alchemist was included in a 1532 German edition printed in Augsburg. For some time this woodcut was attributed to the artist Hans Weiditz (before 1500–*ca.* 1536), but since the early twentieth century the artist has been referred to simply as the Petrarch 'Master'. This image is significant because it appears to be the first effort by an artist to depict in some detail an alchemical laboratory. It is illustrated in G. Friederich Hartlaub, *Kunst und Magie: Gesammelte Aufsätze*, ed. Norbert Miller, Hamburg 1991, p. 176, and A.A.A.M. Brinkman, 'Der Petrarca Meister' and 'Brueghel's Alchemist and its influence, in particular on Jan Steen', in A.A.A.M. Brinkman, *De Alchemist in de Prentkunst*, Amsterdam 1982, pp. 12 and 45 respectively.

7 Geoffrey Chaucer, 'The Canon's Assistant's Tale', in *The Canterbury Tales*, translated by David Wright, Oxford 1985, p. 430. Alchemy was also condemned for religious reasons, particularly during the

 JANE RUSSELL CORBETT

medieval period. See Roslynn D. Haynes, *From Faust to Strangelove: Representations of the Scientist in Western Literature*, Baltimore 1994, pp. 10–11. Later, most Calvinist and Puritan clergy criticized alchemy. See Keith Thomas, *Religion and the Decline of Magic*, Harmondsworth 1971, p. 321. Martin Luther, however, who condemned astrology, was quite sympathetic to alchemy, as will be discussed later.

8  On Bruegel's drawing see Charles de Tolnay, *The Drawings of Pieter Bruegel the Elder*, London 1952, no. 56, plate 56, and Matthias Winner, 'Zu Bruegels "Alchimist"', in *Pieter Bruegel und seine Welt, ein Colloquium*, ed. Otto von Simson and Matthias Winner, Berlin 1979, pp. 193–202. On the print see F.W.H. Hollstein, *Dutch and Flemish Etchings, Engravings and Woodcuts, ca. 1450–1700*, 57 vols., Amsterdam 1949–2001, III, p. 296, no. 197; René van Bastelaer, *The Prints of Peter Bruegel the Elder*, translated and revised by Susan Fargo Gilchrist, San Francisco 1992, pp. 263–67, nos. 197 and 198; and Peter Dreyer, 'Bruegels Alchimist von 1558: Versuch einer Deutung *ad sensus mysticum*', *Jahrbuch der Berliner Museen*, XIX–XXII, 1977, pp. 69–113. On the influence of the print see Jacques van Lennep, 'L'Alchimiste', *Revue Belge d'Archéologie et de l'histoire de l'art*, XXXV, 1966, pp. 152–53 and A.A.A.M. Brinkman, 'Breugel's Alchemist and its influence in particular on Jan Steen', in Brinkman, *op. cit.* (note 6), p. 44. To my knowledge, the earliest dated painting of an alchemist at work produced in the Netherlands is *The Alchemist* by Cornelis Saftleven (1631, panel, 49.2 × 74.2 cm, De Boer, Amsterdam). It is very much indebted to Bruegel's drawing, and is the only known Netherlandish painting of an alchemist which includes in the background the later episode in the life of the alchemist and his family in which they are shown approaching the poorhouse, as depicted in Bruegel's drawing.

9  While Arnold Houbraken gives 1616 as Wyck's year of birth, no documents have been found substantiating this. Arnold Houbraken, *De Groote Schouburgh der Nederlantsche Konstschilders en Schilderessen* [Amsterdam 1718–21] 3 vols., Maastricht 1943–53, II, p. 325. On Wyck see Bernhard Schnackenburg, 'Die Anfänge von Thomas Adriaensz. Wyck (um 1620–1677) als Zeichner und Maler', *Oud Holland*, CVI, 1992, pp. 143–56.

10  Wyck is known to have returned to the Netherlands by 1642, as he was registered in St Luke's guild in Haarlem in that year.

11  Although Wyck signed most of his paintings he was not in the habit of dating them.

12  The collection of the Gemäldegalerie Alte Meister at Kassel has three of Wyck's alchemy pictures that conform to this general pattern. See Bernhard Schnackenburg, *Staatliche Museen Kassel: Gemäldegalerie Alte Meister, Gesamtkatalog*, 2 vols., Mainz 1996, I, p. 333, nos. GK 332, GK 333, GK 334, illustrated II, plates 140 and 141. Arnold Houbraken praised Wyck's alchemy scenes, noting that they were "alle zoogestig van hem bedacht, konstig geschikt, vast geteekent, vet, toetzende, en gloeijende geschildert zyn, dat dezelve konst een hooger prys verdient, dan zy thans gelden mag" [all conceived by him in such a lively way, artistically composed, solidly drawn, thickly painted, in touches and glowing, that this art deserves a price higher than it presently receives]: Houbraken, *op. cit.* (note 9), II, p. 14.

13  There is a curious work in the collection of the Marquess of Salisbury entitled *Philosopher Punishing an Intruder* (panel, 40 × 34.3 cm, Hatfield House) which depicts the same type of room with objects similar to those shown in the alchemist scenes (globe, suspended lizard, manuscripts, and containers of various types) but in which the man is shown standing, holding an opened book in one hand while lifting up a stick as if about to strike a young boy kneeling before him. See Erna Auerbach, C. Kingsley Adams, *Paintings and Sculpture at Hatfield House*, London 1971, p. 237, no. 358; illustrated p. 307. In contrast to the suggested violence of this painting are those versions in which Wyck includes

the alchemist's wife tending to an infant as her husband works; an atmosphere of calm pervades these scenes.

14 There is, however, at least one other painting of alchemists with the figure of Death: Pieter Quast, *Alchemists at Work, visited by Death and by Beggars*, copper, 20 × 29 cm, location unknown).

15 The trumpet often symbolizes death and the seven angels present at the Last Judgment hold trumpets. (It should be noted, however, that according to one author trumpets in alchemical texts often proclaim the arrival of a supernatural being: Rowena and Rupert Shepherd, *1000 Symbols*, London 2002, p. 300.

16 See Volker Manuth *et al.*, *Wisdom, Knowledge and Magic, The Image of the Scholar in Seventeenth-Century Dutch Art*, exh. cat., Agnes Etherington Art Centre, Kingston, Ontario, 1996, p. 88, no. 37 (entry by Dianna Beaufort).

17 This is based primarily on Allen Debus's discussion in Allen G. Debus, *The Chemical Philosophy: Paracelsian Science and Medicine in the Sixteenth and Seventeenth Centuries*, 2 vols., New York 1977, I, pp. 205–06. See also Stanton J. Linden, 'Alchemy and Eschatology in Seventeenth-Century Poetry', *Ambix*, XXXI, 1984, p. 103. While it is an assumption held by several historians of chemistry it is undoubtedly a simplification of a very complex issue. Principe and Newman criticize this position and identify the source of the idea in the work of Carl Jung: Principe and Newman, *op. cit.* (note 2), pp. 407–08. The present author, while acknowledging the problem, holds that there is sufficient evidence to support the generalization as such.

18 This trend in alchemy reflected a general shift in the early modern period regarding what kind of questions were asked by those engaged in natural philosophy. There was a move away from more holistic questions to much more specific ones; from questions such as 'What is matter?' to 'What makes blood flow through the veins?' Victor F. Weisskopf, 'Art and Science', in Boris Otovic *et al.*, *Universitas: Art from the Collection of the University of Copenhagen*, Copenhagen 1996, pp. 38–39.

19 It must be pointed out, however, that Paracelsus and many of his followers, such as the Flemish physician Johan van Helmont (1577–1644), combined an interest in medical alchemy with religious and philosophical concerns.

20 Betty Jo Teeter Dobbs, *Alchemical Death and Resurrection: The Significance of Alchemy in the Age of Newton*, in *Science, Pseudo-Science, and Utopianism in Early Modern Thought*, ed. Stephen A. McKnight, Columbia, Mo., 1992, pp. 69–70.

21 Martin Luther, *Table Talk*, translated and edited by William Hazlitt, London 1857, p. 326. See also Betty Jo Teeter Dobbs, *op. cit.* (note 20), p. 72.

22 Betty Jo Teeter Dobbs, *The Foundations of Newton's Alchemy; or 'The Hunting of the Greene Lyon'*, Cambridge 1975, pp. 57–60.

23 According to Lindsay Stainton and Christopher White, Wyck was definitely in London by 1665, as he produced a drawing of the Waterhouse with Old St Paul's in the background. The Waterhouse was destroyed in 1665 and Old St Paul's succumbed to the Great Fire of London in 1666, a disaster which Wyck depicted in more than one picture. Stainton and White suggest that he arrived in England around 1663: Lindsay Stainton, Christopher White, *Drawing in England from Hilliard to Hogarth*, exh. cat., British Museum, London, 1987, p. 119, nos. 83 and 84.

24 P.K. Thornton, M. Tomlin, *The Furnishing and Decoration of Ham House*, London 1980, pp. 66 and 76; illustration fig. 75. Harry T. Mount suggests that Wyck was in England until about 1673, no doubt on the basis of the paintings by him acquired around that time by the Duke of Lauderdale: Harry T. Mount, 'The Reception of Dutch Genre Painting in England, 1695–1829', diss., University of Cambridge, 1991, p. 234.

25 Horace Walpole, *Anecdotes of Painting in England*, 4 vols., New York 1969, II, p. 234. These pictures were also praised by Houbraken: see the quotation given in note 12.

26 Mount, *op. cit.* (note 24), p. 16. On the basis of his survey of Dutch and Flemish

genre paintings in English sales catalogues between 1689 and 1692, Mount lists 15 paintings of alchemists and 18 of "conjurors" and or Faust: *ibid.*, p. 235.

27 *Ibid.*, pp. 16–17.

28 According to Arnold Houbraken, Dou refused Charles II's invitation either because court life did not suit his personality, or because his friends advised him against it: Houbraken, *op. cit.* (note 9), III, p. 25.

29 The Royal Society was founded in 1660. On Charles II's interest in scientific matters see Simon Werrett, 'Healing the Nation's Wounds: Royal Ritual and Experimental Philosophy in Restoration England', *History of Science*, XXXVIII, 2000, pp. 377–99, and Stephen Coote, *Royal Survivor: A Life of Charles II*, London 1999, pp. 258–59.

30 Werrett, *op. cit.* (note 29), pp. 385–86, and Lisa Jardine, *On a Grander Scale: The Outstanding Career of Sir Christopher Wren*, London 2002, pp. 114–15. Charles's cousin, Prince Rupert (1619–1682), also had an alchemical laboratory.

31 Walpole, *op. cit.* (note 25), II, p. 234, and George Vertue, *Vertue Note Books*, vol. V, *Walpole Society*, XXVI, 1937–38, p. 43.

32 For example, the antiquarian and founding member of the Royal Society, Elias Ashmole (1617–1692), who had strong connections with the royal court, combined an interest in experimental science with hermeticism: *Elias Ashmole (1617–92), His Autobiographical and Historical Notes, his Correspondence, and Other Contemporary Sources Relating to his Life and Work*, ed. Conrad Hermann Josten, 7 vols., Oxford 1966, I, 'Biographical Introduction', pp. 130–47. Ashmole was responsible for the immensely influential *Theatrum Chemicum Britannicum* (1651), a collection of annotated fourteenth- to sixteenth-century English alchemical texts. This interest in hermeticism and magic appears not to have been associated with any particular religious denomination or group. Robert Schuler identifies three different manuscripts that link an interest in spiritual alchemy to moderate Anglicans, orthodox Calvinists and radical Puritans respectively: Schuler, *op. cit.* (note 1), pp. 293–318. See also Charles Webster, *From Paracelsus to Newton: Magic and the Making of Modern Science*, Cambridge 1982, especially pp. 48–74, and Thomas, *op. cit.* (note 7), pp. 264–71, on magical practice in England during the seventeenth century.

33 Thomas, *op. cit.* (note 7), pp. 319–20.

34 *Ibid.*, p. 320; *The Book of Examinations and Depositions, 1622–44*, ed. R.C. Anderson, 4 vols., Southampton 1929–36, II (1931), pp. 104–05.

35 George Lyman Kittredge, *Witchcraft in Old and New England*, Cambridge, Mass., 1929, p. 185.

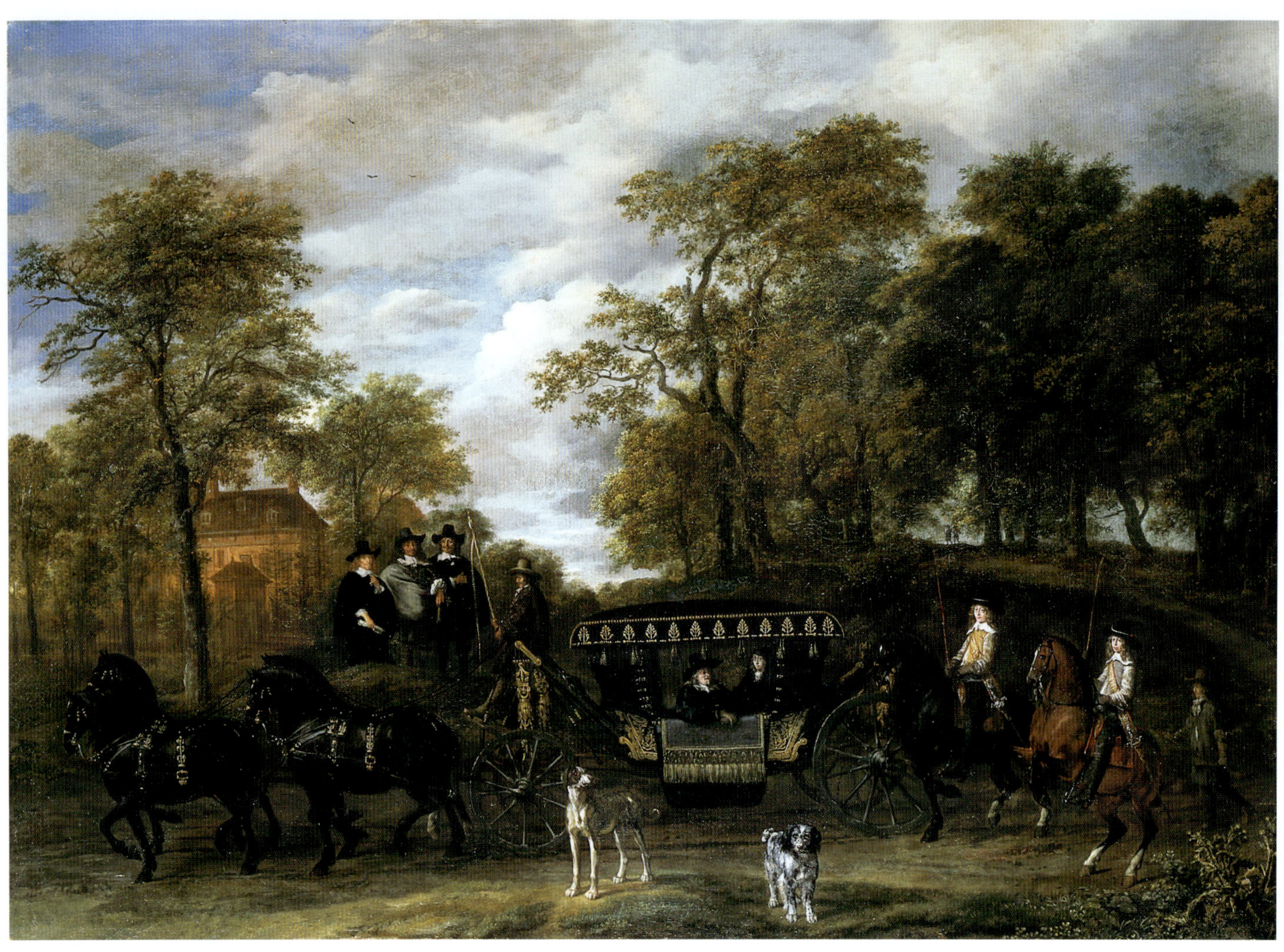

# Jacob van Ruisdael's Clientele

SEYMOUR SLIVE

When we recall that in our time more than eight hundred works by Jacob van Ruisdael (1628/29–1682) have been identified, it is astonishing to consider that virtually nothing at all is known about the way they were acquired by his contemporaries. We can only guess if he kept a stock on hand to sell directly to clients or worked through dealers – of course there is no reason to maintain he did not do both.

The ground is a wee bit firmer when we consider his commissions. At least one patron's name is known. He was the extremely wealthy and powerful Amsterdam burgomaster Cornelis de Graeff (1599–1664), Heer van Zuidpolsbroek, Purmerland and Ilpendam. Ruisdael's effort for him can be spotted in the National Gallery of Ireland's painting of de Graeff and members of his family arriving at Soestdijk, his country estate about fifteen kilometers from Utrecht (fig. 1).[1] The picture, however, is not solely by Ruisdael. It is a collaboration between him and Thomas de Keyser (1596/97–1667), the leading Amsterdam portraitist before Rembrandt arrived there in the early 1630s. De Keyser did the lion's share of the group portrait, which qualifies as an early example of a conversation piece – the prominent figures, the richly appointed carriage, the horses and dogs. Ruisdael was responsible for the landscape and country house in the background. The ages of the family members portrayed as well as the style of the figures and landscape date the picture about 1660, three or four years after Ruisdael moved from his native Haarlem and settled in the principal metropolis of the Netherlands.

De Graeff played a key role in his city's and the new republic's politics. Indeed, during the last decades of his life he was the guiding political force in Amsterdam and the close advisor and confidant of Johan de Witt (1625–1672), Holland's leading statesman; but no attention is called to these aspects of his life in the artists' joint effort.

In 1660, about the time the picture was painted, Joost van den Vondel (1587–1679), the pre-eminent seventeenth-century Dutch poet, published his verse translation of Virgil's *Aeneid*, which he dedicated to De Graeff. In *Parnasloof*, the work's dedicatory poem, Vondel wrote that De Graeff sought welcome

fig. 1 JACOB VAN RUISDAEL
*The Arrival of Cornelis de Graeff and Members of his Family at Soestdijk, his Country Estate, ca.* 1660
Oil on canvas, 118.2 × 170.5 cm
Dublin, National Gallery of Ireland

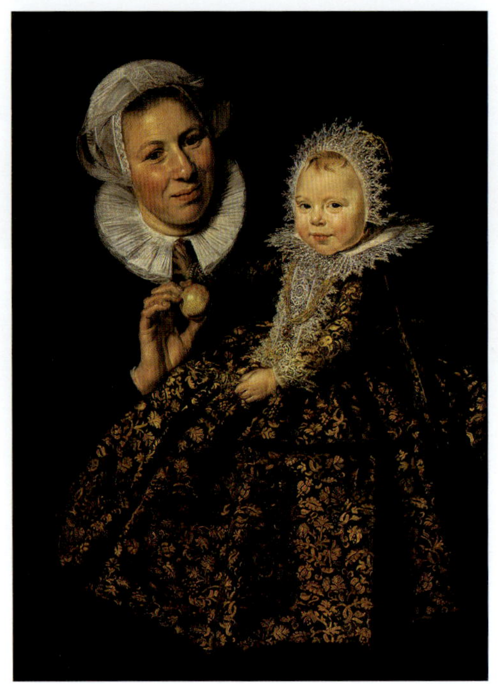



relaxation in Soestdijk's bucolic setting after slaving day and night at the service of his city and country in the burgomasters' chamber of Amsterdam's town hall.[2] De Graeff must have felt equally at home in the glorious New Town Hall. It was not only the seat of his power. He was a member of the committee that planned its programme and served on the one that selected Jacob van Campen (1595–1657) as its architect. He also gave financial support for its construction and composed the inscription on the panel in its high court chamber that commemorates the laying of its cornerstone.

The Dublin picture shows De Graeff in his carriage (monograms that include the letter G are employed in its decoration) with his second wife Catharina Hooft (1618–1691). Their two sons follow behind on horseback: first Pieter (1638–1707) and then Jacob (1642–90).[3] The latter son inherited Soestdijk from his father and, in turn, sold it to the stadholder Willem III, later William III, King of England (1650–1702). A Dutch royal palace still stands at Soestdijk.

As for the painting, it found a home in Pieter de Graeff's Ilpendam manor, a seigniory (*heerlijkheid*) the elder son inherited from his father. In 1670, among the notes he made in his East India Company (V.O.C.) almanac regarding the few pictures he had at the estate, he gave the painting's dimensions and described it as a landscape by De Keyser of Soestdijk, with his late father, his state carriage and a few other portraits.[4] Pieter did not say a word about Ruisdael's contribution.

Neither De Keyser nor Ruisdael is mentioned by the compiler of the 1691 estate inventory of Catharina Hooft, Pieter's mother; at the time of her death the picture was mounted in Ilpendam's salon called the *Johan de Wittzaal*.[5] The



SEYMOUR SLIVE

sympathetic double portrait by Frans Hals (*ca.* 1581/85–1666) of a nurse and a young child (fig. 2), now in Berlin, was displayed in the same room. Like the Dublin portrait it is a family portrait; Hals's picture is a portrayal of Catharina Hooft, about the age of two, with her nurse[6] – perhaps the double portrait was part of young Catharina's dowry when she married Cornelis de Graeff in 1635. And like the Dublin painting, Hals's double portrait was inherited by Pieter – according to Dutch custom, family portraits normally pass to the eldest son.

In 1709, two years after Pieter's death, inventories were made of his effects at Ilpendam manor and his grand home on the Herengracht in Amsterdam. The Dublin painting was still in the manor, described in an inventory, without mention of either of its artists, as in the *Roozaal*:

> 1 large painting with portraits of the late Burgomaster Cornelis
> de Graeff, his wife, and two sons.[7]

The posthumous inventory made of Pieter's effects in his Amsterdam home tells us that he owned two additional depictions by Ruisdael of de Graeff estates:

> One painting of Zuidpolsbroek by Jacob Ruijsdael    36 guilders
> One ditto of Soestdijk                        36 guilders[8]

These paintings are now unidentified or untraceable, but they, as well as the Dublin picture, offer a precious clue to a category of commissions Rusidael received. They establish that at least one family owned views by Jacob van Ruisdael of their properties. It is evident that the de Graeff family had a penchant for views of this type. In addition to those by Ruisdael, Pieter de Graeff's 1709 inventory lists almost a dozen others, including two by Isaac de Moucheron (1667–1744) – one of Ilpendam, the other of Zuidpolsbroek.[9]

No monetary appraisal is given in Pieter de Graeff's inventory for the painting now in Dublin, but, as noted above, his lost views of Zuidpolsbroek and Soestdijk were valued at 36 guilders each. Their valuation was not particularly high. However, each was appraised more than Frans Hals's double portrait of *Catharina Hooft and her Nurse*, which was also in Pieter de Graeff's 1709 inventory; it was valued at merely 30 guilders. The inventory also lists a gold bell that was appraised at 57 guilders, 18 stuivers,[10] almost twice the price of Hals's painting as well as Ruisdael's lost views of two De Graeff estates. It could very well have been the fine gold rattle Pieter's mother holds in her fist in Hals's picture.

Ruisdael's work on a painting of Soestdijk and inventory references to two additional pictures of De Graeff's estates that are either lost or unidentified raise a reasonable question. Are there other works by the artist that can be identifed as commissioned portraits of specific properties? Several candidates come to mind but, as we shall see, none offer open and shut cases.

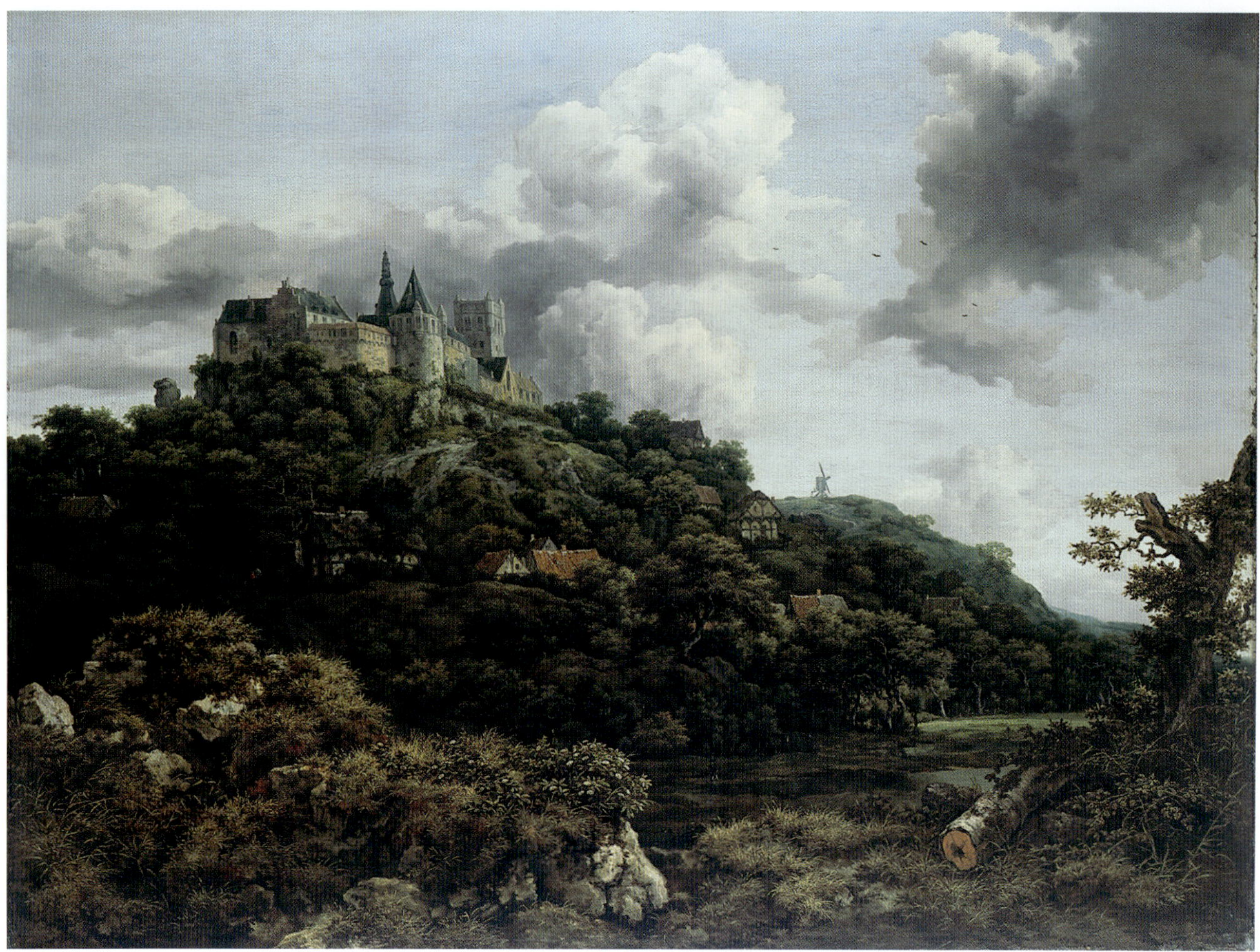

fig. 3 JACOB VAN RUISDAEL
*Bentheim Castle*, 1653
Oil on canvas, 110.5 × 144 cm
Dublin, National Gallery of Ireland

For example, John Smith, who compiled the pioneer catalogue of Ruisdael's paintings, published in 1835, wrote of the artist's majestic *Bentheim Castle* (fig. 3), now a major accent in the National Gallery of Ireland: "Tradition states it to have been painted expressly for the Count of Bentheim, in whose family it is said to have remained until the entrance of the French into Germany, about which time (*ca.* 1792–94) it was taken to Paris ...".[11] To my knowledge there is not a shred of evidence to support the tradition that a Count of Bentheim commissioned the mighty masterwork, and it is apparent from Smith's carefully worded account of the painting's early provenance that he had none either.

During recent decades Ruisdael's painting at Dublin of Bentheim Castle and more than a dozen of his other pictures which include the castle have been given various symbolic interpretations (*e.g.* an allusion to the cardinal sin of pride; a reference to the eternal city of Zion).[12] Some of Ruisdael's contemporaries may have entertained such notions, but an image of Bentheim must have conjured up other thoughts in the minds of the Dutch merchants who imported Bentheim limestone from Westphalian quarries to Amsterdam. During the first



SEYMOUR SLIVE

half of the century it was used as a building material in the city and as such it reached its peak when, along with Italian marble, it was favoured for Amsterdam's New Town Hall. Merchants who handsomely profited by providing hundreds of tons of Bentheim limestone used in the construction of "the world's eighth wonder" had good reason to have fond memories of the site.

The earliest documented reference I know to a painting of Bentheim was made two years before Ruisdael died. It is found in the posthumous inventory, dated 2 May 1680, of the effects of Pieter van Lutsen (*ca.* 1612–1679): "*1 schilderij het huis van Benthem*".[13] Although no artist's name is cited, in view of the rarity of paintings of the castle other than those by Ruisdael, the chance that the inventory refers to one of his pictures seems better than even. As for Van Lutsen, it is known that he was an affluent Amsterdam merchant with international contacts and his family's business may very well have originated in the eastern Netherlands not far from Bentheim.[14] But, in the end, we can only speculate if part of his wealth was related to Bentheim limestone transactions and if his painting of Bentheim Castle was in fact by Ruisdael.

What is known about the history of the Manor Kostverloren in Ruisdael's day raises the possibility that the artist's intriguing painting of its reconstruction,

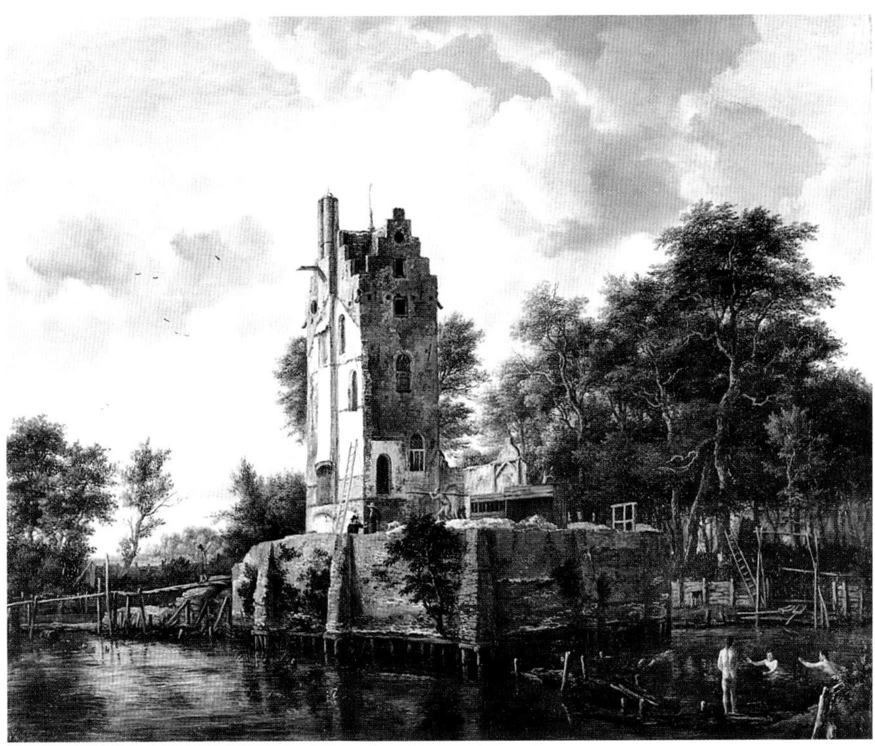

fig. 4 JACOB VAN RUISDAEL
*Reconstruction of the Ruins of Kostverloren, ca.*1658
Oil on canvas, 62 × 75 cm
Amsterdam, Historisch Museum

now at the Amsterdam Historical Museum (fig. 4),[15] was a commissioned work. The bald facts are these. In about 1650 the old manor was badly damaged by fire; however, the fabric of its tower remained sound. In the spring of 1658 the executors of an estate administered by the trustees of an Amsterdam orphanage bought the manor and its grounds. The executors petitioned the trustees to permit them to restore the tower and rebuild the house to make it habitable. They proposed to rent it and thereby derive income for the estate. Their petition was granted. Work on the house was finished quickly — before the end of 1658.[16]

Was the Kostverloren painting commissioned from Ruisdael by the executors of the estate to serve as a record of the beginning of their project? Possibly. But I agree with Bob Haak, who first published the painting, that it is unlikely that they ordered a view of an initial phase of the reconstruction of a rental property.[17] More probable is the hypothesis that the painting was made in response to the artist's own impulse to paint a landscape that incorporated a record of the beginning of the manor's new life when pristine white paint formed a wondrous pattern on a side of its naked tower. Ruisdael's addition of three naked men cavorting in the manor's moat adds an unusual note to the landscape. In Dutch pictures of the period naked male figures who are not gods, saints or heroes are almost as scarce as hen's teeth.

Another possible contender for a work that was made to order is Ruisdael's untraceable drawing known from an etching entitled *De Heer Huydecoepers* [sic] *Huis van achteren* (Mr. Huydecoper's house from the rear) by Abraham Blooteling (1640–1690; fig. 5). In my opinion, however, the lost drawing can be dismissed as a non-starter. It hardly qualifies as a commission given to the artist by Mr. Huydecoper or another person with a special interest in the house, since it is one of a series of Blooteling's six etched *Amstel-Gesichjes door Jacob van Ruisdael* (Small views of the Amstel by Jacob van Ruisdael).[18] The print's unmistakable emphasis is on the large site where workmen are preparing land for Amsterdam's dramatic expansion in about 1663. Like other identifiable Amsterdam structures in etchings of the *Amstel-Gesichjes* series, Mr. Huydecoper's house is an element in a broad topographical view, not the subject of the print.

It is tantalizing to think that some of the artist's celebrated panoramic views of bleaching fields with the skyline of Haarlem on the distant horizon may qualify as commissioned works. Extensive bleaching grounds in Ruisdael's *Haarlempjes* are generally seen adjacent to the buildings of a bleachery — a lye house, a dairy, living quarters and stables. Some of the bleacheries have been identified,[19] but it has not been possible to determine if any of the pictures of them were ordered by their proprietors. Portraits of properties are not common in seventeenth-century Dutch art, but we have seen they exist; Cornelis de

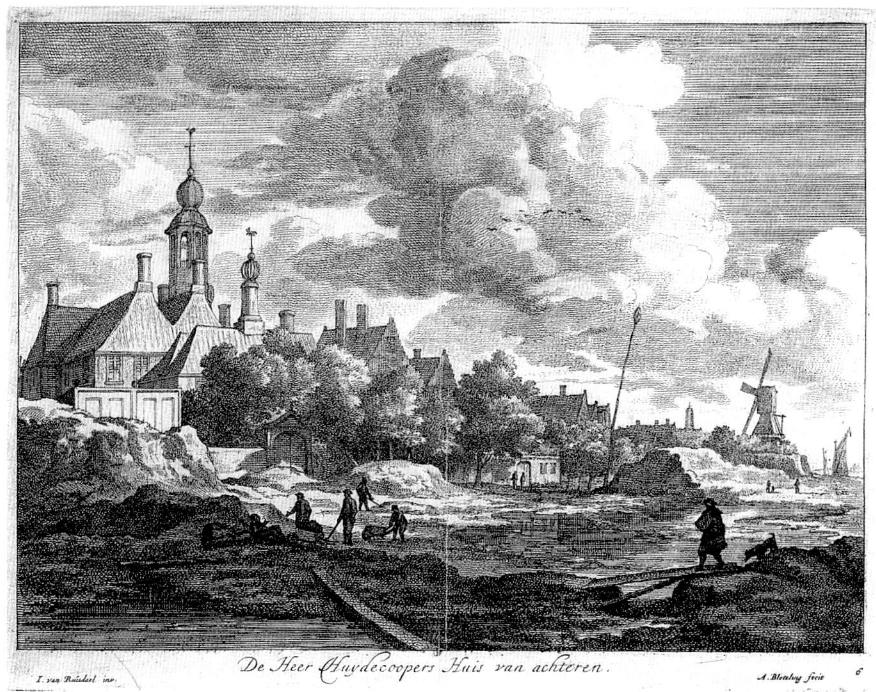



fig. 5 ABRAHAM BLOOTELING
*Rear View of Mr. Huydecoper's House,*
*ca.* 1663–64
Etching, 16.4 × 21.5 cm
Amsterdam, Rijksmuseum

Graeff's painting of his estate at Soestdijk has been mentioned and so have those owned by his son Pieter. Probably the most unusual one is the large, meticulous "pen painting" Jacob van Matham (1571–1631) did in 1627 of Johan van Loo's brewery 'De Drie Lilien' on the Spaarne in Haarlem and of his country manor; in the painting the manor is transported from its actual site about five kilometers from the city to a spot a stone's throw from Van Loo's brewery.[20] Considering the interest of some Dutch patrons in property portraits (in the nineteenth and twentieth centuries the appetite for them spread to other countries and was satisfied by an international group of photographers), it is conceivable that the Rijksmuseum's grandiose *Windmill at Wijk bij Duurstede,* Ruisdael's most famous picture, was commissioned as a portrait of the great mill by its proud owner.

Finding material to support the hunch cited above is exceedingly difficult. The mill depicted in the painting no longer stands, the name of its owner in about 1670 when the masterpiece was painted is unknown and nothing unequivocal can be stated about its provenance until it was purchased by Adriaan van der Hoop from Albertus Brondgeest for 4,000 guilders as late as 1833.

As for pinpointing a view by Ruisdael of a Haarlem bleachery commissioned by its owner, there is little reason to be optimistic. Not a single painting by the artist of the subject is listed in Pieter Biesboer's exhaustive study of Haarlem inventories compiled from 1572 until 1740 (naturally only those dated in 1646, the year Ruisdael burst on the scene in Haarlem, or later, are pertinent here).[21] By contrast, eight are cited in Amsterdam inventories made from 1664 until

1740.[22] The dates are not surprising. The artist only began to depict *Haarlempjes* in the early 1660s – less than a decade after he moved from Haarlem to settle in Amsterdam – and he continued to paint them until his final years. Unexpected, however, is the indication that Amsterdamers had a greater interest in his views of Haarlem than citizens of his native city. Whether any Amsterdamers who had *Haarlempjes* in their possession owned or had investments in Haarlem bleacheries remains to be determined.

Finally, a word about proposals that Ruisdael's magisterial versions of *The Jewish Cemetery* at Dresden and Detroit were commissioned works. Wilhelm Martin suggests they were probably ordered specifically as portraits of the tombs and that their obvious symbolic references were added for good measure.[23] Ernst Scheyer also notes that the artist may have received commissions for them and that one of the versions may have been ordered by the family of Eliahu Montalto (died 1616), the famous doctor of Ferdinand I, Grand Duke of Tuscany (1549–1609) and then of Marie de' Medici (1573–1642), whose white marble sarcophagus is the prominent one in both paintings. Scheyer adds that the other version (and perhaps a third untraceable one) was probably ordered afterwards by another member of Amsterdam's Jewish community.[24]

Martin's and Scheyer's proposals that the cemetery paintings may have been commissioned will remain hypothetical until evidence is found regarding the relation between the artist and the person or persons who acquired them. Once again, there is hardly reason to believe it will turn up soon. Nothing firm is known about the early ownership of the Dresden version until it is recorded in a Dresden inventory of 1754. The Detroit picture's history is more elusive; the earliest solid reference to its existence is in a 1828 London auction catalogue. We can say, however, it is highly unlikely that the paintings were done for Jewish patrons, as Scheyer suggests, because the inscriptions on the pictures' tombs (apart from Ruisdael's own beautiful signature on gravestones in the lower right of each painting) are painted in pseudo-Hebraic letters, not Hebrew. It is improbable that members of Amsterdam's Jewish community would have commissioned or accepted works with gibberish inscriptions instead of faithful transcriptions of the Hebrew texts on the sarcophagi.[25]

The little that is offered in these remarks on Ruisdael's clientele appears to be in the nature of the beast. Put another way, in some areas of art history frontiers of knowledge are reached with almost lightning speed. A consolation which I know Alfred Bader, to whom this essay is warmly dedicated, shares is that slim and even negative findings have a place in the order of things.

1  Seymour Slive, *Jacob van Ruisdael:
A Complete Catalogue of His Paintings,
Drawings and Etchings*, New Haven and
London 2001, pp. 106–08, no. 80.

2  Ed. J.F.M. Sterck *et al.*, *De Werken van
Vondel, Volledige geïllustreerde tekstuitgave*,
10 vols. and index, Amsterdam 1927–40,
VI (1932), pp. 83–87.

3  S.A.C. Dudok van Heel kindly informed
me (private communication) that the
three standing men on the left are possibly
portraits (reading from left to right) of
Cornelis de Graeff's brother-in-law Pieter
Trip (1597–1655; hence a posthumous
portrait), his brother-in-law Willem
Schrijver (1608–1661) and his younger
brother Andries de Graeff (1611–1678).

4  "*4 voet en 2 duim hoog en 6 voet lang van de
schilderije van Keyser, sijnde een landschap van
Zoestdijck met mijn vader Sal. karos en eenige
conterfeijtsels.*" The note, dated 1
November 1670, is in Pieter de Graeff's
V.O.C. almanac, Amsterdam Municipal
Archives, De Graeff archives; S.A.C.
Dudok van Heel, 'In presentie van
de Heer Gerard ter Borch', *Essays in
Northern European Art Presented to Egbert
Haverkamp-Begemann on His Sixtieth Birthday*,
Doornspijk 1983, p. 68, note 12. Dudok
van Heel's 1983 publication confirms the
doubts expressed in Seymour Slive,
*Jacob van Ruisdael*, exh.cat., Mauritshuis,
The Hague, and Fogg Art Museum,
Cambridge, 1981, pp. 23–24, regarding
the probability that the lost Soestdijk
painting by Ruisdael cited in note 8
below is identical with the Dublin
picture.

5  "*1 groot stuck waarin de heer burgemeester
Cornelis de Graeff met desselfs huysvrouw
Catharina en beijde haare soone d'heeren Pieter
en Jacob de Graeff noch jongh sijnde*"; estate
inventory, 27 October 1691, Amsterdam
Municipal Archives, De Graeff family
archives, no. 605, item 32.

6  S.A.C. Dudok van Heel, 'Een minne met
een kindje door Frans Hals', *Jaarboek
Centraal Bureau voor Genealogie*, vol. 29,
1975, pp. 146–59, establishes the identity
of the sitters and the painting's early
provenance. Also see the entry on the
Berlin double portrait in Seymour Slive *et
al.*, *Frans Hals*, exh. cat., National Gallery
of Art, Washington, D.C.; Royal
Academy of Arts, London; Frans Hals
Museum, Haarlem, 1989, no. 9.

7  8 March 1709: "*1 Groote schilderije waarin
Pourtraicten van wijlen d'Hr Burgemeester
Cornelis de Graeff, sijne vrouw en twee
zoonen*"; Amsterdam Municipal Archives,
NA, M. Servaes 5001, fol.511; see Dudok
van Heel, *op.cit.* (note 4), p. 68, note 12.

8  8 March 1709: "*Op de kamer van Vrouwe
Agneta de Graeff* [Pieter's daughter]: *Een
schilderij van zuijdpolsbroek door Jacob
Ruijsdael f.36. – Een dito van Soesdijk f.36*";
Amsterdam Municipal Archives, NA,
M. Servaes 5001, fol. 485; A. Bredius,
"Iets over de copie van Gerrit Lundens
naar Rembrandt's '*Nachtwacht*'", *Oud
Holland*, XXX, 1912, p. 199; see Dudok van
Heel, *op. cit.* (note 4), p. 68, note 12. One
of Cornelis de Graeff's properties was a
seigniory at Zuidpolsbroek (also
Polsbroek). Ruisdael's painting of it may
be an existing landscape which we fail to
recognize as the place. In the attempt
to identify it (which, in the end, was
fruitless), consideration was given to his
paintings of country houses constructed
in a classicizing style that are set in
gardens embellished with fountains. They
are at Berlin, Los Angeles (The Fisher
Gallery of the University of Southern
California), Washington, D.C; and one
surfaced in the anonymous sale, Vendue
Huis der Notarissen, The Hague , 25
April 2002, no. 327 (see Slive, *op. cit.*
[note 1], nos. 554, 576, 588, 573, respectively). As noted, nothing was found to
link any of them with Polsbroek. A bit of
information provided by the indefatigable
Amsterdam archivist I.H. van Eeghen
(private communication), which may help
students who want to resume the search,
is that the house at Polsbroek was not
large. On 24 July 1674 Pieter de Graeff
notes in his V.O.C. almanac that he
contracted with Ruisdael before a notary
to repaint and improve his landscapes of
Soestdijk and Polsbroek, the former for
30 guilders, the latter for 40 guilders.
("*met Ruysdael, schilder, in presentie van de
notaris Padhuysen afgesproken om twee land-
schappen, 't een van Zoesdijck 't ander van
Polsbroeck door hem te doen overschilderen en*

*hebben op 't eene toe af tot verberingh geboden f.30 – gl. en op 't tweede f.40 – gl. 't saeme 70 gl.*"); Amsterdam Municipal Archives, de Graeff family archives, no. 194; see Dudok van Heel, *op. cit.* (note 4), p. 68 note 12. The Soestdijk painting that was valued at 36 guilders in 1709 is probably identical with "*Een dito* [schilderije] *van Soesdijk*" cited in an inventory, dated 10 October 1710, which lists pictures given to Jacobus de Fremeri in the name of Cornelis de Graeff (Pieter's son, died 1719; since the son was said to be mentally incompetent, Fremeri probably received them on his behalf): ". . . *aan de heer Jacobus de Fremeri voor de Ed. heer en mr. Cornelis de Graeff, heer van Purmerland en Ilpendam . . . . Een dito* [schilderije] *van Soesdijk.*"

9 "*Een schilderije van de heerlijkheid van Ilpendam en 't Hof, door de jonge Moucheron f.20 – Een dito van de heerlijkheid van Zuid Polsbroek*"; Amsterdam Municipal Archives, NA, M. Servaes 5001, fol. 485; Bredius, *op. cit.* (note 8), p. 199.

10 Dudok van Heel, *op. cit.* (note 6), pp. 157, 159, note 20.

11 John Smith, *A Catalogue Raisonné of the Works of the Most Eminent Dutch, Flemish and French Painters*, 9 vols., London 1829–42, VI (1835), pp. 81–82, no. 258.

12 Slive, *op. cit.* (note 1), p. 25, and for the sources of the different interpretations see p. 27, note 10.

13 Amsterdam Municipal Archives, NAA 2636 (film 2663); notary Gerrit Steeman (private communication from Burton B. Fredericksen, Getty Provenance Index).

14 Data about Pieter van Lutsen (also Lutzen, Lutselen) and his family was kindly provided by Marten Jan Bok, who combed Amsterdam's archives for references to him.

15 Slive, *op. cit.* (note 1), pp. 99–100, no. 73.

16 See I.H. Van Eeghen, 'Rembrandt aan de Amstel', *Rembrandt aan de Amstel*, published by Genootschap Amstelodamum, Amsterdam 1969 (unpaginated). For the view that the cause of the manor's disrepair about the middle of the century was the rotting piles of its foundations, not a fire as stressed by van Eeghen, see Boudewijn Bakker *et al.*, *Landscapes of Rembrandt: His favourite walks*, exh. cat., Amsterdam Municipal Archives, Amsterdam, and Institut Néerlandais, Paris, 1998–99, p. 282.

17 Bob Haak, 'Het Huis Kostverloren aan de Amstel, Jacob van Ruisdael, 1628/29–1682', *Vereniging Rembrandt, Nationaal Fonds Kunstbehoud*, 1981, p. 93.

18 See Slive, *op. cit.* (note 1), pp. 506–07, under no. D17.

19 Pieter Biesboer, 'Topographical Identification for a Number of "Haerlempjes" by Jacob van Ruisdael', in *Shop Talk: Studies in Honor of Seymour Slive*, ed. Cynthia P. Schneider, Alice I. Davies and William W. Robinson, Cambridge, Mass., 1995, pp. 36–39.

20 Pen and brown ink on panel, 71 × 116 cm, Frans Hals Museum, Haarlem, no. 206 Illustrated in Slive, *op. cit.* (note 1), p. 516, fig. D30a.

21 Pieter Biesboer, *Collections of Paintings in Haarlem, 1572–1745*, Documents for the History of Collecting. Netherlandish Inventories 1. The Provenance Index of The Getty Research Institute, ed. Carol Togneri, Los Angeles 2001.

22 The inventory of the estate of Laurens Mauritsz. Douci, assessed at Amsterdam, 18 January 1669, lists "*een Haerlempje van Ruysdael*" (Abraham Bredius, *Künstler-Inventare: Urkunden zur Geschichte der holländischen Kunst des XVIten, XVIIten und XVIIIten Jahrhunderts*, 8 vols., The Hague 1915–22, II (1916), p. 425. Seven more paintings of views of Haarlem are cited in Amsterdam inventories in a compilation of Dutch inventories made from 1664 to 1740 in a Getty Provenance Index print-out, dated 26 June 2002, helpfully provided by Patricia A. Teter. In the Getty print-out not one is listed in inventories compiled in Haarlem. It is pertinent to add that in 1995 Biesboer wrote that he had "found the title 'Haerlempje' specifically identifying a painting by Jacob van Ruisdael in a Haarlem inventory" (Biesboer, *op. cit.* [note 19], p. 38, note 1). He also stated he had found a reference to a *Haarlempje* by Ruisdael in a Haarlem inventory dated

as early as 1663 (see Slive, *op. cit.* [note 1], p. 51). Yet no *Haarlempje* by Ruisdael is listed in Biesboer's *Collections of Paintings in Haarlem 1572–1740* (*op. cit.* [note 21]).

23  Wilhelm Martin, *De Hollandsche schilderkunst in de 17de eeuw*, 2 vols., Amsterdam 1935–36, II (1936), p. 304.

24  Ernst Scheyer, 'The Iconography of Jacob van Ruisdael's *Cemetery*', *Bulletin of the Detroit Institute of Arts*, vol. 55, no. 3, 1977, p. 138.

25  Concern for literal transcriptions of Hebrew inscriptions by Jewish patrons is found in the drawing Romeijn de Hooghe (1647–1708) made in 1668 of a group portrait of a Jewish family in a richly appointed interior of a circumcision scene (see W.H. Wilson, '"The Circumcision", A Drawing by Romeyn de Hooghe', *Master Drawings*, vol. 13, 1975, pp. 250ff., pls. 22, 23). De Hooghe's transcription of a Hebrew inscription over the doorway in the interior is clearly legible. Mirjam Alexander-Knotter, 'An Ingenious Device: Rembrandt's Use of Hebrew Inscriptions', *Studia Rosenthaliana* 33, 1999, pp. 131–59, offers a fine survey and bibliography on the use of Hebrew inscriptions in Netherlandish Biblical paintings and prints. As her title indicates, her emphasis is on Rembrandt; however, she also considers some of his contemporaries and predecessors. She notes artists used both meaningless letters and correct Hebrew characters that occasionally make no sense. Readable inscriptions are found in biblical works that incorporate the Tetragrammaton, trilingual accusations pinned to the Cross, on garments and headgear, tablets of the law and texts that are part or provide a gloss on biblical themes. Ruisdael's cemetery pictures were not part of Alexander-Knotter's brief.

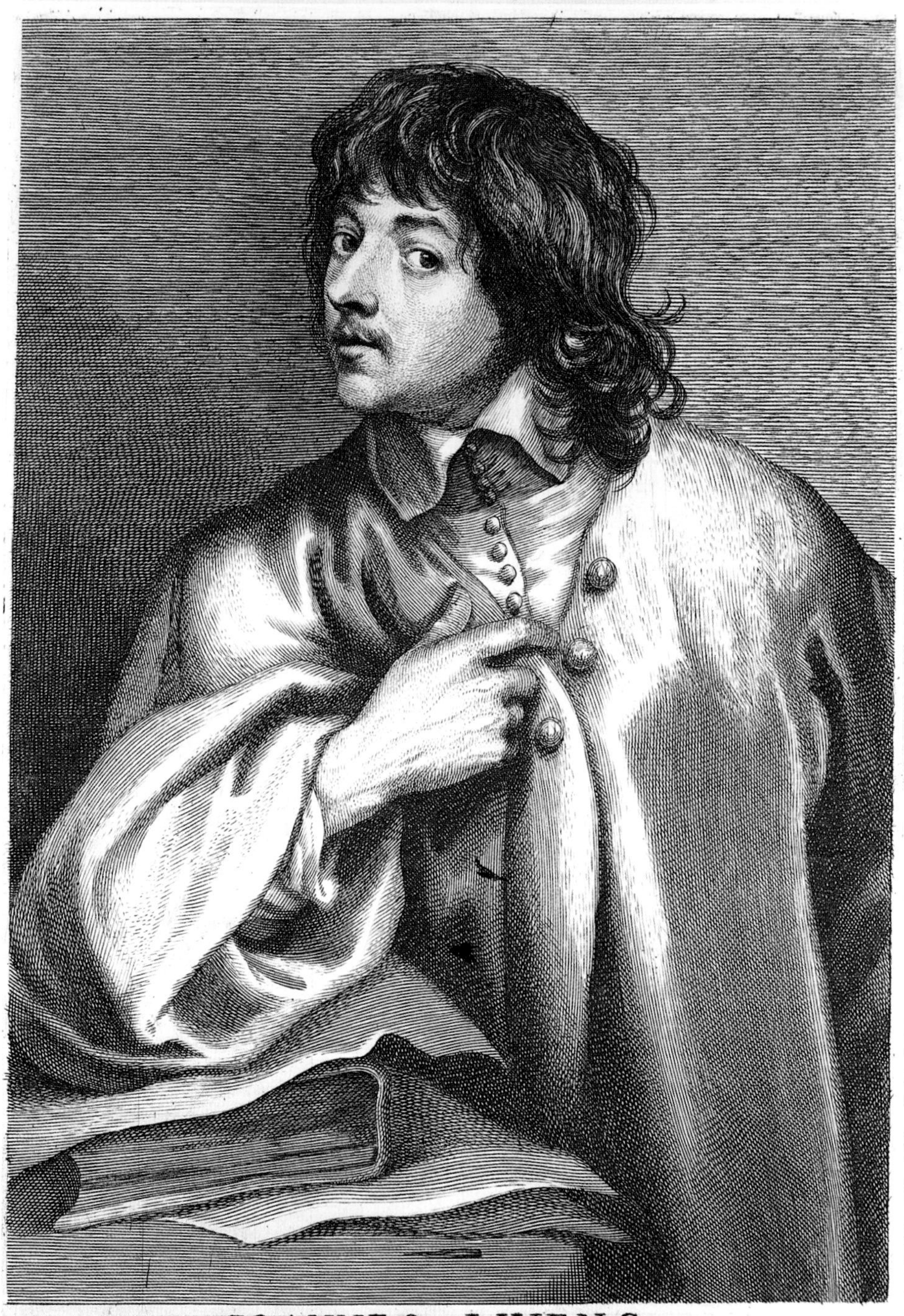

# IOANNES LIVENS

PICTOR HVMANARVM FIGVRARVM MAIORVM LVGDVNI BATTAVORVM.

# Crossing the 'North-South Divide': The Young Lievens, Van Dyck, Rubens and Rembrandt; Connections and Influences

J. DOUGLAS STEWART

No justification is needed for presenting an essay on Jan Lievens (1607–1674) as a tribute to Alfred Bader.[1] Lievens is one of his favourite artists. Alfred has not only lectured passionately and eloquently on Lievens, helping to remove him from 'the shadow of Rembrandt' (1607–1674), but he has also long been an assiduous collector of Lievens's work. He and Isabel have most generously donated three – and promised four more – important Lievens paintings to Kingston's Agnes Etherington Art Centre at Queen's University, Alfred's *alma mater*. In his lectures Alfred always has special praise for Lievens's masterpiece, the 1631 *Job*, once in a British private collection but since 1933 one of the greatest treasures of Canada's National Gallery at Ottawa.[2] This work (only one hundred miles north of Kingston) together with Alfred's past and future donations to Queen's University will make this region the richest location anywhere for the study and appreciation of Jan Lievens as a painter.

This essay gives me the opportunity to present further evidence for the case concerning Lievens's early trip to Antwerp which I put forward in an article in *The Hoogsteder Mercury* in 1990.[3] I will also try to answer those critics who have responded to that piece.[4]

In 1990 my case was based on the engraving by Lucas Vorsterman (1595–1675) after a lost portrait of Lievens by Anthony Van Dyck (1599–1641; fig. 1). Van Dyck remained in his birth-place, Antwerp, until his sojourn in England from November 1620 until February 1621. He resided in Antwerp again from February until November 1621, when he went to Italy. There he remained until 1627, when he returned to Antwerp, where he stayed until 1632, when he finally went back to

fig. 1 LUCAS VORSTERMAN
after ANTHONY VAN DYCK
*Portrait of Jan Lievens*
Engraving, Mauquoy-Hendricx 85,
state V, 24.2 × 15.8 cm
Haarlem, Teylers Museum

England. Traditionally, the Van Dyck image of Lievens was thought to have been created when both artists were in England, between 1632 and 1634, or slightly earlier, during Van Dyck's second Antwerp period. However, I argued in 1990 that these dates were impossible on stylistic grounds, the Vorsterman image fitting into Van Dyck's first Antwerp period, but none of his later periods. I suggested that the image was probably created right at the end of the first Antwerp period, *ca.* 1620–21, when Lievens was only thirteen–fourteen years of age.

This may seem an impossibly young age for Lievens to have travelled from his native Leiden to Antwerp. However, his biographer, Jan Jansz. Orlers (1570–1646), states that Lievens became a pupil of Joris van Schooten (1587–1651) of Leiden when about eight, *i.e. ca.* 1615, staying with that master for about two years. Then, according to Orlers, at the age of ten Lievens was sent to Amsterdam to study with Pieter Lastman (1583–1633), with whom he remained for two years, after which he returned to Leiden, *i.e.* about 1619–20.

Having studied in Leiden and then in Amsterdam, it would have been logical for the young Lievens to wish to see the work of, and perhaps study with, the greatest master of the Southern Netherlands, Peter Paul Rubens (1577–1640), whose international fame had been growing by leaps and bounds since his return from Italy in 1608. Lievens's father, Lieven Hendricxz. (died 1612), had himself been born in Ghent, in Flanders, and there may still have been relatives in the area. The Twelve Years Truce, which would have facilitated travel between the north and the south, remained in effect until 9 April 1621.[5]

The first responses to my proposal were letters from the doyens of Rubens and Van Dyck studies respectively, Julius Held and Sir Oliver Millar. Both scholars noted the moustache on the Vorsterman engraving of Lievens and argued that no thirteen or fourteen year old would have had such facial hair. There are several possible replies to this objection. The young Lievens may have been as precocious physically as he was artistically. Van Dyck, himself a precocious painter, might have 'improved' his sitter's appearance, to make him look older and more mature. Of course, as with most attempts to correlate the features of a portrait with a sitter's actual appearance, this is all speculation.

The first published reaction to my 1990 article came in 2001 from Stephanie Dickey, who wrote:

J. Douglas Stewart has proposed that Lievens had already made a trip to Antwerp in 1620–21, while still a young student of thirteen, and met Van Dyck there. This theory is based on Lievens's youthful appearance in the *Iconography* and on a drawing, signed *I. L.*, based on a head study by Rubens (Vaduz) which Stewart believes Lievens must have seen in Rubens's studio.



J. DOUGLAS STEWART

However, these connections are not conclusive. Contacts with Antwerp already mentioned, including Van Dyck himself, could have made the Rubens drawing [*sic*] accessible in Leiden or The Hague. And while the printed portrait does have a youthful look, it accords well enough with Lievens's appearance in the later 1620s, as recorded in the profile self-portrait of about 1626, and with Constantin Huygens's description, in his biography of *ca.* 1630, of Rembrandt and Lievens as "beardless youths". (Lievens is clean-shaven in the first state of his portrait in the *Iconography*, but sports a moustache in the final version.)[6]

Let me make two immediate points in response to Dickey. Firstly, my theory was based primarily on stylistic analysis. Stylistically, the Lievens portrait seems to me to be a Van Dyck of the first Flemish period, *i.e.* before 1621. Parallels for Lievens's expressive, but awkward pose are found in Van Dyck's early *Apostles, e.g.* the *St Matthew* (formerly at Althorp) and Van Dyck's Metropolitan Museum *Self-portrait* of around 1621. In November 1621 Van Dyck went to Italy, where he gradually learnt to set his forms in space more mellifluously. Well before he returned to Antwerp in 1627 the awkwardnesses of his first Flemish period had entirely disappeared. However, Lievens never went to Italy. Thus I argued in 1990, and still do, that the *Iconography* portrait of Lievens cannot derive from a post-Italian Van Dyck portrait, *i.e.* after 1627.

A second response to Dickey's critique of my theory concerns the Lievens drawing which I identified as a copy of Rubens's painting (not a "drawing"), *Head of a Bearded Man*, now at Vaduz. As a head study of substantial size (65.7 × 49.7 cm) of *ca.* 1617, it is likely that it remained, along with other such studies, in Rubens's studio until his death. [7] It seems very unlikely that it would have found its way north to Leiden or The Hague. On the other hand, if Lievens had visited Rubens's studio in around 1620–21, he might easily have seen it and been inspired to make a copy of it.

Another published response to my argument came from Bernhard Schnackenburg in 2001 in his essay 'Young Rembrandt's "Rough Manner": A Painting Style and its Sources'. In a section of his essay entitled "Jan Lievens' early contact with Antwerp" Schnackenburg writes:

> J. Douglas Stewart's suggestion that Lievens may have been apprenticed in Antwerp already in 1620–21 is somewhat too daring, but it is indeed plausible to see the eighteen-year-old [1625] in the city, where he could visit the studios of Peter Paul Rubens and Jacob Jordaens and study their works and methods.

Douglas Stewart has already provided a piece of evidence for Lievens's special interest in Antwerp, where his youth and quest for (artistic) knowledge was surely met with openness and sympathy. He discovered a drawing with Lievens's monogram showing the head of a bearded man after a painted head study by Rubens. *It appears that whilst in Antwerp Lievens was less concerned with the famous compositions of the great master, which were known through prints, than with the studio practice, the study material and the recipes for paint* [my italics: I will return to this passage later].[8]

In a later section of his essay, 'Van Dyck's early head studies and their influence,' Schnackenburg continues:

> [. . .] in spite of Van Dyck's absence [in 1625] Lievens could still have had the opportunity to study his early work [. . .]. Lievens captured Van Dyck's attention following the latter's return from Italy. The Flemish artist executed his colleague's portrait [*ca.* 1630] and included it in his *Iconography* [. . .].[9]

Thus, Schnackenburg, unlike Dickey, accepts my proposal that Lievens made an early visit to Antwerp (but in 1625 rather than 1620–21), and at that time made his drawn copy of the Rubens head study now in Vaduz. But, like Dickey, Schnackenburg fails to answer my stylistic arguments about the Van Dyck portrait of Lievens, like her giving it the traditional date of *ca.* 1630.[10]

Dickey did point to a piece of evidence of which I had overlooked the significance in 1990, viz. the first state of Vorsterman's engraving, an example of which is preserved in the Lugt collection (fig. 2). That state of the print shows a highly finished face without a moustache.

Ger Luijten, in his illuminating essay 'Prints in progress: proofs in the seventeenth and eighteenth centuries' of 1999, states:

> A number of the cursory etchings by Van Dyck have previously been classified as proofs awaiting completion, but it is clear that too many impressions were printed of them to make this a plausible theory. All the facts point to the existence of an inner circle of connoisseurs [. . .] art lovers for whom the *non-finito* was a quality in its own right. Van Dyck himself did not do any more to these prints; if they were further elaborated it was by someone else [. . .] under the supervision of the publisher Gillis Hendricx [. . .]. The proof of the portrait of [. . .] Jan Lievens [. . .] – before the moustache and without the profusion of hair in the final state – fits the pattern outlined above [. . .]. The head is there, and a few drypoint lines indicate the rest, for which the engraver would have to rely on the oil sketch or painting [. . .].[11]

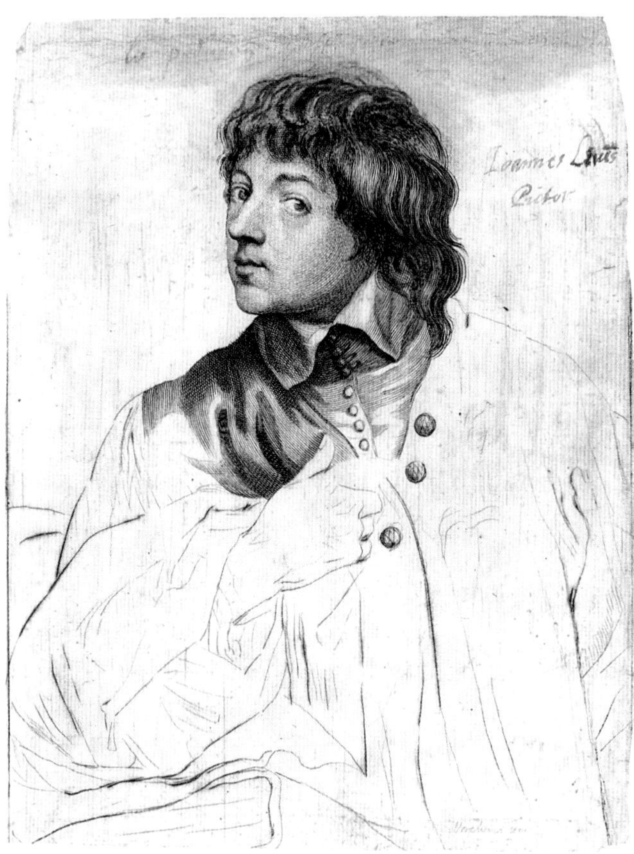

fig. 2 LUCAS VORSTERMAN
after ANTHONY VAN DYCK
*Portrait of Jan Lievens*
Engraving, Mauquoy-Hendricx 85,
state I (proof), 24.2 × 15.8 cm
Paris, Institut Néerlandais,
Collection Frits Lugt

Thus it seems clear that when Van Dyck provided Vorsterman with his model for the portrait of Jan Lievens, the young man from Leiden was not wearing a moustache. Vorsterman would not have produced a proof state of a Van Dyck portrait of Lievens depicting him without a moustache if he had actually worn one at the time.[12] This surely removes the objections of Julius Held and Oliver Millar, as cited above. The later states of the engraving which show Lievens with a moustache presumably reflect an actual change, *i.e.* his growth of a moustache.

Dickey, in her essay quoted above, states that the youthful look of the Van Dyck portrait of Lievens "[…] accords well enough with Lievens's appearance in the later 1620s, as recorded in a profile self-portrait of about 1626 [...]".[13] That profile portrait is at the Statens Museum for Kunst, Copenhagen (fig. 3). The painting is on panel and is signed but not dated. It has been dated to 1626–27 by various critics, but, as there are no early dated pictures by Lievens, the dating remains hypothetical. A remarkable feature about the Copenhagen Lievens *Self-portrait* is that seven copies of it are recorded, one of which, incidentally, once belonged to Alfred Bader.[14]

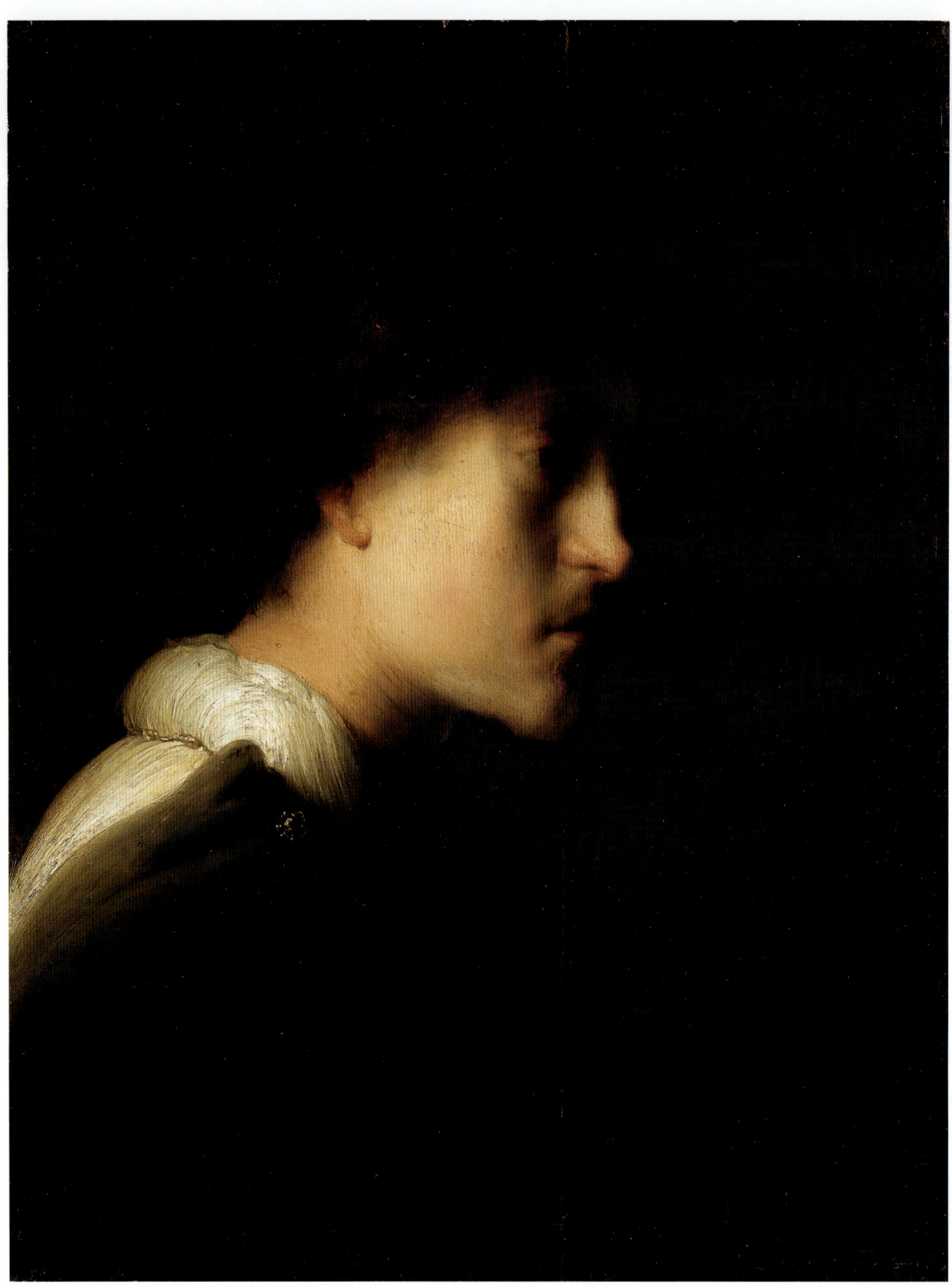

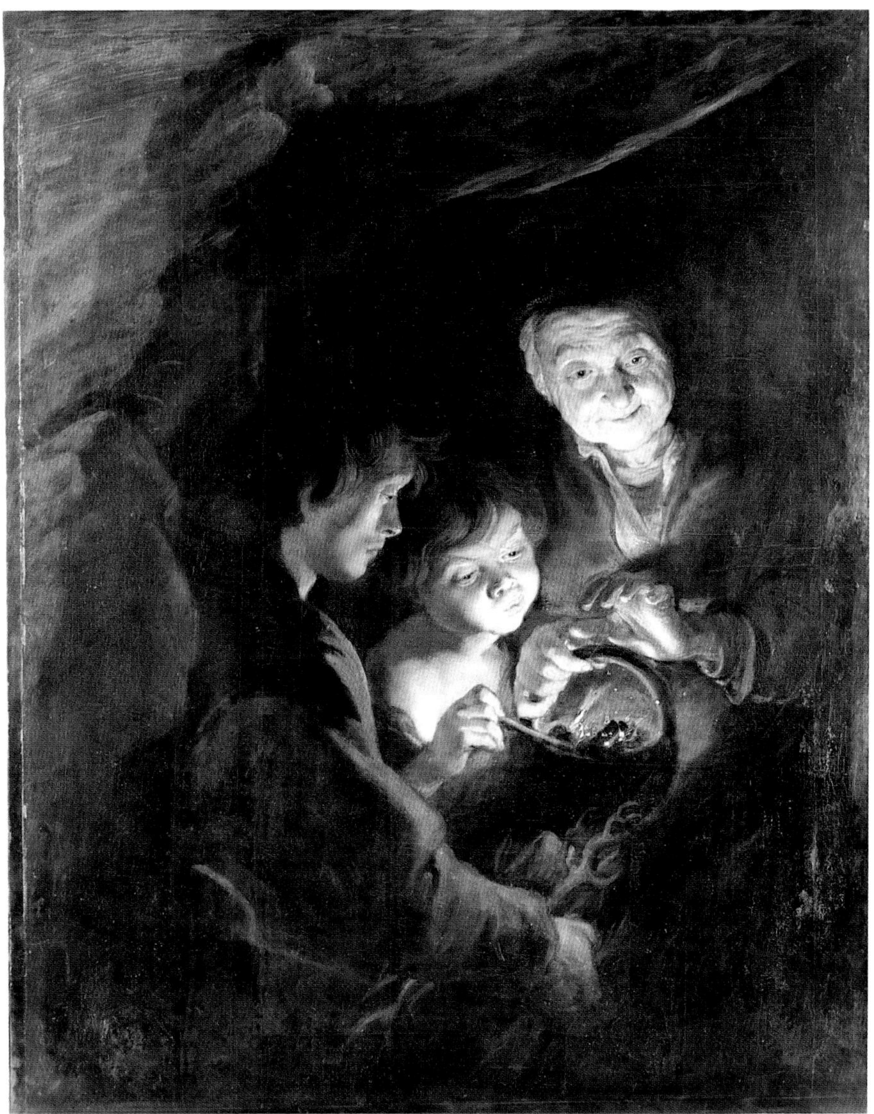

fig. 4 PETER PAUL RUBENS
*Old Woman with Two Boys and
a Coal Pot*, *ca*. 1618–20
Oil on panel, 115 × 92 cm
Dresden, Staatliche
Kunstsammlungen

Something which seems never to have been remarked upon is the striking similarity between the Copenhagen Lievens *Self-portrait* and the youth seen in profile in Rubens's *Old Women with Two Boys with a Coal-Pot* of *ca*. 1618–20 in the Gemäldegalerie Alte Meister, Dresden (fig. 4).[15] But why would the Flemish painter use the young Dutchman as a model?

In his essay 'Puer Sufflans Ignes' (Boy blowing upon fire), Jan Białostocki focused his discussion on two early paintings by Lievens in the Muzeum Narodowe, Warsaw.[16] In one a boy blows on coals dying out in a pot, in order to light his pipe. In the other a boy is lighting a torch with a burning coal which he holds with a pair of tongs; he also blows on the coal. The two paintings, obviously a pair, are both signed *J. Livius*, the Latinized form of Lievens's name.

fig. 3 JAN LIEVENS
*Self-Portrait* (?) *in Profile* , *ca*. 1620
Oil on panel, 52 × 40.5 cm
Copenhagen, Statens Museum
for Kunst

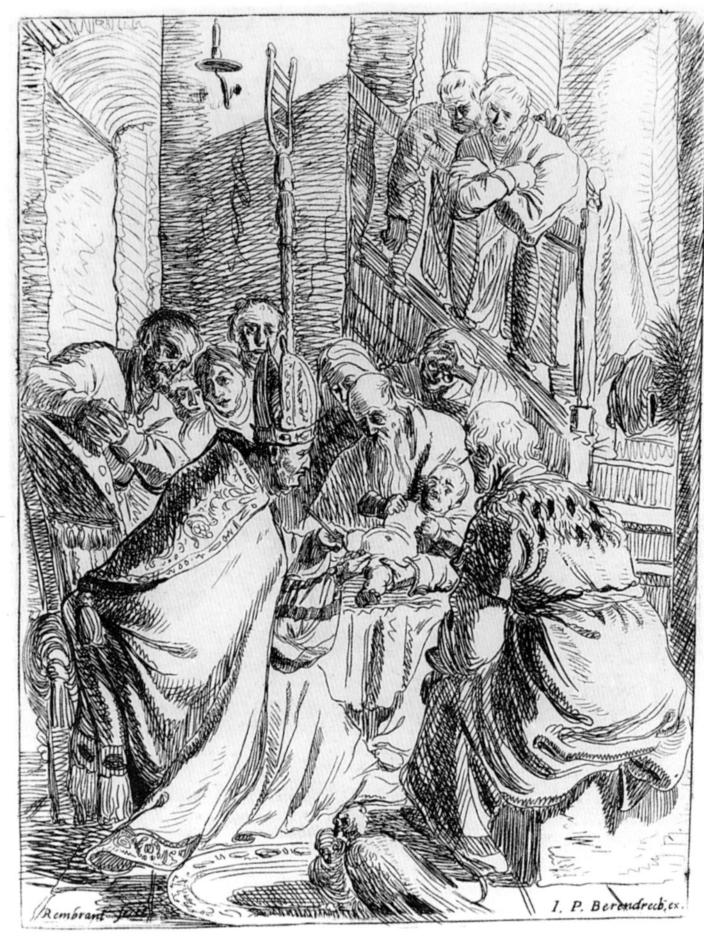



fig. 5 REMBRANDT
*The Circumcision in the Temple,*
*ca.* 1626
Etching, state II, 21.4 × 16 cm
Amsterdam, Museum het
Rembrandthuis

fig. 6 PETER PAUL RUBENS
*The Adoration of the Magi, ca.* 1618–20
Oil on canvas, probably transferred
from panel, 384 × 280 cm
Brussels, Musées royaux des
Beaux-Arts de Belgique

Białostocki suggested that the Warsaw paintings were inspired by passages in Pliny's *Naturalis Historia* praising a sculpture of "a boy blowing a dying fire" and a painting of a boy blowing fire. The sculptor's name was "Lycius". Białostocki wondered "whether the similarity in sound between the name *Lycius*, the literary source of the *puer sufflans*, and *Livius* is wholly accidental, or whether Lievens-Livius may not have also wanted in this way to follow in the footsteps of his ancient predecessor?"[17]

Of course Białostocki was aware of a thematic connection between the Dresden Rubens and the Warsaw pictures. But if, as I have suggested, Rubens included young Lievens in his Dresden picture, perhaps it was Rubens himself, the most learned artist of the age, who thought of the Lycius-Lievens connection, and included the young Leiden artist for this very reason. Certainly, as far as we know, Lievens himself was not especially learned. But if he had learned

   J. DOUGLAS STEWART

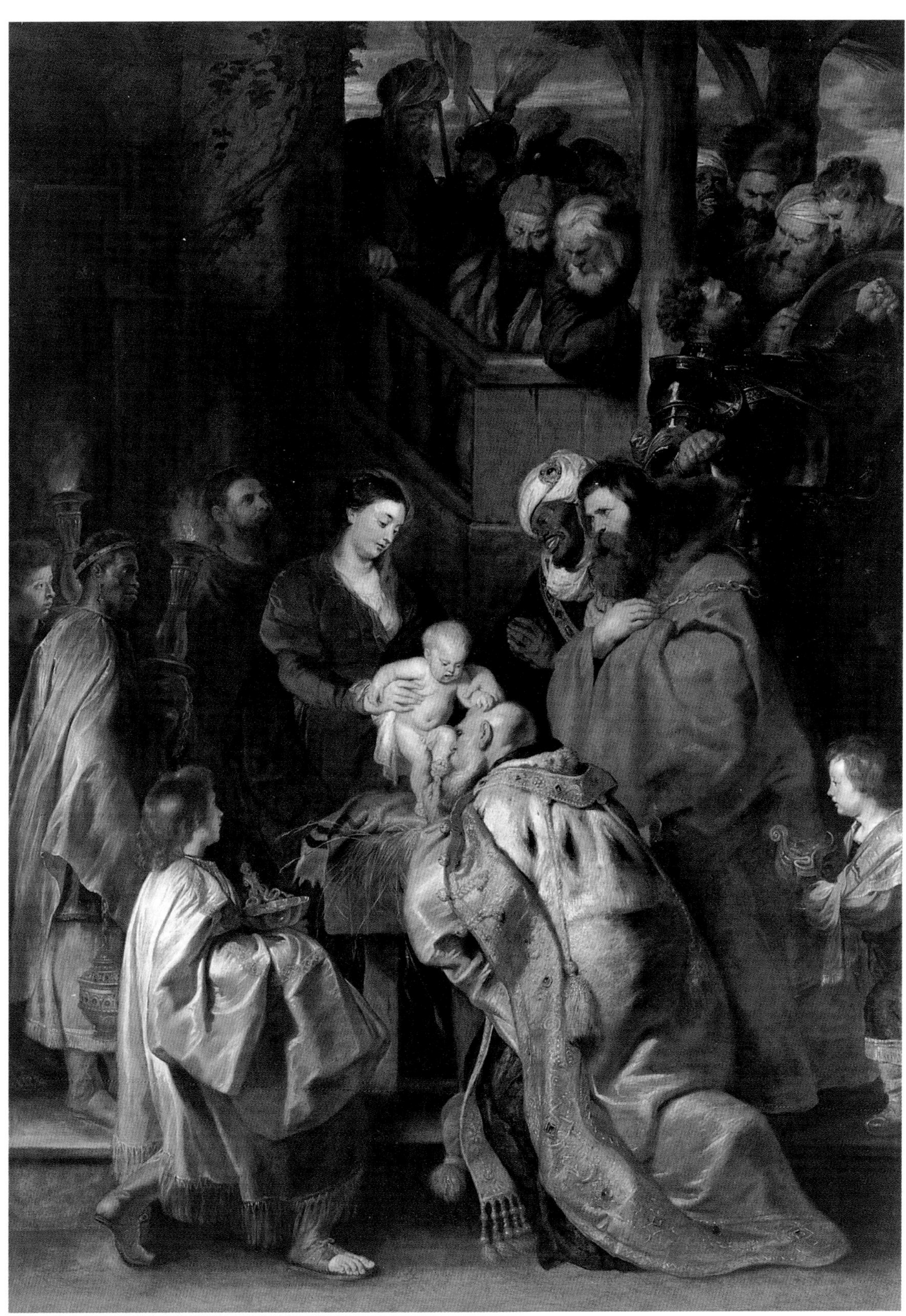

about Lycius-Lievens from Rubens this could also explain his use of the Latinized form of his name, Livius. It should also be noted that the inscription on the proof etching of Van Dyck's portrait of Lievens uses the Latinized form of his name, in a shortened form, *Ioannes Livus / Pictor.*

Finally, I wish to return to Schnackenburg's statement that "[. . .] whilst in Antwerp Lievens was less concerned with the famous compositions of the great master, which were known through prints [. . .]".[18] There seems to be at least one important exception to this statement. Around 1626 both Lievens and Rembrandt made their first etchings. Rembrandt's is a multi-figured composition, *The Circumcision* (fig. 5), showing that event in a grand, high-columned hall, with a stair-case containing two spectators in the rear. The most recent cataloguer of this etching states that "two figures on a raised platform [the staircase] observe the scene. A similar arrangement of figures is found on the right-hand side of [Rembrandt's] *The Stoning of St Stephen*."[19] However, the figures in that picture are shown on a hillock at some distance from the main action. In *The Circumcision* the figures are bent over a staircase balustrade, quite close to the main event.

Moreover, although it has remained unnoticed, the source for the composition of *The Circumcision* is Rubens's *Adoration of the Magi* (fig. 6), now in the Musées Royaux des Beaux-Arts de Belgique, Brussels, but painted originally *ca.* 1618–20 for the Capuchin convent at Tournai.[20] Not only does Rubens's picture show a staircase, with similar balusters, with spectators leaning over it at the upper right; but the vaulted architecture at the left is also similar. A final very telling connection is that between the ermined cloaks of Rubens's kneeling king in the right foreground and the seated figure at the right of Rembrandt's etching.

Rubens's *Adoration of the Magi* in Tournai was engraved by Nicholas Lauwers (1600–1652), but almost certainly long after Rembrandt's etching.[21] In any case, the engraving reverses the painted composition, while Rembrandt's etching follows the direction of the painting. The vaulted architecture at the left of the etching is close to that of the painting, whereas Lauwers considerably altered this passage. Thus it would appear that Rembrandt's knowledge of Rubens's altarpiece came through a drawing after it. Rubens's painting was probably in his Antwerp studio *ca.* 1618–20.[22] Then it went to Tournai, a remote provincial centre, 100 kilometres to the south-west of Antwerp. It seems most likely that it was Jan Lievens who made the drawing during part of the time that I have proposed for his early Antwerp visit, *i.e.* in 1620.[23] (The figure of Joseph in the Rubens altarpiece is the same distinctive model, seen from a different angle, as in the Vaduz *Head Study* of which Lievens made the drawing.)

Rembrandt's borrowings from Rubens's Tournai *Adoration of the Magi* mark, perhaps, the earliest instance of the major influence of a Rubens composition on the Dutchman. In his *David with the Head of Goliath before Saul* of 1627, now in Basle, Rembrandt apparently borrowed again from another Rubens *Adoration of the Magi*. But that borrowing was restricted to a single motif.[24]

To sum up, there is increasing evidence for a journey by Jan Lievens to Antwerp around 1620–21. He was painted or drawn by the young Van Dyck before the latter went to Italy in November 1621. Lievens seems to appear in Rubens's *Old Woman with Two Boys with a Coal-Pot* in Dresden, a picture usually dated *ca.* 1618–20, but hence perhaps closer to the latter date. Lievens definitely made a drawn copy[25] of a Rubens *tronie*, now in Vaduz, a painting he almost undoubtedly saw in Rubens's studio. But Lievens also seems to have been interested in Rubens's large compositions. It can now be demonstrated that the young Rembrandt, in his earliest etching, was influenced by a Rubens altarpiece of *ca.* 1620. Rembrandt's knowledge of the Rubens composition came, not from an engraving, but most likely from a drawing made by his friend Jan Lievens.

Why are these important connections and influences only being discovered now? The answer lies in much of the art historiography of the nineteenth and twentieth centuries, which stress the differences between the "Northern" and "Southern" Netherlands. But, as Hans Vlieghe has argued:

> [. . .] the artists who were active in the Southern Netherlands between 1585 and 1700 must have felt that only to a limited extent did they belong to an artistic tradition that was any different from that in the Northern Netherlands. This is most clearly shown by the fact that both branches of the history of art of the Low Countries are regarded as a single entity by seventeenth-century art historiography.[26]

The converse is also true. Early seventeenth-century Northern Netherlandish artists like Lievens and Rembrandt must have been eager to see, and adapt the discoveries and ideas of their Southern Netherlandish contemporaries, Rubens and Van Dyck, who were developing their own versions of the new international Baroque style.

1  I am indebted to Victoria Pollard and
Venetia Stewart for reading several
versions of this essay and for their very
helpful comments and suggestions.

2  See *Catalogue of the National Gallery of
Canada, Ottawa: European and American
Painting, Sculpture and Decorative Arts*, I,
*1300–1800*, ed. Myron Laskin, Jr and
Michael Pantazzi, 2 vols., Ottawa 1987,
I (text), pp. 165–66. The *Job* was
acquired as a gift from the National
Arts Collection Fund in 1933. Despite
its name, the donating body was not
Canadian, but British; and this gift is
especially remarkable considering the
date (Canada had long since been a
nation in its own right) and the fact that
Britain's own National Gallery still does
not have a Lievens to match Ottawa's.

3  See J. Douglas Stewart, 'Before
Rembrandt's "Shadow" fell: Lievens,
Van Dyck and Rubens: Some
Reconsiderations', *The Hoogsteder
Mercury*, vol. 11, 1990, pp. 42–47.

4  I should like to take this opportunity
also to clarify some confusion about my
name which has in the past led to some
bibliographic errors. My family name is
Stewart; my given names are John and
Douglas. I call attention to this because
in the most recent (2001) response to
my 1990 article, the article is cited in the
bibliography under "Douglas Stewart" –
alphabetically under D, rather than S:
Ernst van de Wetering, Bernhard
Schnackenburg, *The Mystery of the Young
Rembrandt*, exh. cat., Gemäldegalerie Alte
Meister, Staatliche Museen Kassel, and
Rembrandthuis, Amsterdam, 2001,
p. 404. The first example known to me
dates from 1999: Carl Depauw, Ger
Luijten, *Anthony van Dyck as Printmaker*,
exh. cat., Museum Plantin-Moretus,
Antwerp, and Rijksmuseum, Amsterdam,
1999, p. 239, note 1, and p. 392, both
citing my 1979 review of the Princeton
exhibition as "Douglas Stewart".
However, my essay in the 1990 Van
Dyck exhibition catalogue (Arthur K.
Wheelock, Jr *et al.*, *Anthony van Dyck*,
exh. cat., National Gallery of Art,
Washington, D.C., 1990) is cited
correctly on p. 208, note 6, as well

as in the bibliography on page 397,
together with my article on Pieter Thys
of 1997. If I allow this matter to proceed
unchecked I risk becoming lost in biblio-
graphical limbo or at best becoming a
split personality!
    Depauw, Luijten, *op. cit.* above, p. 208,
note 6, referring to Van Dyck's *Mary
Ruthven* (Madrid, Museo del Prado), state:
"[…] the painting's symbolism was
interpreted by Stewart 1990–91,
p. 72, who also stated that the oak was
part of the crest of the Ruthven family,
but we have been unable to confirm this
[…]". *Mea culpa*. I offer sincere apologies
for the confusion. I should rather have
said that the oak *leaves* are part of the
Ruthven coat of arms. See *Flemish Drawings
of the Seventeenth Century, From the Collection
of Frits Lugt, Institut Néerlandais, Paris*,
exh. cat., Victoria and Albert Museum,
London, 1972, pp. 47–48, note 13, with
earlier references.

5  Jonathan Israel, *The Dutch Republic: Its
Rise, Greatness, and Fall 1477–1806*, Oxford
1995, p. 473. For Lieven Hendricxz.'s
death date see *The Dictionary of Art*, ed.
Jane Turner, 34 vols., London 1996, XIX,
p. 348.

6  Stephanie Dickey, 'Van Dyck in Holland:
The Iconography and its Impact on
Rembrandt and Jan Lievens', in *Van Dyck
1599–1999: Conjectures and Refutations*, ed.
Hans Vlieghe, Turnhout 2001, p. 296.

7  Julius Held, *The Oil Sketches of Peter Paul
Rubens: a Critical Catalogue*, 2 vols.,
Princeton 1980, I, p. 597, and
no. 445; Reinhold Baumstark *et al.*,
*Liechtenstein: The Princely Collections*, exh.
cat., The Metropolitan Museum of Art,
New York, 1985, no. 203.

8  Van de Wetering, Schnackenburg, *op. cit.*
(note 4), p. 107.

9  *Ibid.*, p. 109.

10  My thanks to Bernhard Schnackenburg
for very kindly providing me with a copy
of his unpublished paper 'The Stylistic
Development of Jan Lievens as a Painter
1625–28 and His Interaction with
Rembrandt', given at the final symposium
of the exhibition *The Mystery of the Young
Rembrandt* in Amsterdam on 26 May 2002.

11  Depauw, Luijten, *op. cit.* (note 4), p. 24.

12  I am very grateful to David de Witt
    for helpful discussions on this point. In
    contrast to the *Jan Lievens*, the first state
    of Vorsterman's *Francisco de Moncada*
    after Van Dyck shows a very schematic,
    unfinished face – but his moustache is
    clearly indicated. See Depauw, Luijten,
    *op. cit.* (note 4), fig. 21, p. 25.

13  Dickey *op. cit.* (note 6), p. 296.

14  Werner Sumowski, *Gemälde der Rembrandt-
    Schüler*, 6 vols., Landau 1983–94, III,
    p. 1800.

15  *Gemäldegalerie Alte Meister Dresden*, *Katalog
    der ausgestellten Werke*, 6th edn, Dresden
    1987, p. 284, no. 958.

16  Jan Białostocki, 'Puer Sufflans Ignes', in
    Jan Białostocki, *The Message of Images:
    Studies in the History of Art*, Vienna 1988,
    pp. 139–44, 264–65.

17  *Ibid.*, p.144.

18  Van de Wetering, Schnackenburg, *op. cit.*
    (note 4), p.107.

19  Ed de Heer in Van de Wetering,
    Schnackenburg, *op. cit.* (note 4), p. 250.

20  Frans Baudouin, *Rubens*, New York 1977,
    pp. 190, 192, 195 and 376, note 23 (earlier
    references).

21  For the Lauwers engraving see M. Rooses,
    *L'Oeuvre de Rubens: Histoire et description
    de ses tableaux et dessins*, 5 vols., Antwerp
    1886–92, reprint 1977, I, pl. 54, p. 207.
    The engraving is inscribed *Cum privilegiis
    Regis Christianissimi Principum Belgii et
    Ordinum Bataviae*. Rooses concluded that
    the engraving must have been executed
    in 1620 because Rubens obtained his
    Dutch authorization in that year, and
    the Archduke Albert died in 1621 (*ibid.*,
    p. 208). However, Julius Held notes
    that after the death of the Archduchess
    Isabella on 2 December 1633 the Belgian
    privilege (naming only the "*Serenissima
    Infans*" after the Archduke's death)
    was reinstated in its original form
    ("*Principum Belgii*"). Moreover, according
    to Held, "in the years around 1620, only
    [Lucas] Vorsterman worked for Rubens
    as engraver" (Julius Held, *op. cit.* [note 7],
    I, p. 463). Nicolas Lauwers only became
    a master engraver in 1619/20. It seems
    most unlikely that Rubens would have
    entrusted him with such an important
    commission at the very beginning of his
    career. (In Josua Bruyn, Bob Haak, Simon
    H. Levie, Pieter J.J. van Thiel, Ernst
    van de Wetering, *A Corpus of Rembrandt
    Paintings*, vols. I–, Foundation Rembrandt
    Research Project, The Hague, Dordrecht,
    Boston and London 1982–, II (1986),
    p. 598, it is stated that the Lauwers
    engraving of Rubens's Brussels *Adoration
    of the Magi* dates from "1620/21".)

22  Baudouin, *op. cit.* (note 20), pp. 190, 195.
    Baudouin claims that Rubens painted
    the altarpiece with the help of Van Dyck,
    but gives no evidence for this.

23  In turn Govert Flinck may, in 1656, have
    made use of the drawing by Lievens of
    Rubens's Tournai *Adoration of the Magi*
    for the composition of his great painting
    for the Amsterdam Town Hall *Marcus
    Curius Dentatus*. See Sumowski, *op. cit.*
    (note 14), II, no. 638, pp. 1026, 1070.

24  See *Corpus*, *op. cit.* (note 21), I, no. A9,
    p.134: "[. . .] the figure of Saul with the
    motif of the trainbearer(s) is taken from
    Rubens's Lyon *Adoration of the Magi*, via
    an anonymous engraving copied from
    Lucas Vorsterman's print".

25  Sale Sotheby's, London, 10 October 1974,
    lot 361.

26  Hans Vlieghe, *Flemish Art and Architecture
    1585–1700*, New Haven and London 1998,
    p. 1. Vlieghe expanded these views in his
    essay 'Flemish and Dutch Painting in the
    Seventeenth Century: Changing Views
    of a Diptych', in A.W.F.M. Meij, *Rubens,
    Jordaens, Van Dyck and Their Circle: Flemish
    Master Drawings from the Museum Boijmans
    Van Beuningen*, exh. cat. Museum Boijmans
    Van Beuningen, Rotterdam, 2001, pp.
    23–29. (I am very grateful to Bram Meij
    for sending me a copy of this volume.)
    Vlieghe notes (p. 25) that Rubens, from
    shortly after his return from Italy, began
    making use of Dutch engravers from the
    school of Goltzius, and indeed actively
    recruiting them to come to Antwerp.
    Amongst these artists was Lucas
    Vorsterman, the engraver of the
    *Portrait of Jan Lievens* after Van Dyck
    (figs. 1 and 2).

# Jerusalem, Du Schöne!

ASTRID TÜMPEL

Das Flugzeug startete pünktlich, rollte an, rollte weiter, blieb stehen, um bald wieder anzurollen, weiterzurollen und endlich zu beschleunigen, volle Kraft voraus – und dann das erste, kaum merkliche Schwanken, das die Überwindung der Schwerkraft anzeigt. Wenig später ging die Stewardeß durch die Polsterreihen, Newspaper, Madame, aus dem angebotenen Zeitungspacken wählte ich die Jerusalem Post, vertraute Lektüre, vertrauter Blick auf bauschige Wolkenfelder: ich fliege heim ins Gelobte Land, habe ich auch in einem anderen Land mein zu Hause.

Jerusalem ist gelb, sage ich, andere sagen, Jerusalem ist grün und blumenbunt. Ich aber sehe die gelben Quader, aus denen die modernen Häuser gebaut sind, die Synagogen, die Altstadt und die Klagemauer. Vielleicht macht man Jerusalem so grün, so blumenbunt, weil es in Wirklichkeit gelb ist. Gelb waren auch die Judensterne.

Doch ich bin im Mishkenot. Es hat eben zu regnen aufgehört, Regen im Mai, ein Ereignis, vom Taxifahrer fröhlich als Segen Gottes begrüßt. Ich öffne meine Verandatür, lasse die duftende Nacht von Jerusalem herein, die auch die nahe Wüste Juda tröstet, und trinke vom roten Karmelwein, während ich mich auf Terry und Elena vom Israel-Museum freue. Am nächsten Tag, Schalom, umarmen sie mich, führen mich durch den grauen, fensterlosen Gang des Verwaltungstraktes in das schmale Zimmer, und wir haben viel zu bereden über die Ausstellung, die erst in meinem Museum in Amsterdam, und dann hier gezeigt werden soll, genieße es, mein altvertrautes Hebräisch zu sprechen. Es ist erst gegen vier, als wir fertig sind, und ich beschließe, noch eine Weile ins gegenüberliegende Bibel-Museum zu gehen, Bilder tanken, Augenlust, gegenwärtige Geschichte. Kaum Besucher, mein Schritt hallt auf dem Steinfußboden. Vor einer Vitrine machte ich halt. Auf grauem Sockel eine Kuh, eben zwei Handspannen lang. Mit aller Kraft stemmt sie sich gegen den Boden, mit zierlichsten Beinchen, aber gewaltigem Hintern. Der wölbt sich vom Nacken bis zum Schwanz, so ein bockiges Vieh, mit diesem fabelhaften Hintern kriegt sie keiner von der Stelle – doch da rührt sich was vom Eingang her, klappernd nähern sich mir Schritte, ich spüre einen Körper dicht neben meinem.

Widerwillig löse ich meine Augen von dieser Kuh, die seit fünftausend Jahren
bockt. Ich schaue in ein Paar leuchtende Augen, einen rotgemalten, sich gerade
öffnenden Mund und sehe eine Hand, die sich meiner entgegenstreckt:
„Schalom, Frau Haizman, nein, daß ich Sie aber auch treffe . . . hab' Sie so lang
nicht gesehen, wie geht es Ihnen?" Meine Hand wird ergriffen, meine Gestalt in
Wiedersehensfreude eingetunkt. „Was macht Ihre Arbeit, wie geht's Salomon,
ich meine, Ihrem Mann?" Ich stemme meine Füße auf den Fußboden wie die
Kuh. Will meine Hand wiederhaben, starre abweisend ins fremde Gesicht.
„Aber ich bin nicht Frau Haizman", stottere ich, „ich bin Rachel van der Geer,
ich kenne Sie nicht." Der rotgemalte Mund klappt zu. Stille. Ratlosigkeit in den
Augen, die mich eben noch anlachten. „Aber das gibt es doch nicht. Erkennen
Sie mich denn nicht? Ihre alte Sara?" Dabei lacht sie ein bißchen über ihren
Witz, denn diese Sara ist höchstens 25 Jahre alt. Ich schüttle energisch den Kopf,
recke mich, um mich in meiner ganzen Größe zu zeigen, vielleicht wirke ich
auch beleidigt. „Ich habe keinen Mann", höre ich mich sagen. „Na", ruft die
Frau verkrampft, „macht nichts. Nichts für ungut", kneift die Augen zusam-
men und läuft an meiner Kuh vorbei in eine andere Abteilung.

Ich blicke wieder auf die Kuh. Sie ist einmalig. Ich bin anscheinend ein
Duplikat von Frau Haizman. Frau Haizman? Was treibt die? Hat offenbar einen
Mann. Was für einen Mann hat die? Die bockige Kuh hat auch einen Mann, der
kauert brav in der nächsten Vitrine mit einem Zettel vor der Brust: Liegender
Bulle, sumerisch-mesopotamische Zeit.

Ich habe keinen Mann.

Jetzt rollen die Gedanken, rollen hin und her zwischen Amsterdam und
Jerusalem. Flüchtig gleitet mein Blick über ein syrisches Mosaik mit einer Szene
aus der Ilias: Mann und Frau auf einem Sofa. Römische Zeit.

Ich habe keinen Mann.

Mein Vergnügen an der störrischen Kuh ist erloschen. Auch der Schönheit
des Mosaiks kann ich nichts mehr abgewinnen. Ich gehe. Die Beete entlang der
King David-Street werden neu gestaltet. In der Nachmittagshitze sind vier
Leute damit beschäftigt, zwischen den Bewässerungssschläuchen kleine Kuhlen
zu graben und blühende Stecklinge sorgsam hineinzusetzen. Eine Frau steht
daneben und gibt Anweisungen. Es ist schön, dem Pflanzen zuzusehen. Ich gehe
etwas langsamer. Ja, Jerusalem ist gelb und grün und blumenbunt. Ich schaue
die Frau an. Sie lächelt mir zu. Es ist schön, angelächelt zu werden. Oder hält
auch sie mich für Frau Haizman? Ich nehme die Treppe zum Künstlerviertel
hinunter, Richtung Mishkenot, doch auf der Höhe der Windmühle kehre ich
um und biege wieder in die King David-Street ein. Kurz darauf betrete ich
die belebte Halle des King David-Hotels. Hier gibt es genau so viele Bilder
zu tanken wie im Bibel-Museum, denke ich, warum hast du es so fluchtartig

     

verlassen, Augenlust. Und die meisten Bullen hier haben auch ihre Zettelchen mit eindeutigen Angaben – in der Brieftasche, versteht sich, und mit denen weisen sie sich aus wie der Bulle im Museum. Verrückte Ideen, schimpfe ich, Klimawechsel, Schlafdefizit, und nehme auf einem Sofa Platz. Die vielen Bilder verweben sich langsam zu einem Teppich in gedämpften Farben, ich spüre wieder, daß ich in Jerusalem bin, Schalom, Jeruschalaim, und ich bestelle ein Glas roten Karmelwein.

Ich lächle vor mich in, und der Teppich wird zu immer wieder neuen Bildern gewebt.

Ein Mann lächelt zurück. Links von mir. Gewissermaßen da, wo der Teppich in Fransen endet. Ich schaue weg. Doch der Mann steht auf, ein Glas in der Hand und kommt auf mich zu. „Schalom, Frau Haizman", ich traue meinen Ohren nicht, „wie schön, Sie zu sehen, darf ich mich zu Ihnen setzen?" Auf dem Mosaik ein Mann und eine Frau auf einem Sofa.

Ich habe keinen Mann.

„Sie irren sich, ich bin nicht Frau Haizmann. Überhaupt nicht. Nicht im geringsten. Ich bin Holländerin." Der Mann betrachtet mich mit Wohlwollen. „Ich bin jemand ganz anderes", rufe ich laut. Der Mann nimmt endlich seine Augen von mir, blinzelt und sagt freundlich: „Täuschend, diese Ähnlichkeit, bitte, verzeihen Sie." Er stellt seinen Drink aufs Mahagonitischchen, legt ein paar Schekel dazu und geht, nicht ohne sich noch einmal umzusehen.

Amsterdam so weit fort. Amsterdam so nah. Die gleichgültig grauen Wasser der Grachten – Wasser, die nie aufschäumen. Die den Schatten der in schwarze Seide gekleideten Kaufleute verschluckt haben, welche Pfeffer, Koriander, Kardamon und Curry importierten und zusammen mit Ziegeln und Tuchen weit ins Land hinein verschifften. Die ihre Wohnräume, Schlafzimmer, Kontore mit kostbarsten Bildern schmückten, um von aller Welt bewundert zu werden. Bewundertwerden ist schöner als Reichsein. Und die Backsteinhäuser der Kaufleute stehen immer noch entlang der Grachten, jedes mit seinem unverwechselbarem Antlitz, das eine im Rot weinerglühter Wangen, das andere im fahlen Rosagelb eines unheilbar Kranken. Sieht und sagt bloß keiner. Doch alle sorgen dafür, daß die Häuser hübsch in der Senkrechten bleiben.

Ich sitze in meinem Büro, blättere in Katalogen und Sachbüchern, schreibe, beeile mich, denn gleich kommt Besuch. Da meldet die Sekretärin ihn schon, eine kleine, alte Frau mit verschossener, honiggelber Perücke trippelt durch die Tür, schleppt ein mittelgroßes Bild auf mich zu, das in ein blaugrünes Plaid gehüllt und sorgsam mit Spagat verschnürt ist: Frau Rosenbaum, sie wolle mir etwas zeigen. Solche Besuche sind mein täglich Brot und meist unergiebig. Umständlich löst sie Knoten um Knoten, erzählt ohne Übergang von ihrem Leben und wie sie das Bild vor den Deutschen versteckt hat, mit viel Glück, das

Bild von Salomon, seit Jahrhunderten in der Familie ihres Mannes, nur Salomon, der Familienname verschollen, aber ein Frauenheld, endet sie mißbilligend. Das Plaid fällt.

Aufmerksam blickt Salomon mich aus dem schwarzen Rahmen an. Blitzende Glanzlichter in den dunklen Augen. Kastanienbraunes, gelocktes Haar fällt auf den kostbaren Spitzenkragen. Atmende Haut. Der linke Mundwinkel spöttisch hochgezogen, die Lippen weich und voll. Gekleidet ist er in das bekannte schwarzseidene Gewand, dessen Ärmel sich vor dem grünlichen Hintergrund bauschen. Salomon, sichtlich entstiegen den gleichgültig grauen Wassern der Amsterdamer Grachten, um erneut Bewunderung zu erringen. Ich untersuche das Bild sorgfältig, den Firnis, die Pinselstriche, die kaum verzogene Fuge zwischen den beiden Holzplanken, die abgeschrägten Kanten der Rückseite.

„Ein bemerkenswertes Bild", sage ich, „Rembrandtzeit, aber vermutlich ein anonymer Meister", und weiß, daß ich der alten Frau damit nichts Neues sage. Sie nickt, „ich möchte, daß das Bild in dieses Museum kommt, nicht auf eine Versteigerung – ich will nicht viel dafür, bin alt, habe mein Auskommen." Ich lobe das Bild noch einmal, bekunde Interesse für das Museum und verspreche, sie zu benachrichtigen, sobald wir einen Entschluß gefaßt haben. Sie vertieft sich erneut in die Vergangenheit, konnte fliehen in den bösen Zeiten, den Sohn hat sie versteckt bei einer katholischen Familie in Friesland, die ihn als wiedergefundenen Verwandten ausgab, ohne daß die flachsblonden Nachbarn ihr dies angesichts des schwarzgelockten Knaben abnahmen, erst recht nicht, als er bei der Austeilung der Hostie von der hintersten Bank aus fröhlich schmetterte: „Ich will auch ein Stück Mazze", aber Gott hat seine Hand über ihn gehalten wie über Isaak, und derweil faltet sie das Plaid zusammen, rollt die Schnur auf, als wüßte sie, daß diese endgültig ihre Dienste getan hätten und gibt mir ihre Adresse.

Ich schloß die Tür hinter ihr, lehnte das Bild in eine Ecke und machte mich wieder an meine Arbeit. Ich nehme meine Arbeit ernst. Was nicht bedeutet, daß ich keinen Spaß an ihr hätte. Oder eher an der Bewunderung, die sie mir einbringt? Ständig gebe und kriege ich Küsse, auf die Wangen, immer drei nach holländischer Sitte. Auch von meiner Mutter, die mit niemandem mehr spricht, weil der Schrecken der Vergangenheit sie verwirrt hat, aber nach jeder Mahlzeit feststellt, „jetzt ist der Höhepunkt des Tages überschritten", ohne erkennen zu geben, ob dies Erleichterung oder Bedauern bedeutet.

Meine Erinnerung an den einen letzten Kuß anderer Art ist ein Schatten, und den haben die gleichgültig grauen Wasser der Gracht verschluckt, an der ich wohne. Diese sind unendlich tief. Sieht und sagt bloß keiner.

Mein Blick streifte das Bild, und ich fand ihn erwidert. Das weiche Licht des vergehenden Tages löschte den spöttischen Zug und verwandelte ihn in etwas wie eine seltsam gelassene Heiterkeit. Eine Heiterkeit, die von weit herkam und doch genau mich meinte. Ja, Salomon, dachte ich, so ist es, und plötzlich schien er meine Unsicherheit zu sehen und zu verzeihen, die ich hinter meiner Sachkenntnis verstecke, und meinen geheimen Neid auf alle diejenigen, die mit Pinsel, Stift und Feder ihre Zukunft erobern, während ich der Vergangenheit hinterherrenne. Ich gehörte ins Museum, war Teil des leblosen Inventars. So ist es. Salomon war offenbar gänzlich anderer Meinung.

Ich sitze auf meinem Sofa in der Halle des King David-Hotels, und eine Vielzahl lebendigster Menschen summt um mich herum. In Amsterdam bin ich einigermaßen bekannt. Hier bin ich Frau Haizman. Frau Haizman hat ihren Salomon. Salomon?

Ich winke dem Ober und bitte um das Telefonbuch von Jerusalem.

Ich werde nachdrücklich dafür plädieren, daß wir Salomon kaufen. Wenn er auch nicht der erste Frauenheld in unserer Sammlung sein wird.

Da habe ich auch schon gefunden, was ich suchte: Haizman, Salomon, Investments, ein Büro mit zentraler Adresse und ein Privatanschluß in einem Außenbezirk. Ich notiere das und gehe zur Rezeption, Schalom, die Empfangsdame lächelt, ja, sie wird für mich mit Salomons Sekretärin telefonieren, die wird die Botschaft an Salomon weitergeben, daß ich, seine Frau, mich mit ihm im King David treffen möchte, ja, sogleich, einfach so, fahr' gar nicht erst nach Hause, Salomon, bitte. Vielen Dank, die Empfangsdame lächelt zurück, durchs Gesumm finde ich wieder auf mein Sofa und zu meinem Glas, Amsterdam so weit, ich bin in Jerusalem, du schöne.

Und bin lebendigster Teil einer höchst gegenwärtigen, höchst belebten Hotelhalle.

Ich wartete.

Wer wartet, wird eingegrenzt. Unweigerlich findet er sich in einem Tunnel, der den Blick spannt und vorwärts zwingt. Ich aber wartete ohne Ungeduld. Ließ mich tragen von dem Gefühl wohltuender Zeitlosigkeit, war jetzt selber eingewoben in diesen Teppich mit beständig wechselndem Muster.

Ein dunkler Fleck zeichnete sich ab im Eingang zur Halle. Dann formte er sich zu einem männlichen Umriß. Im Zeitraffer kommt ein Mann auf mich zu, mit sicherem Schritt, winkt fröhlich, ist schon ganz nah, lacht mich aus dunklen Augen an und streicht eine kastanienbraune Locke aus der Stirn. Ich weiß, er ist es, ich lächle, er stockt, und seine erhobene Hand beschreibt eine unsichere Linie, malt ein Fragezeichen in die Luft. Sein Lachen weicht einer Ratlosigkeit, die ihn zu verwirren scheint. Was er offenkundig nicht gewohnt ist. „Seltsam", sagt er statt Schalom, seine Augen gehen über mein Gesicht, meine Haare, mein Kleid, meine Beine, meine Schuhe. „Schalom, Schalom, Salomon", sage ich und

betrachte ihn weniger gründlich als er mich, habe ich doch nichts zu vergleichen
wie er, weiß ich doch längst, daß er mir gefällt.

„Setz' dich, Salomon", lade ich ihn ein und weise auf das Sofa.

Zögernd, doch nicht unwillig nimmt er Platz, mich weiter musternd, inzwischen höflich unauffällig. „Ich bin verblüfft", teilt er mit. Doch sein Interesse an dieser zweifellos verrückten Situation wächst, wenn er es auch nicht offen zeigt, ja, und ein freundschaftliches Wohlwollen steigt vom Grund seiner dunklen Augen auf – wie für ein Kind, dem man den Streich verzeiht, weil er so überaus pfiffig war. In sein fragendes Schweigen hinein fange ich an zu erzählen, die Verwechslungen vor der störrischen Kuh und hier im King David, gelange zu meinen schweigsamen Bildern, meinen Forschungsarbeiten, die gedruckt werden auf Seiten weiß und kalt wie Schnee, wer bis ganz oben Karriere macht, atmet eine dünne Luft – natürlich sage ich das alles ganz anders. Salomon ist nicht mehr stumm wie am Anfang, er fragt, er lacht, er erzählt von sich, ich lache.

Der Tag verlischt, die Erde dreht uns in ein anderes Licht, und die Lämpchen an den Wänden glimmen auf. Und siehe, das Licht ist schön und spiegelt sich in Salomons dunklen Augen. Er schuf das Licht, und in seinem Licht schuf er sie einen Mann und ein Weib. „Sie sind tatsächlich ein Abbild meiner Frau", sagt Salomon, „aber sie und ich leben in einer anderen Welt als Sie", und er legt seine Hand tröstend auf meine Schulter, um mich herüberzuholen in seine Welt.

Ein Mann und eine Frau auf einem Sofa. Jetztzeit.

Immer noch redeten wir, lachten, redeten wie ein altes Ehepaar, das sich immer noch was zu sagen hat. Die Wärme seiner Hand dringt durch den Stoff auf meine Haut. „Wollen wir essen gehen?" fragte Salomon, und wir verlassen das King David, fahren aus der Stadt heraus auf eine Schotterstraße, die in die Berge führt. Ein schmaler Weg geht ab, ich finde mich am gedeckten Tisch eines Restaurants, das genau so belebt ist wie die Halle des King David.

Wir essen vom Ziegenböcklein, das der begehrliche Juda seiner Schwiegertochter Thamar nach dem Beischlaf sandte, und vom Linsengericht, für das Esau sein Erstgeburtsrecht an Jakob verkaufte. Als Dessert bestelle ich gedünsteten Apfel, und nach dem ersten Bissen schiebe ich Salomon die süße, saftige Frucht hin, mit der auch Eva Adam verführte.

# Das Wesen der Dinge

ASTRID TÜMPEL

Fuchsmann war nicht mehr jung, zwischen fünfzig und sechzig vielleicht. Eisgraues Haar, zum Igel geschoren. Ein entschlossener Mund, doch seltsam weiche braune Augen, die etwas zu fragen oder zu suchen schienen. Viertel nach neun, wir hatten schon Papier aufgespannt und standen hinter den Staffeleien bereit, das Modell saß ausgezogen auf seinem Schemel, betrat er den Aktsaal. Steil aufgerichtet erschien er in der hohen Tür, mit dem rechten Fuß fest auftretend, den linken leicht nachziehend. „Guten Morgen, Kinder", rief er, wir alle, ob Student oder Studentin, waren für ihn „Kind" und wurden geduzt. Hinter ihm watschelte Dolores in den Saal, eine unsägliche Promenadenmischung, fett, krummbeinig, das eine Ohr spitz aufgerichtet, das andere schlapp herunterhängend, schütteres braunschwarzes Fell mit kahlen Stellen an den Flanken und, als sei da etwas wettzumachen, dicken, verfilzten Zotteln am zu langen Schwanz, der sich wie ein Fragezeichen über den Rücken krümmte. Wir hatten meist dasselbe Modell, „Gnädigste" genannt, dieser Titel erübrigte den Namen. „Gnädigste" entstammte der Generation Fuchsmanns, verblüht, aber sichtlich einmal geblüht. Um Augen und Mund zogen sich unübersehbar Falten, die in seltsamem Widerspruch zu ihrem makellosen Körper standen. Mund, Finger- und Fußnägel leuchteten karminrot, immer karminrot, ihr schulterlanges Silberhaar band sie jedesmal, nachdem sie sich ausgezogen hatte, mit einer riesigen schwarzen Samtschleife zusammen, die fast Schulterbreite erreichte. Sie war eine Meisterin in der Erfindung von Positionen, und sie war in ihrem Körper zu Hause. Selbstbewußt und mit Genuß dehnte und spreizte sie ihre Gliedmaßen, was mich einigermaßen verwirrte und faszinierte. Dolores war ein stolzer Hund. Uns Studenten verachtete sie. Streckte einer die Hand aus, flüsterte lockend, komm, Dolores, komm, zog sie die Lefzen hoch und ließ ein abgründiges Grollen vernehmen. Doch sobald sie allmorgendlich hinter Fuchsmann den Saal erreicht hatte, machte sie einen Satz an ihm vorbei und wackelte, die Krallen tickten auf dem Linoleum, auf die Gnädigste zu. Die beugte sich herunter, ihre Brustspitzen berührten die Schenkel, und kraulte abwechselnd das hochstehende und das schlappe Ohr. Das Untier fiel platt auf den Boden, seufzte und schloß hingebungsvoll die Augen. Fuchsmann seinerseits trat auf die Gnädigste zu, ergriff ihre Hand und küßte sie, was angesichts der Nacktheit einigermaßen komisch wirkte, doch niemand lachte. Dann schob er das elektrische Heizöfchen hin und her, erkundigte sich fürsorglich, ob es der Gnädigsten nicht zu heiß oder zu kalt sei. Fuchsmann siezte sie, sie duzte ihn und nannte ihn Professorchen, was immer klang, als stünde er in der Rangfolge um einiges unter ihr. Trotz dieser gewissen Spannung schien irgend etwas die beiden zu verbinden. Fuchsmann verehrte sie, das war klar, erging sich in Komplimenten. Sie ließ sich die kontinuierliche Verehrung gefallen, ohne sie jedoch besonders ernst zu nehmen. Wir nahmen von dem sich täglich wiederholenden Spiel kaum Notiz, waren viel zu sehr mit uns selbst beschäftigt. Nach der Begrüßungszeremonie nahm die Gnädigste gekonnt ihre erste Position ein, und je nach Mut und Selbstvertrauen warfen wir unsere dünnen grauen oder dicken schwarzen Kohlestriche aufs Papier. Fuchsmann machte die Runde, verkündete das Prinzip der wahren Kunst, nämlich das des Konstruktivismus: „So, Kind, hier hast du den Hintern, ein Kubus, hier den Brustkasten, noch ein Kubus, hier die Brüste, zwei Pyramiden." Mit einem Kohlestummel, den er aus seiner ausgebeulten Rocktasche holte, fuhr er über die Rundungen, zog hier eine Gerade, dort eine Gerade und verband sie zu stereometrischen Gebilden. Dann baute er sich neben der Gnädigsten auf, rief: „Apperzeption! Abstraktion! Reduktion", machte eine Kunstpause und schloß: „Konstruktion, das Wesen der Dinge!" Wir wußten, daß er in einer Zeit, in der alle Welt Farben scheinbar wahllos auf die Leinwand spritzte, schleuderte, schüttete, ein hoffnungslos Gestriger war. Er stellte nie aus. Hin und wieder führte er den einen oder anderen öffentlichen Auftrag aus. Ein Mosaik an der Gartenseite eines abgelegenen städtischen Pflegeheims, in dessen Genuß die allesamt bettlägerigen Insassen nie kamen, oder ein Relief an einer Autobahnbrücke außerhalb der Stadt, das die Autofahrer – beschäftigt mit Überholen, Gasgeben, Wieder-Einfädeln – niemals wahrnahmen. Und doch erwuchs bei seinen Korrekturen aus seinen Würfeln, Kugeln, Zylindern und Pyramiden etwas, das uns das Wesen der Gnädigsten erahnen ließ. Hatte er unsere krummen Linien in seinem Sinne verbessert und uns über das Wesen der Dinge aufgeklärt, grub er wieder in seiner Rocktasche und förderte ein schwärzlich angestaubtes Stück Hundekuchen zutage. „Dolores! Rolle!" rief er, und der fette Bastard schmiß sich auf den Boden, um sich über seinen gekrümmten Schwanz hinweg dreimal um seine Längsachse zu drehen. Dann rappelte er sich mühsam auf, machte Männchen und schnappte gierig nach dem Brocken. Die Gnädigste, die sonst nie eine Miene verzog, lächelte, und Fuchsmann freute sich.

Vom Konstruktivismus, der Gnädigsten und Dolores nahm ich nach Abschluß der Grundklasse Abschied, sah mich in verschiedenen Klassen verschiedenen allein seligmachenden Weltsichten ausgesetzt und fand mich schließlich im eigenen Atelier mit mehr Fragen als Antworten. Kulissenmalen half über die Anfänge, bald fand sich ein Verlag, der meine Gemälde und Zeichnungen für seine Cover verwandte, ein Glücksfall, ich strich hübsche Summen ein und bekam meine Werke zurückgeliefert, nachdem sie fotografiert waren, ja, und dann Erfolge, Ausstellungen – Museen und Sammler zeigten sich interessiert, waren wohl der Meinung, ich hätte das Wesen der Dinge getroffen, bis sich eines Tages der Leiter vom Kunstverein der Stadt, in der ich studiert hatte, bei mir meldete. Ich war jetzt gut zwanzig Jahre tätig, hatte viel verkauft, noch mehr stand in den Holzverschlägen auf dem Spitzboden über meinem Atelier. Ich kroch zwischen den Leinwänden herum, zog diese, jene hervor, der Mensch vom Kunstverein wählte aus, machte sich Notizen. Unvermutet stieß ich auf ein riesiges Gemälde: die Gnädigste! Überlebensgroß. Der blühende Körper in einer aufsteigenden Schräge angeordnet, rosig, atmend, gekrönt von der riesigen schwarzen Schleife, weich schimmernder Samt, der zum Anfassen verlockte. Und vorn, auf dem Boden, Dolores, einmalig in ihrer Scheußlichkeit. Dunkel erinnerte ich mich, daß ich das Bild Jahre nach meinem Abschluß gemalt hatte, erfüllt von Wut auf meine Lehrer, die über ihrer eigenen Weltsicht uns übersehen hatten. Im Hintergrund waren Tische, Hocker und Staffeleien angeordnet, sichtlich konstruktivistisch dargestellt, und ich wußte, es war ein gutes Bild. Mein Besucher klatschte in die Hände, großartig, ja, das kommt auch in die Ausstellung. Nachdem alles abgeholt war, vergaß ich das Bild. Monate später war ich zur Eröffnung geladen. Mein Besucher stand am Pult, redete, was weiß ich, die Luft war erfüllt vom Dunst der vielen Menschen, ein junger Mann rollte die Augen und schrie wirre Gedichte gegen die grün bespannten Wände, an denen meine Bilder hingen. Danach war ich umringt von perfekt geschminkten und frisierten Frauen, die ihren auffälligen Schmuck gekonnt auf ihre Kleider abgestimmt hatten, und von Männern, die reich aussahen, obwohl nicht auszumachen war, weshalb. Meine Bilder schienen das Publikum nicht zu interessieren, niemand stellte Fragen, vielmehr überschüttete man mich mit Bemerkungen, die eine intime Kenntnis der augenblicklichen Kunstszene beweisen sollten und bei mir gleiches voraussetzten. Ich floh. Die Treppe hinunter ins Foyer. Dort war es still. Ich lief an dem Verkaufsstand mit Büchern, Prospekten, Katalogen und Broschüren vorbei zum Ausgang. Neben der Tür hingen dicht an dicht Ausstellunsplakate der örtlichen und umliegenden Museen. Ein Puzzle aus unzusammenhängenden Formen und Farben. Davor stand ein Mann. Als ich eben an ihm vorbeiging, drehte er sich um, stutzte, sah mich offen an. Dann lächelte er, ein um Verzeihung bittendes Lächeln. Aus seltsam weichen, braunen Augen, die etwas zu fragen oder zu suchen schienen. Ich blieb stehen. „Sie sind die Künstlerin?" fragte er freundlich. Es klang eher beiläufig, nicht aufdringlich. Ich nickte. Er hob den Arm und wies auf die Plakatwand. Dort sah ich plötzlich inmitten des Puzzles die Gnädigste. Mit Dolores. Hatte mein Besucher also dies Bild für die Werbung verwendet. Nun gut. Warum nicht. „Sie haben hier studiert?" fragte der Mann, und ich nickte. „Ich habe des Bild oben gesehen. Ich verstehe nichts von Kunst. Bin auch kein Sammler. Habe mit anderen Dingen zu tun. Aber ich möchte es kaufen. Nennen Sie mir einen Preis. Ich zahle, was Sie wünschen." Der Mann sah nicht so schreiend reich aus wie die da oben. Ich zögerte. Das schien er zu spüren. „Das ist Dolores, nicht wahr?" sagte er unvermittelt. Ich war verblüfft. „Woher wissen Sie das?" Er lächelte, schien aber etwas zurückzuhalten. Dann holte er Luft und sagte rasch, wie um es hinter sich zu bringen, „das Modell war meine Mutter". „Ach, was", entfuhr es mir, und ich ärgerte mich, daß mir nichts besseres einfiel. Außerdem starrte ich den Mann auf unhöfliche Weise an. „Haben Sie Fuchsmann noch gekannt?" fragte er. „Ja, sicher, ich hab' ihn in der Grundklasse gehabt, und das Modell, und Dolores, ein Jahr lang." Der Mann lächelte jetzt wieder. „Fuchsmann war mein Vater." Ich fuhr zusammen, – die Gnädigste und Professorchen, ein Paar? Und dabei doch kein Paar? In den Mann kam Bewegung. „Meine Eltern waren nicht verheiratet. Meine Mutter wollte nicht. Aber mein Vater hat bis zu seinem Tod auf sie gehofft, nun, sie wollte frei sein." Er seufzte, „dabei hat sie ihn gemocht, aber heiraten – nein. Er kam regelmäßig, ein guter Vater, geduldig, hatte immer eine Meinung, mir aber nie Ratschläge erteilt. Hat mir mein Studium bezahlt, ja, der größte Wunsch in meinem Leben war, daß meine Eltern heiraten würden. Verkaufen Sie mir das Bild?" Ich nickte und nannte eine mittlere Summe. Der Mann strahlte, griff in seine Brusttasche und überreichte mir seine Visitenkarte. Ein anderer Name als Fuchsmann. „Ich werde alles veranlassen, Sie können das Bild nach dem Ende der Ausstellung hier abholen." Der Mann griff nach meiner Hand, hob sie empor, als wollte er sie küssen, doch dann langte er erneut in seine Brusttasche. Wenig später hatte ich einen Scheck in der Hand. Wir verabschiedeten uns, und ich ging zur Tür. Schon halb draußen, drehte ich mich noch einmal um und fragte über die Schulter: „Und was machen Sie beruflich?" Der Mann rief, und es klang wie ein Triumph, „Ingenieur! Brückenbauer! Konstruktion – das Wesen der Dinge!"

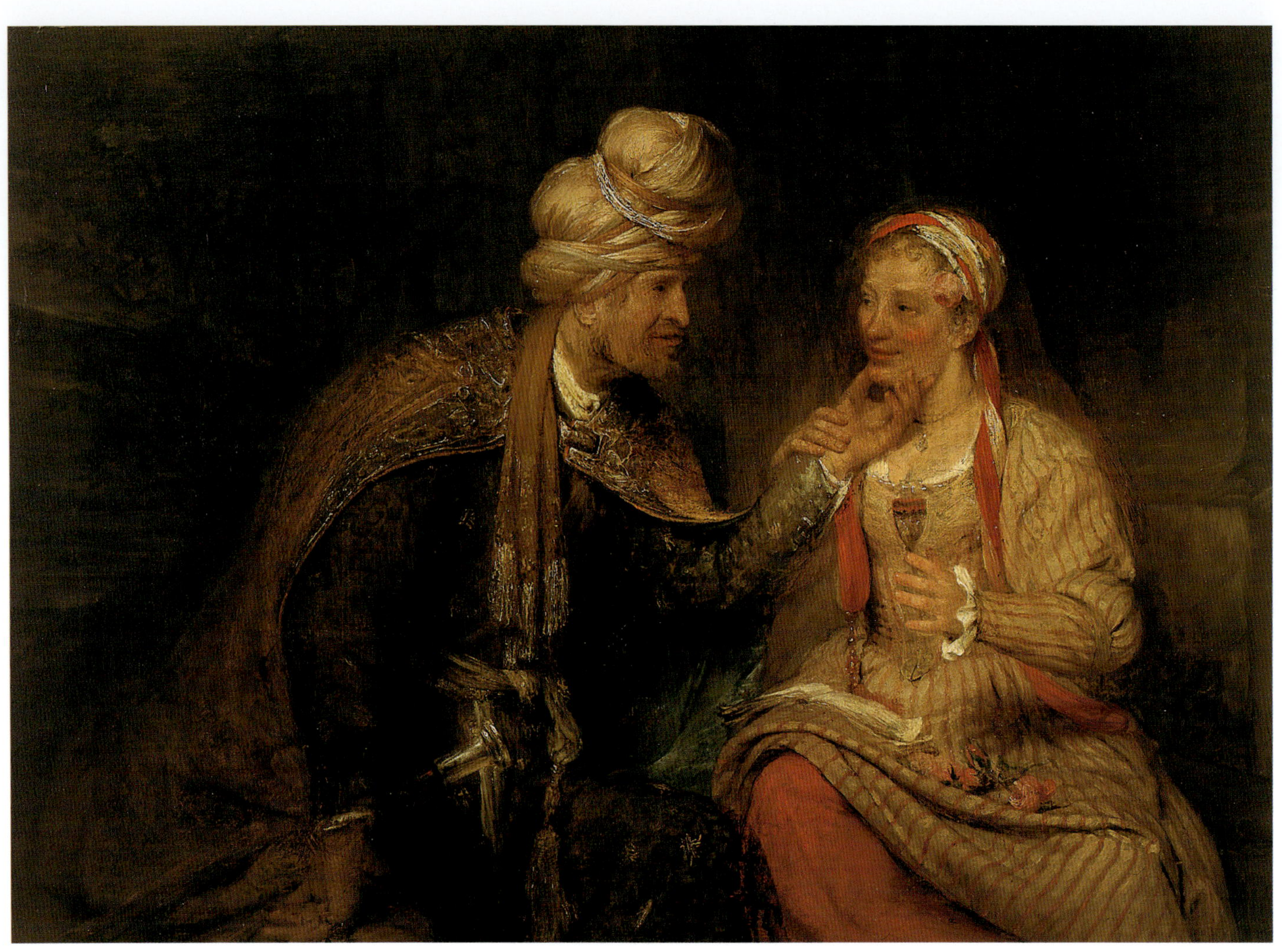

# Arent de Gelder's Religious Iconography

CHRISTIAN TÜMPEL

Arent de Gelder (1645–1727) was primarily a history painter, whose main subject was the Bible. Of his extant paintings of biblical subjects, scenes from the Old Testament form the largest group. He painted more Old Testament scenes than Rembrandt (1606–1669). It was only in the eighteenth century, towards the end of his life, that he began to pay more attention to the New Testament, when he painted a large cycle of the Passion of Christ. In addition to biblical stories, he also depicted scenes from ancient history and mythologyas well as a few allegories, almost two dozen portraits and a small number of genre paintings.

De Gelder's choice of subjects was clearly inspired by his teacher Rembrandt (notably his etchings and late paintings), by members of the Rembrandt school as well as the Pre-Rembrandtists, and by sixteenth-century reproductive prints which provided him with models for the creation of new themes. His range of subject-matter, however, pales compared with the sheer diversity of Old and New Testament themes which appear in the work of the Pre-Rembrandtists, Rembrandt and some of his pupils, as does his range of media. The older master, followed by many of his pupils, drew extensively on the subjects favoured by the famous engravers of the sixteenth and seventeenth centuries, whose ideas he adapted in his etchings and drawings, while his paintings owe much to the Pre-Rembrandtists, Peter Paul Rubens (1577–1640) and the Caravaggisti. Arent de Gelder on the other hand expressed himself almost exclusively through the medium of paint, hence his much smaller oeuvre. And whereas the Pre-Rembrandtists and Rembrandt, together with his studio, drew inspiration from all narrative parts of the Old Testament (including the Apocrypha), De Gelder concentrated on a select number of books only: Genesis (Moltke 1–17), Samuel and Kings (Moltke 19–24), Tobit (Moltke 43–45) and, above all, Esther (Moltke 25–41).[1] His choice of subjects from the New Testament was equally restricted, since he depicted almost exclusively scenes from Christ's youth (Moltke 46–51), Passion and Resurrection (Moltke 58–72).

fig. 1 ARENT DE GELDER
*Judah and Tamar*
Oil on canvas, 102.7 × 147.5 cm
Kingston, Ontario, Agnes
Etherington Art Center, Gift of
Drs Alfred and Isabel Bader

## General themes

Arent de Gelder was apparently content to restrict himself to a select number of themes. Like Pieter Lastman (1583–1633) and Rembrandt before him, he favoured scenes showing meetings in which a Prophet or king encounters a biblical hero in a moment of crucial importance (*Judah pleading with Joseph*, Moltke 16;[2] *Ahimelech gives the Sword of Goliath to David*, Moltke 20; *King David and the Prophet Nathan*, Moltke 22). Of those themes which appear in Rembrandt's work, some assumed a central role for De Gelder: the ability to recognize someone or not (*Judah and Tamar*, Moltke 11–13; *Joseph Weeping*, Moltke 14; *Judah pleading with Joseph*, Moltke 16–17);[3] being frightened or unaffected, speaking or listening, the appearance of heavenly or godly bodies (*Jehovah and the Angels visit Abraham*, Moltke 1; *Jacob's Dream at Bethel*, Moltke 9, 10; the Angel Gabriel as the unrecognized companion of Tobias, Moltke 44; *Simeon in the Temple*, Moltke 47, 48; *Christ on the Mount of Olives*, Moltke 59, 60; *Christ appears before the Two Maries*, Moltke 71). Some subjects treated by Rembrandt appear only sporadically – those physically blind but gifted with vision (*Homer Dictating*, Moltke 76), sacrifices (*The Sacrifice of Isaac*, Moltke 6); others are avoided altogether, for example female nudes (*e.g.* Susanna, Bathsheba, Diana and Andromeda).

In those areas where De Gelder was not influenced by his teacher one finds a completely different range of interests. One which appears to have captured his imagination is the relationship between the sexes, as witnessed by his numerous representations of Lot and his Daughters (Moltke 2–4) and Judah and Tamar (Moltke 11–13), as well as the many depictions from the Book of Esther (Moltke 25–41).[4] *Sarah complaining to Abraham about Hagar* (Moltke 5), *Boaz and Ruth* (Moltke 18) and *Bathsheba reminding David of his Promise to name Solomon his Successor* (Moltke 23) should also be seen in this context.


## Variations on Rembrandt paintings

De Gelder maintained a lifelong admiration for Rembrandt's work, and many of his own paintings are variations of the master's. Even when his style changed at the beginning of the eighteenth century, his narrative principles and compactness continued to be modelled on those of his teacher. But De Gelder would have known only a small section of Rembrandt's painted oeuvre. The works from the period before 1656 had been auctioned in that year. Accordingly, during his time in Rembrandt's studio he would have known only later works, predominantly those executed shortly before or during his apprenticeship (*ca.* 1661–63), *e.g. Homer* (The Hague, Mauritshuis), *Haman and Ahasuerus at the Feast of Esther*



CHRISTIAN TÜMPEL

(Moscow, Pushkin Museum), as well as drawings, such as that showing David and Nathan in the Metropolitan Museum of Art, New York.[5]

During later visits to Rembrandt's studio De Gelder would have seen works done after 1663, such as *Isaac and Rebecca* (Amsterdam, Rijksmuseum) and *Self-portrait as Democritus* (Cologne, Wallraf-Richartz-Museum).[6] In addition, he may have known paintings in private collections or on the art market. Many of Rembrandt's works continued to be of interest to De Gelder decades later, and he proved to be particularly adept at varying the subject-matter. It is likely that he owned reproductive engravings or drawn copies, or that he had access to the collections in which these works were to be found, such as that of his friend Jakob Moelaert (1649–1727).

The composition and colouring of the painting *Ahasuerus and Esther* (Amiens, Musée de Picardie, Moltke 30) was inspired by Rembrandt's treatment of the same subject (Moscow, Pushkin Museum).[7] This painting positively glows with colour, yet it is built around only three hues – brown, red and gold. Because of the brownish-black background, the comparatively colourful figures, of whom Esther is the most beautiful, appear almost like silhouettes.

Depicted is the moment when Esther accuses Haman of wanting to destroy the Jewish people, including herself, for she reveals that she, too, is a Jew. Although her husband King Ahasuerus has not yet delivered his judgement, he has already turned to look at Haman. Rembrandt indicates the imminent downfall of the once-powerful but now silent Haman by placing him in the shadows on the far left, that is on the periphery of the picture. In doing so he anticipates the outcome of the story: Esther remains queen, the Jewish people are saved and Haman is executed. The outwardly peaceful scene veils the drama caused by the mounting tension prior to Ahasuerus's decision. The painting comes alive by capturing the ambivalence of the moment and by the glorious palette of melting colours.

De Gelder removes all uncertainties from his painting. Rather than appearing lost in thought, as in Rembrandt's picture, the king expresses his distress at Esther's account by staring accusingly at the hunched-up figure of Haman, who guiltily bows his head and clasps his hands. De Gelder avoids the transitional moment. Equally, he adopts the richness of Rembrandt's palette but opts for a more clearly defined use of the individual colours. In another painting of the same subject (Melbourne, National Gallery of Victoria, Moltke 31), De Gelder illustrates a slightly later moment, focusing on Ahasuerus's reaction as he clenches his hands in rage. Haman collapses and hides his face behind his hands.

Among Rembrandt's early works which influenced De Gelder, although he could not have known the original, is the painting *David playing the Harp for Saul* from about 1629/30 (Frankfurt, Städelsches Kunstinstitut).[8] This picture had already been etched in 1633 by Willem de Leeuw (1603–*ca*. 1665) from Antwerp. Sitting at the feet of the king, the young shepherd plays his harp in an attempt to soothe the grim-faced Saul, who has been befallen by an evil spirit. A central motif of the painting is the way in which Saul's fist tightens around the spear he is holding – the story goes that he was so jealous of David's achievements that he hurled his spear at him. Rembrandt uses Saul's fist and sinister, brooding countenance to illustrate his despair and envy. David is completely immersed in his music, his subordinate status evident as he kneels in the left corner. All we really see of him is his head, the harp and the hands plucking the strings.

Although De Gelder also shows Saul grasping the spear (1682, Bremen, Kunsthalle, Moltke 19), he prefers to focus on the king's contemplative mood. He is shown leaning forward out of his chair, his head in his right hand (the characteristic pose of the melancholic) as he listens with a heavy heart to David's music. From the corner of his eye he watches the boy who faces him. David stands in the middle ground on the right, partly hidden by the podium on which Saul's chair is placed. In the right foreground lies Saul's turban with its large feather, a motif introduced by De Gelder to indicate that a change of power is about to take place. On the whole, De Gelder heightens the psychological struggle between Saul and David, but tempers the former's aggression by making him appear more melancholic. He incorporates David's apprehension into the composition.


## De Gelder's translation of Rembrandt's etchings into paintings

De Gelder modelled roughly one eighth of all his history paintings on etchings by Rembrandt. Instead of the Caravaggesque half-figure paintings favoured by Rembrandt during his late period, the majority of his etchings illustrate many-figured history subjects, particularly those found in sixteenth- and seventeenth-century prints. De Gelder used Rembrandt's etchings as the basis for his history scenes with small figures in the style of Rembrandt's paintings from the 1630s and 1640s. He would have learned from Samuel van Hoogstraten (1627–1678) how to approach this task and what aspects to take into consideration. A particularly interesting example of such a transformation is De Gelder's *Ecce Homo* of 1671 in Dresden (Gemäldegalerie Alte Meister, Moltke 66). This is a variation of the third or fourth state of Rembrandt's famous etching of 1655 (Bartsch 76) with additional motifs derived from the 1636 etching of the same subject (B. 77).[9]

The changes De Gelder introduced in the painting demonstrate his method of adaptation while at the same time providing us with a clear idea of his artistic and iconographic concerns. Most notably, he thins out Rembrandt's crowded group on the platform. By moving Pilate to the left he increases the distance



CHRISTIAN TÜMPEL

between him and Christ, who now stands alone except for his guards, and thus dramatizes the situation. Compositionally, Pilate is balanced, on the right, with a soldier leaning against the balcony. A series of motifs adopted from Rembrandt's earlier etching (B. 77) enables us to interpret the scene: Pilate, in the chronology of the biblical narrative, has left his throne and now stands, indicating with his right hand that the decision should be left to the crowd; a bust of the ruling emperor decorates the niche of the town hall, symbolizing worldly power (in the etching it is a herm); soldiers wearing the uniforms of contemporary Dutch civic guards, armed with halberds and broad swords, provide a topical reference. Furthermore, De Gelder added a *Caritas* figure in relief on the balustrade to the right.

The people standing below are divided into two groups: on the one hand are those who demand the death of Christ, mainly the angry Pharisees, on the other the ordinary people, including children, who seem to be far more interested in the barking dog in the foreground than in Christ's fate. Such secondary motifs, of which De Gelder introduced several in the foreground, can be classified as genre elements. They allowed the artist to show the great variety of reactions of which a large group of people is capable, especially when not all are interested in the problem facing Pilate. Nevertheless, the numerous genre motifs do not distract from the actual subject, especially since the principal figures are emphasized by the light of the evening sun.

In addition to scenes of mass assembly (relatively rare in the artist's oeuvre), De Gelder frequently used etchings by Rembrandt for his compositions with limited numbers of people. In two depictions of *The Rest on the Flight into Egypt* (Boston, Museum of Fine Arts, and Kettwig, Girardet Collection, Moltke 49 and 50 respectively) he went back to Rembrandt's late etching of the same subject (B. 58). There, Mary and Joseph sit on a small mound of earth. Mary lifts the wrap from the baby's face so that Joseph can see it as he peels some fruit. While De Gelder's Boston painting (Moltke 49) shows the same grouping as the etching, the actions of the protagonists are completely different. On the left Mary holds the Christ Child close to her breast, which she touches with her left hand so that he can drink; but instead the child sleeps. Joseph has apparently come across a reference in his Bible to Christ as the Saviour. With his finger still placed on the word, he looks astonished at the child who is the subject of the text. In a series of works by Rembrandt from the 1640s Joseph is characterized as a man who has no role in the process of salvation and from whom the true nature of the birth of Christ is hidden. De Gelder, on the other hand, shows him as one who recognizes God's will by reading the Bible.[10]

De Gelder twice turned for inspiration to Rembrandt's etching *The Presentation in the Temple* of *ca.* 1639 (B. 49), in a painting of 1684, now in the Art Gallery of Hamilton, Ontario (Moltke 48), and in a later painting in The Hague (Mauritshuis, Moltke 47). In the earlier work he transformed the oblong format of the etching into an upright one, possibly inspired by Rembrandt's earlier etching of the same subject of 1630 (B. 51). Simeon kneels in the centre of a lofty temple giving praise to God for the child. In front of him Mary has fallen to her knees, as has the female companion next to her. Behind Simeon an old man bends forward slightly. De Gelder took this central group – reversed – from Rembrandt's etching (B. 49). The remaining figures on the right are more or less adopted from Rembrandt's crowd, although De Gelder reduces the number of witnesses who listen with scepticism or interest to Simeon's praise. The light streaming through the window falls on the child and the head of Simeon, thereby underlining Christ's role as the Light of the World. In Rembrandt's etching the Prophetess Anna is illuminated by the Holy Ghost as she approaches. By showing Anna with the unusual motif of the dove in a nimbus hovering above her, Rembrandt departed from the text of the Bible, which states that the dove was above Simeon. De Gelder shows the dove above both Anna, who approaches from the left, and Simeon. On the left is a steep staircase, which is clearly adopted from Rembrandt's earlier etching (B. 51). When, about fifteen years later, De Gelder turned again to Rembrandt's etching of *ca.* 1639 (B. 49), he removed the principal figures from the narrative context. In doing so he made use of a popular seventeenth-century artistic device, which I have called '*Herauslösung*' (isolation). Apparently De Gelder also knew Rembrandt's late painting of the subject (Stockholm, National Museum) showing only the figure of Simeon, the Christ Child and Mary.[11]


## '*Herauslösung*'

In order to capture the psychological content of a scene, sixteenth- and seventeenth-century artists adopted a pictorial method already in use in the Middle Ages, which I have called '*Herauslösung*' (isolation). In the early fourteenth century artists often focused on individual biblical figures or groups rather than on the overall narrative context in which they belonged. Caravaggio's followers, primarily when painting scenes with half-length figures, tended either to concentrate on the protagonists of the story or alternatively to isolate a group of figures from a scene with a multitude of characters. Rembrandt made use of both options and Arent de Gelder followed his lead. In his paintings *Lot and One of his Daughters* (Brussels, Musées Royaux des Beaux-Arts de Belgique, Moltke 3), *Jacob's Dream at Bethel* (Winterthur, Sammlung Oskar Reinhart, Moltke 10), *Judah pleading with Joseph* (Heidelberg, Kurpfälzisches Museum, Stiftung Posselt, and Schlangenbad, Sammlung Hohenbuchau, Moltke 16 and 17 respectively), *Belshazzar's Feast* (Los Angeles, J. Paul Getty Museum, Moltke 42), and *Let the Children come Unto Me* (Cassel, Gemäldegalerie Alte Meister, Moltke 57)[12] he limited his depiction to the most important antagonists while leaving out those figures and motifs that would otherwise further clarify the context. In his paintings *Joseph holding the Cup* (present whereabouts unknown, Moltke 15), *The Enraged Ahasverus* (private collection, Melbourne, Moltke 25) und *Esther* (private collection, Pewaukee, Moltke 40, and present whereabouts unknown, Moltke 41) he focused exclusively on one of the protagonists. However, since fragments of paintings may fortuitously resemble such '*Herauslösungen*', one should first determine whether the above-mentioned paintings have survived fully intact and that their unique compositions indeed reflect De Gelder's intentions.


## Variations on the works of other artists

In about one third of his history paintings, De Gelder resorted to themes which had been rendered by artists from the school or circle of Rembrandt, as well as by the Pre-Rembrandtists, frequently in paintings, less often in drawings. They include such subjects as *The Engagement of Isaac and Rebecca* (Moltke 8), *Judah and Tamar* (Moltke 11–13), *Christ and the Woman taken in Adultery* (Moltke 55), and *David and Nathan* (Moltke 22). In the case of *Christ and the Adulteress* and *David and Nathan*, subjects also treated by Rembrandt, it would appear that the older artist's works were not known or not available to De Gelder, so that he had to rely on drawn or painted variations by pupils.

De Gelder painted the story of Judah and Tamar (Genesis 38) at least three times. Judah was Tamar's father-in-law; his eldest son was her husband. After his death, Tamar married her husband's brother, as was the custom. When he, too, died, Judah promised Tamar his third son, but kept postponing the marriage. This was contrary to Jewish law, as Tamar was left a widow without adequate protection. In order to get her due, she resorted to a trick. She disguised herself as a harlot and waited outside the city for Judah to return from sheep shearing. Judah propositioned her and promised her a goat as payment. Tamar demanded his staff, his ring and his cord until the goat would be delivered to her.

The subject was popular in Rembrandt's circle, as witnessed in paintings by Lastman, Ferdinand Bol (1616–1680) and Gerbrand van den Eeckhout (1621–1674), all of which illustrate the handing over of one of the pledges. Characteristically, De Gelder chose to depict an earlier moment. In two of his paintings (private collection, Europe, Moltke 11, and The Hague, Mauritshuis, currently on loan to the National Gallery, London, Moltke 12), De Gelder shows the more dramatic moment when Judah tries to force himself on Tamar before they have agreed on the terms. In the Hoogsteder version Judah brutally grabs hold of the woman's throat, but Tamar defiantly tries to remove his hand while still using her left hand to bargain with. Her gesture is equally clear in the picture in the Mauritshuis, where she is almost lying on the ground while Judah leans over her. The third painting, which once belonged to Alfred Bader (now Kingston, Ontario, Agnes Etherington Art Centre, Moltke 13; fig. 1) shows the couple sitting next to one another. This time Judah touches Tamar's chin gently, but again she is determined first to clarify the terms of their agreement. The staff which Judah soon is to hand over as a pledge hangs from his belt. Tamar's pose indicates the outcome of the story, but the continued dispute between them shows that not all questions have been clarified. In all three representations De Gelder chose to depict the moment preceding the episode found in the older pictorial tradition.

The opportunity of depicting an earlier moment in the story is one which De Gelder frequently takes advantage of. It permitted him to use compositions which relied on thematic constellations particular to that moment. Moreover, it had the advantage of allowing him to disguise his pictorial sources while simultaneously providing his own interpretation of the story.

An interesting example of this approach is *Christ and the Woman taken in Adultery* (Thyssen Collection, Madrid, Moltke 55). The scene is usually illustrated by showing Christ bending down and writing on the ground (*e.g.* Bruegel's grisaille in the Courtauld Institute Galleries, London). Rembrandt, in his *Woman taken in Adultery* in London (National Gallery), chose to depict Christ at the moment when he says to the Pharisees: "He that is without sin among you, let him first cast a stone at her".[13] This picture was inspirational for a number of paintings by members of his school, for example Gerbrand van den Eeckhout,[14] and it was these works which became important for De Gelder. They show Christ standing among the Pharisees, pointing to the repentant adulteress kneeling on the ground. Arent de Gelder also shows her kneeling, but chooses an even earlier moment in the story. The text (John 8: 2) states: "And early in the morning he [Christ] came again into the temple; and all the people came unto him; and he sat down, and taught them." It is only in verse three that the adulteress is brought to Christ. De Gelder shows Christ sitting in the temple teaching. He bases his composition on Van den Eeckhout's *Christ teaching in the Synagogue of Nazareth* (Dublin, National Gallery of Ireland),[15] which shows Jesus sitting among the Pharisees, discussing the law. By using this compositional arrangement as a point of departure for his own painting, De Gelder emphasizes Jesus's role as teacher and calls to mind his dispute with the Pharisees. Their conception of the law is challenged by the teachings of Christ.

Interestingly, in those instances where De Gelder uses the works of artists other than Rembrandt as a source of inspiration for his own compositions, he generally adopts a much freer approach than to those of the great master. While his fluent colouristic style is reminiscent of Rembrandt's late period, his approach to narrative is more drastic, less ambiguous, sometimes even vulgar compared to that of Rembrandt who favoured subtlety, and frequently was content with mere allusions. In some of his paintings De Gelder departed from the episode traditionally represented, particularly when he wished to depict an unusual subject.


## Unusual subjects

A small part of De Gelder's oeuvre is devoted to subjects which hitherto had been depicted only in sixteenth-century prints. The formulation of the subject-matter of his paintings, like those of the Baroque period generally, was determined by sixteenth- and seventeenth-century graphic art. His later works also show knowledge of eighteenth-century prints. He frequently drew on those print series, for example by Maerten van Heemskerck (1498–1574), Maerten de Vos (1532–1603) and Jan van der Straet, known as Stradanus (1523–1605), in which the Bible or individual books from it are illustrated as a whole. Also popular were series dealing with biblical heroes such as Joseph, David and Esther. The illustrations, taken in the main from the Old Testament, were sometimes bound together as Picture Bibles. The Haarlem Mannerists, the Pre-Rembrandtists from Amsterdam as well as Rembrandt and his pupils began to paint these unusual scenes.

De Gelder was probably introduced to prints and their richness as iconographic source material, especially with regard to the Old Testament, by Hoogstraten and Rembrandt. Through these prints, often iconographically old-fashioned, he would have learnt how to present a story from the point of its intention, psychological situation and narrative style.[16] It is most impressive to see how the most modest illustrations of the stories of Joseph, David, Tobit and Esther inspired De Gelder to paint moving scenes, such as *Joseph Weeping* (Copenhagen, Statens Museum for Kunst, Moltke 14), *Judah pleading with Joseph* (Moltke 16 and 17), *Edna blessing Tobias* (Groningen, Groninger Museum, Moltke 45), and *Christ brought to the House of the High Priest* (Amsterdam, Rijksmuseum, Moltke 62).

From the story of David, De Gelder chose two scenes which previously had been illustrated in prints only: *Ahimelech giving the Sword of Goliath to David* (Los Angeles, J. Paul Getty Museum, Moltke 20) and *Bathsheba asking David for the*

*Crown for Solomon* (private collection, Switzerland, Moltke 23). In both cases he probably was inspired by the series of engravings by Benito Arias Montano (*ca.* 1527–1598) and Philips Galle (1537–1612; Plantin, Antwerp, 1575, nos. 46, 47), since these were used by Rembrandt and other artists of his school as iconographic models. While other artists from Rembrandt's circle also turned to the story of Bathsheba demanding from David the crown for her son Solomon (*e.g.* Van den Eeckhout), De Gelder's depiction of *Ahimelech giving the Sword of Goliath to David* (Moltke 20) remains unique in painting.

Fleeing from Saul, David meets the priest Ahimelech. In response to David's request, the priest gives him some of the holy bread, whereupon David asks for a spear or sword to defend himself from one of Saul's shepherds. Ahimelech hands him the sword that once belonged to the Philistine Goliath. Philips Galle depicted David and Ahimelech in full length, seen in profile, at the moment of exchanging the sword. De Gelder chose a more complicated half-figure composition. Wearing the robes of a priest, Ahimelech proffers the horizontally held sword, which David takes with both hands. While Galle identifies David by showing his harp attached to his belt, De Gelder is content to illustrate the unusual scene simply by showing a priest giving a powerful weapon to a young man.

## New subjects

According to theoretical writings on art, artists were not supposed to prove their ability by devising new themes, but instead by creating variations on existing ones, or finding new ways of representing subjects rarely illustrated. It seems, however, that some artists from Rembrandt's 'academy' sought to depict scenes which, as far as we know, had never been visualized before, not even in prints. These artists were inspired both by direct knowledge of the Bible passage and by the fact that the story as a whole had been illustrated in print-series, from which they borrowed a number of iconographical features. But instead of selecting the episodes found in the prints, they frequently chose to depict moments which either preceded or succeeded those shown in their prototypes.[17]

This method of choosing scenes suitable for visual representation was also applied by De Gelder. A good example is provided by his numerous depictions from the Book of Esther. The source of much of his Esther iconography was a series by Philips Galle (1537–1612) after Maerten van Heemskerck (1498–1574), which also was important for Rembrandt.[18] Following the advice of art theorists to create variations on existing themes, De Gelder painted *The Toilet of Esther* three times (private collection; Potsdam, Sanssouci, Gemäldegalerie; Munich, Alte Pinakothek, Moltke 27–29), thus taking up a subject that had been painted by Rembrandt and his circle, even though it had not appeared in Heemskerck's prints.[19] But he also chose scenes which had not previously been depicted. It appears that, although the possibility cannot be entirely excluded that he had at his disposal graphic works no longer extant, De Gelder, instead of using prints which are no longer known, simply invented the iconography himself. Such new subjects include *Ahasuerus with Mordecai and Esther* (Copenhagen, Statens Museum for Kunst; Leipzig, Museum der Bildenden Künste, Moltke 33 and D4 respectively) and *Esther and Mordecai writing to the Jews* (Dresden, Gemälde-galerie Alte Meister; Buenos Aires, Museo Nacional a Bellas Artes; Providence, Museum of Art, Rhode Island School of Design, Moltke 36–38).

Heemskerck's series concludes with a reference to Haman's death on the gallows. It does not include scenes showing the salvation of the Jews and the destruction of the foe at the instigation of Esther and Mordecai. The salvation of the Jews begins when Mordecai takes Haman's place, *i.e.* after he receives Haman's ring and assumes the latter's functions (Esther 8: 2), as shown by De Gelder in his painting in Copenhagen (Moltke 33). This is followed by two decrees, authorized by Ahasuerus and written by Esther and Mordecai, which enable the Jews to take revenge on their enemies. The act of drawing up these Purim letters was chosen by De Gelder as the subject of three paintings, now in Providence, Buenos Aires and Dresden. Of these the picture in Providence (Moltke 38) is especially successful in its combination of meaning and form: Mordecai holds the pen in his right hand while gesturing with his left; Esther holds the letter aloft so that the text is visible. In recognition of its contextual importance, the letter is prominently displayed in the centre of the picture.


## De Gelder's pictorial language

Both Hoogstraten and Rembrandt were instrumental in the development of De Gelder's pictorial language. From the former he learned to express emotions through gestures, from the latter the ability to structure the great variety of emotions and reactions found in his many-figured history scenes. Moreover, Rembrandt taught him how to capture the essential features of histories in half-figure compositions with the means of only a few elements.

In the picture *Joseph and Judah with the Returned Cup* (Heidelberg, Kurpfäl-zisches Museum, Moltke 16) De Gelder has reduced the story to two figures: Joseph stands with his right hand resting on a table while Judah, intervening on behalf of his younger brother Benjamin, bows respectfully before him. Only the cup found in Benjamin's sack, and now in Joseph's left hand, identifies the scene. Although using the minimum of characters, motifs, action and gestures, De Gelder nevertheless creates a painting full of psychological tension. A shadow falls on part of Judah's face, his head is bowed, his hands, also shaded, are extended in a pleading gesture. Joseph's expression is equally serious; his eyes, partly in shadow, are fixed on his older brother's face. De Gelder would have learned both the compositional type and the pictorial language from Rembrandt, who is responsible for another, unusual motif in the painting. The Bible tells us that Pharaoh rewarded Joseph with a ring and cloak because he had interpreted Pharaoh's dreams. As both of these objects are too general to be of use as identifying attributes, especially in such a rarely depicted scene, De Gelder gives Joseph a chain of honour as symbol of the Pharaoh's favour.

The same motif appears in *Joseph Weeping* (Copenhagen, Statens Museum for Kunst, Moltke 14), the scene that follows Joseph's encounter with Benjamin. The chain of honour reflects a practice of sixteenth- and seventeenth-century rulers, who with its endowment showed their appreciation of painters (*e.g.* Charles V and Titian, Charles I and Rubens and Van Dyck). Frequently, the chain carried a medallion with the ruler's portrait. Hoogstraten, De Gelder's first teacher, received such a chain from the Emperor Ferdinand II (1578–1637). Rembrandt depicted Aristotle (384–322 BC), the teacher of Alexander the Great (356–332 BC), wearing a chain of honour complete with portrait medallion (see Walter Liedtke's essay in this volume, and his fig. 1).[20] This motif was immediately understood by seventeenth-century viewers as one denoting honour bestowed on a subject by a king. Such a motif in his pictures of Joseph makes clear that De Gelder was more interested in using a readable pictorial language than offering an exact depiction of a specific event.

Similarly, in his representations of Judah and Tamar, De Gelder shows Tamar with a book (private collection, Europe, Moltke 11; Kingston, Ontario, Agnes Etherington Art Centre, Moltke 13; here fig. 1) or, more appropriately, with a scroll (The Hague, Mauritshuis, currently on loan to the National Gallery, London, Moltke 12), in reference to her legal rights, which were being violated by Judah. In other paintings De Gelder also stresses the legal implications of a situation, for example of marriage, as in the *Marriage Contract of Tobias and Sarah* (Brighton, Art Gallery and Museum, Moltke 44), in which he depicts the moment when the terms of marriage are entered in a book. Similarly, many of the paintings of episodes from the Book of Esther show the laws of the Jews being written on scrolls.

 CHRISTIAN TÜMPEL

Arent De Gelder's use of the *Statenbijbel* and of *The Jewish Antiquities* by Flavius Josephus

Arent de Gelder followed traditional iconography, sometimes of expressly Catholic origin, occasionally combined with motifs which indicate his awareness of Counter-Reformation changes. However, many of his paintings show that he did not solely rely on the established pictorial repertoire but went back to the biblical text directly. Under 'New Subjects' I discussed how De Gelder created scenes which had not been depicted before by expanding on the visual repertoire found in sixteenth-century print-series, for example in his paintings of the writing of the Purim letters, which were inspired by the Esther series by Maerten van Heemskerck.

Other iconographical innovations can only be explained by De Gelder's knowledge of the Reformed *Statenbijbel*. Early Dutch translations of the Apocrypha were based on Luther's German translation which, in turn, was based on the Vulgate. The *Statenbijbel* or *Statenvertaling*, which appeared in 1637, was different in that it was based not on the Vulgate but on the Septuagint, the Greek translations of the Hebrew Bible. It also included, in an appendix, the apocryphal books for which there were no Hebrew texts and which also were translated from the Septuagint.[21] In many important points the Septuagint deviates both textually and contextually from the Vulgate. Only with the appearance of the *Statenbijbel* was it possible for an artist to read a Dutch translation of the Septuagint version.

De Gelder is one of the few artists to have used the *Statenbijbel*, as can be shown in his much-disputed painting in Utrecht (Museum Het Catharijneconvent, Moltke 45). Van Fossen and Janssen identified its subject as Hanna (Edna in the Septuagint),[22] the wife of Raguel, giving Tobias and Sarah her blessing, citing Tobit 7: 15 from the Vulgate as the text source. Sumowski has pointed out that it is not Edna but her husband Raguel who blesses his daughter and son-in-law, and that consequently De Gelder must have deviated from the text in order to incorporate the figure of Hanna.[23] Instead he suggested Anna blessing her son Tobias and Sarah upon their return to Nineveh (Tobit 11: 18). According to all versions of the biblical text, however, their arrival was very different and has a completely different iconography.

According to the Septuagint, on which the *Statenbijbel* is based, Raguel's blessing of the young couple is followed by Edna making a short speech to Tobias, at the end of which she entrusts her daughter Sarah to him.[24] This is the subject of De Gelder's painting. Edna takes Tobias's hands in her own as she talks to him. He inclines towards her, while Sarah stands next to him and her mother. This arrangement is reminiscent of a mourning scene, all the more so because of the finality of the gesture of Edna who emphatically entrusts her daughter to Tobias and requests only that he protect her from any distress. Raguel is present in the background.

Another painting of the story of Tobias, in Brighton (Moltke 44), also demonstrates that De Gelder used the *Statenbijbel* as textual source rather than the Vulgate or translations based on it. The picture illustrates the marriage contract between Tobias and Sarah. According to the Vulgate, Raguel took Sarah by the hand and gave her to Tobias with his blessing. They took a scroll, on to which they wrote the marriage contract.[25] This is the scene depicted by De Gelder, but his painting includes the figure of Edna looking at a document while Raguel writes in a book. Neither Edna nor the book is mentioned in the Vulgate. These are details which are specifically referred to in the *Statenbijbel*, which is more comprehensive in its description of the marriage: "*Ende by* [Raguel] *riep Edna / sijn wijf / ende name een boecksken / ende schreef een handtschrift ende versegelde dat. Ende sy begonden te eten*" (Tobit 7: 16–17).

Both paintings from the story of Tobias show clearly that Arent de Gelder used the *Statenbijbel*. But they also show that he did not share the negative opinion of the Reformed Church regarding the Apocrypha, which appeared in the *Statenbijbel* only as an appendix, complete with critical commentary. De Gelder's choice of subject-matter places the Apocrypha on an equal footing with the stories from the Bible. It is essential that we rid ourselves of the idea that the artistic output of seventeenth-century artists adhered strictly to the teachings of the leaders of their respective churches. Artists like De Gelder and Rembrandt, who repeatedly turned to the Book of Tobit, were not influenced by the criticism of the Apocrypha. On the contrary, in their paintings, drawings and etchings of biblical scenes they showed a marked preference for episodes rich in narrative content for which the Apocrypha provided a rich source.

Poets and painters of the sixteenth and seventeenth centuries considered the *Jewish Antiquities* of Flavius Josephus (AD *ca.* 37/38–*ca.* 100) as an important additional literary source when dealing with stories from the Bible, as I have discussed elsewhere.[26] Arent de Gelder occasionally also borrowed motifs from it.

In his painting *Sarah complaining about Hagar to Abraham* (private collection, Germany, Moltke 5) De Gelder adopts Josephus's characterization of Abraham as a man knowledgeable in astronomy, which leads him to recognize the will of God through the observation of nature. Abraham is shown sitting in the foreground listening to Sarah who kneels before him. Texts are piled on the sofa; more scrolls and books are on the table. Together with the two globes in the background, they characterize Abraham as a man of learning, a man for whom science and faith merge as natural theology.[27] The Bible portrays Abraham as an obedient, though repeatedly doubting, believer, one who continues to survive only through God's intervention. For Josephus, on the other hand, he is a humanist whose knowledge and moral integrity enable him to use natural theology and monotheism to overcome polytheism.[28]

As one of the most important Dutch painters of biblical histories, Arent de Gelder is to be credited with maintaining well into the eighteenth century his own distinctive interpretation of the most characteristic features of Rembrandt's art – his choice of subjects and themes, and variations on them, his sensitive characterization and ability to use chiaroscuro, his brilliant and fascinating use of structure and colour to emphasize important features while barely hinting at less important aspects, and his development of Rembrandt's palette into his own characteristic colour scheme.

When I visited the home of Alfred Bader in 1974 we discussed extensively the iconography of his *Judah and Thamar* by Arent de Gelder (Moltke 13) in front of the original. Ever since we have had many discussions on the iconography of Dutch biblical paintings. For this reason I would like to dedicate to Alfred this essay from 1993, which is being published here for the first time in a reduced version. The English translation has been provided by Kristin L. Belkin. In the meantime Volker Manuth has also written an essay on this subject that has been published in Dutch and German ('"De voorwerpen van zyn Historische vertooningen zyn meest Bybelstof . . .". De bijbelse historiestukken van Arent de Gelder: keuze van onderwerpen en iconografie', in *Arent de Gelder. Rembrandts laatste leerling*, exh. cat., Dordrechts Museum and Wallraf-Richartz Museum, Cologne, 1999, pp. 51–69). He arrives at similar conclusions while adding other aspects and a number of important details.


1  Throughout the text I shall be identifying Arent de Gelder's paintings with the numbers from J.W. von Moltke's catalogue of the artist's works: J.W. von Moltke, *Arent de Gelder. Dordrecht 1645–1727*, Doornspijk 1994.

2  Here the painting is called *Joseph and Judah with the Returned Cup*.

3  In many of the paintings in which Arent de Gelder depicts a scene of recognition or realisation he went directly back to compositions or interpretations by Rembrandt, *e.g. The Circumcision* (Moltke 46), *Simeon in the Temple* (Moltke 47, 48), *The Holy Family* (Moltke 49, 50).

4  Of the paintings mentioned above many have more than one theme: the story of Judah and Tamar revolves not only around the relationship between male and female but also around the consequences of recognizing someone or not.

5  Abraham Bredius, *Rembrandt. The Complete Edition of the Paintings*, revised by Horst Gerson, London 1969, nos. 483, 539; Christian Tümpel, *Rembrandt, Mythos und Methode*, Königstein 1986, nos. 12, 30; for the drawing see Otto Benesch, *The Drawings of Rembrandt*, 6 vols., 2nd edn, revised by Eva Benesch, London 1973, V, no. 948, fig. 1159.

6  Bredius, *op. cit.* (note 5), nos. 416, 61; Tümpel, *op. cit.* (note 5), nos. 32, 177.

7  Bredius, *op. cit.* (note 5), no. 530; Tümpel, *op. cit.* (note 5), no. 30.

8  Bredius, *op. cit.* (note 5), no. 490; Tümpel *op. cit.* (note 5), no. 5; Josua Bruyn, Bob Haak, Simon H. Levie, Pieter J.J. van Thiel, Ernst van de Wetering, *A Corpus of Rembrandt Paintings*, vols. I–, Foundation Rembrandt Research Project, The Hague, Dordrecht, Boston and London 1982–, I, no. A25, pp. 258–65.

9  The reference numbers for the Rembrandt etchings mentioned here and below in the text have been taken from Adam Bartsch, *Catalogue raisonné de toutes les estampes qui forment l'oeuvre de Rembrandt, et ceux de ces principaux imitateurs*, Vienna 1797.

10  De Gelder's Joseph does not mistrust Mary. On the contrary, in the Berlin *Holy Family* he alludes to her role as the second Eve by tenderly laying his arm around her shoulder and offering the child a piece of fruit.

11  Bredius, *op. cit.* (note 5), no. 600; Tümpel, *op. cit.* (note 5), no. 73.

12  I prefer this title to von Moltke's title, *Christ blessing the children*, because De Gelder actually painted this proverb.

13  Bredius, *op. cit.* (note 5), no. 566; Tümpel, *op. cit.* (note 5), no. 63.

14  Werner Sumowski, *Gemälde der Rembrandt-Schüler*, 6 vols., Landau 1983–94, II, nos. 441, 442.

15  *Ibid.* no. 428.

16  De Gelder seems to have been inspired by his graphic models to create in paint such unusual subjects as *Sarah complaining to Abraham about Hagar* and *Joseph Weeping*, both from Genesis (Moltke 5, 14).

17  For example, Jan Victors (1619–after January 1676) depicted the scene where the Prophet Elisha returns the son of the Shunammite woman to his mother after having brought him back to life (2 Kings 4: 36), the episode which follows the more commonly depicted miracle (2 Kings 4: 34–35): cf. Tümpel, *op. cit.* (note 5), pp. 170–71; for an illustration see Sumowski, *op. cit.* (note 14), IV, no. 1772.


   CHRISTIAN TÜMPEL

18  F.W.H. Hollstein, *Dutch and Flemish Etchings, Engravings and Woodcuts, ca. 1450–1700*, 57 vols., Amsterdam 1949–2001, VII, p. 74, nos. 39–46, VIII, p. 243, nos. 248–55; ed. Ger Luijten, *The New Hollstein Dutch and Flemish Etchings, Engravings and Woodcuts, 1450–1700*, Maarten van Heemskerck, Part I, compiled by Ilja M. Veldman, Roosendaal 1993, pp. 132–38, nos. 151–58.

19  Rembrandt (Ottawa, National Gallery of Canada: Bredius, *op. cit.* (note 5), no. 494; Tümpel, *op. cit.* (note 5), no. 8; *Corpus, op. cit.* (note 8), no. A64), Willem de Poorter (Dublin, National Gallery of Ireland, and private collection: Sumowski, *op. cit.* [note 14], IV, nos. 1627, 1628).

20  Bredius, *op. cit.* (note 5), no. 478; Tümpel, *op. cit.* (note 5), no. 108. See especially Julius S. Held, *Rembrandt's Aristotle and other Rembrandt Studies*, Princeton 1969, and Walter Liedtke's essay in this book, pp. 72–87.

21  On this subject see also Volker Manuth's essay in this volume, especially pp. 100–01.

22  D.R. van Fossen, 'The Paintings of Aert de Gelder', unpubl. Ph.D. thesis, Harvard University, Cambridge, Mass., 1969, no. 39; A. Blankert *et al.*, *The Impact of a Genius. Rembrandt, His Pupils and Followers in the Seventeenth Century*, exh. cat., Waterman, Amsterdam, 1983, p. 168, no. 39.

23  Sumowski, *op.cit.*, (note 14), II, under no. 762.

24  Tobit 10: 13 (*Statenbijbel*). The scene is not in the Vulgate and the translations based on it.

25  Tobit 7: 15–17: "*Et apprehendens dexteram filiae suae, dexterae Tobiae tradidit, dicens: Deus Abraham, et Deus Isaac, et Deus Jacob vobiscum sit, et ipse conjungat vos, impleatque benedictionem suam in vobis. Et, accepta charta, fecerunt conscriptionem conjugii. Et post haec epulati sunt, benedicentes Deum.*"

26  W. Forster, 'Josephus, Flavius', in *Die Religion in Geschichte und Gegenwart. Handwörterbuch für Theologie und Religionswissenschaft*, ed. K. Galling, 6 vols., Tübingen 1957–65, III, col. 868f (with bibliography); Tonio Hölscher, 'Josephus der Schriftsteller', in *Real-Encyclopädie der classischen Altertums-wissenschaft*, ed. A.F. Pauly, G. Wissowa, 68 vols., 15 suppl. vols., 2 index vols., Stuttgart 1894–1980, IX (1916), cols. 1934–2000.

27  Pieter Lastman alludes to Abraham's knowledge of the stars by illustrating an astrolabe in Abraham's baggage in the painting *God appears to Abraham on his Way to Sichem* (St Petersburg; Astrid Tümpel, *Pieter Lastman. Rembrandts Lehrer. Seine Zeit und sein Werk*, forthcoming, no. 5). See Christian Tümpel. 'De Receptie van de "Joodse Oudheden" van Flavius Josephus in de Nederlandse Historieschilderkunst', in *idem, Het Oude Testament in de Schilderkunst van de Gouden Eeuw*, exh. cat., Joods Historisch Museum, Amsterdam 1991–92, pp. 194–206, with previous literature.

28  Flavius Josephus, *Jewish Antiquities*, I, VII, 1–2.

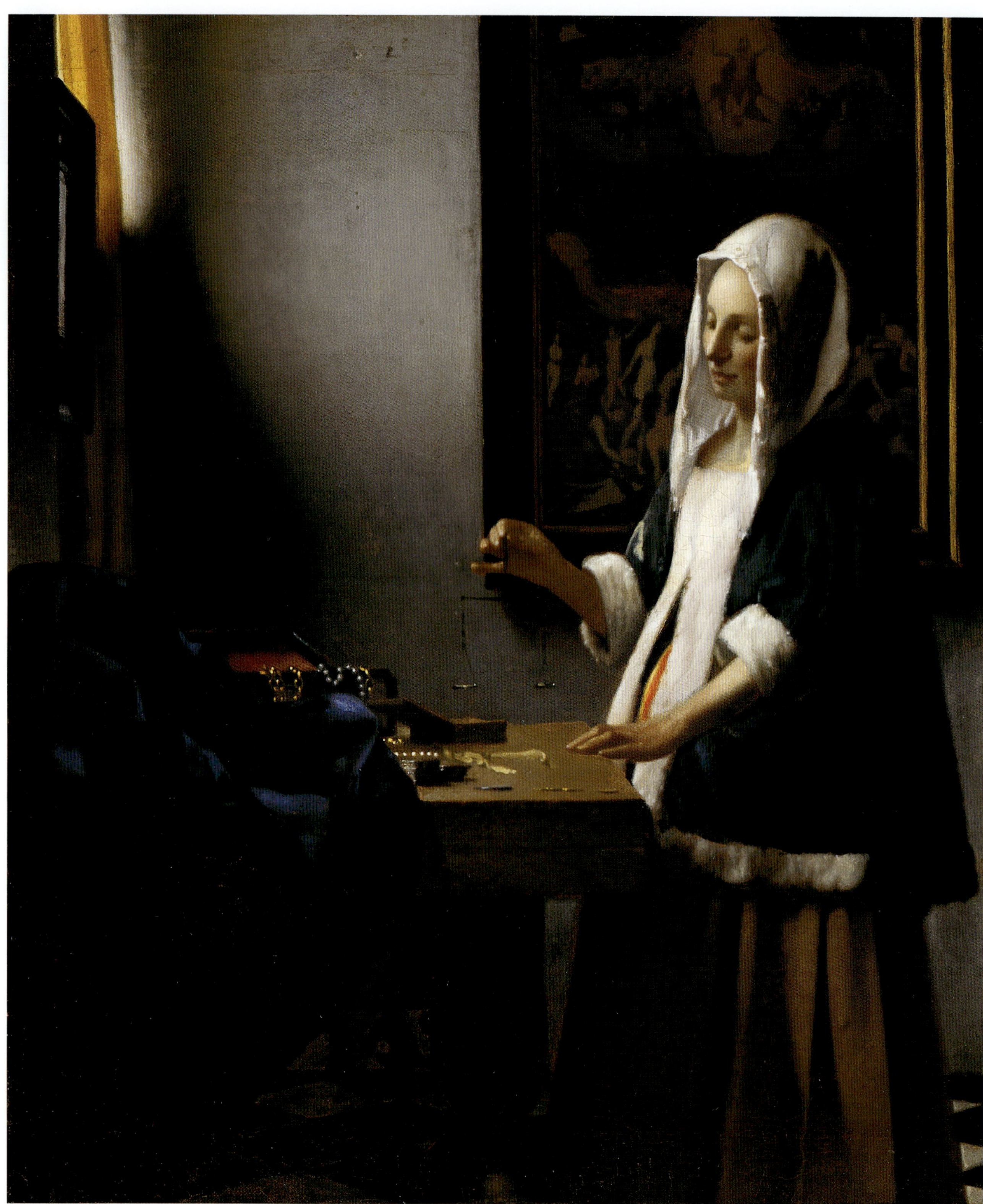

# The Framing of a Vermeer

ARTHUR K. WHEELOCK, JR

Johannes Vermeer's *Woman holding a Balance* (fig. 1) hangs at the National Gallery of Art, Washington, D.C., in a seventeenth-century black ebony frame that the Gallery acquired in 1994. The simple profile of the frame is of the type that one could imagine surrounding the work when it hung in a Delft collection were it not for the fact that a seventeenth-century document indicates that the painting originally had an entirely different framing solution. This document is an Amsterdam sale catalogue from 1696, where the painting was described as: "A young woman weighing gold, in a box by J. van der Meer of Delft, extraordinarily artful and vigorously painted".[1] Of the twenty-one works by the artist mentioned in the sales catalogue, *Woman Holding a Balance* is the only one described as being in a "box".[2]

While this reference has often been noted, no serious efforts have been made to determine why Vermeer had placed *Woman holding a Balance* in a box. Was it a device merely designed to keep light and dust away from the surface or did it have some other function? Was it a framing solution that Vermeer had envisioned from the beginning or was it one that was arrived at once the painting had been completed? Although Vermeer left behind no written documents that explain his artistic ideas, certain stylistic and thematic aspects of the painting suggest that this framing solution was one he consciously planned.

A clue to Vermeer's artistic intent comes from a document related to one of his contemporaries, the Leiden painter Gerrit Dou (1613–1675). Dou, who was twenty years older than Vermeer (1632–1675), and renowned for his detailed manner of painting, was so famous during his lifetime that an exhibition of his works – perhaps the first monographic exhibition ever organized – was held in a private house in Leiden in 1665. Of the twenty-seven works exhibited, twenty-two were in cases.[3] One can only imagine what it would have been like to enter that exhibition room almost three hundred and fifty years ago to see twenty-two closed cases, a few of which had painted shutters, hanging on the wall. Only upon opening the shutter doors of the individual cases could one see the jewel-like paintings Dou had created. Each experience, thus, could become a private moment of discovery and contemplation.

fig. 1 JOHANNES VERMEER
*Woman holding a Balance*, ca. 1664
Oil on canvas, 40.3 × 35.6 cm
Washington, D.C., National Gallery
of Art, Widener Collection

When the exhibition on Gerrit Dou was held at the National Gallery of Art in 2000, it became clear that the cases that once surrounded Dou's paintings served an important function for properly viewing the master's works.[4] The cases forced the viewer to come close to the paintings to open the doors. From this predetermined vantage point the artist's careful, even meticulous, rendering of his scene could be fully appreciated. As in *An Interior with Young Violinist*, 1637, from the National Gallery of Scotland, Edinburgh (fig. 2), Dou often depicted his figures gazing directly at the viewer, almost as though they were surprised to see the doors of the case open. Dou, moreover, quickly draws the viewer into the interior space with a perspective system designed for an unusually close vantage-point.[5] Consequently, the cases Dou used to create self-contained environments for his paintings enabled him to create effective illusionistic images, even at a small scale, that fully engaged his viewers.

The framing devices utilized by Vermeer and Dou raise fascinating questions about the ways in which Dutch artists presented their paintings. Some artists, including Gerard Houckgeest (*ca.* 1600–1661), depicted illusionistically painted frames around their works, suggesting that such images were hung unframed.[6] Artists occasionally enhanced illusionistic effects by painting design elements such as ribbons or curtains on to the surrounding frame, furniture or wall.[7] In some instances the extensions were painted on panels or canvases cut to the shape of the object to be represented.[8]

The artist who was most renowned for shaping his panels and canvases was Samuel van Hoogstraten (1627–1678), who discreetly placed illusionistically painted images around his home to fool the unsuspecting visitor. Some were set into pieces of furniture, but, as Hoogstraten's friend the painter and art theorist Arnold Houbraken (1660–1719) noted, others were free standing:

> I have seen what still remains of these [illusionistic images] in his house: here an apple, pear or a lemon in a dishrack, there a slipper or shoe painted on a board, sawed out, and placed in the corner of the room or under a chair. There were also dried salted fish painted on gessoed canvas, cut out and hung here and there on nails behind a door that were painted so deceptively that one could easily mistake them for actual dried plaice.[9]

The various ways in which seventeenth-century Dutch artists presented their works of art are rarely to be found today. Very few Dutch paintings retain their original frames, and virtually all of these works have been divorced from their original settings. Nevertheless, even if documentation of the original appearance of paintings is scarce, many artists certainly sought to enhance illusionistic effects through their framing solutions. Through such means they could enhance the pictorial ideals praised by, among others, Philips Angel (*ca.* 1618–1664). Angel,

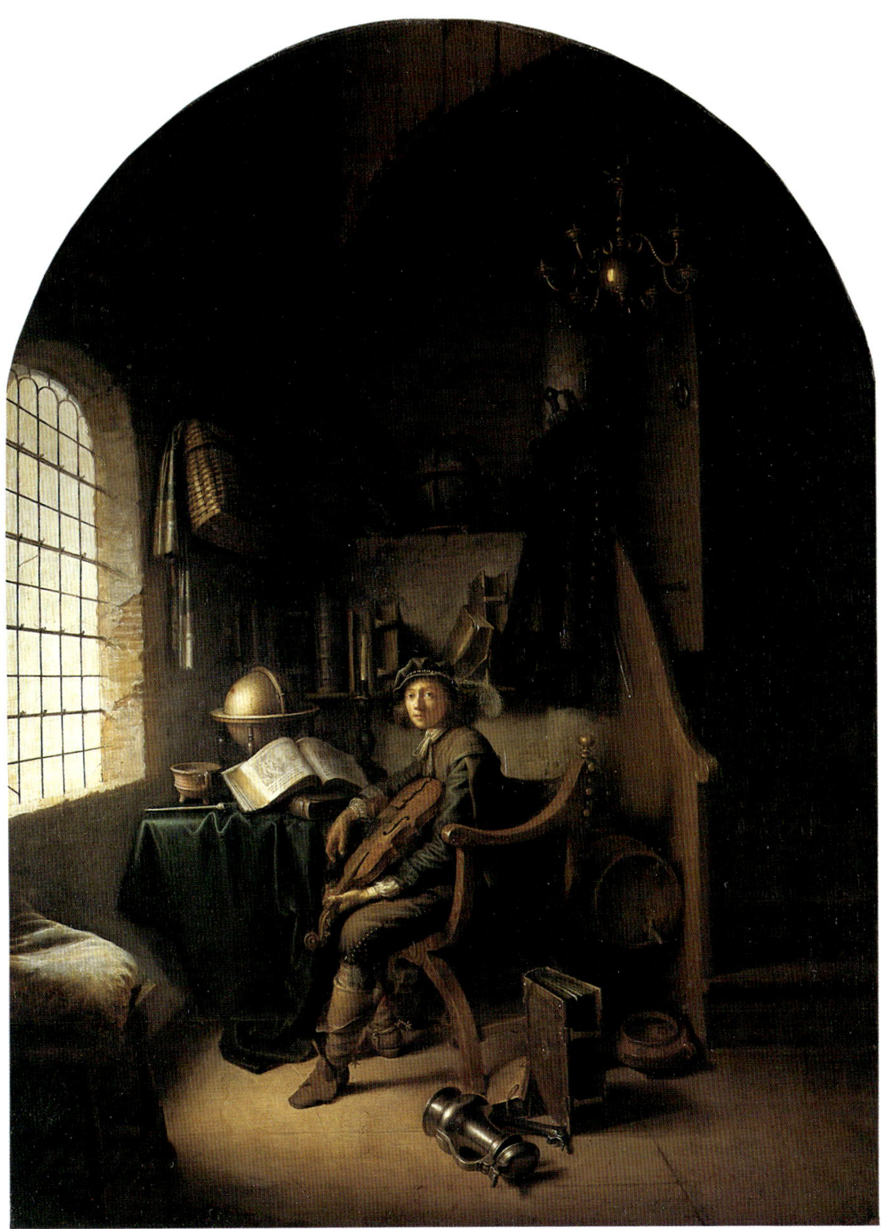

fig. 2 GERRIT DOU
*An Interior with Young Violinist*, 1637
Oil on panel, 31.1 × 23.7 cm
Edinburgh, The National Gallery
of Scotland

in his lecture 'In Praise of Painting' (*Lof der Schilder-Konst*), delivered in 1641 to the St. Luke's Guild in Leiden, argued that if "an artist manages to imitate life in such a way that people judge that it approaches real life without being able to detect in it the manner of the master who made it, such a spirit deserves praise and honour and shall be ranked above all others".[10] Almost certainly, as with Dou's small-scale paintings, Dutch viewers seem to have approached illusionistically conceived paintings with "a willing suspension of belief", which allowed them to accept depictions of reality as reality itself.[11]

The physical relationship between the viewer and the work of art was crucial for works with pronounced perspective effects, such as architectural paintings. For example, when Jan van der Heyden (1637–1712) painted the Town Hall in Amsterdam from an oblique angle strictly according to the laws of linear perspective, he attached a device to the frame, probably to establish a fixed eye point, for indicating the correct distance and vanishing-point for viewing the image. From this vantage-point, the distortions in the shape of the cupola of the Town Hall, which are quite noticeable when the painting is viewed directly, disappear entirely.[12]

Pieter Saenredam (1597–1665) must have also carefully considered the viewer's vantage-point when constructing his interior views of churches. In some instances, as in *The Interior of the Grote Kerk at Haarlem* of 1637 in the National Gallery, London (fig. 3), spatial effects, created primarily by the overlapping of forms and by differences in scale and lighting, can be appreciated from virtually any viewing point. On the other hand, the rapidly receding barrel vault in Saenredam's small-scale *St Anthony's Chapel in the St. Janskerk in Utrecht*, 1645, in the Centraal Museum, Utrecht (fig. 4), only succeeds spatially when the viewer is situated at the proper distance point and directly opposite the vanishing-point.[13] That Saenredam consciously created this effect is evident by comparing the painting to the compositional drawing, where the recession of space is far less pronounced.[14] One wonders whether Saenredam presented this

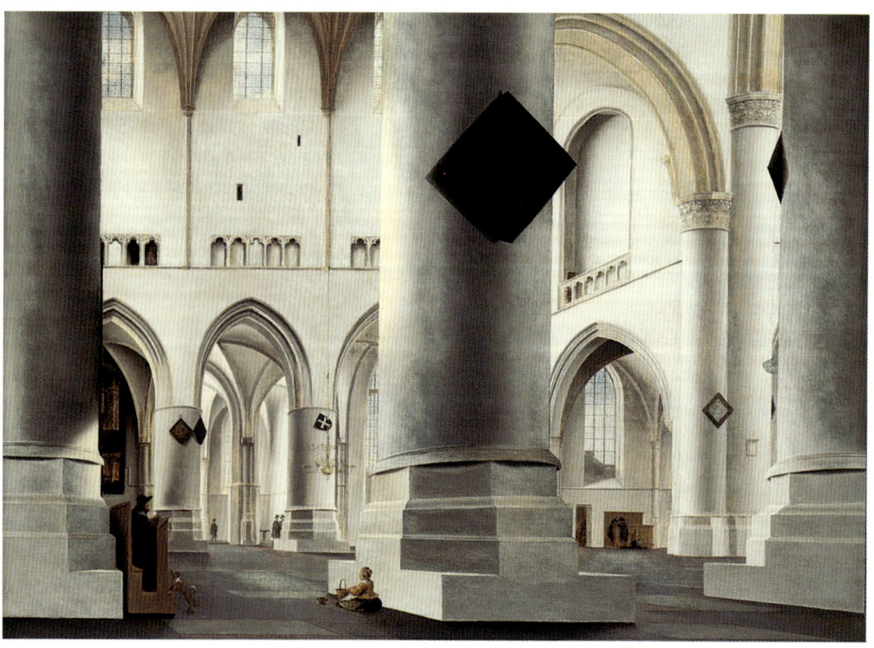

fig. 3 PIETER SAENREDAM
*The Interior of the Grote Kerk at Haarlem*, 1637
Oil on oak, 59.5 × 81.7 cm
London, The National Gallery



ARTHUR K. WHEELOCK, JR

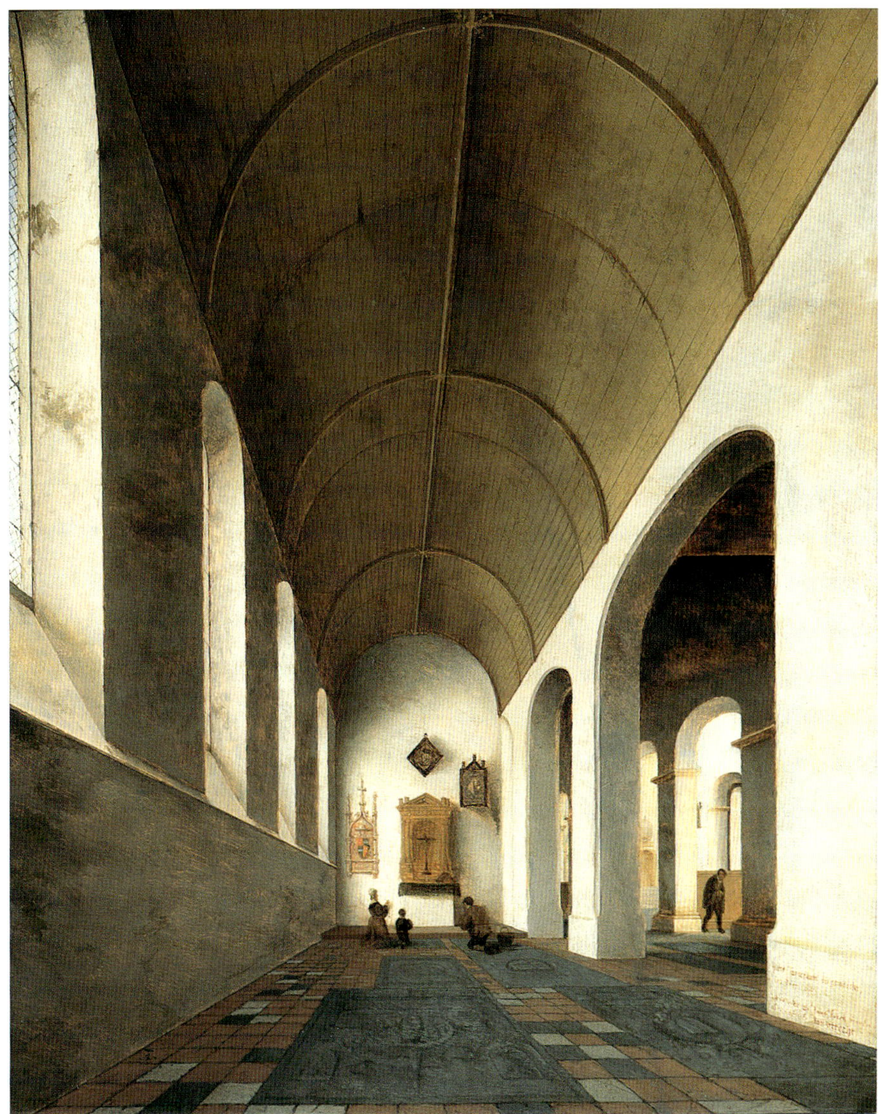

fig. 4 PIETER SAENREDAM
*St. Anthony's Chapel in the*
*St. Janskerk in Utrecht*, 1645
Oil on panel, 41.7 × 34 cm
Utrecht, Centraal Museum

small-scale painting in a case or box similar to those that once enframed paintings by Dou and Vermeer. In this manner he would have forced the viewer to consider the image from the correct distance point, where the perspective system almost magically draws the viewer to the altar at the end of the chapel's deep vault-like space.

Vermeer must have situated *Woman holding a Balance* in a box to establish the viewer's relationship to the painting, but it seems unlikely that his primary intent was to enhance the illusionistic character of the scene. As opposed to Dou, Vermeer did not engage the viewer with the direct gaze of the woman nor did he encourage the viewer visually to enter the room. Instead, when the doors of the box containing *Woman holding a Balance* were opened, the viewer would have stood transfixed by the quiet moment the artist had recorded. In Vermeer's world of gentle equilibrium, no movement occurs, only the woman's silent contemplation as she waits for the empty scales of her balance to come to rest. Vermeer's wondrous light fills the space both physically and psychologically. As it passes by the orange curtain hanging before the window, light entering the room creates a subtle orange glow on the gray wall before it accents the gold and pearls on the jewelry box, the fingers of the woman's poised right hand, and the scales she holds. The woman's left arm resting on the table extends the flow of light, carrying it upwards past her fur-trimmed jacket until it comes to rest on her serene countenance.

By contrast to Dou and Saenredam, Vermeer's compositional focus lies at the front of the picture plane. Freed from the necessity of creating the illusion of a quickly receding interior space, the master employed his perspective primarily to enhance the thematic significance of the scene. He did so by insuring that the orthogonals of the receding edges of the table and mirror merged at a vanishing point at the exact center of the composition, adjacent to the extended little finger of the woman's right hand. The location of the vanishing-point, which Vermeer marked with a pin prick that is still visible on the surface of the painting, brought added visual significance to the balance she holds. As the young woman stands calmly and serenely before a painting of the *Last Judgment*, she is aware that she must balance her life by moderating her own actions, ensuring that transient worldly treasures, symbolized by the gold and pearls on the table, do not outweigh lasting spiritual concerns.[15]

The box within which Vermeer placed *Woman Holding a Balance* would have indicated that the painting had special significance. It was not a work to be viewed every day, as one passed back and forth while busy with mundane activities. Rather, the decision to contemplate this painting would have been consciously made, reserved for those quiet moments when one yearns for inner peace and is in search of spiritual guidance for the conduct of one's life.[16] Although Vermeer's original case has long since disappeared, one can imagine the experience of encountering this radiant image upon opening its doors. In the process, the viewer's eye, located directly opposite the vanishing-point, would have been drawn to the symbolic core of the composition. The experience would have been a private one, a timeless moment for both visual and spiritual enrichment as one contemplated the allegorical themes of balance and harmony that underlie this work.

The love of Dutch art among men of science has always been a great inspiration to me. For their stimulating ideas I would like to thank Professor Robert Dorfman at the University of Maryland and especially Dr Alfred Bader, for whom this article has been written.

1   For the paintings listed in the Jacob Dissius sale, see John Michael Montias, *Vermeer and His Milieu: A Web of Social History*, Princeton 1989, pp. 255–56, 363–64, doc. 439.

2   Vermeer, however, apparently painted other works that were placed in boxes. An inventory of 1683 lists three of Vermeer's paintings in boxes. See Montias, *op. cit.* (note 1), p. 359, doc. 417.

3   Wilhelm Martin, *Gerard Dou*, London 1902, pp. 145–47. See also Ronni Baer, 'The Life and Art of Gerrit Dou', in *Gerrit Dou 1613–1675: Master Painter in the Age of Rembrandt*, ed. Arthur K. Wheelock, Jr, exh. cat., National Gallery of Art, Washington, D.C.; Dulwich Picture Gallery; Mauristhuis, The Hague, 2000, pp. 30–31.

4   I discussed the importance of this framing device for understanding the character of Dou's specific painting techniques and perspective considerations in the session I led at the 'proseminar', or study day, held at the Gallery at the opening of the Dou exhibition in Washington in April 2000.

5   As was discussed at the 'proseminar' (see note 4), a prime example of the perspective distortions Dou made to accommodate the close distance point is the basin and ewer in the foreground of *Lady at Her Toilet*, 1667 (Museum Boijmans Van Beuningen, Rotterdam), a work that is documented as being exhibited in a case with opening doors. For this work, see *Gerrit Dou, op. cit.* (note 3), pp. 128–29, ill.

6   See, for example, Houckgeest's *The Interior of St Gertrude in Bergen op Zoom*, 1655, Statens Museum for Kunst, Copenhagen; see ill. in Sybille Ebert-Schifferer, *Deceptions and Illusions: Five Centuries of Trompe l'Oeil Painting*, exh. cat., National Gallery of Art, Washington, D.C., 2002, p. 128.

7   For example, Jacobus Biltius (1633–1681) occasionally painted dead game hanging from an illusionistic nail painted on an illusionistic frame.

8   See, for example, works by Cornelis Gijsbrechsz. (active *ca.* 1659–*ca.* 1675), among them *A Hanging Wall Pouch, ca.* 1677, in Ebert-Schifferer, *op. cit.* (note 6), pp. 302–03, ill.

9   Arnold Houbraken, *De Groote Schouburgh der Nederlantsche Konstschilders en Schilderessen*, 3 vols., Amsterdam 1718–21; 2nd edn, Amsterdam and The Hague 1753, II, pp. 156–57. The English translation is taken from Celeste Brusati, in Olaf Koester, *Illusions. Gijsbrechts, Royal Master of Deception*, exh. cat., Statens Museum for Kunst, Copenhagen, 1999, p. 55.

10  Philips Angel, 'Praise of Painting', trans. Michael Hoyle, introduction by Hessel Miedema, *Simiolus*, vol. 24, no. 2/3, 1996, pp. 227–58, esp. p. 248. Angel's lecture was first published in Leiden in 1642.

11  This concept is discussed by the present author in his essay 'Illusionism in Dutch and Flemish Art', in Ebert-Schifferer, *op. cit.* (note 6), pp. 80–81.

12  Jan van der Heyden, *Dam Square*, 1668, Galleria degli Uffizi, Florence, illustrated *ibid.*, p. 84. For a discussion of this device, see Arthur K. Wheelock, Jr, *Perspective, Optics, and Delft Artists Around 1650*, New York and London 1977, pp. 168–69.

13  See *Pieter Saenredam, The Utrecht Works: Paintings and Drawings by the 17th-century Master of Perspective*, exh. cat., ed. Liesbeth Helmus, Centraal Museum, Utrecht, 2000, pp. 265–67, ill.

14  The drawing is in the Museum Boijmans Van Beuningen, Rotterdam. See *ibid.*, pp. 262–64, ill.

15  For a fuller discussion of this work, see Arthur K. Wheelock, Jr, *Vermeer & the Art of Painting*, New Haven and London 1995, pp. 97–103.

16  As Marguerite Glass has remarked to me, the effect would have been very much in the tradition of religious scenes within a triptych, which would have been opened only on special occasions.

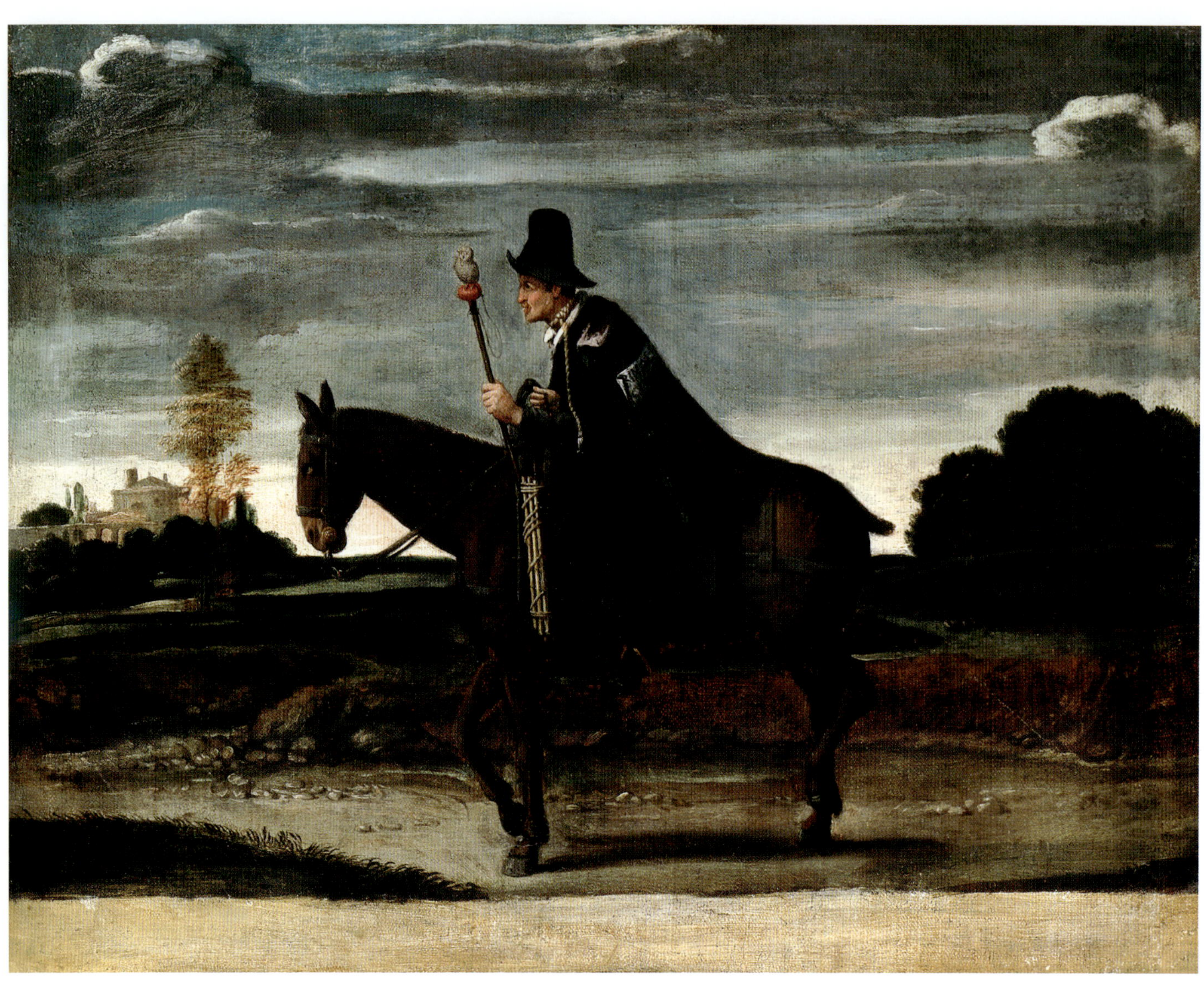

# A Name for a Ridiculous Man

CLOVIS WHITFIELD

Among a number of caricatures by the Carracci Donald Posner noticed the recurrent features of a man whose long nose continued the line of his forehead, with a whiskery moustache and beard, and a mole on his cheek that sported facial hair. No wonder that, of the many *ritrattini carichi* that Annibale Carracci (1560–1609) is said to have done, many did not survive their destruction by the victims of his humour or were ruined by being laughed about so much, as Carlo Cesare Malvasia (1616–1693) suggested.[1] Perhaps as a result, most of the surviving caricatures have usually been associated with Agostino (1557–1603), although there were obviously collections of Annibale's examples, the group assembled in a volume by Don Lelio Orsini, Principe di Nerola, being referred to both by Malvasia and by Giovanni Pietro Bellori (1613–1696).[2] But the gift that Annibale had was more noted in his own time than his brother's, and in particular his ability to reduce a scene to its essentials, with four strokes, or to illustrate a scene like a Capuchin friar asleep in the pulpit, or the exaggerated comical features of his friends. He would illustrate burlesque verses with suitable images, as Bellori says,

> And, to make known Annibale's ingenuity in accommodating burlesque verses to his drawings, he wrote under the portrait of an ill-looking courtier with a long nose who gave himself airs:
>
> > Nature was anxious not to leave the outcome to chance,
> > She widened the mouth and lengthened the ears,
> > But she forgot to redo the nose.[3]

Giulio Mancini (1558–1630) is the first to refer to this habit of the artist, in his *Life* of Annibale:

> He [Annibale] was of pleasant manner, but withdrawn, sharp in speaking and amusingly cutting, as also of very singular *gusto* when portraying someone with a deformity [a gusto accompanied by humour, the whole of which he brought off in 4 strokes, so, for example, if someone had a long nose or a squint, in a portrait he would do in pen, in four strokes, he

fig 1. Here attributed to
ANTONIO CARRACCI
*Messer Rinaldo Coradino on an Ass*
Oil on canvas, 53 × 67.9 cm
Sale Christie's, London,
9 April 2003, lot 103

expressed him with such similitude that you could recognize him, and with humour, exaggerating the lameness or the deformity, and by making him do some action, made it funny.], as one sees in many portraits, and particularly [by his own hand] of Rinaldo Coradino [Coradino, a man ridiculous in himself and well known to him for that reason].[4]

A painting that recently came on to the London market of a *Man on an Ass* (fig. 1) sheds light on the subject.[5] The man in a black cloak and soft hat is stolidly looking forward, traversing the flat bed of a dry stream, and wearing a halter round his neck, a staff surmounted by an owl and a bundle of *fasces* at the saddle. The landscape with a 'Bolognese' castle and trees on the skyline locates it in the first decade of the seventeenth century, stylistic ingredients that point to Annibale's close entourage. It is the label that he carries, like a dunce, on his back that identifies him as *Rinaldo Corad. . .*, and it is clear that this is Messer Rinaldo Coradini, the man who was naturally ridiculous, whose features are known from the Carracci caricatures. Donald Posner realised that he is portrayed twice in the very beautiful drawing from the Ellesmere collection and now in the J. Paul Getty Museum, Los Angeles, of *The Adoration of the Shepherds and other studies* (fig. 2),[6] then attributed to Agostino but more recently, by Catherine Loisel Legrand,[7] to Annibale. Posner noted that the profile turned to the right, the first of three juxtaposed heads, was a 'normal' likeness of the same man who was seen in three-quarters profile to the left, with his whiskery mole and facial hair, and that these features were further exaggerated in the Windsor study with the *Head of St Gregory* (fig. 3) associated with the lost altarpiece of *St Gregory praying for the souls in Purgatory* originally painted for the Salviati chapel in San Gregorio Magno in Rome, consecrated in 1603 (the picture was at Bridgewater House and was destroyed during World War II). It is not clear when this altarpiece was completed, but the finished compositional study that belonged to Padre Resta and is now at Chatsworth, Derbyshire, has all the characteristics of the hand of Antonio Carracci (?1589–1618), suggesting that he was already playing a role in his uncle's studio soon after arriving in Rome (1602).[8] It is in 1604 that we have mention of Rinaldo Coradini, from a document of the Accademia di San Luca.[9] Here he is a *compagno* of the Caravaggesque painter Giovanni Antonio Galli, called Lo Spadarino (1585– after 1651), in a valuation of work "*A di 4 febbraio 1604. E a dì detto o ricevuto schudi quattro di moneta da miser Rinaldo Coradini e Jacomo ditto Spadarino compag*[n]*i per una stima di lavori fatti in casa del Maurela al Bufalo dove che dita stima la fat*[t]*a Giovanpietro ala moneta . . .*".

His features, as we know them from the painting recently sold at Christie's, appear in Carraccesque drawings no less than seven times; and his profile was



CLOVIS WHITFIELD

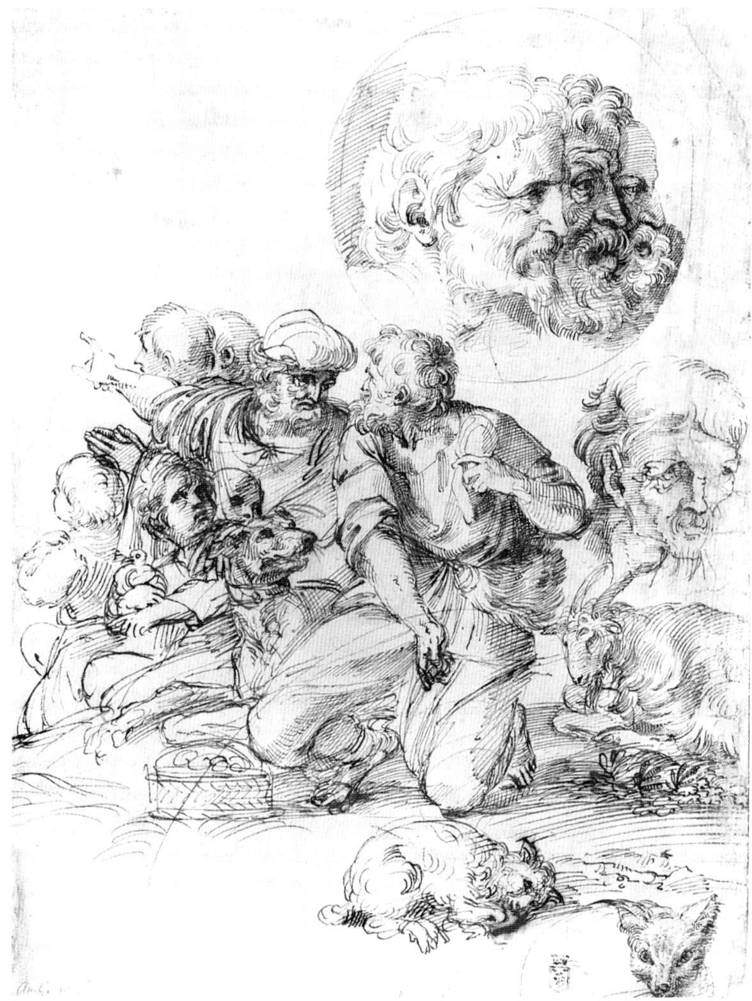

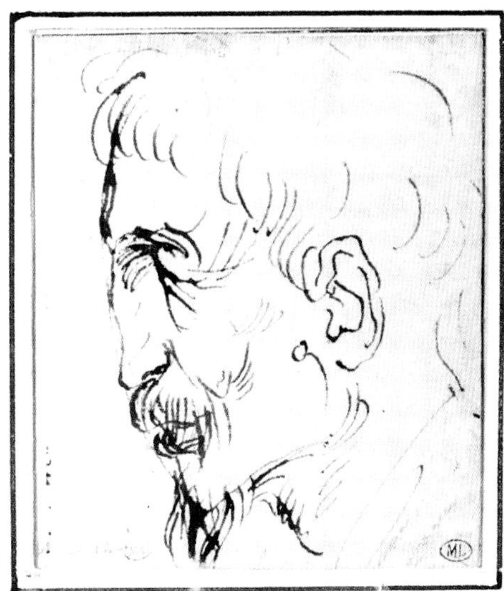

fig. 3 ANNIBALE CARRACCI
*Messer Rinaldo Coradini*
Pen and brown ink, 92 × 80 mm
Paris, Musée du Louvre, Cabinet des Dessins,
inv. no. 7393

fig. 2 ANNIBALE CARRACCI
*The Adoration of the Shepherds and other studies*
Pen and brown ink, 405 × 308 mm
Los Angeles, J. Paul Getty Museum

obviously a classic 'ridicule' in the studio. The profile head in the Pope Gregory
drawing at Windsor (where Coradini is also shown playing bowls and a red-
chalk detail exaggerates his nose, moustache and beard) is repeated in a single
drawing in the Louvre that looks as if it is from Annibale's hand (fig. 4),[10] and
the same profile is found in the Oppé sheet of caricatures.[11] The Oppé sheet,
which looks very like the upright sheet of caricatured heads in the British
Museum,[12] bears the signature of Agostino Carracci and the date 20 October
1594, and, although this seems early for Agostino's presence in Rome, a letter
of 21 February 1595 from Cardinal Odoardo Farnese (1573–1626) to his brother
Ranuccio, Duke of Parma and Piacenza (1569–1622), records a visit of the Carracci
brothers to Rome "several months ago" in the context of the Cardinal's decision
to have them decorate the Sala Grande at Palazzo Farnese with the life and
*imprese* of their father, Duke Alessandro (1545–1592).[13] So the Carracci must
have met '*l'uomo redicolo*' Coradini quite early on in Rome. The subsidiary profile

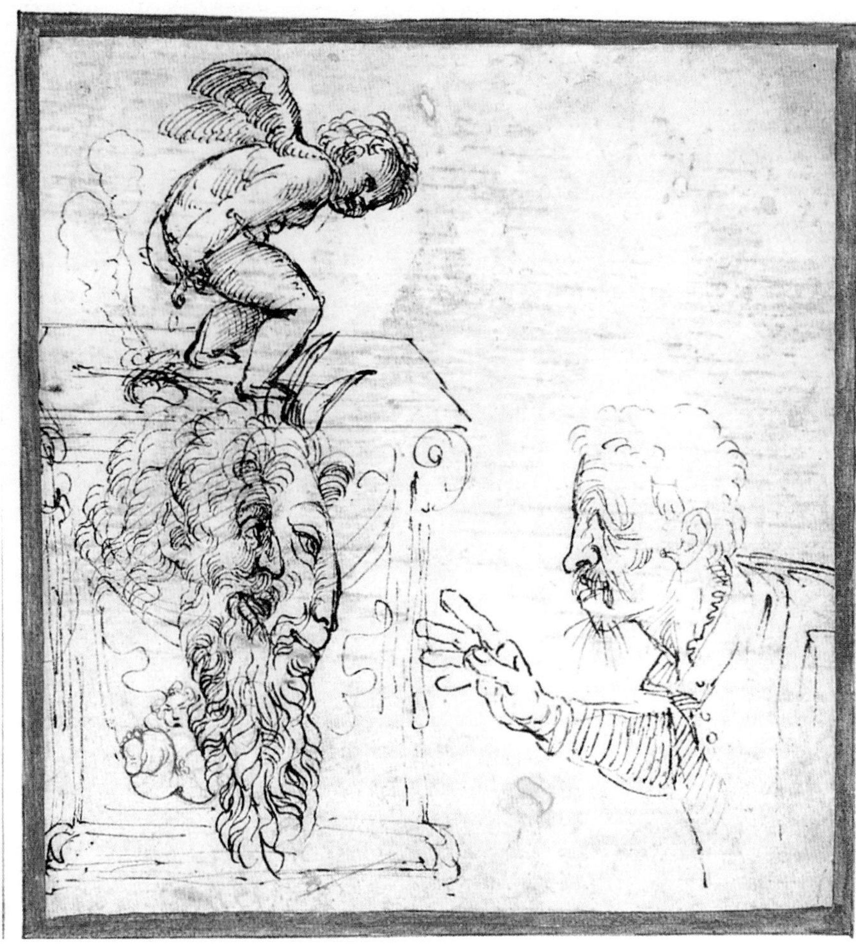

fig. 4 Here attributed to
ANNIBALE CARRACCI, with
addition by ANTONIO CARRACCI
of a figure in profile
*Sheet of Studies*
Pen and brown ink on cream paper,
176 × 163 mm
London, The British Museum,
inv. no. P.p. 3–12

in the British Museum sheet (fig. 5)[14] is a tentative elaboration that looks close to the handling of the painting, and may well be by Antonio even if other parts of the same sheet, like the Cupid defecating on the altar, seem to have Annibale's tongue-in-cheek. The collar, vest and jacket, and perhaps the noose around Rinaldo's neck in the painting, are also anticipated in the drawing. This study is one of many drawings from the world of the Carracci where additions seem to have been introduced by others, during the course of their use in the studio that Annibale left behind.

Bellori tells us that "Annibale had another way of doing physiognomy, transferring a human appearance to animals" and this is of relevance in the two profiles to the left of Rinaldo Coradini in this British Museum sheet, which mimic the resemblance of the old man to the goat behind him, whose ears are cocked forward like a satyr's. Here the origin of the comparison may well be a playful reminder that men grow to resemble their pets, as Ellis Waterhouse used to say, but also has to do with the contemporary debate on physiognomy. This was led by Giovanni Battista Della Porta (*ca.* 1538–1615), whose *Della Fisionomia*



CLOVIS WHITFIELD

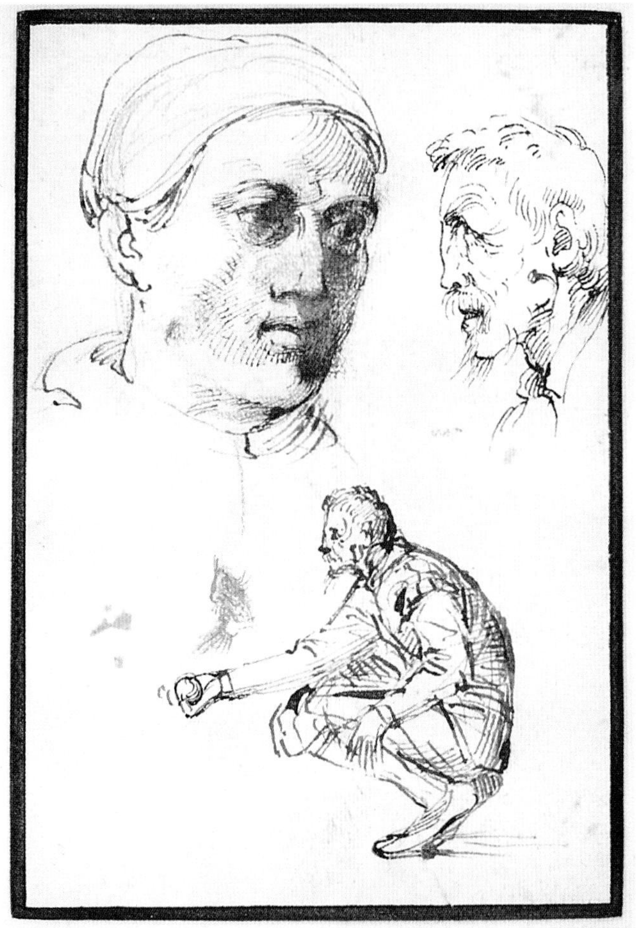

fig. 5 Here attributed to
ANNIBALE CARRACCI and
ANTONIO CARRACCI
*Study for the Head of St Gregory
with a Man bowling*
Pen and two shades of brown ink
over black chalk (upper left only)
on beige paper, 173 × 117 mm
The Royal Collection
© Her Majesty Queen Elizabeth II

*dello huomo* . . . was published in 1598 under a pseudonym. It was the *edizione volgare* of Della Porta's *De Humana Physiognomonia* (Vico Equense 1586), and in Book II, p. 113, Della Porta makes the comparison of the ram's head with that of an old man, to make the point of correspondences between the animal kingdom and the world of mankind. This is an old, medieval way of thought, that Della Porta elaborated and played upon in various guises, including the correspondence between the forms of plants and their relevance to the similar shapes of human body parts. The interest in physiognomy was of great importance at the time, and the expressive exploitation by Caravaggio (1571–1610) of the grimace of *A Boy bitten by a Lizard* (National Gallery, London) owes much to the concern with reading the soul through outward appearances that became a fundamental subject of enquiry in the Seicento. Antonio's concern with caricature and the link with Della Porta is interesting, and he includes in the *Man on a Ass* other fantastical elements like a pet owl on the wand, a symbol of folly, as well as a halter round his neck, to emphasize the *redicolo*. It is almost as though the profile of the ram's head is transformed in the painting to that of the ass, and its waving ears. The evolution of a type of '*paese con figure piccole*' in Annibale's workshop in the years of his decline is also illustrated by these paintings in which much attention is given to narrative, with all the details being intelligible to those in the know. The combination of the landscape background, however Roman it now appears to us – and the turrets and arches are as reminiscent of Grottaferrata as of anywhere else – must have appeared quite novel in early Seicento Rome, and a part of the new fashion for naturalistic, Venetian decoration, that Guercino (1591–1666) would also mimic when he came to Rome a little later.

The ass is a symbol of ignorance for Ripa, who uses the authority of Petrus Valerianus in Book XII of *Hieroglifice*: the "head of the ass demonstrates the same ignorance, as we already said the mother of obstinacy, and ignorance is figured in the head of the ass, since this animal is very stolid, tolerating equally every good or every ill, proving insensible to whips or knotted rope, quite differently to other animals".[15] The expressive exaggeration of the features of Rinaldo Coradini was probably used to accompany some burlesque verse, and indeed the painting has a strip some 3 cm wide at the foot that would have provided room for this text, although there is now no trace of it.

The landscape, and skyscape, are precisely the kind of shorthand that Antonio uses in the little *Rape of Europa* that the Pinacoteca Nazionale in Bologna bought recently,[16] while the pebbles in the foreground are just like others in the little copper of the *St John preaching* that belonged to Elisabeth Vigée-Lebrun's husband,[17] or in the little copper of the *Stoning of St Stephen* in the Louvre.[18] The sky has the same formula of clouds as is to be found in many of Antonio's pictures, like the *Death of Absalom* in the Louvre.[19] It is interesting to observe the transformation of Annibale's ideas by his young nephew, who remained in his studio for seven years up to the end in 1609, and who inherited its contents, much to the annoyance of his uncles, who arrived in Rome too late and found he had already spirited away most of the chattels. We have to take his exploitation of the material he inherited seriously, and indeed look for the impact of his personality on the subsequent reputation of Annibale himself.

1 Carlo Cesare Malvasia, *Felsina Pittrice*, edn Bologna 1841, I, p. 335.

2 *Ibid.*, and Giovan Pietro Bellori, *Vite dei Pittori*, 1672, p. 75; for the *Vita di Annibale Carracci*, see the modern edn, ed. E. Borea, Turin 1976, p. 86.

3 Bellori, *op. cit.* (note 2), p. 75: "*Et accioché sia noto l'ingegno di Annibale in accommodare versi burleschi a' suoi disegni, sotto il ritratto di un brutto e nasuto cortigiano che faceva il bello, scrisse questi versi: Temea Natura di non farlo a caso, / Slargò la bocca, ed allungò gl'orecchi, / Ma si scordò di rassettargli il naso.*"

4 Giulio Mancini, *Considerazioni sulla Pittura*, ed. A. Marucchi and L. Salerno, Rome 1956, p. 220: "*Fu* [Annibale] *di costume piacevole, ma ritirato, acuto nel parlare e mordace con piacevolezza, come ancor, nel ritraher con deformità qualcheduno, di singo-larissimo gusto [accompagnato con il ridicolo, che il tutto faceva con 4 segni, come per esempio se uno avess'auto il naso lungo o fusse stato guercio, nel ritratto di penna, con quattro segni, l'esprimeva con similtudin tale che si riconosceva, e con il redicolo, augumentandogli lo stroppio e deformità e col fargli far qualch'atto, lo faceva ridicolo.], come si vede in molti ritratti et in particolare [di sua mano] di Rinaldo Coradino [Coradino huomo per natura redicolo e per tal rispetto gl'era familiarissimo.].*"

5 Sale Christie's, London, 9 April 2003, lot 103, canvas 53 × 67.9 cm. Formerly in the collection of Colonel Norman Colville, M.C. (1893–1974), the picture was in a sale at Christie's, London, 18 July 1924, as "Velasquez", sold for 8 gns to Spink.

6 Donald Posner, *Annibale Carracci*, 2 vols., London 1971, I, pp. 66–67.

7 In the exhibition catalogue, *The Drawings of Annibale Carracci*, National Gallery, Washington, D.C., 1999–2000, p. 258, no. 82.

8 Ann Sutherland Harris suggested this attribution (oral communication) and the tell-tale hands of the Pope are quite obvi-ously those of the younger artist. Padre Resta had a number of Antonio drawings: see Jeremy Wood, 'Padre Resta as a Collector of Carracci Drawings', *Master Drawings*, vol. 34, 1996, pp. 3–71. The drawing at Chatsworth (inv. no. 455), first ascribed to Annibale by Jonathan Richardson, was in *Drawings by the Carracci from British Collections*, exh. cat., Ashmolean Museum, Oxford, and Hazlitt Gooden & Fox, London, 1996–97, no. 93.

9 Of 4 February 1604, quoted by Salerno in Mancini, *Considerazioni*, *op. cit.* (note 4), II, p. 48.

10 Inv. no. 7393; R. Bacou, *Dessins des Carrache*, exh. cat., Musée du Louvre, Paris, 1961, no. 19, as by Agostino. Philip Pouncey (note on mount) attributed this to Agostino.

11 Repr. by Posner, *op. cit.* (note 6), fig. 56.

12 *Drawings by the Carracci from British Collections*, *op. cit.* (note 8), no. 71.

13 Sir Denis Mahon kindly pointed out this reference to me, in the article by Hans Tietze, 'Annibale Carraccis Galerie im Palazzo Farnese und seine römische Werkstätte', *Jahrbuch der Kunsthistorischen Sammlungen des allerhöchsten Kaiserhauses* (*Wiener Jahrbuch*), XXVI, Heft 2, 1906, p. 54.

14 Inv. no. P. p.3-12; *Drawings by the Carracci from British Collections*, *op. cit.* (note 8), no. 38.

15 Cesare Ripa, *Iconologia*, Rome 1603, p. 397.

16 *The Rape of Europa*, panel, 68.3 × 48.8 cm, in *Classicismo e natura*, *La lezione di Domenichino*, exh. cat., Gallerie Capitoline, Rome, 1996–97, no. 11.

17 Oil on copper, 28.8 × 39.7 cm; sold Christie's, London, 11 December 1992, lot 415. For the Lebrun provenance see William Buchanan, *Memoirs of Painting . . .*, 2 vols., London 1924, II, p 323. The picture was in a sale in Paris, 7–8 July, 1817, lot 13, and then passed to Edward Gray of Haringey. The picture is referred to by Richard E. Spear, *Domenichino*, New Haven 1982, pp. 315–16. There does not seem to be any basis for the attribution of the Boston version of this composition to Badalocchio; it has more the character of one of the versions that G.F. Grimaldi was much called upon to produce for French patrons.

18 Inv. no. 203; S. Loire, *Ecole italienne, XVIIième siécle, I, Bologne*, Paris 1996, pp. 146–48 (as "*Annibal Carrache et atelier*").

19 See Clovis Whitfield, 'Antonio Carracci', in *Studi di storia dell'arte in onore di Denis Mahon*, ed. M.G. Bernardini, S.D. Squarzina and C. Strinati, Milan 2000, pp. 132–52.

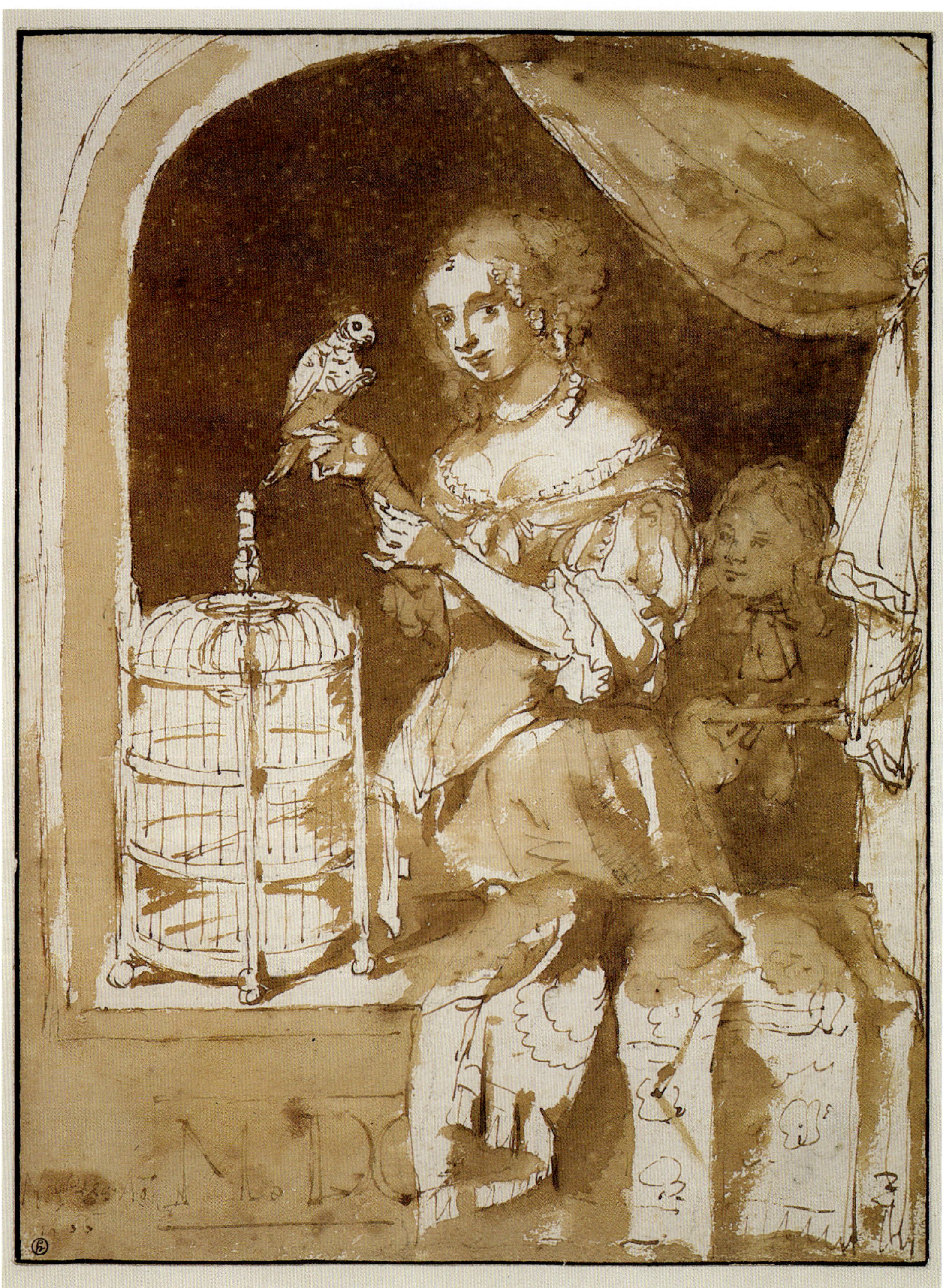

# Paper Trails: Drawings in the Work of Caspar Netscher and his Studio

MARJORIE E. WIESEMAN

Caspar Netscher (1635/36–1684) is known as a painter of genteel 'high life' genre scenes and small-scale portraits that celebrate the exquisite materialism of the Dutch patriciate during the final decades of the Dutch Golden Age. He is less well known as a draughtsman, yet his drawings are fluent and sure, and varied in both technique and purpose. About forty-five drawings by Netscher have been identified, ranging from cursory explorations of pose and gesture to expressive and highly finished drawings in pen and wash and finely detailed portrait studies. Most can be directly related to specific paintings. Inscriptions on many drawings by Netscher and artists in his atelier provide unique insight into the role drawings played in the operation of a successful artistic practice. Among the most interesting and unusual are a series of *modelli* and *ricordi* made to document finished paintings. Annotations on several sheets provide information about the genesis of a painting, its commission or sale, as well as the mechanics of adapting a composition for reuse. This study surveys a selection of drawings by Netscher and artists in his immediate circle, focusing on the function of these drawings and their relationship to finished paintings.

The 1694 inventory of the estate of Netscher's widow, Margareta Godijn, lists at least fifteen sketchbooks and large portfolios of drawings and prints, easily numbering into thousands of sheets.[1] Some of the drawings and sketchbooks are specified as being by Netscher's hand; other volumes of drawings and prints (as well as a quantity of illustrated books) were used as reference material in composing paintings, or as examples for young pupils to copy.

The importance of drawing in the artistic process would have been impressed upon Netscher while he was a pupil of the inveterate draughtsman Gerard ter Borch (1617–1681) in Deventer during the mid 1650s. The rich trove of drawings that survive by the young ter Borch, by his father Gerard the Elder (1582/83–1662) and half-siblings Gesina (1631–1690), Harmen (1638–1677),

fig. 1 CASPAR NETSCHER
*Woman feeding a Parrot*, 1666
Pen and wash in bistre,
243 × 186 mm
London, The British Museum,
inv. no. 0.0.11-250

Moses (1645–1667) and cousin Jan (now Rijksprentenkabinet, Amsterdam), is a vivid demonstration of the emphasis placed on draughtsmanship and the close observation of nature in developing technical and creative facility.[2] The majority of drawings by Gerard ter Borch included in the studio estate are copies after graphic works by other artists or life studies (both clearly part of the pedagogical process), preliminary compositional sketches, or more finished presentation drawings. Few correspond directly to a specific painting by the artist, but in a more general way record his process of observing and composing individual figures and motifs, and his concern with the formal relationships between figures and between figure and setting.[3]

In contrast, a high proportion of Netscher's drawings can be directly and very precisely linked to his paintings. Only a handful seem to be completely unrelated to known paintings, or intended as finished works in their own right. The apparent discrepancies between Gerard ter Borch's graphic oeuvre and that of his erstwhile pupil do not necessarily reflect differing ideas about the role of drawing in the artistic process, but rather the vagaries of survival. As many of Netscher's surviving drawings can be classified as 'working drawings' and seem to have been retained in the studio as aids for developing other paintings, it seems plausible that sketches unrelated to paintings were less likely to have been preserved. On the other hand, the drawings by Gerard ter Borch included in the studio estate were gathered by his half-sister Gesina during his lifetime, and were thus heavily weighted towards youthful works, and those drawings for which the artist had little practical use in his daily artistic practice.

The drawings associated with paintings by Caspar Netscher fall generally into three categories: quick compositional sketches; detailed studies of individual compositional elements; and a remarkable group of drawings comprising both *modelli*, which served to show ideas for a painting to a prospective patron, and *ricordi*, which document a finished painting. The latter group of drawings (it is often difficult to distinguish between the two functions) were executed in a variety of media by both Netscher and, from the mid 1670s, by members of his studio.

Quick sketches track Netscher's initial explorations of figural groupings and gestures before he settled on the final design for a portrait or subject piece. Two such sheets are known for the *Card Party* of about 1665 (Metropolitan Museum of Art, New York).[4] On the verso of a double-sided sheet in Paris is probably the artist's first conception of the composition, a *croquis* in which the four figures are indicated by no more than a series of loops, but which clearly sets out the basic relationships between the figures.[5] In a second sketch on the recto of the sheet, the general distribution of light and shadow within the scene is blocked out in broad areas of wash. A sketch in Leiden develops the composition somewhat further, recording minor adjustments in the poses and gestures of the figures.[6] Other sketches presumably followed, as the painting differs somewhat from all of these preliminary sketches, most notably in the pose of the woman at the left of the scene, who turns her back to the viewer in the final version. Executed with swift and lively strokes of the pen, these sketches are similar in spirit and technique to ter Borch's few surviving drawings for his own genre paintings of the 1650s and 1660s.[7]

Elaborating upon the basic framework developed in these initial conceptions, individual features of the composition were worked out in more detailed studies. In addition to designs for decorative garlands and other bits of *bijwerk*, several extant sheets bear studies of women's hands and arms in various poses.[8] Listed among the volumes of prints and drawings in the 1694 inventory is "*een bruijn portfeuilje mette letter A. sijn 92 teyckeninghe, ongeveer de helft handen in allerhande postuyr*" (A brown portfolio with the letter A., being 92 drawings, about half are hands in various positions). A drawing of a woman's arms now in the Rijksprentenkabinet, Amsterdam, annotated on the verso with the letter A, probably once formed part of this volume; the pose was adopted in Netscher's *Portrait of Elizabeth Bebber*, dated 1677 (Mauritshuis, The Hague).[9] These highly finished drawings of hands and arms served not only as preparatory studies for corresponding elements in Netscher's paintings, but also, as specified elsewhere in the 1694 inventory, as examples for pupils to copy ("*dienende voor discipulen om na te teijckenen*"). Several copies after Netscher's drawings of hands and arms have also been preserved, by different hands and in varying degrees of competence.[10]

By far the most intriguing of Netscher's drawings are his numerous *ricordi*, often annotated with dates, prices, notes regarding colour and composition, and (more rarely) the names of sitters or buyers. This seems to have been an unusual, if not unique practice among seventeenth-century Dutch artists. There are certainly examples of drawings with the same sort of autograph annotations,[11] and some isolated examples of *ricordi* in other artists' oeuvres,[12] but apart from a sketchbook by the architectural painter Daniel de Blieck (died 1673), which contains drawings after his own paintings,[13] I am aware of no Northern parallels to this series of more than twenty surviving drawings in Netscher's oeuvre. Similar drawings by other artists – detailed drawings closely related to painted compositions – were more usually made either as *modelli* or as finished works of art (possibly for sale), and are generally not inscribed with more than the artist's signature and date.[14] On the other hand, those drawings which bear lengthier inscriptions are typically more documentary in nature, with inscriptions intended to clarify or confirm the veracity of a landscape view, a figure's identity or an historic event. Netscher's drawings are often annotated with working notes; they were made for his own use, either by himself or by an assistant, and remained in the studio. In many respects they are the visual equivalent of the written studio memorandum books compiled by artists such as Jacob de Wet the Elder (1610–1671), Adriaen van der Werff (1659–1722), Philips Tiedeman (1657–1705) or Henrik van Limborch (1681–1759), which record cursory descriptions of the painting, the client's name, prices and/or the amount of time spent working on a given piece.[15]

The most famous example of this sort of *ricordi* drawing in the seventeenth century is of course the *Liber Veritatis* of Claude Lorrain (1600–1682), begun in about 1635 and maintained by the artist until his death in 1682. Consisting of 195 sketches originally bound in a single volume, Claude's drawings systematically record virtually all of his paintings, and are inscribed with his signature and the date, and often the title of the work and name of the patron.[16] Unfortunately, Netscher's surviving *ricordi* do not provide such a tidy or thorough documentation of his paintings. They exist in a variety of media on assorted papers, apparently record only a portion of his oeuvre, and are only irregularly annotated. It is not clear that they ever formed a single comprehensive sketchbook or series of sketchbooks.[17] Nonetheless, they offer a valuable record of lost paintings, they inform us about dates and prices for individual works, and more generally shed light on Netscher's studio practice.

A significant portion of the *ricordi* associated with Netscher's genre paintings of the mid-1660s are drawings in wash, or pen and wash.[18] Netscher's choice of this more painterly medium may have been influenced by the exquisite wash drawings produced by Jan de Bisschop (1628–1671), Christiaan Huygens (1629–1695) and other amateur artists working in The Hague during the 1650s and 1660s.[19] Interestingly, many of De Bisschop's wash drawings from the 1660s also reproduce paintings. Although they may have been related to his contemporary interest in the development of the mezzotint technique, the drawings themselves quickly gained status among collectors as independent works of art.[20] For both Netscher and De Bisschop, opting for the characteristically lush wash technique reflects a desire to translate – by the most vivid means possible – a painting's saturated palette and rich chiaroscuro into a monochromatic graphic format. It is surely not coincidental that Netscher's paintings from this period are among his most dramatic expressions of intense color and bold lighting effects.[21]

The inscriptions on Netscher's *ricordi* – particularly those which document his genre scenes – give a rare glimpse of the prices commanded by these paintings during the artist's lifetime. Although some of the prices inscribed on the drawings have been obliterated by a later hand, those that remain legible include 50 guilders, for the *Woman with a Letter and a Medallion* in Kassel, dated 1667; 80 guilders, for the *Man bringing a Letter to a Woman* of 1662 (present whereabouts unknown) and the *Fortune Teller* of 1664; 100 guilders, for the *Woman feeding a Parrot* in Wuppertal, dated 1666 (fig. 1); and (possibly) 140 guilders, for the *Self-portrait with Wife and Children* of 1664, now in the Uffizi.[22] These prices are certainly respectable, if well below the famously extravagant prices commanded by the *fijnschilders* Gerrit Dou (1613–1675) or Frans van Mieris (1635–1681).[23] The lengthy autograph inscription on the verso of the drawing for the *Self-portrait*, moreover, provides considerably more information than just the price: *Casper Netscher: geschijldert en voleyndet: / int Jaer 1668. vercoght aen den hertogh van florensen zijn soon. / prijns van Toscannen. daenmaels inden haege. was. voor [?140] guldens* (Casper Netscher painted and completed [this]: / in the year 1668 sold to the son of the Duke of Florence / prince of Tuscany who was then in The Hague, for [?140] guilders"). The inscription confirms that the painting was indeed purchased directly from the artist by Cosimo III de' Medici (1642–1723) on his trip through the Netherlands in 1668–69 just before he became Grand Duke of Tuscany, and further indicates Netscher's justifiable pride in documenting this princely honour.[24]

Whether *ricordi* from the early portion of Netscher's career had a function in the studio beyond the documentation of a painting which had been sold is difficult to ascertain. While for portraits of the 1670s and 1680s concrete evidence does exist to indicate that such drawings were used as the basis for subsequent painted variants (see below), there appears to be little direct correlation between the existence of a *ricordo* drawing for a genre painting and the existence of a painted copy or variant likely to have been produced in the studio.[25]

Netscher's own drawings for or after his portrait paintings number proportionately far fewer than those related to his genre scenes. For the most part, they are quick sketches in red or black chalk indicating the basic lines of a composition, occasionally annotated with the date of execution and/or colour notes. They were probably not all made as *ricordi*, however. In fact, given the frenetic productivity of Netscher's portrait practice during the 1670s and early 1680s, which would seem to have left him little time for the leisurely documentation of finished works, many of the autograph portrait sketches were probably created as preliminary *modelli* to show a prospective patron his ideas for a commission. Netscher's drawings for the 1680 *Portrait of a Man*, or the *Portrait of Mevrouw Keneyes* of around 1676, both annotated with colour notes on the recto, are examples of such *modelli*; the latter is also inscribed with the name and address of the sitter.[26]

Many of the *ricordi* from the latter part of Netscher's career were executed by other artists associated with his atelier. Theodoor Netscher (1661–1728), Caspar Netscher's oldest son and an accomplished painter in his own right, produced detailed *ricordi* in red chalk as part of his youthful training. Aged

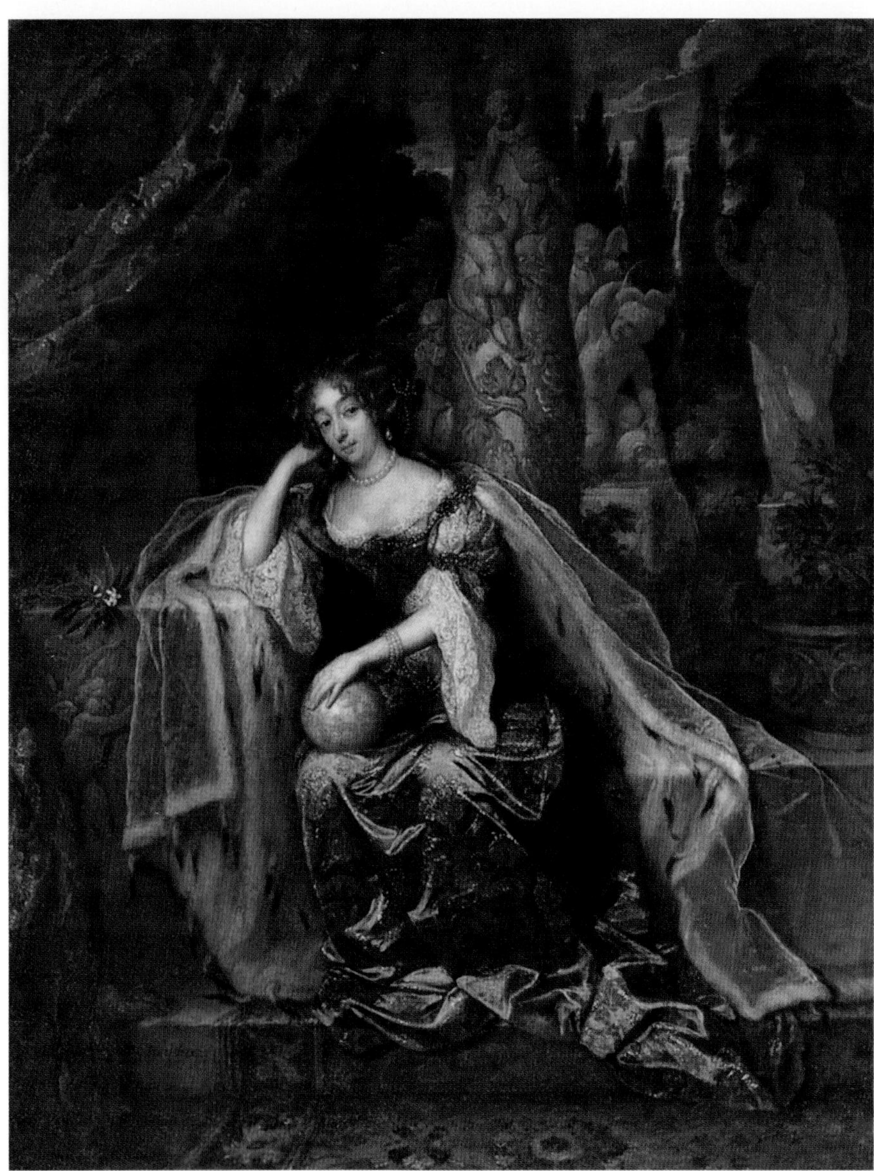



sixteen, he meticulously copied a now lost portrait of a young man in armour in a drawing inscribed: *CNets inv / TNets del. 1677*; a similar drawing from 1679 is signed *C.N. 1679 / T.N.*, and inscribed by a later hand (probably Mattheus Verheyden), *Na 't Portret van Gaspar Netscher. door desselfs zoon Theodorus Netscher . . .getekent* (After the portrait by Caspar Netscher. Drawn by his son Theodorus Netscher).[27] Other hands – most as yet unidentified – were also active in producing drawings after Netscher compositions, both during his lifetime and on into the eighteenth century: not surprisingly, many drawings currently attributed to Netscher are in fact by followers or artists associated with the atelier. Some of these copies and *ricordi* remained the property of the studio, while others were probably retained by individual artists for their own use. Jan



MARJORIE E. WIESEMAN

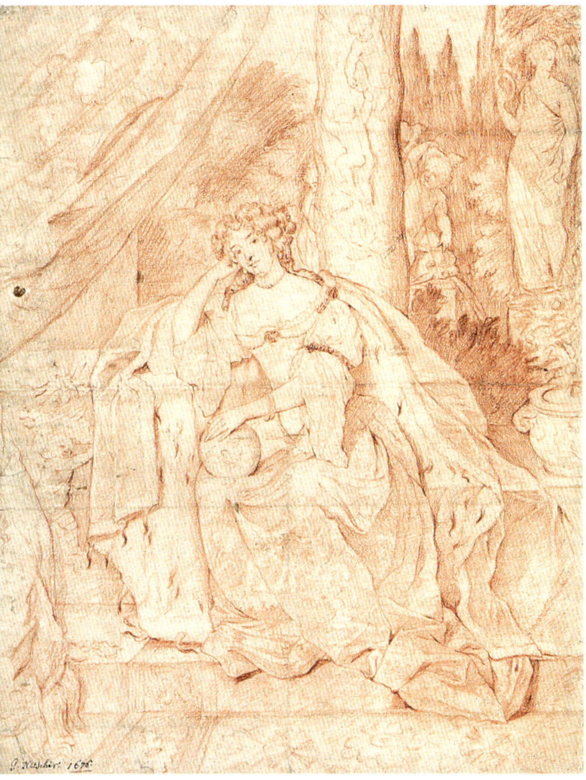

fig. 3 THEODOOR NETSCHER
*Portrait of a Princess*
Red chalk, 466 × 363 mm
Sale Christie's, Amsterdam,
10 November 1999, lot 105

van Gool (1687–1763) notes that Mattheus Verheyden (1700–1776), a pupil of Constantijn Netscher (1668–1723), borrowed some painted sketches ("*geschilderde schetsen*") by Constantijn's father, which he then copied with great attention in pencil or pen. Many of Verheyden's mature portrait compositions are visibly indebted to works by Caspar and Constantijn Netscher.[28]

This process of imitation and adaptation is evident in a group of works related to the *Portrait of a Princess (called Mary II Stuart)*, a full-length likeness of a woman engulfed by an ermine-lined cloak and seated in a lush garden terrace. The only known version of the painting, signed and dated 1676, is largely the work of Netscher's studio and may be a second version of a lost original (fig. 2).[29] A cursory black chalk drawing in Stuttgart probably represents Netscher's early conception of the design,[30] and the finished painting is carefully recorded in a red chalk drawing by Theodoor Netscher (fig. 3), inscribed by him on the verso: . . . *met omber en goude blomme / De Tabbert blauw met Goude blomme / De mantel bl* [crossed out] *Root fulp de voerich / hermine een tapijt op de vlour. / CNet. pix TNet. del. 1676* (. . .with brown and gold flowers / The gown blue with gold flowers / The cloak red velvet the lining / ermine a carpet on the floor.). This drawing also bears an inscription in pen on the recto by Mattheus Verheyden, whose familiarity with the composition is revealed in his own variation on the theme, a drawing in Bremen which modifies and updates Netscher's original design.[31]

For portraits at least, the *ricordi* and *modelli* that remained part of the Netscher studio served not only to document a given painting, but also as models for later works which utilized the same basic composition. A drawing for a man's portrait, which can be linked to at least three works originating in the Netscher studio, is a veritable palimpsest of studio practice (fig. 4).[32] The drawing was apparently a *modello* for the *Portrait of Jacob Scott* of about 1683, a work probably commissioned from Caspar Netscher but largely, if not wholly, executed by the studio.[33] The verso of the sheet bears an inscription specifically related to this painting: *De Rock blau met / zilvregoude Bloemen de / onslagh klarse paarse* [?] *lack achte / weerschyn de Stoel root* ("The robe blue / with silver-gold flowers the / reverse purple [?] lacquer-like / sheen the chair red"). The basic design for the portrait was also used for another painting issuing from Netscher's studio, a *Portrait of a Man* also of about 1683. The latter painting differs from the drawing in several respects: there is no dog, the background is changed, and the sitter's robe is russet *changeant* silk lined in blue, rather than the blue with gold and silver flowers specified in the inscription.[34]

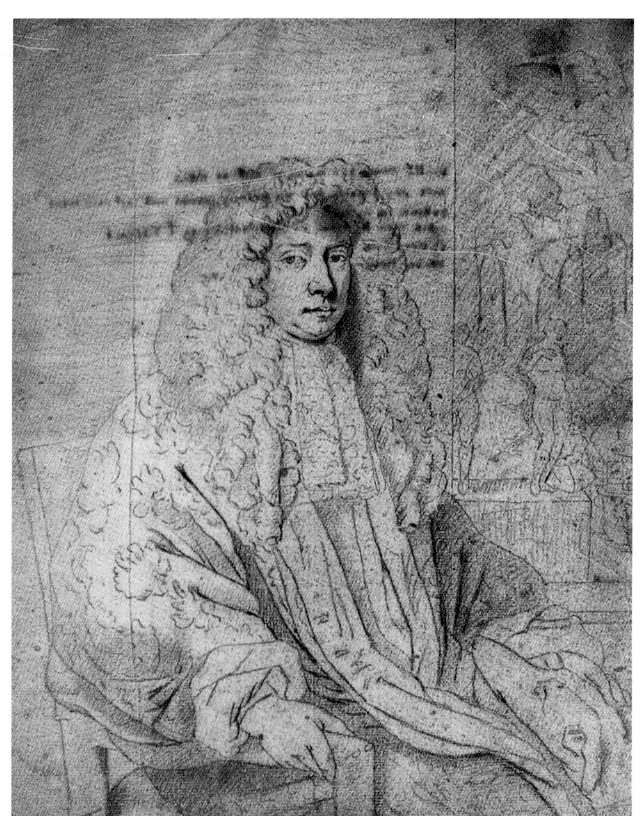

fig. 4 Attributed to CASPAR NETSCHER
*Portrait of Jacob Scott*
Red chalk over sketch in black chalk, 302 × 244 mm
Amsterdam, Gemeentearchief, inv. no. KD66-221

A second inscription on the back of the sheet is written in a different (later) hand: *De Hr Buys zal moghen geschildert werden / met een japonse Rok van paersch, gevoert met ligt fillemort / zittende op een stoel, / agter zich Hebbende een Bibliotheeq in 't vehrschiet / is voor hem – / zonder Hond* (Mr Buys shall be painted / with a purple Japanese robe, lined in light brown / sitting in a chair / a library behind him in the distance / for him – / without the dog). A decade after the original was painted, Netscher's son Constantijn adapted this same composition for his *Portrait of Paulus Buys*, dated 1693; here the sitter is clad in a solid robe, rows of books form a backdrop, and his left hand rests on his knee rather than on the head of a dog.[35]

The fertile accumulation of drawings that were once the cornerstone of Netscher's artistic practice are now randomly preserved and widely scattered. Yet those that remain offer vivid insight into the operation of an active and successful studio during the closing decades of the seventeenth century. To keep pace with the constant demand for his work, Netscher developed an efficient and effective production system grounded in assiduous draftsmanship: first plotting the composition in a series of quick, intuitive sketches and detailed studies; developing a working *modello* to offer to prospective patrons; and finally documenting the completed painting in an annotated *ricordo*. The resulting 'paper trail' became a permanent resource of the Netscher atelier, ensuring patrons a high standard of quality and a consistently elegant presentation well into the eighteenth century.

1 Marjorie E. Wieseman, *Caspar Netscher and Late Seventeenth-century Dutch painting*, Doornspijk 2002, p. 147, doc. 100. Portions of the inventory were published by Abraham Bredius in 'Een en ander over Caspar Netscher', *Oud Holland*, V, 1887, pp. 263–74.

2 On the drawings of the ter Borch family, see Alison McNeil Kettering, *Drawings from the TerBorch Studio Estate*, 2 vols., The Hague 1988.

3 The only drawings that can be tied to existing paintings are a handful of compositional sketches for genre scenes, which are among the latest works included in the group, and executed many years after ter Borch left Zwolle and established himself as an independent artist. Certainly there would originally have been many more of these drawings produced in developing the subtle and sophisticated genre compositions for which the artist is known. See Kettering, *op. cit.* (note 2), I, pp. 89–90 and 148–50, nos. GJr 87–90.

4 Wieseman, *op. cit.* (note 1), p. 199, no. 48.

5 Pen washed with bistre; Musée du Louvre, Cabinet des Dessins, Paris, inv. no. 495; Wieseman, *op. cit.* (note 1), fig. 53.

6 Pen and ink, Prentenkabinet der Rijksuniversiteit, Leiden, inv. no. PK 1704; Wieseman, *op. cit.* (note 1), fig. 54.

7 See Kettering, *op. cit.* (note 2), I, pp. 148–50.

8 For example, in the Rijksprentenkabinet, Amsterdam, and the Graphische Sammlung der Staatsgalerie, Stuttgart.

9 Wieseman, *op. cit.* (note 1), no. 155.

10 Rijksprentenkabinet, Amsterdam, inv. no. 1894.3720; and École des Beaux-Arts, Paris, inv no. 34.607. See Peter Schatborn, in *Dutch Figure Drawings from the Seventeenth Century*, exh. cat., Rijksprentenkabinet, Amsterdam, and National Gallery of Art, Washington, D.C., 1981–82, p. 98; and Van Gool's comments on Mattheus Verheyden cited in note 28 below (a drawing by Verheyden of a woman's arm, dated 1725, is in the Prentenkabinet der Rijksuniversiteit, Leiden, inv. 2026).

11 Compare, for example, Adriaen van der Werff's preliminary drawing for his *Samson and Delilah* of 1693, inscribed with color notes on the recto (Rijksprentenkabinet, Amsterdam); Barbara Gaehtgens, *Adriaen van der Werff 1659–1722*, Munich 1987, fig. 42a. Most of van der Werff's drawings of this nature seem to be preliminary studies, and many are squared for transfer.

12 A problematic drawing of a woman making sausages, traditionally attributed to Gerard Dou, is signed and dated 1650 and inscribed *verso* in a seventeenth-century hand: *Geschildert voor den / Keurvorst van Ments / en verzonden den 13 Augustus* (Musée du Louvre, Cabinet des Dessins, Paris, inv. no. R.F. 663); it apparently records a lost painting by Dou sent to the Elector at Mainz. The sheet may have remained in the artist's studio as a model for creating replicas. A painting by Schalcken is partly based on the drawing; see Thierry Beherman, *Godfried Schalcken*, Paris 1988, pp. 262–63, no. 166 and p. 382, no. D34. Beherman proposed that the Louvre drawing is a preliminary study by Schalcken for this painting; Ronni Baer (in correspondence) has rejected the drawing from Dou's oeuvre, thus casting doubt on the veracity of the inscription on the verso.

13 De Blieck's sketchbook, which dates to the 1650s, contains seventy sketches after paintings of church interiors (Rijksdienst voor de Monumentenzorg, Zeist); see Jeroen Giltaij, in *Perspectives: Saenredam and the architectural painters of the 17th century*, exh. cat., Museum Boijmans Van Beuningen, Rotterdam, 1991, pp. 309–13. Some drawings are dated, but otherwise there are few annotations.

14 Willem van Mieris made several large, highly finished drawings after his own compositions, but these were intended for sale, rather than as studio documentation. See Emke Elen-Clifford Kocq van Breugel, 'Tekeningen van Willem van Mieris (1662–1747) in relatie tot zijn schilderkunst', *Leids Kunsthistorisch Jaarboek*, III, 1985, esp. pp. 154–58; and Albert J. Elen, '"Ongemeen uitvoerig op Perkament met sapverven behandeld." De gekleurde tekeningen van Willem van Mieris uit de collectie Willem Witsen', *Delineavit et Sculpsit*, XV, 1995, pp. 1–24.

Examples of portrait *modelli* include
Rembrandt's drawing (British Museum,
London, inv. no. 1891-7-13-9) for the
*Portrait of a Woman, called Maria Trip*,
dated 1639, now in the Rijksmuseum.
Pentimenti in the painting suggest that
the drawing was done when the painting
was at a fairly advanced stage, to work
out changes later effected in the portrait
itself. See Martin Royalton-Kisch,
*Drawings by Rembrandt and his Circle in the
British Museum*, exh. cat., British
Museum, London, 1992, p. 78. Michiel
van Musscher's pen-and-wash drawing of
*Michiel Comans and his Wife*, dated 1667
(Rijksprentenkabinet, Amsterdam) was
probably also intended to give the client
an explicit idea of the proposed painting;
see P.J.J. van Thiel, 'Michiel van
Musscher's vroegste werk naar aanleiding
van zijn portret van het echtpaar
Comans', *Bulletin van het Rijksmuseum*,
vol. 17, March 1969, esp. p. 9.

15   Jacob de Wet's sketchbook contains notes
pertaining to the sale of paintings, a list
of pupils, and several sketches unrelated
to known paintings; see Abraham Bredius,
'Het schetsboek van Jacob de Wet', *Oud
Holland*, XXXVII, 1919, esp. pp. 215–19,
and Werner Sumowski, *Drawings of the
Rembrandt School*, 10 vols., New York,
1979–92, X (1992), nos. 2353–72. Van der
Werff's memorandum documents the
hours he and his brother Pieter devoted
to paintings executed between 1716 and
1722; see Gaehtgens, *op. cit.* (note 11),
pp. 442–44, doc. 6. Tiedeman's notes offer
a brief description of works and record
observations on clients and commissions;
see Peter J. Schoon, 'Een notitieboekje
van Philip Tiedeman (1657–1705), Leven
en werk van een zeventiende-eeuwse
Amsterdamse kunstenaar', *Oud Holland*,
CIV, 1990, pp. 31–46. Van Limborch's
memorandum book describes paintings
completed between 1716 and 1732, and
the time devoted to each; see Guido
M. C. Jansen, 'De *Notitie der dagelijxe
schilderoeffening* van Henrik van Limborch
(1681–1759)', *Bulletin van het Rijksmuseum*,
vol. 45, 1997, pp. 27–67.

16   Michael Kitson, *Claude Lorrain: Liber
Veritatis*, London 1978, p. 17.

17   References in the 1694 inventory to
sketchbooks and portfolios of drawings
do not offer enough information to form
any conclusions. The album of drawings
by Caspar Netscher and other artists now
in the Rijksprentenkabinet, Amsterdam
(inv. no. 1894.3720) was probably
assembled by Mattheus Verheyden; the
fifteen sheets now in the Graphische
Sammlung der Staatsgalerie, Stuttgart,
all from the collection of Edward Habich,
are described in the 1899 sale of his
collection as "Skizzenblätter", and not
as a bound book.

18   See Wieseman, *op. cit.* (note 1), figs. 56,
57, 58, 59, 60 and 61, and the comments
included under the respective catalogue
entries: nos. 23, 31, 28, 32, 52, 54, and 62.

19   Netscher's wash drawings have often
been attributed to de Bisschop, and de
Bisschop's have occasionally been attrib-
uted to Netscher (for example his wash
drawing after Netscher's portrait of
Johan de Witt in the Fitzwilliam Museum,
Cambridge). Christiaan Huygens the
Younger's wash drawings (which also
included drawings after paintings and
sculptures) were also strongly influenced
by de Bisschop; see *Met Huygens op reis:
Tekeningen en dagboeknotities van Constantijn
Huygens jr. (1628–1697)*, exh. cat.,
Rijksprentenkabinet, Amsterdam, and
Museum voor Schone Kunsten, Ghent,
1982–83, esp. pp. 32–33.

20   On Jan de Bisschop's drawings after
paintings, see Michiel Plomp, in
*Episcopius: Jan de Bisschop (1628–1671),
advocaat en tekenaar*, exh. cat., Museum
Het Rembrandthuis, Amsterdam, 1992,
pp. 38–39.

21   Netscher also made less finished *ricordi*
sketches in black or red chalk. Despite
their abbreviated character, they may be
distinguished from preliminary drawings
by their precise mimetic relationship to
the finished painting, and by inscriptions
which specifically note the date of the
composition and price for the finished
work.

22   Respectively: black chalk, Graphische
Sammlung der Staatsgalerie, Stuttgart,
inv. no. I/2062 (Wieseman, *op. cit.* [note 1],
no. 60 and fig. 65); black chalk, Wallraf-

Richartz-Museum, Cologne, inv. no. Z1774 (*ibid.*, no. 17); brush and brown ink with wash and white heightening, private collection (*ibid.*, no. 28 and fig. 60); pen and wash in bistre, British Museum, London, inv. no. 0.0.11-250 (*ibid.*, no. 54); pen and ink over graphite, Staatliche Graphische Sammlung, Munich, inv. 1951.48 (*ibid.*, no. 33 and fig. 66). For additional examples, see *ibid.*, nos. 23, 26, 31, 54, 62, and 93.

23  In 1675, five paintings by Netscher belonging to the Amsterdam art dealer Gerrit Uylenburch were valued between 140 guilders and 500 guilders; see Wieseman, *op. cit.* (note 1), pp. 132–33, doc. 48; the document was first published by S.A.C. Dudok van Heel ('Het "Schilderhuis" van Govert Flinck en de Kunsthandel van Uylenburgh aan de Lauriergracht te Amsterdam', *Jaarboek Amstelodamum*, vol. 74, 1982, pp. 84–87). For a survey of prices paid for paintings by Dou, Mieris and other Leiden school artists in the seventeenth century, see Eric Jan Sluijter, 'Schilders van "cleyne, subtile ende curieuse dingen"; Leidse "fijnschilders" in contemporaine bronnen', in *Leidse Fijnschilders*, ed. Eric Jan Sluijter, Marlies Enklaar, Paul Nieuwenhuizen, exh. cat., Stedelijk Museum De Lakenhal, Leiden, 1988, pp. 36–45. To cite a more relevant comparison, of the seventeen genre paintings by Johannes Vermeer that were included in the 1696 sale of the Dissius collection in Delft, twelve were valued between 40 guilders and 80 guilders – roughly commensurate with the prices noted on Netscher's *ricordi*. See John Michael Montias, *Vermeer and his Milieu: A Web of Social History*, Princeton 1989, pp. 363–64, doc. 439.

24  As the inscription is dated 1668, it seems plausible that the drawing was executed when the painting left the studio, although it cannot be ruled out that it was made upon the completion of the painting in 1664, and subsequently inscribed.

25  See Wieseman, *op. cit.* (note 1), nos. 54, 60 and 62.

26  Black chalk with annotations in red chalk, Rijksprentenkabinet, Amsterdam, inv. no. 1894:3720, fol. 12; and blue-black chalk with annotations in red chalk, Graphische Sammlung der Staatsgalerie, Stuttgart, inv. no. I/1073; see Wieseman, *op. cit.* (note 1), under nos. 187 and 156.

27  Red chalk, sale Sotheby's, London, 17 June 1976, lot 69, ill.; and red chalk, Rijksprentenkabinet, Amsterdam, inv. no. 1894.A3000, respectively.

28  "*Leenende hem . . . de portretschilder* [Constantijn] *Netscher eenige geschilderde schetsen van deszelfs vader, die hy alle met veel oplettentheit met het penseel of tekenpen copiëerde*" (Johan van Gool, *De nieuwe schouburg der Nederlantsche Kunstschilders en schilderessen*, 2 vols., The Hague 1750–51, II, p. 282). Several drawings after paintings by both Caspar and Constantijn Netscher (in the Prentenkabinet der Rijksuniversiteit, Leiden, and the Rijksprentenkabinet, Amsterdam) have been attributed to Verheyden. Verheyden probably also assembled the volume of drawings by Caspar Netscher and other artists now in the Rijksprentenkabinet (inv. no. 1894.3720); several of the drawings bear annotations in his hand. He seems to have adopted the practice of compulsively annotating his own *ricordi* drawings as well. On Verheyden as a draughtsman, see Esther Daems, 'Twee Zwitsers in Staatse dienst getekend door Mattheus Verheijden', *Delineavit et Sculpsit*, III, June 1990, pp. 24–27.

29  A lesser copy of the painting is in the Staatliche Kunsthalle, Karlsruhe, inv. no. 2032.

30  A more detailed drawing in red chalk over graphite (Iris and B. Gerald Cantor Center for Visual Arts, Stanford University, Stanford, inv. 1974.202) is probably by a member of Netscher's studio.

31  Theodoor Netscher, red chalk, sale Christie's, Amsterdam 10 November 1999, lot 105; and Mattheus Verheyden, pen and brush with grey ink on blue paper, Kunsthalle, Bremen, inv. no. 1967/520.

32  *Portrait of Willem Buys* [sic], red chalk, over sketch in black chalk, Gemeentearchief, Amsterdam, inv. no. KD66-221 (as by Caspar Netscher).

     MARJORIE E. WIESEMAN

33  Wieseman, *op. cit.* (note 1), no. C178.

34  Wieseman, *op. cit.* (note 1), no. C228*bis*.
This version is the only one with a
pendant portrait of a woman; a *ricordo*
in red chalk for this latter painting (The
Art Museum, Princeton University,
Princeton, inv. no. x1948-933) is inscribed
on the verso: *de Rock blauw / de Serp wit
met / goude bloemen / de gardijn doncker /
fuljemort met goude / bloemen* (the Skirt
blue / the Scarf white with / gold flowers
/ the curtain dark / brown with gold /
flowers).

35  Wieseman, *op. cit.* (note 1), no. C122
(collection Pauw van Wieldrecht,
Leersum, inv no. 98N).

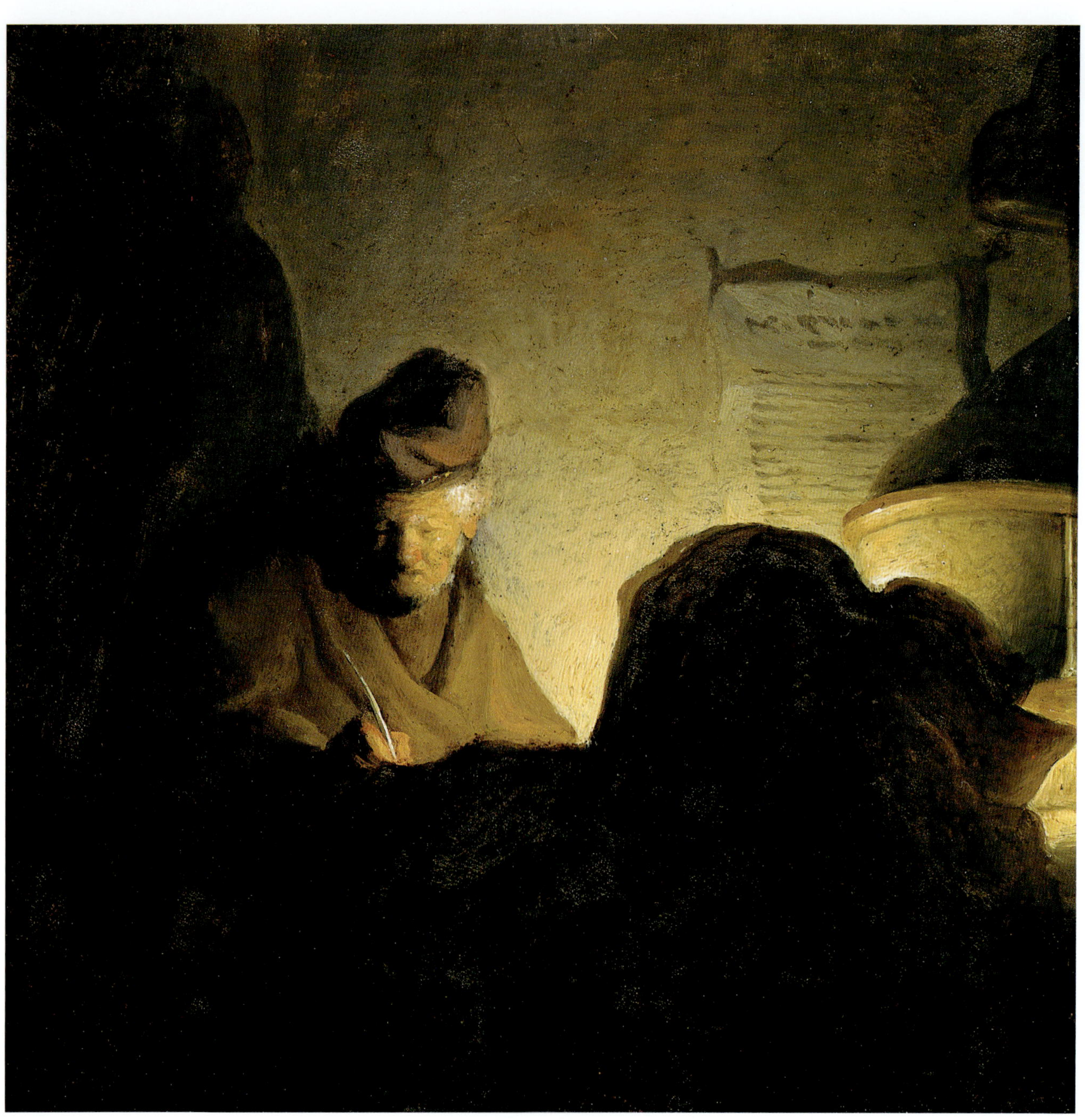

# *The Scholar by Candlelight* and Rembrandt's Early Transition

DAVID DE WITT

The small painting on copper of a *Scholar by Candlelight* in the Bader Collection once formed part of the oeuvre of Rembrandt (1606–1669), but, ever since Horst Gerson cast doubts on it in 1969, it has been excluded from the accepted body of his works (fig. 1).[1] It is a modest scene, featuring an old man in a dark interior. He is seated to the left of centre, at a writing table, behind a large book that looms in the foreground. To the right, piled on a table against the wall, is a scholarly still life, including a globe, an item which could identify the man more precisely as an astronomer. On the back wall hangs a piece of paper bearing text that is indicated only with cursory linear strokes of dark colour. Especially noticeable is the rough style in which the old man's head is painted. Recently scholars have revisited Rembrandt's development of a rough or loose manner in his early years in Leiden, and in this context this work has attracted renewed attention, although not yet a thorough reconsideration.

The strikingly loose handling of the figure's head as well as the overall dramatic effect of this tiny painting tend to draw attention away from its refinements. What is generally overlooked is that some passages feature a smooth manner and very thorough and powerful description, especially relative to the work's very small size. The contours around the shaded book in the foreground, for example, are masterfully modulated to suggest the undulating paper surfaces and the penetration of light through the leaves peeling away at the top and sides. A close look at details in the dark shaded area in the foreground reveals careful description and modulation that have remained beautifully intact. The cloak of the scholar is painted thickly and smoothly, with rounded folds and edges, suggesting a heavy fabric. This simple garb alludes to the earlier tradition for the depiction of scholars, based on hermits such as St Jerome.[2] Light hatching articulates the gown's rough surface texture. By contrast, the fleshiness of the scholar's head is generated through rougher, layered, semi-transparent brushstrokes. The flesh and fabric in the *Scholar by Candlelight* likely reflects Rembrandt's growing sophistication in handling paint

fig. 1 Attributed to REMBRANDT
*Scholar by Candlelight*, *ca.* 1627–28
Oil on copper, 13.8 × 13.8 cm
(originally 15.5 × 13.8 cm)
Milwaukee, Wisconsin, collection of
Drs Alfred and Isabel Bader

to describe various materials and surface textures. It advances well beyond the metallic smoothness of Rembrandt's teacher Pieter Lastman (1583–1633), which is often hard in its effect. Not surprisingly, the above mentioned subtleties have been passed over in the more recent, generally dismissive scholarly discussion of this painting. In what follows, it will be argued that its combination of rough and smooth manners suggests that this painting relates to Rembrandt's development around 1627/28.

For most of its known history, this picture had been accepted as a work by Rembrandt. He was identified as its author in the earliest secure trace of this work, the inscription to a print after it (with reversed composition) by J.B.P. Lebrun of 1790 (fig. 2).[3] Nonetheless, curiously, some time after 1823 the owner of the painting had the initials G.D.F. added to the paper on the wall, to

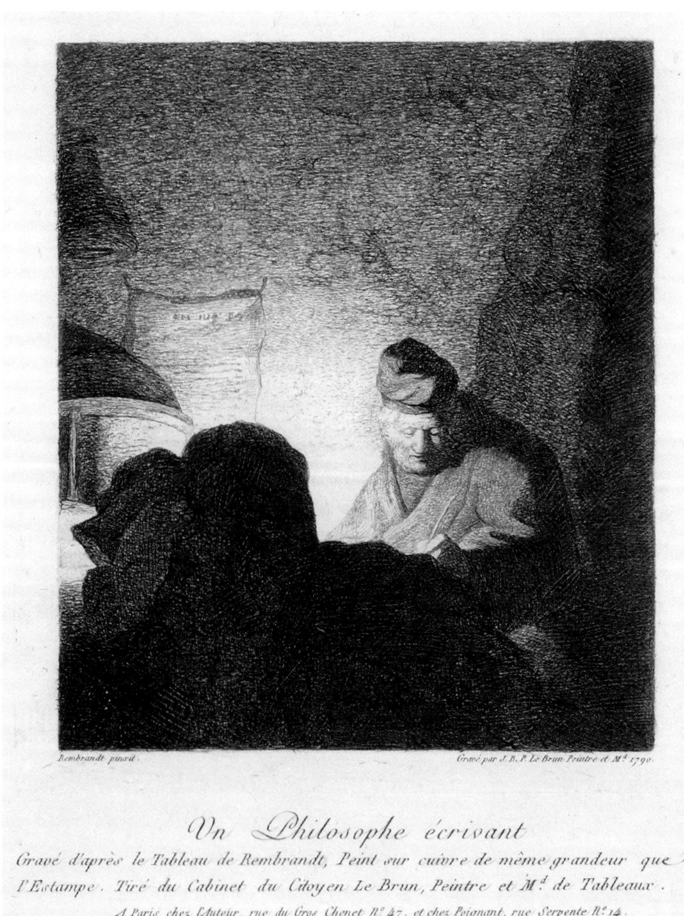



fig. 2 J.B.P. LEBRUN after REMBRANDT
*Scholar by Candlelight*, 1790
Etching, 15.7 × 13.8 cm (image)
The Hague, Rijksbureau voor Kunsthistorische Documentatie



DAVID DE WITT

indicate Gerard Dou (1613–1675) as the artist.[4] This modification is testimony to the popularity of Dou during the first half of the nineteenth century.[5] The false monogram was largely ignored when the painting resurfaced seventy years later, and was once more accepted as a Rembrandt.[6] It was easily removed with light solvents during a cleaning of the painting in 1958.[7]

In 1969, the Rembrandt attribution was cast into doubt by Horst Gerson in his revised edition of Abraham Bredius's book on Rembrandt.[8] Shortly afterwards, in 1972, the then newly formed Rembrandt Research Project (RRP) studied the painting and published it ten years later in the first volume of their *Corpus of Rembrandt Paintings*, rejecting the attribution to Rembrandt and assigning it to the C-category.[9] In its analysis of the picture, the RRP pointed to the use of a copper support as evidence against an attribution to Rembrandt. More specifically, the problem lay with the ground layer, which is of a light grey colour. There are, of course, three other paintings on copper that have been considered possibly to be by Rembrandt.[10] They date to around 1629–30. Nearly identical in dimension, the three pictures feature a ground layer consisting of gold leaf. Rembrandt probably acquired these three sheets of gilded copper at the same time from the same supplier. Although the height of the *Scholar by Candlelight* was probably similar before it was trimmed at the top, it is a centimetre wider. While there is no suggestion that the present picture has anything to do with the other three works, they may serve to illustrate the fact that Rembrandt had used copper as a support for his paintings and that he therefore may well have acquired another sheet, without any gilding. More importantly, the three accepted paintings show a remarkable range of handling. The *Laughing Soldier* in the Mauritshuis, The Hague, is one of the key examples of Rembrandt's early experimentation with loose brushwork.[11] By contrast, in his *Head of an Old Woman* in Salzburg he applied a very fine manner, while the so-called *Self-portrait* in Stockholm hovers somewhere in between these styles. As a group, these three early paintings on copper suggest a moment in Rembrandt's career during which he experimented with supports and different modes of paint handling. It is against this background of artistic experimentation that the small copper panel from Milwaukee should be considered.

In 1996, in the catalogue to the exhibition *Wisdom, Knowledge & Magic*, held at the Agnes Etherington Art Centre, Kingston, Ontario, Volker Manuth upheld the RRP's doubts regarding the work's authorship.[12] More recently, the painting has been included in the major exhibition *The Mystery of the Young Rembrandt* in Kassel and Amsterdam, where it was once again catalogued as by an early follower of Rembrandt rather than by the master himself.[13] Yet by this time the case seemed no longer straightforward. In one of his essays in the exhibition catalogue Ernst van de Wetering revisits the long-recognized

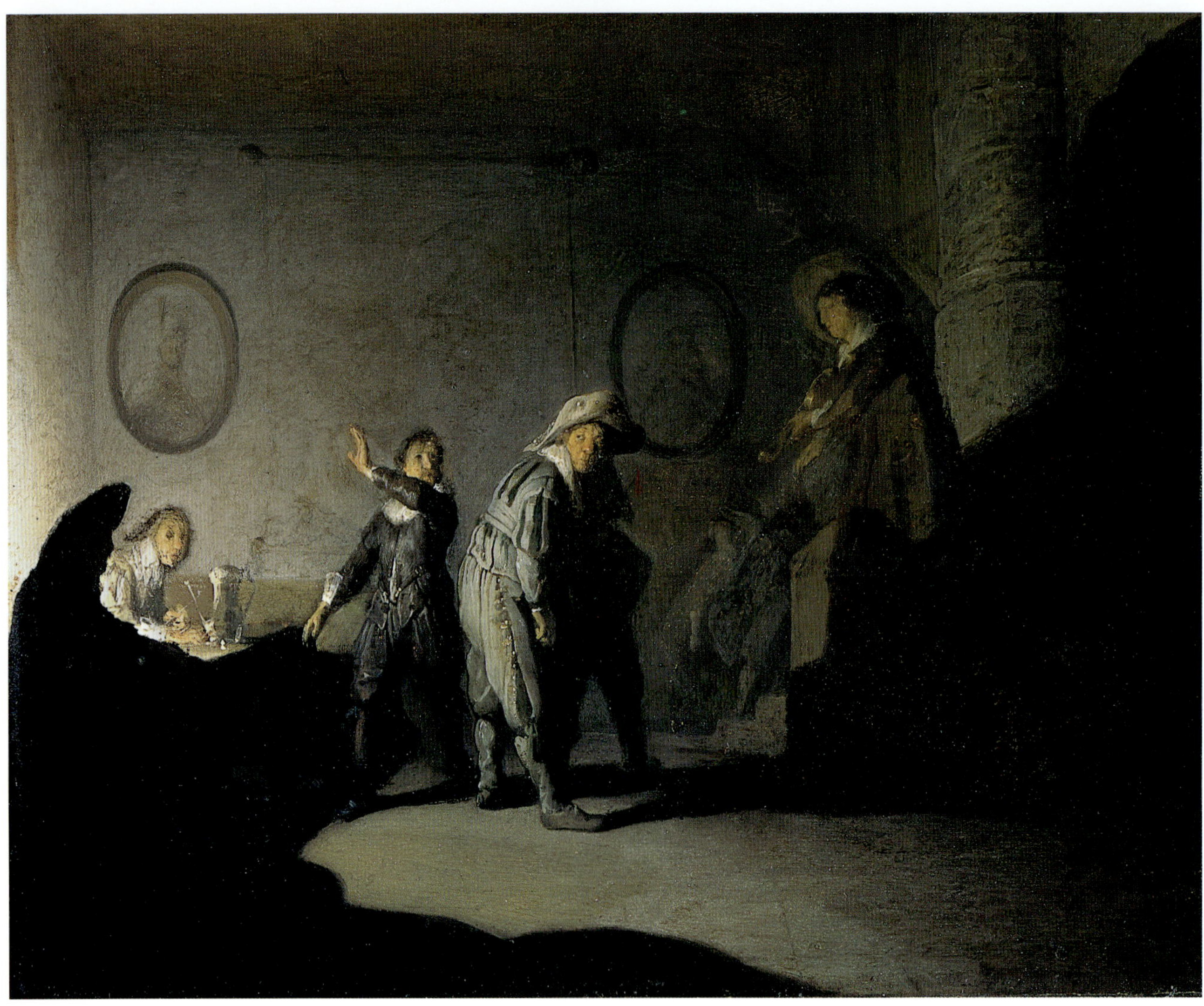

fig. 3 REMBRANDT
*Clap-hands, or La Main Chaude*
Oil on panel, 20 × 26 cm
Dublin, National Gallery of Ireland

connection between the *Scholar by Candlelight* and two other works, the *Flight into Egypt* in Tours and the genre scene known as *Clap-hands* or *La Main Chaude*, in Dublin (fig. 3).[14] The author makes a case for the re-attribution of these hitherto rejected works to Rembrandt himself. In his argument Van de Wetering draws a connection between *Clap-hands* and another early work, the *Artist in his Studio* in Boston.[15] Yet the Boston painting is comparatively smoothly painted; the rough paint handling of *Clap-hands* relates more closely to what appears in the *Supper at Emmaus* of 1629 in Paris (fig. 4).[16] The reattribution of *Clap-hands* to Rembrandt, as Van de Wetering further points out, forces a reconsideration of the attribution of the Bader painting.[17] Yet, regrettably, the author does not pursue the question any further. The author of the catalogue entry, Bob van den Boogert, on the other hand does not engage at all with Van de Wetering's suggestion, but

   DAVID DE WITT

rather writes the painting off as a derivative of the *St Paul in Meditation* in Nuremberg, dating it to *ca.*1629/30.[18]

In his catalogue entry Van den Boogert unfortunately does not examine an alternative possibility, namely that the Milwaukee painting might have been painted by Rembrandt just before the *St Paul* in Nuremberg, in 1628. The Nuremberg painting marks the moment when Rembrandt had adopted elements of a looser or rougher style. It followed upon a painting of 1627 known as the *Money-changer*, or *The Parable of the Rich Man*, in Berlin, which shows a single figure seated in a candlelit interior, painted in an emphatically fine and smooth manner.[19] Regardless of the authorship, it might be argued that the Milwaukee painting reveals a transitional style, comprising elements of both a fine and rough manner that one could imagine Rembrandt to have used between painting the night scenes in Berlin and Nuremberg. It seems that this sequence appears more convincing than the suggestion that the Milwaukee painting was painted after the Nuremberg one. An artist imitating the Nuremberg picture – which shows an overall rough manner – would have had little reason to paint

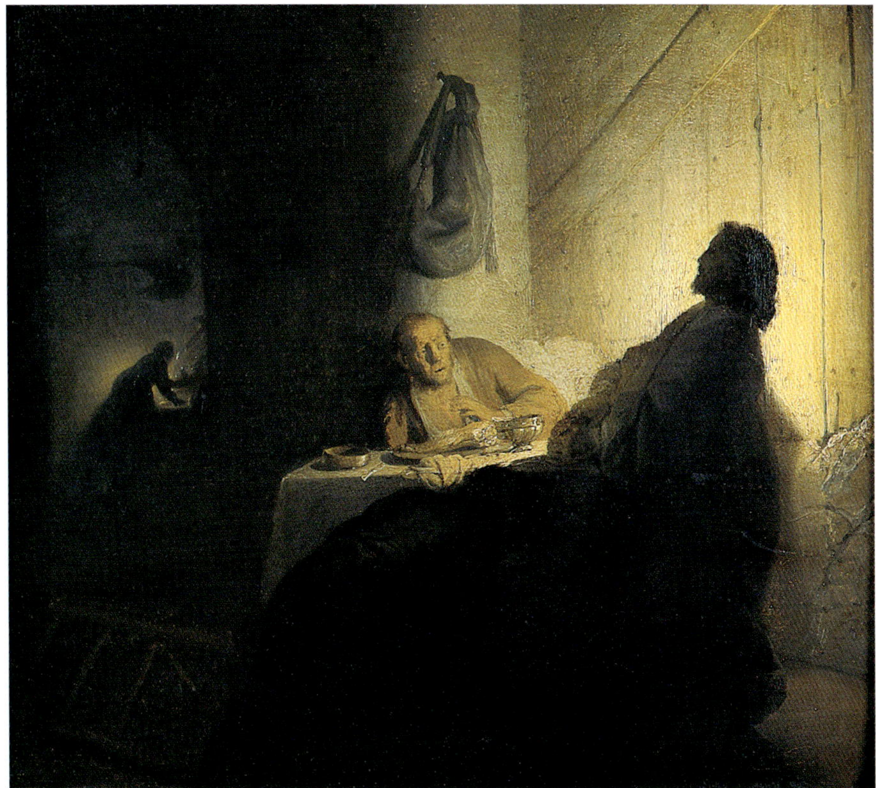

fig. 4 REMBRANDT
*The Supper at Emmaus*
Oil on paper laid down on panel,
37.4 × 42.3 cm
Paris, Institut de France – Musée
Jacquemart-André

some areas in a smooth and precise way. In the scenario suggested above the *Scholar by Candlelight* would reflect a transitional stage in Rembrandt's style, using a rough manner only partially in order to experiment with its evocative and suggestive effects.

Having discussed this shift in Rembrandt's style of the late 1620s, it may be worth considering what may have prompted his change in approach. Following his tutelage in Amsterdam under Pieter Lastman – and probably also Jan (*ca.* 1581/2–1631) or Jacob Pynas (1592/93– after 1650) – Rembrandt spent only a short time following his teachers' model closely. Paintings such as his *Stoning of St Stephen* in Lyons, the unidentified *History Piece* in Leiden and the *Baptism of the Eunuch* in Utrecht exhibit powerful chiaroscuro in brilliant outdoor light, the hard and smooth modelling of flesh, and the high-keyed palette that Lastman and the Pynases had derived from the work of Adam Elsheimer (1578–1610) in Rome. These works display the high ambitions that Lastman's practice, focused entirely on history painting, had inspired in his young pupil. They furthermore reveal the considerable development of Rembrandt's style from a series of much-debated genre paintings attributed to him from the time before he went to Lastman. Those works have been identified as part of a series of the Five Senses, and are mostly interior scenes with large-scale figures. Their style most likely reflects the approach of Jan Lievens (1607–1674), which Rembrandt had observed in Leiden before he went to Amsterdam.[20] Once he had returned to Leiden, Rembrandt revisited the motif of the dark interior illuminated by an artifical light source, this time with considerably greater ambition and complexity and with fresh eyes for other sources, some of which he had probably encountered in Amsterdam's bustling art trade. Elsheimer's works, which Rembrandt could have known through Hendrick Goudt's masterful prints, remained an important influence. Goudt beautifully evoked Elsheimer's night scenes through the richness of his etched black lines. Rembrandt also absorbed the Caravaggism of prominent Utrecht artists, in particular the dramatic light effects achieved by Gerrit van Honthorst (1592–1656). (We will come back to this aspect shortly.)

These already acknowledged sources do not, however, entirely elucidate Rembrandt's transition in the years 1627/28. Around 1629 he painted the remarkable scene of *The Supper at Emmaus*, now in Paris (fig. 4). This picture is characterized by two striking features: the emphatic expression of one of the disciples and – as we have mentioned earlier – the rough handling of the paint. Bernhard Schnackenburg had suggested the free facture of Anthony van Dyck (1599–1641) as the source for the loose handling of the Paris picture, comparing it to a work in the museum in Cassel.[21] This analogy, however, does not seem entirely convincing, as Van Dyck's approach is more fluid and rather unlike



DAVID DE WITT

the abrupt, sharp hatching applied by Rembrandt. Instead it may be worth considering a different influence, suggested by earlier scholars, namely the genre specialists from Haarlem. In 1959 Egbert Haverkamp-Begemann pointed out the way in which Rembrandt looked to the work of the Haarlem painter Willem Buytewech (1591/92–1624) for the composition of his 1626 *Tobias and Anna* in the Rijksmuseum.[22] In the recent exhibition on the young Rembrandt in Cassel and Amsterdam the painting known as *Clap-hands* from Dublin has also been connected in a general way to the work of Buytewech, David Vinckboons (1576– before 1633), Esaias van de Velde (1587–1630) and Pieter Codde (1599–1678), who had developed the subject of the Merry Company, containing groups of small, fashionably dressed figures set deeply into elegant interiors.[23] Although Rembrandt's figures pursue similar leisurely activities and wear equally fashionable attire, they present themselves much less elegantly than Buytewech's fops.

In his 1960 analysis of the early Rembrandt Kurt Bauch pointed to another trend that affected the young artist – the Bruegellian peasant mode as rejuvenated by artists like Adriaen Brouwer (1605/06–1638), who probably spent some time in Frans Hals's workshop in Haarlem.[24] Bauch's remarks, however, have received only marginal attention since. Brouwer is the key figure in the rise of peasant subjects in Dutch painting. This genre, with its origins in the work of another nominal Dutchman, Hieronymus Bosch (*ca.* 1450–1516), had survived into the seventeenth century in the work of the followers of its greatest champion, Pieter Bruegel the Elder (*ca.* 1525–1569), in Antwerp.[25] When Adriaen Brouwer picked it up in the 1620s (probably having trained in it before moving to the Northern Netherlands), he was carrying forward a tradition that was still being practised by Bruegel's own descendants (albeit as an archaization), and for which there was still a healthy market.[26] Brouwer was active in the northern provinces between 1625 and 1631. He first stayed in Amsterdam in 1625–26 before moving to Haarlem – presumably as a fully trained artist.[27] Although he may have worked in Frans Hals's studio, he never adopted Hals's style but instead inspired a whole generation of Dutch genre painters with his own approach. It has been observed that Brouwer introduced greater concentration, creating groups of just a few figures and placing them in spare interior spaces. For this he may have drawn on the work of Buytewech. He also developed a wide vocabulary for emotional expression, moving well beyond his forebears in subtlety and observation. It may well be possible that Rembrandt had encountered Brouwer and his work during his training with Pieter Lastman in Amsterdam.[28] Rembrandt certainly had an interest in Brouwer. We know that one of Brouwer's earliest paintings, dating to the beginning of his Dutch period, had been acquired by Rembrandt. A reference in his inventory of 1656 can be connected to a "Pancake Baker" by Brouwer, which is probably his *Old Woman making Pancakes*, now in Basle (fig. 5), as he clearly developed its composition in his own etching of the same subject in 1635.[29] Listed at the very beginning of the inventory, it seems to have had a place in the most conspicuous room of his house, the semi-public entrance hall.[30] Rembrandt owned three further paintings and some drawings by Brouwer, and in this respect he may have anticipated Peter Paul Rubens (1577–1640), who came to know of Brouwer only after the latter artists had moved back to Antwerp in 1631, and who would come to own at least seventeen works by Brouwer.[31]

The precise extent of Brouwer's Dutch oeuvre that Rembrandt could have known around the time he was painting *Clap-hands* and *The Supper at Emmaus* is as yet unclear, but it would be useful to attempt a more accurate assessment. Konrad Renger has pointed out that a number of paintings given to the artist's Antwerp period do not bear the city's stamp mark on the reverse of their panel support, which may suggest that some of them had indeed been painted earlier, in the north.[32] The problem is exacerbated by the fact that Brouwer rarely signed and never dated his own works. More generally, until now the dating of Haarlem genre pictures has not received as much attention as their interpretation and the tracing of their printed sources, and neither has the specific context of the revolutionary decade of the 1620s.[33] Although Brouwer's *Woman making Pancakes* does indeed not reveal the artist's fully developed powers of expression, suitable examples of his mastery can be found among the accepted works of his Dutch period which Rembrandt could have known, such as his *Fighting Peasants* in the Rijksmuseum.[34]

Instead of Van Dyck, it thus seems that one should rather consider the style of Brouwer as an important precedent for Rembrandt's *Supper at Emmaus* in Paris and the closely related *Clap-hands* from Dublin. Ironically, Kurt Bauch, who had drawn the link between Rembrandt and Haarlem, resisted the attribution of *Clap-hands* to Rembrandt.[35] These paintings of the period between 1627 and 1630, however, show Rembrandt keen to match powers with Brouwer and his followers in Haarlem who specialized in genre painting. This stylistic connection to genre painting is indeed a groundbreaking aspect of the Paris picture. It also derives from the *boerengezelschap* or peasant low-life scene practised by Brouwer, by way of its vulgar types, the awkward and inelegant poses, and rough paint handling.[36] Most importantly, Rembrandt seized upon Brouwer's candid facial expressions, which convey *emotion*, rather than the *pathos* dictated by theory for history paintings. These breaches of academic decorum would be the earliest of many for Rembrandt. They permitted him a wide range of expressions, and of expressive types, unencumbered by the demands for idealization imposed by Italian, especially Tuscan, models for history painting, a



DAVID DE WITT

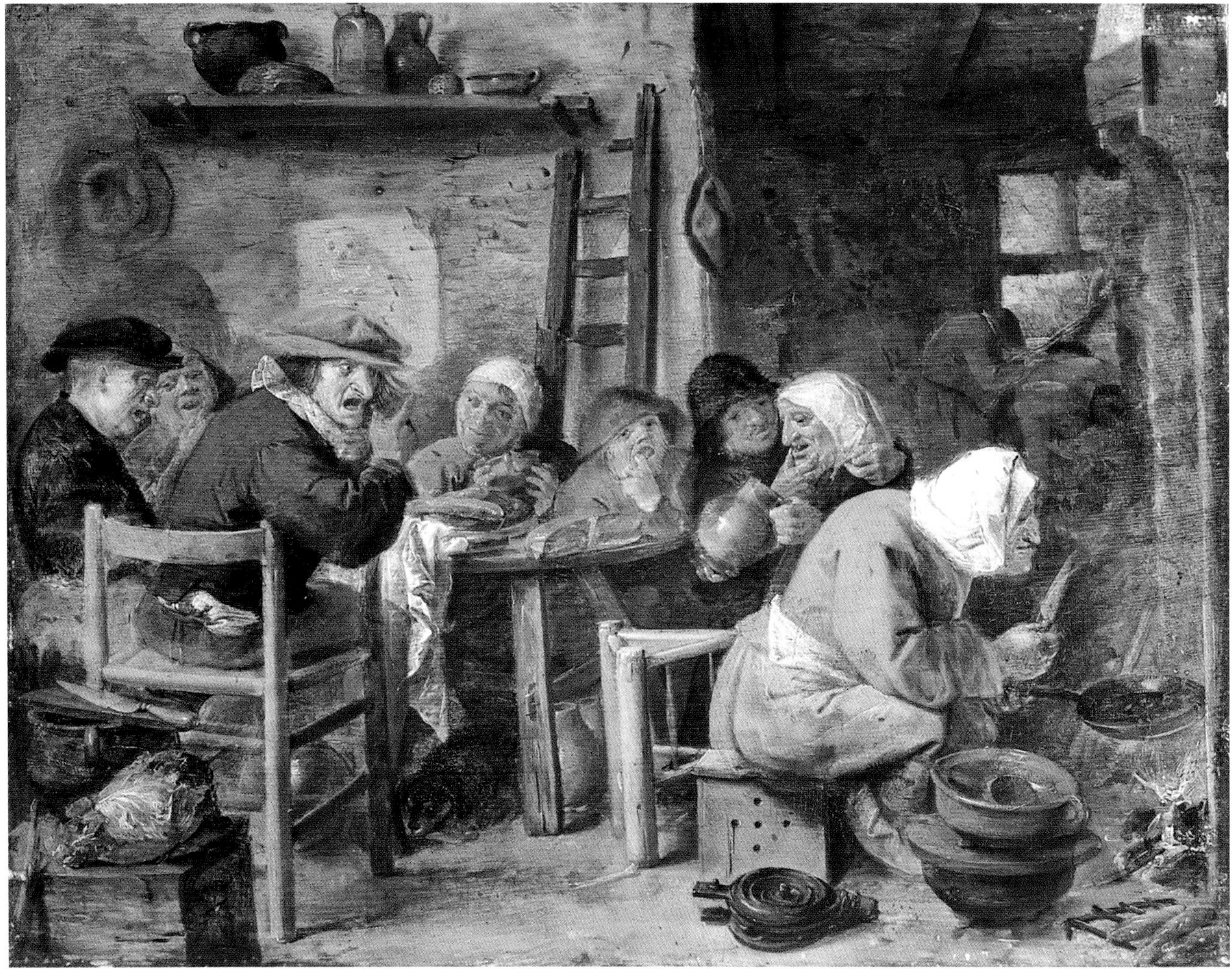

fig. 5 ADRIAEN BROUWER
*Old Woman making Pancakes*
Oil on panel, 29.2 × 36.3 cm
Basle, Kunstmuseum Basel

requirement most famously specified by Giorgio Vasari (1511–1574) in his *Lives* of 1550 and 1568.[37] Rembrandt's interest may in part be related to Karel van Mander (1548–1606), who praised the elder Pieter Bruegel's genius highly in his *Schilder-boeck*, not the least because he himself also painted genre subjects in Bruegel's manner.[38] Van Mander in turn cajoled the aspiring history painter to master all subject-matter, his theoretical ideal of *verscheydenheyt*. This concept also included the genre painter's mastery of candid expressions of the emotions. Rembrandt probably absorbed the mastery of emotional expression from genre painting. It helped him to earn his early reputation, but it would later exasperate academically oriented critics like Arnold Houbraken (1660– 1719), who sought a fixed and defined vocabulary of expressions that could be taught systematically.

Considering these relationships, I would argue that the *Scholar by Candlelight* also reflects Rembrandt's interest in Brouwer's works, adopting some of the undignified roughness and expressiveness of the Fleming's peasants as well as his satirical approach. More broadly, this painting reflects the synthesis of various artistic models Rembrandt was exposed to around 1627–28. His chiaroscuro, with various compositional elements caught in strong light was inspired by the settings of the Caravaggesque painters from Utrecht. In the present picture the artist even incorporates the characteristic device of a *repoussoir* by hiding the source of the illumination, a candle, behind the large book on the lectern. The hidden candle is probably derived directly from Rembrandt's *Parable of the Rich Man* in Berlin. There the light source casts inky-black shadows on the back wall, in an effect similar to that seen in *Clap-hands*. In this dark, intimate interior scene, with its dramatic lighting and secular subject, the artist further modified a pictorial type of the 'scholar in his study' that had already been refined by Jan Lievens in the mid 1620s in Leiden, as exemplified by his *Quillcutter*, last in Kreuzlingen, and his *Scholar in his Study*, last in Paris.[39] A critical contrast, however, between the two painters' works is the figure scale. Compared to Lievens's typically monumental, looming figures, the old man in the Bader picture is very small. In this respect he is closer again to the peasants in Brouwer's interior scenes. By following the Brouwer tradition Rembrandt eventually parted ways with his fellow *Leidenaar* Lievens, who concentrated more closely on the work of the Utrecht Caravaggisti, Van Dyck and Rubens.

There are, furthermore, a few less immediately noticeable aspects that link some of Rembrandt's early paintings. Van de Wetering points to the motif of expressive hand gestures Rembrandt used in *Clap-hands*, *Christ at Emmaus* and the *Artist in his Studio*.[40] The tensed hand plays a similarly distinctive role in the *Scholar by Candlelight*. Over the edge of the book, we see the scholar's proper right thumb is shown crooked sharply around his pen. Efficiently described in a few thick strokes, and strongly emphasized by the light falling on it, this element forcefully expresses the old man's rapt absorption in profound thought. Alongside this expressive element, the distinctive painterly effect of the linear, thin impasto highlight is a technical device common to Rembrandt's early paintings. The scholar's pen in the Bader painting is drawn in one stroke of white paint that forms a bead on the painting's surface. Fluid and tapering, this type of accent also appears throughout *Clap-hands*, and in the figure of Joseph and the donkey in the foreground of the *Flight into Egypt* in Tours. Significantly, it also appears in the Paris painting of the *Supper at Emmaus*. Attention to such traits is not what one would expect of an imitator. They are secondary devices that make a subtle contribution. Such exploitation of detail was pursued doggedly by Rembrandt, yet rarely by his followers, who tended to devote themselves to the more obvious, general characteristics of his works.

Another connection between the Milwaukee picture and Rembrandt's works can be observed in his early drawing and etching of the *Apostle Paul*, where he adopted a similar general composition that isolates the head and torso of the saint and incorporates an internal light source behind a large book.[41] It may be suggested that these works draw on the Bader *Scholar by Candlelight* and lead to the Nuremberg *St Paul*. Undated, they would thus be placed around 1628/29. Moving into the next decade, the same arrangement appears in two of the prints of Jan Gillisz van Vliet (*ca.* 1610–1668), his *Mathematician* and *Geographer*, from his series on the trades of around 1635. By this time Van Vliet had ceased his collaboration with Rembrandt, who nonetheless remained his primary influence, and these prints underscore the suggestion that the Bader painting that served as their model is indeed either an autograph work by Rembrandt or a close and sensitive copy of a lost painting by him, of *ca.* 1628.

The present analysis embraces various elements of early seventeenth-century Northern Netherlandish painterly practice that were synthesized by the young Rembrandt, working in Leiden around 1628. The existing scholarly model, pointing to Lastman, Lievens and the Utrecht Caravaggisti as influences, is here expanded by introducing the notion that Rembrandt also looked to the vibrant approach to genre painting in Haarlem, which owed much to Pieter Bruegel. Artists such as Adriaen Brouwer are a probable source for Rembrandt's attention to low-life characters, and spontaneous, undignified emotional expressions, also in his history paintings. In such works these elements went against the usual expectation of grandeur and refinement. These aspects of Rembrandt's early practice form a likely context for the creation of the *Scholar by Candlelight*, with its combinations of rough and smooth handling, of high subject-matter and crude characterization of a hermit type passionately engaged in thought and writing. This work reflects clearly the master's formative period as a painter.

1  For Gerson's opinion see Abraham Bredius, *Rembrandt. The Complete Edition of the Paintings*, revised by Horst Gerson, London 1969, p. 588, no. 425.

2  See David de Witt, Jane Russell Corbett, Sandra Richards, 'The Scholarship and Spirituality of Saints and Hermits', in Volker Manuth *et al.*, *Wisdom, Knowledge & Magic: The Image of the Scholar in Seventeenth-Century Dutch Art*, exh. cat., Agnes Etherington Art Centre, Queen's University, Kingston 1996; and more specifically Russell Corbett's contribution on 'The Pictorial Development of St Jerome c. 1500–1700', pp. 13–14.

3  J.B.P. Le Brun, etching, 15.7 × 13.8 cm (image), inscribed below: *Rembrandt pinxit Gravé par J.B.P Le Brun Peintre et M̱d̲ 1790 / Un Philosophe écrivant / Gravé d'après le Tableau de Rembrandt, Peint sur cuivre de meme grandeur que l'Estampe. Tiré du Cabinet du Citoyen Le Brun, Peintre et M̱d̲ de Tableaux. / A Paris chez l'Auteur, rue du Gros Chenet No. 47, et chez Poignant, rue Serpente No. 14*, in *Galerie des peintres flamands, hollandais et allemands*, 3 vols., Paris 1792–96, II, p. 2 (the print). The painting is mentioned on p. 5 as sold to Robert de Saint-Victor. Theodor von Frimmel pointed to a sale reference of 1739, although noting that the lack of precise measurements made a positive identification impossible. See 'Wiedergefundene Bilder aus berühmten alten Sammlungen', *Blätter für Gemäldekunde*, II, 1906, pp. 21–23 (with illustration). Von Frimmel cites from Gerard Hoet "*Een schryvend Mannetje*", sold in an anonymous auction in Amsterdam on 15 April 1739, lot 88 (as Rembrandt); see Gerard Hoet, *Naamlyst van Schilderijen . . .*, 2 vols., The Hague 1752, I, p. 581. The Rembrandt Research Project (see note 9) drew a connection to a sale reference of three years earlier: sale Jan van Loon, Amsterdam, 18 July 1736, lot 26 (for 105 guilders); see Hoet, *op. cit.* (as above), II, p. 391; and sale J. van der Marck, Amsterdam, 25ff. August 1773, lot 261.

4  The painting appeared at a subsequent sale as a Rembrandt, with no mention of the initials: sale Robert of St Victor, Paris, 26 November 1822, lot 69; cited by Theodor von Frimmel, 'Ein Rembrandt aus der Galerie Le Brun', *Blätter für Gemäldekunde*, I, 1905, p. 21. Von Frimmel states that Hofstede de Groot had noted that the monogram had been added after the Paris sale of 1822. The painting's history in the ensuing years is not documented; von Frimmel placed it in the collection of a Mr Dubois, theatre director in Vienna, before it moved on to the Mayer collection.

5  For more on this subject see Arthur K. Wheelock, Jr, 'Dou's Reputation', in Ronni Baer, *Gerrit Dou 1613–1675: Master Painter in the Age of Rembrandt*, exh. cat., ed. Arthur K. Wheelock, Jr, National Gallery of Art, Washington; Dulwich Picture Gallery; Mauritshuis, The Hague, 2000, pp. 12–24.

6  Wilhelm von Bode, Cornelius Hofstede de Groot, *Rembrandt Tentoonstelling*, exh. cat., Rijksmuseum, Amsterdam, 1898, no. 1 (unpaginated).

7  Letter from Josef Hasjinek, Chief Conservator of Paintings, Kunsthistorisches Museum, Vienna, 8 September 1958, on file with Drs. Alfred and Isabel Bader, Milwaukee: "*Umseitiges Ölbild ist auf Kupfer gemalt und hat eine Grösse von 13.9 × 13.9 cm. Es zeigt den Zustand, bevor ich das Bild reinigte. Bei Anwendung eines ganz leichten Putzmittels wurden die Initialen "G.D.F.", die sich, wie das Foto zeigt, auf dem an die Wand gehefteten Brief befanden, leicht weggeputzt. Diese Initialen erwiesen sich also als eine spätere Zutat. Prof. Josef Hasjinek, Hofrestaurator d. Gem. Gal. des Kunsthist. Museums / Wien, 8 September 1958.*"

8  Bredius, *op. cit.* (note 1), p. 588, no. 425.

9  Josua Bruyn, Bob Haak, Simon H. Levie, Pieter J.J. van Thiel, Ernst van de Wetering, *A Corpus of Rembrandt Paintings*, vols. 1–, Foundation Rembrandt Research Project, The Hague, Dordrecht, Boston and London 1982–, I, pp. 554–557, no. C18.

10  Rembrandt, *Laughing Soldier*, oil on gilded copper, 15.4 × 12.2 cm, The Hague, Mauritshuis, inv. no. 598; Rembrandt, *Old Woman at Prayer*, *ca.* 1629, oil on gilded copper, 15.5 × 12.2 cm, Salzburg,

　　　DAVID DE WITT

Salzburger Landessammlungen-
Residenzgalerie, inv. no. 549; Rembrandt,
*Self-portrait*, signed and dated 1630, oil on
gilded copper, 15.5 × 12.0 cm, Stockholm,
Nationalmuseum, inv. no. NM 5324
(stolen in 2001).

11 Justus Lange has recently noted a
connection to the work of Brouwer, but,
curiously, cited works painted later,
in the 1630s, which could not have
directly influenced Rembrandt. See
Ernst van de Wetering, Bernhard
Schnackenburg, *The Mystery of the Young
Rembrandt*, exh. cat., Staatliche Museen
Kassel and Rembrandthuis, Amsterdam,
2001, pp. 366–68. This painting is
traditionally dated to *ca.* 1629/30, on
the basis of the date appearing on the
Stockholm *Self-portrait*, but it is naturally
difficult to compare to known dated
works, on account of its unusual
handling.

12 See Volker Manuth's entry on the
painting in Manuth *et al.*, *op. cit.* (note 2),
pp. 50–51, no. 14.

13 See Bob van den Boogert's entry in
Van de Wetering, Schnackenburg, *op. cit.*
(note 11), pp. 298–301, no. 59.

14 Rembrandt, *Clap-hands, or La Main Chaude*,
Dublin, National Gallery of Ireland, inv.
no. 439; see Homan Potterton, *National
Gallery of Ireland. Illustrated Summary
Catalogue of Paintings*, Dublin 1981, p. 136;
and *The Flight into Egypt*, panel, 27.5 ×
24.7 cm, Tours, Musée des Beaux-Arts;
see *Corpus*, *op. cit.* (note 9), I, pp. 478–82,
no. C5.

15 Rembrandt, *The Artist in his Studio*, oil
on panel, 24.8 × 31.7, Boston, Museum
of Fine Arts, inv. no. 38.1838.

16 Rembrandt, *The Supper at Emmaus*, paper
laid down on panel, 37.4 × 42.3 cm, Paris,
Musée Jacquemart-André, inv. no. 409;
see *Corpus*, *op. cit.* (note 9), I, pp. 196–201,
no. A 16 (with illustration).

17 Ernst van de Wetering, 'Delimiting
Rembrandt's Autograph Œuvre – an
Insoluble Problem?', in Van der Wetering,
Schnackenburg, *op. cit.* (note 11), pp. 77–78.
Van de Wetering offers a counter-
argument, comparing this work with the
Berlin *Money-changer*, which, however,
ignores, even contradicts, his argument

about *Clap-hands* and the development of
a looser style in Rembrandt's early work.

18 Van de Wetering's suggestion of revisiting
the attribution of *The Scholar by Candlelight*
was unfortunately also not discussed at
the symposium at the end of
the exhibition in Amsterdam.

19 Rembrandt, *The Parable of the Rich Man* ,
signed and dated 1627, oil on panel,
31.9 × 42.5 cm, Berlin, Staatliche
Museen zu Berlin, Gemäldegalerie,
inv. no. 828 D; see *Corpus*, *op. cit.* (note 9),
I, pp. 137–42, no. A 10 (with illustration).

20 The connection was revisited in the
exhibition in Kassel and Amsterdam
in 2001–02 (Van de Wetering,
Schnackenburg, *op. cit.* [note 11],
pp. 150–9, nos. 9–11). Rembrandt's
observation of Lievens during this
period is particularly evident in no. 9,
*The Three Singers (Hearing)*, oil on panel,
21.6 × 17.8 cm, London, collection of
W. Baron van Dedem; see also Peter C.
Sutton, *Dutch & Flemish Paintings. The
Collection of Willem Baron van Dedem*,
London 2002, pp. 199–201, no. 42 (with
colour illustration); this painting of
*ca.* 1625–26 takes its main figure from the
*Singing Man* of *ca.* 1625 by Jan Lievens in
the collection of the Agnes Etherington
Art Centre: oil on panel, 90.2 × 76.2 cm,
acc. no. 34-020.06. For the Lievens see
Werner Sumowski, *Gemälde der Rembrandt-
Schüler*, 6 vols., Landau 1983–94, III,
p. 1791, no. 1224, p. 1863 (with colour
illustration).

21 Bernhard Schnackenburg, 'Young
Rembrandt's "Rough Manner",
A Painting Style and its Sources', in
Van der Wetering, Schnackenburg,
*op. cit.* (note 11), pp. 92–121.

22 Egbert Haverkamp-Begemann, *Willem
Buytewech (1591/2–1624)*, Amsterdam
1959, p. 6.

23 Van de Wetering, Schnackenburg, *op. cit.*
(note 11), pp. 308, 310, no. 62; the entry
draws a connection to a significantly later
painting by Jan Miense Molenaer, of
*ca.* 1649.

24 Kurt Bauch, *Der frühe Rembrandt und seine
Zeit*, Berlin 1960, pp. 30–37.

25 Recent reminders of the scale and
longevity of the Bruegel phenomenon

have been the exhibitions *Pieter Breughel der Jüngere – Jan Brueghel der Ältere. Flämische Malerei um 1600, Tradition und Fortschritt*, exh. cat., ed. Klaus Ertz and Christa Nitze-Ertz, Kulturstiftung Ruhr, Villa Hügel, Essen; Kunsthistorisches Museum, Vienna; Koninklijk Museum voor Schone Kunsten, Antwerp, 1997; and *Brueghel Enterprises*, exh. cat., ed. Peter van den Brink, Bonnefantenmuseum, Maastricht, and Musées Royaux des Beaux-Arts de Belgique, Brussels, 2001.

26  Konrad Renger, *Adriaen Brouwer und das niederländische Bauerngenre 1600–1660*, Munich 1986, p. 45.

27  Abraham Bredius, *Künstler-Inventare: Urkunden zur Geschichte der holländischen Kunst des XVIten, XVIIten und XVIIIten Jahrhunderts*, 8 vols., The Hague 1915–22, III, pp. 804–05.

28  Ben Broos, 'Rembrandts eerste Amsterdamse periode', *Oud Holland*, CXIV, 2000, pp. 1–6.

29  Adriaen Brouwer, *Old Woman making Pancakes*, monogrammed, Basle, Kunstmuseum, inv. no. 909; this painting or a version of it (*e.g.* Philadelphia, Museum of Art, Johnson Collection, no. 680) appears in Rembrandt's inventory of 1656: "*Een stuckie van Ad. Brouwer sijnde een koekebacker*" (A little piece by Adriaen Brouwer, being a pancake maker); see Walter L. Strauss and Marjon van der Meulen, *The Rembrandt Documents*, New York 1979, p. 349, no. 1. The other paintings are cited on pp. 349 and 357, the drawings on p. 371. The print by Rembrandt, *The Pancake Maker*, signed and dated 1635, etching and drypoint, was catalogued by Adam von Bartsch in *Le Peintre-graveur*, Vienna 1803–21, under no. 124. For the connection between the painting in Rembrandt's possession and the print see Holm Bevers's entry on the print in Holm Bevers, Peter Schatborn, Barbara Welzel, *Rembrandt: the Master and his Workshop, Drawings and Etchings*, exh. cat., Altes Museum, Staatliche Museen Preussischer Kulturbesitz, Berlin; Rijksmuseum, Amsterdam; National Gallery, London, 1991, no. 10, pp. 192, 194, note 3.

30  See Strauss, van der Meulen, *op. cit.* (note 29), p. 349, no. 1.

31  *An Inventory of Pictures found in the howse of the late Sr Peter Paul Rubens Knt: after his death: Inprimis pieces of Italian Mrs.*, in Jeffrey Muller, *Rubens: The Artist as Collector*, Princeton 1989, pp. 139–42, nos. 272–88 (no. 281 consists of two paintings).

32  Renger, *op. cit.* (note 26), pp. 48, 123, note 15.

33  See *ibid.* and Hans-Joachim Raupp, 'Adriaen Brouwer als Satiriker', in ed. Henning Bock, Thomas W. Gaehtgens, *Holländische Genremalerei im 17. Jahrhundert. Symposium Berlin 1984. Jahrbuch Preussischer Kulturbesitz*, IV, 1987, pp. 225–52; and more recently Elmer Kolfin, 'Een geselschap jonge luyden: productie, functie en betekenis van Noord-Nederlandse voorstellingen van vrolijke geselschappen 1610–1645', diss., Rijksuniversiteit Leiden, 2002. Renger's volume of 1986 incorporates the most intensive study to date of the chronology of Brouwer's work, largely adhering to the already recognized small oeuvre of surviving works from Brouwer's Dutch period.

34  Oil on panel, 25.5 × 34 cm, Amsterdam, Rijksmuseum, inv. no. A65; see Margret Klinge, *Adriaen Brouwer & David Teniers the Younger*, exh. cat., Noortman & Brod, New York and Maastricht, 1982, p. 34, no. 2 (with colour illustration).

35  Bauch, *op. cit.* (note 24), p. 243.

36  Renger posited influence in the other direction, although he did not analyse specific works from this period by Rembrandt. See Renger, *op. cit.* (note 26), pp. 39–41.

37  In discussing Vasari's interest in the ideal, Erwin Panofsky singled out Vasari's discussion of *disegno* with respect to painting. See Giorgio Vasari, *Le vite de' piu eccellenti pittori, scultori ed architettori*, Florence 1550, ed. Gaetano Milanesi, Florence 1878–85, I, pp. 168–69. For the discussion see Erwin Panofsky, *Idea. A Concept in Art Theory*, translated by Joseph J.S. Peake, Columbia 1968, pp. 60–63.

38  Karel van Mander, *Lives of the Illustrious Netherlandish and German Painters. From the first edition of the "Schilder-boeck"*, ed.



DAVID DE WITT

Hessel Miedema, translated by Michael
Hoyle, 6 vols., Doornspijk 1994–99, I,
pp. 190–96, fol. 233r–34r. On his
appreciation for Bruegel, see Hans-
Joachim Raupp, *Bauernsatiren. Entstehung
und Entwicklung des Bäuerlichen Genres in der
deutschen und niederländischen Kunst ca.
1470–1570*, Niederzier 1986,
pp. 304–05, 322–24.

39  Jan Lievens, *Quillcutter*, canvas, 127 ×
107.5 cm, formerly Kreuzlingen, collection of Heinz Kisters; see Sumowski,
*op. cit.* (note 20), III, p. 1794, no. 1235
(with illustration p. 1874); *A Scholar in
his Study*, panel, 91 × 71 cm, formerly
Paris, Charles Sedelmayer; see Wilhem
R. Valentiner, *Rembrandt. Wiedergefundene
Gemälde*, Klassiker der Kunst, vol. 27,

Stuttgart and Berlin 1921, pp. XXVI, 109
(with illustration, as Rembrandt; given
by Hofstede de Groot to Lievens). In his
review of Valentiner's book, Abraham
Bredius attributed the work instead to
Lievens; see *Zeitschrift für bildende Kunst*,
LV, no. 7/8, 1921, p. 6.

40  Van de Wetering, Schnackenburg, *op. cit.*
(note 11), p. 73.

41  *The Apostle Paul, ca.* 1628, etching, 23.8 ×
20 cm; see Bartsch, *op. cit.* (note 29),
no. 149/2. For the drawing of *ca.* 1628
(red chalk and wash heightened with
white, 23.6 × 20.1 cm, Paris, Louvre,
inv. no. 22.887) see Otto Benesch, *The
Drawings of Rembrandt*, ed. and enlarged
by Eva Benesch, 6 vols., London 1973,
I, no. 15.

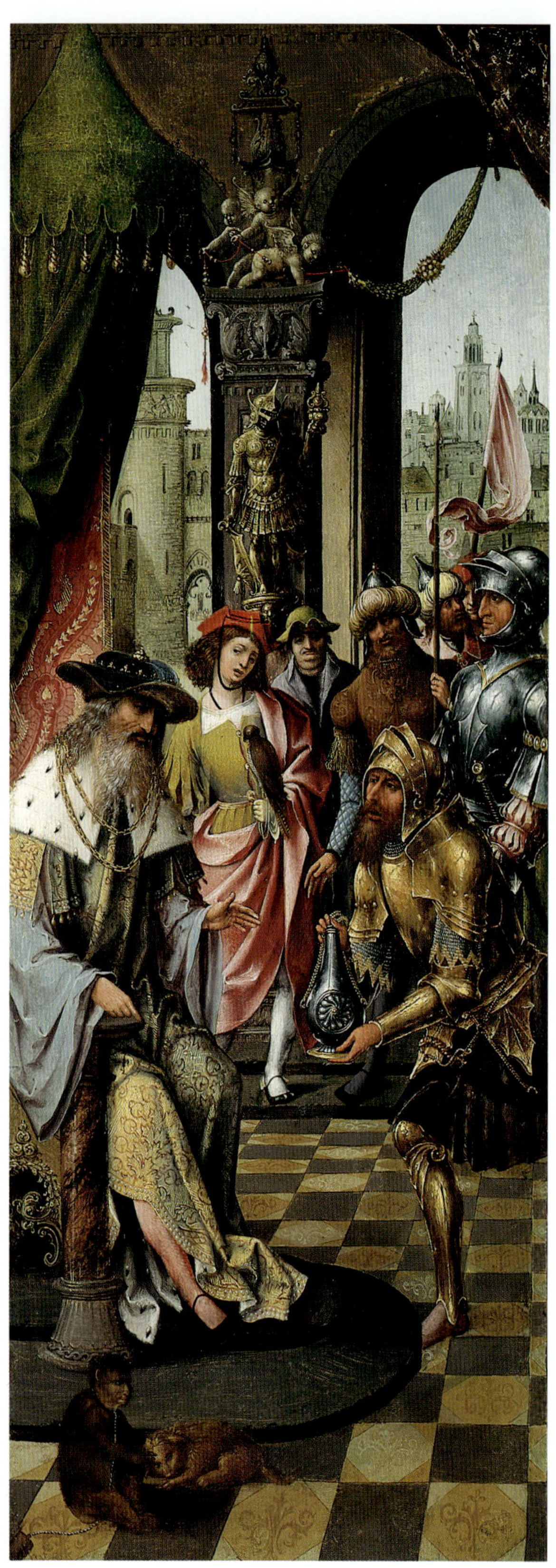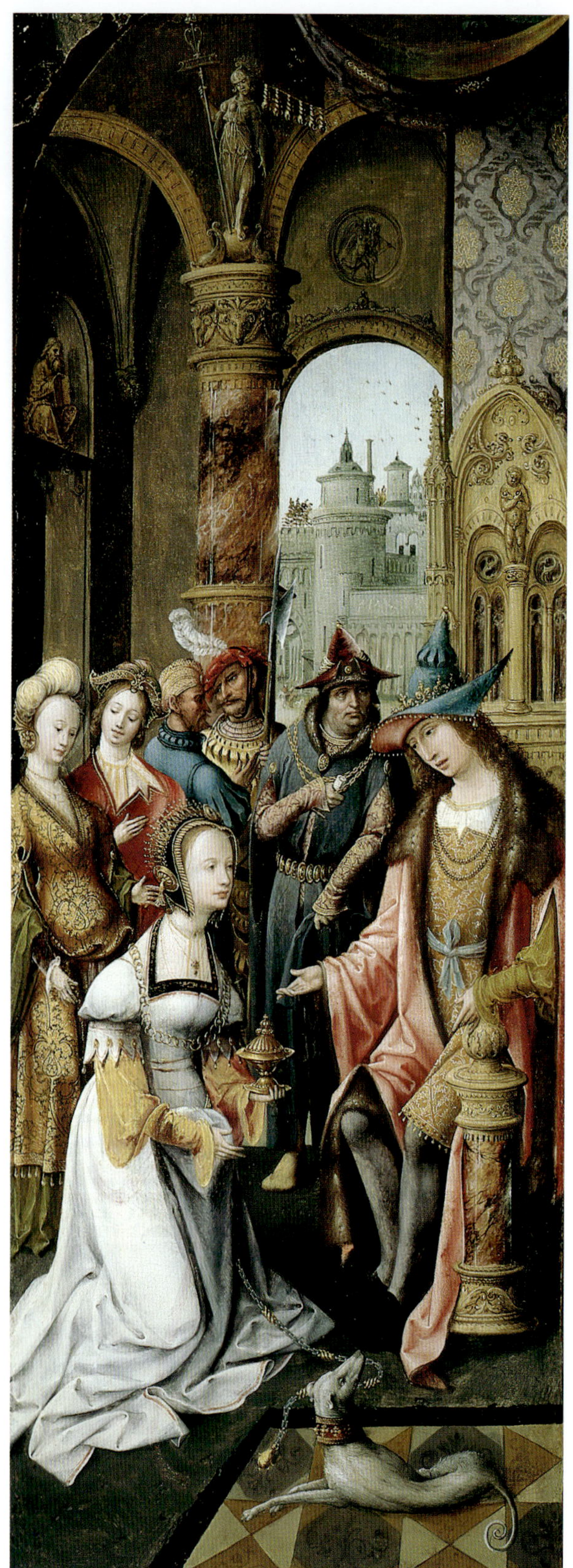

# Hebrew Kings and Antwerp Mannerists

MARTHA WOLFF

At the Art Institute of Chicago we consider ourselves fortunate to have Alfred Bader as a neighbour and honour his energy, his keen eye and his love of Dutch painting, not to mention his vast knowledge of subjects drawn from the Hebrew scriptures. Thus I hope he will be pleased with this fresh look at two long-neglected paintings in Chicago that represent kings of Israel.

*King David receiving the Cistern Water of Bethlehem* and *King Solomon receiving Gifts from the Queen of Sheba* (fig. 1) once formed the wings of a small triptych and were painted about 1515 to 1520 in the flamboyant Late Gothic style known as Antwerp Mannerism. When Charles Hutchinson, President of the Board of Trustees of the Art Institute of Chicago, bought them in 1890, the top of each scene, originally arched, had already been cut and simplified into a rectangle. The panels were cradled by the Paris dealer Durand-Ruel before being sent out to Chicago, and they were transferred from panel to canvas after they entered Hutchinson's collection.[1]

Despite these interventions, the two paintings are in excellent condition. A venerable King David and a youthful King Solomon are each enthroned under a rich canopy in a lofty hall. The palace settings are not represented as rational spaces; rather the middle of each composition is filled up with a row of courtiers blocking the recession into depth, and the upper portions of the wings are elaborated with screens of arches, heroic sculpted figures, putti and hybrid ornament. Though the kings are distinguished by fur-trimmed robes, gold chains and crowns barely visible on their fanciful hats, the general welter of pattern and colour threatens to overwhelm them and the gift-givers who kneel before them. It is chiefly the tall, brocade canopies and the stone platforms of their thrones that set these figures apart and emphasize their regal status.

The triptych wings in Chicago were not mentioned by Max J. Friedländer, who established the grouping of hands still used to characterize Antwerp Mannerism at the same time as he gave the style a name. Friedländer did, however, describe a number of related works that are key to an understanding

fig. 1 ANTWERP
*King David receiving the Cistern Water of Bethlehem, King Solomon receiving the Queen of Sheba*
Oil on panel, transferred to canvas, 72.7 × 26.8 cm and 72.7 × 27 cm
Chicago, Art Institute of Chicago, Gift of Mr Charles Hutchinson, 1936

of the Art Institute's pair and their function as the wings of a triptych. Since some of these works disappeared from view after the publication of the relevant volume of Friedländer's *Die altniederländische Malerei* in 1933 and have only recently resurfaced, it is helpful to describe them again. A diminutive triptych in the Prado (fig. 2) shows *King David receiving the Cistern Water of Bethlehem* and *King Solomon receiving Gifts from the Queen of Sheba* on wings flanking an *Adoration of the Magi*. The Adoration takes place in the ruined palace of David, a structure almost rivalling in height and richness the palaces on the wings. Friedländer attributed the Madrid triptych to the so-called Pseudo-Blesius, one of the more creative personalities among the Antwerp Mannerists, and he derived

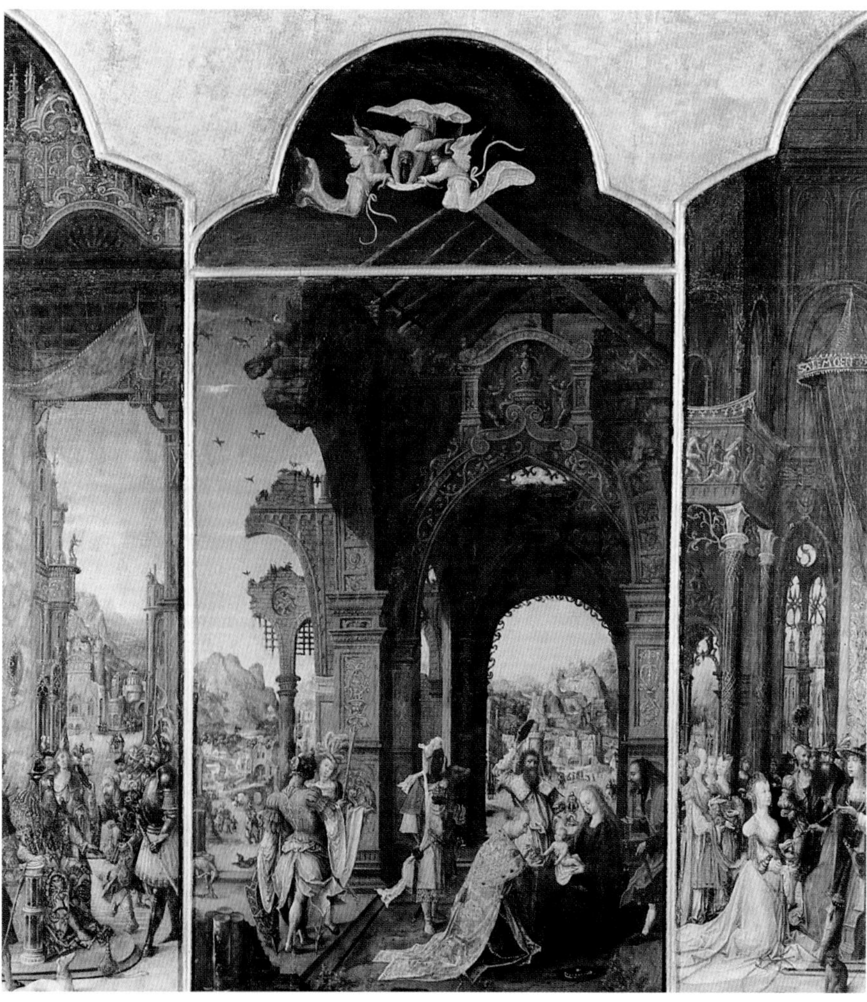

fig. 2 Attributed to
'PSEUDO-BLESIUS'
Triptych: *King David receiving the Cistern Water of Bethlehem*, *The Adoration of the Magi*, and *King Solomon Receiving Gifts from the Queen of Sheba*
Oil on panel, 58 × 54 cm
Madrid, Museo del Prado



MARTHA WOLFF

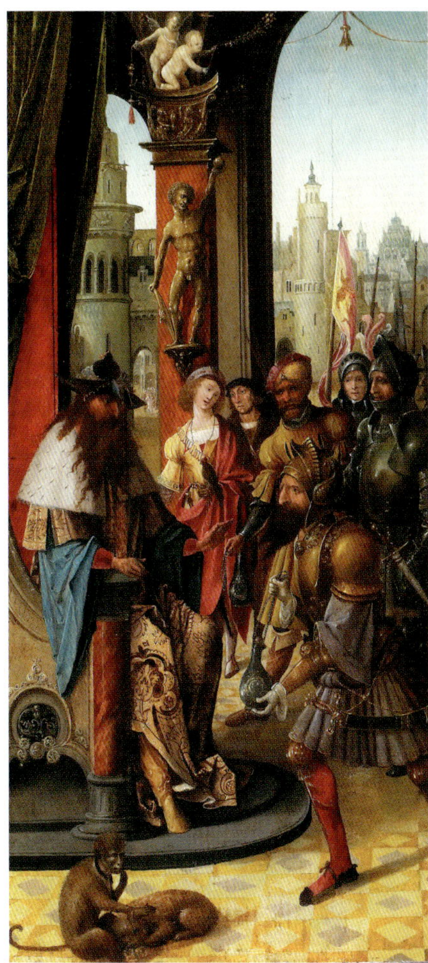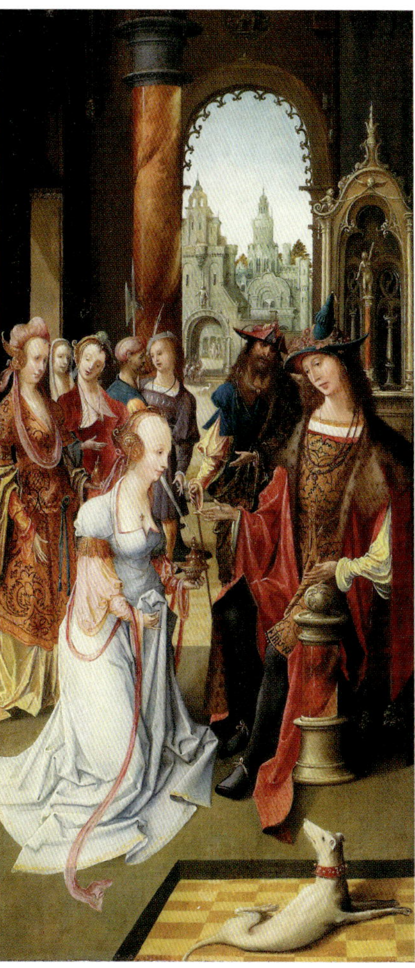

fig. 3  Attributed to
'PSEUDO-BLESIUS'
*King David receiving the Cistern Water*
*of Bethlehem, King Solomon receiving*
*Gifts from the Queen of Sheba*
Oil on panel, 55.3 × 24.7 cm
and 55.4 × 25 cm
Gift from the collection of
Dr Anne Tanenbaum to the
Government of Ontario, on
long term loan to Toronto,
Art Gallery of Ontario

the painter's awkward name from another *Adoration of the Magi* in the Alte Pinakothek, Munich, that formerly bore the spurious inscription *Henricus Blesius fecit*.[2] Friedländer also assigned a pair of diptych wings of the same subjects, then in the Portalès collection, Paris, to the Pseudo-Blesius. After passing through several sales, the Portalès wings entered the Tanenbaum collection and are now on long-term loan to the Art Gallery of Ontario (fig. 3). The design of this pair is very closely related to the Art Institute wings; coincidentally, the wings in Toronto have also lost their central panel and been cut at the top.[3] Related in subject and composition is a larger triptych that Friedländer described in the Von Groote collection, Schloß Kitzburg. He associated a large group of Antwerp Mannerist paintings with the Master of the Groote Adoration, whom he named after this important altarpiece. Though the triptych was later considered lost, it remains in Kitzburg near Cologne and was recently studied and published by Jochen Sander and Peter van den Brink.[4] Other triptychs combining the same subjects include one that has been in the church of St Peter and St Ildefonso in

Zamora since the middle of the seventeenth century.[5] A grisaille *Annunciation* decorates the reverse of the wings of the Zamora triptych; in the other variants the exterior of the wings is lost, blank or inaccessible. Finally, a pair of wings in the Musée d'art religieux et d'art mosan, Liège, appear to be relatively recent copies of the Chicago wings made after they had been cut down; they are the same size and the upper corners, which were always rectangular, repeat the design of the extended and repainted tops of the Chicago wings.[6]

The repetition of these subjects as triptych wings shows that the Art Institute paintings must also have flanked an *Adoration of the Magi*. The homage paid by the three kings to the infant Jesus was a favourite subject of Antwerp Mannerist painters and their patrons. As the centre of a triptych the *Adoration of the Magi* was frequently flanked by other scenes from the infancy of Christ or by standing saints. Sometimes two of the three kings were distributed across the wings, as though taking on the supporting role of patron saints. The triptychs with David and Solomon thus form a distinct type within a larger group of Antwerp Mannerist paintings of the *Adoration*. The paintings in Madrid, Toronto, Chicago and Kitzburg are also especially fine examples of Antwerp Mannerism, without the air of routine production that often dulls the impact of paintings in this style. Through them it is possible to examine the interconnections between different workshop trends and to speculate on the role of subjects drawn from the Hebrew scriptures in the painting of this period.

In the triptychs illustrating David and the cistern water and Solomon and the Queen of Sheba, the narratives from the Hebrew scriptures serve as proto- types amplifying the notions of kingship and homage in the central panel. The episode of David and the cistern water occurs at the end of the Second Book of Samuel. David had expressed a longing to drink the water of the well of his native town of Bethlehem, then occupied by a Philistine garrison. Three of his mighty men broke through the guard and brought him the desired water, but he would not drink it. Saying, "Is not this the blood of the men that went in jeopardy of their lives," he poured it out as an offering to the Lord (2 Samuel 23: 14–17). After Solomon had succeeded his father as king and completed the construction of the Temple, the Queen of Sheba came with her court to test what she had heard of his fame. Being persuaded of his wisdom and the splendour of his kingdom, she presented him with gifts, saying, "Blessed be the Lord thy God, which delighted in thee, to set thee on the throne of Israel" (1 Kings 10: 1–10).

A precedent for representations of David and Solomon as commentary on the Adoration of the Magi exists in illustrations to the *Speculum Humanae Salvationis*. This early fourteenth-century treatise, written in Latin but subsequently trans- lated into several vernacular languages, presented a sequence of events from the

     MARTHA WOLFF

life of Christ and the story of salvation, each followed by three prefigurations. Frequently each set of four images and their corresponding explanatory text was organized across a page opening with text below each image. Alternatively the four images might be placed one above the other on a page opening with the text on the following page.[7] The chapter for the Adoration of the Magi begins with the Three Kings presenting gifts and continues with the following prototypes: first the meeting of the Three Kings, then the three strong men bringing David the water of Bethlehem, and finally the throne of Solomon. The text interprets the three mighty men as prefigurations of the Kings, entering Bethlehem without fear of the Philistine garrison, just as the Kings would not fear Herod.[8] The fourth image is explicated by a description of the characteristics of the throne of Solomon as a metaphor for the Virgin Mary; the Queen of Sheba and other visitors presenting gifts are mentioned only in passing.[9] Similarly, the illustration in the *Speculum Humanae Salvationis* is a symbolic representation of Solomon's throne rather than a narrative. The Queen of Sheba may be included as an ancillary figure or omitted altogether, but the clear depiction of Solomon's throne with its steps and lions is the most important part of the illustration.[10] Another typological text, the so-called *Biblia Pauperum*, places a greater emphasis on narrative, with both text and allegorical elements playing a less prominent role than in the *Speculum*. The image sequence of the *Biblia Pauperum*, particularly as it was spread through late fifteenth-century printed editions, features two prototypes from the Hebrew scriptures on either side of a Christian antitype in an arrangement very like a triptych.[11] Flanking the representation of the Adoration of the Magi are, on the left, Abner kneeling before David as he pledges to help unite the Israelites under his rule and, on the right, the Queen of Sheba presenting her gifts to Solomon. In blockbook versions of the *Biblia Pauperum*, the repetition of the thrones and of gestures of presentation in each prototype underlines the analogous throne-like setting of the Virgin and Child as well as the homage rendered by the kings (fig. 4). These two episodes from the *Biblia Pauperum* sequence were used in a late fifteenth-century altarpiece by the Brussels Master of the Saint Barbara Legend, now divided between New York and Rome.[12]

It seems likely that the inventor of the programme found in the Antwerp Mannerist triptychs conflated the prototypes used in the *Speculum* with the formal symmetry and the emphasis on the Sheba narrative found in the *Biblia Pauperum*. By the second half of the fifteenth century it is not uncommon to find subjects from the Hebrew scriptures and a typological structure transferred from illustrated texts to devotional paintings as well as tapestries and other media. Many of these appear to have been commissioned works.[13] Thus the Master of Saint Barbara's Adoration triptych based on the *Biblia Pauperum*

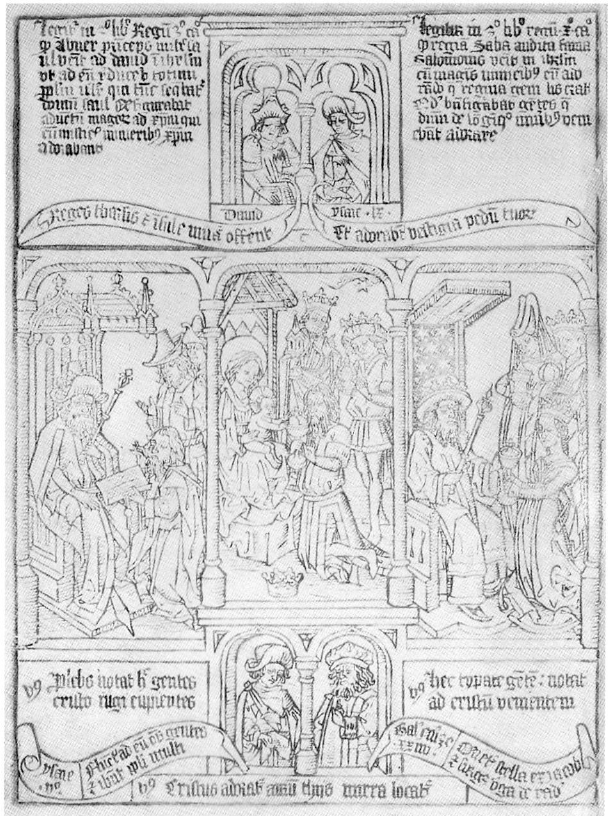

fig. 4 GERMANY
*Biblia Pauperum: The Adoration
of the Magi*
Woodcut, 28.5 × 21.7 cm
London, The British Museum,
inv. no. 1845-8-9-4

mentioned above was made for members of a confraternity or corporation who kneel in the foregound of the wings. In the Antwerp Mannerist triptychs discussed here the subjects have become conventional, repeated from one version to the next. The sources in the tradition of illustrated typological books have been adjusted to stress narrative, visual symmetry and elaborate courtly settings, as in the preference for the story of the Queen of Sheba over the overt mariological symbol of the throne of Solomon. The chance to exploit exotic costumes and numerous secondary figures may have made these stories particularly appealing to Antwerp mannerist painters and their clientele, and the compositions could be put together from more or less stock elements of gesticulating figures and architectural ornament. The political significance of David and Solomon as anointed kings dedicated to God, effectively evoked elsewhere in the years around 1500, does not seem to operate here.[14]

The interconnections between the triptychs or fragments in Madrid, Toronto, Chicago and Kitzburg show the division of design, underdrawn layout and painting among different artists – an economy of production that may reflect the reality of the open market. It is possible to get a sense of this division of labour through the underdrawn preparation, visible with infrared reflectography. This technique is a very promising tool for the study of Antwerp Mannerism, one that Peter van den Brink employs systematically in a

     MARTHA WOLFF

forthcoming study.[15] The drawing in the Chicago *David and the Cistern Water* shows relatively few changes and employs diagonal or gently curved strokes of parallel hatching and occasional cross-hatching, usually within long lines defining the edges of forms (fig. 5).[16] Contour lines are frequently repeated. The underdrawing for *Solomon and the Queen of Sheba* includes many changes and has an experimental character, but uses the same linear vocabulary (fig. 6). The organized underdrawing and open network of hatching used in the David panel in particular is analogous to the underdrawing that Peter van den Brink found in the Kitzburg triptych by the Master of the Groote Adoration and which he considers to be characteristic of this group altogether.[17] The underdrawn layout of the Chicago *Solomon and the Queen of Sheba* is clearly based on the design of the Toronto *Solomon*. This is most evident in the background where the distant buildings were underdrawn as they appear in the Toronto painting (figs. 6 and 3). Other details based on the model of the Toronto painting but changed in the paint stage include the ornamental back of the throne and the placement of the Queen's pink sash, now only visible as a pentiment in the Chicago painting. The style of the underdrawing of the Toronto wings differs markedly from that of the two Chicago paintings and the Groote Adoration. In the *Solomon* panel it is much more nervous, displaying less interest in volume or the clear delineation of the boundaries of forms (fig. 7).[18] In the drapery, shadows are indicated by broad, imprecise areas of hatching unconnected to the abrupt, squiggled lines marking the folds. In the Toronto wings a single artist seems to have been responsible for both drawing and painting. Thus the highlights applied with the point of the brush to the sleeve of the courtier behind David have a fluttering, nervous quality that is strikingly similar to the squiggles of the underdrawn drapery. This consistency of execution is not present in the Chicago wings, where the drawing looks like that of the Master of the Groote Adoration, but the paint layers appear to be by a different hand. Certainly the wings in the Art Institute are painted with more exuberant colour and pattern, and a more delicate, active touch than the work associated with the Kitzburg triptych.

These comparisons reveal several artists or, perhaps more accurately, several workshop sub-trends involved in the production of closely related variants. The overall conception of the scenes can be associated with the Pseudo-Blesius, whose brilliant but brittle figures and fondness for fantastic, towering architectural settings are reflected in the miniature Madrid triptych and the larger Toronto wings (now substantially cut down). This concept and also the details of the Toronto wings served as the basis for the underdrawn layout of the Chicago wings, probably put in place by the Master of the Groote Adoration. But the Chicago wings were painted in a style closer to the so-called Master of the Antwerp Adoration, as is evident from a comparison of the facial types of

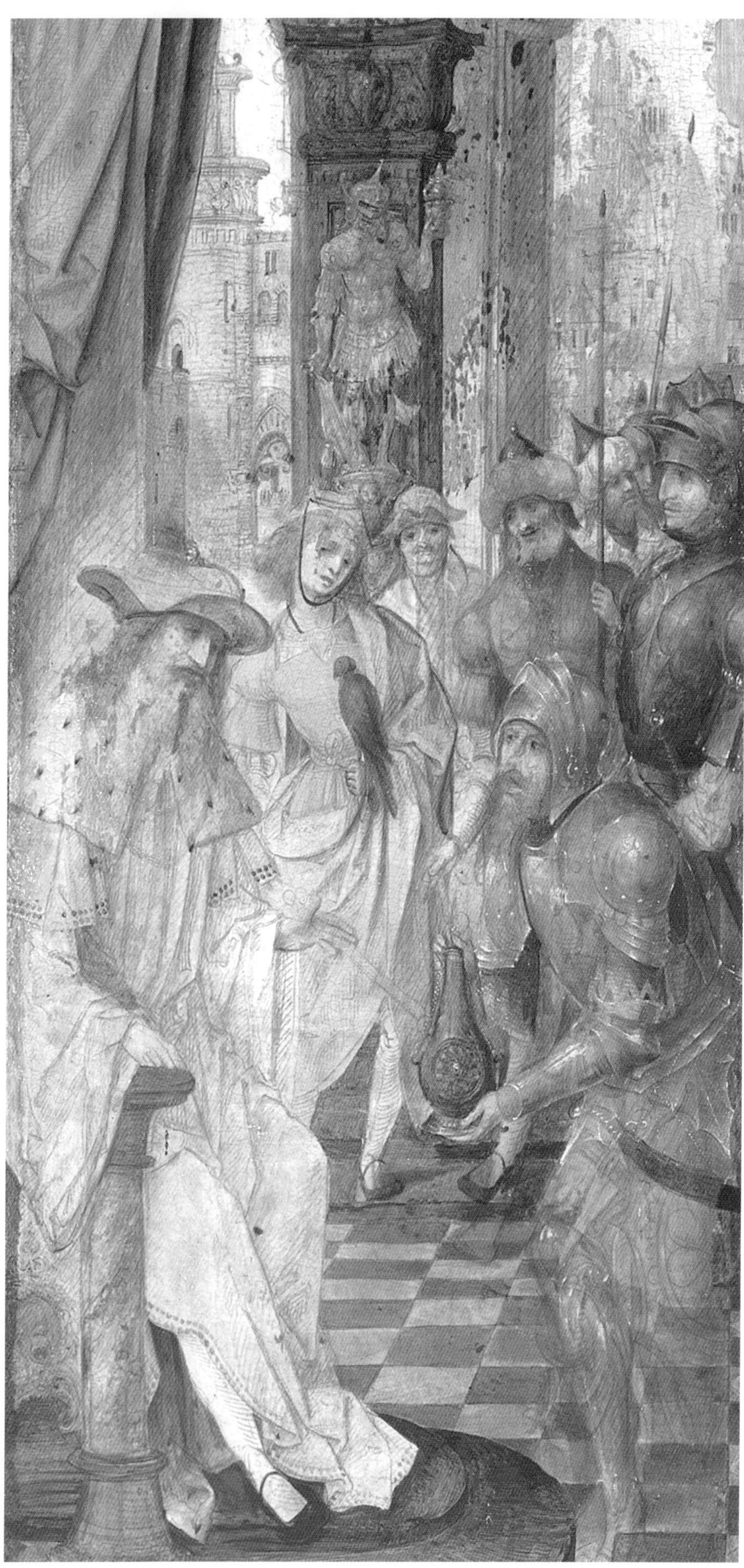

fig. 5  Detail of infrared reflectogram mosaic of Antwerp, *King David receiving the Cistern Water of Bethlehem*, Art Institute of Chicago

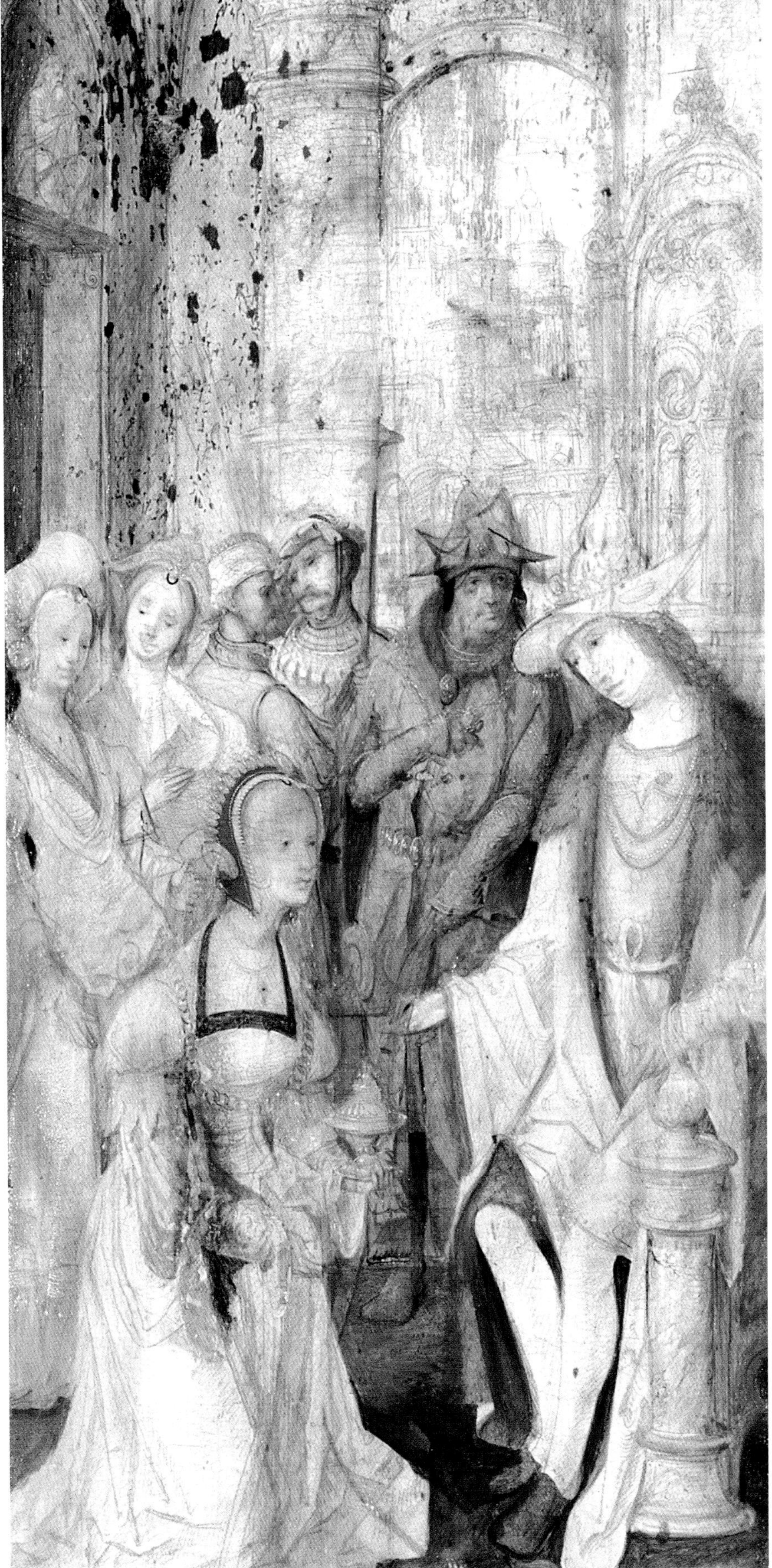

fig. 6  Detail of infrared reflectogram mosaic of Antwerp, *King Solomon receiving Gifts from the Queen of Sheba*, Art Institute of Chicago

the queen and her courtiers in the Adoration triptychs in Antwerp and Brussels.[19] In addition to laying out the underdrawn design of the Chicago wings, the Master of the Groote Adoration also worked out his own imposing and distinctive variation on the typological subject in the triptych from the von Groote collection, with its more sombre and weighty figures and more legible spatial arrangement. This triptych composition thus provides evidence for the close association of three of Friedländer's groups, named by him the Pseudo-Blesius, the Master of the Groote Adoration and the Master of the Antwerp Adoration. Friedländer himself confessed to difficulty in telling the workshops of the Master of the Groote Adoration and the Master of the Antwerp Adoration apart. This is an issue particularly for the more routine productions, and the underdrawn styles do differ.[20]

The evidence for collaboration and transmission in a relatively unusual subject makes these Adoration triptychs a revealing case study in the combination of artistic personalities typical of Antwerp Mannerism. The choice of the stories of kings of Israel taken from an earlier typological tradition also raises the broader question of the subjects favoured by Antwerp Mannerists. On the whole, they treated subjects with wide appeal, suitable for devotional works produced speculatively rather than on commission – the Crucifixion, the Adoration of the Magi, the Nativity, the Virgin and Child with saints and angels. Those few Antwerp Mannerist works with clear evidence of the special instructions of a patron are of exceptional quality. An example is the *Adoration of the Magi* triptych in Antwerp, showing a donor with St Catherine on one wing and St George on the other. The Master of the Antwerp Adoration was named after this commissioned triptych, and it is telling that none of the associated works rises to its exquisite level of quality.[21] The Adoration triptychs and fragments with David and Solomon are all executed with care and refinement, but they do not now show signs of having been commissioned works. Indeed, the repetition of related or identical compositions in itself argues against a commission. These depictions of David and Solomon can be contrasted with the apparently unique arrangement of a triptych in the Mauritshuis in The Hague in which the story of Solomon occupies the centre as well as the wings. In this splendid work a central image of Solomon's idolatry is flanked by wings showing Solomon and the Queen of Sheba and the repentance of Solomon in a sequence that has a narrative and didactic, rather than typological function. That the Mauritshuis triptych conveyed a moralizing message is underscored by the debt of the central scene to Lucas van Leyden's woodcut of Solomon's idolatry, itself part of a series devoted to the Power of Women. It has been plausibly suggested that the triptych, with its admonitory subject, was made in connection with the marriage in 1521 of Willem Simonz., Lord of Stavenisse and Cromstrijen

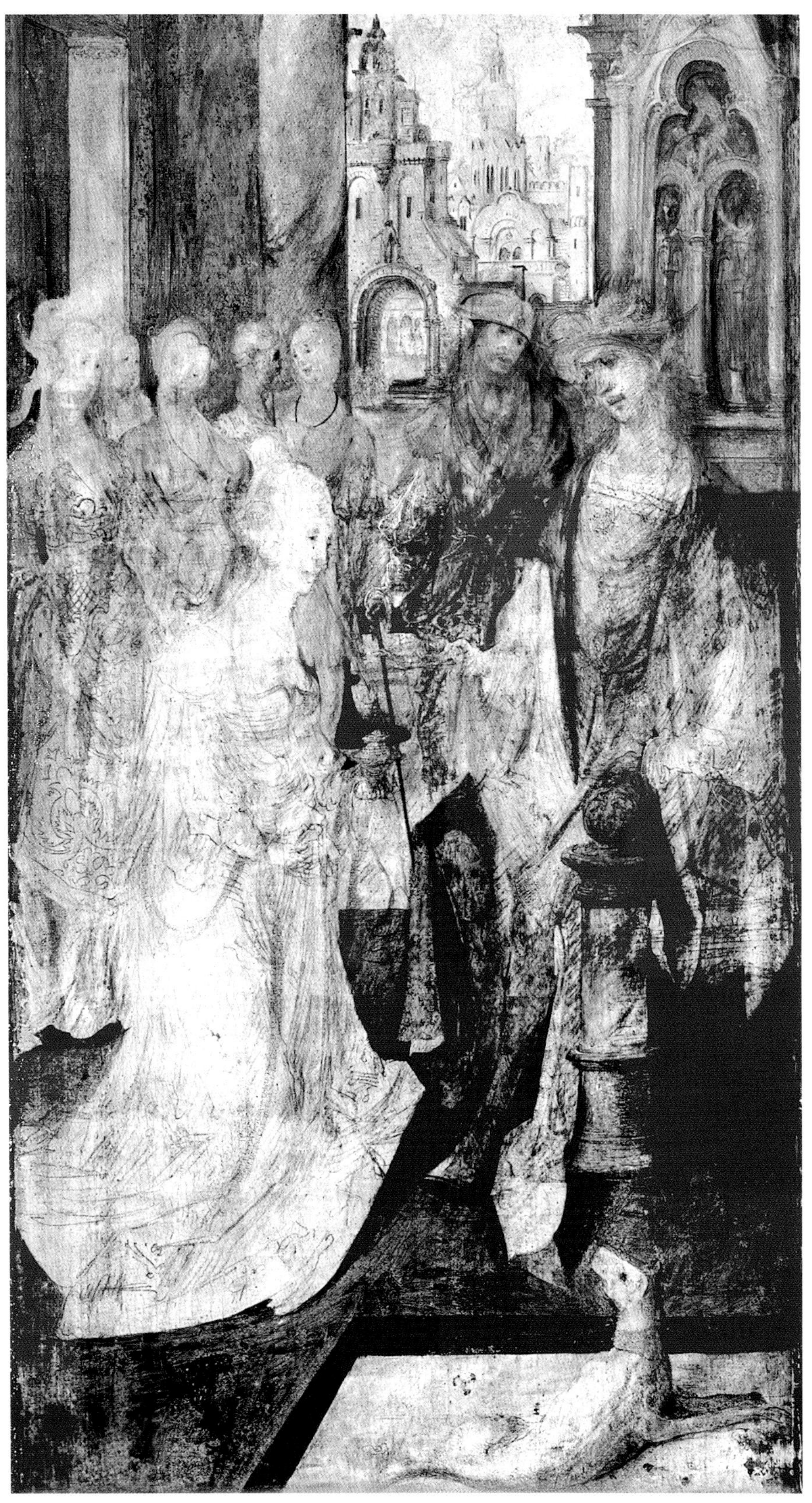

fig. 7 Detail of infrared reflectogram mosaic of Antwerp, *King Solomon receiving Gifts from the Queen of Sheba*, on loan to Toronto, Art Gallery of Ontario

(1498–1557), and his wife Adriana van Duyveland (1506–1545), since their arms carried by putti decorate the back of the wings.[22] The use of a scene from the Hebrew scriptures for the centre panel in an altarpiece format is not entirely unprecedented in the first decades of the sixteenth century, but it is very rare. Other examples include an Antwerp Mannerist triptych in the Pinacoteca Nazionale, Bologna, with several episodes from the story of Esther on the central panel and wings, and Cornelis Engebrechtsz.'s *Elisha at the River Jordan healing Naaman* in the Kunsthistorisches Museum, Vienna.[23] They must signal a shift in the way these paintings were used, a shift towards works that were not strictly devotional, but were at once moralizing and made for visual pleasure, probably in a domestic setting. The Antwerp Mannerists' recasting of typological conventions was most likely part of this broader tendency.

In the past the baffling fluidity of the workshops producing paintings in the Antwerp Mannerist style has discouraged scholars interested in an individual painter's evolution – even though painters as important and diverse as Jan Gossaert (*ca.* 1478–1532), Joos van Cleve (active 1507–40/41), Bernard van Orley (*ca.* 1488–1541), Cornelis Engebrechtsz. (1460/65–1527) and Jacob Cornelisz. van Oostsanen (*ca.* 1470/75– by 1533) show connections to this trend at some point in their careers. With new interest in workshop production as a response to the art market, Antwerp Mannerism has received fresh attention and some of the paths for the dissemination of the style have been sketched.[24] Clearly, the subjects treated by these painters and the way their choices may relate to new audiences deserve further study.

1 The present image size is 72.7 × 26.8 cm
and 72.7 × 27 cm; the wings originally
had curved tops to cover what must
have been the ogee-arched profile of the
central panel. Each panel was made into a
rectangle by the insertion of a triangular
segment in the upper inner corner. An
undated photograph in the Durand-Ruel
archive shows that the paintings were
already cut and the inserted segments
repainted before 1890. When the wings
were last restored, in 1981, the inserts
were not repainted. Underdrawing with
architectural decoration on these inserts
suggests that they were made from
segments of the top of the altarpiece,
either from the wings or the lost centre.
A receipt from Durand Ruel for conservation work dated 12 July 1890 includes
a charge for "cradling and repairing a
diptych"; Archives, Art Institute of
Chicago. The wings must have been
transferred from panel to canvas by 1908
since they are mentioned as transferred
in John La Farge, 'Art in America: Two
Works Formerly Attributed to Herri
met de Bles', *The Burlington Magazine*,
XII, 1908, p. 387. The wings were also
published by Salomon Reinach, *Répertoire
de peintures du moyen âge et de la renaissance
(1280–1580)*, 6 vols., Paris 1905–23, II,
p. 13, no. 1, ill. (as belonging to Durand
Ruel). Recently, they were briefly
discussed by Peter van den Brink in
his contribution to Jochen Sander,
*Kabinettstücke. Gold, Weihrauch und Myrrhe.
Die "von Grootesche Anbetung der Heiligen
Drei Könige" – ein wiederentdecktes Meisterwerk
der Renaissance in Antwerpen*, exh. cat.,
Städelsches Kunstinstitut und Städtische
Galerie, Frankfurt, 2001, p. 60, ill.
pp. 58 and 61.

2 Inv. no. 1361 from the Escorial. The
open triptych is mounted on a secondary
support and cradled, measuring 58 × 54 cm
in this form. I am very grateful to María
Pilar Silva Maroto for enabling me to
examine the triptych in the reserves of
the Prado. See Max J. Friedländer, *Die
altniederländische Malerei*, 14 vols., Berlin
and Leiden 1924–37, rev. edn Leiden and
Brussels 1974, II, pp. 14–15, 67, no. 2,
pl. 2. The Munich *Adoration of the Magi*

is *ibid.*, II, p. 67, no. 1, pl. 1.

3 *Ibid.*, p. 67, no. 3, pl. 3; see sale, Drouot
Rive Gauche, Paris, 21 November 1977,
lot 8 and sale Sotheby's, Monaco,
2–3 December 1988, lot 617. The wings
were then joined into a single panel and
cradled. They have since been separated
and the cradles removed; their painted
surfaces measure 55.3 × 24.7 cm and 55.4
× 25 cm respectively. They have narrow
unpainted edges at the sides, but are
trimmed within the painted image at
both top and bottom. The amount cut
away is probably rather substantial at
the top, since the baldachins topping
the thrones as well as the terminations
of some columns and arches are now
missing. I am most grateful to Martha
Kelleher and Sherry Philips of the Art
Gallery of Ontario for permission to
examine the wings.

4 Friedländer, *op. cit.* (note 2), II, pp. 24, 70,
no. 27, pl. 27. Sander, *op. cit.* (note 1),
gives the dimensions with the original
frame as 114.6/90.5 × 84.8 cm and
illustrates numerous details in colour.
The upper edges of these wings have also
been cut. I am grateful to Peter van den
Brink for the information that the backs
of the wings are unpainted.

5 José Ángel Rivera de las Heras, in *Las
Edades del hombre. Remembranza*, exh. cat.,
Iglesia de El Carmen de San Isidoro and
Catedral di Zamora, Zamora, 2001,
pp. 587–591, no. 16, figs. 16–1 to 16–5.
A variant of this triptych is in the town
hall of Marsala, Sicily; see Giovanni
Carandente, *Les Primitifs Flamands.
Répertoire. Collections d'Italie I. Sicile*,
Brussels 1968, p. 14, no. 6, pl. 4b.

6 The Liège *David receiving the Cistern Water
of Bethlehem* is illustrated in Cyriel Stroo
and Pascale Syfer-d'Olne, *The Flemish
Primitives, Catalogue of Early Netherlandish
Painting in the Royal Museums of Fine Arts
of Belgium*, vols. 1–, Brussels 1996–, I,
fig. 110.

7 For the arrangement of text and image in
the *Speculum*, see Bert Cardon, *Manuscripts
of the Speculum Humanae Salvationis in the
Southern Netherlands (c.1410 – c.1470)*,
Louvain 1996, esp. pp. 32–45. The
episode from the story of salvation

occupying the first place was sometimes distinguished from the three successive scenes by formal means; thus in a mid-fifteenth-century Flemish manuscript in Glasgow, the antitype is in colour and the successive images are painted in grisaille (University Library, MS. Hunter, 60, Cardon, no. XII).

8  *Speculum Humanae Salvationis. Texte critique, traduction inédite de Jean Miélot (1448)*, ed. Jules Lutz and Paul Perdrizet, 2 vols., Mülhausen and Leipzig 1907–09, I, pp. 128–29. The three mighty men went to fetch the water David requested, whereas the kings traveled *"pour avoir de l'eaue de la grace eternele"*.

9  *Ibid.*, p. 129; the relevant portion of the longer text is, *"... Le roy Salomon se seoit en ung trosne du yvoire treffin et net, et estoit vestu de fin or tresprecieusement. Tous les roys terriens desiroient veoir le roy Salomon, et lui portoient divers dons tresriches et tresprecieux. La royne Sabba entre les autres lui offrit telz et si grans dons que paravant on n'avoit veu en Jherusalem pareils. Le throsne du vray roy Salomon est la vierge Marie ...."*

10  For images of the prototype of Solomon's throne in the *Speculum*, see Cardon *op. cit.* (note 7), fig. 58; Adrian Wilson and Joyce Lancaster Wilson, *A Medieval Mirror. Speculum humanae salvationis 1324–1500*, Berkeley, Los Angeles and London 1984, colour pl. II-1 and pp. 158–59, and Evelyn Silber, 'The Reconstructed Toledo *Speculum Humanae Salvationis*: the Italian Connection in the Early Fourteenth Century', *Journal of the Warburg and Courtauld Institutes*, XLIII, 1980, pls. 9b, 10a and b. In the late fifteenth-century Dutch printed *Speculum* the Queen of Sheba is omitted altogether; see the illustration in Wilson and Wilson, *op. cit.* (above), pp. 158–59.

11  For the evolution of the layout of the *Biblia Pauperum* and its relation to other illustrated typological texts, see Gerhard Schmidt, *Die Armenbibeln des XIV. Jahrhunderts*, Graz 1959, pp. 1–8, 88–104.

12  The wings are in the Metropolitan Museum of Art and the centre in the Galleria Colonna, Rome; see Walter S. Gibson, 'A New Identification for a Panel by the St. Barbara Master', *Art Bulletin*, XLVII, 1965, pp. 504–06, figs. 1–3.

13  Bert Cardon noted that typological imagery is frequently used in books of hours for an élite clientele, 'Typologische beeldvoorstellingen in de late 15de en de vroege 16de eeuw', in *Dirk Bouts (ca. 1410–1475), een vlaams primitief te Leuven*, exh. cat., Sint Pieterskerk and Predikherenkerk, Louvain 1998, pp. 97–105, esp. p. 104.

14  See Robert W. Scheller, 'Imperial Themes in Art and Literature of the early French Renaissance: the Period of Charles VIII', *Simiolus*, XII, no. 1, 1981–82, pp. 57–60 and *idem*, 'Ensigns of Authority: French Royal Symbolism in the Age of Louis XII', *Simiolus*, XIII, no. 2, 1983, pp. 99, 116–20 and figs. 22 and 23, for these kings as political symbols. Of the David and Solomon wings only the triptych in Zamora may include contemporary political symbols in the form of an eagle pattern in the floor tiles of *Solomon and the Queen of Sheba*. Matthias Weniger suggests that the Zamora Solomon is an idealized likeness of the young Charles V (review of the exhibition at Zamora, *op. cit.* [note 5], in *The Burlington Magazine*, CXLIV, 2002, p. 167), though his features do not differ from those of the related Solomon figures and none wears the insignia of the Golden Fleece.

15  This is his forthcoming dissertation for the University of Groningen, 'Ondertekening en andere technische aspecten bij schilderijen van de "Antwerpse manieristen" 1515–1525' as well as an exhibition planned for 2005. His work will show that Friedländer's groupings remain the basis for study of the style, but that the dynamic relations between workshops can be mapped in more detail. I am most grateful to him for enthusiastically sharing his archive of underdrawings.

16  Cynthia Kuniej Berry, the conservator for the forthcoming catalogue of early Netherlandish paintings at the Art Institute, recorded the underdrawing on both Chicago wings in July of 1999 using an Inframetrics InfraCAM and

  MARTHA WOLFF

a Macintosh computer with a MAC
capture board. It was assembled with
Adobe Photoshop 5.0.

17  Peter van den Brink in Sander, *op. cit.*
(note 1), ill. pp. 46, 48–54.

18  The panels at the Art Gallery of Ontario
were examined by Cynthia Kuniej
Berry and Martha Wolff on 27 and 28
November 2001 using an Inframetrics
InfraCAM and were recorded using a
PCMCIA Video Acquisition Card and
a portable personal computer. The
Toronto *David receiving the Cistern Water
of Bethlehem* has a much more minimal
underdrawing; it is noteworthy that in
both the Chicago and Toronto wings the
episode of the Queen of Sheba received
more attention. Unfortunately, there is
little underdrawing in the paintings
attributed to the Pseudo-Blesius available
for comparison. The few attributed works
have either not been surveyed or show
only minimal drawing with infrared
reflectography.

19  See Friedländer, *op. cit.* (note 2), II,
nos. 46 and 52, pls. 49, 50 and 52.

20  *Ibid.*, p. 26. The underdrawing of a Magus
from the Brussels Adoration clearly
exemplifies the Master of the Antwerp
Adoration's underdrawing style, with its
more tense, rhythmic curves closely
allied to the linear pattern of Dürer's
woodcuts; see Godehard Hoffmann, 'Der
Annenaltar des Adrian van Overbeck in
der Propsteikirche zu Kempen – Werk
und Werkstatt eines Antwerpener
Manieristen', in Wilfried Hansmann
and Godehard Hoffmann, *Spätgotik am
Niederrhein: rheinische und flämische
Flügelaltäre im Licht neuer Forschung,*
Cologne 1998, fig. 37.

21  Friedländer, *op. cit.* (note 2), XI,
no. 46, pls. 49 and 50.

22  Ariane van Suchtelen in *Art on Wings,
Celebrating the Reunification of a Triptych
by Gerard David,* exh. cat., Mauritshuis,
The Hague, 1997, pp. 72–74, no. 7, ill.

23  Pinacoteca Nazionale, inv. no. 204; Licia
Collobi Ragghianti, *Dipinti fiamminghi in
Italia 1420–1570. Catalogo,* Bologna 1990,
p. 172, no. 344, ill. pp. 174 and 175, as
'Pseudo-Blesius' (?); and Friedländer, *op.
cit.* (note 2), X, no. 67, pls. 54 and 55.

24  In addition to the work of Peter van
den Brink mentioned above, important
recent studies include Hoffmann, *op. cit.*
(note 20) and Guy-Michel Leproux,
*La peinture à Paris sous la règne de François
Ier,* Paris 2001.

# List of Art Historical Publications
by Alfred Bader

'Aert de Gelder's "Forecourt of a Temple"', *The Burlington Magazine*, CXII, 1970, pp. 691–92

'A New Interpretation of Rembrandt's Disgrace of Haman', *The Burlington Magazine*, CXIII, 1971, p. 473

'An Unknown Self-Portrait of Michael Sweerts', *The Burlington Magazine*, CXIV, 1972, p. 475

*Selections from the Bader Collection*, privately printed, Milwaukee, Wisconsin, 1974

*The Bible Through Dutch Eyes. From Genesis Through the Apocrypha*, exh. cat. Milwaukee Art Centre, Milwaukee, Wisconsin, 1976

*The Detective's Eye: Investigating the Old Masters*, exh. cat. (with Isabel Bader), Milwaukee Art Centre, Milwaukee, Wisconsin, 1989

*Adventures of a Chemist Collector*, London 1995

Arranged chronologically by year. Prefaces to exhibition catalogues are not listed.

# Photographic Credits

Amsterdam, Rijksmuseum, pp. 65, 94, 183: © Rijksmuseum-Stichting Amsterdam
Basle, Kunstmuseum, p. 271: © Öffentliche Kunstsammlung Basel, Martin Bühler
Berlin, Staatliche Museen zu Berlin, Kupferstichkabinett, pp. 118, 123: © Staatliche
    Museen zu Berlin, Kupferstichkabinett; Foto: Jörg P. Anders
Boston, Museum of Fine Art, p. 18: © 2004 Museum of Fine Art, Boston
Chicago, The Art Institute of Chicago, pp. 278, 286, 287: photographs © 2002,
    The Art Institute of Chicago, all rights reserved
Cleveland, The Cleveland Museum of Art, p. 45: © The Cleveland Museum of Art, 2004
Detroit, The Detroit Institute of Arts, p. 46: © 1989 The Detroit Institute of Arts
Dublin, The National Gallery of Ireland, p. 266: © courtesy of the National Gallery
    of Ireland
London, Courtauld Gallery, p. 144: photograph Witt Library
London, The National Gallery, pp. 82, 234: © National Gallery, London
New York, The Metropolitan Museum of Art, p. 23: All rights reserved, The Metropolitan
    Museum of Art; p. 72, The Metropolitan Museum of Art, Purchase, Special contributions
    and funds given or bequeathed by Friends of the Museum, 1961 (61.198).
    Photograph © 1993 The Metropolitan Museum of Art
Paris, Musée du Louvre, p. 20 © Photo RMN – Jean Schormans; p. 42: © Photo RMN –
    Hervé Lewandowsky; p. 77: Réunion des Musées Nationaux/Art Resource, NY; p. 243:
    © Photo RMN
Tyntesfield, Somerset, The National Trust, p. 105: © Christie's Images, Ltd 1999
Utrecht, Centraal Museum, p. 237: Collectie Centraal Museum, Utrecht
Washington, National Gallery of Art, p. 232: © 2004 Board of Trustees, National Gallery
    of Art, Washington

Christie's, pp. 240, 255: © Christie's Images Ltd, 2002
The Royal Collection, pp. 148, 155, 245: The Royal Collection © 2004, Her Majesty
    Queen Elizabeth II
Sotheby's, p. 110: © Sotheby's, Amsterdam